SYSTEMS THEORY
VS
EVOLUTIONARY THEORY

ADRIAN MOIR

BALBOA.PRESS

A DIVISION OF HAY HOUSE

Balboa Press books may be ordered through booksellers or by contacting:

Balboa Press
A Division of Hay House
1663 Liberty Drive
Bloomington, IN 47403
www.balboapress.com.au
AU TFN: 1 800 844 925 (Toll Free inside Australia)
AU Local: (02) 8310 7086 (+61 2 8310 7086 from outside Australia)

Scripture quotations marked NKJV are taken from the New King James Version. Copyright © 1982 by Thomas Nelson, Inc. Used by permission. All rights reserved.

Print information available on the last page.

ISBN: 979-8-7652-0043-8 (sc)
ISBN: 979-8-7652-0042-1 (hc)
ISBN: 979-8-7652-0041-4 (e)

Library of Congress Control Number: 2024919420

Balboa Press rev. date: 09/13/2024

CONTENTS

(* Indicates that it's resourced material).

Citations, Online References, and External Links are listed on the last Page.

DISCLOSURE

The contents of this book is in relation to the subject of human equality with a strong focus on interpreting the human conscience, morality, and law. The book contains references to theological terms from the Holy Bible, as well as scientific references to systems theory and systems science. The book is intended to empower the individual with knowledge concerning the basic rights of a human being, whilst exploring the implications of the evolutionary theory in society from both a theological and scientific viewpoint. The book also contains references to quantum theory, the matrix, war, conspiracy, the Holocaust, Communism, New Atheism, politics, nudity, sexual immorality, animal cruelty, hell, and racism from a Christian perspective. This book is not recommended for individuals under the age of 18. All views within this book are within the spectrum of the law concerning freedom of speech, so as to not break the law, nor infringe upon a person's basic rights as a human being.

GENEALOGY

The Moir family has a long and outstanding history involving knighthood, construction, finance, sport, education, law, and politics, beginning in Scotland with Sir Kenneth Moir, and later in Australia with the arrival of Joseph James Moir. The author of this book (Adrian Donald Moir) is a direct descendant of Joseph James Moir, who was the first Moir to move to Australia in 1829 from his homeland of Scotland.

Joseph James Moir (1809 - 1874) was the Australian ancestor of Alan John Moir (1903 - 1981) who was also the great-grandson of Sir Graham Berry (1822 - 1904). Alan John Moir was a close relative of the late Ian Donald Moir (1947 - 2015), the father of Adrian Donald Moir who has authored this book. Adrian Donald Moir was born in Lithgow, New South Wales, Australia, in 1982, and has earned a trade qualification in engineering. As of 2023, Adrian Moir works for an engineering and construction firm on the Eastern side of Brisbane, Australia, where this book was written in honour of our Lord and Saviour, Jesus Christ.

The surname Moir was first founded in Aberdeenshire (Gaelic: Siorrachd Obar Dheathain), a historic county, and present day Council Area of Aberdeen, located in the Grampian's region of North-Eastern Scotland, where they held a family seat from early times. The family name Moir first appeared on the early census rolls taken by the early Kings of Scotland who knighted Sir Kenneth Moir as a champion knight. In the year 1330, Sir Kenneth Moir rode with James Douglas, Lord of Douglas, and the Catholic Crusaders to Spain with the heart of Sir Robert the Bruce to defeat the pagan Moors who had laid siege to the Spanish fortress at the Battle of Teba in Andalusia. Sir Kenneth's surname was forever changed from De La More to Moir, from the Scottish Gaelic for: "brave and mighty one."

The earliest Moir armorial bearing displaying the Family Crest depicts a shield beset with laurels under a knight's Templar helmet. Larger than the helmet above is a skull scrubbed clean with two leg bones in a cross position under the skull to represent a secret Order of Knights Templar. Today, the fraternity of Skull and Bones at Yale University has chosen this symbol to represent their secret society. The skull and crossbones symbol was also used by the former Nazi regiment of SS Officers in conjunction with the Cross of Malta, an older more widely depicted Knights Templar, British Royal, and Freemasonic symbol that began with Emperor Constantine in the year 312 AD.

The Moir Family Crest is not one of triumphant victory, nor does the author of this book promote such symbolism, instead, the Moir Family Crest is a grim reminder of a best forgotten past that has derived from an occult society of Knights Templar who ultimately faded into obscurity through history's pages. The Moir skull and crossbones Family Crest is one of the most mysterious, yet significant symbols in AD history with its earliest recorded origins dating back to Sir Kenneth Moir of Scotland during the late Crusades.

Joseph James Moir was a prominent Freemason, ironmonger, citizen, and Shot Tower manufacturer in 19th century Tasmania, Australia. Joseph James Moir was born in the Scottish border town of Kelso in 1809, where he learned his trade as a Master Mason. Joseph James Moir began his colonial life in the land of Australia as a Master Builder, constructing houses and Churches around Hobart, Tasmania, and acquiring land and property. He established a strong reputation for notable buildings, such as St Mark's Anglican Church, Pontville, and was appointed to the civic position of Clerk of Public Works for the early Australian colony in 1834.

In 1870, Joseph James Moir, together with two other Masons, constructed a Shot Tower at Queenborough Glens, using dressed curved sandstone blocks quarried at an abandoned Convict Probation Station nearby. The Shot Tower in Taroona, Tasmania, served as a munitions manufacturer for the colonial police force and the Royal Army, and is the most distinctive and important landmark of Tasmania. The shot tower built by Joseph Moir is also one of Tasmania's most historical industrial buildings with a National Trust Classification (A), and remains open to the public as a Museum of early Australian colonial history.

As a former Melbourne solicitor, Alan John Moir KCMG of the Melbourne establishment firm Gillott, Moir and Winneke that is now referred to as: Minter and Ellison, was a prominent lawyer and Company Director who held various other positions, including President of the Victorian Institute of Law (1939 - 1940). Alan John Moir was also the Director and Chairman of GTV 9 and Director of David Syme and Co Limited where he played an important role in the formation of Syme as a public company in 1948. Alan John Moir received a Companion title Order of Saint Michael and Saint George (CMG) in 1971 for his services to the racing industry as a relative to Henry Albert Underwood of the Underwood racing family. The Melbourne A J Moir Stakes was named after Alan John Moir who was the former Chairman of the Moonee Valley Horse Racing Club in Melbourne.

Sir Graham Berry KCMG, was elected to the Australian Legislative Assembly for East-Melbourne at a State election in 1861. When Charles Gavan Duffy (1844 - 1917) formed a strong Australian liberal government in June 1871, Sir Graham Berry became the Treasurer for the Australian Liberal Party. Sir Graham Berry later accepted the office as Chief Secretary and Postmaster General of the Australian coalition government in 1883. In 1886 Berry resigned from Parliament and was appointed Victorian Agent General in London, then an important and prestigious post. He was also appointed Executive Commissioner to the Colonial and Indian Exhibition for his services to the British empire and was officially appointed Knight Commander of the Order of St Michael and St George (KCMG). In 1897, Sir Graham Berry was elected as a Victorian delegate to the Constitutional Convention that drafted the Australian Constitution which was put into effect on January 1, 1901.

INTRODUCTION

In systems theory, a system is defined by its parameters, which are the rules that govern the system, and the evolutionary interpretation is that systems are self-existing, which is postulated without proof by members from the scientific community, because rules are always inferred, rather than deriving from materials alone. Yet the theory of evolution has been taken so seriously by its proponents that any doubts that are urged against the theory are met with a vicious barrage of insults and abuse, which has only amounted to being a statement of their faith, rather than being evidence from science.

The argument between Biblical creation and the evolutionary theory is one of origins, but because modern physics has derived from the interpretation of thermodynamic systems, it will mean that a thermodynamic system requires a correct explanation through the curriculum in order for the argument of origins to be settled satisfactorily. The second aspect of this argument concerning origins is one of discernment concerning the difference between a supernatural process, and a natural process. The proof that a supernatural process has occurred in terms of origins is entirely due to the existence of the human conscience, which cannot be interpreted in terms of naturalism due to the nature of conscience, which is for our understanding of morality, as well as law and order.

So, for the purpose of this book I will attempt to explain the supernatural, as well as the scientific method as an integrated system at work, because in order to interpret a law in science or society, then rules are required, which is what the human conscience is for; Interpreting rules and morality. Morality is by definition rule based on the basis of ethics, which not only defines our system of law and order in terms of its legal structure and commitments to public safety, but also, science, because science is governed by ethics, rather than by scientists. If we are to allow scientists to dictate the law, as from a secular premise, then morality and law will be lost in obscurity, because laws are for the benefit of an individual's protection within the system, rather than to protect a pet theory.

The scientific basis for the evolutionary theory is that all processes, whether artificial or not, have derived from a natural process, which in turn, defines evolution in terms of a theory. Thus, the theoretical basis for the evolutionary theory is the same as it is for philosophical materialism, in that all processes have derived naturally, that is to say, that all processes have derived from energy and matter alone. Yet according to systems theory and systems science, a system is defined by its parameters, which are the rules that govern the system, and rules are always inferred, rather than deriving from materials alone, which is the very thing that brings the evolutionary theory into question as a legitimate scientific practice.

The pseudo-scientific practice of the evolutionary theory from secular science attempts to define all life as the result of a natural process only, which has only amounted to being a desperate attempt to deny the supernatural, because both an artificial process, and a supernatural process, cannot be explained in terms of naturalism or philosophical materialism, which is a limitation of the evolutionary theory, rather than an expedience. No living system can self-emerge from materials alone due to the law of probability, and the principles of entropy, which states that order will decline into disorder over time within a thermodynamic system due to randomness within the system.

Entropy is the product of random decay from order, which means definitively that disorder cannot produce an orderly system over time, because you cannot have disorder without first having an orderly system in place to define disorder with, otherwise, there would be nothing to define that which is orderly in terms of a procedure. This principle can be summed up by the following axiom: Anything random will remain random unless a method is applied, which then defines the process as a procedure due to the application of a method. Thus, the universe began as orderly, rather than disorderly, because any process that tends toward disorder over time will only increase in disorder in a matter of time, which is in accordance with the law of probability.

A thermodynamic system will always be the result of a method in place, otherwise, there would be no causality for a procedure, because all thermodynamic systems tend toward disorder over time due to the principles of entropy, and the law of probability, which applies to all thermodynamic processes, including DNA RNA transcription. The purpose of the evolutionary theory is to define all processes as a natural process only. Yet according to systems theory, a natural process is simply the normal workings of a system in place. So, in order for a normal process to occur, then there needs to be a system in place first that is operating according to plan, only then can something abnormal occur by reason of the fact that something normal was occurring to begin with, which is self-explanatory.

According to the laws of physics, ordered complexity cannot derive at random from disordered complexity, otherwise, there would be nothing to define that which is orderly, because ordered complexity derives from taking rules into account, which in turn, gives rise to a procedure. So, in order for a procedure to occur that is orderly, and therefore, predictable, then a method is required first, which is why a system is defined as a method due to the presence of a procedure. Any process that is occurring according to a cycle in place, such as the water cycle or the reproductive cycle for example, is by definition a procedure, and is therefore evidence of a system.

So, my challenge to the atheist community is to provide evidence of a system's causality without relying on a method to do so, because the moment that a method is implied is the same moment that creativity is inferred, and therefore, a Creator as well, because a method is by definition, specific. And there is only specified and unspecified to choose from, which limits the definition of evolution to being a creation, rather than a natural process, because there have been a number of rules applied to the theory in order to assume intellectual authority over the human being from a secular premise. So, in order to be specific here concerning the debate between creation and evolution, then a method of identification is required first, which cannot derive from a natural process only, because a natural process will always be limited to the number of specifics there are in place to define the process with, while any additional specifics to a given process must occur by design by definition of the word, create.

One does not need to present the Almighty to an atheist in order to satisfy the atheist's conclusions, but rather, one only needs to prove that life is a creation. And the final proof that life is a creation derives from the existence of genetic instructions, because anything that derives from instructions, is by definition a creation. So, in order to introduce the Creator to the reader, I will attempt to interpret the Holy Bible as the founding and governing source of our knowledge concerning His nature, as well as His creation.

The empirical method of identification from the practice of both science and law has derived from the interpretation of systems, that is to say that creation science and the common law is to be interpreted using Biblical theology for the benefit of the people, as well as the system. Our universal system of common law was founded upon the judicial verdict that all human beings are born free and equal, and are endowed with conscience by their Creator, and that natural law has derived from the Creator who stands above His creation, as well as a part of His creation, for God breathed life into His creation, as well as offering His blood for the redemption of sin. Blood has no other causality apart from a supernatural process, because blood cannot be replicated in a laboratory, and because blood derives from an instructional system, such as DNA RNA transcription, which cannot be denied due to the existence of genetic instructions, which is empirically verified.

The theory of evolution cannot be empirically based, because the evolutionary theory cannot be empirically verified due to the sheer number of evolutionary changes that are said to have occurred over a 13.8 billion year history without a single eyewitness account concerning the history of the Earth, as well as mankind in terms of origins. The Holy Bible presents the history of the Earth, as well as mankind from the viewpoint of eyewitness accounts, which is the strongest form of physical evidence there is before a court of law when in writing, because no exhibit in a courtroom can be interpreted on its own. Our universal dating system derives from a Biblical timeline from BC to AD, which has been established on the basis of eyewitness accounts concerning the history of the Earth, while the evolutionary timeline is based entirely on human conjecture for the purpose of theory.

So, in order to differentiate between theory and fact, then the correct word definitions are required first that act as a table of facts, which is essential to any debate in both science and law. No theory in science or law can be based on human conjecture alone, because word definitions are in place in order to correct an individual with; Meaning that it is the correct word definitions in place that are authoritative when describing a given theory or phenomena. Natural phenomena cannot always be explained in terms of philosophical materialism by definition of the word, system, because a system is defined by its parameters, which are by definition rule based, and rules are always inferred, rather than deriving from materials alone, which is both self-explanatory, as well as self-evident on the basis of observation and empirical verification.

There is no other causality for the existence of orderly systems apart from the inference of rules by definition of the word, order. Thus, an orderly thermodynamic system at work is defined as a creation due to the presence of rules, such as physical laws, which constitute as a system in itself, because physical laws are by definition rule based the same as morality is rule based for the purpose of law and order. So, in order to correctly define a system, then rules must be inferred, and there is no other way to interpret systems apart from the inference of rules, because rules derive from systems by the application of a method, which is the evidence that systems have derived from a supernatural process. Thus, systems were in place before any theory in science or law could be established, which is the evidence of supernatural creativity due to the presence of rules, such as physical laws, which cannot be self-existing, because a rule is also equal to an order or command.

God the Creator has spoken all things into existence by an audible vibrational command, which forms the only causality for the existence of orderly systems by definition of the word, order. And it was the actions of man that brought disorder into the world when the one rule was broken in the garden that God did create, thus leading to the extension of more rules in order to correct the system that God had created for man. And it is a cardinal principle in systems theory that the more rules a system has, the more likely the system will fail, which is in accordance with the law of probability. So, in order to correct the system we live by, then rules are required, thus constituting the purpose of a legal system, while it is the purpose of the evolutionary theory to cause the individual to espouse some form of freedom from rules by likening a human being unto that of an animal.

The purpose of this book is to create awareness of the depravity and unethical conduct by individuals who hail from the evolutionary theory, while at the same time, providing the reader with an alternative theory, because if the theory of evolution goes unchallenged, then the lawful premise for human equality will erode into nothing more than just a concept. If the evolutionary theory is to bring the lawful definition of person into question before the law by attempting to define a human being as a type of animal, then it is the evolutionary theory that must be called into question by the law, rather than the individual's basic right to be defined as a created human being, which is self-explanatory. So, for the purpose of this book I will discuss the system we live under as a legal system, as well as the scientific method of empirical verification in order to further outline the proof of God's creation as an integrated system at work.

Systems theory and applied systems science is modern science, while evolution is primarily a racial theory due to the racial terms in use, such as Homo-Sapien, Neanderthal, Negroid, and primate, which are by definition derogative in relation to a person's ancestry, and are therefore, unlawful. The only way for humanity to progress into a future based on human rights and equality, is by the teaching of systems theory and systems science, and with a correct theology, because science and law cannot be taught without a system of morality from a universal principle due to ethical reasons.

According to the New Atheist movement and the evolutionary theory, a human being is to be defined as a type of animal, rather than a person with rights. So, the primary reason why the New Atheist movement has failed humanity on the issue of human rights and equality, is because the atheist cannot admit that they are fully human without detracting from their atheism in turn, which is a crime against humanity on the basis of equality. The idea that the definition of a human being shares its definition with the term, animal, derives from Linnaean taxonomy and the theory of evolution, rather than law.

The term used by the evolutionary theory to describe a person as an animal derives from the Linnaean definition of a mammal, which applies to any organism with a mammary gland as being in the same phylum or group. But what the word, mammal, does not take into account, is a species method of reproduction, which must be taken into account in order to define a species with in terms of a breeding group or phylum. The other aspect of a breeding group that must be taken into account, is their method of communication, because communication is essential for mating.

One of the origins of scientific racism can be traced to Linnaeus' work on the classification of man, which had devastating and far-reaching consequences for humanity. Linnaeus' work on the classification of man forms one of the 18th century roots of modern scientific racism. Linnaeus did two things that changed our understanding of humans. He decided man was an animal like any other, and put Homo-Sapiens in the animal kingdom alongside other animals. This paved the way for Darwin's theory of evolution a century later.

This page aims to look at Linnaeus' works in detail, both printed and in manuscript, to trace the development of an idea which became fundamental in the history of anthropology and has had devastating and far-reaching consequences for humanity, including the dehumanisation of non-Europeans and the justification of evils like slavery and indigenous genocide. Linnaeus was the first naturalist to include man within the animal kingdom. In 1735, the class into which Linnaeus inserted man was called Quadrupeds, and the order, Anthropomorpha. These names Linnaeus would change to Mammals and Primates later on in his career. The order of Anthropomorpha contained the genera Homo (humans), Simia (apes) and Bradypus (sloths). Systema naturae was edited 12 times in Linnaeus' life.

As each edition was amended, corrected and augmented, Systema naturae grew in scope and content. For the first 9 editions (1735-1756), Linnaeus' classification of man remained stable, with the human species divided into four types, or "varieties," as he called them in Latin. By the 10th edition of Systema naturae, Linnaeus switched the order in which the varieties appear yet again, and chose to place Americanus first, possibly influenced by ideas of the 'noble savage.' One variety never varied in this hierarchy, however, Africanus consistently remained at the bottom of the list. Moreover, in all editions, Linnaeus' description of Africanus was the longest, most detailed and physical, and also the most negative. - Source: The Linnaean Society of London (Linnaeus and race).

According to United States Federal Law under Title VI Section 601 of the Civil Rights Act of 1964, the United States government is prohibited from discriminating against a person based on their race, colour, or national descent in programs or activities that receive federal financial assistance, which does include public education. Thus, the United States federal government is committing a human rights violation by the promotion of the evolutionary theory from public education due to the enforcement of the Linnaean/Darwinian definition of man within public school textbooks, which forms the philosophical basis for scientific racism, and the race war that still continues to this day.

So, in order for students to be adequately informed concerning the correct definition of what a person is, and what the endowed human conscience is for, then the secular standard for public education must be lifted, because it is the universal law of human equality that is of a higher legal standard than scientific theory due to international agreement. According to international law, the burden of proof is upon the individual who is challenging a lawful instruction, such as the lawful definition of person, because a human being is not to be denoted as an animal from the viewpoint of Linnaean taxonomy and the evolutionary theory for reasons relating to the correct interpretation of human rights and equality.

Human rights and equality is the universal indivisibility of law and order, so that any law which caters to the Linnaean/Darwinian definition of man as a lower animal, (as enforced by the United States government at the tax payers expense) is by definition, a crime against the people who shall be defined as persons without distinction for the benefit of the legal system to operate effectively through a just deliberation of the law. Thus, the federal government of the United States is required by federal law to repeal the enforcement of the evolutionary theory from public education in order that justice should be served to those who have suffered the injustice of racial discrimination through public education for long enough, for it is the will of the people that systemic racism should be abolished from the premise of law.

This action requires public understanding of the fraudulent nature of secular science, which is not a saving grace to all of mankind as the United States government assures, but rather, it is the sole cause for race riots, racial hate speech, and racial segregation policies. The United States government is bound by federal law to due deliberation of the law in regards to Section 601 of the Civil Rights Act in order that the government should not be publicly liable in this matter. The official reason why the United States government has refrained from removing the Linnaean/Darwinian terms and classification system from public education, is solely due to the lack of a viable option, which is where the teaching of systems theory as a new standard model comes into act as a viable option, which cannot be rejected on the basis of secular science, because it is secular science that has caused this issue to begin with by the reinterpretation of conscience.

According to international human rights legislation, the human being has been defined as distinct from the animals due to the existence of the human conscience, which is legally incontestable before international law for reasons relating to the correct interpretation of human rights and equality. The definition of person from international law has derived from the use of the word, conscience, which is a theological term from the Holy Bible historically, and from the United States Constitution legally, and not from biology or taxonomy, because the human conscience is a non-physical aspect of the human mind called the psyche or soul.

Science is not an authority concerning the human being, because science is governed by ethics, and ethics derive from morality and law, which means that law and morality are forever intertwined, and neither one can be interpreted without the other. No individual has sufficient cause to reinterpret the correct definition of what a person is before the law for reasons relating to a moral obligation by the law to uphold the virtues of human rights and equality as a legal standard for civil rights. And the correct definitions are the lawful definitions, from which, a person's basic rights are preserved as universal and inalienable for the benefit of an individual's protection within the system.

The escalation of youth crime and increased rates in incarceration within Australia, the United States, and the United Kingdom is solely due to the inability of public school students to learn about their Creator, as from law. So, for this reason, it is the highly immoral and unethical conduct by the New Atheist movement that must be brought into question by the law, rather than the existence of God the Creator, because if the atheist is to deny their humanity on the basis of evolution, then it is the evolutionary theory that is putting the basic rights of the people in jeopardy, rather than the faithful in God our maker.

So, in order to build a case for the purpose of defending the universal definition of man, then evidence is required, which is why defining yourself, or others, as an animal, constitutes as evidence that is self-incriminating, and therefore, cannot be used as a defence before the law. And the reason why it is self-incriminating to define yourself or others as having derived from the animals, is because the animals are legally defined as property. So, because of this legal status, it is unlawful to regard a human being as a type of animal via their ancestry so that every person may exercise their basic rights as a created human being.

The human conscience has been defined as being endowed to all of mankind by their Creator according to United States Constitutional law, and Commonwealth theology, and as self-evident, which means that there is no legal obligation for any individual to try and refute the existence of the Creator before the law from the viewpoint of any science, because the common law has recognized the Creator as being the source of inalienable rights, for all are endowed with conscience by their Creator for the purpose of human rights and equality, and human freedom thereby. The theological terms from international law that are used to define a person with are defined as incontestable and not-without-standing in their legal defence, because the law of human equality has been signed by 192 nations under the Universal Declaration of Human Rights and Equality (UDHR).

According to the United Nations High Commissioner's Office, human equality has been defined by "religious teachings," rather than the evolutionary theory, which means that the universal definition of person has derived from Biblical theology due to the use of the word, conscience, to define a person as distinct from the animals. The lawful term, conscience, is an ecclesiastical term from Latin that has derived from Biblical theology, which is also where the term, science, has derived from historically; Meaning to know or have knowledge of. The lawful term, conscience, is universally protected under international law as not-without-standing in its legal defence for the benefit of an individual's protection within the system. Under the UDHR, a person has the universal right to be defined as a "living soul" on the basis of conscience and reason.

This means that the New Atheist movement is committing an international human rights violation by the reinterpretation of conscience to meaning that of an animal, which is not a religious test before the law, but a moral one instead. Any scientific argument by atheism that attempts to dismiss the Creator before the law will be defined as "Scientific Atheism," and therefore, Communism, which is entirely due to the academic definition of Scientific Atheism. According to academics, Scientific Atheism is the core doctrine of Communism, which goes unabated from the public education system with the consent of the law.

The issue with Communism, as from the views presented by the author of Communism, Karl Marx, is that it's an open conspiracy to throw the whole of Western civilization into disrepute with God in Heaven through the indoctrination of Scientific Atheism, and by the reinterpretation of property. The principles of Scientific Atheism from the New Atheist movement has called our basic freedoms into question by the reinterpretation of the lawful term, conscience. Thus, the New Atheist movement is by definition a Communist front that attempts to call our basic freedoms into question by the reinterpretation of conscience in order to stifle the due process of law.

> *Quotation: ─────────────────────────
> "The democratic concept of man is false, because it is Christian. The democratic concept holds that each man is a sovereign being. This is the illusion, dream, and postulate of Christianity. Communism is for us not a state of affairs which is to be established, an ideal to which reality will have to adjust itself. We call Communism the real movement which abolishes the present state of things. The conditions of this movement result from the premises now in existence." - Karl Marx, founder of Communism. Source: Works of Karl Marx On The Jewish Question. Deutsch-Französische Jahrbücher. (Documented in February, 1844).

If inalienable rights derive from nature, then man is thereby the property of the State, because both nature, and the animals, are legally defined as property, which forms the basis for human slavery. But if inalienable rights derive from the Creator, then man is thereby independent of the State in terms of ownership, and is therefore, sovereign. Thus, the evolutionary definition of man as animal forms the unlawful basis for human slavery and subjugation by the reinterpretation of property, while the Biblical definition of man forms the lawful basis for human rights and equality by the legal definition of conscience. And an individual may choose whether they believe in God the Creator or not, but there are no protections under international law when it comes to the denial of conscience, because the legal definition of person is universal, rather than institutional.

So, all it takes to be truly enlightened is to understand your basic rights as a created human being, and then to stand upon these rights in the face of adversity, which is the very thing that gave America its independence within the world as a nation under God. The greatest political achievement by atheism was to create a Communist State. While the greatest political achievement by Christianity was to create a Constitution that protects the people's right to life and liberty, which has become the international standard for human rights and equality, and has also led to the independence of 65 other nations including Canada, New Zealand, and Australia. The United States Constitution was never to be interpreted using secular terminology only, but with a correct theology instead, because it was the founding fathers of America who further outlined a Commonwealth system or Christian coalition, rather than the New Atheist movement.

The lawful term, conscience, can only be described by its correct definition in use, which is in place so that each individual should have freedom of belief and religion, as well as protection of person before the law. Freedom of conscience is a religious liberty that cannot be overruled from the viewpoint of a science without incurring the burden of proof in return, because it is the human conscience that is defined as self-evident before the law, rather than scientific theory. The idea that evolution is a fact of nature, and is therefore incontestable holds only one value, and that is to stifle the religious orientation of the United States from a Christian based democracy to that of a secular society, which is a Communist ideal, rather than a Constitutional practice.

So, for this reason, the United States public education system must include the correct definition of what a person is from a lawful interpretation regardless of the religiosity of the legal definitions used. Otherwise, there will be sufficient cause for reasonable suspicion and Class Action against the United States government to reform the public education system to include the Constitutional definition of man as a created being, thereby replacing the teaching of evolution with the teaching of systems theory as a new standard model for public education, because the theory of evolution cannot be taught from public education without the inclusion of scientific racism as a negative consequence.

Any theory that attempts to divide mankind into a racial hierarchy of less evolved to more evolved is by definition a racist concept, because one group will always be seen as biologically inferior to the rest, which is a crime against humanity on the basis of equality. Systems theory and systems science is modern science, and is not in opposition to the lawful terms used to describe a person with, as from international law under the UDHR.

According to international law, all human beings have been endowed with conscience in order to understand a moral obligation, which forms the basis of a legal obligation, and every human being has a lawful obligation to acknowledge the human conscience before the law for reasons relating to the correct interpretation of human rights and equality. No human being can be defined as having derived from the animals before international law since 1948 under the UDHR, because an animal is defined as property before the law, which means that the theory of evolution is doing more to enslave humanity by equating mankind with the animal kingdom, rather than freeing the people by the truth that sets us free. And the one truth that sets a person free from subjugation, whether foreign or domestic, is that all human beings have been endowed with conscience by their Creator, which forms the basis for human freedom by the rights of conscience.

So, in order for students to reach their full potential as individuals within society so that they too can contribute with a fair outcome, then the theory of evolution must be challenged from the premise of law, because it is our basic freedom as created human beings that is at stake here due to lobbying efforts by the New Atheist movement involving a pseudo-definition of man that is being propagated from the public education system with the consent of the law. All human beings have a universal right to be defined as persons without distinction so that no human being is discriminated against or unfairly treated before the law in accordance with freedom of conscience, which does not include any protections under the law for unbelief in regards to the lawful definition of person.

The United States government has no Constitutional right to deny creation science to its students on the basis that it's a religious concept any more than they have the right to deny the religiosity of the legal definitions used to describe a person with, because the Creator is defined as self-evident before the law for reasons relating to the correct interpretation of inalienable rights and human equality. The lawful definition of person derives from the theological term, conscience, which is legally incontestable under international law for the purpose of equal rights, and is based on theological terminology in order for the legal definitions to be universal in their interpretation, because it is morality that defines what is universal for ethical reasons, rather than science. The term, secular, as from law, is a neutral term, which is not to be misappropriated as being anti-religious in any way so that freedom of religion can be exercised as a right, rather than a privilege.

According to international law under the UDHR, the ability to govern is defined as a privilege, rather than a birthright, while the right to be defined as a created human being with a human ancestry is defined as an inalienable right, because all human beings are endowed with conscience before the law. The term, endowed, from law, is that which is a birthright, which forms the basis of an inalienable right. So, because the ability to govern from a secular premise is defined as a privilege, rather than a birthright, while the universal definition of a human being is defined as inalienable, it will mean that no secular government has a lawful obligation to teach that man is animal from the public education system for reasons relating to the correct interpretation of human rights and equality.

In order for human equality to be taught from its institutional roots, then the theory of evolution must be overruled from the premise of law in order for the secular standard for public education to be returned to the people, to whom, it rightfully belongs, because it is the theory of evolution that denies the universal definition of what a human being is all on the theoretical basis that man is animal. And it is for this reason above all other reasons that the theory of evolution is a form of subjugation upon the human mind, because the theory of evolution conflicts with the human conscience due to a confliction between the law and public education. The correct definition of person as a created human being is the very thing that liberates the human mind from subjugation, which is a form of liberation as defined by the principles of liberty itself.

*Quotation: ————————————————————
"Our nation is founded on the principal that observance of the law is the eternal safeguard of liberty, and defiance of the law is the surest road to tyranny." - John F. Kennedy. Source: Radio and Television Report to the Nation on the Situation at the University of Mississippi. (Documented September 30, 1962).

If society is to improve, rather than spiral out of control to the point of no return, then the theory of evolution must be challenged from the premise of law, because no scientist has the right to redefine what the human being is before the law for reasons relating to the correct interpretation of human rights and equality. In order for human equality to be exercised as an inalienable right under international law, then a universal definition of person is required, and the universal definition in place to define a person as distinct from the animals, as from law, derives from the Holy Bible, rather than from secular ideology or science due to the use of the theological term, conscience, to define a person as distinct from the animals.

Thus, any scientific or theological argument by the New Atheist movement that attempts to define belief in God our maker as a form of subjugation upon the people is without merit, nor justification, because in order to be liberated from subjugation, then you must first be defined as a created human being with a human ancestry so that freedom of conscience can be exercised as a right, rather than a privilege. And the one law that liberates the human mind from subjugation is the universal law of equality, because it is human equality that defines our basic freedoms in accordance with freedom of conscience. So, for this reason, it is the New Atheist movement and the evolutionary theory that has subjugated the minds of the people to a form of tyranny by the teaching that man is animal, and by the reinterpretation of conscience, while it is the Creator Himself who has liberated the people by the rights of conscience.

This liberty is inalienable on the basis that human rights and equality cannot be used as a justification to define man as animal without calling the rights of conscience into question, because the rights of conscience is the lawful premise for human freedom, which is a religious liberty, rather than an atheist ideal. So, for this reason, no human being is legally obligated to teach that man is animal from the public education system without raising reasonable suspicion through due process, because the due process of law applies to human beings only, rather than the animals.

Under international agreement from the UDHR, no animal can be cross-examined before the law due to their lack of conscience, which is why defining yourself, or others, as an animal raises reasonable suspicion, because if man is animal, then laws do not apply, which is the philosophical basis for lawlessness, anarchy, rebellion, and Communist revolution. The only thing that is required when interpreting the universal law of equality, is belief, which is legally protected under international law as freedom of conscience, or freedom of belief. Thus, unbelief in the human conscience does not constitute as a right under international agreement, nor does the reinterpretation of conscience as defined by international law under the UDHR.

The universal law of human equality is not just a concept, but a self-evident reality instead, because all human beings have been endowed with conscience by their Creator, and it is from the conscience that our convictions derive from, which is how we make a moral decision, and our decisions are subject to the Biblical principles of universal morality, which cannot be justified by nature, because nature is defined as property, legally speaking. The human conscience is self-evident before international law, because in order to receive a conviction of truth, then you must also have a conscience to reason from, and the ability to reason derives from the ability to ask questions, of which, separates mankind from the animal kingdom.

An inalienable right cannot be defined as a privilege under international law, because a privilege requires merit, while an inalienable right is from birth; Hence the legal term, endowed. So, that which is endowed, such as the right to be defined as a created human being with a human ancestry, is by definition, inalienable, because it is a birthright, rather than a privilege alone. While the privilege of being a created human being is one of compassion, because the human conscience desires compassion on all grounds. Compassion can also be interpreted as concern, which is a form of love that the human conscience desires most. And God the Creator has shown His compassion to all of mankind by the gift of His Spirit, for God is word, as well as Spirit, which also happens to be the correct definition of the lawful term, conscience; A source of word or spirit.

A leading argument by the New Atheist movement is the separation of Church and State, which was enacted so that the government of the United States did not create a universal religious institution, which was in opposition to a Commonwealth system in terms of practice and theology under the common law. The common law is of common interest to the people, rather than secular science, because it is the principles of law and order that human freedom was defined, as defined by the United States Constitution and Commonwealth theology.

*Quotation: ————————————————

"They (the founding fathers) were intent upon establishing a Christian Commonwealth in accordance with the principles of self-government. They were an inspired body of men. It has been said that God sifted the nations that He might send choice grain into the wilderness. Who can fail to see it in the hand of destiny? Who can doubt that it has been guided by a divine providence?" - Calvin Coolidge. Calvin Coolidge was an American attorney and politician who served as the 30th President of the United States from 1923 - 1929. Source: Presidential Speech titled - The Destiny of America. (Documented on Memorial Day, May 26, 1923).

The Commonwealth system derives from the practice of English common law, that is to say that the common law has derived from Christian ethics and teachings so that a system of equality can exist between all nations, which has led to the creation of the UDHR by the United Nations, because the legal definition of conscience under Commonwealth theology, and the UDHR are the same. The United States has led the world in human rights and equality by declaring their independence from British rule, which is why the United States does not partake in the Commonwealth games.

Yet the indivisibility of the common law in practice and observance acts as a common ground for the good of the people who are subject to the system. Thus, it is our universal system of common law that shall prevail over the cultural debate, because a person's national heritage is secondary to our national trust. And we are collectively as a people forbidden to abandon the common law in favour of a cultural debate, because cultures shift, but the premise of common law is as eternal and immutable as morality itself. The premise of common law derives from previous verdicts that act as a legal precedent or standard. And it is Biblical creation as a legal standard from the premise of common law that has paved the way for human rights and equality by the correct interpretation of the human conscience.

According to systems theory, a standard must always be inferred according to a set of rules, thus constituting Biblical creation as a legal standard that is universal in its interpretation, by which, the courts must follow under the common law in order to be consistent with a prior judicial verdict that derives from Biblical theology as a legal precedent. The former legal precedent within the United States that all men are created equal has been overruled by the Supreme Court in order to pave the way for the evolutionary definition of man, thus leading to the subjugation of the people in the form of indoctrination, which is a Communist ideal, rather than an American liberty.

The United Nations Declaration of Human Rights and Equality (UDHR) is a continuation of the former United States revolution against pro-slavery by the rights of conscience. Thus, any pro-revolutionary movement that calls the lawful definition of conscience into question will lead humanity into a new age of slavery by a shift in culture. The shift in culture that we are seeing today within the United States and the Commonwealth nations is one from a Christian based democracy to that of a secular society, which is a danger to humanity due to the reinterpretation of conscience. Thus, it is the sovereign duty of every citizen within the system to uphold the lawful definition of person, as defined by international agreement, so that a return to slavery does not occur with the consent of the law.

The New Atheist movement has attempted to challenge a lawful instruction that is universal in its interpretation, such as the universal definition of person, as well as calling for a new age scientific revolution in place of the previous, which is the official reason why the New Atheist movement should be called into question by the law, rather than our God given humanity. If the lawful definition of person is to be called into question by the evolutionary theory, then it is the evolutionary theory that should be called into question by the law, rather than a person's right to be defined by a human ancestry, which is self-explanatory. Mankind has had religion since the beginning of time, and any attempt at removing religion altogether is a crime against humanity, because every culture around the world was built upon religion, and to destroy culture, and re-write history is a tyrant's game, and not a patriot's aim.

When a crime is committed, or when a nation is at war, civil rights are superseded for reasons relating to national security. So, your civil rights are removed when there is a national crisis, or when you are convicted of a crime. But, that which is inalienable is also endowed; Meaning from birth. So, it is by definition a birthright that you are defined as a created human being in order that you should have rights in the first place, which may be taken from you if you disobey the law, or, if you are an enemy of the State on the grounds of war. So, for this reason, the New Atheist movement constitutes as an enemy of the State on the basis that the New Atheist movement has reneged their rights by the reinterpretation of conscience, which is where your inalienable rights derive from according to international law.

Only those who are by definition, sovereign, retain their civil rights in the event of a national crisis, such as the government of a nation, or an individual who has legally declared their sovereignty with Washington D.C. And it is for this reason that the royal family of England retains their basic rights in the event of a national crisis, because they have legally declared their sovereignty in order to subjugate the people as a form of property under the rule of law. The rule of law is a form of subjugation upon the people who shall be self-governed under a universal system of morality, because it is Biblical morality that defines a law as just, rather than the legislator for ethical reasons. The idea that law and order can be maintained without religion only paves the way for a fascist dictatorship, just as we've seen by the rise of Communism, and by a rise in the cost of living with every additional piece of new technology we create.

Science will one day destroy humanity on the basis that science is leading humanity into a new age of slavery, whereby an individual is enslaved to a device in order for the scientific establishment to profit from the public, which then leads to the creation of debt, and then onto bond slavery as we are seeing today by the rise of taxation, and Federal Reserve interest rates, whereby a person is born into debt with the promise to repay government spending, which is a Communist ideal, rather than a virtue of human freedom. The other leading factor that will cause the destruction of mankind, is the evolutionary practice of cloning humans with animals, which must stop immediately for the safety of mankind, or we will see the human population go extinct by the rise of zoonotic viruses, such as COVID 19.

International law has derived its definition of what a person is from the United States Declaration of Independence, because the legal definition of conscience therein, is the same. Thus, the United States Declaration of Independence is a universal statement of truth that is legally binding under United States Federal law, and Constitutionally protected as self-evident. Thus, it is the duty of every individual to acknowledge their Creator, as defined by the Holy Bible, because it is freedom of conscience that defines our basic freedoms, of which, derives from Biblical theology under the common law, rather than the evolutionary theory of ape to man, which forms the philosophical basis for the individual's denial of conscience.

Inalienable rights are clearly defined as universal on the basis of conscience and good reason, because that which is endowed is by definition from birth, which forms the lawful basis for the rights of conscience. Thus, any and all arguments by the New Atheist movement that inalienable rights are non-existent derives from a theological dispute with the universal law of equality, which is entirely due to the individual's denial of conscience, as defined by international agreement. The universal law of human equality is in place so that each and every person should have protection of person within the system, rather than to protect a pet theory, which is why the evolutionary theory failed to convince at the trial at Nuremberg for the same reason that Social Darwinism failed to convince.

*Quotation: ——————————————————
Social Darwinism, the theory that human groups and races are subject to the same laws of natural selection as Charles Darwin perceived in plants and animals in nature. Social Darwinism declined during the 20th century as an expanded knowledge of biological, social, and cultural phenomena undermined the theory, rather than supporting its basic tenets. - Source: Encyclopedia Britannica (Social Darwinism).

The United States government has a legal obligation to uphold the lawful interpretation of what a person is for the benefit of an individual's protection within the system, so there is no moral cause that is sufficient enough to refute the Creator before the law, because the preservation of inalienable rights and human equality by the rights of conscience is a moral obligation, as well as a legal one. So, for this reason, the United States government must include the correct definition of what a person is from the public education system regardless of the religiosity of the definitions used, because every individual person is to be defined by a human ancestry before the law for reasons relating to the correct interpretation of human rights and equality.

The idea that the lawful definition of person can be overruled by the evolutionary theory on the basis that our legal system is a man-made construct is without sufficient cause, because, the evolutionary theory is also a man-made construct on the basis of theory, and is thereby subject to a higher authority in itself. The legal standard for human rights and equality, as from international law, is of a higher legal standard than scientific theory. While the legal standard by international law is also subject to a higher standard in itself, such as moral law, which forms the basis for ethical conduct. Morals are by definition personal, while morality is by definition universal, because morals are an opinion concerning right and wrong, while morality is the standard in place to define good and evil. And morality is indeed universal, otherwise, there would be no universal definition to define corruption with, as well as unethical conduct.

Every individual person has a universal right to be defined as a "living soul" with a human ancestry at all times under Article 6 of the Universal Declaration of Human Rights and Equality (UDHR) in order that no individual should ever be subjected to unfair treatment or discrimination before the law. The universal law of human equality is in place so that we each have security of person before the law, because without security of person before the law, then laws cannot protect you as an individual. Under the common law, the burden of proof is upon the individual who is challenging a lawful instruction, such as the right to be defined as a created human being with a human ancestry, which is not only inalienable under international law according to Article 6 of the UDHR, but also, it is protected as self-evident for reasons relating to the correct interpretation of human rights and equality.

Laws in society do not define what is good or evil, because laws are governed by ethics, which in turn, derives from Biblical morality under the common law. So, for this reason, laws in society cannot be defined as a legal obligation unless there is a moral obligation first, which means that morality is above the law from a Biblical premise, because it is Biblical morality that defines what is good and evil, rather than law. A human being is not to be enslaved by the laws we create, because if there is one thing that will enslave mankind faster than anything else, then it is the adoption of rules that simply do not apply. And the evolutionary theory has applied a number of rules to society and law in order to assume authority over the human being from a secular premise, which is a crime against humanity on the basis of reason, because the one thing that cannot be reasoned with here on Earth, is a nihilist who has denied their conscience in favour of a pseudo-definition of man.

Each human being is entitled by international law to be self-governed under the universal law of human equality in order that each person may exercise their basic rights freely, such as the right to freedom of religion and belief. So, for this reason, atheism itself constitutes as a belief, because in order to reject a belief, then an alternate belief is required first, because that is what a belief is, a set of preferences that forms the basis of an opinion. Faith is thereby an integral part of the scientific method and law, because that is what a theory is, a belief or notion that is conjectured on the basis of an opinion or observation.

So, if there is one thing that science cannot refute on the basis of theory, then it is faith, because faith is established on the basis of a belief the same as any theory in science or law, and there are no protections under international law for any theoretical assertion that denies the human conscience for reasons relating to the correct interpretation of human rights and equality. So, for this reason, the New Atheist movement is in a de-facto relationship with the universal law of human equality due to the reinterpretation of conscience, which is a crime against humanity on the basis of equality. The New Atheist movement has attempted to define the human conscience as an animal instinct only, while international law has defined the human conscience as the sole basis for human rights and equality, which does not include any protections under the law for the reinterpretation of conscience.

The official reason why the New Atheist movement is in denial of the human conscience, is because the word, conscience, is a theological term from the Holy Bible, which cannot be replaced by a scientific or secular definition without destroying the lawful basis for human rights and equality. If religion is to be a saving grace for all of mankind, then a correct theology is also required when interpreting the law, because a legal obligation is defined by a moral obligation, which must derive itself from a system of morality that is by definition, universal.

Otherwise, there would be no official basis to define a legal obligation as universal by the law, and every human being has a lawful obligation to acknowledge one another as equal in rights on the basis of conscience, rather than science, because science is governed by ethics, which in turn, derives from a system of morality. So, in order for a law to be made universal in its interpretation, then a system of morality that is universal is also required, which cannot derive from secular science, because science is subject to ethics, which in turn, derives from a system of belief. Thus, a system of belief is required when interpreting the law, which automatically implies that a religion is required so that a standard for public morals can be applied to society, which is essential for the practice of law and order, because the fastest way to destroy law and order, is by a system of non-belief.

The purpose of the evolutionary theory is to apply a system of non-belief in relation to the Creator God of Genesis, which in turn, causes the individual to deny their conscience, which is a crime against humanity on the basis of equality. The New Atheist movement and the United States Supreme Court has attempted to remove the inalienable right of citizens to be defined as created human beings with a religious test in place that is designed to reject Biblical creation with an automatic dismissal on the basis of secular science. But, the problem with denying Biblical creation as a legal standard with an automatic dismissal, is that human freedom has been defined by theological terminology, rather than secular science.

Human freedom is measured by freedom of conscience, which is a religious liberty, rather than a secular ideal, which means that any reinterpretation of this freedom will lead to a return to human slavery by the denial of conscience. America is not a secular society that owes its allegiance to a secular government, because that is Communism. But rather, America is a Christian based democracy that is to scrutinize the secular government, which is why freedom of conscience, and freedom of the press are defined as inalienable.

The United States government has cited Secularism as their right and justification to deny Biblical creation to their students, which is a crime against humanity, because the ability to govern is not defined as a right, but rather, it is defined as a privilege according to the freedom of the voting constituency. So, the removal of Biblical creation from public education should only occur through a public referendum, because it is the people's liberty that is at stake here due to the evolutionary theory that challenges the lawful basis for self-governance under the common law. According to online legal resources, the common law, historically, has derived from Biblical theology, that is to say that the common law is to be interpreted by theological terminology, rather than secular science.

Historically, America is a Christian based democracy that is to scrutinize the secular government in order that the government should be a servant to the people, rather than a mechanism for human enslavement. The founding fathers greatest achievement by the introduction of inalienable rights and the rights of conscience derives from self-governance under the Biblical principles of Judeo-Christianity, rather than from Secular Humanism, which has now denied the Biblical premise for self-governance by the introduction of the evolutionary theory from society and law.

So, for the United States government to remove creation science from the public education system on the basis of Secularism, is in fact, an act of neutrality, because the United States Constitution, the Bill of Rights, and the Declaration of Independence was enacted in order for a Christian democracy to be protected by so that the voting constituency should be convicted by their conscience in regards to a moral obligation by the law to uphold the Constitution when called upon. The United States Constitution is to be interpreted by Biblical theology, because the lawful term, conscience, is a theological term, rather than a secular one.

If public school students in America are prevented from learning about their Creator, as defined by the Declaration of Independence under Constitutional law, then America will have nothing in which to combat Communism with as a political ideology, because all it will take for Communism to succeed, is for inalienable rights to fail. And the fastest way for inalienable rights to fail is for the rights of conscience to be denied on the basis of the evolutionary theory, which is why protecting the lawful definition of a human being as distinct from the animals, is by definition, an inalienable right.

According to United States Constitutional law under the First Amendment: "Congress shall make no law respecting the establishment of a religion, or, prohibiting its free exercise thereof." Yet the United States Supreme Court has done exactly that by banning creation science to public school students from the premise of Secular Humanism, which is by definition a religion according to the United States Supreme Court. The United States Supreme Court has acted as a religious authority, or institution, with a religious test in place that is designed to dismiss Biblical creation with an automatic dismissal from the premise of Secular Humanism, and has thereby invented a religion in opposition to the Constitutional definition of the Creator. When it is the Creator God of Genesis who is defined as self-evident in accordance with Constitutional law under the Declaration of Independence, where a person is defined as endowed by their Creator with certain inalienable rights, such as the rights of conscience.

In an often cited footnote to a 1961 decision, Torcaso v. Watkins, 367 U.S. 488, 495 No. 11 (1961), the Supreme Court listed Secular Humanism as one of several non-theistic religions practiced within the United States. Thus, Secular Humanism is by definition a religion on the basis that Secular Humanism attempts to define morality as an animal instinct, which cannot be justified legally due to the rights of conscience. The rights of conscience cannot derive from nature or the animals without defining a human being as property at the same time, which is entirely due to the lawful definition of property. Freedom of conscience is a religious liberty that grants protections for both Secular Humanism, as well as Biblical creation, yet it is Biblical creation as a legal standard that defines our human freedom by a correct interpretation of the human conscience.

The Declaration of Independence clearly outlines that the inalienable rights of the people have derived from the Creator God of Genesis, and it is the United States Constitution that grants protections for the Declaration of Independence, so that the teaching of a universal Creator God, (as from the Holy Bible) is Constitutionally protected as universal under the common law. The common law has derived from previously settled cases in that a verdict has been reached, such as the verdict as to whether man was created or not, which cannot derive from nature or the animals without defining man as property at the same time. The New Atheist movement has cited the separation of Church and State as their right and justification to deny their Creator, as from United States Constitutional law, whilst invoking a new religion in turn, such as Secular Humanism.

But, without a universal system of morality, then a law cannot be made universal in its interpretation, because a legal obligation is defined by a moral obligation, which in turn, requires a system of morality that is by definition, universal. And the one thing that atheism cannot offer is a system of morality that is by definition, universal, which is entirely due to the correct definition of atheism; Meaning no theism. So, in order to be consistent when interpreting United States Constitutional law, then a Creator God is a requirement in order to define both morality and inalienable rights as universal in their interpretation.

Secular Humanism attempts to define morality as having derived from nature and the animals, but if man is to look to the animals, or nature, as a source of morality, then there will be no obligation by the individual to carry out a lawful instruction, because nature, and the animals, are unaware of morality. Morality can only derive from moral teachings, which forms the basis for moral law. But if man is to look to the animal kingdom as a source of morality, then there will be no lawful basis for right and wrong, because the animals are without a sufficient level of conscience in order to receive a conviction of truth before the law, which is why no animal can be cross-examined under the common law.

Thus, it is the human conscience that is to be explained factually to students who are entering a legal system with their own experience, because morality and law can only derive from a source of conscience, which cannot be attributed to nature or the animals without defining man as property in turn. Morality is therefore above the law from a Biblical premise due to the rights of conscience, and the correct interpretation of the Creator under the common law, because the endowed human conscience derives from the Creator God of Genesis, rather than nature.

The idea of an infallible government derives from the principles of Communism, as set forth by Karl Marx, while the principles of self-governance under the common law derives from Judeo-Christian ethics, and Biblical theology. So, in order for a government to be defined as infallible when interpreting the law, then the Judeo-Christian faith must be overthrown from the premise of law, which is why protecting the lawful definition of conscience as self-evident, is by definition, an inalienable right. The Antisemitism that follows the evolutionary theory from the practice of Social Darwinism is a stain on the theory that cannot be washed away by the reinterpretation of conscience, nor can a secular standard for public education correctly inform the people of their inalienable rights.

Thus, under reasonable suspicion and reasonable grounds, there is sufficient cause for Class Action and litigation against the United States government to include the Constitutional definition of man within public education regardless of the religiosity of the legal definitions used, because the Administration has sworn a public oath to uphold the said Constitution, the Bill of Rights, and their Declaration of Independence by placing their right hand upon the Holy Bible so that the administration should be publicly liable, which is in accordance with judicial proceedings under the common law in criminal cases.

*Quotation: ————————————————
"Let it simply be asked where is the security for property, for reputation, for life, if the sense of religious obligation desert the oaths, which are the instruments of investigation in Courts of Justice? And let us with caution indulge the supposition that morality can be maintained without religion. Whatever may be conceded to the influence of refined education on minds of peculiar structure, reason and experience both forbid us to expect that national morality can prevail in exclusion of religious principle." - George Washington. Source: Presidential Farewell Address. (Documented September 17, in the year of our Lord, 1796).

Washington directly links religion and morality to private and public protection as the foundation of a civilized society. Washington writes, and he warns against, the idea that the nation's morality can be maintained without religion. So, the more secular society becomes as a result of evolution being taught by the State, the more freedoms the people will lose, because the rights of conscience derive from the Creator God of Genesis in accordance with Commonwealth theology under the common law, while Secular Humanism is in opposition to this universal principle due to the evolutionary definition of man. And it is for this reason above all other reasons that the theory of evolution must be challenged from the premise of law, because the dictates of the people must first be well informed of the dangers of the evolutionary theory in order to make an informed decision by the rights of conscience.

The purpose of the Commonwealth system is to unite the nations under a Judeo-Christian democracy so that an equality can exist between all nations, which was the crowning achievement by the forefathers of America, England, and the United Kingdom, which have a strong alliance on the basis of Christianity, which is of a common interest to the people, while secular science is not. This in turn requires a system of theology and morality that is universal in its interpretation, which is formerly known as the Commonwealth system or Christian alliance. A coalition force of democratic Christian nations shall endure through strife and retribution by their enemy, and shall never cease to deliver the word of God to the nations on the basis of conscience and equality.

Therefore, laws in society should reflect upon the universal principles for human equality from a Biblical interpretation in order to sustain a population peaceably under the common law, because international human rights legislation has acknowledged the human conscience as the sole basis for human rights and equality, and human freedom thereby. So, because the word, conscience, derives from the Holy Bible, and because the human conscience is legal proof of the human mind, soul or spirit, it will thereby serve as proof that mankind is to be self-governed under the Biblical principles of universal morality, because we owe our human equality to no one save the Creator Himself who has endowed each person with conscience and with rights.

LEGAL REFERENCES

*What is Commonwealth Theology?

Commonwealth Theology describes itself as a consolidation of mainstream Christian theologies that better conforms the relationship between the Christian Church and today's Israel to the relationship prophesied in the Old Testament and confirmed by the writings of the Apostolic Age Church. - Source: Wikipedia Encyclopedia (Commonwealth Theology).

*Christianity and the Common Law:

The history of the English common law, from which, the American, Australian and other common law jurisdictions originated, owes much to the influence of Christianity in its origins and development. It is indeed not possible to grasp the full development of the common law without first exploring its profound religious dimensions, and its motivating faith. Until at least the early 19th century, the common law was heavily influenced by Christian theology. This theology holds that there is a natural or divine reason for the existence of basic laws, and that these laws stand above human legislation, thus reflecting universal and unchangeable principles according, too which, everyone ought to live. - Source: The American Law Registry - Christianity and the Common Law. (Documented May, 1890).

*Article by the United Nations Human Rights Office of the High Commissioner - (Module 1 Freedom of Conscience):

Conscience shapes human choices and distinguishes human beings from other creatures. Freedom of conscience is imperative and larger than the freedom of religion or belief. It covers all ethics and values a human being cherishes, whether of religious nature or not. There are no admissible limitations to this freedom, as long as personal convictions are not imposed on others and do not harm them. The Universal Declaration of Human Rights and Equality (UDHR) is a milestone document in the history of human rights. Drafted by representatives with different legal and cultural backgrounds from all regions of the world, it set out, for the first time, fundamental human rights to be universally protected.

Our most fundamental responsibility is to stand up and act for everyone's right to free choices and particularly for everyone's freedom of thought, conscience, religion or belief. We affirm our commitment to the universal norms and standards, including Article 18 of the International Covenant on Civil and Political Rights, which does not permit any limitations whatsoever on the freedom of thought and conscience or on the freedom to have or adopt a religion or belief of one's choice. These freedoms, unconditionally protected by universal norms, are also sacred and inalienable entitlements according to religious teachings. - Source: The Universal Declaration of Human Rights and Equality (UDHR).

Article 1 of the UDHR:

All human beings are born free and equal in dignity and rights. They are endowed with reason and conscience and should act towards one another in a spirit of brotherhood.

Article 6 of the UDHR:

Everyone has the right to recognition everywhere as a person before the law.

Article 18 of the UDHR:

Everyone has the right to freedom of thought, conscience and religion. This right includes freedom to change his religion or belief, and freedom, either alone or in community with others and in public or private, to manifest his religion or belief in teaching, practice, worship and observance.

Word definitions used:

*Definition of (Commonwealth) by Oxford Languages:
  1. An independent country or community, especially a democratic republic.
  2. An international association consisting of the UK together with states that were previously part of the British Empire, and dependencies.

*Definition of (conscience) by Oxford Languages:
  A person's moral sense of right and wrong, viewed as acting as a guide to one's behaviour. Similar: moral sense, inner voice.

*Definition of (morality) by Oxford Languages:
  Principles concerning the distinction between right and wrong or good and bad behaviour. Similar: ethics.

*Definition of (law) by Oxford Languages:
  The system of rules which a particular country or community recognizes as regulating the actions of its members and which it may enforce by the imposition of penalties. Similar: rules.

*Definition of (ethics) by Oxford Languages:
  Moral principles that govern a person's behaviour or the conducting of an activity. Similar: morality.

*Definition of (psyche) by Oxford Languages:
  The human soul, mind, or spirit. Similar: soul.

*Definition of (person) by Oxford Languages:
  A human being regarded as an individual. Similar: living soul.

*Definition of (faith) by Oxford Languages:
  Complete trust or confidence in someone or something. Similar: belief.

*Definition of (purpose) by Oxford Languages:
  The reason for which something is done or created or for which something exists. Similar: motive.

*Definition of (creativity) by Oxford Languages:
The use of imagination or original ideas to create something; inventiveness. Similar: innovation.

*Definition of (Scientific Atheism) by Wikipedia Encyclopedia:
Scientific Atheism may refer to: Marxist–Leninist Atheism, a Communist doctrine and philosophical science formerly promoted in the Eastern Bloc. New Atheism, a 21st century atheist movement.

*Definition of (system) by Oxford Languages:
1. A set of things working together as parts of a mechanism or an interconnecting network; A complex whole. Similar: order.
2. A set of principles or procedures according to which something is done; An organized scheme or method. Similar: method.

*Definition of (system) by Wikipedia Encyclopedia:
A system is a group of interacting or interrelated elements that act according to a set of rules to form a unified whole. A system, surrounded and influenced by its environment, is described by its boundaries, structure and purpose and is expressed in its functioning. Systems are the subjects of study of systems theory and other systems sciences.

STATEMENT OF FAITH

Blessed is the Lord our God who has created the Heavens and the Earth, and has endowed all life with ability, but unto His own image the gift of conscience, with which, to reason from so that all may know His ways of truth and life. God has established all things by His word and has come down to mankind in bodily form in order that He may bear witness of the Gospel message of hope, for all who call upon the Lord shall be saved, and confession unto salvation is by the grace of God alone who has shown His mercy to all of mankind by the gift of His Spirit, for all are endowed with conscience for the purpose of human rights and equality, and equal justice thereby.

God is a righteous God and He has given mankind justice by the provision of His moral law, which is do unto others as you would have them do unto you, and, to love the Lord your God with all of your own being, for God has put an eternal merit on faith and love, for He has established all things with faith in love, so that all may know that God alone is their maker, and that God alone is truly good. The Father in Heaven has sent His only begotten Son into the world, and has brought the Gospel message of hope and salvation to the world from the Heavens above, and He alone was made sin for us and His body broken for the transgressions of the world.

The Earth was created void and without meaning until the Spirit of God breathed life into man, thereby establishing His covenant with man as Holy here on Earth. All living creatures were made by God who is, and who was, and who is to come, the Almighty, so that all living creatures are subject to His word, each according to their own ability, for the Lord has given each person a measure of faith, which is not to be forsaken, for the gift of the spirit is the gift of life. The glory of God is seen in all that He has made, so that we should have life everlasting in the kingdom to come, for the Lord is a good shepherd who will not lead His flocks astray. May the Spirit of the Lord be with you as you read this testimony, for the salvation of the Lamb is without number in the Heavens above, for He alone has conquered death by giving His life upon the cross of cavalry, and by His resurrection from the dead.

Therefore, He has been raised above the Heavens forevermore, and He alone will judge with all of His might on the day of wrath once the Shepherd comes like a thief in the night. We thank You dear Heavenly Father for Thy Gospel message of hope in Your Son, Jesus Christ, who alone shepherds the way to life everlasting by the confession of faith, and by the proclamation of the Gospel message of hope and salvation which You have prepared for all that love You forever. Amen

*Quotation: ──────────────────────────
Ephesians 2:11-18
Jew and Gentile Reconciled Through Christ:
Therefore, remember that formerly you who are gentiles by birth and called "uncircumcised" by those who call themselves "the circumcision" (which is done in the body by human hands) remember that at that time you were separate from Christ, excluded from citizenship in Israel and foreigners to the covenants of the promise, without hope and without God in the world. But now in Christ Jesus you who once were far away have been brought near by the blood of Christ.

For He Himself is our peace, who has made the two groups one and has destroyed the barrier, the dividing wall of hostility, by setting aside in His flesh the law with its commands and regulations. His purpose was to create in Himself one new humanity out of the two, thus making peace, and in one body to reconcile both of them to God through the cross, by which He put to death their hostility. He came and preached peace to you who were far away and peace to those who were near. For through Him we both have access to the Father by one Spirit. - Source: The Holy Bible.

A MESSAGE TO THE ATHEISTS

Atheism is defined as the denial or lack of belief in God, rather than the evidence for His non-existence. So, because atheism receives the same protections as a religion for reasons relating to freedom of belief, it will mean that atheism also requires physical evidence the same as any religious person. According to law, the strongest form of physical evidence there is derives from an eyewitness testimony, which becomes physical evidence when in writing so that no exhibit in a courtroom can be interpreted on its own.

Writing is a highly distinct physical trait because we apply meaning to the words used, which means that purpose derives by intention, which is the very reason why something random is without purpose or meaning until someone applies a meaning to it. So, because life has meaning due to the existence of love, and because meaning is always intentional, and therefore cannot derive at random, it will mean that life has a universal purpose regardless of anything an atheist might say to the contrary. Because if life has had meaning applied to it intentionally, which it has, then life is by definition a creation, otherwise, there would be no purpose to life, when life serves as the purpose for the universe itself, because without life, the universe would be void without meaning.

According to the definition of the word, purpose, anything that exists has a reason to exist, whether it be an object or a living creature, the principle remains the same, because purpose always derives by intention, and therefore, cannot derive at random. The meaning of life is to love one another as Christ Jesus has loved us, which gives all life purpose and meaning due to the existence of love. Therefore, God is not a magician, nor is He a murderer, because the meaning of life is to love one another as He loves us, which gives us hope in times of need, as well as purpose when faith is relied upon. So, I urge you to acknowledge your maker who is ready to receive you with thanksgiving's and earnest prayer, because God is not a kinsman unto hatred, but unto love instead.

The existence of hell is because morality exists, and the Biblical principles of universal morality cannot be broken without a negative consequence occurring, because this is sin. While obeying the Biblical principles for universal morality will produce a positive effect within an individual for others to benefit from in terms of morality, because a moral cause that is sufficient for everyone should always be determined by the universal rules for morality, rather than by opinion alone. So, because the most extreme offences require the most extreme forms of punishment, it will mean that hell is for real, because no man or woman has the right to deny the Biblical principles of universal morality as they are fixed the same as all physical laws are a constant, which gives stability and reliability to humanity and the system of the universe.

And yes, death is an issue that we all face, but there is no justification for death unless a law has been broken, whether it be a moral law or a physical law, the principle remains the same, as both moral law and physical laws are for sustaining the system that God has created. So, because the existence of morality is self-evident, then so also is moral law, and moral law is defined as being universal on the basis that each human being has been endowed with conscience in order to understand morality with, which means there is a universal lawgiver. And it is for this reason that we have laws regarding the sexual conduct of individuals, because no one is free to do as they feel, sexually, for reasons relating to morality; Meaning that there is a universal standard in place concerning marriage, which in turn, defines gay marriage as amoral, and therefore, unlawful.

The Biblical principles of universal morality is not only the ethical standard for right and wrong, but also, the Biblical principles of universal morality is the sole basis for individual human freedom, because freedom of conscience is the basis for freedom of thought and belief, and the human conscience is defined as having derived from the Creator, rather than the animals. So, for this reason, human beings are to be self-governed under the Biblical principles of universal morality, rather than by instincts alone, because it is illogical to deny the existence of universal morality when the existence of the human conscience is self-evident. And God alone will decide who is worthy of rest for their faith in Him, and who is unworthy of rest for denying the Spirit of the Lord His rest, and the Lord does rest on the truth of a matter, and none other.

According to the Holy Bible, God is the source of moral law and of love, and the fulfilment of the law is found in the fulfilment of love, so that faith in love is equal to faith in God, for Christ Jesus did not come to Earth to execrate God's wrath on mankind, but rather, He came in order to reveal the love of the Father, because it is love that will conquer evil in due time, rather than hatred, and it is according to faith that love will succeed.

So, all that is required of a person, is to have faith in love, for the love of God has overcome the world through His Son, Jesus Christ, so that all who believe in Him are justified by their faith, having accepted God's love toward them, because it is by faith that we understand the things of God to be true according to the Holy Spirit, and by reason of confession and belief. So, we know by faith that love is justice to the downtrodden, because it is love that shows compassion, and it is compassion that the people require in their darkest hour. May faith preside within you as you preside within His mind in accordance with the love you have received by the will of His Spirit, and by the word of the Gospel message of hope that sets us free from the fear of the things to come.

*Quotation: ──────────────────────────
Romans 5:8-11
Reconciliation through Christ:
God demonstrates His own love toward us, in that while we were still sinners, Christ died for us. Much more then, having now been justified by His blood, we shall be saved from wrath through Him. For if when we were enemies, we were reconciled to God through the death of His Son, much more, having been reconciled, we shall be saved by His life; And not only that, but we also rejoice in God through our Lord Jesus Christ, through whom, we have now received the reconciliation. - Source: The Holy Bible.

A PRAYER FOR THE ATHEIST

May the Lord bless you and may the Lord shine on you even though you reproach Him who alone lives forever above the heights of the Heavens. The Lord is a Good Shepherd and He will not lead you astray. His love is kind and His mercies are endless toward those who do not take His worthy name in vain. Let not your heart be troubled, for you are important to Him, and you are a special creation whom He has loved by the giving of His spirit to those around you with great joy that you may know His favour is for them who believe in Him.

For the word of the Lamb has come down to you that you may open your eyes and see with your heart the loving grace that is of the Father and of the Spirit in order that you may understand that He has loved you with all of His heart. God has known you since before you were born and He has given you life here on Earth that you may share in His good word with faith from above. I pray thee that you will turn from your wicked ways and find Him who alone protects the ways of the meek, for the Lord is their Shepherd, and He alone is their peace.

May you find forgiveness of sin for the haughty eyes of men, and their lust for power, God hates. So, be of good cheer this day for the love of the Father has come forward to you before you meet Him who will hold you to your word, as you have held others to their own. May peace be upon you this hour, and may the light of the Gospel message flood your mind with godly wisdom and with the power of prayer, for the love of the Father in Heaven is upon those who acknowledge Him as their Lord and Saviour, for He alone shepherds the way to life everlasting. May faith preside within you as you preside within His mind, for the Lord watches over all things and is ready to receive you with thanksgiving's and earnest prayer.

In the name of Jesus His Son, I pray that you will find it in your heart to forgive Him who has weaved you together from the womb and has placed within you a measure of faith that you should find in Him a loving Saviour and a caring Father, for the Spirit of Hope yearns for you to know Him as the Lord your God who has delivered you this prayer today through the kindness of His eternal Spirit, and by the grace of His merciful heart. In Jesus' worthy name, please forgive your enemies today, and God will have mercy on your soul, for the condemnation of the wicked will be fulfilled in accordance with God's love for the meek. Amen

CHAPTER 1

Systems theory

A SYSTEM IS DEFINED BY ITS PARAMETERS WHICH ARE THE rules that govern the system, and rules are always inferred having derived from a method initially, so that the amount of functionality within a system is specific, rather than random. The purpose of systems theory is to analyse existing systems in order to discover how each system relates to one another for the purpose of identification and comparison so that a system can be assessed for weaknesses. No system can self-emerge from materials alone because a set of parameters in place that act according to a set of rules is evidence of creativity. While any group of primary mechanisms within an operational system must rely on an overall method to be in place in order for the system to be integrated.

There are no physical examples of a group of primary mechanisms within an operational system having derived by pure chance, because a group of primary mechanisms within an operational system must be pre-specified according to an overall plan. Otherwise, the individual mechanisms cannot be combined into a single mechanism called a system. An irreducibly complex system is where each primary mechanism within the system has a designated function, so that the removal or failure of any individual primary mechanism will result in a total systems failure. And every operational system has a level of irreducible complexity, because all operational systems are comprised of a group of primary mechanisms.

An orderly system cannot occur at random over time, because an orderly system will always be governed by a procedure in place that derives from the application of a method, which is the only causality there is for a cycle in place that is both repeatable under observation, as well as predictable under demonstration, in accordance with the law of probability.

The law of probability applies to any sequence or series of events, whether numerical or otherwise. And it is a rule from the law of probability that anything random will remain random unless a method is applied, which then defines the process as a procedure due to the application of a method. In order for a group of events to be relative to each other, resulting in an algorithm or procedure, then a method is required first, because that which is relative is also that which is specific. So, in order for a group of events to be predictable in accordance with the law of probability, then a cycle is required, so that anything that is operating according to a cycle in place, is by definition, predictable. While that which is random is by definition, unpredictable, due to the lack of a cycle in place that is repeatable under observation.

So, anything that is occurring according to a cycle in place, is by definition, specific, while anything that is outside of a cycle is by definition, unpredictable. And it is for the purpose of a cycle that systems exist, because anything that is occurring according to a cycle in place, is by definition reliable. Any system that is operating according to a cycle in place cannot occur at random over time, because any system with a cycle in place, is by definition, specific. And that which is specific is the diametric opposite of that which is random; Meaning that specifics cannot occur at random over time.

So, the relationship between systems in systems theory is relying on each system to be relative to another, resulting in an integrated system whereby everything is relative to physical laws, because physical laws are by definition a system on the basis that each physical law is relative to the next, resulting in an irreducibly complex system whereby the removal of one physical law will result in an immediate systems failure. This principle is a universal principle that applies not only to a thermodynamic system, but also, morality, because morality derives from moral law, which in turn, gives order and stability to the system of the universe, as well as law and order.

The amount of energy for an operational system must derive from outside of the system itself prior to its designated function, and if the arrangement is not pre-specified to ensure the functionality of the system is going to work, then the energy input will be wasted, which reduces the level of efficiency a system has over time, rather than increasing a system's level of efficiency in a matter of time. So, it will always be a method that initiates the process for a systems formation, because there is a step-by-step procedure in place that cannot occur at random.

A procedure is defined as the succession of one event after another according to a series of events that are relative to each other, which can also be referred to as a method due to the presence of an algorithm. An algorithm is any process or set of rules that are to be followed in series which gives rise to a procedure or sequence that is used for solving a particular problem, or for establishing a typical system or cycle.

For example: The human body is a biomechanical system that is comprised of numerous primary mechanisms that work together in synchrony to form a complex whole, such as the nervous system, the skeletal system, and the muscular system just to name a few. No individual system within the human body can specify for the body's system as a working whole, which means that each individual system must be incorporated according to an overall plan. Otherwise, there would be nothing to combine each of the primary systems into what's known as a complex system. A complex system is any system that is incorporated according to multiple primary systems that combine to form a single mechanism or system.

The human body is also divided up into left and right according to the placement of the limbs and the internal structures, such as the skeletal system and the organs, which must be predetermined in order for the left side of the body to be compared with the right side in terms of a single system. The reason that the body has a left hand along with a right hand, is because a method has been applied in order to give the body functionality. The genetic instructions for a right hand cannot specify for the instructions needed for a left hand, and neither can the left rib cage specify for the right rib cage.

So, in order for either one to occur, then a set of specifics are required according to an overall plan before either one has any survival value whatsoever. The amount of energy the body requires must also derive from outside of the body prior to its designated function as a result of food and oxygen intake, which must be pre-specified or pre-determined before the system of the body can begin its growth cycle, which is evidence of creativity due to a set of parameters in place that act as a standard for biological consumption.

According to Oxford Languages, a parameter is defined as: 1) "A numerical or other measurable factor forming one of a set that defines a system or sets the conditions of its operation. Similar: specifications." While the term, specifications, refers to: 1) "An act of identifying something precisely, or, of stating a precise requirement." So, that which is governed by a cycle in place, such as the circulation system within the human body, is also that which is governed by a set of parameters, because any series of actions that are repeating themself according to a cycle in place that is predictable, is by definition, specific. A system is defined by its parameters, which are by definition, inferred, because any set of actions in series that are specific in relation to each other, resulting in a cycle or procedure, are by definition, planned.

The growth of an organism into maturity is governed by a cycle that is both repeatable under observation, and is therefore predictable under demonstration, which means that the growth of an organism into maturity is by definition, specific. And that which is specific is also that which has been specified; Meaning that living systems show evidence of design. The growth cycle of an organism occurs as a predictable pattern, so that the pattern development of an organism into maturity is occurring according to a predictable cycle, which is evidence of a system. So, because the pattern development of a particular organism occurs as a sequence, and because each interval within the sequence is relative to the next resulting in a life cycle or system, it will mean automatically that a method is involved due to the presence of a procedure that, is by definition, predictable, which cannot occur at random over time in accordance with the law of probability, because that which is predictable, is by definition, orderly.

The amount of oxygen intake that's required for the body to function efficiently must have been pre-specified according to an overall plan, otherwise, the system of the body would immediately begin a shutdown procedure in order to conserve oxygen. So, for this reason, the body must rely on an algorithm to be in place in order to set the parameters needed for energy storage and consumption, because energy consumption cannot begin without a supply of stored energy first, and stored energy cannot be regulated without the need for consumption, so both are thereby operating according to a method in place that is by definition, integrated.

Any system that is integrated cannot occur at random in accordance with the law of relativity, because that which is relative, is by definition, specific. The specifications for any living system requires an overall plan, because in order to integrate a system, then a method is required first. The oxygen levels within the body must also remain at a particular level or the system will automatically shut down in order to conserve oxygen, which means that there is a set of parameters in place that could not have occurred at random, because the parameters for breathing are specific in relation to the hearts rhythm, as well as oxygen storage and consumption.

A living organism that survives on either oxygen or carbon dioxide cannot begin its growth cycle unless there is a source of oxygen and carbon dioxide first, which in turn, derives from living organisms, which means that life could not have begun as a single organism. The evolutionary theory assumes that life began as a bacteria, such as an RNA virus, or as an autotroph, and has slowly evolved over millions of years into a more complex biological form. But the problem with this theory is that an RNA virus cannot self-replicate without the need for a host cell first in order to utilize its DNA.

So, life could not have begun as an RNA virus, because a DNA template is required first in order for RNA synthesis to occur. And life could not have begun as an autotroph, because an autotroph manufactures its own food through photosynthesis and by carbon dioxide absorption, while oxygen is a by-product of this process. Photosynthesis converts carbon dioxide and water into oxygen and glucose so that the organism can use glucose as a food source whilst disposing of waste products like oxygen. So, because oxygen is a waste product of photosynthesis, while carbon dioxide is a requirement, it will mean that life could not have begun as an autotroph, because there is no way for an autotroph to engage the process of oxygen absorption, which would be required in order to convert an autotroph into an organism that requires oxygen respiration.

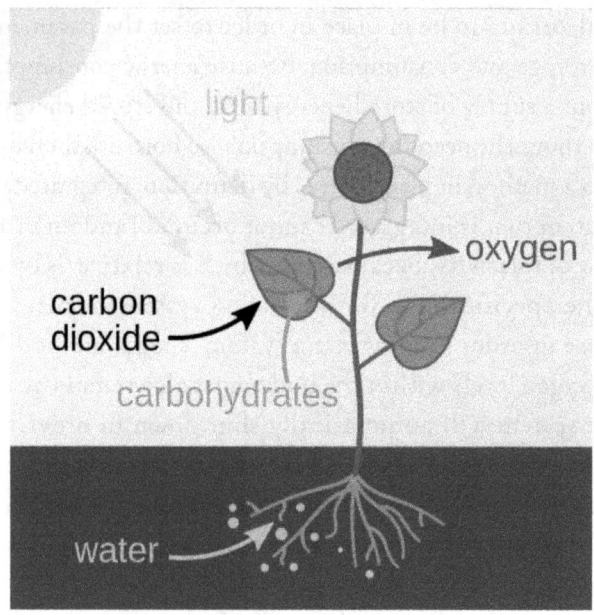

(Above) Illustration of photosynthesis.
Source: Wikipedia Encyclopedia.

According to the correct definitions in use, adenosine triphosphate (ATP) is the primary source of energy for cellular respiration involving oxygen storage and consumption. The structure of ATP is a nucleoside triphosphate consisting of a nitrogenous base known as adenine, which is a ribose sugar or carbohydrate, and three serially bonded phosphate groups. So, there are essentially three parts to the ATP molecule which are: 1) Adenine nucleoside, which is a base molecule or sugar. 2) Ribose, which is a five-carbon sugar found in RNA known as ribonucleic acid. And 3) Triphosphate, which is a three stage bonded phosphate or group, hence the prefix, "tri" meaning three. ATP is often referred to as the energy source of oxygen respiration and can be compared to storing fat cells within the human body. ATP is primarily used to store energy for future cellular reactions, or it can be used to burn energy during oxygen respiration.

So, because an autotroph cannot produce mitochondria, which is essential for oxygen respiration, it will mean that an autotroph cannot convert oxygen into carbon dioxide via a citric acid cycle, also known as the Krebs cycle, or, the tricarboxylic acid cycle. The oxidation process uses enzymes and molecular oxygen for its reactions. However, the fermentation process does not use molecular oxygen for its reactions, and it only uses enzymes. The process of fermentation from pyruvate fermentation results in the formation of lactic acids, which then leads to a breakdown of materials, rather than a build-up of organization. When two low-energy waste products occur during oxygen respiration, such as H_2O and CO_2, the H_2O will act as a radiator liquid in order to exchange heat with its surroundings the same as sweating from your forehead, because as oxygen respiration occurs during a Krebs cycle, oxygen is burnt, which then expels CO_2 as a by-product, as well as H_2O.

The CO_2 that is released during a Krebs cycle then becomes a source of respiration for an autotroph resulting in a continuous breathing cycle between oxygen dependent organisms and autotrophs. So, because the breathing process between an oxygen dependent organism and an autotroph is occurring according to a cycle in place, it will mean that a method has been applied due to the presence of a procedure that is both repeatable under observation, as well as predictable under demonstration. And anything that is repeatable under observation, as well as predictable under demonstration, is by definition, orderly, due to the presence of a procedure or cycle. A thermodynamic cycle that obeys a procedure cannot occur at random over time in accordance with the law of probability, because a thermodynamic process begins as orderly, and will therefore decline into disorder over time in accordance with the second law of thermodynamics. The second law of thermodynamics applies to all thermodynamic processes, which is a law in science that forbids the formation of an orderly process from occurring at random over time. This principle is known as entropy law.

A thermodynamic instructional system, such as DNA RNA transcription, cannot self-improve over time due to entropy law, and the problem of aging. Time and chance on a thermodynamic instructional system is equal to entropy, because an instructional system cannot self-improve, as the specifics for the arrangements must derive from planning so that biological entropy is equal to aging, which automatically results in accumulative mutations over time within an instructional system. Entropy is defined as being the unavailability of a system's thermal energy that is wasted due to a lack of order within the system, and is interpreted as the degree at which a system will decline into disorder from a state of ordered complexity.

An instructional system cannot self-improve over time, because parameters are by definition, inferred, and are therefore, specific. So, for this reason, entropy law not only applies to a thermodynamic system, but also, entropy applies to all instructional systems by reason of the fact that no instructional system can be self-existing. Thus, living systems show evidence of design, because all living systems are instructional systems, which in turn, defines a reproductive system as an instructional system that incorporates a set of parameters that are by definition, inferred.

According to the principles of thermodynamics, all living systems are defined as open systems that exchange energy and matter with their surroundings, and all living systems are instructionally based from their DNA, rather than chemically based from the elements alone. So, by definition, all life has been inferred, because the only way for an instructional system to occur, is by the action of creativity, either directly or indirectly, and there are no examples of instructions occurring at random over time, because an instruction is by definition, specific. DNA RNA transcription is a thermodynamic instructional system, because the process of transcription is chemically based that incorporates a proofreading mechanism to govern the method of transcribing from DNA to RNA, which also limits the amount of mutations that can occur at random, thereby making the system efficient.

So, the more efficient a system is, the more specifics there are in place in order to conserve thermal energy, which means that specificity is equal to efficiency. While inefficiency during a thermodynamic process is interpreted as the degree of disorder within a system due to a loss of heat during a thermal reaction that was unused to complete a specific task. So, in order for a thermodynamic system to utilize the energy input, then there must first be a set of specifics in place that act as a set of parameters, or the energy input is wasted due to a lack of order within the system. This means that ordered complexity derives from taking rules into account, (such as physical laws) by way of inference in order to generate the specifics needed, which in turn, sets the parameters for a system's operation.

A common argument by evolutionists is that entropy can be reversed, because it is entropy law that stands in the way of ordered complexity deriving at random. And an example that an evolutionist will use in order to describe entropy reverse would be a simple snowflake that stores ordered complexity in the form of a geometric shape. Evolutionary theorists assume that the process of entropy can be reversed, because a snowflake has ordered complexity that supposedly derives from disordered complexity via a natural process. Yet the process by which a snowflake stores thermal energy is at subzero temperatures with a maximum state of disorder occurring when the water vapour has frozen. Entropy is at its maximum state of disorder when the temperature unit reaches absolute zero, because in order for entropy to be offset, then thermal energy must be conserved. Residual entropy is the difference in entropy between a non-equilibrium state and crystal state of a substance close to absolute zero. So, in other words, residual entropy is that which is remaining before a gas or a liquid reaches thermal equilibrium, which is defined as non-equilibrium.

This principle concerning residual entropy is a part of the third law of thermodynamics, which states that the complexity of a thermodynamic system at thermal equilibrium is in a state of maximum entropy, or maximum disorder, so that any snowflake which is frozen in its shape is thereby conserved in a state that is approaching maximum disorder. So, because a snowflake is in a state of residual entropy according to the principles of entropy law, it will mean that the ordered complexity of water approaches a maximum state of disorder when frozen into an ice-crystal. Thus, the entropy of a snowflake cannot be reversed unless the snowflake melts, because non-equilibrium approaches a state of maximum disorder when a liquid or gas approaches a constant temperature below zero. And in any event, the formation of a snowflake is a far-fetched example when describing a biological process that is also subject to entropy law.

The entropy of a living system is equal to the amount of thermal energy that is wasted compared to that which is used by a complex mechanism, which is why entropy cannot be reversed as evolutionists have claimed, because once the process has occurred, there is no way to reverse the process that has already occurred. The only way to offset the rate of entropy within a thermodynamic system, is by the application of a method, whereby a mechanism that has been pre-specified can be put into place in order to conserve thermal energy into the conversion of useful work. This means that entropy is a constant unless a method is applied, because the conversion of thermal energy into useful work must first be designated by an internal mechanism that has been pre-specified according to an overall plan. This principle constitutes as evidence for design, because the complexity of any given system must always be inferred according to a set of rules that acts as a set of parameters, thereby establishing the limitations of a system at work.

The purpose of entropy is to expel thermal energy in order to regulate a system's internal temperature, so that entropy is the result of ordered complexity, rather than the cause. The thermodynamic efficiency of any given system will always be due to the amount of thermal energy that was conserved during a thermodynamic reaction, whether chemical, mechanical, or biomechanical, the principle remains the same, because ordered complexity is relative to design, while disordered complexity is relative to random decay. This means that random decay can only occur once a thermodynamic system is established first, only then can something random occur by definition of the fact that something orderly was occurring to begin with, which is self-explanatory.

A second common argument by evolutionists concerning entropy law, is that the entropy of the Earth will decrease by the application of sunlight, which is argued for three main reasons. First; Because sunlight provides warmth in the form of thermal energy, and is thereby, conserved. Second; Because all plant life relies on sunlight in order for growth to occur, which is essential for efficiency. And thirdly; Because sunlight is also potential in energy for electrical power use and energy transformation in accordance with the third law of thermodynamics involving energy transformation. But what the evolutionist has not taken into account is the second law of thermodynamics, which states that the entropy of an isolated system remains at a constant, and the Earth, sun, moon, and stars all exist inside of an isolated system with its internal temperature reaching absolute zero.

This means that entropy of the sun and the Earth remains at a constant due to the dispersion of heat throughout space, which is reflected by the Earth's atmosphere back into outer-space. So, because the Earth is reflecting solar radiation, it will mean that the Earth is in a state of entropy due to a loss of thermal energy by the sun, which cannot be reversed once the process has already occurred. Thus, entropy reverse is entirely theoretical on the basis that once an action has occurred, there is no way to reverse the process due to the forward motion of time.

According to the second law of thermodynamics, all thermodynamic systems tend toward disorder over time; Meaning that disorderly states are the most probable. So, in order for sunlight to be conserved, then a mechanism is required first, otherwise, the thermal energy is wasted and will increase in disorder over time, rather than increasing in ordered complexity in a matter of time. And the Earth does act as a complex mechanism in order to conserve thermal energy for the purpose of energy consumption, which means that the Earth must have been created before the sun, because the purpose of the sun is to provide warmth to the Earth, and not the other way around.

For example: The purpose of a gas heater in your bedroom is to provide warmth to yourself, but without yourself, then the heat is wasted. So, in order for a gas heater in your bedroom to serve a purpose, then a person is required first, otherwise, the heat is wasted. This principle implies that a complex mechanism is required first before any thermal energy can be conserved for a particular purpose. And it is a universal rule that everything has a purpose, which implies automatically that everything was created by definition of the word, purpose.

According to Oxford Languages; "The reason for which something is done or created, or for which something exists," defines the word, purpose. So, in other words, all things have derived by intention, otherwise, the universe would be void without meaning. In the book of Genesis chapter 1, God created the oceans on day one, and the Spirit of God hovered over the face of the deep and the Earth was void without meaning. While on day 6, God breathed life into man and he became a living soul. Thus, life serves as a purpose for the universe itself, otherwise, the Earth would be void without meaning. The Holy Bible also states in chapter 1 that the sun and moon were created on day 4, while the Earth was created on day 1. Thus, the Holy Bible has taken a thermodynamic system into account by the interpretation of a procedure that is both logical, as well as orderly, in terms of process.

The purpose of living systems is applicable to the ecosystem, whereby all living systems are incorporated into a more larger system, and the smaller the mechanisms are within the system, the more complex the overall system is, because ordered complexity within a system is also equal to data compression, and all methods for data compression rely on planning in order to generate the specifics needed. When we think of compressed data storage, we tend to think in-line of computing, but the amount of data storage capacity within DNA is equal to 215 petabytes worth of data per gram, which is equal to 215,000 1 terabyte hard-drives worth of storage capacity within 1 drop of DNA. This means that DNA is the most compressed form of data storage there is known to man, and it is the level of compression for the data stored that makes DNA the most complex instructional system there is, so nothing can be compared to DNA in terms of its physical complexity.

The information within DNA is stored as an encoded sequence that is made up by four chemical bases: adenine (A), guanine (G), cytosine (C), and thymine (T). So, because DNA coding can store up to 215 petabytes worth of data per gram, in sequence, it will mean that DNA has been pre-arranged according to an overall plan. Otherwise, the sequence would have to occur by chance, and the longer the sequence is, the more times it must be multiplied by itself in order to gain a probability factor for the likelihood that the sequence could occur by chance. The law of probability applies to any sequence or series of events that are specific in relation to each other, such as the word, create, in relation to the word, Creator, which is also applicable to biology as well, because a genetic sequence for a protein must be specific in relation to other proteins, or they will not combine to form a functional cell.

A cell is made-up by multiple proteins that each have a specific function within the system of a cell, and are thereby integrated according to an overall plan or design so that each protein is working in conjunction with other proteins in order to engage the process of protein manufacture and genomic replication. So, because each of the proteins that make-up a living cell are specific in relation to each other, it will mean automatically that a method has been applied in order to combine each of the proteins into a working cell that is integrated. The human genome stores all of the genetic instructions needed to form a complete human body, which cannot be the result of time and chance, because all of the usable instructions within the genome are specific in relation to each other, and therefore, cannot derive at random over time in accordance with the law of probability.

The human genome comprises of approximately 3.2 billion nucleotides of DNA, which must be multiplied by 2 in order to include both the DNA sequence and the RNA sequence, which is equal to 6.4 billion chemical letters in total. The odds of the human genome forming by mere chance over time has been equated by mathematicians as being a statistical impossibility, because when you multiply 6.4 billion with itself in order to gain a probability factor, the odds turn out to be 1 in 4.096e+19. The number (e), also known as Euler's number, is a mathematical constant approximately equal to 2.71828 which can be characterized in many ways. It is the base of the mathematical logarithms and it is also the limit of (n). (1 + 1/n)n is characterized by (n) and the number (n) approaches infinity (∞) for numbers according to the principles of mathematics. So, by following the rules of probability, the odds of the human genome forming by mere chance over time is a statistical impossibility, because the only way to overcome these odds in terms of probability, is for a method to be applied.

For example: Joan Ginther is an American four-time lottery winner, while the odds of winning one U.S lottery game is equal to 1 in 18 septillion. But the fact that she has earned a PhD from Stanford University as a statistician means automatically that she has applied her knowledge in relation to probability, and has therefore applied a system in order to increase the likelihood of winning, because when you multiply 18 septillion by 4 in order to gain a probability factor for the overall event to occur, the odds turn out to be 1 in 7.2e+25. If a person is caught cheating during a game of cards then it is usually because they have an unfair advantage, which is most often exposed when a group of events occur that are highly unlikely; Meaning that the law of probability will always catch a person out at some point in time.

So, in order for a group of events to occur that are specific in relation to the next, then a method is required, otherwise, there is no way to increase the likelihood of the overall event occurring. So, the law of probability is mathematical evidence for supernatural creativity, because there is no natural process that can cause a thermodynamic instructional system, such as DNA RNA transcription, to occur at random, which means definitively that a method has been applied to life. There are only two possibilities for the existence of life; Either life is self-existing, or life was created, but because the likelihood of the human genome forming by chance over time has been equated as being a mathematical impossibility, it will mean automatically that life was created, because anything that has had a method applied to it, is by definition a creation. The only example of a causality for instructions that one can provide derives from the action of creativity, because an instructional system must be pre-specified according to a set of rules in order for an instruction to convey a meaning.

The only way in existence to increase the likelihood of an instructional system occurring is by the application of a method, because in order for an instruction to proceed, then a method of communication is required first. This principle implies that a standard for communication is required first before an instructional sequence can proceed, otherwise, the instructions received cannot be interpreted. Thus, a send and receive mechanism is required first the same as a standard for communication is required at the beginning of the process.

The evolutionary idea that a living system can self-emerge over time from chemicals alone via a natural process is without a reasonable explanation from science, because a natural process will always be limited to the number of specifics there are in place to define the process with. While any increase in the number of specifics that a process has will always be the result of a method having been applied, which in turn, defines the process as a procedure. While a random process will always be according to a set of variables within a system, otherwise, there would be no causality for a random event.

In order for a random process to occur, then there needs to be an orderly system in place first in order to define what the random process is, otherwise, there would be no way to define that which is orderly. This means that systems were in place before any random event could have occurred, because a random process will always be the result of a method in place, either directly or indirectly, rather than the cause of one. So for this reason, a system is referred to as a method or a procedure, and there is definitively no other causality for a method or a procedure apart from the action of creativity, because both a method and a procedure are by definition, specific. In order for a random event to occur, then there needs to be a system in place first that is operating according to plan, only then can something abnormal occur by reason of the fact that something normal was occurring to begin with.

A natural process is simply the normal workings of a system in place, while a random process is any variable within a typical system, such as a random fluctuation. So, in order for a random event to occur, then a system is required first, otherwise, there would be no causality for a random fluctuation or variation. The proper definition of perfect, is any system that is working according to plan, rather than because of its level of efficiency, because no system is ever 100% efficient. And the reason that no system is ever 100% efficient, is because a system is defined by a set of parameters that are subject to fluctuation (or change) in accordance with the number of variables there are within the system, because that is what a random variable is; A random fluctuation within a system.

For example: Linear and angular momentum are defined as a physical law in science because they act according to a set of rules that are universal under demonstration and interpretation. In physics, linear and angular momentum are equal to a set of parameters that can alternate, or fluctuate, from one to the other. Such as a particle or object in motion that comes into contact with another particle or object resulting in a change of direction or rotation. This principle is not only a law in physics known as energy transformation, but also, it is a principle in law concerning morality, because laws will fluctuate depending on the situation resulting in a consequence that is unpredictable until a verdict is reached, thereby setting a legal precedent or premise. This means that both moral law and physical laws give definition to reality in terms of a single system that is both orderly, as well as specific due to the presence of rules.

An operational system will always be subject to physical laws that act as a set of rules, or parameters, that governs a thermodynamic system as a working whole, and, sets its limitations. Parameters are never by random chance, because they must always be inferred the same as any set of rules. So, for this reason, no system that is by definition orderly can derive at random, because an orderly system is defined by a set of parameters that are equal to a set of rules, and the level of order that a system has (whether it be a thermodynamic system, or a system of law and order) will always be equal to the number of rules that have been taken into account, such as physical laws, or moral law, which in turn, sets the parameters for a system's operation.

An instructional sequence in place will always be the evidence of creativity having been applied, because an instruction is equal to a message or a command, hence the term, messenger RNA (mRNA). Any set of instructions can be interpreted into words, because there is a sequence in place that has a meaning applied to it in order to convey a message, and the arrangements for the sequence must be pre-specified according to a standard for communication just as words do in order for the sequence to convey a meaning, which in turn, defines the sequence as orderly. So, it is never the sequence itself that defines the sequence as orderly, but rather, it is the standard in place for communication to occur that defines whether the sequence is orderly or not according to a set of rules that act as a set of parameters.

For example: The definition of a standard is the extent to which something is orderly, which means that it is the standard in place for communication to occur that defines a word or method as orderly. But in order for a standard to be defined as orderly, then a method is required first, such as the English alphabet system which acts as a standard or method of communication, while English grammar acts as a set of parameters. So, because a method or standard in place will always be inferred according to a set of rules so that a set of parameters can be established, it will mean that all instructional systems are by definition inferred, rather than deriving from materials alone due to the presence of an instructional command.

And the rule with any set of instructions, (such as genetic instructions) is that they must derive from a source of communication, whether binary or not, because in order for an instruction to convey a meaning, then the instructions must be pre-specified according to a set of rules that act as a standard for communication to occur the same as words do. So, because an instructional system of communication derives from a method, and because all methods of communication derive from a standard in place, it will mean that all systems of communication have derived from a source of conscience (word).

*Quotation: ————————————————————
John 1:1-5
The Word Became Flesh:
In the beginning was the Word, and the Word was with God, and the Word was God. He was in the beginning with God. All things were made through Him, and without Him was not anything made that was made. In Him was life, and the life was the light of men. The light shines in the darkness, and the darkness has not overcome it. - Source: The Holy Bible.

In order to speak then a voice is a requirement, yet no animal has a voice, but rather, they have a distinct calling sound, because the ability to speak derives from an inner voice or conscience, and the ability to reason, while the ability to obey derives from understanding. So, for this reason, we as human beings act as a voice for the animals, rather than the animals acting as a voice for human beings. Thus, the ability to speak derives from an inner voice or conscience, and because speaking is equal to a language, it will mean that the human conscience has derived from a source of word, because that is what the human conscience is: An inner voice or word. And there is no other causality for human speech apart from a source of conscience, because the ability to speak requires the ability to reason, and the ability to reason derives from the ability to ask questions in the form of a language or word.

So, for this reason, one cannot argue that the human ability to speak has derived from the animals, because, A) The ability to speak requires the ability to reason and ask questions. B) Because an animal has no understanding of morality, which is what the human conscience is for. And C) The ability to speak derives from a source of word, rather than a mating call by the animals. When Jesus said to Peter in the Gospel of Matthew 16:23 "Get behind Me Satan," He was: A) Referring to Satan, rather than Peter. B) He was referring to Satan through Peter. And C) He was giving an order. So, from the Scriptures we find the introduction of a mystery, which is in relation to a spiritual dimension that all human beings are a captive to whether they desire it or not, because the ability to speak derives from a source of conscience, rather than from materials alone.

The human ability to ask questions means automatically that each human being has been endowed with reason and with conscience, because the ability to ask questions derives from a method of reasoning, which is in accordance with the first Article of the Universal Declaration of Human Rights and Equality which states that: "All human beings are born free and equal in dignity and rights. They are endowed with reason and conscience and should act towards one another in a spirit of brotherhood." So, from the Universal Declaration of Human Rights, we find that the ability to reason derives from a source of conscience, rather than from the animals.

The human ability to reason and ask questions is a unique trait that cannot be defined as a physical trait, because the ability to reason derives from a source of conscience, and nowhere else. So, it is for this reason that there is no clinical basis for any psychiatric disorder, because the conscience is a non-physical aspect of the human mind called the psyche or soul. The ability of the human mind to cope with psychological stress derives from having a strong conscience, because it is your reasoning ability that is able to apply a method of psychology in turn, and therefore, a system. A system of language is equal to a form of communication, and we interpret a language in the form of an instruction, message, or command.

A language is specifically for conveying a message or an instruction, while communication is specifically for signalling. Instructions rely on a standard to be in place for the information to be interpreted by, while data is information stored, and the data stored will always represent some kind of arrangement, whether naturally occurring or planned, and it is the formation of the materials into an arrangement that provides the information stored. So, information is always found in the arrangement of something, but instructions will always display intent, because instructions are not only passive, but they're also active as well through communication. And this is why rocks do not communicate, but we do interpret data from rocks that we convert into words for our own understanding. But if instructions were found in rocks, such as a carving with inscriptions for example, then we can assume automatically that it has derived from someone, rather than just somewhere?

Animals communicate with each other in many ways, but no animal can invent a language, because all forms of language have derived from a source of conscience or word, rather than from the animals. When an instructional sequence is given, it is called the directive or order, and when instructions are stored they are called passive instructions, and it is when the instructions become a directive that an action will occur, but the directive will always be sent, either directly or indirectly from a source of conscience. The human conscience is the only thing we have for inventing words so that a language can be established, because all forms of language derive from some form of word. So, because DNA is being transcribed into messenger RNA via a proofreading mechanism, which is equal to a virtual communications system with a standard for definitions in place, it will mean that DNA RNA transcription was initiated by a source of conscience or word.

Yet nature is not consciously aware of anything, nor does nature have a conscience to reason from, which leaves only one other possibility for the origin of genetic instructions, and that is from a source of word due to the presence of instructions. So, in other words, all life has derived from a source of conscience, because that is what the conscience is, a source of word or instruction, and though an animal can obey a word, and thereby understand a command or an instruction in the form of a voice, sound, or signal, they cannot establish a method of communication for themselves or others, because an animal is unable to invent a word.

So, when a person invents a word, it derives from their conscience directly, while an animal's ability to communicate derives indirectly from a source of conscience, such as the Creator of a word. The proof that no animal has a conscience, is due to the fact that no animal suffers from a guilty conscience, because the human conscience is aware of who you are, rather than just what you are, which is the reason why no animal can express a name for itself by itself, because a name is relative to a word.

So, both language and communication have derived from a source of conscience in order to establish a standard that governs the method of communication within a group of species, and between each kind of creature, that is interpreted independently in terms of a personal interpretation, whether it be a human being or an animal, the principle remains the same, because each species of animal will interpret another species method of communication independently of the other, the same as each person will interpret a method of communication independently of others.

The ability to communicate (whether it be a human being or an animal) has derived from a source of conscience in order to establish a method or standard for communication, which is why an animal's calling sound is fixed, while human beings are able to invent a method of communication or word, because a human being is endowed with conscience, while the animals are not. So, because rules have been inferred in order for instructions to occur, and because an instruction is equal to a message or command, it will mean that God the Creator has established all things by His word, and has created every living creature, each according to their own kind, so that all living creatures are subject to His word, each according to their own ability.

*Quotation: ─────────────────────

"I have often expressed my sentiments, that every man, conducting himself as a good citizen, and being accountable to God alone for his religious opinions, ought to be protected in worshipping the Deity according to the dictates of his own conscience." - George Washington. Source: Address of the General Committee representing the United Baptist Churches in the State of Virginia, and assembled in the City of Richmond. (Documented May 8, 1789).

A natural process can only be defined as the normal workings of a system in place, while the inventing of a system must derive from a method, and a method always derives by design as a rule, because a method is by definition, inferred, and this is why living systems have not self-emerged over time via any natural process, because a natural process will always be limited to the number of specifics there are in place to define the process with, while any increase in thermodynamic efficiency must derive from an increase in specificity, because that which is orderly is also specific.

So, living systems are not self-improving with age due to hereditary mistakes, nor can living systems be self-existing either, because all living systems rely on other living systems in order to coexist, which in turn, gives purpose to every living creature within the ecosystem, so that all individual living systems, no matter how large or small, are symbiotic, and are fully reliant on other living systems in order to coexist. So, because all living systems are symbiotic, it will mean that an overall plan or method has been applied to the ecosystem, because each living creature is specific in relation to other living creatures, which cannot occur at random due to the law of relativity, and the law of probability.

The evolutionary theory assumes that all life has derived from an RNA virus, and has slowly evolved over millions of years into a more complex form. But what the theory of evolution has not taken into account is that all viruses are parasitic, which means that a virus has no designated function without pre-existing life. Thus, a virus or parasite is the direct result of entropy law where the amount of ordered complexity within the ecosystem is wearing down over time, rather than building up in terms of ordered complexity.

All biological systems tend toward disorder over time in accordance with the second law of thermodynamics, and the law of probability, which is why diversification leads to speciation, because as a particular kind is diversifying, the amount of variability is reducing itself with each new species. The purpose of speciation is to have an open breeding population that is free to integrate, while a closed breeding population will always be subject to an increase in hereditary mutations. And it is the build-up of hereditary mistakes that leads to biological disorder over time in accordance with entropy law, and the law of probability.

The law of probability applies to any group of events that are relative to one another resulting in what's known as a series or consequence, so that any series of actions that work together as a single process in order for a procedure to occur will be defined as specific, such as the relationship between bees and flowers, which produces honey as an end product. The likelihood of a group of bees producing honeycomb without the flowers first is an absolute zero, because the process of making honey is occurring according to a procedure or plan, which is the same in reverse, because bees are required in order for pollination to occur. This means that there is a set of parameters in place that could not have occurred at random, because each step during the procedure for making honey is specific in relation to the next, resulting in an algorithm or cycle.

So, the process of honey manufacture is governed by a series of steps that occur as a cycle, such as a life cycle, which could not have occurred at random over any length of time by definition of the fact that there are multiple processes working in combination with each other in order to produce an end product or desired effect. This principle also applies to the human body, because there are multiple processes working together in synchrony in order to form an end product or desired effect, such as blood, as well as waste products, such as urine. So, as a rule, any group of processes that work together for a single purpose will be defined as specific in accordance with the law of relativity. In systems theory, any group of processes that work together in synchrony, are by definition, relative, due to the presence of a procedure. While a random process will always be the result of a system in place, rather than the cause, because ordered complexity cannot occur at random in accordance with the law of relativity, and the law of probability.

The law of relativity is applicable in this case, because any group of events that can be quantified will also be relative, rather than random. A random process will always be defined by a lack of predictability, which is why the only way to increase the likelihood of a cycle occurring that is both repeatable under observation, and therefore predictable under demonstration, is by the application of a method. In order for thought to occur, then there must first be a source of memory, which is why the human mind is defined as a processing unit that can be tasked to complete a complex function, like interpreting instructions, which matter and energy alone cannot cause to occur inside any length of time proposed.

The human mind is specifically for processing instructions from memory, while the information stored within the mind is where memories derive from, because thoughts are processed from memory, which the brain interprets as an instruction that leads to an action. So, unless there is a standard in place to define the instructions with, then the action of processing instructions cannot occur, which is why a language will always have a standard in place in order to specify whether the sequence is orderly or not according to a set of rules; Meaning that the human body has also been pre-specified according to a standard in place in order for communication to occur throughout the body.

For example: The human brain is processing instructional information at every moment via electrical and chemical signals from multiple regions of the body simultaneously, such as the body's heart rhythms, hearing, taste, sight, hunger, and so on, which enables the bodies reflex response to respond immediately with a course of action via the nervous system. This means that the human brain is processing a combination of chemical, vibrational and electrical signals beyond the speed of light in order for the brain to process all of the instructional information simultaneously within and around the body, which is required in order for the brain to interpret its surroundings in real time.

Any form of instructions can be translated into words, while non-readable instructions require additional specifics in order for the instructions to be processed. The human brain is processing instructional information beyond the speed of light from multiple sources of communication within and around the body, which means that the human brain has derived supernaturally, because the speed of light is the limit of all physical interactions. So, because the human brain will interpret instructional information from each region of the body simultaneously via the nervous system and the brain, it will mean that there is a universal standard in place for all of the body's electrical and chemical signals to be interpreted by, which is evidence of design, rather than evolution, because a standard in place will always be inferred according to a set of rules.

The concept that an instructional system can self-emerge over time from materials alone has not taken into account that all systems are by definition rule based, which means that rules must be taken into account before the specifics can be generated, which in turn, gives rise to a procedure or method. So, in order for a set of specifics to be conveyed, then a method of communication is required first, and communicating instructions is the last thing that nature can do, because materials alone do not communicate with each other. The evolutionary theory of the human brain having derived from material substances alone over billions of years is without a proper explanation from science, because energy and matter are not self-aware.

No amount of chemical reactions can ever become self-aware over time from materials alone, because in order for an instructional sequence to occur, (such as DNA RNA instructions) then a standard for communication is required first. Otherwise, there would be nothing to define a sequence as orderly, which is required in order for a meaning to be conveyed. So, in order for genetic instructions to convey a meaning, then a standard for the instructions to be interpreted by is required first before an instructional command can be processed. And a standard for communication will always be the evidence of creativity having been applied, either directly or indirectly to the materials used, because a standard will always be inferred according to a set of rules that acts as a set of parameters for communication to occur.

A self-replicating or reproductive system will always be instructionally based from its DNA RNA, which means that there are no examples of any living system having derived from materials alone, because in order for instructions to occur, then a method of communication is required first. A thermodynamic instructional system cannot self-improve over time, because a natural process cannot take future conditions into account in order to generate the specifics needed. So, in order for any level of improvement to occur to an instructional system, then additional specifications are required first. Otherwise, the improvements will be unspecified, and will therefore advance into decay, rather than improving a system's level of efficiency.

For example: A spare tire on the back of a vehicle will add weight to the vehicle, reducing its overall performance and fuel efficiency, but when the vehicle has a flat tire, the spare tire will be needed, which must be predetermined in order for a fifth wheel to be of any importance to a vehicle that only requires four. And this is the same for a typical gene sequence, because when a genetic sequence is forming using the four base intervals, such as adenine (A), cytosine (C), guanine (G), and thymine (T), the sequence will be encoded according to each base interval. While another chemical character called uracil (U) will be required at the end of a gene sequence in order to direct the sequence to stop.

So, a thermodynamic instructional system cannot be improvised at any point due to the overall level of efficiency that is required at the start of the procedure, which must be predetermined in order for the total number of chemical letters to be present at the start of an organism's function. Otherwise, there would be nothing for the selection process to select from in terms of chemical characters. And this is evidence that creativity has been applied to genetic sequencing, because there is no way to reduce the number of chemical characters that are required in order for a typical gene sequence to occur without reducing the systems level of efficiency, which means that there is a standard in place for genomic replication to occur that is both universal, as well as inferred.

DNA RNA transcription is a thermodynamic instructional system that incorporates a proofreading mechanism in order to convey a genetic instruction or command. This means that genetic instructions are governed by a procedure that is by definition, specific. This instructional system cannot be improved upon in terms of its thermodynamic efficiency, because a DNA sequence is limited to the chemical characters in use, while any additional chemical characters require additional specifics in order for the instructions to convey a meaning.

This means that the chemical characters that are used to define a genetic sequence are fixed according to a set of parameters that act as a standard for genomic replication to occur. So, in other words, DNA RNA sequencing is governed by a set of specifics that cannot be reduced or multiplied without the need for additional specifics, and is thereby limited to the number of chemical characters in use, which is evidence of design due to a standard in place that is both efficient, as well as inferred.

Ordered complexity is defined as being orderly due to the presence of a procedure, or due to a systems level of organization, or due to a standard for definitions, giving the system a typical quality or function. While disordered complexity is defined as a state of complexity that is unorganized due to a process that was unspecified. And the difference between ordered complexity, and disordered complexity, is that ordered complexity is by definition, specific, while disordered complexity is by definition, unspecified. So, the process of an organism growing into maturity is an orderly thermodynamic process at work due to a procedure in place that is pre-specified, and therefore, specific. While a biological mutation is the result of an orderly process at work that has failed due to a copying mistake within the DNA RNA proofreading process, or as a result of damage to the cell's instructions, and is thereby, disorderly, due to a reduction in terms of specifics.

Disordered complexity is the direct result of ordered complexity in a state of random decay, known as entropy law, which means that ordered complexity cannot occur at random, otherwise, there would be nothing to define that which is orderly. Entropy is defined as the measurement of a system's thermal energy per unit temperature that was unused to complete a specific function, and entropy is also defined as a constant during any thermodynamic process that exchanges heat with its surroundings, because no thermodynamic system is ever 100% efficient due to a loss of thermal energy whenever a task is completed.

Entropy within a thermodynamic instructional system is represented by reductionism, which means that the more time and chance takes its toll on a thermodynamic instructional system, the more the system will decline into disorder over time, which is what biological aging is due to accumulated mutations over time. And accumulated mutations over time will indeed build-up within the overall gene pool of a particular kind, which is entirely due to diversification and speciation, because the more a particular kind diversifies, the lower a species ability is to diversify because diversification has already occurred resulting in a reduction in terms of survivability, rather than an increase. The purpose of speciation is to preserve a particular kind by having an open breeding population that is free to integrate, which in turn, offsets the rate of biological entropy by the sharing of chromosomes, which are hereditary.

So, it is for this reason that an open breeding population is necessary in order for a thermodynamic instructional system to be efficient, because a closed breeding population will always result in an accelerated rate of hereditary mutations, thus leading to an increase in the rate of entropy, rather than a decrease. There are three types of thermodynamic systems, which are open, closed, and isolated systems, and entropy law affects each type of system in different ways due to the transfer of thermal energy via inputs and outputs of the system.

For example: An open system is any set of boundaries that has both an input and output feature for the transfer of thermal energy or mass. This means that entropy will affect an open system from within and around its boundaries due to inputs and outputs of the system. And an example of an open system would be the human body, which has inputs and outputs in order for the flow of particles to move through the body whilst disposing of waste products at the same time. So, because energy and mass are being absorbed as well as expelled from the body's system due to the process of consumption and temperature regulation, it will mean that entropy law affects an open system from within and around its boundaries due to inputs and outputs of the system. While the particles within a closed system are separated from its environment while the system is closed, but can be made transferable through a single opening.

In this way, the conservation law occurs within a closed system while the system is closed, but the entropy of a closed system will occur when mass or thermal energy is being transferred either in or out of the system via a single opening that can be shut off. The internal decay of a closed system is thereby relative to the internal decay of an isolated system while the system is closed. Entropy law will also affect a closed system from around its boundaries, because no closed system is ever 100% impermeable to its environment unless it is an isolated system. The purpose of a closed system is to temporarily isolate its contents within its boundaries in order to conserve mass or thermal energy. While the purpose of an isolated system is to permanently prevent the contents of the system from escaping its boundaries in order to conserve mass or thermal energy while the system is in a state of isolation, because there are no inputs or outputs of the system.

An isolated system will always be subject to entropy law from within its boundaries, rather than around its boundaries, because an isolated system has no inputs or outputs to exchange thermal energy or mass, and is thereby impermeable to its environment. So, whether the system is open, closed, or isolated, the principles of conservation will remain in effect, but when the transfer of mass or thermal energy through inputs and outputs of the system occurs, the principles of entropy will begin to take effect due to a loss of thermal energy or mass.

The internal decay of a closed system is thereby relative to the internal decay of an isolated system while the system is in a state of isolation. This principle implies that ordered complexity cannot occur at random over time within an isolated system, because the transfer of thermal energy or mass has stopped, thus resulting in a maximum state of entropy known as thermal equilibrium. Thermal equilibrium is the condition under which two substances in physical contact with each other exchange no heat or energy. Two substances in thermal equilibrium are said to be at the same temperature.

The first law of thermodynamics states that the total amount of energy and mass within an isolated system remains at a constant, because energy and mass can neither be created nor destroyed, but energy and mass can be transformed from one form of energy to another. And this is where the imaginations of those who hail from the evolutionary theory begin to run wild, because the assertion here is that if energy can transform from one type to another, then both a living system, and a solar system, can transform from one type to another in an upward progression in terms of efficiency.

But when energy transformation occurs from one form to another, it will always be the result of a system in place, such as a hydroelectric dam that transforms the kinetic energy of water into electrical energy for energy manufacture, or when matter is converting into thermal energy through a thermal reaction, such as nuclear fusion for example. Nuclear fusion reactions power the sun as well as nuclear power stations through the process of nuclear fusion. In a fusion reaction, two light nuclei merge to form a single more heavier nucleus, or core, resulting in a thermal exchange that produces thermal energy.

This fusion process releases thermal energy and mass, because the total mass of the resulting single nucleus is less than the mass of the two original nuclei when combined; Meaning that the process of nuclear fusion is subject to entropy law whereby a loss of thermal energy and mass has escaped the process or system. So, the release of mass during nuclear fusion has derived from a portion of the two nuclei when combined, rather than deriving from pure energy itself. Positron annihilation lifetime spectroscopy (PALS) is a commonly used technique for the investigation of the electronic properties of condensed matter. The first application of positrons in condensed matter was in the study of electronic structures of metals and in the characterization of defects in solids.

A positron has the same mass and spin as an electron, whilst retaining an opposite polarity. If a positron is surrounded by one or more electrons, the positron may annihilate with one of the electrons, i.e. Both particles disappear and their masses are transformed into energy, which is emitted as γ quanta. This principle states that mass can become energy, rather than energy becoming matter. So, the idea that energy can become matter via a natural process is postulated without proof by the Schwinger Effect theory.

The Schwinger Effect theory is an evolutionary or origins theory which assumes that when a positron and an electron combine, mass is released, thereby establishing a natural causality for the existence of matter through energy conversion. Yet according to the principles of (PALS): When positron annihilation lifetime spectroscopy occurs, γ quanta is produced, which is a form of radiation called "gamma rays," rather than a form of matter. So, the Schwinger Effect theory has not taken into account that: A) The first law of thermodynamics, which states that matter and energy cannot be created or destroyed via a natural process and that the amount of energy and mass within an isolated system remains at a constant. B) That γ quanta is a form of radiation, rather than a form of mass. And C) Entropy law will take affect when thermal energy is released during nuclear fusion or by positron annihilation lifetime spectroscopy.

> *Quotation: ————————————————
> "Science is incompetent to reason upon the creation of matter itself out of nothing. We have reached the utmost limit of our thinking faculties when we have admitted that because matter cannot be eternal and self-existing, it must have been created." - James Clerk Maxwell. Source: Nature, vol 8, No: 209. (Documented October 30, 1873).

A second example of energy transformation, is that the total amount of usable energy (such as liquids, solids, and gases) are being transformed through the conversion of thermal exchange during any thermal reaction, so that solids can transform into liquids, and liquids can transform into gases or vice versa, while the total amount of mass and energy has not changed due to the law of conservation within the isolated system of the universe. Thus, matter and energy can transform from one type to another, but the total amount of energy and mass remains the same, and will increase with entropy over time unless a method is applied in order to conserve thermal energy or mass. The conservation principle of thermodynamics remains in constant effect, which limits energy transformation to being a form of entropy that leads to an increase in disorder over time in accordance with the second law of thermodynamics.

The second law of thermodynamics states that the entropy of a thermodynamic system will always increase over time, because there will always be a loss of thermal energy or mass that has escaped the process or system during any thermal reaction. The principles of energy transformation from the first law of thermodynamics is limited to being a process of exchange that can convert energy from one form to another, and thereby increases with disorder over time when energy or mass is wasted or expelled from the system during a thermodynamic process, because the conservation of thermal energy into useful work will always be the result of ordered complexity, rather than time and chance.

Adding time to a process that tends toward disorder over time will only increase the level of disorder there is in a matter of time, rather than increasing in ordered complexity as the evolutionary theory assumes is occurring via energy transformation. The law of entropy that disorder will always increase over time applies to any form of energy transformation that was unspecified, because energy can only transform from one form to another via a method. This principle implies that energy transformation increases with disorder over time unless a method is applied. So, the only way for energy transformation to become orderly, and therefore, efficient, is by the application of a method.

Solar energy is a type of energy that will increase with entropy over time, because solar radiation is dangerous to the environment, which is why there are mechanisms in place that reflect sunlight, such as the atmosphere and the magnetosphere, so that plants can convert ultraviolet radiation into usable energy, the same as a solar panel that requires an inverter in order to transform DC electricity into AC electricity for the purpose of energy consumption; Meaning that the only way to offset the rate of entropy a thermodynamic system has, is for the system to conserve thermal energy via a mechanism that has been pre-specified, otherwise, there would be no definition for efficiency during a thermodynamic process. The level of thermodynamic efficiency a system has will always be the result of specificity, (rather than time and chance) because specificity is relative to efficiency, while time and chance is relative to disorder.

The second law of thermodynamics states that a thermodynamic system will always be found in a state of disorder or moving towards it, because there are far more random probabilities than ordered ones during any thermodynamic process; Meaning that an orderly system cannot derive at random over any length of time proposed, because a process that tends toward disorder over time cannot increase in ordered complexity in a matter of time. Another example of energy transformation would be linear and angular momentum, which can transform from one form to the other by the transfer of momentum and direction. But the change of potential energy will not be a progressive type of energy transformation in terms of efficiency unless the process has been pre-specified first according to a method or procedure.

For example; When a baseball has been pitched, the direction of travel and rotation can be altered from one direction to the other via a method, such as a curve ball effect. This principle also applies to any object in motion, yet the outcome is unspecified unless a method or procedure has been applied; Meaning that the only way to control an object in motion in terms of speed, direction and rotation, is by the application of a method. An object in free fall will obey the laws of conservation unless acted upon by another force or object, so that any object in motion retains its direction of travel until the object is at rest, or if the object is acted upon by another force or object. So, the only way for energy transformation to be made efficient, is by the application of a method, otherwise, the process will tend towards disorder over time in accordance with entropy law, and the law of probability.

According to astrophysics, the sun acts as a centre of gravity for the solar system as a working whole, so that the direction of each planet's orbit around the sun is governed by the sun's immense gravity and rotation that spins in one direction. However, the direction of rotation for each planet is not governed by the sun's speed and direction of travel due to variations in rotational direction. This means that the sun's gravity could not have pitched the planets into their direction of rotation over time, because there are two planets that spin backwards, such as Venus and Uranus, which is evidence that a method has been applied to the solar system due to the presence of a curve ball effect.

A curve ball effect will always be the direct result of a method in place, because in order for a curve ball effect to occur, then a procedure is required first, which is evidence of design, rather than evolution. A second aspect of the solar system that goes unacknowledged from the evolutionary theory, is that a solar system operates according to seasonal cycles, which is perpetual in motion in terms of speed and direction of travel or rotation while the system is in motion. Thus, a solar system is evidence of design due to a cycle in place that is both repeatable under observation, as well as predictable under demonstration, which cannot occur at random over time in accordance with the second law of thermodynamics.

The second law of thermodynamics is applicable to the law of probability, in that a thermodynamic system will tend toward disorder over time, while a sequence or cycle in place is evidence of design due to the presence of a procedure. Any system or process that is operating according to a procedure in place will be defined as specific due to the application of a method, which in turn, defines the purpose of a system, because in order for a cycle to occur, then a method is required. Thus, the presence of seasonal cycles is evidence of design by definition of the word, procedure, which shares it definition with the term, method, in that a system has occurred intentionally. So, it is for the purpose of reliability that systems exist, because a random process cannot be relied upon in accordance with the law of probability.

*Quotation: ———————————————————
"This most beautiful system of the sun, planets and comets, could only proceed from the counsel and dominion of an intelligent and powerful Being. This Being governs all things, not as the soul of the world, but as Lord over all. And on account of His dominion He is to be called; Lord God or Universal Ruler." - Sir Isaac Newton. Source: The Principia, Mathematical Principles of Natural Philosophy. (Documented July 5, 1687).

The third law of thermodynamics states that the entropy of a closed system at thermodynamic equilibrium approaches a constant value when its temperature approaches absolute zero. A system that is in a state of maximum disorder will be any closed system with an internal temperature at absolute zero, which is defined as thermodynamic equilibrium. Only when a closed system has reached a point of thermal equilibrium will entropy begin to stop, because the flow of thermal energy has also stopped, and has thereby reached a point of maximum disorder in terms of its internal temperature and configuration. Absolute zero is the lowest limit of the thermodynamic temperature scale, and is defined as a state at which the entropy of a pressurized or refrigerated gas reaches its minimum temperature, which is equal to zero kelvin, or minus 273.15 degrees Celsius.

An isolated system obeys the principles of conservation, because the total amount of energy or mass remains at a constant level within the system. While a closed system obeys the law of conservation while the system is closed, thereby isolating its contents from its surroundings. And an open system obeys the conservation principle due to stored energy within the system, or by the transfer of thermal energy through inputs and outputs of the system in order to regulate the system's internal temperature. So, it does not matter whether it's an open, closed, or isolated system, the laws of thermodynamics involving the principles of thermal conservation and entropy still applies as long as there is a thermal process of exchange at work.

The evolutionary theory assumes that all types of change are by definition, evolution, whether it be an increase in ordered complexity, or a decrease. But the problem with this definition is that a method of identification is required first in order to define whether an increase in efficiency has occurred compared to when it hasn't, which cannot be defined by a single term, because entropy and efficiency do not share the same meaning. So, for this reason, the term "spontaneous evolution" has been used in an attempt to define all change as evolution, which cannot be defined as a logical definition, because the definition does not take into account that specificity and randomness are polar opposites of one another.

The counter argument here is that the definition of evolution has a negative and a positive meaning according to a negative prefix, such as de-evolution, compared to the positive term, evolution. But what the term "de-evolution" does not take into account is that ordered complexity is required first before random decay can begin to occur, which means that ordered complexity must have derived before disordered complexity could occur. This principle implies that creation has occurred, rather than evolution, because random decay cannot occur unless ordered complexity has already occurred; Meaning that systems began as both orderly and complex, rather than disorderly and perplexed.

The other aspect of "spontaneous evolution" implies that entropy cannot be reversed due to the forward motion of time, which automatically disqualifies evolution as an innovative process, because anything that tends toward disorder over time cannot increase in ordered complexity in a matter of time. The concept that the second law of thermodynamics may be formulated by the observation that the entropy of an isolated system left to "spontaneous evolution" means automatically that spontaneous evolution tends toward disorder over time, and is therefore a failed mechanism for biological improvement in accordance with the law of probability, and the principles of entropy law.

According to the second law of thermodynamics, a system will always be found in a state of disorder or moving towards it in accordance with the law of probability, which is the very thing that forbids an orderly process from occurring at random, because the process of random decay from order begins with an orderly process at work, rather than a disorderly process evolving by itself into a more orderly process with time. A system that has been pre-specified implies automatically that specifics were required, which is applicable to any orderly process or cycle. The evolutionary theory assumes that all change is by definition, evolution, whether it be a change in ordered complexity, or a change in disordered complexity, the definition remains the same. Yet the definition for an increase in ordered complexity must derive from an increase in specificity, while an increase in disordered complexity requires time, because all thermodynamic systems tend toward disorder over time.

This means that adding time to a process that tends toward disorder over time will only increase the amount of disorder there is in a matter of time, rather than increasing in specificity. Specificity on the other hand requires a mechanism for improvement, which cannot be time itself, because all thermodynamic systems tend toward disorder over time. So, because specificity is relative to ordered complexity, and because specificity always derives by design, it will mean that the only way to increase a system's level of ordered complexity, is by the application of a method.

The transformation of one form of energy to another will always be the result of a system in place, rather than the cause of one, because any loss of thermal energy that was unused to complete a specific task will be defined as entropy; Meaning that entropy cannot occur unless there is an orderly system in place first, which cannot occur at random over time, otherwise, there would be nothing to define that which is orderly in terms of a thermodynamic process. The universe is an isolated system according to the laws of thermodynamics, which means automatically that the universe began as orderly, rather than disorderly, because the progression of entropy is a state of decline from ordered complexity into a state of disordered complexity, and not the other way around.

This principle in thermodynamics establishes the universe as both orderly and complex from the start of its function, rather than occurring at random over time via a natural process, because anything random will remain random unless a method is applied, which then defines the process as a procedure due to the application of a method. Yet the universe could not have begun as a random process, because a random process will always be the result of a method in place, rather than the cause of one; Meaning that systems were in place before a random or natural process could have occurred.

The physics principle of entropy leaves all evolutionary theories of simple to complex via a random or natural process as false from the moment of assertion, because, A) Ordered complexity cannot derive at random, otherwise, there would be nothing to define that which is orderly. B) Because a natural process will always be limited to the number of specifics there are in place to define the process with, while any additional specifics to a given system must derive from a method of innovation. And C) Because any process that has not derived by design, is by definition, random.

The evolutionary idea that systems have derived from a natural process serves only one purpose, and that is to deceive the laity, because purpose always derives by intention, or in other words, the evolutionary theory was designed to deceive the people on purpose, rather than to educate the individual. So, because a natural process will always be limited to the number of specifics there are in place to define the process with, it will mean that a natural process is evidence of a creation, because specifics derive from taking rules into account, which is evidence of design, rather than evolution.

Thus, specificity is relative to design, rather than evolution, because evolution defines itself as a natural process only, which cannot share its definition with an artificial process by definition of the fact that a natural process, and an artificial process, do not share the same meaning. There are only three types of processes that can occur in order to define a given process with, which are natural, artificial, and supernatural processes. But because the solar system cannot be attributed to a natural or artificial process, it will mean automatically that a supernatural process has occurred by design due to the presence of a cycle in place, (such as seasonal cycles) that are both repeatable under observation, as well as predictable under demonstration, which cannot occur at random over time in accordance with the law of probability.

This principle implies automatically that a Creator God is required when interpreting the existence of systems, because a system is defined by a cycle or procedure in place, which cannot be attributed to a natural process only, because a natural process is simply the normal workings of a system in place, rather than the cause. The only causality there is for a set of specifics, is by design, because a set of specifics must always be inferred according to a set of rules. So, for this reason, there is no other way to define a procedure apart from a method, and the universe does display the presence of a procedure, because the universe is defined as an isolated system, which implies automatically that a supernatural process has occurred by design.

An isolated system displays properties of design that cannot occur at random, because in order for an isolated system to be established, then a set of parameters are required first, which cannot be attributed to a natural process only due to specificity, which is the evidence of design. And all systems, whether naturally occurring or not, display properties of design due to the presence of a procedure. For example; Wind erosion will always occur according to a natural process, which in turn, gives rise to variation via a fluctuation within a more larger system, such as the weather system in conjunction with the ecosystem.

Thus, a natural process is simply the normal workings of a system in place, rather than the cause, because a natural process will always be limited to the number of specifics there are in place to define the process with, while any additional specifics to a given system must occur by design by definition of the word, specific. And specifics are indeed a requirement when establishing a typical system, because in order for a system to occur, then a procedure is required first, which is the evidence of design by definition of the word, method. A method in place will always be the evidence of design, because a method is by definition, specific, due to a set of parameters in place that are inferred according to a set of rules.

A random fluctuation within a typical system gives rise to variation over time, which cannot be attributed to a natural process only, because in order for a procedure to occur, then a set of parameters are required first, which in turn, sets the limitations of a system's operation. The other leading factor of a typical system is that when a process has occurred, there is no way to reverse the process that has already occurred due to the forward motion of time. And time itself is relative to random decay unless a method is applied, because all things tend toward disorder in accordance with the law of probability.

Thus, the entropy of any given system will always be relative to time, which is the official reason why adding time to a given process will result in further decay unless a method is applied. This principle can be summed up by the following axiom: Anything random will remain random unless a method is applied, which then defines the process as a procedure due to the application of a method. So, for this reason, a system is defined as a method due to the presence of a procedure.

*Quotation: ───────────────────

"The law that entropy always increases holds, I think, the supreme position among the laws of nature. If someone points out to you that your pet theory of the universe is in disagreement with Maxwell's equations; Then so much the worse for Maxwell's equations. If it is found to be contradicted by observation, well, these experimentalists do bungle things sometimes. But if your theory is found to be against the Second Law of Thermodynamics, then I can give you no hope; There is nothing for it but to collapse into the deepest humiliation. The beginning of the universe seems to present insuperable difficulties unless we agree to look on it as frankly supernatural." - Sir Arthur Stanley Eddington. Arthur Stanley Eddington was an English astronomer, physicist, and mathematician. The Eddington limit, is the natural limit to the luminosity of stars, which provided one of the earliest confirmations of general relativity in 1919. Source: The Nature of the Physical World by Sir Arthur Stanley Eddington. (Documented January 1, 1920).

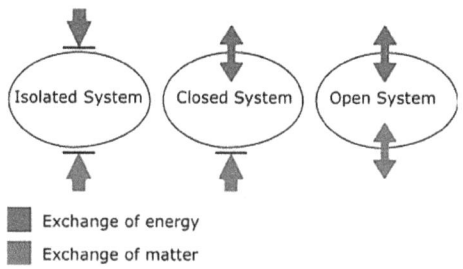

Exchange of energy
Exchange of matter

(Above) Visual Illustration of open, closed, and isolated systems. Source: Wikipedia Encyclopedia.

In systems theory, an action from an orderly molecular motion that is being directed by instructions will always be the result of a procedure in place, because the amount of entropy within a thermodynamic instructional system will be equal to the number of random variables there are within the system. While anything random during a thermodynamic process will decline into disorder over time due to the law of probability unless a method is applied. A typical system will always be limited by a set of parameters that can fluctuate, which not only leads to variation over time, but also, entropy, because entropy is the direct result of a system in a state of random decay, so that a random fluctuation within a given system will lead to an increase in disorder over time unless a method is applied.

A random process will always be the result of a system in place, either directly or indirectly, rather than the cause of one, because in order for a process to be defined as random, then a specified process is required first in order to define what the random process is, otherwise, there would be nothing to define that which is specific. A random process is by definition unpredictable in accordance with the law of probability, while a procedure is by definition predictable due to a cycle or system in place. So, by definition, a random process and a procedure cannot share the same meaning, yet both are the result of a system in place, either directly or indirectly due to the presence of a system.

When biological variation occurs from generation to generation, the amount of variation that can be expressed by an organism will be reduced over time due to the DNA RNA copying process, because every living organism is limited to being a variant of the first copy that its genome began replication with. So, each time replication occurs from the genome, the amount of variability that is passed down to the individual hereditarily is reducing itself with each successive generation, because all of the variability was with the first copy that its genome began replication with, rather than the variant.

So, for this reason, biological evolution is not occurring on any level, because each successive copy from its original will have a lowered ability to pass on variation, which is what diversification and variation is, because diversification results in the separation of a particular kind into separate species or breeding groups. Thus, diversification, in biology, refers to a particular kind that is diversifying into separate breeding groups or species in order for an open breeding population to occur that is diverse. The purpose of speciation is to preserve a particular kind, while a closed breeding population will have an accelerated rate of hereditary mutations due to the problem of inbreeding.

So, speciation is thereby the result of a thermodynamic instructional system that is diversifying over time into separate breeding groups so that an open breeding population can exist, because any closed breeding population will be subject to an increase in hereditary mutations, which must be offset by having a breeding population that is diverse, as well as open. And it is for this reason that diversification leads to a reduction in terms of survivability for a particular species, whilst maintaining a particular kind, because as diversification occurs within a particular breeding group, the breeding group will spread out into distinct groups in order to preserve their biological kind while certain species will go extinct during this process. Each time replication and procreation occurs, only a portion of the total amount of variation can be passed down hereditarily, because DNA RNA synthesis and biological reproduction are a copying process, which means that each successive copy is simply a variant of its original.

The term, variant, in biology, is specifically in reference to a type within a kind. While the term, variability, is in relation to how much variation a variant can express, and variability is always inherited, rather than deriving from within the organism itself, because a variant will always be limited to being a type or sort within a kind due to the limitations of the copying process. A set of biological features that an organism has, will always be limited to its basic format, because each of the organisms physical features have derived from a standard in place to define the organism in terms of a variant within a kind.

The best example of a biological kind, would be mankind, because each human being is a variant of one kind, as defined by the genomic template which acts as a standard for each person to be defined by in terms of a variant within a kind. And the proof that mankind is only one kind is due to the action of procreation, because human beings cannot procreate with any other creature apart from human beings. And though each person is a variant within a kind, mankind remains as one species, because all groups of humans can interbreed.

So, the rule with any copying process, is that each successive copy will only be a variant of its original due to the limitations of the copying process. The amount of variability that an organism has must derive from a predecessor that was similar to itself, rather than from within the organism, because variability is always inherited. Otherwise, there would be nothing for the selection process to select from in terms of physical traits, because DNA RNA transcription is a copying process. This means that all of the variability for a particular kind has derived from an original breeding pair, which is evidence that God has created every living creature, each according to their own kind. DNA RNA transcription is a copying process, and the rule with any copying process is that each copy must derive from an original copy, which in turn, defines each copy as a variant within a kind.

DNA proofreading works by selecting from a genomic template that acts as a standard for each variant to be defined by, so that the amount of variation a variant can express derives from an original genomic template, rather than from the environment surrounding it. So, in order to analyse an operational system, then the system as a whole must be broken down into smaller stages that can be studied independently, or as a complex whole. And a rule in systems theory is that an operational system cannot be defined by its individual mechanisms, because a single mechanism for a system cannot specify for the system it is for as a working whole. This means that a system is incorporated according to an overall plan, rather than occurring at random from any individual mechanism within the system.

A chemically based thermodynamic instructional system is evidence of creativity having been applied, because there are instructions present, such as DNA RNA instructions, which specify for the biomechanical features that an organism has. A biomechanical system must be defined as a creation, because any group of primary mechanisms that derive from instructions, must occur by design. The method for a thermodynamic instructional system will always be according to a set of parameters, which are not a part of the mechanisms for the system, and have therefore derived from outside of the system's componentry by way of inference, otherwise, a genetic instruction would have no meaning or purpose.

Any system consisting of a group of primary mechanisms working together as a unified whole cannot self-emerge, because each of the mechanisms used require an overall plan first in order to combine each of the mechanisms into a single mechanism called a system, which in turn, gives each primary mechanism purpose within the system, and therefore, meaning. The rule with any system that is comprised of a group of primary mechanisms is that each primary mechanism must be in place before the system can begin to perform its primary function, while any loss or failure of a primary mechanism will result in an immediate systems failure, which in turn, defines an operational system as an irreducibly complex system due to a group of primary mechanisms that are working together for a single purpose.

For example: A mouse trap has five main parts; A hammer, which kills the mouse; A spring, which snaps the hammer down on to the mouse; A hold-down bar, which holds the hammer in the cocked position; A catch, which holds the end of the hold-down bar and releases it when the mouse connects with the catch; And a platform, to which everything else is attached. And each mechanism for the mouse trap must be of a specified size and shape so that they will fit together which gives the system functionality and purpose, which does not occur at random, but by design, because purpose always derives by intention, rather than by pure chance.

So, we already know that the probability is extremely low for a mouse trap to occur by chance, because specifications are required first. But the probability would be even smaller again if the mouse trap was to be shrunk into a molecular trap, because compressing a device is equal to increasing its complexity. And even though the parts are few for a mouse trap, there is still specified complexity involved that could not have occurred at random, as each component has a primary function within the overall system resulting in an irreducibly complex system.

The overall set up of a mechanical system requires the components to be specific in relation to each other in order for the system to have a designated function, so specificity is required prior to the formation of an operational system in order to set the parameters in place, which in turn, sets the limitations of a particular system. And the rule with any system that is made up by a group of primary mechanisms (like the human body for example), is that the primary mechanisms must have had creativity applied to them either directly or indirectly in the form of a plan or method in order to combine each individual mechanism into a single mechanism called a system.

So, the human body can be compared to an irreducibly complex system, because the system of the body is made up by a group of primary mechanisms, such as the skeletal system, muscular system, nervous system, cardiovascular system, respiratory system, the digestive system, and so on, which cannot be removed nor fail without causing a total systems shutdown procedure to occur automatically. This means that there is a level of irreducible complexity with any operational system due to the combination of multiple primary mechanisms that work together for a single purpose. The biological purpose of the human body is to maintain oxygen levels and nutrients within and around the body in order to maintain the body's overall level of efficiency. While the meaning of life is relative to the ecosystem whereby every living creature is integrated into a larger more complex system so that each living creature is symbiotic, and is therefore relying on other living creatures in order to coexist, which in turn gives every living creature purpose within the ecosystem.

In physics, the definition of a molecular trap has been defined as: 1) "The interception of a reactive molecule or reaction intermediate so that it is removed from the system, or converted into a more stable form for study or identification." So, the process of identification will always involve a method with a standard in place, so this does not occur at random, but via a procedure instead, which in turn, defines the process of identification as a method or system. And the human body is endowed with a system of inspection and identification with a trigger mechanism in place, because the body will keep a long record of previous infections in order to fight future infections, which is evidence of design due to the presence of a molecular trap known as immunological memory. Immunological memory works by having a trigger mechanism in place in order to trigger a secondary immune response, which in turn, derives from a system of identification the same as a molecular trap in physics relies on a method of identification before the system can respond with a course of action.

Immunological memory, as a process, relies on a trigger mechanism to be in place along with a method of identification, which cannot be paired together without the application of a method, simply because there is a procedure in place. So, in order for a method of identification to be coupled with a trigger mechanism, then a procedure is required, which cannot be attributed to a natural process only, because the system is integrated with multiple primary features that work together for a designated purpose. This means that there is a physical law in place that forbids the formation of an integrated system from occurring at random, such as the law of probability.

The law of probability stands in the way of evolution for three main reasons. First; Because evolution defines itself as a natural or random process only. Second; Because a natural process will always be the result of a system in place, rather than the cause of one. And thirdly; A random process will always tend toward disorder over time in accordance with the law of probability. A natural process cannot give rise to new specifications by reason of the fact that a method is required first, which cannot be attributed to a natural process, because a method must always be inferred according to a set of rules that act as a set of parameters, thereby establishing a typical system or process.

The idea that physical laws and scientific principles just appear at random through identification is without a proper explanation from science, because physical laws do not just spring into existence by themselves, and it is theory that attempts to explain an action and its cause. Every physical law in science is described by an action in order to give demonstration to the principles in use, and though the principles do derive from theory, the physical laws themselves do not, because physical laws are always based on a measurable action, rather than by theory alone.

According to Oxford Languages, a principle in science is defined as: 1) "A fundamental truth or proposition that serves as the foundation for a system of belief or behaviour, or, for a chain of reasoning." While a law in physics is defined as: 1) "A fact, deduced from observation, to the effect that a particular phenomenon always occurs if certain conditions are present." So, the difference between physical laws and scientific principles, is that physical laws derive from an observable action, while a principle derives from a belief, and the truth of a principle will always be subject to repeatability and reliability.

So, because physical laws act according to a set of principles, it will mean that physical laws were inferred, which cannot be attributed to science alone, because modern science has derived from the interpretation of physical laws, and not the other way around. Each physical law gives a description of a particular action or phenomenon so that all physical laws are in relation to each other, resulting in an irreducibly complex system whereby the removal of one physical law from the system would result in a total systems failure. The purpose of an integrated system is to have a designated function which cannot be self-existing on the basis that a designated function must be pre-specified according to an overall plan. Otherwise, there would be nothing to integrate the system, which is required in order for functionality and efficiency to occur.

This means automatically that DNA has not derived from nature alone, but has originally derived from a method instead, which is evidence of a miracle, rather than evolution, because a method is by definition, inferred. And this limits the origin of life as having only one origin, which is by supernatural creativity due to the lack of a natural process that can cause blood to occur without pre-existing blood. So, because blood is manufactured by the body from an instructional procedure, and is thereby an end product of a cycle in place, it will mean automatically that blood is evidence of supernatural creativity, because blood cannot be replicated in a laboratory, and because blood derives from a biological process that is instructionally based.

Anything that is defined as an end product of a cycle in place, is by definition, manufactured, which includes any blood products as well due to the presence of an instructional procedure. An end product that is the result of a cycle in place, such as rainfall, sunlight, or blood for example, is by definition, manufactured, because there is a procedure in place that is occurring according to a cycle or process that is repeatable under observation, and therefore, predictable under demonstration.

For example: Magma is less dense than the surrounding rock which causes it to rise. When magma reaches the surface it is then called lava, and the eruptions of lava and ash produce volcanoes. The lava that reaches the Earth's surface will harden and become igneous rock, and this occurs as a sequence that produces land formations called islands, which means that rocks do not produce rocks any more than islands produce islands. So, the process of island formation has therefore occurred as a sequence, and the process began with something other than what was produced, which is an equivalent to a manufacturing method that produces an end product according to a cycle in place.

Anything that is produced repeatedly via a cycle in place, is by definition manufactured, whereby an end product is produced according to a procedure, which is the evidence that a method has been applied either directly or indirectly. And the Earth itself was manufactured at some point in history, because there are many examples of other planets within our solar system and beyond. But no planet could ever give rise to another planet, because a planet is not self-replicating, as all self-replicating systems are instructionally based. According to the cosmic theory of evolution, the Earth formed over 4.6 billion years ago out of a mixture of dust and gas around the sun. It then supposedly grew larger thanks to countless collisions between dust particles, asteroids, and other growing planets, including one last hypothetical impact that threw enough rock, gas, and dust into space to form the moon.

Thus, the standard explanation from secular science assumes that the Earth is the result of particle and asteroid collisions over time, and that life has derived from other worlds that supposedly contain water and organics due to meteor fragments on Earth that contain sea water and bacteria. Yet the Earth could not have derived from particle and asteroid collisions over time due to the force of the sun's gravitational effect, which is far greater than any object within the solar system by orders of magnitude. This means that a group of particles and asteroids cannot collect together to form a single cluster in proximity of the sun, because a gravitational effect greater than the sun is required first. Otherwise, there would be nothing to gather the particles and asteroids into a single location near the sun to form the Earth due to the sun's immense gravitational effect.

The current assertion by Big Bang cosmologists is that particles and gases formed the Earth via electrolysis, but because particles and gases have mass, it will mean that they cannot form into a cluster in proximity of the sun's intense gravity, which is self-explanatory. According to Genesis chapter 1, God made the Earth on day one, while the sun and the moon were created on day four, which means that the Holy Bible has taken the sun's gravitational effect into account, while the Big Bang theory has not. And the sun's gravity must be taken into account, because no planet could be formed whilst being in the proximity of the sun's immense gravity.

So, because there are no examples of a planet having derived from particle and asteroid collisions due to the sun's immense gravity, it will mean that they have derived from supernatural creativity instead, which is equal to being a miracle, because there is no natural process that can generate a planet from particle and asteroid collisions over time within the sun's proximity due to the sun's intense gravitational field, which exceeds any object within the solar system by orders of magnitude.

No planet could be formed by particle collisions in proximity of the sun due to the sun's immense gravity, which means automatically that the Earth must have been formed before the sun, which confirms the Biblical account, rather than the Big Bang theory. And the fact that sea water and bacteria are found within meteorite fragments means automatically that the fragments have derived from Earth, rather than from another world. The evidence that meteor fragments containing sea water and bacteria have derived from Earth is due to the Mid Atlantic Ridge, which is a giant crack beneath the Atlantic Ocean that has sealed over and stretches over a distance of more than 40,000 miles around the Earth.

Scientists from NASA have discovered that beneath the Earth's crust is a subterranean ocean. This subterranean ocean was released during the formation of the Mid Atlantic Ridge causing the fountains of the deep to burst forth from their chambers under the ground with enough force to send rock and debris hurtling into orbit. So, the meteor fragments that are falling to Earth have in fact derived from the Earth initially, rather than from another planet, which explains why there are microbes and sea water within the meteor fragments.

This theory is known as the Hydro-plate theory, which was first announced by Walt Brown, who is a retired army officer with a degree in mechanical engineering, and this is the most probable cause for the existence of microbes and sea water within meteorite fragments. The Hydro-plate theory also explains the tilt of the Earth, because the forces involved when the Mid Atlantic Ridge occurred was enough to tilt the Earth onto its axis as a direct result of hydro-jet propulsion, giving rise to two additional seasons, such as Autumn and Spring. Before Noah's flood, the Earth only had two seasons, such as Summer and Winter, which is according to the historical account recorded within the book of Enoch, who was seventh from Adam and lived prior to Noah's flood.

So, from the book of Enoch we find an explanation for the tilt of the Earth, which could not have occurred any other way apart from hydro-jet propulsion, because, A) An asteroid collision forcing the Earth to tilt onto its axis, would in turn, create a crater 40,000 miles wide, rather than a 40,000 mile long crack beneath the Atlantic ocean. B) The Earth is over 75% water, which means that water is not in short supply for hydro-jet propulsion to occur, while an asteroid the size of a continent is in short supply here on Earth. And C) The Earth is made up by tectonic plates that broke apart during the formation of the Mid-Atlantic Ridge, rather than by meteor fragments that have clumped together over millions of years.

A method is a requirement in order to explain the origin of something, because any process that gives rise to an end product will always be the result of a procedure in place. So, the only way to interpret a process, whether random or specified, is by the application of a method, which means that all processes, whether random or not, have derived from a method, either directly or indirectly. The solar system itself is an end product of a supernatural process, because the arrangement and configuration of the planets constitutes as a system or cycle whereby a method has been applied, which could not have occurred via a natural process, because a natural process will always be the result of a method, rather than the cause of one.

The purpose of the solar system is due to the measurement of time, which is occurring according to a sequence in place due to the effect of seasonal cycles. So, because the solar system is operating according to a cycle in place that is both repeatable under observation, and therefore, predictable under demonstration, it will mean that the solar system is orderly, and could not have occurred at random over any length of time proposed due to the law of probability. The law of probability will always take effect as long as there is a sequence in place, whether it be a numerical sequence, or a sequence of events, the principle remains the same, because the only way to increase the likelihood of a given event to occur, is by the application of a method, which is how a procedure comes into effect.

A random process will always be according to a set of variables within a system that is governed by a method or a procedure, because there are physical laws in place that will govern the limitations of a random outcome, such as the law of probability. Physical laws are by definition specified, having derived from a method initially, because physical laws are specific in relation to each other resulting in an irreducibly complex system whereby the removal of one physical law would cause a chain reaction resulting in a total systems failure.

Physical laws not only constitute as a system in place, but also, physical laws are a creation, because any set of rules that are specific in relation to each other cannot occur at random over time due to the law of probability. So, in order for a sequence of events to occur that are specific in relation to each other, then an overall method is required first, because a method is by definition specific the same as a group of events that are specific in relation to each other. So, as a rule, a random process cannot give rise to a method, because a random process will always be the result of a method in place, rather than the cause of one.

For example: There are 36 numbers on a Roulette wheel that are arranged into a specified sequence in order to generate a random outcome based on the numbers provided. While the probability of a Roulette wheel producing an orderly sequence from 1 to 36 is infinitely improbable due to the selection process being random. But because there is a method in use, it will mean that the random outcome was the direct result of a system in place, which is designed to fluctuate according to a set of variables that are limited by a set of parameters. While a typical gene sequence has at least 100 nucleotides that are arranged into an order that must be specific so that a group of proteins can work together in combination with each other to form a functional cell.

Therefore, life cannot be the result of a random process, because there is a set of sequences in place that are combined to determine the outcome as specific in order for the final outcome to be defined as orderly. And this is applicable to systems biology, because all of the body's rhythms will fluctuate according to a set of high to low variables that are limited by a set of parameters, which in turn, sets the limitations of a biological process. This means definitively that life has had meaning applied to it, because life is the result of a system in place that is both specific, and supernatural, rather than random or natural. Any increase in specificity must derive from a method of innovation, because that which is specific is the diametric opposite of that which is random.

So, a random process will always be according to a set of variables within an operational system that are governed by physical laws, which in turn, sets the limitations of a system's operation. Any process that produces a sequential outcome that is orderly, (such as a numerically ordered sequence from 1 to 100 for example) will always be the result of a method in place that defines the sequence as orderly, and therefore, specific. And the longer the sequence is, the less likely that the sequence could have occurred at random in accordance with the law of probability.

The law of probability can be applied to any physical process, because a process is defined by a sequence of events that are either specific in relation to each other, or not, depending on the process. But it will always be a method or standard in place that defines the process as orderly, rather than the sequence itself, because an orderly sequence in place will always be the result of a method, rather than the cause of one. The law of probability is equal to a method that allows for a prediction to occur; Meaning that the only way to differentiate between that which is orderly, and that which is not, is by the application of a method.

For example: Each term within a sequence that is specific in relation to the next will always have a numerically ordered place according to a method or procedure in use that defines the sequence as orderly. But the sequence itself is never responsible for the method in place, because a numerically ordered sequence will always be the result of a method, rather than the cause of one. So, the longer an orderly sequence is, the lower the probability is for the sequence occurring by chance, because a sequence that is orderly according to a method in place will always be specific in relation to another sequence. And an example of how long an orderly sequence can be, would be DNA instructions, because one drop of DNA can store enough information, in sequence, to reach the moon and back.

Yet there is a longer sequence in place that is rarely ever mentioned, such as time sequences, because the solar system acts as a mechanism for time to be measured by within the vacuum of space, and the speed at which time passes is not increasing or decreasing over time, because the solar system is perpetual; Meaning that the level of order there is within the solar system is equal to its sequential nature as the system orbits the sun perpetually. This means that the solar system is a type of clock that required configuration at the start of its function, otherwise, the system would not be perpetual according to its seasonal cycles.

So, the concept by naturalism concerning a self-emerging universe is not only false, but also quite ridiculous as a train of thought, because it is not a practical concept to teach that a natural process can increase the level of ordered complexity that a system already has. A natural process cannot be responsible for the formation of the universe, because a method has been applied due to the presence of a procedure. The evidence that a procedure has been applied to the isolated system of the universe, is due to the constant of time, because the universe acts as a mechanism for time to be measured by within a vacuum, which is in constant effect. Time is in constant affect within the isolated system of the universe as a mathematical constant, and any system that operates according to a mathematical constant, is by definition, orderly.

Thus, the ordered complexity of the universe is dependent on time as a mathematical constant, such as the speed of light within a vacuum, which acts as the limit of time to be measured by. The speed of light within a vacuum, commonly denoted as (c), is a universal and mathematical constant that is equal to 299,792,458 metres per second. Thus, the universal constant of time is governed by three main factors. First; Time is in constant effect within three dimensions of space. Second; Time has a limit in terms of speed, which is governed by the speed of light within a vacuum that acts as a mathematical constant for the measurement of time. And thirdly; Anything that is for the purpose of measuring time, is by definition, orderly, as well as calibrated. Thus, the isolated system of the universe displays properties that are relevant to calibration in terms of a time constant with an input and output effect that is governed by the three dimensions of space.

According to Oxford Languages, the definition of (time) is defined as: 1) "A plan, schedule, or arrange when something should happen or be done. Similar: schedule." So, according to the world's foremost dictionary, Oxford Languages, we find that time is the result of a plan, and is thereby inferred according to a set of rules that act as a set of parameters which sets a limit on time. And it is for this reason that time has a limit, which cannot be extrapolated into a theory involving billions of years without first having a plan in place, which is the evidence that the evolutionary theory was invented, rather than discovered, due to the use of planning.

The entire purpose of secular science, in terms of a theory, is to try and debunk the existence of the supernatural by inferring a natural process. But the problem with this logic, is that time is the result of a supernatural process at work by definition of the fact that time is the result of a plan in place, otherwise, time would have no purpose. And it is a rule in linguistics that anything which exists has a purpose within the system by definition of the word, purpose, because everything was created. According to linguistics, the term, (purpose) is relevant to a creation, which is why the theory in secular science concerning the supernatural attempts to defeat the purpose of a creation, which has ultimately backfired by defeating the purpose of life, which is to serve. And it is for the purpose of rules that justice should be served, which is the reason why the Creator will judge His creation.

The evolutionary theory cannot determine a causality for systems via a natural process, because a natural process will always be the result of a system in place, rather than the cause of one. So, for this reason, all living systems are different as opposed to nature and material substances alone, because an instructional method has been employed in order to give rise to the process of genomic replication. Thus, the evolutionary theory assumes that all processes have derived at random, which is the only evolutionary explanation for a natural process. But the problem with the evolutionary in terms of a theory, is that a random process will remain random unless a method is applied, which is the only causality there is for a natural process. Thus, a natural process must occur by design due to the application of a method.

According to modern evolutionary theories, a random change in allele frequencies over time results in evolution, which is the current model by secular science to explain variation, as well as biological improvement. This theory is better known as "genetic drift," because as one species drifts from one phenotype to another, the genotype is expressed in terms of a variant. Genetic drift is a change in allele frequencies in a given population that occurs due to random chance events. So, to be more exact, genetic drift is any biological change that is due to a mistake in selecting the alleles for the next generation from the gene pool of the current generation that affects the following generation, and is more commonly referred to as a genetic mutation.

The biology term "allele" is an abbreviation of the term, "allelomorph" meaning "another form." This term in biology was first announced by British geneticists, William Bateson and Edith Rebecca Saunders in the early days of genetic research to describe various forms of gene detection within different phenotypes or species. But the problem that goes unacknowledged from the theory of genetic drift, is that a random change or fluctuation within allele frequencies leads to biological disorder over time by definition of the word, random. Any process that is by definition, random, will decline from order into disorder over time in accordance with entropy law, and the law of probability, which is the official reason why the theory of evolution has no working mechanism for biological improvement by reason of the fact that anything random will remain random unless a method is applied, which then defines the process as a procedure due to the application of a method. Biological reproduction occurs according to a cycle in place, such as the reproductive cycle, which is evidence of an integrated system at work.

Any process that produces an end product according to a cycle in place, will always be the result of a method in use, and the only causality we have for a method, is by design. So, the only causality there is for a system, is also by design, because a system is defined as a method due to the presence of a procedure. And this is the same for any manufacturing method whereby an end product is produced according to a cycle or procedure in place, because a cycle or procedure that is repeatable under observation, is also predictable under demonstration, and therefore, cannot derive at random over time in accordance with the law of probability.

The term, manufacture, refers to the process of turning raw materials or parts into finished goods via a method or procedure for the purpose of producing an end product or desired effect, which in turn, defines the purpose of a system. Everything is a product of a cycle in place, but the efficiency of the process will depend on the number of specifics there are in use. Yet nature cannot plan specifics in advance, because specifics derive from taking rules into account, such as physical laws. This means that physical laws are equal to a standard in place for specifics to be defined by in terms of thermodynamic efficiency, because the level of ordered complexity that a system has will always be equal to the number of specifics there are in place to define the process with.

According to Oxford Languages, the term, specific, in physics, refers to being: 1) "Of or denoting a number equal to the amount of properties a given substance has compared to the value of the same number of properties from some other substance used as a reference." Such as water for example, which is defined as a good conductor of electricity. So, a set of specifics can be generated based on the properties that water has in order to use as a reference for other substances.

While a vacuum, such as outer-space for example, has poor insulating properties to conduct electricity, and the amount of insulation a substance has is referred to as the "specific dielectric strength." So, the term, specific, in physics, is denoting a physical quantity expressed in terms of a unit of mass, volume, or other measure, in order to give a value independent of the properties known, which encompasses the full scale of the particular system studied. A set of specifics is equal to the value or number of rules that have been taken into account in order for a given process to occur so that an end product or desired effect can be established, which will always be in relation to a method or procedure in place for the specifics to be defined by in terms of a process or system.

Specific dielectric strength is measured as the maximum voltage required to produce a dielectric breakdown through a material, and it is expressed as volts per unit thickness. For example: The dielectric strength for Plastic material varies from 1 to 1000 MV/m, and the higher the dielectric strength, the better the insulation properties are, and insulation is necessary for efficiency, because any loss of thermal energy during a thermodynamic process is equal to entropy.

So, as a rule, the more efficient a thermodynamic system is, the better its insulating properties will be, and the higher the value is for the insulation in terms of efficiency, the greater the number of specifics there are in place. And the more specifics there are in place, the greater the amount of ordered complexity there is within the system, which is why specificity is equal to efficiency, as well as ordered complexity. Entropy is the loss of thermal energy during a thermodynamic process that was unused to complete a complex function, which is why disorder cannot produce an orderly system over time, because specifications are required first in order to utilize the energy input, otherwise, the energy is wasted.

Specific conductance is the ability of a substance to conduct electricity, and it is the reciprocal of specific resistance. Conductance in physics means the flow of current through a liquid conductor, which is applicable to biology, because the unit of specific conductance for the volume of a cell is equal to $ohm^{-1}cm^{-1}$ while an equivalent conductance is defined as the conductance of all the ions produced by a one gram equivalent of an electrolyte in a given solution.

But without the correct medium in place for the solution to react in, then the insulation's efficiency for the conservation of thermal energy is reduced, and this is due to a poor form of insulation within the system. While a vacuum is a poor insulator for the purpose of free flowing thermal energy, which means that thermal energy cannot be stored within the vacuum of space without a mechanism in place first, because a vacuum has no insulating properties. And this is why a star could not have derived naturally, nor can the energy and mass output of a supernova produce another star within the vacuum of space, because there is nothing in the vacuum of space to insulate the thermal energy and mass output of a chain reaction.

The insulating properties of iron within a star's core is extremely high, and the iron present requires the input from a stronger source of energy than what the nuclear fusion process is within a star in order for a star to have begun its life cycle, because nothing can fuse with iron. A star cannot produce another star, because iron is a stable element that cannot form naturally, and because there is not enough insulating properties within the vacuum of space to cause a chain reaction to be isolated without an iron core first.

Iron is one of the most stable elements on the periodic table, and because iron is stable and cannot be fused with any other element, it will mean that iron cannot form naturally or synthetically via any fusion process. And though iron can be welded using either thermal or arc welding processes, the process is still not fusing iron with any other element, because thermal welding with iron results in a bond called intergranular penetration, rather than atomic fusion. While arc welding iron requires the presence of iron within the weld metal used, because any lighter elements will bond intermolecularly, which is why iron cannot be fused atomically with any other element apart from iron.

So, because the thermal output of a star must be insulated within a vacuum in order for a chain reaction to be isolated, it will mean that iron is required first in order for a star to have a gravitational effect that causes a chain reaction to be insulated within a vacuum. The standard explanation from secular science that iron is forming from hydrogen via nuclear fusion within a star has not taken into account that iron is required first in order for a star to have a gravitational effect, which is required in order for a chain reaction to be isolated within a vacuum.

When a star dies the thermal output is increased, but the dispersion rate is also increased at the same time, because there is no natural process that can cause a thermal reaction to be insulated within a vacuum. And though some dwarf stars, and supernovas share material with each other, the process is still not generating a new star, because the thermal output is being dispersed, rather than collected, so the universe is therefore limited to the number of stars present. The sun is not hot enough, even at its centre, to make iron by the fusion of lighter elements, and there is only one iron atom for every 31,600 hydrogen atoms, which is why hydrogen bonds cannot account for the presence of iron, because there is not enough hydrogen within the universe to account for the amount of iron there is. So, not only is iron a stable element, but also, iron is a limited element the same as gold and silver.

In the year 1941, gold was synthesized from mercury by neutron bombardment, but the isotopes of gold produced were highly radioactive. German scientist, Adolf Miethe, reported achieving the same feat, but after various attempts around the world it was deemed an experimental failure. The isotopes of gold produced were highly radioactive, and therefore, unstable, and will eventually decay back into mercury after a certain number of years. This means that no amount of particle collisions over time is ever going to produce a single gram of gold, because gold is a stable element, rather than an unstable radioactive isotope. The idea by evolutionary scientists that a stable element, such as iron, gold or silver can be produced synthetically, is based entirely on modern alchemy, rather than the scientific method, because iron, gold and silver cannot be replicated naturally or synthetically, and are therefore a limited element within the system of the universe.

All a star can do concerning iron, is to purify iron within its core the same as a foundry purifies precious metals in order to remove any impurities, which in turn, increases the density of iron resulting in a star's collapse once the iron core has reached its maximum payload. While anything lighter than iron that bonds intermolecularly will be defined as an alloying element, which gives iron a variety of properties for industrial and commercial use. Evolutionary scientists and Big Bang cosmologists assume that stars are born from nebulas. Yet a nebular cannot produce a star over time, because a nebular is a gas cloud, which is not only a poor insulator for thermal energy, but also, the expansion rate in outer-space is equal to dissipation, which limits the ability of a nebula to form into a solid object, because the pressures involved within a nebular are slowly expanding, rather than condensing.

According to physics, gases are the result of a liquid evaporating due to heat, or from a solid undergoing thermal expansion which releases the particles. Gases are always the result of thermal energy either produced by a chemical reaction, or by thermal energy being applied to a given substance. But when hydrogen gas is compressed, it will then become a liquid with a constant temperature below zero. This means that hydrogen gases cannot form into iron even if the gases were to be compressed due to a gravitational effect, because iron requires a thermal process in order to reduce the amount of hydrogen there is, resulting in a low hydrogen bond.

Cold fusion is a hypothetical type of nuclear reaction that requires atomic particles to be fused at subzero temperatures, and would be required in order for hydrogen atoms to fuse into iron under an immense gravitational effect, because any thermal fusion process involving heat will cause the particles to expand, rather than contract. There is currently no accepted theoretical model that would allow cold fusion to occur, because all fusion processes generate heat, and are therefore subject to entropy law.

The iron present within a star's core could not have derived via any thermal, gravitational, or fusion process, because iron is a stable element that cannot be fused with any other element. So, because iron cannot be fused with any other element apart from iron, it will mean that no other group of elements can fuse into iron. This means automatically that the number of stars we have today has derived by the action of supernatural creativity directly due to the lack of a natural process that can cause iron to occur.

A method or standard is based on a set of principles, and we do apply principles to laws in physics based on theory, but it is the physical laws in place that are the higher standard, and not the theories we invent that give rise to the principles in use. So, because physical laws are a standard in physics, and because a standard or method is equal to a set of principles, it will mean that physical laws were inferred according to a set of principles by the application of a method. And there is no other causality for the existence of physical laws, because a standard in place will always be inferred according to a set of rules.

Anything that has had inference applied to it, is by definition a creation, and physical laws are by definition inferred, because physical laws are specific in relation to each other resulting in an irreducibly complex system that is rule based. So, it does not matter how strong the individual's faith is in evolution, because no amount of time and chance can produce the specifics needed for an orderly system to be established at random, as all methods originate from planning due to the presence of a procedure. So, physical laws must be the result of a method in place, because, A) All physical laws have a primary function within the system. B) Because all physical laws are specific in relation to each other. And C) Because physical laws are rule based, which is evidence of design.

The purpose of physical laws is to act as a universal standard to define a thermodynamic system with the same as morality is in place to define good and evil with. So, because both morality and physical laws are by definition universal, it will mean that there is a universal standard in place for both to coexist. The universal interpretation in place to define physical laws derives from systems science and systems theory, which in turn, derives from Baconian and Newtonian creation science, rather than the evolutionary theory. While the universal standard in place to define morality with, as from common law, derives from a source of conscience; Meaning that morality has derived supernaturally the same as physical laws due to the presence of rules. Rules are always inferred, rather than deriving from materials alone, so that no amount of secular science or philosophical materialism can explain the causality of systems, because a system is by definition rule based, and rules are always inferred.

> *Quotation: —————————————————————
> "Just because science so far has failed to explain something, such as consciousness, to say it follows the facile, pathetic explanations which religion has produced somehow by default must win the argument is really quite ridiculous." - Richard Dawkins, former Oxford professor for public understanding of evolutionary science and co-founder of the New Atheist movement. Source: Radio Interview by Steve Paulson with Richard Dawkins. (Documented October 13, 2006).

Conscience, according to Darwin's theory of evolution, looks backwards and judges past actions, inducing that kind of dissatisfaction, which if weak we call regret, and if severe, remorse. And this is one reason why Dawkins cannot explain the existence of the human conscience as an atheist from the principles of Darwinism, because Darwin never said that he was an atheist. Thus, Dawkins' attempt to so eloquently refer to the human conscience as "consciousness," is a direct result of his atheism, rather than because of any evidence on his part. And the reason that Dawkins cannot admit that human beings have been endowed with conscience by their Creator is solely due to his atheistic worldview, as the human conscience is specifically related to the existence of morality and the human soul or spirit, which is something that atheism has rejected entirely in favour of a pseudo definition of man.

The more the theory of evolution continues to spread, the more problems society will face, because we live within a legal system that is governed by universal law. And the one law that all must acknowledge, is the universal law of human equality, because it is incontestable and not-without-standing in its legal defence under the agreement of 192 nations, and is therefore the highest legal standard in the world for the lawful interpretation of human rights and equality.

God the Creator has endowed all life with ability, but unto His own image the gift of conscience, with which, to reason from, but the one thing that cannot be reasoned with here on Earth is a nihilist who has rejected the existence of the human conscience by employing a pseudo-scientific reason. And it is for this reason that the theory of evolution is a danger to any society that is based on human equality and law, because the theory of evolution is in opposition to the universal law of human equality due to a theological dispute with the word definitions in use to define a human being with. So, because this is a theological dispute, rather than just a scientific one, it will mean that a correct theology is required, otherwise, there would be no way to interpret morality before the law.

The existence of human equality is self-evident and universal, because all human beings have been endowed with conscience by their Creator, and it is from the conscience that our convictions derive from, which is why proof of conscience is required before the law in order to make a case or enter a plea, and this is also why no legal obligation can be placed on an animal due to their lack of conscience to understand its moral implications. So, walking into a courtroom and claiming that you evolved from an ape like creature is not only unjustifiable legally, but also, it is highly unreasonable due to the sake of others who shall be defined as persons without distinction before the law regardless of any scientific theory or enterprise that might arise in order for human rights and equality to be exercised as a right.

In order to have a fair system of public education, then there must first be an acceptance by the establishment for the existence of morality as being universal from the premise of law, and there must also be an acceptance of an individual's basic right to be defined as a created human being at all times. And these rights do not leave the individual when entering a private or public establishment, because these rights are inalienable, as well as universal. No school, courtroom, or workplace has the right to deny a person their basic rights by equating them as an animal of some description via their ancestry based on any set of rules they have set in place for themselves or their establishment, because the lawful definition of conscience is in place so that we each have protection of person under international law.

The evolutionary theory defines all persons as animals from the use of certain terms, such as: mammal, primate, lower animal, and so on, which is the very thing that deprives an individual of their inalienable right to be defined as a created human being before the law. And this is also why those who hail from the evolutionary theory should be restricted from lobbying to government for rights to be removed from citizens in order to grant privileges to themselves, because it is the theory of evolution that is in opposition to the lawful premise for human rights and equality.

Any opposition to the theological definitions from law that are used to describe a person with is a crime against humanity on the basis of equality, which in turn, defines the evolutionary definition of man as unlawful in accordance with international agreement. The official reason why the theory of evolution is in practice from society and law is solely due to the denial of Biblical creation as a legal standard, which is the very thing that stands in the way of the evolutionary definition of man. In systems theory, a system can only handle that which it was intended for, which is why a system of equality cannot be used to define man as animal, otherwise, the system will fail. And it is for the purpose of systems theory that overlapping systems can be assessed for weaknesses so that further strategies can be better applied in order to improve or disable a particular system.

If the theory of evolution goes unchallenged before the law, then we will see our basic right to human equality slowly disappear under pretended legislations that attempt to cater to all from a secular premise. When nothing can enslave mankind faster than to deprive the people of their God given humanity by redefining the individual to being that of an animal. But because the universal law of human equality defines a person as distinct from the animals on the basis that all human beings have been endowed with conscience, it will mean that no individual has a legal or moral obligation to reject the existence of the Creator before the law, because all human beings have a legal obligation to acknowledge the human conscience before the law for reasons relating to the correct interpretation of human rights and equality.

*Quotation: ———————————————————

The United States Supreme Court has denied creation science to its students for reasons relating to Secularism, which is why the theory of evolution has become dominant from public education. And this is a danger for society, because evolution is a racial theory by the inclusion of inferior and superior human races based on a supposed animal ancestry. While systems theory is not a racial theory, and is also defined as modern science according to the principles of thermodynamics, which cannot be justified by the evolutionary theory, because a system will always be inferred according to a set of rules that not only defines a system as a creation, but also, it is the rules in place that sets the limitations of a system's operation.

Evolution is a failed theory in science, because living systems are not self-improving, and is clearly defined as an immoral social practice that lacks empathy, because natural selection is defined as survival of the fittest whereby the weak are taken advantage of by the strong. While any system of belief that lacks empathy is to be highly scrutinized, and should never be equated as being a fact of nature, nor should it be an official standard for the public education curriculum in any way, because individuals are governed by ethical conduct which bears responsibility on the individual's conscience, and this is a moral aspect of reality, as well as a physical one.

The more the theory of evolution continues to be taught from public education, the more human beings will be enslaved by a theory that attempts to challenge the universal law of human equality, because inalienable rights are defined by the common law as being endowed to mankind by our Creator, which is an opposing view to the pseudo-scientific theory of evolution that defines man as a lower animal. Under international agreement, a human being is to be defined as endowed with conscience in accordance with religious teachings, which is why the New Atheist movement is contrary to a lawful obligation that is in place to uphold the virtues of human rights and equality, as defined by international law.

So, in order to be consistent when interpreting the universal law of equality, then a Creator God is a requirement, because inalienable entitlements have been defined by religious teachings. And this also means that systems science and creation science are a lawful practice, while a racial theory, such as evolution, is by definition unlawful due to the nature of the racial terminology used to describe a person with. Systems theory and systems science is creation science, which can be used for good or for evil, but the only way to define whether the practice is good or evil, is by moral law, which in turn, sets a lawful premise for Biblical creation as a legal standard that is universal in its interpretation. And it is the unethical conduct by individuals who hail from the evolutionary theory that should be brought into question by the law, rather than a person's universal right to be defined as a created human being, which is self-explanatory.

The idea that evolution can be equated as being a fact of nature, and therefore incontestable, is a requirement for atheism in order for the theory to never be questioned, which is in the best interests of those who wish to define man as an animal in order to espouse some form of freedom from rules. And this is also why the inalienable rights of citizens is in great jeopardy around the globe, because if the American government continues to promote evolution through the public education system, then the universal definition of person will erode with each passing generation.

The universal definition of person has derived from the theological term, conscience, rather than from biology or taxonomy that defines man as a lower animal. The United States Constitution gave rise to the universal definition of man in accordance with freedom of conscience so that inalienable rights should be defined as universal in their interpretation, rather than institutional. But if America continues to teach that man is animal through the public education curriculum, then human equality will one day be lost due to a pseudo-definition of man that was without merit or sufficient cause.

Today, the pseudo-definition of man from the theory of evolution is the root cause of inequality along with the race war that still persists within the United States and other parts of the world. No scientific theory that defines man as an animal is with sufficient cause to argue before the law for reasons relating to the preservation of human rights and equality, so that no individual is subjected to inhumane treatment or torture; Meaning that the universal definition of man is in place so that we each have security of person before the law.

Yet the United States government has endorsed the torture of human beings who are seen as enemies of the State, which is a crime against humanity on the basis of equality. Every human being has an inalienable right to a fair hearing that includes a trial by jury so that a person may give a defence that is not coerced. So, the denial of the human conscience by the evolutionary theory in practice has only paved the way for human and animal torture, which is the reason why we must protect our inalienable right to be defined as created human beings, because it is the Creator who has endowed each person with conscience and with rights so that our basic rights should be preserved as inalienable.

*Quotation: ————————————————————

"The exceptions here or elsewhere in the Constitution, made in favour of particular rights, shall not be so construed as to diminish the just importance of other rights retained by the people, or as to enlarge the powers delegated by the Constitution, but either as actual limitations of such powers, or as inserted merely for greater caution. No State shall violate the equal rights of conscience, or the freedom of the press, or the trial by jury in criminal cases. And that the said Constitution shall never be construed to authorize Congress to infringe upon the just liberty of the press, or the rights of conscience." - Samuel Adams, American Statesman and a founding father of the United States. Source: Debates of the Massachusetts Convention. (Documented January 9, 1788).

Under United States Federal law according to Title VI Section 601 of the Civil Rights Act of 1964 - 78 Statutory (252: 42 U.S.C 2000d) a person is not to be excluded from receiving factual information from the public education system on the basis of their nationality or religion, and: "No racial, ethnic, or ancestral epithets, or slurs, are to be made against any individual." Yet defining a human being as a primate, mammal, lower animal, higher animal or as genetically inferior at some point in their ancestry is a crime against humanity, because this deprives the individual of their inalienable right to be defined as a created human being with a human ancestry.

Thus, depriving an individual of their basic right to obtain factual information regarding their true origins as a person through the public education system in accordance with the lawful definitions that are in place to correct an individual with, is a crime against humanity, because the individual is being told one thing by the public education system, while being told another thing by the law. So, there is in fact a discrepancy between the lawful definitions of what a human being is, which derive from Biblical theology under United States Constitutional law, and the standard definitions from public education, which derive from Linnaean taxonomy and the theory of evolution.

But because the individual is entitled to be defined as a person before the law despite whatever belief that is in place by the secular government, it will mean that every individual is legally entitled to the correct definitions regarding what the endowed conscience is, and where it is from, because it pertains to a person's inalienable right to be defined as a created human being, which is a universal right that is in accordance with international law. And the correct definitions are defined as being the lawful definitions in order for human equality and inalienable rights to be defined as universal.

A human being is not to be denoted as having derived from any other ancestry apart from human ancestry so that human equality should apply to all human beings from every culture, which means that there should be no confliction between the lawful definitions for what a person is, and that which is to be taught through the public education system in regards to human origins, because no human being, legally, is to be told that they're a mammal by their education minister, and are therefore an animal of some description, as this deprives the individual of their God given humanity, and their right to factual information in accordance with United States Federal law under Title VI Section 601 of the Civil Rights Act.

The self-evident and self-explanatory word definitions from law is what's authoritative when building a case under the common law, rather than theory alone, because lawful definitions are equal to a lawful instruction, while theoretical conjectures concerning the past are secondary to any lawful obligation. And this is why any dispute over man's origins must be settled by the law, because the lawful definition for human equality is what's at stake here due to lobbying efforts by those who hail from the evolutionary theory. If mankind is to have human equality, then the lawful definitions are to be equated as being a lawful instruction, and not the racist, pseudo-scientific, Linnaean classifications from taxonomy or Darwinism, which has now flooded the school textbooks within the public education system.

Yet the only thing that's required for this injustice to end, is for the United States Supreme Court to demand that the theory of evolution and the Linnaean taxonomical terms be denied from future textbooks for the purpose of introducing the lawful definitions as a continuous and sustainable standard for public education, because the only reason that school textbooks include a racial theory, such as evolution and Linnaean taxonomy, is because the Supreme Court has denied creation science to their students. The theory of evolution could be replaced overnight by simply employing the teaching of systems theory and systems science as a new standard model, because systems theory is a non-racial theory, and is not reliant on the Linnaean taxonomic terms which are the sole basis for Social Darwinism, the evolutionary theory, and scientific racism.

According to international law, everyone has the right to express their opinion under freedom of speech, but a racist opinion should always be invalidated on the basis that we have human equality from the premise of law, which is the basis for equal justice and equal rights to preside from for the benefit of an individual's protection within the system. The preservation of human rights and equality, as defined by the legal definitions in use, are in place so that we each have protection of person before the law in despite of any scientific theory, enterprise, or ambition.

Evolutionists have not only defined man as an animal, but also, they have attempted to merge human DNA with animal DNA in order to try and vindicate the theory of evolution at the taxpayer's expense, and now they're on the way to merging the human brain with a microchip. Scientific enterprise lobbies the heaviest to government for funding inhumane social experiments on the public, such as the pharmaceutical industry for example, which lobbies to government the heaviest in order to have psych drugs forced onto adults and children for the sole purpose of profiteering from the public when there is no clinical basis for any psychiatric disorder due to the nature of conscience.

The level of naïve ignorance and blatant stupidity that it takes to accept the theory of evolution is without a doubt, unsustainable, because as we progress into the future, it will be the love of many that will grow cold due to the propagation of a scientific theory that challenges the very system we live under. And we do live within a legal system which every member of mankind has a stake in according to the universal law of human equality and systems theory. All are required to acknowledge the universal definition of person before the law for the sake of human rights and equality, rather than the theory of evolution that defines man as a lower animal, of which, the legal system cannot cater for, because our entire legal system is based on human rights and equality, which cannot define man as an animal without detracting from the lawful definition of what a person is as a negative consequence.

According to the principles of systems theory, each person within the system should be represented in its management, thereby catering to human rights and equality. While evolution, as a system of belief, caters to no one on the basis of equality due to the evolutionary definition of man, which forms the basis for human slavery by a reinterpretation of the lawful term, conscience. Human freedom is not measured by word definitions that are intended to try and relate a human being with the animal kingdom, but from the existence of the human conscience instead, because human freedom is defined by freedom of conscience, which is a religious liberty, rather than a secular ideal.

The lawful definition of "person," according to online legal studies, is an individual who is able to act in his or her own right, and is capable of undergoing legal rights and liabilities that include individuals, (such as natural persons) and corporate organisations (which are legal fictions). While the definition of "person" from Oxford Languages is defined as "a living soul," which automatically implies that a Creator God is required when interpreting the law due to the rights of conscience. According to international law under the agreement of 192 nations, the human being has been defined as distinct from the animals on the basis of conscience and good reason, because it is the human conscience that is able to take on a moral obligation, which forms the basis of a legal obligation.

The correct definition of a natural person is any individual who is endowed with conscience, which applies to every individual human being, while the definition of a legal fiction is defined by a corporation. A company is a legal entity considered as a fictional person in law, that is distinct from its members and with separate company rights and liabilities. As per the fiction theory, a corporation exists only as an outcome of fiction and metaphor. Thus, the personality that is attached to these corporations is done purely by a legal fiction.

The legal fiction "person" is created only in the eyes of the law for reasons relating to public liability. A natural person on the other hand is a living human being with a living soul that is endowed with certain rights from birth. Legal duties to natural persons can occur without their express consent, which can be used for good or for evil, but it will always be morality that defines what is right or wrong, rather than law due to ethical reasons. Thus, a system of morality is required when interpreting the law due to ethical reasons, which cannot derive itself from a philosophical conjecture, otherwise, there would be no standard in place to determine the truth.

So, for this reason, morality is above the law from a Biblical premise, because it is Biblical morality that acts as a legal standard under the common law for the benefit of the people who are equal in rights. Thus, equal justice is defined by morality as universal regardless of philosophy, because it is equal justice that defines our equality. In jurisprudence, a natural or physical person is a person who has their own legal personality, and is regarded as a "living soul," while jurisprudence is the theory or philosophy of law. Common law has been developed by judges on a case by case basis in order to build on the legal precedent or interpretation of earlier court decisions. Thus, under common law jurisdictions, jurisprudence is a philosophy that is based on potential truths or principles that act as a legal standard for the interpretation of civil rights.

So, for this reason, a system of morality is a requirement for any system of law and order, or there would be no legal standard to define a law as just. The United States and the Commonwealth nations have favoured a system of morality that is based on Biblical creation as a legal standard from the New Testament, because it is Jesus Christ who has ushered in an age of human rights and equality, and human freedom thereby in accordance with Biblical teachings. The lawful premise for self-governance under the common law derives from Biblical teachings as a legal precedent, because it is Biblical theology that defines human freedom by the rights of conscience, rather than the teaching of evolution, which is the primary mechanism for human enslavement by the teaching of man's descent from the animal kingdom.

Our universal system of common law was founded upon the Biblical principles of human equality and equal justice for all, because all have been endowed with conscience by their Creator for the purpose of human rights and equality. Scientific endeavour on the other hand is the direct result of personal endeavours that can be used for good or for evil, and scientists do lobby to government the heaviest for funding, so it is usually the taxpayer who is paying for the personal ambitions of a scientist, even though most of the promises by scientists are short lived. Such as the promise that a cure for cancer would be ready after ten more years of research, which was announced to the public from the international news reports over 25 years ago... And this is the main reason why there are more people profiting from cancer research than there are people dying from cancer; Meaning that cancer research is one of the most profitable types of research undertaken due to a continuation of obliged donations and unfulfilled promises.

In the year 1769, when the early settlers began to settle in New Zealand, they became self-sufficient on a quarter-acre block of land, but today, most people live from the refrigerator inside small apartment blocks that are powered by coal power stations, which has led to an explosion in human population levels that is unsustainable for mankind due to an industrial monopoly. Mankind is not the problem however, but scientific endeavour to make billions of dollars is, and we will see the destruction of humanity as the wealth of a nation is concentrated into the hands of a few due to corruption within the system we live in. And we do live within a legal system which every member of mankind has a stake in according to the lawful definition of human equality that defines all individuals as having been endowed with conscience by their Creator.

So, we have freedom today according to the lawful definition of what a person is, but the more evolutionary scientists continue to try and merge mankind with the animal kingdom, the more we will see our basic human rights removed, all on the basis of a racial theory that defines man as a lower animal, of which, a system of equality cannot cater for due to the rights of conscience. Every time mankind has reached a peak in population levels a mass extinction suddenly occurred, such as the flood of Noah's day, the bubonic plague, and by genocide just to name a few. And the Holy Bible does predict that a mass extinction will occur when the mark of the beast comes into effect, and the idea by evolutionary scientists to clone man with the beasts of the field is most certainly an end game scenario for all of mankind.

The purpose of systems theory is to identify and compare different systems in order to understand and evaluate how each system relates to one another in order to asses a system for weaknesses so that a system can be improved or disabled. This means that all systems are integrated either relying on a primary feature within the system, or from an alternative system. Evolution, as a system of belief, is contrary to a lawful instruction that is universal in its interpretation, such as the universal definition of person. While creation science is not in opposition to the lawful definition of person due to theological consistencies that relate Biblical creation to the common law.

This means that evolution, as a secular theory, is inconsistent with human rights and equality on the basis that each person is defined as a living soul, rather than an animal of some description. If evolutionary theorists continue in their attempts to try and merge mankind with the animal kingdom, then mankind will one day be extinct due to a pseudo-scientific definition of man that was without merit, nor justification, because the one thing that cannot be defined as an animal under the rights of conscience, is a human being.

CHAPTER 2

Systems Engineering

S YSTEMS ENGINEERING, OR SYSTEMS DESIGN, IS THE DISCIPLINE OF
design and development that incorporates many fields of engineering,
and combines them to form a process in order to evaluate a system,
and improve the system. Risk management and assessment is an ongoing
process within systems engineering, and with all digital and mechanical
systems maintenance, because design and maintenance forms the main
purpose of systems engineering. Systems engineering involves discovering
faults within a particular system by having an ongoing assessment strategy
in place, which is designed to reduce risks to persons and equipment, and
to correct faults within the system by implementing controls and ideas to
the system based on an overall strategy, which is defined as the hierarchy
of control.

The hierarchy of control is a system for controlling risks by implementing
a step-by-step approach to eliminating or reducing risks for any given system,
and it ranks risk control as the highest priority. The hierarchy of control is
broken into 5 stages with the first priority being: Elimination. Elimination
is important because a hazard or fault within a system is best removed before
an incident occurs. Elimination is the first level of control, and eliminating a
fault or hazard within a system can be as simple as a routine clean-up, or as
time consuming and complicated as removing a malware program from the
database of a large mainframe terminal. Elimination is also a continuation

of step 5 within the hierarchy of control, which is assessment, because the procedure is a continuous management plan.

Second to elimination is: Substitution. Substitution is where elimination has occurred, and a substitute mechanism is to be put in place in order to keep the system operational, because the previous mechanism has failed, and this will always involve the replacement of the mechanism with a substitute mechanism. The third step for the hierarchy of control is: Engineering controls. Engineering controls are defined as being an engineered improvement by design, rather than by substitution alone, which was only temporary. And an engineered improvement will always be subject to the application of a designing technique, which in turn, gives rise to new engineering specifications and innovations. And the level of improvement will depend on the number of new specifics that have been introduced to the system, so that no system can self-improve, because engineering controls are required in order for innovation to occur.

The fourth step for the hierarchy of control is: Administrative controls. Administrative controls are training programs, procedure implementation, policy creation, and shifts in the design for a system, and this step is governed by the administrative body, which is where the orders for the system as a whole have derived from. Systems engineering relies primarily of administrative controls in order to implement controls and ideas, and this occurs as a procedure that is done according to a method so that no system can self-improve unless a method is applied. The fifth step for the hierarchy of control is: Assessment. Assessment is an ongoing process, because any new parameters for the system must be assessed for functionality in order to ensure the overall system is operating according to plan. And if a fault is discovered within the system then the process of implementing controls begins again starting with elimination, which means that this is a continuous management plan involving systems checks, and systems design, and the entire process relies primarily on communication with each step for the purpose of implementing controls and ideas.

Systems engineering is an engineering process that relies primarily on planning and communication in order to establish, improve, or disable a particular system, which means that this is a design, implement, and evaluate procedure that is done according to a method. So, because the specifics for a procedure must derive from planning as a rule, it will mean that evolution has played no role in a systems formation, because, A) Evolution defines itself as a natural process only. B) Systems engineering is by definition a design process, and is therefore an artificial process, rather than a natural process. And C) Because a natural process cannot be, at the same time, an artificial process, which limits the definition of evolution to being a theoretical postulation only due to the lack of a mechanism for innovation to occur.

A natural process cannot cause innovation to occur, because a natural process will always be limited to the number of specifics there are in place to define the process with. While any additional specifics to a given system must derive from a method of innovation, otherwise, there would be no causality for an increase in specificity. And it is the hierarchy of control that acts as an engineering design, hazard elimination, and systems assessment procedure in order to assess a particular system for weaknesses so that improvements can be made to the system based on future designs. This means that we as individuals can assess a design and deduce automatically that a system in place is evidence of creativity by definition of the fact that a system must derive by design. Otherwise, there would be no causality for innovation to occur due to the lack of a procedure that is by definition, specific.

In order for the standard for public education to adapt to new information, and then make efficient changes with the new information received, then there needs to be a correct standard in place that gives adequate explanations and definitions for that which is required, and pertinent facts require an explanation. If the hierarchy of control is blocked at any stage, then the administrative controls are required to engage the problem, and that is because the orders for the system have derived from the administrative body, which is what governs an engineered system as a working whole. Thus, accountability is also required when explaining the cause of a problem within an engineered system, and a legal system is by definition an engineered system, because a legal system is based on law, and laws are evidence of design. So, for the purpose of this chapter I will discuss an economic and industrial system in terms of an engineered legal system in order to detect faults prior to the system's failure.

An engineered system will always be subject to failure, because no system is ever 100% efficient due to fluctuations within the system, which means that systems assessment is an ongoing process. If the system of education is to be the blame for increased rates in incarceration, which it is, then so also is the standard in place, because the system is based on the standard to begin with. And it is the secular standard for public education that should be brought into question, and not the students who are subject to the system, because the standard for public education itself must be self-explanatory with minimal enforcement.

Otherwise, there will be the injustice of indoctrination caused by the enforcement of a particular standard that was false from its own assertions, and therefore, gave little value to the students who must carry the experience with them for the remainder of their life. And the one pertinent fact that requires an explanation to every student, is where does the human conscience come from, and what is it for? Because science has spent the last two and a half centuries trying to figure out how the human conscience arrived, rather than interpreting what the conscience is for.

According to Oxford Languages, social engineering is defined as: 1) "The use of centralized planning in an attempt to manage social change and regulate the future development and behaviour of a society." 2) "The use of deception to manipulate individuals into divulging confidential or personal information that may be used for fraudulent purposes." So, the issue of social engineering can have a positive or negative effect, resulting in a social trend that is predictable, but it will always be due to a plan in place that is either designed to succeed, or designed to fail. Social Darwinism is a political ideology that attempts to incorporate the theory of evolution into society, which forms the basis for systemic racism due to a pseudo-definition of man that is propagated from the public education system with the consent of the law.

In opposition to Social Darwinism, there is Biblical creation which was the former system for public education before the theory of evolution took over. The former system for public education within the United States involving Biblical creation as a legal standard, is by definition, Constitutional, because inalienable rights are defined as having derived from the Creator due to the lawful definition of conscience. While the increased rate in incarceration among citizens within the United States and elsewhere is entirely due to the implementation of the evolutionary theory into public education, because if the education system has failed to interpret the lawful definition of conscience, then a person's basic rights have been put into harm's way.

The increased rates in incarceration within the United States and elsewhere is entirely due to the introduction of the evolutionary theory from society and law, which cannot be removed through elimination without first having a substitute method. Thus, Biblical creation is a substitution to the theory of evolution for three main reasons. Firstly; Biblical creation is not in conflict with the universal law of equality. Second; Biblical creation was the former model for public education within the United States. And thirdly; Biblical creation acts as a legal standard that is self-evident under the common law for the benefit of an individual's protection within the system.

The teaching of systems theory is by definition an engineered improvement compared to the teaching of evolution, because both systems theory and systems science can only be defined by creation science by definition of the fact that a system is rule based. So, because the evolutionary theory is unlawful due to an open conflict with the lawful definition for human equality, and by a denial or reinterpretation of conscience, it will mean that substitution is required in order for society to be properly educated concerning a lawful instruction that is universal in its interpretation.

The former system for public education within the United States derives from Biblical creation as a legal standard, which many claim has failed as a mechanism for learning due to the introduction of the evolutionary theory into public education and law. But in reality, it was Biblical creation as a legal standard that led to the correct interpretation of inalienable rights, and the rights of conscience. While the secular standard for public education involving the enforced education of the evolutionary theory has utterly failed as a mechanism for improvement due to an open conflict with the universal law of equality. Thus, it is not Biblical creation as a legal standard that has failed as a mechanism for learning, while the secular standard has, because it is the secular standard for public education that brings the rights of conscience into question due to a theological dispute.

Evolution, as a theory, is the leading cause for systemic racism due to a continuation of the Linnaean definition of man, which forms the philosophical basis for scientific racism, and the theological dispute with the law of equality. Thus, the evolutionary theory in practice from a secular premise has utterly failed as a system of education due to an opposition to the universal law of equality, because according to the theory, human beings have evolved from the animals. When according to international law, a human being must be defined by a human ancestry in accordance with international agreement for reasons relating to the correct interpretation of human rights and equality.

According to international law under article 1 of the Universal Declaration of Human Rights and Equality (UDHR), all human beings have been endowed with conscience, with which, to reason from, which is the very thing that separates mankind from the animal kingdom, because the ability to ask questions derives from the ability to reason from a source of conscience, of which, the animals do not share, which is both self-explanatory, as well as self-evident in terms of a legal precedent or standard. The secular interpretation of human rights and equality derives from the theory of evolution and Linnaean taxonomy that defines man as a lower animal by the reinterpretation of conscience, when it is the correct interpretation of conscience that forms the basis for human rights and equality.

The lawful term, conscience, is a theological term from the Holy Bible that has been used by international law to define a person as distinct from the animals for reasons relating to the correct interpretation of inalienable. The Holy Bible from the New Testament clearly teaches that Christ Jesus has ushered in an age of human rights and equality by His death upon the cross, and by His resurrection from the dead, which is referred to as the "Age of Grace" in terms of Christian theology. According to the Gospel of Ephesians 2:11-18 Jew and gentile are reconciled together by the blood of Christ. His purpose the Bible says was to create in Himself a new humanity out of the two, thus making peace, and to reconcile them both to God through the cross by one Spirit.

The universal law of human equality is of a higher legal standard than scientific theory, while international law is subject to a higher authority in itself, such as moral law, otherwise, there would be no universal definition to define corruption with, as well as unethical conduct. Thus, morality is above the law from a Biblical premise, because it is the verdicts reached from the contents of the Gospel message of hope that outlines the lawful premise for human rights and equality under the common law by the rights of conscience. Historically, the rights of conscience has derived from Biblical creation as a legal standard by which the courts must follow under the common law, which is where international law has derived its definition of human freedom due to the use of the Biblical term, conscience, to define a person as distinct from the animals. So, for this reason, any theory that attempts to define man as animal is by definition, unlawful, which must be contested from the premise of law in order for the people to exercise their basic rights as created human beings.

The United States legal system has led the world in human rights and equality by the introduction of inalienable rights as having been endowed by our Creator, which forms the basis for human rights and equality under freedom of conscience. Systems engineering and applied systems science is modern science, which can only be explained in terms of creation science by definition of the word, design. While the evolutionary theory attempts to deny the evidence of design by defining every process as a natural process only, when there is nothing natural about designing and engineering by definition of the fact that designing and engineering are both an artificial process. So, for this reason, the secular standard for public education has failed as a mechanism for learning due to the reinterpretation of conscience, while Biblical creation was the former system for education and law that led to the creation of the United States Constitution.

According to the First Amendment under the United States Constitution, the right to petition the Government for a redress of public grievances is protected as an inalienable right. And it is the theory of evolution in practice from society and law that acts as a public grievance for reasons relating to the universal definition of man, which cannot be contested for reasons relating to the preservation of human rights and equality. So, in order to be consistent with a lawful instruction that is universal in its interpretation, such as the universal definition of person, then the theory of evolution must be challenged from the premise of law, because the right to be defined as a created human being with a human ancestry is defined as inalienable in order that our basic rights are protected as inalienable.

Proponents from the New Atheist movement who hail from the theory of evolution have attempted to refute the existence of inalienable rights due to an open conflict with the theological terms from law that are in place to protect an individual with so that their conscience is not in conflict with the lawful instruction. If a human being is to denote themselves as an animal, and then to deny the existence of inalienable rights, then they cannot be reasoned with as an individual, nor can they receive a conviction of truth before the law for reasons relating to the reinterpretation of conscience.

The evolutionary definition of man forms the basis for systemic racism due to the use of certain terms, such as Homo-Sapien, Negroid, mammal, lower animal, and so on, in order to try and relate mankind with the animal kingdom. And this is a crime against humanity on the basis of equality whereby every person has a birthright to be defined as a created human being at all times with a human ancestry regardless of any scientific theory or enterprise. Thus, it is inalienable that each person should be defined as created in the image of God for reasons relating to the correct interpretation of conscience.

The legal standard for interpreting the human conscience, as from international law, is of a higher legal standard than scientific theory, and it is the theory of evolution that is in question here as a method, because if the evolutionary theory is to bring our humanity into question before the law by attempting to define a person as a type of animal, then it is the evolutionary theory that is to be brought into question by the law, rather than our God given humanity, which is self-explanatory. The human conscience has been defined by international law as endowed, rather than evolved, and that which is endowed, according to law, is also a birthright.

According to international law under the UDHR, every person has a birthright to be defined as a created human being without distinction by definition of the word, person. While any scientific theory that attempts to redefine the human being in order to suit a given theory, is a crime against humanity, because without a definition for a human being that is universal in its interpretation, then human rights cannot be interpreted as inalienable. The Universal Declaration of Human Rights and Equality has out-lined that freedom of conscience is the most sacred of all rights, which automatically implies that freedom of religion and belief is inalienable. So, because freedom of religion is inalienable, and because the term, conscience, derives from theology, it will mean that a Creator God is required in order to be consistent with human rights legislation under international law.

The social trend that is occurring within America and other parts of the world today is a predictable trend from one of human freedom under the law, to one of human enslavement with the consent of the law. And what I mean by this, is that our basic freedoms as human beings is slowly being removed by the teaching of evolution from the practice of public education and law, because it is the theory of evolution that is in opposition to a lawful instruction that is universal in its interpretation, such as the universal right to be defined as a created human being with a human ancestry. The theory of evolution, along with Social Darwinism, is contradictory to international law, because each human being is entitled to be defined by a human ancestry, which cannot derive from the animals without detracting from a legal obligation to uphold the virtues of human rights and equality.

Individuals who hail from the evolutionary theory are required by international law to recognize the basic rights of a human being, which does not involve defining a person to being that of an animal. Yet public education providers have done exactly that by referring to a human being as a type of ape, which is without merit, nor justification, before international law for reasons relating to the correct interpretation of human rights and equality. So, in order for public education, and public education providers to be correctly informed regarding a lawful instruction that is universal in its interpretation so that a human rights violation does not occur against the public, then the theory of evolution must be overruled from the premise of law in order to accommodate for human rights and equality regardless of the religiosity of the legal definitions used.

Anything that has derived from instructions, such as the human body or written law, is by definition, engineered, because the process of formation began with instructions, resulting in a group of mechanisms that work together as a unified whole, which is evidence of design, rather than evolution. Thus, both systems engineering and creation science are not in opposition to a lawful instruction that is universal in its interpretation, while the theory of evolution has brought our humanity into question by a reinterpretation of the theological term, conscience. So, because we live within a legal system that is based on human rights and equality, and because a legal system is by definition an engineered system due to the application of a design or plan, it will mean that engineering controls are required to be put in place by the administration for the benefit of an individual's protection within the system, otherwise, laws cannot protect us as individuals.

No engineered improvements can be made to the theory of evolution without causing a contradiction to the theory in turn, because that which is engineered, is by definition, designed. So, because systems engineering is by definition a design, evaluate, and implement procedure, while evolution is not, it will mean that engineering controls can be put into place using systems theory and systems science without causing a contradiction to the theory. And the reason why no engineered improvements can be applied to the theory of evolution without causing a contradiction to the theory in turn, is because evolution defines itself as a natural process only, while systems engineering and systems design is an artificial process by definition of the word, create.

In order to evaluate and assess a particular system for weaknesses, then a method of identification is required first, which cannot be self-contradictory or the method will fail. And it is the secular standard for public education that has utterly failed to identify a particular problem that is self-contradictory, which only exacerbates the problem over time, because if there is one thing that cannot be observed using secular science, then it is Biblical creation. So, for this reason, the theory of evolution is the greatest theoretical set-back in all of modern science, because the only thing that can be observed using secular science, is philosophical materialism.

Philosophical materialism is the core philosophy for secular science, which is self-contradictory on the basis of naturalism, and the reason why naturalism is self-contradicting, is because not all processes are by definition, natural. The sole purpose of secular science is to deny the supernatural, when the supernatural cannot be dismissed under any set of rules, because rules are always inferred the same as any creation. So, in order to distinguish between a natural process, and a supernatural process, then a method of identification is required first, which cannot derive from pure naturalism due to a contradiction between that which is natural, and that which is not. And it is for the purpose of identification that a supernatural process is required to be explained factually to students on the basis that a natural process cannot be used to explain the causality of conscience.

The official reason why a natural process cannot be used to define the causality of conscience, is solely due to the limitations of a natural process, which is simply the normal workings of a system in place that is operating according to plan. So, because a natural process has derived from a plan in order for the process at work to occur independently of the Creator of the process, it will mean that a supernatural process must be inferred in order to correctly explain the causality of conscience, because the human conscience is the only thing we have to invent a rule or system. And this does not constitute as a religious test in order to dismiss evolution as a theory, but rather, it is a method of identification, which is essential to any theory in both science and law.

A supernatural process must be inferred in order to explain the causality of conscience for three main reasons. First; Because the human conscience is neither material nor natural, and thus, cannot derive from nature or the animals. Second; The human conscience is for our understanding of morality, while nature and the animals are unaware of morality. And thirdly; Morality is rule based, and rules must always be inferred in order to interpret a system or process. Otherwise, there would be no method of identification in regards to a natural process compared to an artificial process, because in order to distinguish between the two, the a method is required, which is the evidence of a creation by definition of the word, system. The term (system) is interchangeable with the term, (method) in that a procedure has been inferred, which is the only way to interpret a process, whether natural or not.

The second aspect of naturalism from secular science that leads to a contradiction in regards to the lawful definition of conscience, is the lawful and common definition of person, which is defined as a "living soul." So, in order to differentiate between an animal and a human being, then proof of conscience is required, which in turn, requires the ability to reason and ask questions in the form of a language or word. A name will always be relative to a word, and it is for the purpose of identification that each person is given a name, while no animal has ever expressed a name for itself by itself due to their lack of conscience.

The process of identification works as a sequence, because the entire purpose of identification is to identify a sequence in order for a prediction to occur, which forms the basis of a theory or trend. And the social trend that is occurring within America, and other common law districts, is a trend from a Christian based democracy to that of a secular society. America is not a secular society that owes its allegiance to a secular government, because that is Communism. But rather, America is a democratic republic that is to scrutinize the secular government, which is why freedom of the press, and freedom of conscience are defined as inalienable.

An Executive Order is one where the president of a nation is able to apply a strict directive so that an effective change can occur. This means that the president of the United States has the authority to remove the racial terms from public education so that a substitution can be put in place in order to improve communication between the law and students. And the racial terms from the evolutionary theory are indeed, unlawful, rather than Biblical creation, because it is Biblical creation as a legal standard that led the United States of America to human freedom and independence from foreign subjugation by the rights of conscience.

So, in order for an engineered control to be put in place by the administrative body in relation to systemic racism within public education, then the theory of evolution must be overruled from the premise of law so that a person's basic rights are protected as inalienable. Rights such as: freedom of conscience, thought, and belief are an inalienable right, while any system of belief that allows for racial terms to be included within the context of law and education must be reformed in order to cater for human rights and equality, which is a fundamental right in accordance with international law under Article 1 of the UDHR.

According to statistics, the United States spent $563 billion on importing goods from Communist China in 2022, which in turn, is being funnelled into the Communist Party's military. A war with Communist China is indeed a reality and will inevitably occur over time unless trade reform with China occurs first. In the year 2022, the American government spent $876 billion on its military whilst providing $563 billion to Communist China, which means that America will inevitably lose the war against Communist China unless the American government diverts spending towards a stronger manufacturing base within the borders of their own country, because the war against Communist China is a trade war, rather than a political dispute alone.

The Free Trade Agreement, (according to its own interpretation) is a treaty between two or more countries that is designed to reduce or eliminate certain barriers to trade and investment, and to facilitate stronger trade and commercial ties between participating countries, which happens to be the positive spin. But the negative result by the Free Trade Agreement in effect is a continuation of the former British-American slave trade agreement that has mutated itself into the Free Trade Agreement, which has only amounted to being a global financial disaster by the introduction of a trade war with Communist China, which is expedient for the military industrial complex of Communist China, but not for the American tax paying workers who bare the financial brunt of it all.

The counter claim here is that the introduction of Communist China into the Free Trade Agreement with America has resulted in more exports from America to China. When in reality, exports from America to China in 2022 were $195.5 billion, while America's imports from China during 2022 was equal to $562.9 billion according to the United States Government Trade Representative. This over representation of imports from China to the United States equates to being an economic disaster due to spending almost three times what the system is producing in only one year. And no economic and industrial system can maintain its level of imports over time by spending more than what the system is producing, because the end result is extreme poverty due to the creation of debt.

If the Free Trade Agreement between America and Communist China continues unabated, then the end result is a global financial meltdown, as well as a global war, because the United States government has committed itself to supporting the Communist government of China through the Free Trade Agreement, rather than the American people. The American dream of owning your own home, paying your taxes, and sustaining a reasonable quality of life has converted itself into an economic and industrial nightmare with the consent of the law. So, it is for this reason that the Free Trade Agreement is a continuation of the former slave trade agreement whereby a person is born into debt with the promise to repay government spending with each tax declaration that is created.

The former British-American slave trade agreement allowed Britain and America to exploit the working capacity of the poor in order to sell to the wealthy, which is also the same as competing the spending and borrowing power of the United States with the working class of China. If America is to continue as a global superpower, then the Free Trade Agreement between China and America must be overruled in order for

America to rebuild its manufacturing base, and to allow for more jobs, which in turn, increases the likelihood of the American dream becoming a reality for each and every citizen.

The issue of a nation importing more than it exports is not only an economic problem for the United States, but also, for Canada, New Zealand, Australia, the United Kingdom along with many other nations, which is being done in order to create the right conditions for global war. Global war is an inevitable consequence of the Free Trade Agreement having been put into effect, because the Free Trade Agreement is designed to fail resulting in an engineered financial crisis. The reason that this is being done globally is to instigate a final social cataclysm by design due to a major shift in social and economic trends, which has been instigated on purpose by Communism and Marxism by the use of social engineering techniques resulting in a shift in culture from one of human freedom, to one of moral and social decay.

According to the principles of Marxism, the working class must be forced to purchase more and more expensive goods until the debt becomes unbearable due to an unnecessary amount of spending and borrowing, which must in some way funnel itself into a Communist industrial system. So, because the Free Trade Agreement is for the express purpose of funnelling money into a Communist industrial system, it will mean that the Free Trade Agreement is a Communist trade agreement that leads to human slavery by the creation of debt, rather than human freedom by the creation of jobs.

The Free Trade Agreement between Communist China and America will inevitably fail over time due to the number of American jobs that are lost to Communist China, and because of American imports from China weighing in at almost three times the amount that America is exporting in return, it will mean that we are facing a global economic disaster, which is the equivalent of an engineered financial crisis that is unavoidable for America and the rest of the world at this time. The purpose of systems engineering is to detect faults prior to a systems failure and to engage in effective communication so that an engineering control can be put in place by the administration before a major incident occurs. And the major incident of a global conflict with Communist China is unavoidable unless an engineered control involving trade reform with China occurs first by the Administrative body in accordance with the will of the people.

So, in order for substitution to occur so that an engineered control can be put into effect, then elimination is required first, which is why abandoning the Free Trade Agreement with China will lead to the creation of an engineered control, but substitution is required first, which must derive itself from the will of the people, rather than the administration alone, because the administration has already failed the people by leading the people into global economic upheaval. And the correct way to apply a substitute method is with a previous mechanism, such as the former United States industrial system that catered for individual human sovereignty, whereby the worker was paid in full, and the company produced a product, which was the founding and governing principle by the people of the United States that made America the financial superpower that it is today.

If mankind is to proceed into a future based on human rights and equality, then the theory of evolution must be challenged from the premise of law, otherwise, we will slowly lose our basic rights as human beings due to a theory that attempts to cater to all from a secular premise, whilst failing to yield to a lawful instruction that is universal in its interpretation for the benefit of an individual's protection within the system. A person cannot be defined as both a human being and an animal before the law without detracting from the legal definition of person, because a person is to be self-governed under the law, while an animal is to be defined as property. And if you wish to challenge this principle, then the final result is human slavery due to the legal definition of property.

A human being is not to be denoted as an ape, primate, or mammal before international law, because these definitions are derogative in relation to a person's ancestry, rather than literal. The theory of evolution attempts to equate a human being with the animal kingdom in order to define the progression of mankind in terms of a human-animal ancestry. Yet no human being can be defined as having derived from any other ancestry before the law apart from a human ancestry for reasons relating to the correct interpretation of human rights and equality.

If society is to be self-governed under the principles of universal law by the rights of conscience, then the education system must agree with the lawful definitions in place that are designed to protect our basic freedoms, or there will be contradictions between that which is lawful, and that which is not. So, because the human conscience is defined as being the lawful basis for human rights and equality, and because human equality is the lawful basis for equal justice and universal rights to be defined by, it will mean that the human conscience must be interpreted to students for the benefit of a legal system to operate effectively, whereby each person understands the correct lawful definitions without contention.

Historically, when the United States Union, under Abraham Lincoln, was at war with the South during the American Civil War, the facts needed to be explained to the citizens correctly, because the citizens were depending upon the truth of the overall situation from the administration in order to make a moral decision as to whether or not they should continue fighting the war. So, because the war was essential for ending the infamous British-American slave trade, and for maintaining the principles for human equality set forth by the Declaration of Independence, it will mean that the people were already well informed concerning the existence of their endowed conscience. Therefore, they understood full well how important it was to defend the Constitution in order to protect their inalienable right to freedom of conscience, and individual human independence thereby.

Proof of conscience is a requirement before the law in order to be defined as a human being, rather than an animal or a thing, which are both defined as property, legally speaking. No individual can deny the existence of the human conscience before the law, because human slavery has been abolished under international agreement, which is why defining yourself, or others, as an animal cannot be justified under international agreement from the premise of law, because no human being, legally, can be defined as property. The creation of the Universal Declaration of Human Rights and Equality is a direct result of the United States Declaration of Independence, because both documents outline that freedom of conscience is inalienable.

The social trend towards humanity by the teaching of evolution from public education has amounted to being a form of systemic racism that cannot be eliminated from law and education without a substitute method first, such as Biblical creation. So, as we progress into the future, we will see a rise in minority groups who challenge basic public morals due to the application of the evolutionary theory within society that acts as a social experiment that is engineered to fail, thereby leading to the collapse of America and the rest of the world by the reinterpretation of conscience. A denial of conscience can and does include the reinterpretation of conscience to meaning that of an animal, which is propagated from the public education system with the consent of the law.

The idea that science is in authority derives from the Enlightenment period whereby faith was to be replaced by science. Whereas today, we are to be self-governed under international law by the universal law of human equality, which has taken its legal definition of what a person is from the United States Declaration of Independence and their Constitution that defines all individuals as having been endowed with conscience by their Creator, which is also the lawful basis for inalienable rights to be defined by in accordance with Biblical teachings under the common law.

If inalienable rights derive from man, then man has enlightened man, but if inalienable rights derive from the Creator, then God has enlightened man. And the individual may choose whether they believe in God the Creator or not, but as from law, the decision is made for them for the purpose of inalienable rights to be made universal in their interpretation. The true meaning of what it means to be enlightened, is that you understand what your inalienable rights are as an individual, and then to stand upon these rights in the face of adversity, which is the very thing that gave America its independence within the world as a nation under God.

An engineered system cannot be explained in terms of materialism, because the very word engineering means to "create" or "design." So, for this reason, engineering is not a natural process by definition of the fact that designing is an artificial process. This means that it requires an extremely dishonest individual with a gold medal in mental gymnastics to try and explain how an engineered system could arise either directly or indirectly from materials and energy alone, because an engineered system requires planning in advance the same as instructions do in order for a method to be established.

So, when the standard explanation from secular science does not live up to the lawful definitions that are in place to define a human being with, then it is the secular standard for public education that must be replaced, and the members from that industry must not be allowed to interfere with the functions of government, which includes lobbying to government for rights to be removed from citizens in order to grant privileges to the minority of people who were denying the lawful definitions for human rights and equality in the first place.

An engineered crisis will always be the result of a plan in place, either directly or indirectly, and the level of chaos that is produced will always be relative to the number of people who have been affected by the crisis directly. And an example of an engineered crisis, would be residential construction in China, which has had numerous apartment buildings collapse due to a poor adherence to international safety standards; Including the illegal addition of extra floors whilst failing to provide reinforced steel bars; As well as decaying infrastructure, such as underground gas pipes, which has led to explosions in apartment areas resulting in building collapses.

Yet these engineering issues could have been easily prevented if the government was not taking bribes from major building and construction firms. An engineered crisis will always be the result of a plan in place, whether deliberate or not, which means that an engineered crisis can occur by accident, or on purpose. And the main crisis that is occurring in America today, is the issue of racism, which is a mixture of both foreseen and unforeseen factors.

According to United States Federal law, it is illegal to refer to a person by the Linnaean/Darwinian term, Negroid, because this type of terminology is racially motivated, and therefore, derogative in relation to what a human being is. Yet there is no law requiring school textbooks to refrain from using certain terms, such as Neanderthal, Homo-Sapien, mammals, and primates, which are indeed racial terms by definition of the fact that they are in regards to a person's ancestry. Racial inequality in the United States is by definition an engineered crisis, because the terminology used to regard certain groups of people as genetically inferior according to their ancestry is a direct result of the theory of evolution and Linnaean taxonomy. And it does not matter whether the administration is aware of it or not, because the end result is systemic racism and social inequality from public education and law.

A legal representative or local member of government is an individual's representation within a legal system, because every individual has a stake within the system according to systems theory and the law of equality. The system we have is a universal system based on human rights and equality from the premise of law, so that each person has an inalienable right to a fair hearing, and equal justice thereby. And international law has given protections to freedom of belief from the UDHR, while there are no protections under international law for unbelief in regards to the lawful definition of conscience, because all are required according to their endowed conscience to recognize the universal rights of others, and unbelief does not constitute as a right under this universal declaration.

All human beings are required by international law to acknowledge the lawful definition of person for reasons relating to the preservation of human rights and equality, and no one is to deny the lawful interpretation of what a human being is for the benefit of an individual's protection within the system. The human being has been defined by the endowed human conscience for the purpose of human rights and equality, which is something that science, in all of its brilliance, has failed to interpret from the viewpoint of the evolutionary theory, because the term, conscience, is a theological term, rather than a secular one.

But unfortunately, this has led to a society based on science fiction, rather than law, because people are far too busy studying what's on free to air TV, rather than reading what the correct definitions are from a responsible source of information. And the system of a legal society will break down over time if communication breaks down due to a confliction between freedom of information through a non-legal representative, and information gained through a lawful representative, such as a local member of government who is responsible for the individual's protection through the provision of factual information.

For example: If an individual was to watch a film or documentary on TV that defined the human being as a mammal, and therefore an animal, then this would be an offence before the universal law of human equality. But because individuals have freedom to information does not mean that corporations, and public education providers have the luxury of misinforming the public concerning a lawful instruction. And if John Doe appears before court, and wishes to argue that he came from a fish, then that is because of a failure in communication on the system's part due to the evolutionary standard for public education being non-factual, and not the individual who is simply repeating what he has learned from his stake within the system.

Today, more people are getting dumber rather than smarter due to an inevitable conflict between the lawful interpretations for human equality, which derive from theology, and the educational material that is freely available to them via programs that are run for free, which in turn, derives from a secular premise, and the evolutionary theory. But because freedom of information must be factual if it claims to be factual before the law, then it is the lawful definitions that are to be regarded as factual, rather than the random opinions of a naturalist scientist from a university who is to irresponsible to give someone the time of day, let alone interpret what the human conscience is for, because the human conscience is for the benefit of the student who is being introduced to an engineered system that is based on human rights and equality, rather than science.

An engineered system is any system that has been designed, which includes a legal system by definition of the word, create. Thus, it is the creation of laws that constitutes as a system by design, and it is for this reason that physical laws and moral law are also designed for the benefit of the individual who is being introduced into the education system. In systems theory, a system can fluctuate from one set of rules to another due to a set of parameters that can vary, which is what a random variation is. But if a random variation is to be used as a mechanism for improvement, then the only improvement to the system, is random decay.

Social and moral decay within the system we live by is the direct result of a system that is fluctuating from one social trend to another in terms of a progression. And the progression of an engineered system will lead to failure if the administration is unaware of a major incident. Hazard elimination and incident reports are in integral part of systems engineering, because the orders for the system as whole have derived from the administrative body. If the administrative body is unaware of a major incident, then an engineered control cannot be established. Thus, hazard identification is integral part of systems engineering the same as hazard reports, which means that no major incident can be swept under the rug without causing further incident. And the major incident that has occurred within America, is the rise of minority groups that question basic public morals on the basis of fictional beliefs.

The theory of evolution is the most widely used theory in science fiction films; Meaning that the theory of evolution is the world's most fictional theory in the history of cinema. Especially when you take into account that ancient mythology is defined by the belief in half-human half-animals from a secular premise, which historically, forms the basis of Greco-Roman mythology. While our universal dating system from BC to AD is based on a Biblical timeline, rather than an evolutionary timescale, because the Holy Bible is based on recorded eyewitness events, while the theory of evolution is postulated without proof due to a lack of eyewitness accounts concerning the history of the Earth. Evolutionary scientists are attempting to create half-human half-animals in the laboratory through cloning methods, which is in fact evidence of design, rather than evolution, because half-human half-animals do not occur naturally, and are always the result of a bioengineering technique.

In order for an engineered system to be established, then there must also be an effective method of communication, which not only relies on control measures to be in place, such as the hierarchy of control, but also, rules, or an engineered system cannot operate effectively due to an inevitable breakdown in communication. So, in order for laws and lawful definitions to be interpreted to students in order that they too can contribute to the system with a fair outcome, then there can be no confliction between the lawful definitions of conscience, and the standard definitions from public education. Any materialistic or secular standard for public education by the United States that denies the lawful interpretation of what the human conscience is, and where it is from, based on the assertion that no explanation is needed, must be reformed, otherwise, the system will inevitably fail the students who should be made fully aware of the engineered legal system they're entering into according to the proper definitions in use for the purpose of maintaining their individual protection within the system.

For example: In the United States, the Supreme Court has ruled that: "The teaching of Biblical creation as a science in public schools is unconstitutional, irrespective of how it may be purveyed in theological or religious instruction." But the United States Constitution, the Bill of Rights, and the Declaration of Independence has defined human freedom by the existence of inalienable rights, which are defined as being endowed to every individual by their Creator on the basis of conscience and equality. So, the religiosity of creation science is no different to the religiosity of the legal definitions used to describe a person as distinct from the animals, so that creation science is Constitutional, while the theory of evolution is not.

Freedom of conscience is a religious liberty embodied within the First Amendment of the United States Constitution known as: The First Liberty, because this liberty grants freedom of thought and belief; Prohibits the establishment or interference of religion by the government; And implicitly acknowledges the United States as a place that accommodates for religious pluralism. Public school students within the United States, legally, should never be informed by their government that creation science cannot be taught on the basis that it was religious, only to replace the Biblical standard for public education with a secular standard that is by definition, substandard.

The similarity between systems engineering and the United States legal system derives from the correct interpretation of Biblical creation as a legal standard for both law and public education, because an engineered system can only occur by design. The founding fathers of the United States foresaw the collapse of America before it began to occur, and they attributed this failure to the alteration of government powers. Every time a new law is created, a new bureaucracy is created also, which then leads to an increase in taxation in order to make an effective change, which can either be an increase in fines by the increase of penal offences, or it can be due to oversized government, which can and does lead to an increase in financial hardship, which must be offset by having a strong manufacturing base. A strong manufacturing base within an industrial system is the only true safeguard against financial hardship due to the creation of jobs, because creativity is the source of all wealth.

For example: When a product for market is manufactured or made, it will always begin with raw materials that must be laboured in order for the end product to occur. Thus, adding labour to the process of manufacturing is the only way for wealth to be created, which is not only expedient for the bureaucracy, but also, the working class, because when labour is applied to raw materials, the creation of wealth also increases. This principle is a law of creation in that creativity is the source of all wealth, rather than the ownership of property, because you borrow from your assets as collateral, while labour increases the ownership of assets, such as raw materials.

Systems engineering is thereby a creation process in accordance with the law of creativity, which cannot be attributed to a natural process, because the process began with labour, while raw materials have already been supplied by our Creator. In order for an increase in raw materials to be made available, then labour is required first, otherwise, the raw materials can be refined. And it is for this reason that the theory of evolution places an unnecessary constraint upon the people by the reinterpretation of conscience, because freedom of conscience is the lawful basis for individual human sovereignty, whereby a worker is paid in full, and the company produces a product.

If the human conscience has derived from the animals, then man is simply a beast of burden like the cattle of the field, which is a Communist ethic, rather than an American ideal. So, for this reason, it is the correct definition of conscience that will sustain us as free individuals within the system, because a legal system is dependent upon each person to first understand a lawful obligation before they can obey a lawful instruction. A lawful obligation can only be defined by a moral obligation, otherwise, a person's conscience will be in conflict with a lawful instruction, which then leads to self-exclusion from the law, as well as anarchy. If the correct interpretation of the human conscience, as well as morality, is restrained from the system of public education, then the legal system will also become restrained due to a conflict of interest that sets itself against the law.

Thus, the only true safeguard we have against lawlessness and extreme poverty, is with a correct theology, which cannot be constrained to the point of physical and moral exhaustion without creating a global rebellion in turn. This issue is well understood by those who hail from the political and industrial viewpoint of absolute Marxism, because the sole purpose of Marxist philosophy, according to Karl Marx himself, is to dethrone God, and to destroy what he calls "Capitalism," which is a Marxist term, rather than a political and economic venture by the founding fathers of the United States.

*Quotation: ————————————————————
"Religion is the general theory of this world, its encyclopedic compendium, its logic in popular form, its spiritual point d'honneur, its enthusiasm, its moral sanction, its solemn complement, and its universal basis of consolation and justification. It is the fantastic realization of the human essence since the human essence has not acquired any true reality. The struggle against religion is, therefore, indirectly the struggle against that world whose spiritual aroma is religion. Religious suffering is, at one and the

same time, the expression of real suffering and a protest against real suffering. Religion is the sigh of the oppressed creature, the heart of a heartless world, and the soul of soulless conditions. It is the opium of the people.

The abolition of religion as the illusory happiness of the people is the demand for their real happiness. To call on them to give up their illusions about their condition is to call on them to give up a condition that requires illusions. The criticism of religion is, therefore, in embryo, the criticism of that vale of tears, of which, religion is the halo. Capital is money, capital is commodities. By virtue of it being value, it has acquired the occult ability to add value to itself. It brings forth living offspring, or, at the least, lays golden eggs." - Karl Marx, founder of Communism. Source: Deutsch-Französische Jahrbücher - A Contribution to the Critique of Hegel's Philosophy of Right. (Documented February 10, 1844).

According to Marxist philosophy, the abolition of religion is the abolition of all morality, and he is basing his ideas upon his disdain for the wealthy, that is to say, America, which is a global economic superpower by the rights of conscience involving the law of creativity. In Marx's own words, he has stated that capital has acquired the "occult" ability to add value to itself, which is simply an atheistic way of condemning creativity as the source of all wealth. Thus, Karl Marx was fully aware that America's capacity to become a global economic superpower is owing to the practice of religious principle, in that the rights of conscience has led America to economic victory, as well as self-defeat, because freedom is abused by the abuse of power. But if religion is to be the blame for the abuse of power, and oversized government debt, then so also is human freedom, because human freedom is measured by freedom of conscience and belief, rather than spending and borrowing power.

The United States Supreme Court has no more rights to deny the religiosity of the legal interpretations from their Constitution, any more than they have the right to remove factual information from the public by citing a secular standard for public education as their right and justification, because both the legal definition of person, and the legal definition of conscience, are protected as inalienable, as well as universal. Under United States Constitutional law and the Declaration of Independence, human independence is defined by inalienable rights, which derive from God the Creator in order for inalienable rights to be defined as universal, otherwise, they must derive from nature, when nature is defined as property by the law.

Thus, the conflict of interest here derives from the interpretation of nature as all powerful, when one needs to be made aware of nature and its limitations, otherwise, nature becomes the source of human rights, which then leads to moral and social decay, because nature is unaware of morality. Morality and law are forever intertwined, and neither one can be interpreted on its own, which means that a correct theology is required when interpreting the law. And a correct interpretation of the law starts and ends with an equality in mind, because it is a founding and governing principle of the United States that men cannot follow the dictates of other men, which means that a source of law is required when interpreting a law as just. So, for this reason, it is moral law that defines a law as just, rather than nature, otherwise, it is nature that is all powerful, rather than morality.

*Quotation: ———————————————
"If man's feelings, passions, etc, are not merely anthropological phenomena in the narrower sense, but truly ontological affirmations of nature, and if they are only really affirmed because their object exists for them as a sensual object, then it is clear that they have by no means merely one mode of affirmation, but rather, that the distinct character of their existence, of their life, is constituted by the distinct mode of their affirmation. In what manner the object exists for them, is the characteristic mode of their gratification.

The meaning of private property (apart from its estrangement) is the existence of essential objects for man, both as objects of enjoyment and as objects of activity. By possessing the property of buying everything, by possessing the property of appropriating all objects, money is thus the object of eminent possession. The universality of its property is the omnipotence of its being. It is therefore regarded as an omnipotent being." - Karl Marx, founder of Communism. Source: A Critique of Hegel's

Philosophy - Economic and Philosophic Manuscripts - The Power of Money. (Documented in 1844).

According to the Hegelian dialect of problem, reaction, solution, an engineered financial crisis will eventually lead to the collapse of religion, which then leads to the collapse of America once money and wealth becomes all powerful through the practice of multinational corporations and false marketing strategies. The idea of allowing multinational corporations to dictate the needs of the people leads to false advertisement through the love of money, which is an inherent evil that cannot be justified by the universal principles of human morality.

Morality is by definition universal, while morals are by definition personal, which means that morals are refined, while morality is eternal. But if morality derives from nature, then nature itself is eternal, which cannot be a logical definition due to the limitations of nature, which is not self-existing due to the presence of rules. So, in order to interpret nature, then rules are required, which cannot derive from nature alone, because nature is not eternal, while morality is, which means that a universal system of law must derive from the correct interpretation of morality, which in turn, requires a correct theology.

The United States Constitution, and their Declaration of Independence, was never to be interpreted by secular ideology alone, but with a correct theology instead, so that a system of common law should succeed over tyranny and fraud by the rights of conscience. The shift in American culture from one of educational dominance, to one of disrepute, is the direct result of those who challenge Biblical creation as a legal standard before the courts from a secular premise. So, for this reason, it is the secular standard for public education that must be returned to the people, too whom, it rightfully belongs so that a continuous and sustainable standard for public education can be applied to society and law for the benefit of an individual's protection within the system.

If the United States Constitution is to be interpreted by secular ideology alone, then the religious rights of man have been denied without proper due course, when nothing within the Constitution forbids the teaching of God the Creator, but instead, the Constitution promotes Biblical teachings by the rights of conscience, which supersedes any judicial decision for reasons relating to protection of person. The rights of conscience is a religious liberty that cannot be overruled from a secular premise without invoking the principles of human slavery in turn, because human freedom is measured by the rights of conscience, rather than secular science, which forms the philosophical basis for the reinterpretation of conscience.

According to Isaac Newton and the principles of modern physics, any action will result in an equal and opposite reaction, thus leading to the discovery of gravitational systems. Emotions can have a positive or negative consequence, depending on our thoughts, which are bipolar in terms of feelings and vibration; Meaning that we each experience positive and negative thoughts based on the gravity of the situation. So, for this reason, a person's psychology is affected in two ways the same as physics is operates in two separate ways. First; Actions have consequences, which then leads to an emotional experience that is either positive or negative, so that each person is bipolar, depending on the own experiences. And second; Any reaction is a direct result of the previous action, so that everything is relative to both physical laws and moral laws.

So, in order to obtain a correct psychology, as well as a correct theory in both science and law, then the human conscience is required to be explained factually to students who must carry the experience with them for the remainder of their life. This experience of knowing the correct source of conscience is the leading and contributing factor that leads to justice and civil rights, as well as interpreting the world around us by the inclusion of both physical laws and moral laws, which in turn, gives stability to the universe, as well as law and order.

If the atheist is to deny the gift of conscience on the basis of their atheism, then it is the atheist that is reneging their basic rights in order to espouse some form of freedom from rules, which can and does lead to lawlessness by self-exclusion from the law. There is no freedom without the law, because it is the law that defines the limitations of liberty. The limitations of liberty is the direct result of the implementation of rules that are designed to be just in their interpretation, which in turn, defines morality as universal in terms of precepts. Precepts are defined as rules that are intended to influence behaviour and thought, which can have both a negative and positive outcome, depending on the rules in place.

Rules can either free an individual from subjugation, or they can enslave the individual due to the adoption of rules that simply do not apply. And the one rule that simply does not apply, is the rule set in place by the United States government that the theory of evolution cannot be contested for reasons relating to a secular interpretation of the said Constitution, which is a mechanism for human enslavement by the reinterpretation of conscience. The lawful term, conscience, derives from Biblical theology, and stands as self-evident before the law on the basis of reason, because the one thing here on Earth that cannot be reasoned with as an individual, is an nihilist who has denied their conscience in favour of the evolutionary definition of man, which is the sole basis for lawlessness and anarchy.

Systems engineering is a systems design process that is governed by a procedure, such as the hierarchy of control, which is a step-by-step procedure to implement controls and ideas into the legal system that stands as of now. But unfortunately for the system, it will inevitably fail. The reason why the legal system we live in will inevitably fail is due to a failure in communication between the law and students, which is being done on purpose in order to dumb down society for the express purpose of social engineering.

The United States system of government is by definition an ideocracy, that is to say, the system has shifted from one of educational dominance to one of global disrepute. The idea of pitting the weak against the strong derives from the principles of Social Darwinism, which is being done on purpose as a social experiment in order to oppose the previous system of Biblical creation as a legal standard for law and order, which not only forms the basis for human rights and equality by the rights of conscience, but also, it is how students are well informed in regards to their basic rights.

For example; If a group of students were to engage a legal society whilst holding to the viewpoint that man is animal, then their contribution to society has derived from their observations of the animal kingdom. While on the other hand, those who have been properly educated regarding the lawful definition of man as a created human being will be able to apply a system of justice for all by the rights of conscience. An ideocracy within America is the direct result of those who question basic public morals in order to include certain rights for themselves, which will inevitably apply to others in return. Rights such as gay marriage, the right to be defined as an animal, and the right to use racial terminology in order to define other groups of people as biologically inferior to others constitutes as a threat to our legal system as defined by the universal law of equality.

The universal law of human equality firmly distinguishes man from animal on the basis of conscience and reason, which cannot be in conflict with the definitions from public education without bringing the rights of conscience into question, which is a crime against humanity on the basis of equality. The universal law of equality is just in its own interpretations by the rights of conscience, which cannot be overruled by the evolutionary definition of man without using racial terminology in order to define a person's nationality as inferior to another.

Thus, human freedom and human liberty is protected by the universal law of equality, which clearly defines that the rights of conscience have derived from "religious teachings" due to the theological term, conscience, which is both self-explanatory, as well as self-evident before the law for reasons relating to protection of person. The legal system we live under is by definition an engineered system, which means that improvements can be applied to the system using the hierarchy of control, which is designed to reduce risks to persons by implementing controls and ideas, and by a correct interpretation of the law.

A correct interpretation of the law within the education system is our only true safeguard from government tyranny, because it is the action of coercion and speech dictates that forbid a legal system from operating effectively whereby each individual is correctly informed in regards to their human origins and legal obligations. Under international law every human being has a lawful obligation to be defined as a created human being with a human ancestry by definition of the word, person, which in turn, disqualifies evolution as a theory in practice. Biblical creation on the other hand acts as a legal standard that is universal in its interpretation, and is not in opposition to a lawful obligation by the individual to be defined as a person before the law.

The argument between Biblical creation and Darwinian evolution is an argument concerning origins, which must be settled by the law in such a way that liberty is not lost in obscurity, which means that simplification is required in order to teach the students who are subject to the system. The principles of liberty are the principles of human freedom in that just liberties can do no harm, and can be exercised without limitations. While a system of equality is a system of justice that is intended for the justified who are falsely accused. Thus, human liberty is defined by the rights of conscience, which is justice for the weak, and the strength of a nation.

> *Quotation: ———————————————————————
> In this country, where there is no established Church, but where guarantees against an establishment and against religious preferences are found in the Federal Constitution and in every State Constitution, we would not expect to find a general acquiescence in the earlier English view. The cases are numerous where the maxim is broadly asserted upon the authority of the English precedents. In most, if not all of these cases, however, the utterances are pure dicta. Many of them show merely the rhetorical piety of the judiciary. There being, strictly speaking, no common law of the Union, there is no necessity for inquiring as to the interpretation of the maxim as applied to the United States Government. It is significant, however, that almost contemporaneous with the adoption of the Federal Constitution, it was declared by the Senate of the United States that the National Government was not founded on the Christian religion.

In the Treaty with Tripoli ratified by the Senate in 1797 (8 U. S. Statutes at Large 155), occurs this article: Article XI. "As the Government of the United States of America is not in any sense founded on the Christian religion, as it has in itself no character of enmity against the laws, religion or tranquillity of Alusselmen, and as the said States have never entered into any war or act of hostility against any Mahometan nation, it is declared by the parties, that no pretext arising from religious opinions shall ever produce an interruption of the harmony existing between the two countries. Coming to the State Governments, it will be found that the maxim has been altogether repudiated, as applied to their common law by the Supreme Courts of Ohio and Louisiana.

In Bloom v. Richards (1853), Ohio Statutory 387, 390, 391, the Supreme Court of Ohio speaking by Chief Justice Thurman, said no further: "Neither Christianity, or any other system of religion, is a part of the law of the State. Thus, the Statute, upon which, the defendant relies, prohibiting common labour on the Sabbath could not stand for a moment as a law of the State, if its sole foundation was the Christian duty of keeping that day holy, and its sole motive to enforce the observance of that duty." This view was followed in the later Ohio cases, Gatrick V. Wasolz (1855), Ohio Statutory 566, and the Board of Education of Cincinnati (1872) Ohio Statutory 211. In the latter case, the Court held that Christianity was part of the law of the land in the sense that the Constitution and laws were made by a Christian people.

Taking up the more important decisions of the State Courts, (People v. Ruggles) was an indictment for blasphemy. It was decided that blasphemy against God, and contumelious reproaches and profane ridicule of Christ or the holy scriptures, were offences punishable at common law, whether uttered by words or writings. And it was held that wantonly, wickedly and maliciously uttering the following words: "Jesus Christ was a bastard and his mother must be a whore," was a public offence and punishable by the common law of New York.

It was said by Chief Justice Kent: "The people of this State, in common with the people of this country, prefer the general doctrines of Christianity as the rule of their faith and practice, and to scandalize the Author of these doctrines, is not only, in a religious point of view, extremely impious, but even in respect to the obligations due to society, is a gross violation of decency and good order. Christianity, in its enlarged sense, as a religion revealed and taught in the Bible, is not unknown to our law. The statute for preventing immorality consecrates the first day of the week as a holy time, and considers the violation of it as immoral." - Source: The American Law Registry - Christianity and the Common Law. (Documented May, 1890).

In the year 1795, The United States government dispatched diplomats Joel Barlow, Joseph Donaldson, and Richard O'Brien to North Africa and successfully concluded treaties with the States of Algiers, Tunis, and Tripoli. According to Article XI of the Treaty of Tripoli, the United States is not a Christian nation, and would not let the fact that Tripoli is a Muslim region interfere with their political relationship. Historically, the religion of Tripoli is Sunni Muslim, so in order for the United States government to form a treaty with Tripoli, they had to denounce their Christian faith in favour of a pro-slavery treaty.

So, the common argument today by the New Atheist movement that the United States Constitution was not founded upon the Biblical principles of Judeo-Christianity as a result of the Treaty of Tripoli is indeed without merit, because the argument by the New Atheist movement that America is entirely secular based on the Treaty of Tripoli is projected as evidence without the individual ever realizing that Tripoli is a Sunni Muslim region, and that the agreement was set in place due to the sheer number of Sunni Muslim pirate attacks that was affecting the British-American slave trade with North-Africa. The only reason that Christianity was denounced by the Supreme Courts in the Treaty of Tripoli, was to maintain the British-American slave trade with North Africa, which is now heavily outdated.

According to the American Law Registry, the common law has derived from English dicta, that is to say that the common law has derived from judicial proceedings based on a legal precedent that is intended to be just in its interpretation, thus constituting Christianity as the maxim of the common law. However, the Christian faith is not a part of American law anymore than it is a part of the Constitution, yet the United States Constitution was written by men of the Christian faith who adopted the common law of England, whilst retaining their national sovereignty from the British crown.

The actions by the founding fathers of the United States was one of piety to religious principle and the common law by the rights of conscience. The rights of conscience, according to United States Constitutional law, is to allow for freedom of worship, rather than to protect a particular branch of Christianity, such as the Catholic Church of Rome, or the Anglican Church of England. Thus, the adoption of the English common law by the founding fathers of the United States was an adoption of Christian principle, not because the Constitution favoured a particular branch of Christianity, but because individual human sovereignty, and national independence, was reliant on the correct interpretation of conscience within the framework of Biblical doctrine.

The rights of conscience, as defined by the Biblical interpretation of conscience led to the creation of the United States Constitution, the Bill of Rights, and the Declaration of Independence on the grounds by which human sovereignty must be defined, as well as Constitutionally granted in order to have a fair system of justice from the practice of law, thus constituting the common law of England as just in its interpretations, and good for the benefit of the people of the United States that immorality should not be safeguarded by the law for reasons relating to protection of person, and national security.

Chief Justice James Kent, who was seated among the High Courts between 1798 and 1804, delivered the opinion of the unanimous court decision that though the Constitution has discarded religious establishments as authoritative from the practice of law, it does not forbid judicial decisions concerning offences against Christianity and morality, and are punishable by law because they strike at the root of moral obligation, and thereby weaken the security and protection of the nation's people. Protection of person, and national security, is relative to protection of moral obligation by the law to uphold and thereby fulfil the just duties of man and society through due deliberation by judicial decision in order to protect the people from social and moral decay. And it is for this reason that immorality, as defined by Biblical doctrine, leads to social and moral decay, which is not to be protected by the High Courts as a just virtue from the law, because immorality is a mechanism for social injustices that lead to a High Court ruling in order to sustain the peace, which is a common law practice.

Thus, Biblical morality, as defined by the Holy Bible, is in place to protect humanity, rather than enslave as the New Atheist movement has argued from the viewpoint of the evolutionary theory, which has now dominated the High Court's views in place of protection of person, and has led to a national crisis by the rise of social and moral decay by the inclusion of gay rights to marriage, enforced secular education at the tax payers expense, and by the evolutionary definition of man as a lower animal. So, for this reason, it is the High Courts that has failed to deliberate a due verdict that all men are created equal, which not only allows for protection of person, but also, national security.

*Quotation: ————————————————
"When occasions present themselves, in which the interests of the people are at variance with their inclinations, it is the duty of the persons whom they have appointed to be the guardians of those interests, to withstand the temporary delusion, in order to give them time and opportunity for

more cool and sedate reflection. Instances might be cited in which a conduct of this kind has saved the people from very fatal consequences of their own mistakes, and has procured lasting monuments of their gratitude to the men who had courage and magnanimity enough to serve them at the peril of their displeasure.

But however inclined we might be to insist upon an unbounded complaisance in the Executive to the inclinations of the people, we can with no propriety contend for a like complaisance to the humours of the legislature. The latter may sometimes stand in opposition to the former, and at other times the people may be entirely neutral. In either supposition, it is certainly desirable that the Executive should be in a situation to dare to act his own opinion with vigour and decision. The same rule which teaches the propriety of a partition between the various branches of power, teaches us likewise that this partition ought to be so contrived as to render the one independent of the other.

To what purpose separate the executive or the judiciary from the legislative, if both the executive and the judiciary are so constituted as to be at the absolute devotion of the legislative? Such a separation must be merely nominal, and incapable of producing the ends for which it was established. It is one thing to be subordinate to the laws, and another to be dependent on the legislative body. The first comports with, the last violates, the fundamental principles of good government; and, whatever may be the forms of the Constitution, unites all power in the same hands." - Alexander Hamilton, United States founding father. Source: Primary Documents in American History - Federalist Paper Number 71. (Documented March 18, 1788).

A second common argument by the New Atheist movement that Christianity is not the official basis for the common law, is the separation of Church and State, which was first instituted by the United States to further outline the limitations of government in order for freedom of religion to be exercised as a right, rather than a privilege. The separation of Church and State was enacted by Congress so that a person could not be convicted by the law for religious reasons, which not only protects atheists, but also, Christians, because this is a religious liberty, rather than an anti-religious ideal.

The separation of Church and State was enacted to protect American citizens from British imperial rule, as well as Papal inquisitions by the Pope who subjugated protestant Christians and Jews for centuries, because the Roman Vatican sees itself as a "Universal Church," with a universal ecclesiastical jurisdiction over all lands, titles, and property. But because the United States Constitution is a universal statement of truth that is legally binding in order to create a corporation with a National Trust classification, it meant that no particular Church or institution could be recognized without creating a universal religious institution at the same time, which was in opposition to the good of the Commonwealth in terms of practice and theology, because the purpose of the Christian Commonwealth system is to unite the Christian nations under the common law, rather than to divide the world according to a particular institution or sect of Christianity.

The notion by the New Atheist movement that the separation of Church and State was enacted in order to protect atheism based on a secular authority, is in fact, a leading argument by the New Atheist movement. But in order to have protection of person under the common law in accordance with the First Amendment of the United States Constitution, then you must also have a religion or belief, otherwise, your opinion is invalid, because you argue from a premise, rather than by theory alone.

Thus, freedom of conscience forms the basis of our universal system of common law for reasons relating to a legal standard that acts as a lawful premise in which to argue from. So, because of this legal status, atheism is in the same category as religion when it comes to academics and law, because every statistic concerning religion, science, and politics includes a ratio for atheism. So, in despite of the so-called position of non-belief, atheism still constitutes as a belief for three main reasons. First; Is because atheism is protected under the First Amendment according to freedom of belief. Second; In order to reject a belief, then an alternate belief is required. Thirdly; In order to have a valid opinion, then you must also have a belief, otherwise, your opinion has no grounds in which to argue from.

A third example that is commonly used by the New Atheist movement to deny the Creator before the law, is the issue of human slavery recorded in the Holy Bible from the Old Testament, which I will further explain. According to Exodus 21:16 "Whoever steals a man and sells him, and anyone found in possession of him, shall be put to death." (End of quote).

This commandment explicitly states that forcing a person into slavery is unlawful, because a slave in the Old Testament was to be bought with a price. The Old Testament also grants protection for slaves according to Exodus 21:20 which reads that: "When a man strikes his slave, male or female, with a rod and the slave dies under his hand, he shall be avenged." (End of quote).

According to the book of Leviticus chapter 25:8-10 we read that: "You shall count seven weeks of years, seven times seven years, so that the time of the seven weeks of years shall give you forty-nine years. Then you shall sound the loud trumpet on the tenth day of the seventh month. On the Day of Atonement you shall sound the trumpet throughout all your land. And you shall consecrate the fiftieth year, and proclaim liberty throughout the land to all its inhabitants. It shall be a jubilee for you, when each of you shall return to his property, and each of you shall return to his clan." (End of Quote). The year of Jubilee recorded in the Holy Bible was a time where each slave shall be set free and return to their own family. The year of Jubilee occurred every seventh Sabbath year, which is equal to every 50 years.

The year of Jubilee was an economic, cultural, environmental, and communal reset, when the land and the people should rest from harvesting, and all those who were in slavery are to be set free in order to return to their former communities, whether male or female. The nation of Jews did indeed practice slavery, but the laws in place allowed for slaves to be protected, as well as freed after so many years of service, and this practice was tied in with a financial reset during the year of Jubilee. And the reason for a financial reset was to allow for property that was previously sold to be returned to its former owner so that each person should have their ancestral land returned to them for the benefit of the people.

If a person sold their land to another, or bought a slave from another, then both the land that was sold, along with the slave that was bought, should be returned to its former estate, which granted protection for the ownership of land, as well as freedom for the slaves. This ancient practice was a fair system of practice compared to that of other ancient civilizations who treated their slaves poorly by defining a slave as someone else's property for life with absolutely no chance of redemption. The practice of a financial reset every fifty years prevented the people from falling into slavery perpetually, as well as protecting the rights of inheritance, each according to their own clan or tribe so that each person should never be deprived of a homeland for themselves, and their future children.

The practice of a financial reset every five decades is exactly what is required in today's world, because as the years progress with trade and commerce, the level of debt also increases with compounding interest, which becomes unbearable, as well as unpayable. So, in order to be consistent with compounding interest, then there must be a year of Jubilee that allows for debts to be forgiven, and for property to be returned to its former estate. Otherwise, land and commodities will be concentrated into the hands of a few, which then leads to a permanent form of slavery known as bond slavery whereby a person is born into debt. And this is the current financial situation by the Federal Reserve Act, because the Fed sets the interest rates with absolutely no intention of ever forgiving a single debt no matter how poor or vulnerable the people become as a direct result of inflation over time.

Thus, the Holy Bible presents a solution to our current financial crisis by the year of Jubilee, which is not to be misconstrued as being a mechanism for human slavery, but one of human freedom instead. A global economic crisis is by definition an engineered crisis, because as the current trend towards inflation occurs, the more the people will be subjugated by the lender, which leads to human slavery. Each person that is born into debt with a promise to repay through the practice of income tax is thereby subject to a system based on perpetual debt, rather than surplus, which amounts to an open form of bond slavery whereby every tax payer who is born into debt is obligated to repay government spending. While a system of Jubilee not only allows for debts to be forgiven, but also, for land to be distributed evenly among the people, which is a fair system of practice that allows for equality so that the wealth of a nation is not concentrated into the hands of a few.

A fourth example that is used by the New Atheist movement in order to dismiss the Creator before the law is the argument from philosophical materialism that denies the human conscience, which is a crime against humanity on the basis of equality. The human conscience is not a product of nature or the animals, but of God instead who has endowed each person with conscience and with rights. The reinterpretation of the human conscience by the New Atheist movement has paved the way for human slavery, because if a person is to be defined as the product of nature, then mankind is thereby the property of the State due to the legal definition of property. Philosophical materialism denies the existence of the human conscience, simply because there is no materialistic interpretation of the human conscience. Yet, the human conscience is self-evident under the common law for reasons relating to the correct interpretation of human rights and equality.

*Quotation: ————————————————
"The common law does not necessarily conform with international law, but international law is a legitimate and important influence on the development of the common law, especially when international law declares the existence of universal human rights." - Source: International Law and the Common Law in the 21ˢᵗ Century. Published Online by the Australasian Legal Information Institute. Transcript by Professor and Director of the Centre for International and Public Law at the Australian National University. (Documented in 2002).

A fifth common argument by the New Atheist movement concerning the abolition of Christianity are the Roman Inquisitions that led to the death of approximately 9 million people between the year 1542 and finally ended in the year 1859. Only one ministry of the Roman Curia, the Congregatio Sancti Officii, remained as the supervisory authority of the Roman Catholic faith and was dissolved in 1965. The Roman Inquisition, also called the "Suprema Congregatio Sanctae Romanae et Universalis Inquisitionis," which is Latin for the "Supreme Sacred Congregation of the Roman and Universal Inquisition," was a Papal inquisition that was done in order to expand the interests of Rome, rather than the Christian faith.

The Roman Inquisitions have long been a primary subject in the debate between New Atheism and Christianity regarding Roman accusations of heresy, witchcraft, and treason. This is because the Roman Catholic Church sees itself as a "Universal Church" with an ecclesiastical jurisdiction over all lands, titles, peoples, and property with the sovereign duty to wipe out the enemies of Rome under the guise of Christianity. The New Atheist movement argues that the Roman Inquisitional period is cause for revenge against the Christian religion due to the number of deaths involved, and has called for the abolition of all religion in order to promote atheism, humanism, and secularism as a source of morality.

The counter argument here that I am about to present is not one in favour of the Roman Inquisitions, but rather, against, and I will base my argument on the historical fact that Jesus Himself was crucified by the Roman empire. The Roman Catholic Church, according to modern historical resources, is a continuation of the former Roman empire that collapsed in year 476, when the German chieftain Odoacer deposed the last emperor of Rome, Romulus Augustulus. Jesus Christ, according to the Holy Bible, was the Messiah of the Jews, rather than Rome, and was thereby a Jewish saviour, rather than a Roman one. Yet the Roman Catholic Order was unable to abolish the influence of Christianity, and thereby adopted the Christian Faith as a means of universal control in order to continue the Roman empire's ventures that relied on human torture as a means of expanding its sadist ambitions.

So, if one was to argue that Christianity is to blame for the Roman Inquisitions and the atrocities that were committed by Rome and many or Europe's elite, then one can cite the Holy Bible in reference to the crucifixion of Jesus Christ by the Roman empire. The Roman Inquisitions were not a Biblical doctrine, nor was the formation of the Roman Order. Thus, any and all arguments concerning the abolition of the Christian faith from the viewpoint of New Atheism is without merit, not justification, especially when you take into account that over 100 million people have died under Communist rule in the last century, making Scientific Atheism the world's most dangerous belief system bar none.

Every human being has a lawful obligation to acknowledge the human conscience under international law for reasons relating to protection of person before the law. But if the atheist was to admit that they have a conscience, then they have thereby forfeited their atheism. So, it is for this reason that the New Atheist movement should not be allowed to interfere with the functions of government through lobbying efforts in order that our universal right to freedom of conscience should be protected as inalienable in accordance with international agreement.

Common law legal systems can trace their roots back many centuries to England during the Middle Ages, and even today, several countries around the world, including the United States, Canada, India, and Australia continue to rely heavily on the common law when resolving their legal disputes. The only way to define the human conscience from the practice of common law, is that the human conscience is endowed by our Creator for reasons relating to protection of person. So, in order to be consistent with human rights legislation under the common law, then a Creator God is required. A Creator is also required when interpreting international human rights legislation, because according to the United Nations Human Rights Commission, human equality has been defined by "religious teachings" on the basis of conscience and reason, rather than by secular ideology or science.

The lawful definitions used within the Universal Declaration of Human Rights and Equality to define human liberty and inalienable rights with have derived from the Biblical principles of Judeo-Christianity under the common law, because the correct interpretation of conscience has derived from Biblical theology that includes the lawful definition of person, which is why protection of person before the law is defined as inalienable under international agreement. One cannot separate the existence of the Creator from international human rights legislation, and the common law, any more than one can separate ethics from science without detracting from the merit that's required in order to invent a rule, because rules are to be made fair for the good of the people, and for the good of the common law.

Today, one-third of the world's population lives in common law jurisdictions or in mixed legal systems that combine the common law with the civil law. And though India, and other common law jurisdictions do not hold to a Biblical worldview, the common law has derived from the Biblical interpretation of conscience, which in turn, sets a legal precedent under the common law that not only protects the Creator as self-evident, but also, the rights of conscience. The rights of conscience can be exercised by any religion, which forms the basis of an equality between all nations under international agreement. But according to the universal principles of equality, there needs to be equal opportunity. Thus, it is not by the equal distribution of wealth or property that defines a law as just, but rather, it is by the equal distribution of rights.

Equal rights is at the helm of international agreement in order that equal justice should have a lawful premise, which derives itself from the practice of common law, rather than secular ideology or science. The practice of common law is for the common good, which has been so expedient throughout the world that the common law should not be under estimated in terms of its value to all of mankind. Thus, under equal opportunity between all nations, it is the lawful definition of conscience, as from a Biblical interpretation, that has lightened the way to human freedom by a correct interpretation of the law.

A correct interpretation of the law can and does include equal opportunity between both parties in a dispute before the law, whether it be the plaintiff, or the defendant, the principle remains the same, because law is in place for reasons relating to protection of person, rather than to vilify a particular theory in science or law. And it is for this reason that the United States Supreme Court decision to grant Constitutional protections to the theory of evolution that constitutes as a direct threat to our way of life by the reinterpretation of conscience to meaning that of an animal, which is entirely due to the lawful definition of property.

Under United States Federal law, the rights of conscience is both self-evident, as well as Constitutionally protected for the benefit of the people, and their public safety, which cannot be interpreted by a theory in science without invoking a new religion in turn, such as Secular Humanism, which is a violation of the First Amendment where the government has no moral obligation to create a religious institution with a religious test in place that is designed to dismiss Biblical creation as a legal standard with an automatic dismissal. A theory in science will always be subject to a cross-examination before the law due to the lawful definition of theory. While a self-evident proposition or truth in law is legally binding for reasons relating to moral obligation, and due deliberation, such as the self-evident truth that all men are created equal, and are endowed by their Creator with conscience and with rights.

This verdict under the common law has been decided upon many years ago as a legal precedent that is legally binding as a moral obligation, and as just in its interpretation for the benefit of the people; Not to continue assuming the facts, but rather, to establish them for future cases. Thus, the case at hand as to whether man was created or not has been settled with a moral obligation in place to dismiss a religious test before the law, so that freedom of conscience and belief may be exercised with equal opportunity in place. But if equal opportunity has been restricted by law in order to protect a theory in science, then so also has our equality, because equal opportunity and human equality go hand in hand, and cannot be interpreted by a science without invoking a religion in turn. The scientific method is not for the establishment of a religion, but for our understanding of nature and of nature's laws, which are by definition a creation under the common law due to the lawful definition of conscience.

> *Quotation: ─────────────────────────
> According to their views (the founding fathers), as the recognized religion of the country, the duties and injunctions of the Christian religion were interwoven with the law of the land, and were part and parcel of the common law, and to maliciously revile it is a public grievance, in as much so as any other public outrage upon common decency and decorum. Most of the States, however, have recognized that, for some purposes and in some sense at least, Christianity is a part of their common law, the more general view being that it is part of the common law no further than Lord Campell declared it to be a part of the common law of England. In many of the cases that have occupied the courts, involving religious questions, the proposition has been advanced and reasoned from, that Christianity is a part of the common law. - Source: The American Law Registry - Christianity and the Common Law. (Documented May, 1890).

Our universal system of Biblical morality and common law are forever intertwined due to the rights of conscience. So, in order for a lawful instruction to be made a legal obligation, then there needs to be a moral obligation first, which, according to common law proceedings, derives itself from the moral teachings of Biblical Christianity, rather than from Secular Humanism or science. The idea that a secular authority can reinterpret the inalienable rights of individuals on the basis of science is the very thing that amounts to being a global injustice, because the definition of the term, secular, is that it's a neutral term, which is not to be misappropriated in any way as being anti-religious for the purpose of freedom of religion to be exercised as a right, which is a cardinal principle of the common law and international agreement in order that every religion should have equal opportunity, and a fair hearing before the law. Science is not an authority when it comes to the practice of law and order, because in order for laws to be made fair, then a system of morality is required first, while a degree in science is not a requirement.

So, as far as science goes, the secular standard for public education is leading mankind into a new age of slavery, whereby the teaching of inalienable rights endowed by our Creator has been replaced by the teaching of evolution involving ideas concerning the mythical Bigfoot and toad-to-prince gradualism. The idea behind systems engineering is to minimize rework, detect faults prior to a systems failure, and to engage in effective communication, which must require validation and verification for any instructional command to proceed. Otherwise, a janitor for the White House could theoretically change the course of history with the swing of his signature for example. And the process of verification relies primarily on authentication, because there is a hierarchy in place, and the process of authentication will work as a sequence, which is not linear, but curved instead.

For example: At the top of the hierarchy of controls there is the administrative body, which formulates the orders for the system via conceptual ideas that are then translated down into a project framework through planners and engineers who design the project that derived from a concept originally. The project is then broken down into smaller projects, and then down again into individual tasks, which then begins to curve back upward into a project formation whereby the smaller projects are coming together to form a larger more complex whole. And every stage in the process for engineering a system relies primarily on effective communication, so that the definitions for one instruction cannot be followed by instructions for the same thing, but with a different definition in place.

Otherwise, additional specifics are required in order to interpret the new information. And the additional specifics that are lacking in our global society are the lawful interpretations for what a human being is through the public education system, which is equal to a breakdown in communication between the standard for human equality under International law, and public education. This means there is no lawful grounds for the United States Supreme Court to deny creation science to public school students who are engaging a legal system with their own experience that holds to a Biblical interpretation of what a person is based on the theological term, conscience, which forms the basis for an individual's basic human rights.

The United States Supreme Court, and the United States Federal government, was never to interfere with, nor remove, the inalienable right of an individual to be defined as a created human being with a human ancestry based on a secular premise. The actions by the United States Supreme Court has amounted to being a fiat authority based on its own interpretation of the said Constitution, because the right to human equality under a Biblical definition was the founding and governing principle of the United States Constitution, the Bill of Rights, and the Declaration of Independence according to the founding fathers themselves.

> *Quotation: ─────────────────────
> "Our Constitution was made only for a moral and religious people. It is wholly inadequate to the government of any other. The Declaration of Independence laid the cornerstone of human government upon the first precepts of Christianity." - John Adams, 2nd President of the United States. Source: Presidential Address to the Militia of Massachusetts. (Documented October 11, 1798).

The United States Constitution was never to be misconstrued, nor used as being an authority over the people from a secular premise in order to deny an individual their inalienable right to be defined as a created being, which is the very thing that robs an individual of their basic right to factual information regarding their true origins as a person. The United States Supreme Court has cited Secularism as their right, and justification, to deny the inalienable rights of the people through the public education system to be correctly informed concerning their humanity as a person who is endowed with conscience by their Creator.

The just liberties of the people are thereby in danger due to a secular standard for public education that denies the redress of public grievances on the basis that no explanation for the human conscience is required, which is leading America and the rest of the world into a new age revolution by minority groups who challenge basic public morals. And the theory of evolution in practice from society is indeed a public grievance on the basis of conscience and reason, because the one thing that cannot be reasoned with here on Earth, is a person who has denied their conscience on the basis of theory. Therefore, the theory of evolution must be challenged from the premise of law, or we will all wake-up one day to an ideocracy governed by the lawless, rather than a society that is self-governed under the common law.

If the secular government is to bring the inalienable rights of the people into question by defining man as animal, then it is the secular government that must be brought into question by the law, rather than a person's humanity as a created human being, which is self- explanatory. The lawful interpretation for what a person is under United States Constitutional law is required to be explained factually to students according to the lawful definitions set in place by the original Constitution, especially in regards to the lawful definitions used to define a person with. The removal of a Biblical standard for public education by the United States Supreme Court has only paved the way for total enslavement, where the correct definition of person, as from a Biblical interpretation, has been redefined in order to equate a human being with the animal kingdom for reasons relating to Secular Humanism and the teaching of evolution.

America is the land of the free and the home of the brave, because the men and women fought for their right to be defined as human beings endowed by their Creator with conscience in order to establish their independence within the world. And the world itself will follow suit to Americanized public education if the people are not properly informed about the dangers involved with the theory of evolution being taught by the State.

*Quotation: ———————————————————
"The education of all children, from the moment that they can get along without a mother's care, shall be in

State institutions at the expense of the State. Freedom of education shall be enjoyed under the conditions fixed by law and under the supreme control of the State. We know that violent measures against religion are nonsense; But this is an opinion; As socialism grows, religion will disappear. Its disappearance must be done by social development, in which, education must play a part." - Karl Marx, founder of Communism. Source: The Eighteenth Brumaire of Louis Bonaparte. (Documented in 1852).

According to Article 26.2 of the Universal Declaration of Human Rights and Equality: "Education shall be directed to the full development of the human personality, and to the strengthening of respect for human rights and fundamental freedoms." So, according to international human rights legislation, the purpose of free public education is for the development of an individual into a legal system based on human rights and equality. And universal rights, according to the UDHR, are by definition, endowed, rather than evolved. This means that creation science is a lawful interpretation universally, because the term, endowed, in legal terms, means from birth, rather than from nature. And this is the only definition there is to define a person's inalienable rights as being universal, otherwise, they must derive directly from nature, when nature is defined as property, legally speaking.

The theory of evolution, historically, is a racial science that denies human equality based on biological racism and evolutionary phylogeny as we've seen over time with the rise of Social Darwinism that equates man as an animal, and therefore, as property of the State for revenue purposes. Communism can only work if the human being is the property of the State, which in turn, requires students to be denied their inalienable rights as individuals who are endowed with conscience by their Creator.

So, it is for this reason that the theory of evolution from Marxism has equated the individual as the property of the State, because the one thing that does not exist under Communist rule, is the ownership of private property. The longer evolution is taught by the State, the sooner our inalienable rights will vanish into thin air, all because of a minority of people who are denying the lawful basis for human equality by citing evolution as their right and justification to define themselves and others as animals, which is the very thing that lowers a person's conscience, and their ability to be reasoned with as an individual.

According to United States Constitutional law, the lawful definition of, inalienable, is defined as being "endowed by our Creator from birth," which is where the United Nations definition of inalienable has derived its legal definition from historically. And that which is universal and inalienable are the lawful definitions for what a person is that are in place to protect an individual with so that their conscience is not in conflict with the lawful definitions for human rights and equality, which are defined as being universal for the purpose of an individual's protection within the system, rather than to protect a pet theory.

So, it does not matter whether a person believes in God the Creator or not, because the correct definition of what a person is, as from international law, is in place to protect an individual with, rather than enslave them, which is why the United States Supreme Court has no legal grounds whatsoever to redefine what a person is from the viewpoint of the evolutionary theory and Linnaean taxonomy, because a human being is to be defined as distinct from the animals for reasons relating to the correct interpretation of human rights and equality. If the United States government wishes to outlaw creation science to its students for reasons relating to a secular standard, then the United States government has thereby redefined the religious rights of man by citing Secular Humanism as their justification. And this in itself is equal to a form of religious discrimination under the First Amendment, because the Constitutional basis for inalienable rights derives from Biblical theology, rather than from secular ideology.

International law has defined freedom of conscience as inalienable, meaning that the right to a religion is protected as universal. Therefore, creation science has a lawful basis universally, while the theory of evolution does not, because the human conscience is endowed to every individual by their Creator, rather than from nature. The Universal Declaration of Human Rights and Equality has obtained their legal definition of person from Biblical instruction, because the UDHR clearly states that freedom of conscience is inalienable, which is a Biblical doctrine, rather than a secular one.

So, from this designation, a Creator God is a requirement in order to be consistent when interpreting international human rights legislation, because the definition of conscience outlines the need for a Creator God, which must derive itself from Biblical theology under the common law, otherwise, the definition will derive from Islam instead. Islam is also responsible for the continuation of the former British-American slave trade, because the one thing that Islam has perfected over the years, is human trafficking.

The human conscience is specifically for our understanding of morality, and because morality is rule based, it will mean that the human conscience is for understanding rules, and rules are equal to laws. The human conscience is therefore a requirement in order to enter a legal society, while a degree in science is not a requirement. The human being is not to be denoted as being from a savage primate before international law respectively for the purpose of human rights and equality; Meaning that the theory of evolution is by definition a philosophical dogma based on the denial of equality, as defined by international law.

And belief is all that's required in order for a legal system to operate effectively, because laws should derive from the self-explanatory word definitions that are in place to define human equality with, and not from Darwinian evolution or Linnaean taxonomy, which is now heavily outdated by the Universal Declaration of Human Rights and Equality under international agreement. And it is the lawful definition of what a person is that must be upheld before the law within every nation in order for a global society that is self-governed under the universal principles of human equality to operate effectively, rather than the pseudo-scientific definitions that refer to man as an animal, and therefore, property.

The random opinions of a naturalist scientist in regards to their own personal interpretations of what the human being is are secondary to any lawful instruction that is universal in its interpretation, because all are required to acknowledge the inalienable right of others to be defined as a created human being regardless of their own opinions for the purpose of human rights and equality, and human freedom thereby. If the United States government continues to deny creation science to its students for religious reasons, then the United States will have nothing in which to combat Communism with as a political ideology, because all it will take for Communism to succeed globally, is for religious liberty to be denied to students, which in turn, conditions an individual's mindset to being anti-religious, as well as in opposition to the laws that protect our God given humanity.

An engineered system will always be subject to failure, but the level of failure will be equal to the amount of expectation that was placed upon the system as a whole, which not only applies to an industrial system due to a high level of expectations that were set upon the system financially, but also, for any standard of education, because if the expectations from the administration were too high for the education system to cope with, then the system of law will inevitably fail due to an unfair management plan that was inconsistent in regards to a universal interpretation of the law.

According to systems engineering and systems theory, the more expectations that are placed on a system, the more constrained the system will become, because a system is designed to handle only that which it was intended for. And a system based on human equality and law cannot be used to enslave a population theoretically, because that is not what it was intended for originally. And the system with the greatest amount of expectation upon it globally, is the United States economic system and their system of law, because the United States has the world's largest economy, and because the United States has led the world in human rights and equality by the creation of the United States Declaration of Independence, which has led to the creation of the United Nations Declaration of human independence.

The Universal Declaration of Human Rights and Equality (UDHR) has derived its legal definitions from the United States Constitution that defines each individual as having been endowed with conscience, which forms the basis for human rights and equality. But unfortunately, America has relaxed its grip on itself before the world by trying to overextend itself financially as an economic system through the practice of Social Darwinism, which aims to protect its financial interests by exploiting the weak who are lesser off financially by defining each citizen as property for revenue purposes.

Most of America's industrial capacity has been moved offshore to Communist China, because it is illegal to form a workers Union in China, and because China has the lowest number of environmental protection laws of any industrialized system, which is highly profitable for the banking cartel within the United States in the short term, but not for China in the long term, because any rapid influx of financial growth, is historically, unsustainable. And China has had the fastest growing economy for almost 50 years now, which is why a global financial meltdown is virtually imminent due to an unsustainable financial practice.

So, unless the United States shows some constraint in regards to borrowing and spending, then the global standard for trade and commerce will continue to be based on managing debt, rather than surplus. No industrial system can rely on importing more than it exports, which is equal to depreciation over time due to spending more than what the system is producing. And this is why a fractional reserve banking system is an inefficient and unsustainable financial practice, because it produces more cash than it has commodities in reserve, and the profits gained by the Federal Reserve will be concentrated into the hands of a few who are not subject to being audited by the Treasury Department of any nation. Under a Federal Reserve system, money is loaned into existence with the promise to repay, which is where income tax comes into effect. The actions by the Federal Reserve has led to an engineered financial crisis on numerous occasions by preventing loans to banks, thereby restricting the necessary flow of money.

The second biggest lender to the United States, is in fact, China, which is a Communist system and cannot maintain its level of exports to the United States and the rest of the world as well without completely destroying their environment in the process. But this is being done globally in order to prop up a global financial scheme based on debt, because debt equals money due to compounding interest when loans are created. And the longer America continues to exploit China's workforce through the practice of Social Darwinism, and by competing the wealthy with the poor, the higher the poverty rates will be within the United States and in China, because when you compete a worker in China who is on $12 per hour with a worker who is doing the same job in America for $24 per hour, then minimum wages cannot increase over time due to a competition in place that is both financial, as well as political. And this will lead to a global financial crisis over time due to inflation, which in turn, raises the cost of living, and must be offset by a systematic increase in the award wage, otherwise, the financial system will inevitably fail as a direct result of inflation.

*Quotation: ————————————————

"A heavy or progressive or graduated income tax is necessary for the proper development of Communism. Civil servants and priests, soldiers and ballet-dancers, schoolmasters and police constables, Greek museums and Gothic steeples, civil list and services list; The common seed within which all these fabulous beings slumber in embryo is taxation. Taxes are the source of life for the bureaucracy, the army and the court, in short, for the whole apparatus of the executive power. Strong government and heavy taxes are identical." - Karl Marx, founder of Communism. Source: Communist manifesto - Chapter II, Proletarians and Communists. (Documented in February 21, 1948).

The biggest industrial polluter on Earth is China with only 1% of their air quality meeting the global standard for health and sustainability, which is why global trade reform with China is needed before the world's largest economic system fails catastrophically due to an unsustainable economic and environmental practice. The former United States industrial system relies primarily on individual human creativity for the purpose of innovation. While the Communist industrial system in China relies primarily on copyrighting ideas in order to keep the financial gains by the industrial system under Communist control, because counterfeiting engineered designs is the one thing that China has perfected over the years. The former industrial system in the United States was designed to cater for individual human sovereignty, whereby the worker was not being exploited by a heavy and progressive income tax.

In China, a registered business can sell their products to the rest of the world at cost price with the government promising an annual growth of 17% in return; Meaning that all trading in China is run through the government for the purpose of expanding its military. And it is the citizens of China who are the ones that are being exploited the most in this situation, because they cannot form a workers union under Communist rule, when the right to form a labour union is a universal right according to article 23.4 of the UDHR. Chinese citizens also have no legal rights to their own ideas under copyright laws, which the Communist government of China ignores entirely for the purpose of counterfeiting engineered products, which is the very thing that Communist China has perfected over the years under the guise of censorship.

VPN's are outlawed in China because they allow users to jump the governments AI firewall and securely connect to the internet outside of the country while blocking their IP address at the same time, which prevents Chinese citizens from being exposed to arbitrary arrest and persecution under Communist rule. The decision by the Communist Party of China to impose the ban on Google was done because of Google's unwillingness to completely abide by China's censorship regulations, which was regarded as a challenge to China's claim to universal digital sovereignty. Baidu is Communist China's primary search engine on the internet, which was created in the year 2000 by the Communist Party of China hacking and stealing Google's source codes.

The internet restriction by the Chinese government is a desperate attempt to maintain absolute control over freedom of information. Communist China now blocks all Google apps including, YouTube, Blogger, Google Sheets, Google Docs, etc etc... Anything that is owned and hosted by Google is currently inaccessible in China, while the Chinese app Tik Tok is currently under investigation by the United States for spying on American citizens.

Any system of law that claims to give the individual freedom, whilst denying the individual the right to vote at the same time and the right to freedom of information, is by definition, an unfair system, because the individual is believing one thing from international law, whilst being forced to accept another by the Communist government, which maintains a one party preferred system and is heavily engaged in the censorship of publicly documented information. And this is not only an issue for any society under Communism, but also, the United States, because the United States founding fathers have based its entire voting system upon each individual being defined as free according to their God given conscience, rather than slaves under a scientific theory for the sole purpose of financial gain through an immoral social practice, such as Social Darwinism. Freedom of information in regards to a person's true origins as a created human being needs to be explained factually to students who are engaging a legal system that holds to a Biblical definition of man by the rights of conscience, and by the correct interpretation of inalienable rights.

The United States public education system is now entirely secular due to lobbying efforts by atheists and Communists, when the standard for public education was previously in favour of the original Constitution, and the Biblical definitions therein. So, in order for education reform to occur within the United States, then an acknowledgement of the Holy Bible on the administration's part must occur, because the administration has sworn a public oath to uphold the Constitution by placing their right hand upon the Holy Bible, rather than The Origin of Species or Das Kapital, which forms the current philosophical basis for systemic racism and human exploitation.

The Constitutional definition of man is what constitutes Biblical morality as having a lawful premise within the United States under their Constitution, while atheism has reneged their responsibility to the public within the United States to uphold the Constitution by refusing to acknowledge the Biblical definition of man in despite of the fact that the Biblical definition of man is the Constitutional premise for inalienable rights and human equality. The United States Oath of Office is in place so that the Administration is publicly liable, rather than because of a religious test or practice.

So, in order for the United States government to fulfil their Oath to the public's safety by upholding the said Constitution, then an acknowledgement of the Holy Bible is required, because it is the Creator God of Genesis who is defined as self-evident before the law, rather than the legislator, which is why no Administration is infallible when it comes to the interpretation of the law. The idea that the Supreme Court is infallible in regards to the interpretation of the law derives from the practice of Communism, rather than the founding fathers, because the entire purpose of an infallible government derives from the principles of Communism set forth by Karl Marx, which was instigated in order to promote atheism, rather than the common law.

The common law is in place so that each person should have a fair hearing, and so that equal opportunity should exist between both parties in a dispute before the law, which is the lawful premise for equal rights under the rights of conscience. The rights of conscience is a Biblical doctrine in that conscience derives from the Creator, who is defined as both word and spirit from the Gospel of the New Testament, which also happens to be the correct definition of conscience; A source of word or spirit. Thus, every human being is endowed by their Creator with spirit, and it is for the purpose of law that we have a word from above that is not to be misappropriated as a means of protecting the immoral, as from the premise of law.

The United States Supreme Court has tied its own hands by rejecting the Biblical definitions from the Constitution in favour of the evolutionary interpretations from a secular premise, and it is the evolutionary interpretations that have no Constitutional basis whatsoever, while the Biblical definition of man is historically, Constitutional. No amount of Secularism can truly take away the individual's inalienable right to be defined as a created human being who is endowed by their Creator with conscience, which is why public school students must be informed in regards to creation science through the practice of systems theory and Biblical creation by definition of the fact that man was created. Otherwise, America will inevitably lose its independence to Communism as a direct result of the theory of evolution being taught by the State, because the theory of evolution is an integral part of Marxist ideology, rather than United States Constitutional law.

The Holy Bible is foundational to the entire legal system of the United States and Western civilization, rather than the theory of evolution. So, there should be no conflict between that which is lawful, and that which is being taught through the curriculum for public education. And though the United States system of government is secular, the democracy is not, which is why the government has no Constitutional right to deny creation science to its students on the basis that it is religious, because the idea of a secular government by the founding fathers was to maintain a Biblical standard for education and law, which was never to be misconstrued as being anti-religious in any way towards the religious rights of man.

States within the United States use one of two methods to select textbooks that are to be used for public schools. Thirty States allow local agencies or schools to choose textbooks, while a total of twenty States and three territories, known as textbook adoption States, choose at the State level what textbooks can be used. So, because Texas is such a big State, with a large population, it was therefore a large market for textbook producers, because the government was buying roughly 48 million textbooks every year, which is a highly profitable enterprise for publishers.

Publishers wanted their books to be approved in Texas because it meant their sales would be stronger nationwide. State officials and school officials have said that there is no law in Texas for the State education standard requiring the teaching of both evolution and creation. Instead, the State education policy requires students to: "analyse, evaluate, and critique the scientific basis for evolution," even though it is the theory of evolution that opposes the Constitutional definition of a human being.

The States Board of Education (SBOE) sets curriculum standards and reviews, and adopts textbooks based on those standards for Texas public schools. Yet according to statistics, A-levels for exam completions have risen exponentially, because academics claim that the pass rate for students has soared over the past 20 years compared with previous decades. But as a negative result of the education standard being dumbed down to cater for the theory of evolution, the rate of incarceration has thereby increased at the same rate that people are supposed to be getting smarter. As of May 2022, the United States had one of the highest prisoner rates per capita, with 573 prisoners per 100,000 of the national population. So, because the increased rate of incarceration over the years is linked with the introduction of evolution as a standard for public education, it will mean that the theory of evolution is doing more to enslave mankind under a theory, rather than freeing the people by the truth concerning their God given humanity.

The Biblical standard for public education is what made America great, because each individual during the War of Independence was fully informed in regards to their inalienable rights, and their obligation under the law to defend the Constitution when called upon. And the Union under Abraham Lincoln was victorious at the end of the Civil War because there was no contradiction between the lawful instructions given, and the religious education that the individual had received. The American industrial system was not based on the censorship of information in regards to what a human being is, but rather, it was based on human sovereignty as inalienable so that a person should never be defined as property. And it was the correct definition for human equality that the Union was fighting for during the Civil War in America, and not their right to deny the self-evident definition of what a person is before the law, which is exactly what is occurring today by minority groups who question recent history on the basis of a racial theory like evolution.

The leading cause that made America great was not their ability to industrialize the nation, but that the industrial system catered for individual human sovereignty, which is more valuable to a worker than fine gold, because individual human sovereignty is the primary motive force that delivers innovation with a fair outcome, whereby the worker is paid in full, and the company produces a product. So, it was freedom of conscience that made America great, which is based entirely on the Biblical definition of man being endowed by their Creator with conscience and with rights.

Individual human sovereignty, as defined by the United States Constitution, is an inalienable right that has been overruled by the Supreme Court in order to accommodate for a financial system based on income tax, thereby equating mankind as property of the State for revenue purposes. The former American industrial system relied primarily on individual human sovereignty in order to generate ideas freely, which derived from a Judeo-Christian based democracy. While the Communist system of industrialism relies on the individual to be expendable without question, because if their freedom of thought is expressed as a form of individual human sovereignty under God, then they are eliminated due to the totalitarian nature of Communist authority from absolute atheism. And it is the United States Supreme Court that has denied the Constitutional definition of human sovereignty by the inclusion of the 16th Amendment that defines income tax as Constitutional, which is in opposition the founding father's views concerning human independence from the State.

The idea that each individual should be subject to financial institutions in order to obtain spendable commodities is the very thing that leads to human slavery over time, rather than human independence, because as the financial institutions grow in size, the rate of poverty for the people increases with every loan that is created. And this is a direct result of irresponsibility by financial institutions that are engaging in an unsafe and unsustainable financial practice that involves heavy interest on loans in order to maintain a system based on debt, rather than surplus.

The more loans that are created by banks, the higher the surplus is for the institutions, and the lower the spending power is for the people who have an inalienable right to their own property. And money is by definition property, which is not to be taken away by the central bank that has laid claim to all commodities at the expense of the people who have an inalienable right to their own property in conjunction with international law. And the proof that all spendable commodities are owned by the FED is due to the label on money, which clearly indicates that monetary notes are owned by the Federal Reserve system.

The dehumanizing and degradation of individual human sovereignty by financial institutions, the United States Supreme Court, and the mainstream media is an integral part of Communist indoctrination, which is being done in order to maintain a financial system based on direct taxation and human slavery thereby. If government debt is not paid in full with each passing generation, then the burden falls onto the next generation in the form of bond slavery, which is the very thing that leads to human slavery by the reinterpretation of property. When Benjamin Franklin was asked after a session of the Constitutional Convention in May 1775, "what kind of a government have you given us?" he replied, "A democracy, if you can keep it. Our republic is founded on the principle that it will continue only as long as the people keep democracy alive." The founding fathers of America drafted the Constitution in response to a religious people on the moral grounds that a Christian democracy shall succeed over a secular one.

Yet the founding fathers were also aware that a democracy is subject to failure as a result of financial powers that seek to enslave mankind through the practice of usury and government legislation. And I use the term Christian democracy in relation to its foundations within the United States, because Christianity is the longest running system of religion within the United States, and because the ability to vote is according to an informed public, which is why freedom of the press, and freedom of conscience, are an integral part of the United States Constitution in order to cater for a Christian democracy, rather than a secular society. A secular society is no more free than a Communist one, because as Secularism grows, so does the abolition of all religion, which is an integral part of Communist revolution according to the principles of Communism as set forth by Karl Marx.

America was founded upon a Christian democracy, rather than a secular society, because it is the secular government that is to be scrutinized by the voting constituency, and not the other way around, so that the democracy should never be enslaved by the government, which was the founding fathers greatest fear. The separation of Church and State was enacted in order for freedom of religion to be exercised as a right, rather than a privilege, and so that the voting constituency should never be subjected to religious discrimination before the law. And the application of the evolutionary theory from public education has indeed acted as a form of religious discrimination by the denial of conscience, when it is freedom of conscience that forms the lawful basis for the Constitutional definition of man as a created human being.

According to the founding fathers, freedom of religion is an inalienable right, while the term, secular, is in relation to a privilege that cannot be exercised as a right to overrule the people's liberty to freedom of religion and belief. This liberty has been removed from public education on the basis of Secularism, when the founding and governing principle of the United States Constitution derives from the Biblical definition of man as having been endowed with conscience and with rights. Rights such as freedom of conscience are denied on the basis of the evolutionary theory from society and law, which is a crime against humanity on the basis of equality, because if there is one thing that cannot be exercised as a right under philosophical materialism, then it is the rights of conscience, which is a religious liberty, rather than a secular ideal.

The only thing that a person requires in order to become independent as an individual, and therefore, sovereign, is to be properly informed about their inalienable rights, because this is what it truly means to be enlightened; That you understand your inalienable right to be defined as a created human being, and then to stand upon this right as an individual, which is a Christian based ethic, rather than a secular one, because inalienable rights derive from the Creator, rather than from nature. If mankind was endowed by nature with conscience, then man is thereby the property of the State, because nature has a separate legal status compared to that of a human being.

But if mankind is endowed with conscience by their Creator, then mankind is thereby independent of the State in terms of ownership, and is therefore, sovereign, because the human conscience is able to make a moral decision independently of others in order to judge right from wrong, which is how equal justice works from the premise of law in trials by jury under the common law. The process of elimination in regards to the theory of evolution does not involve engaging the education system with another open debate, but more effectively, by challenging the legal system itself, because it is the lawful definitions in use for what a human being is that require protection before the law, rather than the evolutionary definition of man. The evolutionary definition of man is leading the world into a new age of human slavery by the reinterpretation of conscience, which is a crime against humanity on the basis of equality.

The founding and governing principle of human freedom rests upon the correct interpretation of the law, which does not include any legal protections for a scientific theory, because a theory in science will always be questionable before the law. Explaining the correct definition of inalienable rights and human equality to students is the only way to truly defeat Communism, systemic racism, and the evolutionary theory over time, and it is international law that holds to the highest standard in the world for the definition of what human equality is under the UDHR, because it has been signed by 192 nations, and is therefore, not-without-standing in its legal defence.

Thus, by substituting the teaching of evolution in public schools with systems theory and systems science will ensure that a coherent standard from law can be applied, because systems engineering and systems biology is modern science, while Darwinian evolution and Linnaean taxonomy is an age-old racial theory that requires dismantling and removal in order for an engineered control or substitution to be put into effect, and for universal rights to be interpreted to students for the benefit of their protection within the system. The theory of evolution is a failed system of belief based on philosophical materialism, and the main reason why the theory of evolution has failed completely as a pseudo-scientific belief, is because the theory has attempted to challenge the international standard for human rights and equality by equating mankind with the animal kingdom, which is a crime against humanity on the basis of equality.

Systems theory is by no means a religion, but the religiosity of the facts that are presented by systems theory and systems science is no different to the religiosity presented by the lawful definition of man under the common law. And law is fundamental to human freedom, just as much as it is to keeping individuals free from being victimized, incarcerated, exploited, and made to feel stupid by default of the situation they're in, all because of the system in place, which could have been easily prevented had the standard for public education been factual in regards to the lawful definitions concerning what a human being is, and where the endowed human conscience derives from.

The very word system means there is a Creator God, because if a system is defined by a set of rules, which it is, then a system is thereby evidence of a creation, because anything that has had rules applied to it, is by definition a creation according to the law of creativity. And this is the main reason why the theory of evolution, is in itself, a creation, because there have been a number of rules applied to the theory over the years within evolutionary textbooks in order to imply that the theory is authoritative, when nothing robs an individual of their God given freedom faster than the adoption of rules that simply do not apply.

The number one thing that will cause any system of law to fail, is by a breakdown in communication concerning a lawful instruction, which inevitably stops the system from performing efficiently by blocking the hierarchy of control completely. And it is when people start denying that they have a conscience that the legal system we live under begins to break down, because the system was dependent upon every individual to acknowledge a lawful instruction by having their conscience convicted by the truth.

The legal definition for the term, Creator, as from United States Constitutional law, is defined as "Lord, Lord Almighty, or God." While the lawful interpretation of what a person is before international law has defined the individual as having been endowed with conscience in accordance with the United States Constitutional definition of man, because the legal definitions therein are the same for the purpose of inalienable entitlements to be universal in their interpretation. This means that there is no legal or moral obligation for any individual to remove the religious rights for freedom of conscience and individual human sovereignty to exist by under international law in order to protect a racial theory that denies a person their God given humanity.

The lawful terms, endowed, and conscience, are theological terms from the Holy Bible historically, and from the United States Constitution legally, which is where the UDHR derives its legal definitions from. This means that a secular standard to govern the people with must relent for the purpose of freedom of information, because human beings have a universal right to learn about their Creator from a source of reliable information. And that source must be the government of a nation for the benefit of the people to understand the legal system they live in, which is an engineered system, rather than an evolved accident.

So, an acknowledgement of the Holy Bible by the United States Administration is in order, because we owe our human equality and inalienable rights to no one save the Creator Himself who has endowed all life with ability, but unto His own image the gift of conscience, with which, to reason from, so that all may know that God alone is their maker, and that God alone is truly sovereign. The term secular, is by no means a privilege that can be exercised as a right by the government at any time to deny an individual their inalienable right to freedom of information that is factually based upon the lawful definitions under Constitutional law. And no individual should ever be force fed the unlawful pseudo-definitions by the evolutionary theory through the public education system, which was theologically based within the United States to begin with before the evolutionary theory took over.

The United States Supreme Court ruling concluded that Intelligent Design is not science, and permanently barred the board of education from "denigrating or disparaging the scientific theory of evolution," which is the very thing that stops students from learning about human equality as an alternative to the theory of evolution. And this was one of the saddest days in American history, because if one cannot juxtapose two separate theories in school, then there will be the problem of indoctrination through forced education, which is a crime against humanity in itself.

Christian universities and schools do not limit their students to learn only creation science, because students can learn about evolution as well through the curriculum. While public school students are subjected to a one-sided view of science and history from the viewpoint of the evolutionary theory. So, the rule of the day is: He who pays for his education, has a say in his education. But just because public education should be paid for by the State, does not mean that the State has the luxury to deny a student their basic right to a full education. And a full education should always include the lawful interpretation of a person's basic human rights, which includes the universal right to be defined as a created human being.

So, for this reason, public education providers have no legal right, nor obligation, to refer to a student as an animal of some description, because this would be a violation of international agreement under the UDHR where all human beings are to be defined as distinct from the animals for reasons relating to the correct interpretation of human rights and equality. Systems engineering is a practical science with numerous applications for every industry with some of the most important technological advancements in science having derived from applied systems thinking. Systems science is to be interpreted from the viewpoint of creation science, because a system is rule based, and rules are always inferred, rather than deriving from materials alone.

The theory of evolution as a standard explanation from public education could be replaced overnight by the teaching of systems theory and systems science, because systems theory is a non-racial theory, and because systems science is not in opposition to the lawful definitions used to describe a person with, while the theory of evolution is in opposition to the lawful definition of person, and has been at the root cause of inequality and systemic racism since the theory was first established. Systems engineering can only be explained in terms of creation science, because an engineered system relies primarily on design and communication in order for innovation to occur. While the evolutionary definition of systems engineering attempts to define engineering as a natural process only, when designing and engineering cannot be defined as a natural process by definition of the word, design.

The United States Supreme Court decision to eliminate creation science from public education and then to substitute with the teaching of evolution as a theory has led to an engineered social crisis due to the nature of systemic racism. Thus, the only way to combat systemic racism is by the correct interpretation of human rights and equality that involves the theological definition of conscience. The United States Supreme Court has ruled that Biblical creation is an offence before the law on the basis that the theory of evolution is now protected under Federal law, when no theory in science can be defended by Federal law without incurring the burden of proof in return. So, in order for the administration to put an engineered control in place before a major incident occurs, then the evolutionary theory must be challenged from the premise of law, which cannot be overruled or blocked on the basis of any previous legal precedence for three main reasons.

Firstly; Because it is the secular standard for public education that has failed as a mechanism of improvement to public education by defining man as a lower animal from the theory of evolution. Secondly; Because the Supreme Court has no legal obligation to overrule the lawful definition of person from the evolutionary theory. And thirdly; Because it is the inalienable right of the people to decide who is guilty in criminal cases from a trial by jury, rather than being a Supreme Court decision alone. And in this case, it is the Supreme Court of the United States that is publicly liable for neglecting a lawful instruction that is universal in its interpretation, such as the inalienable and universal right for each individual person to be defined as a created human being who is endowed with conscience by their Creator.

The burden of proof in criminal cases is to meet the standard of proof, of which, derives from Biblical creation as a self-evident legal precedent. The universal and inalienable right to be defined as a created human being before international law is by no means a religious test upon the nations, or the Supreme Court of the United States, but rather, it is a moral one that must be complied with in accordance with international agreement, because the preservation of human rights and equality is a moral obligation, as well as a legal one.

So, in this matter, the burden of proof here rests upon the United States Supreme Court for overruling Biblical creation in favour of the evolutionary theory, because it is the evolutionary theory that has failed as a mechanism for learning in regards to a lawful instruction that is universal in its interpretation. While the legal standard for the rights of conscience has historically derived from United States Constitutional law, and is universal in its interpretations under the common law for the benefit of an individual's protection within the system.

So, in order to be consistent when interpreting inalienable rights and human equality to students, then a Creator God is required, because it is the universal law of equality that defines human freedom by the rights of conscience, rather than the evolutionary theory, which is the sole basis for systemic racism, Social Darwinism, and Communist influence. The human conscience can only be interpreted to students on the basis that a Creator God is self-evident, because the word, conscience, is not-without-standing from a legal premise.

So, for this reason, the theory of evolution has amounted to being a public grievance that must be addressed under the common law by the application of a former rule. And the former rule that must apply to the United States Supreme Court derives from a person's basic right to be defined as a created human being who is endowed with conscience and with rights, which is defined by international law as both universal and inalienable for the benefit of an individual's protection within the system. The right to be defined as a created human being is by definition a birthright, rather than a theoretical assertion. Thus, the rights of conscience is the self-evident nature of God who has endowed each person with rights and obligations that derive from Biblical theology, rather than secular science, which has failed as a method of learning due to the reinterpretation of conscience.

*Quotation: —————————————————————
"The moment the idea is admitted into society, that property is not as sacred as the laws of God, and that there is not a force of law and public justice to protect it, anarchy and tyranny commence. If "Thou shalt not covet," and "Thou shalt not steal," were not commandments of Heaven, they must be made inviolable precepts in every society before it can be civilized or made free." - John Adams. Source: Defence of the Constitutions of Government of the United States, Chapter 16. (Documented January 15, 1787).

The decision to deny Biblical creation to public school students by the United States Supreme Court is the main reason why public education in America is failing the students who should be made fully aware of the legal system they're entering into that holds to a Biblical definition of man on the basis of conscience and reason. And the longer the theory of evolution is taught from public education, the faster inalienable rights will erode, which is equal to an engineered social crisis, because it is the Holy Bible that defines human equality, and human independence thereby, rather than the theory of evolution, which forms the basis for the individual's denial of conscience.

So, unless the ban on creation science is lifted, then Communism will inevitably succeed over time as a mechanism of enslavement, because the only way to define a person's sovereignty, is by the Biblical definition of man, which the United States Constitution has acknowledged, while the

Supreme Court has denied. The theory of evolution is the greatest threat to a Christian democracy there is, because the common law system of justice, and the United States system of democracy, is to cast their vote on the basis of a moral obligation to uphold the correct definition of what a person is in order to protect the democracy from legislative intervention, which was the founding fathers greatest fear.

So, what we are seeing in America today is a cultural shift from a Christian based democracy to a secular one, when it is the Christian democracy that is to scrutinize the secular government according to the process of Constitutional law, rather than a secular society owing its allegiance to a secular government, which is the basis for Communism. The evolutionary theory from Marxism and Communism is the greatest threat to the stability of America and the rest of the world today, because as the number of minority groups that spring up from society increases, the more likely that a major revolution will occur. And the one thing we must guard ourselves against is a revolution by minority groups who question basic public morals on the basis of evolution.

The founding fathers of America foresaw the collapse of a Christian democracy long before it occurred, because they understood that the religious rights of man would be denied from within the system, rather than by standing armies. The collapse of a Christian democracy within the United States is in fact equal to an engineered social crisis, because the United States Constitution was founded upon the first precepts of Christianity that include an acknowledgement of the Creator God of Genesis so that a person's basic rights are protected as inalienable before the law. And as the current trend toward Secularism continues throughout society, the more atheism and unbelief will grow as a direct consequence of the theory of evolution being taught from public education, which is exactly how Communism will succeed over time by a shift in culture.

If the theory of evolution be a blessing to anyone, then it would be those who hail from the tyranny of Marxism and Communism, because it is the rise of minority groups who question basic public morals on the basis of evolution that is putting the peace and security of nations into harm's way. And it is the peoples security as created human beings that is at stake here due to lobbying efforts by atheism who attempt to define a moral test as a religious test, which is a crime against humanity on the basis of reason and of logic. If morality is to be tested on the basis of atheism, then there will be no universal premise to define morality with, when a universal system of morality is required in order to define a law as universal.

So, it is thereby illogical, as well as unreasonable for the sake of others to deny the Creator before the law on the basis of theory, because theory also constitutes as a belief, and is thereby subject to moral law on the basis of faith. If morality is to be tested on the basis of atheism, then the people will be led astray into a land of confusion, rather than a place of liberty and justice for all, because without a universal system of morality from the premise of law, then there will be nothing to measure the law, which is the very thing that will forbid the law in the minds of many who's conscience should not be in conflict with a lawful obligation.

Human liberty cannot be measured by science, nor can it be suppressed by pretended legislations that attempt to cater to all from a secular premise, but rather, human liberty is immeasurable on the grounds of human freedom. Human freedom is best expressed as an opposition to tyranny and fraud by the rights of conscience, which was the founding fathers greatest achievement by the introduction of inalienable rights as having derived from the Creator God of Genesis on the basis that each and every individual is a created human being, which is the very thing that liberates a person, and their mind, from all fraud and tyranny that attempts to suppress the people and the laws that sustain our basic freedoms.

*Quotation: —————————————————————

"The general principles on which the Fathers achieved independence, were the only principles in which that beautiful assembly of young gentlemen could unite, and these principles only could be intended by them in their address, or by me in my answer. And what were these general principles? I answer, the general principles of Christianity, in which all these Sects were united; And the general principles of English and American liberty. Now I will avow, that I then believe, and now believe, that those general principles of Christianity, are as eternal and immutable, as the existence and attributes of God; And that those principles of liberty, are as unalterable as human nature and our terrestrial mundane system." - John Adams, 2nd President of the United States. Source: Excerpt from a letter by John Adams to Thomas Jefferson. (Documented June 28, 1813).

The purpose of systems engineering and systems design is to detect faults prior to a systems failure and to engage in effective communication so that a hazard or fault can be eliminated from the system before a major incident occurs. And it is the American system of government that is set to fail over time by the introduction of the evolutionary theory into public education, and by the Supreme Court ban on creation science, because United States Constitutional law derives from Biblical theology under the common law, rather than secular science. So, as far as science goes, creation science is Constitutionally protected as inalienable, while the theory of ape to man is not. And the longer Americanized public education continues to hold sway within the world, the more secular society will become, which inevitably leads to the rise of Communism and socialism by the reinterpretation of conscience. This engineered social crisis has occurred by design, rather than by accident, because the main objective by Communism is to destroy the foundations of America by the rise of minority groups who question basic public morals, thus bring the common law into question.

So, for this reason, it is the inalienable right of every individual to defend the United States Constitutional definition of man in place of the evolutionary theory, because it is the evolutionary definition of man that will allow Communism to succeed over time by a shift in culture. Communist revolution can and does include an anti-religious mindset among the laity, which is a direct result of the evolutionary theory from the practice of education and law. Thus, a correct theology from public education is the only true safe guard against Marxist ideology, Islam, national socialism, and religious terrorism, because it is Biblical creation as a legal standard that forms the basis for the rights of conscience, which is a religious liberty, rather than a secular ideal.

Human freedom cannot be measured by a test tube, nor can human freedom be suppressed by law without causing a rebellion in turn, because human freedom is immeasurable under the rights of conscience, which requires a correct theology, and a correct interpretation of the law. Law is fundamental to human freedom in that a just decision should preside over tyranny and fraud, which means that law is in place to protect the peace, rather than to vilify a particular theory in science that has denied the lawful interpretation of conscience. The lawful interpretation of conscience under the common law is in place so that each person should be convicted by the truth, and the one truth that sets us free from subjugation, whether foreign or domestic, is that all men are created equal for the purpose of human rights and equality.

CHAPTER 3

Systems Biology

S YSTEMS BIOLOGY IS THE STUDY AND DESIGNING OF COMPLEX models that derive from biological systems, such as the model for the skeletal system, which supports the muscular system, which in turn, supports the nervous system. In systems biology, a living system will be broken down into smaller systems that are analysed independently or as a complex whole for the purpose of identification and comparison. The Human Genome Project is an example of applied systems thinking in biology, which is an international scientific research project with the goal of determining the number of base pairs there are that make up the total amount of human DNA, and for identifying and mapping all of the genetic sequences within the human genome so that comparisons can be made according to a comparison chart.

The Human Genome project is outlined by a method of identification for determining all of the different gene sequences there are within the human genome, and then to categorize them individually in order to understand how each of the body's proteins are made. The information gathered from the human genome is analysed to produce the specifics needed for a comparison chart, whereby each of the different gene sequences can be compared with one another for the purpose of identification. The reason why the method of research in systems biology is instructionally based, is because each of the models that are designed derive originally from instructional systems, including not only DNA instructions, but also, the transfer of information around the body via the nervous system and the heart, which is why instructional sequencing is the main focus for research in systems biology.

Systems biology relies primarily on research and analysis in order to develop a method of identification for each of the different sequences there are within the body, because it is the sequences in place that gives repeatability to the results. Each of the body's individual systems work together in sequence, which are then categorized individually for the purpose of identifying faults within the body's overall system in accordance with the specifications that derive from a comparison chart. So, each of the models or diagrams that are used in systems biology are for identification purposes, which is why interpreting DNA is important, because the instructional development from DNA to RNA, and then on to protein manufacture starts and ends with DNA instructions, because proteins arrange DNA sequences, and DNA sequences specify for the arrangement of proteins.

For example: When a protein for hair is being manufactured within the body, the body will require the number of proteins that are needed to form a strand of hair according to a specified amount. The information for manufacturing the proteins for hair is governed by another separate layer of instructions that directs the amount needed for the task so that the overproduction of hair does not occur where it isn't needed. But as the body gets older, and the rate of accumulative mutations increases within the body, the amount of hair a person has will begin to seemingly grow out of control around the body, which is a result of the system's instructions breaking down over time. And this is because the amount of mutations that have accumulated over time will inevitably destroy an organism through aging, rather than improve its genome.

The philosophy that accumulative mutations over time will increase the survivability of an organism derives from the science fiction of Darwinian evolution by natural selection, which asserts that accumulative mutations over time will increase the amount of order there is within the genome. When the truth is that the accumulation of mutations over time leads to a reduction in regards to the amount of order a thermodynamic instructional system has. So, because DNA RNA transcription is a thermodynamic instructional system, it will mean that certain instructions will become unreadable over time as diversification occurs, which is what junk DNA is.

The existence of junk DNA within the human body has been used as an excuse by evolutionary scientists to suggest that life is the result of junk DNA, when the truth is that any set of chemically based instructions that become unreadable over time due to a loss of specifics is equal to a reduction in terms of ordered complexity, rather than an increase. And this is the same for junk files that accumulate over time within a computer's operational software, whereby certain digital instructions become unreadable, because nearly anything you do on a computer requires the system to create a temporary file.

Each file on a computer that is needed to install, run, or execute a request is only needed at the very moment you make the request, but once the final step in the process is completed, the file is no longer needed, so the file then turns into a computer junk file. And this is similar to what DNA RNA transcription is doing because the DNA strand within a double helix spiral is short term and must be discarded once the mRNA sequence is completed. Thus, the human body requires a defragging process the same as a computer does, and DNA junk files within the body are indeed broken down by other proteins which use the DNA from the junk files to make new combinations of DNA instructions, so that little is wasted in terms of material, making the system efficient. And as diversification occurs over time, the rate of accumulative mutations will also increase which reduces a species survivability over time, rather than increasing it.

So, because the total amount of genetic instructions for any kind of creature was with the first copy that its genome began replication with, it will mean that each successive copy is only a variant of its original, so that individual species within a group are broken up into separate types and sorts within a kind. And only the original kind for each copy will have all of the information for variation, while each successive copy will have a lowered ability to pass on variability, which is equal to a reduction over time in terms of survivability.

For example: The specifications for a polar bear to make fur is different to the specifications for a brown bear to make fur, and neither one on their own is an improvement in terms of an overall level of efficiency, because if the specifications to make both types of fur were with one type of bear, then the bear that could specify for both would have a greater chance of survival. So, only a portion of the specifications to make fur will be passed down from generation to generation as diversification occurs, and it will be whatever is most suitable to the type of climate there is that will determine what type of fur is most efficient within a particular breeding group.

So, diversification will always lead to a reduction in survivability over time, because as each species becomes more suited to a given habitat, the less likely it will be able to survive in a different habitat with a different climate, because diversification has already occurred. Diversification is equal to speciation, and speciation is equal to specialization in regards to a given habitat. But the more efficient a breeding group becomes toward a given habitat over time, the less suitable that group will be in regards to a different habitat, which is why speciation is equal to a reduction in terms of survivability, rather than an increase as the theory of evolution assumes.

A species is defined as any breeding group that has derived from a particular kind, while a biological kind is represented by a group of species that have derived from an original version. The purpose of speciation is to provide an open breeding group that is free to integrate, which in turn, offsets the rate of hereditary mutations by having a breeding population that is diverse, thereby increasing the survivability of a particular kind. As diversification occurs over time, species will go extinct due to hereditary mutations, climate changes, and by other leading factors, which then leads to the extinction of a particular kind.

Thus, each particular kind is broken down into smaller groups known as species for the purpose of preserving a particular kind. And it is for this reason that a Darwinian inbreeding program known as evolutionary eugenics is an inefficient and unsustainable way to offset the rate of accumulative mutations, because a closed breeding will share the same chromosomal mutations, which must be offset by having an open breeding population that is free to integrate, or their biological kind will go extinct due to accumulative mutations. DNA RNA transcription is a copying process, and the rule with any copying process is that each successive copy must derive from an original copy, which in turn, defines each successive copy as a variant of its original. And only the original copy of a particular kind will have all of the genetic information for variation and speciation, while each successive copy, or species, will have a lowered ability to pass on variability due to the limitations of the copying process.

Instructions are defined as an order or directive, and that is because the information has been structured into a command, and the rule with any form of instructions is that they can be converted into words, so long as the specifics are in place. And translating DNA from the genome is a process of converting DNA instructions into sequences that we can interpret and understand in order to identify the total amount of instructions that are stored within the genome. DNA coding is the sequence of chemical characters that have been arranged into encoded sequences called gene sequences, which are represented by letters when interpreted into a format design. The characters that represent the DNA coding are adenine (A), cytosine (C), guanine (G), and thymine (T), which are arranged into a double helix spiral with the DNA configuration determining the RNA sequence that is to be conveyed into a protein.

A single strand of messenger RNA (mRNA) can fold back on itself in all directions according to a sequence that is governed by the placement of each chemical character, and this occurs as an interaction between the individual chemical characters within the RNA sequence. mRNA is single stranded, so any hydrogen bonding is intramolecular and can assume a variety of shapes in order to specify for a particular protein. So, because DNA instructions are the commands from the genetic sequences stored within the genome, and because DNA can be interpreted into a binary language, it will mean that they must have a predetermined figure or value, and the value or product of each figure (A, T, C, G) has derived originally from a standard for communication that not only required the chemicals that make-up the arrangement of the DNA sequence, but also, from sound as well.

The existence of multiple electromagnetic vibrational frequencies within a living cell occurs as a rhythm in sequence, and this is what actually governs the process of all of the interactions within the cell at a molecular level, and at an atomic level as well. And this is because the system of the atom is governed by resonant vibrational frequencies that surrounds an atom's core, which are a continuous wave of electromagnetic pulses that forms an atom's structure. The nucleus of an atom is held together by a polar active subatomic force that is produced by the electromagnetic particles that surrounds an atom's core, which is similar to how the solar system works, with the heaviest mass at the centre, and with satellite mechanisms in place to give the system motion, functionality, and structure. Every object has a characteristic frequency, or set of base frequencies, at which it vibrates the most with the least amount of energy input. These vibrations are associated with standing wave patterns called modes.

The arrangement of the mRNA sequence that is to be folded into a protein structure is governed by the DNA sequence, but the folding of the mRNA sequence is initiated by a set of electromagnetic vibrational frequencies, because the chemical group of nucleotides that make-up the mRNA sequence are polar active, and will respond to an electromagnetic field at the right frequency, which then initiates the folding of the mRNA sequence according to the placement of each nucleotide. The pattern development of a protein is not only molecular, but also, subatomic, because the folding of the mRNA sequence is affected at a molecular level from the electrons surrounding the atomic nuclei, which must be synchronized according to a set of base frequency ratios (or rhythm), in order for a protein structure to be stable within its environment.

The mRNA sequence for a protein must be pre-specified according to a method in place that is not only governed by the DNA sequence, but also, it is governed by electromagnetic vibrations that are in tune according to a set of base frequencies in ratio that act as a set of parameters, because the mRNA strand will fold back on itself to form a protein structure according to the placement of each term within an mRNA sequence. And each term within an mRNA sequence is electromagnetic, which means that both the mRNA sequence, and the correct signature frequencies, are working together in synchrony as a single process. Any set of signatures or sequences that work together in unison to form a single process or procedure are by definition integrated, which cannot occur at random over time, because in order to integrate the system, then a method is required first.

The structure of a protein is governed by an mRNA sequence that must be arranged according to the placement of each nucleotide, so that each term within the sequence can fold back in the right direction according to a correct electromagnetic frequency that stimulates the folding process, which is why listening to a rhythm in tune can help stimulate RNA synthesis, DNA proofreading, and protein manufacture. Current scientific research has shown that blood flows more easily through the body when music is played during surgery, which can also reduce the heart rate for the patient and the surgeon, which in turn, lowers blood pressure, decreases stress hormones called cortisol, and increases the production of serotonin and endorphin levels within the blood. Music that is in tune can also elevate a person's mood and boost the brain's production of the hormone dopamine.

So, if one term within the mRNA sequence is out of place, then the protein will be malformed, because there is a set of electromagnetic frequencies present that will cause the mRNA sequence to fold back on itself according to the placement of each nucleotide, which is evidence of design, because, the arrangement of a protein is governed by two separate signatures, such as the mRNA sequence, as well as the frequency signatures. This means that the only causality there is for proteins, is by design, because both the mRNA sequence, and the signature frequencies are working together for a single purpose, which cannot occur at random in accordance with the law of probability. The process of protein manufacture is by definition, specific, and there is only specified and unspecified to choose from; Meaning that anything that has not derived by design, is by definition, random. Yet protein manufacture cannot be defined as a random process, because the process is by definition, specific, and is thereby, specified.

The electromagnetic vibrational frequencies that stimulate the mRNA folding process are by definition, specific, for three main reasons: A) Because the system is integrated. B) Because the system works according to a cycle in place. And C) The frequency ratios have been structured into a rhythm in sequence. Any set of base frequencies that are in ratio with one another according to a rhythm in sequence is by definition, specific, because in order for a rhythm to occur that is in sequence, then there must be a cycle in place that is repeatable under observation. So, the process of protein manufacture is thereby integrated in terms of a system that displays properties in relation to frequency ratios that have been pre-specified according to a set of high to low rhythms that work together in sequence.

In the late 18th century, German physicist and musician, Ernst Chladni, demonstrated how vibrations could be used to create striking geometric imagery by spreading fine sand across the top of a metal plate and then running a violin string along the side of its edge. Chladni's demonstrations show that the sand will settle into distinct geometric patterns depending on the frequency that the sound waves produce by the violin string rubbing against the edge of the metal plate.

When the Chladni plate, for instance, vibrates in one of its modes, a hexagonal geometric pattern appears in the sand on top of the plate, which is why geometric patterns, such as circles and triangles overlapping each other, are found in nature. Centuries later, in the 1960's, a Swiss physician named Hans Jenny built on Chladni's experiments in an effort to study vibrational phenomena, which he called cymatics. Cymatics is a physics term which refers to the study of visible effects that sound and vibrations cause on matter, and everything that is organic or inorganic vibrates at a certain frequency, because the structure of an atom is vibrational.

For example: A snowflake is born when water vapour travels through the air and condenses by changing from a gas to a solid which then forms into an ice crystal. Water is a liquid crystal that holds memory in terms of its geometric shape at a molecular level, and when water molecules are vibrated the molecule will take on the particular shape that the vibration is making, which gives each snowflake a signature pattern. Sound is not only visible in terms of geometric patterns, and is therefore deterministic, but also, the frequencies must be in tune with one another in order for a molecule to be stable within its environment, which is evidence of design due to the presence of a rhythm in sequence that is held in tune according to a standard in place.

A standard base frequency is the frequency at which an atom or molecule will vibrate most, while each base interval in ratio acts as a sequence or rhythm that is held in tune according to scale. In music theory, a scale is any consecutive series of notes that form a progression between one note and its octave, typically by order of pitch or fundamental frequencies known as base frequencies that can be structured into a rhythm in tune.

When musical vibrations are channelled through a malleable medium, (such as a liquid) the vibrations cause the medium to arrange itself into visible geometries with overlapping shapes, and this is what actually causes the unique pattern of a snowflake to form, because as the vapour is solidifying into an ice-crystal, a geometric pattern is formed simultaneously, which is entirely due to the resonant vibrational frequencies that are affecting the particles at a subatomic level. So, because a snowflake can retain its geometric shape, and because the geometric shape is the result of electromagnetic vibrations, it will mean that there is a space for memory that is both vibrational, as well as electromagnetic. This principle in physics is known formally as quantum field, which acts as a space for memory in terms of energy, frequency, and vibrations.

The arrangement of atoms to make up a molecular bond is arranged according to a set of base frequencies from the force of the vibrational resonances that are produced by the electromagnetic polar effect between the positively charged protons and the negatively charged electrons. The signature frequency of each resonant impulse according to a scale of different frequencies in ratio specifies for the arrangement of a molecular structure, which is evidence of creativity, because any set of frequencies that are in ratio with one another according to a rhythm in tune is by definition, specific.

The structure of a molecule must be synchronized according to a set of base frequencies that are in ratio with one another in order for a rhythm to occur that is in tune, as well as in sequence, which is predetermined according to each figure or value that each base frequency has in terms of musical scale or notation, because it is musical scale that acts as a mechanism for tuning to occur in terms of frequency ratios. And atoms must be in tune with one another or they will not bond, which is why atoms were indeed created, because the stability of a molecular structure is depending upon the atoms to be in tune with one another according to a set of base frequencies that are in ratio with one another, the same as it is for musical scale when a group of instruments are working together in synchrony or symphony.

Albert Einstein confessed to thinking about science in terms of music, and often drew his inspiration directly from his experience as a musicianist, and later converting these intuitions into logical theorems, words, and mathematics. Einstein spent much of his career in the development quantum mechanics and special relativity involving the mathematical interpretation of atoms. The structure of an atom is in constant motion, which means that an atom must work according to a rhythm in sequence so that the electrons do not collide with one another.

The structure of an atom also works according to a cycle in place that is repeatable under observation, and anything that is repeatable under observation, is also specific, which cannot occur at random by definition of the fact that anything random will be unpredictable. The cycle of an atom is governed by its orbital structure with the satellite mechanisms in place to give the system motion, which occurs as a vibratory cycle or system. And anything that occurs according to a cycle in place that is by definition, predictable, is therefore, specific.

Thus, anything that works according to a rhythm in sequence, such as a cycle, is by definition, orderly, which is the evidence of design, because the only causality there is for an orderly system, is by the inference of rules that act as a set of parameters, thereby setting the limitations of an atom's structure in terms of vibrations. Musical vibrations operate in the same way with each aspect of a musical piece occurring as a cycle or system that can fluctuate from one cycle to the next in harmony or synchrony, which works as a sequence or rhythm. And an atom's structure must be synchronised with other atoms in order for a molecule to be stable within its environment, otherwise, the molecule will simply fall apart. Thus, the stability of an atom's structure is governed by musical vibrations that are inaudible, yet that they must be in tune, as well as in sequence in order for an atom's structure to be independently stable.

The force that each atom exerts is vibrational, and the pattern development that a group of atoms can form will define the structure of a molecule, which is why molecular bonds are governed by the electromagnetic polarity that each atom has. And this is also why the external vibrations of an atom must be specific at a subatomic level, because the system of an atom must be in rhythm in order for the shape of a molecule to be in tune. And this occurs as a sequential rhythm that is governed by a set of base frequencies that are in ratio with one another in order to act as a standard for tuning to occur the same as it is for musical scale.

For example: Tuning and temperament in music is the adjustment of one sound source to another, such as a voice or string to produce a desired pitch or frequency in relation to a given tone, and the modification of that tuning is used to reduce the level of dissonance or distortion. There are two key reasons why you should tune your instrument. First: Is to ensure that it plays at the correct pitch so that the instrument is in tune with itself. And secondly: To ensure that the instrument is in tune with the other instruments surrounding it.

Musical scale typically uses seven standard or primary notes, such as A, B, C, D, E, F, and G, (along with seven flats, and seven sharps). This means there are seven primary musical notes in the chromatic scale for music that are represented by differences in frequency or pitch, as well as being in ratio with one another according to a universal standard in place for each base frequency at a given interval. So, as an example, the middle-A note has a frequency of 440 Hz and the middle-B note has a frequency of 494 Hz which is measured by a graph with high to low variations called musical scale.

The electromagnetic impulse from an atom's satellite electrons produce vibrational resonances that will govern the whole process of any molecular pattern development that we see from an atomic level, which is governed by the signature frequency for each electromagnetic impulse according to scale, which is equal to a rhythm in tune when a molecule is formed. And the resonant vibrational frequencies for the system of an atom must be in tune in order to give stability to the structure of a molecule, because the subatomic particles surrounding the atom's core are in motion, so they must not collide with one another.

So, in order for the structure of a molecule to be stable, then the atoms need to be governed by an electromagnetic polarity with a polar effect that is produced by the negatively charged electrons that surrounds the atom's positively charged protons, so that the electrons maintain their course of action in sequence, which is required so that the electrons do not collide with one another. And it is the negatively charged electrons in motion that causes the resonant impulse that each atom has, while the electromagnetic field, (or orbit) that each atom produces acts as a space for memory in terms of frequency ratios.

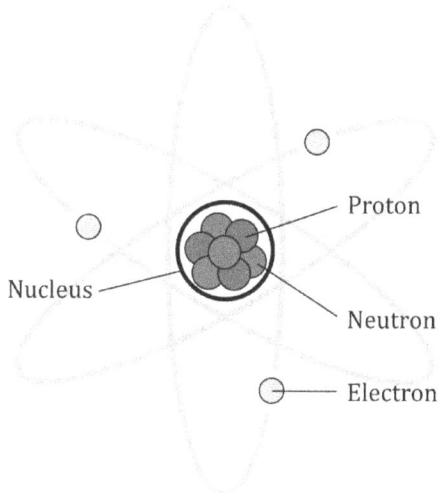

(Above) Illustration demonstrating the system of an atom's structure. Source: Wikipedia Encyclopedia.

The scale of different frequencies for each atom is in ratio with one another according to a universal standard for each base frequency, such as musical scale, which is why musical scale acts as a universal standard for tuning to occur, because each base frequency that an atom produces within the shape of a molecule is in tune with one another, giving each molecule a signature frequency. And though each atom within the shape of a molecule is in tune with one another in order for a molecule to be stable within its environment, it will be the sequential rhythm in place that acts as a musical piece due to the presence of a rhythm in sequence, as well as in tune.

The signature frequency, or set of base frequencies, that each atom has occurs as a rhythm in tune according to the placement of each base interval resulting in a sequential rhythm, (or sequence) that is held in tune by an electromagnetic polarity. In mathematics, a sequence is defined as the succession of one numeral after another that is in order resulting in an algorithm or procedure. A sequence in place can also be defined as a series of events that are in relation to each other, and are thereby, relative. Thus, it is the law of relativity that defines a sequential rhythm or sequence as orderly, which is evidence of design due to a set of parameters that is governed by a standard in place that defines the sequence as specific.

So, in order to define a sequence as orderly, then a set of parameters are required first, which means that a set of rules are required in order to set the parameters in place for tuning and temperament to occur, which is why musical scale acts as a set of parameters (or system) that governs the limitations of a rhythm in tune. Musical scale acts as a universal standard for tuning to occur in order to reduce the level of dissonance, (or disorder) that an instrument has; Meaning that the stability of an atom is governed by a rhythm in sequence, as well as a method of tuning, and is therefore, orderly, in terms of frequency ratios that have been structured into a vibrational command that is universal in terms of cause and effect. Thus, atoms are not self-existing, because the stability of an atom's structure is governed by an electromagnetic polarity that is held in tune according to a cycle in place, which is evidence of design due to the presence of a rhythm in sequence, as well as in tune.

In biology, the human body will generate multiple vibrational frequencies from the heart which effects the circulation system, and it is the key tones and resonances according to a scale of different frequencies that governs the correct flow of circulation within the body, and this occurs as a rhythm, or sequence, that can be interpreted into a model for identification. Defibrillators are devices that send an electric pulse or shock to the heart to restore a normal heartbeat. They are used to prevent or correct an arrhythmia, which is an uneven heartbeat that is too slow or too fast.

So, if the heart is beating too fast or too slow due to an arrhythmia, then the defibrillator can help the heart to stop suddenly, and then begin beating at the correct rhythm again, which means that the heart requires tuning the same as an instrument does. The heart is made up by four chambers that include two upper chambers (atria) and two lower chambers (ventricles). The heart's rhythm is normally controlled by a natural pacemaker called the sinoatrial node, or sinus node, which is located in the upper right chamber of the heart called the atrium. The sinus node sends electrical impulses to the heart that acts as a method of signalling to govern the heart's rhythm which starts each heartbeat and keeps the heart's rhythm in sequence, as well as in tune. However, it's quite normal for a person to have a fast or slow heart rate, because the heart rate may increase with exercise or slow down during sleep.

So, because the heart rate is governed by a rhythm that is fluctuating between a set of high to low variables, it will mean that there is a ratio in place for each of the high to low rhythms, and it is the ratios in place for each of the high to low rhythms that acts as a standard for tuning to occur. And this also means that the heart was made, because the sinus node continuously generates electrical impulses that are equal to an instructional command that is vibrational, thereby setting the normal rhythm and beats per minute for a healthy heart. So, the heart has been tuned according to a set of high to low frequencies that are in ratio with one another, which acts as a standard for cardiologists to study and make assessments based on the frequency ratios.

For example: A digital guitar tuner is a device that measures the frequencies produced by vibrating strings on an electric or acoustic guitar. It then aligns those measurements with notes according to musical scale, and if the frequencies match a particular note, then the tuner will display the name of that note on an LED display. While the digital tuner for a smart TV allows you to receive and display a digital signal, which means that tuning is equal to an instructional command in order for a desired effect to occur. So, because the only way to replicate this ability, is to design a system of digital tuning, it will mean that the human body was also designed, because there is no other causality for a method of tuning to occur except by design. And the electrical signals between the heart, the brain, and the sinus node, are indeed evidence of design, because they are communicating via sensory signals.

An electrocardiograph or ECG is a test used to measure the electrical activity of the heart which is translated into a graphic recording, or model, that shows the electrical impulses generated by the heart muscle. An ECG is used to help diagnose specific cardiac anomalies, such as disturbances of heart rhythm and conduction. And this is a systems study for cardiologists who must interpret the heart's rhythms in order to complete a systems check on the body's overall health based on the individual signatures for each impulse.

The resonant vibrational frequencies in rhythm from the heart is also what stimulates our emotions, as well as thought, because a positive thought will have a positive feeling that affects the heart's rhythms, while negativity will have a negative emotional response from the heart. The human brain can have positive or negative thoughts based on a polar effect within the mind that stimulates the heart's rhythms, as well as our emotions, which means that emotions are vibrational. So, because the vibrational frequencies from the heart are expressed as a rhythm in sequence that is kept in tune by the frequency ratios that derive from the sinus node and the brain, it will mean that there is a universal standard in place for all of the different types of signature frequencies that the heart produces, which can then be translated into a graphical model for interpretation and assessment, which is how a cardiograph works.

Each time there is an abnormality within the body's circulation system, the heart rate will be affected, and this occurs as a sequence with each signature impulse from the heart determining the high to low rhythms, which is then assessed according to a scale of different signature impulses, or set of frequencies, that the heart produces in order for an assessment to be made. And it is the sequence in place that allows for a prediction or diagnosis to be made according to a cardiograph that acts as a universal standard for assessment and interpretation.

So, the human heart also requires tuning and balancing to work the same as an atom requires tuning and balancing, because the heart is impetus due to each heartbeat, which means that the body is always in motion internally, the same as an atom is always in motion externally by the subatomic particles that surrounds the atom's core. And the standard base frequencies in place for each impulse that the heart produces can be interpreted as being either a normal rhythm, or as an abnormality, according to a universal standard for each of the high to low rhythms in ratio, which is how a fault is identified within the body's overall system using a cardiograph or ECG.

This means that the identification process for each of the body's high to low rhythms act according to a scale or standard in place for all of the different signature frequencies that the body produces, which occurs as a set of ratios that are in sequence, as well as in rhythm. And it is the sequence in place that generates the specifics needed for a diagnosis to be made based on a comparison chart where all of the different signature frequencies have been categorized and compared according to a set of ratios that are specific in relation to each other, thereby setting a universal standard for cardiologists to make an assessment. And this is a part of an early detection method that has been engineered to find faults throughout the body's overall system based on the electrical impulses that derive from the body's high to low rhythms.

A standard frequency is defined as the frequency at which a body will resonate if excited by a vibrational force, which is then broken down into a ratio of different frequencies that work together as a standard for tuning to occur. If the frequency ratio is 1:1 the two frequencies will make the same pitch; Meaning that they're in unison. But if the frequency ratio is 2:1 then they are what's known as an octave. And if the frequency ratio is 3:2 then they are referred to as a perfect fifth. A perfect fifth is made up of seven semitones, and this interval is the most consonant of all intervals, which according to music theory, is the base interval of harmony or balance.

In music, an interval ratio is the ratio of a given frequency for pitch, tone, and timbre in a musical interval that is governed by musical scale. Frequency ratios are used to describe intervals in both Western and non-Western music, and they are most often used to describe base intervals between notes tuned using tuning systems, such as Pythagorean tuning, just intonation, and meantone temperament, the size, and duration of which, can be expressed by smaller integer ratios, such as sharps and flats.

For example: The base atmospheric electromagnetic resonant frequency for the Earth is 7.83 Hz, and our atmosphere is continuously resonating with a radio frequency of 7.83 Hz, which is a ratio of 1:1 along with progressively weaker harmonics at around 14.3, 20.8, 27.3, and 33.8 Hz. These oscillations are called the Schumann resonances. According to systems biology, the normal frequency of a human body standing is about 7.5 Hz, while the frequency of the sitting posture is generally between 6 and 4 Hz which is a ratio of 3:2 and is equal to a perfect fifth. A perfect fifth frequency ratio allows the body to be at rest whilst sitting down due to a reduced amount of muscle activity.

So, the standard frequency for the human body is broken up into a set of ratios in rhythm, the same as the Earth's resonant frequencies are governed by a set of ratios in sequence, which is then converted into a model for the purpose of identification and comparison. And these are standard base frequencies which are the resonant vibrations that governs each of the interactions between each part of the body, and the environment surrounding the body. So, in order for each of the body's different ratios of vibrational frequencies to be in sequence with one another, then a rhythm is required.

A rhythm in place that derives from a set of vibrational frequencies that are in tune with one another will always be the result of a method having been applied due to a standard in place for tuning and sequencing to occur, because the outcome of a rhythm in sequence that has been tuned according to a set of frequency ratios, is by definition, specific. And this is applicable to biology, because all of the body's high to low rhythms are in synchrony; Meaning that they're in ratio with one another, as well as in sequence.

So, because the Earth is relying on multiple frequency ratios for each base interval to be in rhythm, as well as in sequence, it will mean that the Earth has had planning applied to it in order for life to be in tune with itself, as well as its surroundings. And this is the same for a group of musical instruments that are to be used in musical notation in order to indicate various aspects of how a piece of music is to be performed in synchrony, because the standard base frequencies of the Earth are in tune with the human body, the same as a group of musical instruments that work together in symphony.

This means that the likelihood of life occurring at random is physically impossible due to the number of specific events that must be multiplied by each other in order to gain a probability factor for the overall event of life forming by chance to occur in terms of frequency ratios, because the ratios have been synchronized together into a rhythm in sequence that is held in tune according to a standard in place, and is therefore, orderly. And the circulation system of an organism does rely on a rhythm in sequence to be in place that is specific in terms of frequency ratios, because any sequence that is for the express purpose of signalling within an organism, is by definition, specific.

The structure of an atom is vibrational according to a rhythm in sequence, and is held in tune by the polar active subatomic force that each atom has, which must be synchronized in order for the structure of a molecule to be stable within its environment. So, because the only causality there is for a vibrational resonance that is held in tune according to a rhythm in sequence is by design, it will mean that God the Creator has spoken all things into existence by an audible vibrational command. Otherwise, there would be no way to define a causality for an atom that is held in tune according to musical scale.

Quantum information from resonant vibrational frequencies are the different levels of vibration according to scale, (or ratio) that occurs as a rhythm, (or sequence) and is held in tune by a standard for tuning that is universal, (such as musical scale) and can be translated into an instructional format known as musical notation. The stability of a molecule is thereby relying on a set of base frequencies in ratio or rhythm, and is governed by the position of each base interval with smaller integer ratios determining the rhythm in sequence.

Thus, the structure of an atom or molecule can be compared to that of a musical piece in terms of frequency ratios, but because atoms are not communicating with one another via instructions the same as a trumpet does not communicate with a violin, yet both atoms and molecules are working together in synchrony according to a sequential rhythm that is held in tune according to musical scale, it will mean that the structure of an atom or molecule is performing according to musical notation. And this is the same for a piano that is to be performed according to the instructions that derive from a music book, only the balancing act of a molecule or atom is performing from memory instead, rather than written instructions, which is evidence of quantum information.

This means that quantum field is storing vibrational information from memory in the form of musical scale that can be structured into a vibrational command known as musical notation. In quantum physics, materials with memory, also referred as materials with hereditary effects, are a class of materials that contain a dependence upon the past history of thermodynamic, kinetic, electromagnetic, or other physical, or non-physical states. Thus, any substance or form of energy that retains its geometric shape or vibration will be defined as a source of memory.

The vibrational rhythm or sequence that each atom has within the shape of a molecule works in symphony, (or synchrony) according to a universal standard for each base frequency, (or interval) that is in ratio, (or tune) and is therefore, specific. So, I am not suggesting that atoms communicate with one another, but what I am suggesting is that atoms are not self-existing, because the rhythm of an atom's motion is in tune, as well as in sequence. So, in order for atoms and molecules to be stable within their environment, then a method of tuning is required first, which cannot occur at random over time, because a method is by definition, specific.

According to Oxford Languages, the definition of purpose has been defined as: 1) "The reason for which something is done, or created, or for which something exists." So, by definition, the word, purpose, is for providing a reason for why something was created, which is the reason why purpose always derives by intention. Otherwise, there would be no reason for life to exist, when life serves as the purpose for the universe itself, because without life, the universe would be void without meaning. In systems theory, the purpose of a system is to have a primary or designated function, whereby each individual mechanism has been incorporated for a specified purpose or primary function.

So, in other words, the primary function of a system must first be designated in order for the primary feature to have a purpose, which is evidence of design, because purpose always derives by intention. This means that life has also derived by intention, because living systems have a primary function, such as breathing. Thus, one cannot argue that life is meaningless without detracting from the purpose of a system, which is to act as a standard or method that is repeatable under observation, and therefore, predictable under demonstration. An atom is by definition a system, because an atom is governed by a rhythm in sequence that is held in tune according to a cycle in place that is repeatable under observation, and is therefore, specific.

The evidence that creativity has been applied to atoms and molecules is the same as it is for any instrument that is in tune with itself, and the instruments surrounding it, so that a desired effect can occur according to each base interval in rhythm or sequence. The frequency ratios produced by a group of atoms within the shape of a molecule must be in tune with one another in order for the structure of a molecule to be stable, which means that there is a universal standard for tuning to occur in terms of vibrations, such as musical scale. Musical scale derives from a source of memory in terms of a universal standard for definitions that are vibrational, because musical scale is governed by a set of base frequencies in ratio in order for tuning and balancing to occur within the shape of an atom or molecule.

Musical scale is a universal standard for tuning to occur, because an atom or molecule is vibrational with an electromagnetic field present that is oscillating according to a set of high to low variables that are in ratio, or rhythm, as well as in tune. So, in order for a standard for tuning to be universal in terms of frequency ratios so that tuning and balancing can occur within the shape of an atom or molecule, then there needs to be a type of medium, or storage mechanism, that is vibrational in order to act as an environment for quantum information to be conserved in terms of a space for memory, which is known as quantum field.

Quantum field theory states that everywhere in this universe, and at every instant of time, there is the existence of different types of fields that we cannot see but can detect, like a magnetic field, electric field, gravitational field, and vibrational field. In quantum field theory, what we perceive as particles are excitations of the quantum field itself. The most practical example of a quantum field is quantum electromagnetism, which exists as two distinct fields, such as electromagnetic field and the electron field. The following theory I am presenting involves quantum field in the form of stored vibrations known as musical scale, which is essential for our understanding of quantum information. Quantum information can be interpreted as instructions via musical notation, because quantum information is stored within a space for memory, such as musical scale, which acts as a universal standard for tuning and balancing to occur within the shape of an atom or molecule.

Quantum field is a plane of existence that we cannot see nor touch, yet a quantum field is required in order to explain stored information in terms of frequency, vibrations, and electromagnetism. Musical notation is governed by a scale of high to low variables that are in ratio with one another, and are represented by musical symbols when translated into an instruction. Musical symbols are instructional in terms of how a piece of music is to be performed in terms of musical notation. Musical scale can be translated into musical notation, which is instructional, as well as universal in terms of frequency ratios. So, in order for tuning and balancing to occur within the shape of a molecule or atom, it will mean that a quantum field is storing vibratory information in the form of electromagnetic frequencies, known formally as musical scale, that can be translated into musical notation or instructions. This means that quantum field is storing instructional information from memory in the form of musical scale, which is evidence of design due to the presence of an instructional system that is vibrational.

A quantum field must also be electromagnetic, as well as vibrational, because the charge of an atom is governed by an electromagnetic polarity that must be maintained within its environment as either positive or negative, depending on the type of charge. This means that the electromagnetic frequency within a quantum field is maintained by an electromagnetic polarity that can alternate in terms of its current capacity, which must derive from an electromagnetic field that encompasses the universe in order to act as a malleable medium for quantum information to be stored in terms of a space for memory. So, in order for musical scale to be universal in terms of a method of tuning, then there must be a hidden medium throughout the universe that is storing vibrational information, such as an electromagnetic field. This field thereby incorporates a steady wave or pattern of electromagnetic vibrations that are stable, as well as constant, in order to act as a standard for tuning to occur within the shape of an atom or molecule. A resonant electromagnetic field that encompasses the universe is required in order to explain atomic particles, because atoms are not only electromagnetic, but also, they're vibrational.

Any sequence or rhythm that is oscillating according to a cycle in place will be defined as evidence of a creation, such as seasonal cycles, internal body rhythms, or electromagnetic waves that derive from an atom's structure. A rhythm or cycle that is repeating itself in sequence under observation is thereby predictable under demonstration, which is the evidence of creativity in accordance with the law of probability, because any sequence that is predictable under demonstration cannot occur at random. The unit of measurement to define an electromagnetic wave that oscillates according to a cycle in place is more commonly known as Hertz. And this is the evidence that creativity has been applied to atoms, as well as the human body, because any rhythm in sequence that is oscillating according to a cycle in place that is repeatable under observation, is by definition, orderly.

Quantum field theory is used in particle physics to construct a theoretical model of the universe. Quantum information, however, is the vibrational information stored within a space for memory known as quantum field. This means that the edge of the universe has an electromagnetic field present that acts as a vibrational medium for atoms to move around inside the perimeters of this field. Quantum field defines the structure of the universe in terms of a vibrational medium for atomic particles to be in tune with one another.

A quantum field is electromagnetic, as well as vibrational in terms of its structure and purpose, because without an electromagnetic field present that is vibrational, then the vibrations of an atom would not be in rhythm, as well as in tune. The electromagnetic field lines that forms a quantum field are the lines of electromagnetic waves that travel in every direction, which acts as a universal standard for base frequencies that are to be held in tune within a space for memory, because in order for one device to be in tune with another, then a standard is required in the form of frequency ratios that act as a universal standard for tuning and balancing to occur.

*Quotation: ————————————————————
Synchronization of Human Autonomic Nervous System Rhythms with Geomagnetic Activity in Human Subjects: A coupling between geomagnetic activity and the human nervous system's function was identified by virtue of continuous monitoring of heart rate variability (HRV) and the time-varying geomagnetic field over a 31-day period in a group of 10 individuals who went about their normal day-to-day lives. A time series correlation analysis identified a response of the group's autonomic nervous systems to

various dynamic changes in the solar, cosmic ray, and ambient magnetic field. There were significant correlations between the group's HRV and solar wind speed, Kpa, Ap, solar radio flux, cosmic ray counts, Schumann resonance power, and the total variations in the magnetic field. In addition, the time series data were time synchronized and normalized, after which all circadian rhythms were removed.

It was found that the participants' HRV rhythms synchronized across the 31-day period at a period of approximately 2.5 days, even though all participants were in separate locations. Overall, this suggests that daily autonomic nervous system activity not only responds to changes in solar and geomagnetic activity, but is synchronized with the time-varying magnetic fields associated with geomagnetic field-line resonances and Schumann resonances. - Source: The National Institutes of Health.gov - Published Online by the National Library Of Medicine. (Documented July 14, 2017).

A quantum field can be expressed as a set of electromagnetic field lines that are storing vibrations in the form of musical scale, because the frequency ratios have been structured into a rhythm in sequence that is held in tune according to a set of high to low variables. This means that a fifth dimension known as memory can be expressed in the form of an electromagnetic field that is storing vibrational information within the field lines, which is required in order for tuning and balancing to occur within the shape of an atom or molecule. When a body or structure resonates at a given interval the vibrational information will be unpredictable unless a rhythm or cycle is occurring under observation, which then defines the vibratory pattern as predictable, and therefore, orderly.

Any set of base frequencies that are in ratio with one another, are by definition, synchronised, which also applies to the human body, because all of the body's rhythms have been synchronised in accordance with an electromagnetic field that is storing vibratory information. Thus, a quantum field is storing vibrational information for the purpose of synchronisation, which is required for tuning and balancing to occur that is universal in effect, leaving only one causality for the existence of the universe as having derived from an audible vibrational command. Otherwise, there would be no causality for the existence of an orderly thermodynamic or dynamothermal system, because all thermal systems are reliant on key tones and vibrations in the form of wave patterns that have been structured into a universal system known formally as quantum field, which acts as a source of memory in terms of frequency, energy, and resonance.

Mechanical waves, and electromagnetic waves, are two very distinct ways that energy is transported. Waves patterns in water, and sound waves through the air are two prime examples of mechanical waves. Mechanical waves are caused by a disturbance, or vibration in matter, whether solid, liquid, gas, or plasma, which act as a type of medium for mechanical waves to travel. These mechanical waves travel through a medium by causing the molecules to bump into each other, such is the case with a domino effect. Mechanical waves cannot travel in the vacuum of space, because there is no medium to transmit these wave lengths.

Electromagnetic waves on the other hand differ from mechanical waves in that they do not require a physical medium to propagate over distances. This means that electromagnetic waves can travel not only through air and other materials, but also, through the vacuum of space. In the late 1860's, a Scottish physicist named James Clerk Maxwell developed a scientific theory to explain electromagnetic waves. He noticed that electrical fields and magnetic fields can couple together to form electromagnetic waves. He summarized this relationship between electricity and magnetism into what are now referred to as: "Maxwell's Equations."

In the year 1887, German physicist, Heinrich Hertz, applied Maxwell's equations to the production and reception of radio waves. The unit of frequency for a radio wave, known as one cycle per second, is named the Hertz, in honour of Heinrich Hertz. The number of crests that pass a given point within one second is described as the frequency of the wave. One wave, or cycle per second, is called a Hertz (Hz), after Heinrich Hertz who established the existence of radio waves. For example: A wave with two cycles that pass a point in one second has a frequency of 2 Hz.

Stored information within a quantum field relies on constant set of vibrations that act as a method of tuning, which is evidence of design, because any set of vibrations that are oscillating according to a rhythm in sequence is evidence of a cycle. And a cycle cannot occur at random, because a cycle is repeatable under observation and therefore, predictable, while that which is random is by definition, unpredictable. So, for this reason, quantum field is by definition, orderly, due to a method of tuning that is vibrational, as well as universal, which is required in order for a rhythm in sequence to be in tune with itself, as well as its environment, which in turn, gives stability to the vibrations of an atom or molecule.

This means that quantum information is stored within a space for memory that is electromagnetic, the same as an atom's electromagnetic field lines represent the orbit of an atom's electrons and is in constant effect, thereby setting a universal standard for tuning and balancing to occur within the shape of an atom or molecule. The balancing act of an atom occurs as a rhythm in sequence that is governed by a cycle in place, while the cycle that is occurring derives from quantum field lines that are storing vibrations in the form of frequency ratios, which then acts as a mechanism for tuning and balancing to occur that is universal in terms of a space for memory, because an atom's cycle performs from memory, rather than written instructions.

Thus, a quantum field is storing vibrational information within a space for memory that acts as a universal standard for tuning and balancing to occur in the form of frequency ratios that have been structured into a set of high to low variables known as musical scale. While musical notation derives from musical scale, which is by definition, instructional, in terms of musical symbols, and is evidence that a quantum field is storing instructional information that has derived from audible vibrational command.

According to Isaac Newton, the relationship between the mass of the Earth and its gravitational effect is caused by the relationship between the sun and its satellite objects, providing some of the first insights into the propagation of light and gravity based on the then theoretical existence of aether. In Aristotle's book, On The Heavens, he stated that celestial spheres made of aether held the stars and planets in their place, which later gave rise to the Medieval term, quintessence.

Quintessence is the Latin name of the fifth element used by Medieval alchemists as a way to describe a medium that makes up the heavenly bodies in terms of a substance or element. The Medieval elemental system consisted of four basic elements that included earth, wind, water, and fire, with quintessence making up the fifth element. By the arrival of the 20th century, Einstein's theory of special relativity followed the Newtonian concept by

Isaac that the existence of aether was able to explain the propagation of light as a pattern of waves in order for light to travel through a vacuum, or medium, the same as sound waves travel through the air, or ripples in a pool.

Fundamental particles, such as atoms, display quantum properties in relation to energetic charge, mass distribution, and momentum. These characteristics are conserved until the particle interacts with another particle due to quantum entanglement, or if the particle radioactively decays, or if a molecule simply falls apart in a chemical reaction resulting in a random distribution of atoms or particles. These products, such as atoms and molecules, preserve quantum information within their structure in the form of vibrations, which is stored within a space for memory due to the principles of conservation involving quantum mechanics.

Quantum field is thereby informational in terms of vibrations, because the standard base frequencies that a quantum field produces acts as a universal standard for tuning and balancing to occur within the shape of an atom or molecule so that its structure is conserved within a space for memory. And this is applicable to any particle, molecule, body, instrument, or structure, because a universal standard for tuning and balancing cannot occur without a universal standard for vibrations that is fixed, such as musical scale. Musical scale is the scale of high to low base frequencies that have been structured into a ratio of high to low rhythms, which are in constant effect due to a space for memory known as quantum field.

So, a quantum field is not only electromagnetic, but also, it is informational, because, A) An atom's structure is vibrational. B) An atom is governed by an electromagnetic polarity. And C) Because musical scale acts as a universal standard for tuning and balancing to occur that is vibrational. This means that the conservation of a rhythm in tune is governed by a vibratory pattern that derives from a quantum field with stored information in terms of a space for memory, so that musical scale is hidden within the fifth dimension known as memory; Meaning that musical scale constitutes as quantum information, because every atom will cycle in sequence according to a rhythm in tune.

This information known as quantum information is thereby specific, because a quantum field is held in tune according to musical scale, and is thereby conserved, which can be interpreted into a language with symbols known as musical notation. Otherwise, there would be no universal standard for tuning to occur in terms of frequency ratios that have been structured into a vibrational command in order for tuning to occur within the shape of a molecule or atom. So, because quantum information is stored in the form of musical scale, and because musical scale is interpreted as musical notation, it will mean that quantum information is specific.

A rhythm in sequence known as cycles per second is the universal standard to define the structure of an atom in terms of frequency ratios. These vibrations have been structured from stored information that is vibrational, which is evidence of a space for memory that is hidden within a quantum field. Quantum field is thereby specific in terms of stored vibrations in order for an atom to be in tune with itself, and its environment. Quantum field acts as a storage mechanism in terms of musical scale, because when a rhythm in tune occurs, it will always be relative to musical scale in terms of frequency ratios that have been structured into a vibrational command in the form of musical notation. And musical scale is indeed instructional, because there are many different types of creatures that will communicate through singing, which in turn, acts as a language or instructional method.

According to online resources, there are at least 200,000 species that sing in ways that are incommunicable to us, such as birds, fish, whales, and frogs, yet they are communicating with each other using vibratory patterns and waves, which is evidence that quantum field is storing instructional information, because quantum field is storing electromagnetic vibrations in the form of musical scale, which: A) Enables each kind of creature to be tune with its surroundings, which is required for biological growth to occur at the correct frequency range. B) Allows for audible communication to occur within a particular breeding group. And C) Allows for different types of structures to be integrated in terms of integrity, which is required in order for a structure to stable within its environment.

So, when an atom performs a balancing act, the information must derive from a set of vibrations that are in constant effect, because there is a cycle in place that is repeatable under observation, and all biological systems operate according to a cycle in place with a rhythm in sequence so that each of the body's organs are working in synchrony. This means that music is the language of biology due to the presence of a quantum field that is governed by a cycle in place that works according to a rhythm in sequence, and is held in tune according to a scale of high to low base frequencies that are in ratio with one another, and is formally known as musical scale, because musical scale acts as universal method of tuning, the same as a quantum field acts as a universal system of tuning for radio frequencies.

According to the study of radio wave propagation, a radio frequency spectrum includes a set of frequencies that forms the electromagnetic framework used by radio communication systems ranging from 30 Hz to 300 GHz. It is divided into several ranges, (or bands) and given labels, such as low frequency (LF), medium frequency (MF) and high frequency (HF), the same as musical scale is broken into seven standard or primary notes, such as A, B, C, D, E, F, and G, along with seven flats, and seven sharps. It is interesting to note here at this point that not only are radio frequencies broken up into seven different ranges, or bands, with three separate labels, such as (LF), (MF), (HF), the same as musical scale is broken up into seven primary notes, along with seven flats, and seven sharps, but also, the number twenty one in mathematics can be divided by seven to equal three.

According to Biblical theology, the number 7 is the number of God the Creator who has applied this number with many of His commandments, such as the year of Jubilee, the seven day week, and the seven Churches of Revelations just to name a few. The second attribute of God the Creator is the number 3, for God is Father, Son, and Holy Spirit, known formally as the Holy Trinity. A third aspect of God's attributes is the human conscience, which can be broken up into three main attributes, such as word, spirit, and, morality, with each of the attributes being relative to a system of law known formally as morality, which is also universal in effect.

God in Heaven has placed His signature upon His creation as seven and three, which is in combination with musical scale, radio waves, and mathematics, along with the human mind, thus acting as a universal standard for vibrations, numbers, and theology. This theology holds that God the Creator is universal, rather than tribal or theoretical, because the Holy Bible has recorded the attributes of God as a universal being who is able to issue an audible vibrational command that all of creation shall obey for the purpose of harmony, balance, and grace.

The body's normal rhythms work together in sequence for the purpose of bodily functions, which is governed by a set of high to low variations that will fluctuate according to a cycle in place, which in turn, provides a sequence in rhythm. Thus, any cycle that is in rhythm or sequence, as well as in tune, will be defined as specific due to the presence of a method of tuning in place, which is evidence of a system. This means that both living systems, as well as atoms were by definition made, because the cycle that is occurring at an atomic level derives from stored information in the form of musical vibrations that acts as a universal standard for tuning and balancing to occur. Quantum field is thereby storing vibrational information that acts as a space for memory in terms of musical vibrations, which are structured into a command for the purpose of tuning and balancing.

The language of biology is music, that is any rhythm in tune, which not only stimulates our emotions, thoughts, and conscience, but also, a rhythm in tune will stimulate biological growth, because a living cell is subject to resonant vibrational frequencies that are electromagnetic, which in turn, stimulates RNA synthesis, DNA proofreading, and protein manufacture. DNA proofreading is governed by an instructional method that is not only vibrational, but also, it is electromagnetic, because in order for DNA proofreading to occur within a living cell, then there needs to be a polarity with a polar effect RNA folding can be stimulated.

When RNA synthesis occurs, the RNA folding is stimulated by an electromagnetic pulse the same as the heart muscle is stimulated by an electromagnetic pulse at the right frequency. This means that the body is in tune, as well as in balance in order for all of the body's rhythms to be in sequence with one another. Thus, the body is governed by two separate signatures, such as the DNA signatures, as well as the frequency signatures that work together as a single process in order for biological growth to occur, and is conserved in terms of a space for memory that not only derives from the genome, but also, quantum field.

Stored information within an electromagnetic field are the differences in frequency ratios that have been structured into a rhythm in sequence known as cycles per second, and is conserved within a space for memory in terms of vibrational information until an external source of energy interacts with these vibrations. Quantum field, in terms of an electromagnetic field, is vibrational in terms of a constant, which is unaffected by an external force, because quantum field acts as an impermeable barrier to all forms of energy, thereby constituting as a universal perimeter, or field of existence that isolates the universe in terms of a system. So, the conservation principle thereby applies to quantum field the same as it does for any other type of energy.

The first law of thermodynamics is defined by the law of conservation of mass and energy, which states that: 1) Energy cannot be created or destroyed via a natural process. 2) The total amount of energy and mass within the universe remains at a constant. And 3) That energy can be transformed from one form to another, or, transferred from one place to another, but the total amount of mass and energy must remain unchanged. While the term, conservation, in physics is defined as: 1) The principle from which the total value of a physical quantity or force (such as mass and energy) or a set of parameters (such as linear and angular momentum) remains at a constant within a system that is not subject to an external influence or disturbance. The conservation of mass can be described in a number of ways, but for the point of emphasis, I will use two simple examples.

The first example of the conservation of mass is that any system that is closed or isolated will retain the same amount of mass within its boundaries. Such as the contents of a closed jar, or the celestial bodies within the universe, and are therefore stored or conserved within a space for memory. And the celestial bodies are conserved, because they exist within the universe, rather than around it, which in turn, defines the universe as an isolated system that is finite, rather than infinite. While the conservation of energy derives from energy stored, which requires a mechanism for space in terms of vibrations known as memory, the same as the conservation of mass requires a mechanism for space known as volume in order to store a material substance, which can either be linear or angular in shape or motion, which is equal to distribution. This relationship can be described in the form of an equation.

Linear momentum is defined as: 1) The product of the mass (m) of an object and the velocity (v) of the object in free fall. The equation for linear momentum is given as: Momentum (p) equals mass (m) times velocity (v). While angular momentum is defined as: 1) The product of any rotating object or particle in motion that produces inertia. The equation for angular momentum is given as: Angular momentum (L) equals mass (m) times velocity (v) times radius (r). A stationary object has memory due to the fact that the object is stationary, and is thereby, conserved. While linear momentum has memory due to a direction of movement that maintains its course of action as direct, or straight, and is therefore conserved, unless acted upon by another force. And angular momentum has memory, because the direction of rotation that it started from results in a direction of travel that is singular, and therefore, conserved, unless acted upon by another force.

Thus, a stationary object, or an object in motion, will retain memory due to: volume (space), position (time), and weight (distribution), unless the object is acted upon by another force, or simply falls apart, which results in the fragments remaining in a linear or angular momentum until the fragments are at rest, or, conserved in their position. So, in order for an object that is either in motion or stationary to be conserved in its location or direction of travel, then there needs to be a mechanism for space, because the conservation principle requires a mechanism for storage, and storage is equal to memory, which constitutes as the fifth dimension known as quantum field.

The existence of the fifth dimension, known as quantum information or memory, is a combination of (space), (time), (distribution), (conservation), and (memory), with memory constituting as the fifth aspect, and is considered as a spatial dimension the same as time, only there is the addition of stored information in the form of a rhythm in tune that is in constant effect, such as musical scale. So, in addition to the first three physical dimensions, such as height, length, and width; There is a fourth dimension, such as position, also known as time or location. The fourth dimension describes a single location (space) in relation to another location (time) in terms of distance travelled (distribution); Hence the term: spacetime distribution.

In this way, the conservation principle of light is broken down into a combination of speed, (time) distance, (travel) and distribution, (space). While the conservation of an object that is stationary, or in motion, is due to a combination of location, (time) weight distribution, (travel), and volume (space). This means that the existence of the fifth dimension known as memory, as well as quantum field, can be described as a principle under demonstration by the conservation of time-travel through space, whether it be energy or mass, the principle remains the same due to the forward motion of time. And we all experience time-travel through space at every moment of the day as time moves forward, rather than backwards; Meaning that we are traveling through a spacetime continuum, rather than a spacetime reversal, because when an action has occurred, there is no way to take it back.

The equation for time-travel through space can be given as: Speed (s) equals distance (d) times time elapsed (t). So, in other words, the speed at which something is traveling can be measured in seconds, which is a variable due to the Shapiro Time Delay, or it can be measured in terms of light speed within a vacuum, which is a constant due to a lack of resistance. So, it does not matter if the speed of light varies when it travels from point A to point B through another type of medium, because the universal standard for time to be measured by as a constant is governed by the limit of speed, known as the speed of light within a vacuum.

The principles of conservation involving the fifth dimension known as memory is applicable to biology, because the direction of movement within, and from an organism is governed by a mechanism for memory in order to repeat a particular process, such as muscle memory for example. Muscle memory is a neurological process that allows you to remember certain skills, such as motor skills, so that the body can repeat these skills without exerting too much conscious effort. While an organism or embryo without a muscular system maintains its course of action from memory in order to complete a given task within a set span of time. So, whether it be an apple seed, a tree, or a piece of fruit, the principle remains the same due to the conservation of stored information within a space for memory that is vibrational in sequence according to a rhythm in tune.

The medium in which resonant vibrations move through the air is well understood to be that of observable particles that bounce or reflect off of one another. This principle is true even for radio-waves that move through a vacuum; Meaning that another type of medium exists in order for radio-waves to travel through space. This medium has been referred to as aether or quantum field, which is electromagnetic in nature in order to store resonant vibrations in the form of musical scale. Otherwise, there would be no way to tune your instrument, whether it be a violin, a radio, or a speaker, the principle remains the same, because anything that resonates will have a peak performance at a given interval or frequency, from which, the device is tuned.

This means that tuning a device is relative to quantum field in that quantum field is storing resonant vibrations that are in constant effect, and will fluctuate according to a set of high to low variables the same as the Earth's electromagnetic frequencies fluctuate according to a set of variables that acts as a standard for tuning to occur. So, for this reason, musical scale constitutes as evidence for the presence of a quantum field that is storing vibrational information in terms of frequency ratios, and is thereby specific in terms of a rhythm in sequence, which is essential for tuning and balancing.

Any sequence that is specific in relation to another sequence, is by definition, relative, whether it be a word, a binary language, or a set of base frequencies, the principle remains the same, because the information has been structured into a command that is by definition, specific. So, for this reason, a quantum field can fluctuate the same as the polarity of an atom can fluctuate from positive to negative. Quantum fluctuation is the difference in frequencies that have been structured into a ratio of high to low variables known as frequency ratios. Thus, tuning and temperament is evidence of design due to a set of base intervals that have been structured into a command, which is applicable to a quantum field the same as it is for musical scale.

Quantum fluctuation gives definition to the vibrations of matter and energy in terms of a rhythm in sequence that is held in tune, or conserved, by an electromagnetic field, or polarity, that can fluctuate from positive to negative, the same as an atom's polarity can also be reversed when a two-atom molecule is formed resulting in the transformation of energy from one polarity to another in accordance with the first law of thermodynamics involving energy transformation. The polarity of atoms can be changed by changing electronegative bonds and by adding another atom. When two atoms are connected, their polarity can be changed by changing the bonded atom. The binding of more than one electronegative atom will result in the change in the bonds polarity. Thus, atoms and molecules can express a change in polarity in accordance with the first law of thermodynamics involving energy transformation.

The aspect of a quantum field involving musical scale, or notation, is that each base frequency oscillates according to a rhythm in sequence that occurs as a cycle in place that is measured in cycles per second known as Hertz. And anything that is operating according to a cycle in place that is both repeatable under observation, as well as predictable under demonstration, is by definition, orderly. Thus, quantum field is a system due to the number of electromagnetic vibrations that are oscillating according to a cycle or sequence in place that is charged by an electromagnetic field in order to maintain an atom's electromagnetic polarity within the perimeter of this field, thereby conserving the polarity of an atom, which can alternate from positive to negative, depending on the type of atomic bond.

So, not only is quantum field electromagnetic, but also, quantum field is specific due to a universal standard for tuning to occur in the form of vibrations known as musical scale, which can be interpreted into a vibrational command in terms of musical notation. Musical notation is a set of visual instructions that are used to perform a piece of music. Learning musical notation also increases memory and awareness, as well as communication skills, because musical notation is bilingual in terms of instructional information.

Musical vibrations that are governed by musical notation stimulates biological growth, as well as elevating a person's mood. While vibratory distortion has a negative effect on the human mind, body, and soul, because not only is the mind and body vibrational, but so also is the spirit. So, the human conscience is not only a source of word, but also, the human conscience is vibratory. This allows the human mind to invent music, as well as lyrics, because the human conscience is a source of word and melody. This is similar to the common nightingale, which is considered as the most pleasant melodic bird that relays a song from the vibrations within their mind.

The difference though between a nightingale and a human being when singing a song, is that human beings are able to invent a word, which derives from the human conscience, which is not only vibrational, but also, the human conscience is spiritual. The nightingale is able to sing purely from memory in order to communicate with their own kind, while a human being is able to read from instructions in order to learn a particular language or skill, such as musical notation. So, because the human conscience desires compassion, and because the human conscience is better expressed through compassion, it will mean that the human conscience desires to love. Love is an instruction from God the Creator, because the Spirit of the Lord desires to be loved the same as any creature that can sing. But because God is Word, and because God is Spirit, it will mean that we can only love God in spirit and in truth.

God the Creator has revealed His word to the world through the love of His Son, Jesus Christ, who gives definition to life by the meaning of parables that are hidden in allegory, but revealed through the love of the Father in Heaven. And the more a person treasures God's word, the more the Spirit of God will reveal that which is hidden. The Heavens above are revealed through the love of the Father, and the Earth is produced by the glory of God. Therefore, the Earth and the Heavens are a vibrational instrument that carries the voice of God, which cries from the wilderness in accordance with the faith we have received, for it is by faith in the Creator above that the things of God are revealed through the love He has shown to the world by the gift of His Son.

*Quotation: ————————————————
Matthew 13:44
The Kingdom of Heaven is like a treasure hidden in a field. - Source: The Holy Bible.

In order for life to occur, then the odds must first be overcome, and there are many types of phenomenon that prohibit life from forming naturally, such as genetic instructions, signal transmission, and protein formation, which cannot occur by chance, because any sequence that is specific in relation to another sequence cannot occur at random in accordance with the law of probability. Any set of sequences that are specific in relation to each other are by definition, relative. And that which is relative is also that which has been designed due to the presence of a procedure that will combine multiple sequences into a single process. The odds of a single protein forming by chance that has a properly folded chain of amino acids joined by peptide bonds has been equated by mathematicians as being equal to 1 in 10^{164}.

This means that on average, you would need to construct 10^{164} chains of amino acids 150 units long in order to expect to find one that is useful due to the number of random configurations there are within a typical gene sequence. So, because the probability of one gene sequence forming by chance that is specific in relation to another sequence has been equated as being a statistical impossibility due to the number of possible random configurations there are, it will mean that proteins have derived by the action of supernatural creativity, because there is no natural process that can cause an instructional sequence to occur by chance that is specific in relation to another group of sequences according to a standard in place for each sequence to be interpreted by in terms of a single process or procedure.

According to the theory of evolution, all processes are by definition, natural in origin, whether artificial or not. When designing cannot be defined as a natural process, because anything that derives by design, is by definition a creation. Evolution, as a theory, has defined itself as a natural process only, which cannot be, at the same time, an artificial process, which limits the definition of evolution to being a theoretical assertion only due to the lack of a mechanism for innovation to occur, because designing is by definition an artificial process regardless of the materials used. And that which has been designed is also that which has been innovated, so that all innovation derives by design, either directly or indirectly.

Evolution, as a theory, defines itself as a "natural process" only, yet evolution, as a process, can only be defined as random selection, because any sequence of events that have not derived by design, are by definition, random. This means that a natural process must derive from a method of design that is specific, otherwise, the process is entirely random. Thus, the theory of evolution attempts to apply the definition of design to the theory in order to give the theory of evolution credence and validity; All because the argument here is about probability, as the likelihood of life occurring at random is an absolute zero.

Without a method for protein manufacture to occur, then the process would not happen inside any length of time proposed, because time is not a mechanism for biological improvement due to the problem of aging. So, because protein manufacture is governed by an instructional method, such as DNA RNA transcription, it will mean definitively that life was made according to a set of rules due to the presence of an instructional procedure. So, the challenge here to the atheist is to try and interpret the causality of instructional systems without relying on a method to do so, because the moment that a method is implied, is the same moment that creativity is inferred, and therefore, a Creator as well.

The fantasia by those who hail from the theory of evolution has postulated that all life derives from smaller organisms, such as bacteria, when bacteria is symbiotic to larger organisms that are multicellular. Thus, a single celled organism has no designated function within the ecosystem without the presence of a more complex biological system, which is required in order for bacteria to break down biological materials that derive from larger more complex organisms. A single celled bacteria relies primarily on larger more complex living systems to be in place before a bacterium can have any purpose within the ecosystem.

For example: Most unicellular organisms live in bodies of water and must move around in a fluid in order to find food, and they must obtain nutrients by eating other organisms, such as plant-like protists, as well as other types of bacteria, but some can make their own food through photosynthesis. Plants are autotrophs, which means they produce their own food. They use the process of photosynthesis to transform water, sunlight, and carbon dioxide into oxygen, and simple sugars that the plant uses as fuel. These primary producers form the base of an ecosystem that provides the fuel for living systems that are more complex.

A Prokaryotic cell, is any organism that lacks a distinct nucleus and other organelles due to the absence of internal membranes which house the nucleus of the cell, and the lack of internal membranes in Prokaryotes is what distinguishes them from Eukaryotes. Prokaryotes are divided into two domains, Bacteria and Archaea, so that organisms with a nucleus are placed into a third domain called Eukaryote. The theory of evolution has postulated that single celled organisms give rise to multicellular organisms over time, because while being unicellular, some Prokaryotes, such as Cyanobacteria, can form large colonies.

Yet these bacterial colonies are still made-up by individual single cells to form a conglomerate mass of organisms, so this is still not proof of any single celled organism evolving into a multicellular organism, because the single celled organisms have grouped together to form a mass of single organisms, which is not defined as being one organism. In order for a group of cells to form a multicellular organism, then each cell must be specific in relation to other cells, which cannot occur at random over time from a group of single celled organisms, because a group of cells that are specific in relation to each other requires an overall method in order to combine each of the cells into a multicellular organism or system, which is evidence of design, rather than evolution.

The concept of a single celled organism evolving into a multicellular organism has been postulated as being a fact, even though there are no physical examples of any single celled organism evolving into a multicellular organism according to observation. And besides the absence of a nucleus, Prokaryotes also lack mitochondria. Mitochondria generates most of the Eukaryotic cell's supply of adenosine triphosphate (ATP), which is used as a source of chemical energy when oxygen is released during aerobic respiration at the inner mitochondrial membrane. Prokaryotic cells are less structured than Eukaryotic cells, and they have no nucleus, so instead their genetic material is free-floating within the cell, which is why Prokaryotes have no mitochondria, and they also lack the many membrane-bound organelles found in Eukaryotic cells.

According to the Encyclopedia, a human being is defined as being in the family of Eukaryotic cells, but because the definition of a Eukaryote is in reference to an individual cell, it will mean that the term, Eukaryote, cannot be used to define a multicellular organism with in terms of a species, because the definition does not take an organism's method of reproduction into account. And an organism's method of reproduction must be taken into account, otherwise, there would be nothing to define a species with in terms of a breeding group or phylum. And the other aspect of an organism that must be taken into account when defining a species, is their method of communication, because communication is essential for mating.

Prokaryotic cells are therefore at the bottom of the food chain, because they can produce their own food through photosynthesis the same as plants do, and there are absolutely no examples of Prokaryotic cells producing a mitochondrial membrane for the production of oxygen respiration, leaving the theory of evolution without a working mechanism for biological innovation that can be demonstrated. Prokaryotic cells are designed to live on nutrients and sunlight as a plant would for the purpose of being a source of energy for living organisms that are more complex.

The evolutionary theory from biology assumes that Eukaryotic cells have derived from Prokaryotic cells through the digestion of complex organic compounds that are found in nature. In terms of carbon metabolism, Prokaryotes are classified as either heterotrophic or autotrophic. Heterotrophic organisms use organic compounds, usually from other organisms, as carbon sources, while Autotrophic organisms use carbon dioxide as their only source of carbon. This means that there are no examples of a Prokaryotic cell morphing into a Eukaryote via the process of digestion, because the Prokaryote relies on carbon dioxide as a source of carbon, while a Eukaryote relies on oxygen respiration which releases carbon dioxide.

The tiny system of the Prokaryotic cell relies on a much larger, more complex system to be in place in order to have a purpose within the ecosystem, because a Prokaryotic cell is for the purpose of being a food source for other more complex organisms. Life is more than just chemistry, because all life is instructionally based from its DNA, so life is also instructional, rather than just chemical. So, because organic material derives from life, rather than from chemicals alone, it will mean that life could not have derived from inorganic matter, because organic material derives from living systems, rather than from inorganic matter. And life could not have derived from organic material either, because organic material derives from living systems in a state of random decay.

The study of systems biology does not incorporate the theory of evolution for two main reasons. First, is the fact that systems are always designed from planning and they do not occur at random over time, otherwise, there would be nothing to define an orderly process at work, because everything would be entirely random. And the second reason is because the biological theory of evolution is primarily a racial theory, and is responsible for the practice of Social Darwinism, evolutionary eugenics, and scientific racism, all of which have been adequately refuted by modern genetic research.

Mankind is broken up into different nationalities, which is not a biological phenomenon as the theory of evolution claims, but a sociopolitical one instead, so the racial theory of evolution has no stake in systems biology. No living system could self-emerge due to the fact that all self-replicating systems are instructionally based from their DNA, so there is no way for natural circumstances to have produced life, because a thermodynamic instructional system is evidence of design by definition of the word, synthesis.

DNA synthesis is the normal or artificial creation of DNA molecules that are made up of nucleotide units that are linked by covalent bonds and hydrogen bonds. DNA synthesis, or DNA proofreading, occurs when these nucleotide units are joined to form a DNA sequence in relation to a DNA template, which can occur artificially (in vitro) or normally (in vivo). So, because the only example that science can give to demonstrate the process of DNA RNA transcription, is to use the term, synthesis, it will mean automatically that life is a creation, because anything that is synthesized from instructions according to an algorithm in place, is by definition, made, whether it be naturally occurring or artificial, the causality remains the same.

An instructional system is not just a sequence in place, because a send and receive mechanism is needed in order to convey an instruction, which is how DNA RNA transcription works, and the information must also be stored when passive, which is what the genome is for. This means that the processing of genetic instructions acts according to a method in place, which cannot occur by chance, because instructions must be specific in order for the processing phase to occur. The evolutionary theory defines itself as being a natural process that requires no input from an intelligent source, but because a system is governed by a procedure, it will mean that systems have derived by design by definition of the word, method. So, the rule here is that a natural process cannot specify for a particular method, because a natural process will always be the result of a method in place, rather than the cause of one. Evolution has played no role in the formation of living systems at any point, because all life is governed by an instructional method, such as DNA RNA transcription, DNA proofreading, and DNA modification.

There is no physical way possible for instructions to occur by natural circumstances alone, because instructions are always the result of a communications method. A natural process is a non-creative process that cannot plan anything into existence by design, because a natural process will always be limited to the number of specifics there are in place to define the process with. While any additional specifics to a given process must derive by design, because that which is specific is the diametric opposite of that which is random; Meaning that specifics cannot occur at random over time.

The normal workings of a system is defined as a natural, or normal process, but the inventing of a system requires an inventor, and this is true for any type of system, because there will always be a method in place that is specific due to the presence of a procedure. So, for this reason, the evolutionary theory cannot account for the existence of systems; Simply because a system is equal to a method, and the only causality there is for a method, is by design, because a method is by definition, specific. And there is no other causality for a system apart from a method, because, A)

A system is defined by its level of order, rather than by its level of disorder. B) Ordered complexity cannot derive at random, otherwise, there would be nothing to define that which is orderly. And C) Because that which is orderly, is also that which is specific, and that which is specific, is also that which has been specified.

Designing is described as being the second stage during the process of creativity, because designing derives from the imagination, and it is the process of contemplation that gives rise to new innovations via planning, so that the action of creativity is therefore governed by a procedure in itself. The third step in the process of creativity is implementation, whereby a design has been planned, and is now ready to be put into effect with a physical outcome, which is the only way for an operational system to occur, because a procedure is required first.

For example: When a system is made, it will always derive by design either directly or indirectly, because there was a level of input in order to initiate the process, resulting in a step-by-step procedure. But when a system forms during a natural process, the system will always be unspecified, because additional specifications are required in order for innovation to occur. And an example of a system that is the result of a natural process, would be a river dam that formed after a flood. But this in no way constitutes as an innovation, because this was a part of a natural process or fluctuation that was already occurring within a more larger system, such as the ecosystem. A flood of water causing a river dam to occur, is simply a random fluctuation within a more larger system, and is thereby subject to a cycle in place, which is evidence of a complex system that is integrated.

So, the formation of a dam wall can occur according to two different types of processes, yet both are by definition made. The first is where no direct input was involved, and the second is where intervention has occurred directly, such as a group of logs that are blocking the flow of a stream or river resulting in the natural formation of a dam wall, which occurs according to the normal workings or fluctuations of a system in place, such as the ecosystem. While the engineered construction of a dam wall that is to be used for a specified purpose will always have a designated function, because the placement of each component for the dam wall must be specific in relation to the next resulting in a procedure. So, both types of dams are by definition made, simply because there is a method in place that has resulted in a procedure.

When a lake occurs, it will always be the result of a method in place due to the presence of a procedure, whether naturally occurring or not. This means that both a natural process, and an artificial process are evidence of creativity having been applied, either directly or indirectly, due to the presence of a procedure. A second example of a natural process that is occurring according to a procedure in place, would be the digestive system. The digestive system works by breaking down solids and liquids that in turn expel gases. So, when solids and liquids are breaking down within the body, there will be a random distribution of particles known as gases that need to be expelled from the body in order to maintain a level of efficiency so that the internal pressure of the digestive system can be regulated.

This process occurs naturally in terms of a procedure, but because there is a cycle in place that is repeating itself in series, it will mean that creativity has been applied at the start of the process, because anything that occurs according to a cycle in place that is repeatable under observation, as well as predictable under demonstration, is by definition, specific. Any process that is working according to a procedure or cycle in place that is repeating itself in series will always be the result of a system in place, which is evidence of design, rather than evolution.

According to Oxford Languages, a cycle is defined as: 1) "Any series of events that are regularly repeated in the same order." While the definition of a system is defined as: 1) "A set of things working together as parts of a mechanism or an interconnecting network; a complex whole. Similar: order." So, from the world's foremost dictionary, we find that a cycle is orderly when a process is repeating itself in series, which is evidence of a system in place, rather than a random occurrence by definition of the word, orderly. But because a system will always be subject to a random fluctuation, it will mean that an orderly process is subject to variation over time. And this is the only way to explain variation, otherwise, there would be nothing for the selection process to select from in terms of physical designs.

Human logic cannot dismiss the need for creativity when explaining the origin of systems, because it is illogical to suggest that a natural process can occur all by itself without the need for a method first. The logical design of a system is the abstract representation for the system's flow of data through inputs and outputs of the system, and this is achieved through the designing of graphical models that are relative to the actual system being studied, so that designs are included in the context of all systems diagrams.

Logical design is defined as being entity-relationship diagrams called ER diagrams, and this is what defines the relationship between a conscious being and the system being studied, because the design of the system was not natural to begin with, but logically deduced from thought via a method of communication, which is how a design is implemented. So, because a diagram for a system must be logically designed, it will mean that all systems have derived from a source of creativity, either directly or indirectly, because the diagram of a system will always derive from the system being studied, therefore, both the system, and the diagram of the system, have derived by design.

So, in other words, the specifics for any given diagram used to interpret a system with is simply the product of the system being studied. This means that an operational system requires a pre-existing system to be in place in order for the system to occur, so that a daughter system is never more complex than the parent system it has derived from. And this is powerful evidence for supernatural creativity, because no daughter system is ever more complex than its parent system.

Anything that is manufactured via a procedure, or deduced from logic, is defined as an end product, whereby a method has produced something other than what the process began with, and this will always be the result of a concept deduced from thought, either directly or indirectly. An end product will always be the result of a system, because anything that is the end product of a cycle in place, is by definition a creation, which is evidence of a Creator due to the presence of a procedure. The ordered complexity of any given system will always be in accordance with the number of specifics that have been applied to the method, which can be broken down individually into a set of parameters, which in turn, sets the conditions for a system's operation.

So, in order for the organised complexity of an operational system to be understood from a limited perspective, then the system needs to be broken down into smaller stages in order for the overall system to be studied. So, because a single mechanism for a system is not comprised of the specifics needed for the system as a working whole, it will mean that all daughter systems have derived from a parent system that was more complex than the daughter system is by itself.

For example: The process of procreation involves the temporary combination of two separate systems called the male and female, which then procreate together in order to produce an end product called a child. So, because every child has derived from two separate systems that were combined temporarily to form a highly complex manufacturing system in order to produce an end product called a child, it will mean that the parent system is far more complex than the daughter system is by itself.

This principle applies to any type of system, whether it be a concept design, or a married couple producing a child, or a manufacturing base that produces a new office building within a city, the principle remains the same, because an end product is never more complex than the method it has derived from. And this is the same for a concept design, because a design is never more complex than the designer, which is self-explanatory. While any unicellular organism that reproduces by itself cannot increase in organized complexity through cellular division over time, because a single celled organism is defined as a thermodynamic system, which means that the thermodynamic principles of entropy applies to all unicellular organisms. So, as a rule, a system must derive by design, either directly or indirectly, due to the application of a procedure so that no system is ever more complex than its Creator.

Therefore, a unicellular organism began as complex, and as accumulative mutations increase over time within the genotype of an organism, the less complex the organism will be compared to the first generation it derived from. Unicellular organisms are not becoming more complex over time through cellular division, because the principles of entropy law must be applied to the process, which means definitively that unicellular organisms began as complex, and as cellular division occurs over time, the rate of entropy is thereby increased due to accumulative mutations.

An end product, such as a concept design, or a thermodynamic system, will always be the result of a method in place in order to produce all of the materials needed for the end product to occur. So, because an end product is never more complex than the method it has derived from, it will mean that the method used to produce the universe was far more complex than the universe is by itself, which is evidence of supernatural creativity, because the universe is the most complex system there is. And the universe is indeed the result of a method, because the universe is defined as an isolated system due to the first law of thermodynamics that includes the law of conservation of mass and energy.

The argument between evolution and creation is one of origins, thus, a causality for the universal numerical standard in place is required to be explained factually in order to have a coherent theory regarding origins. The theory of evolution attempts to define all processes as a natural process only, yet there is nothing natural about numbers on the basis that numbers reach infinity according to the principles of mathematics.

When describing the origin of something, it is referred to as a beginning like a set of numbers starting from 1 and ending in 10. But when numbers reach infinity in mathematics, they are no longer represented as numbers, but as letters instead, and that which is infinite requires no explanation concerning a beginning or an end by definition of the fact that it was infinite in number. So, because the Creator in Heaven is defined as being infinite, it will mean that He does not require a beginning or an end, but rather, He is described as being the cause of the beginning and the end. And the universe must have an end at some point, because the universe is in a constant state of entropy according to the second law of thermodynamics. This means definitively that the universe began as orderly, because as the system of the universe progresses with time, the greater the amount of entropy there will be, and the more entropy increases over time, the less orderly the system will become compared to when it began.

Numbers may reach infinity by the use of letters as an equivalent so as to explain infinite complexity based on limited observations. This principle in mathematics only applies to equations regarding astronomically low probabilities. And the one rule concerning astronomically low probabilities that brings the theory of evolution into question as a legitimate science, is the probability of life forming by chance, which has been equated as the lowest probability in the universe. Biological complexity cannot be broken down into smaller categories in order to shrink the odds, because the odds of one protein forming by chance that is relative to another protein is infinitely improbable.

In order for any sequence, whether numerical or otherwise to be relative to the next, resulting in an algorithm or procedure, then a method is required first. Thus, the only way to increase the likelihood of a given event to occur, is by the application of a method. And a method is by definition, specific, due to the presence of a procedure, which means that a method or procedure in place is the evidence of creativity, and therefore, a Creator as well.

The evidence for a theory must always be based upon the self-explanatory word definitions in use in order to provide a proper demonstration for describing a given phenomenon, rather than just opinion, because evidence cannot be based upon pure conjecture alone, but upon the correct self-explanatory word definitions in use, which is essential to any theory. A system is defined as being a group of parameters that work together according to a set of rules in order to form a complex whole for a particular purpose by design, which in turn, gives rise to a procedure or cycle via a method.

A thermodynamic system is any group of primary mechanisms that work together to form a unified whole for the purpose of insulating energy or matter from its surroundings in order to produce an end product or desired effect. The very definition of what a system is proves that all life was made, because every living system is instructionally based in order for the process of genomic replication to occur independently of the Creator who has set rules upon His creation that act as a set of parameters. And all forms of matter and energy are by definition made, because the structure of an atom is the direct result of a system in place whereby a method has been applied resulting in a cycle that is repeatable under observation, and is thereby reliable under demonstration, which cannot occur at random in accordance with the law of probability.

Life cannot be the result of a random process, because life does not occur at random, but according to a procedure instead. While the inventing of a process that has been specified will always require a method to be established first, simply because there is a step-by-step procedure in place. But the difference between a procedure, and a random process, is due to the fact that a procedure is by definition, specific. While a random process will always be according to a set of random variables within a system that can fluctuate from one set of parameters to another, otherwise, there would be no causality for a random event. So, both a procedure, and a random process, derive from a method initially in order for either process to occur, but the main difference between the two, is that a procedure will always be predictable due to a sequence in place, while a random process, is by definition, unpredictable, in accordance with the law of probability.

Any process with a predictable outcome, is by definition, specific, because there is a procedure occurring in terms of a sequence or cycle that is repeatable under observation, as well as predictable under demonstration, which is evidence of design. While a random process is by definition, unpredictable, due to a set of variables that will fluctuate within a system. So, the more predictable a process is, the more likely that the process is governed by a procedure, while the less predictable a process is, the greater the chance that the process is entirely random. This means that a natural process is evidence of design the same as a procedure, because a natural process will always be the result of a system in place, rather than the cause of one.

The word, design, is in relation to an artificial process, because the process of designing always involves input from a designer, and therefore, a Creator as well. While the origin of systems must also derive by design, but because the origin of systems cannot derive from a natural process, it will mean that the origin of systems has derived from a supernatural process directly instead due to the lack of a natural process that can cause innovation to occur in terms of additional specifics. While evolution, as a theory, was in fact designed, rather than discovered, and the proof that the evolutionary theory was in fact designed, rather than discovered, is due to the fact that there is no law in science to define evolution with in terms of an actual discovery. So, in order for evolution to be defined as a process, then a procedure is required first, which in turn, defines evolution as a creation due to the application of a method. And the number one figure in recent history that is attributed with having first developed the theory was a man by the name of Charles Darwin.

Charles Darwin, according to history, devoted himself to the idea of selective breeding, thereby attempting to distinguish himself as biologically superior to those around him by marrying his first cousin for the same reason that a Pharaoh would marry his own sister, which was to maintain a bloodline of so-called "racial purity." Darwin's theory of evolution was the sole cause of World War II and the Holocaust through the practice of evolutionary eugenics, Social Darwinism, and race based sciences.

Evolutionary eugenics holds to the idea that certain ethnic groups are more evolved than the rest, which is why evolution is by definition a racial theory that is used in an attempt to undermine or exterminate certain racial groups in order to try and preserve their own ethnicity. Yet according to historical resources, three of Darwin's ten children; Anne Elizabeth, Mary Eleanor, and Charles Waring, died during childhood. Six of the surviving seven went on to have long-term marriages, but three of those marriages bore no children, suggesting that his children suffered from infertility. Darwin's first daughter (Annie), died of tuberculosis at age 10. His second daughter (Mary) lived for only 23 days. And his last child (Charles Waring) was born with Down Syndrome, and died of scarlet fever at the age of 18 months.

The evidence that all life was made by God, is due to the fact that all life is instructionally based from its DNA, and the only causality we have for instructions, is by the action of creativity. And the evidence that all matter and energy was made by God is due to the conservation principle, which states that matter and energy cannot be created or destroyed via a natural process, and that energy cannot be converted into matter under normal conditions; Leaving only one other possibility for the formation of matter and energy, which is by supernatural creativity due to the lack of a natural process that can cause energy, such as light, to become organized into a solid object with mass, such as an atom.

Every individual must be accountable for their own actions, and ethical conduct will always be relative to laws that are in place to prevent an individual from exploiting another person or animal, either physically or psychologically. But the practice of animal and human experimentation from the theory of evolution has resulted in the worst forms of human and animal cruelty as a direct result of survival of the fittest being put into practice. The theory of evolution, in practice, is a crime against humanity, because no individual is to be equated as being that of an animal, and no animal is to be subjected to inhumane treatment or torture. The level of intelligence within a given society will always be relative to the level of compassion that is exhibited to not only human beings, but also, to the animals, because animals are living creatures, and are therefore self-aware, so no human being has the right to torture or inhumanely treat an animal.

If the theory of evolution goes unchallenged, then the level of human and animal cruelty will escalate, because natural selection will be taught, and the end result is Social Darwinism in industry and society. The theory of evolution is the biggest hindrance for the progression of any modern society that is to be self-governed under the universal principles of law and morality, because the ethical conduct of an individual must weigh upon their God given conscience. So, for this reason, a scientist must always recognize the endowed human conscience before the law and society, just as every individual must recognize another human being's inalienable right to be defined as a created human being, or their position to have authority over others should be removed.

Technological advancements in the past decade have allowed scientists from MIT to take a close look at the proteomes of living organisms. As a result, more than 120,000 solved protein structures are readily available, and these protein structures can be customized, so they have numerous applications for the medical industry, because if you can manufacture human proteins artificially, then you can test vaccines on the proteins, as well as cosmetics. The process of developing a cosmetic product or a vaccine that is fit for human use can be developed far more efficiently and ethically than the methods in use for human-animal experimentation, because the product can be trialled directly on artificial human proteins, rather than the animals. And this also reduces the clinical trial process for a vaccine from being a ten year period with an average cost of $2.6 billion, down to a six month period as we've seen with COVID 19 vaccines, which took only a matter of months to prepare.

There are only a handful of animal protection laws in the United States that are designed to keep animals safe from being exploited due to the nature of the agricultural industry, and scientific experimentation. The Animal Welfare Act (AWA), was signed into law in 1966, and this is the primary federal animal protection law within the United States. The AWA mainly involves animals kept at zoos, and used in laboratories, as well as animals that are commercially bred and sold like those in puppy mills, and agricultural farming.

The AWA directs the Secretary of the United States Department of Agriculture to set minimum standards regarding the treatment of animals. The AWA itself, as well as its enforcement by the Department of Agriculture, are frequently criticized for allowing inhumane practices to occur against animals under human care. The Preventing Animal Cruelty and Torture Act (PACT), was signed into law in 2019. The PACT law makes some of the most inhumane forms of animal cruelty illegal, specifically: electrocution, crushing, burning, drowning, suffocating, impaling or sexual exploitation.

Under most State and federal laws, animals primarily are regarded as property, and have little or no legal rights of their own. So, because of this legal status, it is upon every individual to do what is in the best interest for the protection of the animal and their welfare in all instances.

Owners are therefore responsible for the animal's care just as they would be with any other form of property, except animals require special care because they are self- aware, and any creature that is self-aware must be treated with dignity and respect. And though federal laws prohibit the torture of animals by citizens, the animals that are kept in laboratories are forced to endure chemicals being dripped into their eyes, injected into their bodies, forced up their nostrils or forced down their throats, and nothing is prohibited in terms of experimentation, so the animals are subjected to drug addiction, and are forced to inhale toxic substances, such as cigarette and marijuana smoke.

Animals under human care are also subjected to maternal deprivation from their mothers, deafened, blinded, burned, stapled, and infected with diseases, viruses, and parasites, such as paralysis ticks. Yet according to the United States Centre for Biotechnology, and the National Library for Medicine: "Animal experiments, no matter what the species is that's used, or the type of disease research undertaken, are highly unreliable, and the method, statistically, has very little predictive value in reducing the risk of harm for humans."

Animal experimentation is typically defended by arguments from evolutionary scientists, saying that animals provide sufficiently good models of human biology. And this is the typical mindset of an evolutionary scientist who believes that humans are animals, and therefore, are subject to the same biology as animals, when humans are very distinct biologically. According to the United States Pew Research Centre for National Statistics: "Animal experimentation often significantly harms humans through misleading safety studies," which was quoted from an article by Research Gate.com under the title: "Wasted Money in the United States - Biomedical and Agricultural Animal Research."

Research from animal experimentation is usually engineered to provide data that is ameliorated by experts to give a positive spin to the method, because without a host, then there would be no practice. Yet animals are trialled on even though they can never represent a human subject for clinical trials, which is why animal testing is inefficient, as well as unethical. Federal law is to uphold the rights of an animal so that animals are not abused, which is not secondary to any type of experiment, clinical method, or trial, that may deprive the animal of their dignity as a living creature.

All animals that have been domesticated to live with humans, such as cats and dogs for example, rely primarily on human care in order to survive, so it is therefore highly immoral to exploit the trust of a domesticated animal in order to harm or torture them. Domesticated animals are usually more trusting than humans are normally, and this is why the animals that are held in laboratories require their dignity and respect as created beings that are endowed with a high level of self-awareness, just as much as the lab technicians are endowed with conscience. Animals are not to be treated as having derived from a virus as the theory of evolution claims, because this is the very thing that robs an animal of its identity and respect.

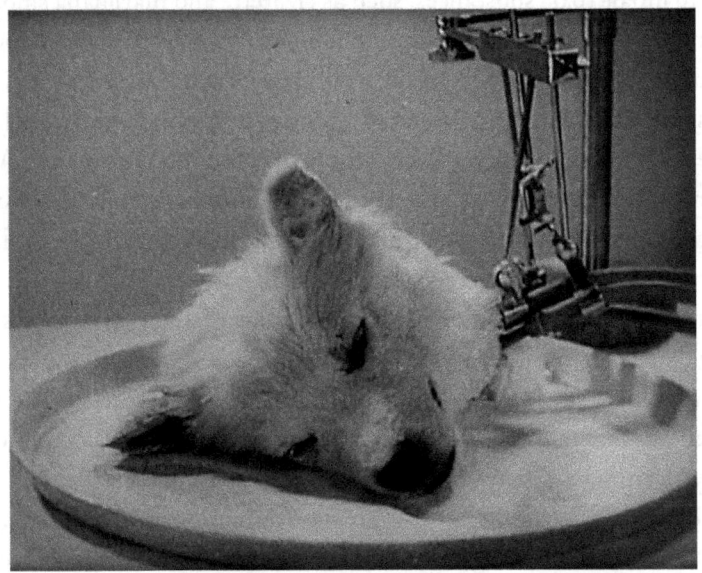

(Above) Image Result of Brukhonenko's decapitation experiment from a 1940 documentary film directed by David Yashin that purports to document Soviet research into the resuscitation of clinically dead organisms. The film depicts and discusses a series of medical experiments. The film was shown in London towards the end of 1942, and then to an audience of a thousand U.S scientists the next year in New York at the Congress of American-Soviet Friendship. Source: Wikipedia Encyclopedia (Brukhonenko's decapitation experiment).

In criminal psychology, a psychopathic personality is a personality construct that is characterized by impaired empathy and remorse, which usually presents itself in its early stages by cruelty to the animals. A loving person will love the animals, while a psychopath aims to harm or mistreat the animals in order to espouse some form of violence without fear of reprisal. This type of behaviour is progressive towards a serial killer who knows no compassion or empathy for other human beings due to the number of animals they have killed during the course of their life. Documented serial killers, such as Jeffrey Dahmer, Ted Bundy, and David Berkowitz killed dozens of innocent people without showing any remorse before the law.

These men (and a significant number of other serial killers) have something very strange in common. Years before turning their rage and psychopathic behaviour on humans, they practiced on animals. Those without sympathy for others, including the animals, are doomed to violence, whether they are aware of it or not. If human beings are to share this world with the creatures that God has created, then an acknowledgement of animal welfare must be taught to students, or there will be contradictions between that which is just, and that which is not. It is unfair to blame religion for all of the world's problems, because the fairest of people have a faith, which is a testimony to the religion they have. So, in order to promote a fair system of human behaviour, then faith will play an integral part whether the individual is atheist or not, because faith works by having a belief in moral values.

The evolutionary theory on the other hand conditions the human mind to lose all respect for other living creatures that are symbiotic to mankind, all on the philosophical basis of survival of the fittest. Evolution, as a scientific theory in practice, is responsible for some of the worst crimes against the animals in human history. If mankind is to be educated regarding human-animal cruelty, then the theory of evolution must also be challenged from the premise of law, because it is the welfare of every species that is brought into question without mercy by those who hail from the evolutionary theory due to a denial of conscience, as well as compassion.

The scientific argument that animals should be trailed on in order to promote human longevity is leading mankind into a system of human-animal cruelty, because in order to gain longevity, according to modern evolutionary science, then the animals are to be put into harm's way so that a person can live a longer life expectancy, when your life expectancy is not owing to clinical research, but to yourself instead. So, for this reason, we are not to torment the animals with scientific experiments in order to promote human longevity, because it is the right of every living creature to live an expected lifespan without interference from clinical research.

Animal cruelty is defined as depriving an animal of food, water, shelter, and veterinary care. Torturing, maiming, or killing animals is also defined as animal cruelty. There are many reasons why people are cruel to the animals, but scientific and clinical research tops the list with millions of animals tortured, maimed and killed every year in the name of clinical trials that are designed in an attempt to try and increase the longevity of human beings. A major ethical concern related to clinical trials is whether the participants are fully informed about the risks entailed with these trials and the likelihood that they will not personally benefit from the research. The clinical and evolutionary practice of cloning human body parts onto the bodies of animals is leading mankind into an age of extinction, rather than an age of longevity.

If mankind is to merge himself with the beats of the field through clinical trials that aim to increase the lifespan of a human being, then mankind will one day be extinct due to an increase in animal hereditaries within the overall gene-pool of mankind. The likelihood of mankind surviving the clinical methods in use from the evolutionary theory in practice is equal to zero in terms of biological improvements, because the more animal hereditaries that occupy the overall gene-pool of mankind, the faster human beings will go extinct.

The clinical practice of exogenous growth hormones being administered to the animals has been shown to affect a variety of physiological processes including growth and lactation. The production of exogenous growth hormones that is to be used on animals has been reported to alter animal growth and metabolism. These clinical trials are ameliorated to give a positive spin to the method of injecting livestock with exogenous growth hormones, which has serious implications to human health and sustainability.

The European Union banned the use of hormone growth promotants (HGP) in meat production in 1989 due to concerns about the possible link between cancer and HGP residues in meat that is intended for human consumption. Yet the use of HGP to increase growth rates is a widespread practice in the country of Australia with around one half of both grain-fed cattle and pasture-fed cattle being inoculated with exogenous growth hormones. Drug companies are currently lobbying to the government of Australia to have exogenous growth hormone injections on live cattle to be made mandatory across the country.

The issue concerning clinical trials on humans and animals not only involves a lack of transparency regarding the risk of harm to humans, but also, clinical trials are opaque in regards to where the trials have derived from, such as animals held in laboratories. There are a million ways to speak about animal cruelty, but there is only one way to act, and that is to educate yourself regarding the issue surrounding clinical trials that aim to increase human longevity, animal production, and meat quality, whilst promising that no harm can be done. The primary reason why obesity is on the rise in Australia, is entirely due to exogenous growth hormones being either fed or injected into cattle, chickens, and even fish.

According to the National Institutes of Health, hormonal residues from exogenous growth hormones were detected in approximately 98% of all farmed fish samples tested. Among the hormone contaminated samples, around 92% of samples contained hormonal residues above the acceptable dietary intake. Exogenous growth hormones increase cattle weight by about 10% on average, which means definitively that clinical trials on animals involving exogenous growth hormones is leading mankind into an age of obesity due to the nature of profiteering and deceitful advertisement.

God in Heaven has endowed all living creatures, each according to their own abilities, just as man has been also, so each animal is therefore entitled to life and liberty the same as any person, which is a respect in return for their service to mankind as a food source, because humans should not eat other humans for a number of good reasons, including the increased likelihood of contracting a degenerative chromosomal mutation, which is physical evidence that humans do not share the same biology as animals. Animals from agriculture that are to be slaughtered are always to be treated humanely during the course of their life, and with due respect for their needs. Otherwise, we will breed a generation of people who have no empathy for God's creatures whatsoever, which is a direct result of the evolutionary theory in practice.

The current situation by leading meat markets and advertisement campaigns aims to promote the eating of animals in order to profit from the public on a global scale, which is in fact an industry of death, rather than sustainability. Yet if each person was to slaughter their own food, then the numbers would be very different indeed. All food derives from plant life either directly or indirectly, because animals that are carnivorous eat other animals that survive on plants. And it is proven through statistical studies that eating carnivorous animals amounts to being a poor dietary habit, which is why modern synergetic farming systems rely on animals that graze freely on plants.

Animals under human care should not be deprived of their basic needs, and they should have lived a life worthy of living, because they are our God given responsibility to uphold and protect against the unfathomable number of odds that they face. And an ecosystem with a feral animal problem, such as the wild boar populations in Australia, which destroy crops are indeed a pest in high numbers, just as locusts are in swarms, but the issue here is not just about the devastation by pests, but rather, how does an ecosystem actually work?

Locusts convert plant material into proteins, such as their bodies, and are enjoyed by many different kinds of other animals. Their eggs, laid in burrows in the ground, are dug up to be eaten by other insects, and the nymphs are caught by small birds and lizards. So, all in all, locusts have a great ecological role to play in the food chain for an ecosystem, which means that we are not to try and control their numbers with highly toxic and mutagenic chemicals, but with a correct ecology instead.

For example: Permaculture is a form of systems study whereby multiple layers within the ecosystem can be broken down and studied individually, or as a complex whole. Permaculture can be used as a growth mechanism for agricultural ecosystems in a self-sufficient and sustainable way. It is a form of agriculture that draws attention to overlapping systems of ecology to develop synergetic farming systems based on crop diversity, resilience, productivity, and most importantly, sustainability.

The process involves establishing a smaller environment using small varieties of plants and animals that can become a sustainable food source for other living systems. And this is an integral part of systems biology, because the layers of complexity within the permacultured environment have derived from planning directly, as each layer of complexity within a permacultured environment has been incorporated according to a method. Permaculture is similar to creating a garden that can be as big as any forest is for example, but the permacultured environment will always be according to a method in place.

The use of permaculture is an effective way to introduce new layers of complexity to an environment slowly so that the system can be studied for weaknesses, and the increase in complexity to the system will always be equal to the number of different species that have been introduced to the system over time. And each plant and creature plays a specific role in the agriculture of a new ecosystem that has derived from planning using the specifics that were already in place from other more complex ecosystems, such as a rain-forest for example, which is the most complex type of ecosystem there is.

Permaculture looks at biodiversity to maintain an ecosystem, and biodiversity is required in order for any individual plant or animal to have a designated function within the overall system. And the more creatures that are introduced to the new ecosystem over time, the more different types of vegetation there will need to be, which is why most permacultured systems start with fast growing legumes in order to create the right soil conditions for larger plants to grow, which in turn, provides food and protection for all of the creatures that are to be introduced to the system over time.

So, areas that are dry and remote usually have a small amount of bird life, which inevitably increases the number of locusts within a dry habitat, such as the Middle-East, which is affected by locusts swarms far more often than forested areas are, because a forested area will always have more birds and reptiles, which significantly lowers the population of locusts and other pests. And every type of living creature within an ecosystem has a designated function within the system, so that an ecosystem is defined by the number of creatures and plants that occupy a particular habitat.

This means definitively that a system was in place before any ecosystem could have been established, because all living systems have been incorporated according to an overall plan, otherwise, there would be no causality for ordered complexity within the ecosystem. Ordered complexity within an ecosystem is relative to the number of plants and animals within the system that are symbiotic. So, in order to control the number of wild boars in Australia the same as locust numbers are kept within a limit, then the introduction of larger animals that eat wild boars is required, because the only way to offset an introduced species is to introduce another type of species. And I am not saying that we should turn the Australian outback into an African Savanna in order to control wild boar populations, but what I am saying is that in order for an ecosystem to be made efficient, then the system needs to be highly integrated.

If animals are to retain their God given dignity and respect, then they must not be treated as being biologically inferior to man, because the belief that a biological hierarchy exists that relates all creatures back to an RNA virus via their genetics has been scientifically refuted by modern genetic research. And it is only the die-hard evolutionists hailing from the theory of evolution who wish to retain the right to abuse God's creatures within a laboratory in order to have a profession. But because the practice of torturing animals for experimentation is no longer viable for the medical industry, it will mean that the practice of human-animal exploitation for clinical reasons should be made a thing of the past.

The teaching of evolution could be replaced overnight by using systems theory as a new standard model for public education, but only if the establishment is willing to trial a non-Darwinian strategy for the purpose of improving the practice of human-animal experimentation, and for improving communication between the law and students, because most of the unspoken crimes that are being committed within society occur in laboratories due to the evolutionary theory being taught as a standard for public education, which demands a materialistic interpretation for everything, including life itself.

> *Quotation: ————————————————————
> "There is no fundamental difference between man and the higher animals in their mental faculties. The lower animals, like man, manifestly feel pleasure and pain, happiness and misery." - Charles Darwin. Source: The Descent of Man. (Documented February 24, 1871).

The main difference between man and ape is due to the existence of the human conscience, which is defined as being necessary for our understanding of morality, and we know animals cannot understand morality, because they do not perceive nudity, while humans do. And nudity is something that we have laws against within society, as well as laws that govern the limitations on human sexual behaviour, which derive from the universal principles of Biblical morality, rather than nature. And the correct interpretation for Biblical morality starts and ends with human equality, because without human equality, then there is no lawful basis for human rights to be universal in their interpretation.

So, in order to be consistent when interpreting the universal law of human equality, then a definition for the human conscience that is universal is required first, which, according to international law, has derived from theology, rather than biology. The human conscience, according to international law, is defined as being necessary for our understanding of morality, which cannot be attributed to the animals in any way for reasons relating to the correct interpretation of human rights and equality, which is in accordance with the Universal Declaration of Human Rights and Equality under Article 6 of the universal treaty.

According to the Biblical principles of Judeo-Christianity, there is to be an equality between each person for the sake of others who are less fortunate, which is why it is better to serve, rather than receive, because there is no reward for receiving something according to the universal principles of morality. If you receive something, then you have your reward, but if you give something, then you reward someone else, which in turn, deserves reward in the afterlife, each according to what they have done. But we are not to reward the wicked for their crimes against humanity any more than we should reward those who do not acknowledge the existence of the human conscience before the law for reasons relating to the correct interpretation of human rights and equality.

*Quotation: ————————————————

2 Corinthians 8:13-15

For I do not mean that other men should be eased, and ye burdened, but that there be an equality; That now at this time your abundance may supply their want; That their abundance may also supply your want; So that there may be equality. For as it is written: "He that had gathered much had nothing left over, and he that had gathered little had no lack." - Source: The Holy Bible.

According to Darwinian theory, man is a lower animal on a hierarchical scale that has descended from an African ape, and Darwin based his idea on the comparative brain size between apes and man. But Darwin was basing his theory on man being similar to a large ape, and not a chimpanzee, as man has been equated too by evolutionists today, even though the human brain is about three times larger than the brain is for a chimpanzee. The part of the brain called the cerebral cortex plays a key role in memory, attention, awareness, and thought, which contains twice as many cells in humans as the same region in chimpanzees.

The skull of a chimpanzee has a heavy brow-ridge that rises upward from the cranium, and by contrast, the brow-ridge of a human skull protrudes outward from the forehead instead. And between the eyes, there is a pronounced nasal bone in the human skull, while a chimpanzee has a flat curve that leads to the nasal opening of the skull instead. And the human skull has 22 bones in total, while the chimpanzee skull has 28 bones, yet they're supposed to be our closest relative genetically, but the amount of physical differences there are between a chimpanzee and a human are biologically vast.

For example: The number and size of the lumbar vertebrae (lower back) in humans is different than in apes, because humans have 5 comparatively larger lumbar vertebrae, while most large apes typically have 4 lumbar vertebrae that are relatively smaller. And though the lumbar region of the spine is smaller in all apes, they are in fact less likely to suffer from back problems during their lifespan, because they are quadrupeds, so they do not have the same amount of stress on their lower back as humans do.

Anatomically, an ape has a back posture set at 45 degrees, while a human's posture is vertical, and this is not only due to the shape of the spine, but also the pelvis, because an ape's pelvis is designed for a quadruped, while a humans pelvis is designed to be bipedal. The ilium which is the top portion of the innominate bone (pelvis) in humans is shorter and broader and it curves around the torso, whereas in apes it is flat against the back of the torso so that it can walk on all fours. And there are no examples of an intermediate between a creature that is bipedal compared to a creature that is a quadruped due to the shape of the pelvis.

Any creature that is bipedal as well as slumped over from its back will always be the result of a mutation that is degenerative, rather than progressive in terms of venturing upright. While any creature that is a quadruped, yet retains the ability to walk upright, does so temporarily, and is most suited to walking on all fours due to the shape of the pelvis and spine. So, there are no examples of an intermediate between a quadruped and a bipedal creature for reasons relating to genetic disease, as well as correct back posture, which must be predetermined at the start of a vertebrates function, or they will suffer from back problems, which is never going to be progressive in terms of hereditary traits.

According to the evolutionary theory, a chimpanzee is man's closest relative, but according to anatomy, a chimpanzee has a bone in their penis in order to penetrate the female during intercourse, while humans do not. And you cannot evolve a penis that doesn't require a bone from a penis that does, otherwise, an evolving creature would have to attempt penetration with only half a bone in its penis, which is never going to be genetically successful amongst a group of chimpanzees.

Apes also have a rounder, more barrel shaped rib cage to support their weight with the centre of gravity being higher up the spine, while the human spine has an S-shape that keeps the head and the torso suspended above the centre of gravity, which in turn, gives the human spine suspension like a shock absorber in order to reduce the likelihood of jarring during certain activities, such as running and jumping. When viewing the human spinal column from the posterior (rear) position, the spine appears vertically straight from the neck to the tailbone, while the normal curves of the spine from the side view are unique to human beings only. But if the curves for the spinal cord are not correct, then we know this is the result of a disorder known as Lordosis and Kyphosis.

Correct back posture allows your nervous system to flow freely from your brain to your organs, muscles, joints, and blood vessels, which allows for freedom of movement and increases circulation in order for the organs to function freely. And when it comes to running, poor posture is seen far too frequently as a cause of fatigue. Poor posture makes running slow and painful, and though the position or angle of the posture may seem comfortable, the progressive issues that lead to back problems are very subtle, and this affects the efficiency of running to a large degree.

Proper running posture helps you breathe and move more efficiently, allowing you to run either as long or as fast as you like. And the trick for maintaining good posture, is to keep your chin up, and make sure you're not leaning too far forward with your shoulders, and not too far back with your waist, which some runners do as they hunch over when fatigued. While all apes, chimps, and monkeys are better suited to being hunched over due to the centre of gravity being further up the spine.

In the world of Mixed Martial Arts (MMA) training and competitive fighting, the fighters find that working towards better posture gives them greater control over their individual fighting stance and techniques, thus leading to more control by the individual whilst reducing the likelihood of injury. Posture is a rarely talked about subject in health, but it is one of the most critical biological elements of any vertebrate. Good posture is important to your overall health and sustainability, because it offers a variety of benefits including reduced back pain, increased energy levels, and greater self-esteem.

Having a good back posture is important to your overall health, because it can help you avoid muscle tension, pain, fatigue, and many other common ailments and medical conditions. This means that the human posture is highly specific, leaving no room for improvement, and this also means the human posture was preset before the first human body began to function, because the one thing that cannot evolve, is a correct back posture. Any change to the human spine would offset the centre of balance by changing the centre of gravity, which requires structural changes that need to be pre-specified first, or immediate damage will occur to the spine and the tissue surrounding the spine when attempting to lift something heavy, or whilst running and jumping.

What about man's DNA being similar to chimpanzee DNA?

The difference between each human being's DNA is between 0.0% to 0.1% of the genome. The human genome has 3 billion nucleotides worth of DNA instructions, which must be multiplied by 2 in order to include the RNA sequence with the DNA sequence resulting in 6 billion nucleotides or 3 billion base pairs. So, 0.1% of 6 billion is equal to 6 million nucleotides worth of DNA RNA instructions, while the difference between a chimpanzee and a human being is 0.1% to 1.2% of the total amount, which is equal to 36 million nucleotides within the human genome sequence that are different to a chimpanzee.

This figure (36 million vs 6 million) equates to being a ratio of 12:1 which indicates that human beings are closely related to each other, while the chances that a chimpanzee is related to a human is 12 times less than that of another human. And this is enough to prove that the difference between a chimpanzee and a human is vast, rather than close, so I will compare these results with a jet airliner that has 6 million parts.

So, by comparison, it would take 12 jet airliners worth of parts compared with just 1 in order to compare the amount of difference there is between a human and a chimpanzee. Now if you could imagine an airport that has 12 jets on the airstrip compared to just 1 jet at the other end of the strip, it will be the same as comparing the difference between a chimpanzee and a human in terms of ratios between 0.1% and 1.2%. But if you place 1 jet beside another twin aircraft with the same parts and design, then it is the same as comparing one human being with another in terms of variation between 0.0% and 0.1% of 6 billion nucleotides.

And what all of this means is that anything greater than 0.1% difference between a human genome sample against an unknown sample is to be considered not human, because all human beings are within 0.0% to 0.1% of each other in terms of genetic differences statistically, and this is because there is a limitation on the amount of variation within mankind that is governed by a set of parameters within the genome. So, in order for humans to express themselves as individuals, then there must be a set amount of variation, but the amount of variation is limited to being within 0.0% to 0.1% of the total amount of genetic instructions within the human genome according to a statistical analysis of the data provided by the National Institutes of Health.

Systems biology has been responsible for some of the most important advancements in the science of human health and environmental sustainability, and it is a holistic approach to deciphering the complexity of biological systems that starts from understanding what the specifics are that forms the system as a working whole. Systems biology is integrated, involving many scientific disciplines, such as biochemistry, bioengineering, biosynthetics, and other disciplines in order to make predictions based on assessments under varying conditions, which is then used to develop solutions to problems within the food and health industry. And this ability to design predictive multi-scale models enables scientists to discover new biomarkers for diseases and biological disorders.

A biomarker is a biological molecule found in blood, or other body fluids or tissues that show signs of an abnormality, which gives an indication for the presence of a condition or disease. A biomarker may be used to see how well the body responds to a treatment for a disease or condition, and they are used as a reference when comparing abnormalities within the body's overall system. Biomarkers can have molecular, histologic, radiographic, or physiological characteristics. Examples of biomarkers include everything from blood pressure and heart rate to basic metabolic studies, as well as x-ray, and genetic tests for blood and other tissues. A biomarker is a measurable indicator of the severity or presence of a biologically diseased state; Meaning that a biomarker is anything that can be used as an indicator for identifying a particular problem within the body.

For example: Glypican-3 (GPC3), is a biomarker for a tumour and is used for the diagnosis of melanoma, especially in the early stages of the disorder. Previously, the most useful prognostic factors in clinical practice for localized melanoma are Breslow thickness, presence of lymph node involvement, and ulceration. In metastatic disease, they're location of metastatic site and lactate dehydrogenase elevation, so the growth of a metastatic site will become pronounced as it begins to protrude outwardly.

Another example of how a biomarker can be detected, is by an electrocardiograph that is used to measure the electrical activity of the heart and make assessments that are based on the signature impulses from the body's heart, just as biomarkers within the blood are used to determine cancerous formations on the body's skin. And it is the biomarkers that highlight the issue, and a problem within the body will always occur as a sequence, so the better the sequence of a progressive state is understood, then the better the early detection method will be, and the easier it will also be to put a control measure in place at an earlier stage during the development of a problem.

A sequence is defined as the following of one thing after another in series according to a succession, or, as something that follows a subsequent event that produces a particular result called a consequence. A sequence can also be a list of numbers in a certain order, and each number in a sequence is called a term, so that each term in a sequence has a position, such as first, second, third and so on... Sequences are useful in a number of mathematical disciplines for studying the likelihood of a given event, because a sequence in place gives predictability to a group of events.

The term, probability, is defined as being: 1) "The quality or state of something being probable, such as the extent to which something is likely to happen or be the case." And a biomarker or ECG signature for example, is the result of a sequence in place; Meaning that a prediction can occur, which then leads to a diagnosis when the specifics are in place. The evolutionary theory, no matter how reasonable the interpretations may sound, is based entirely on random selection, rather than systems design and systems analysis.

So, because the evolutionary theory is based entirely on random selection, it will mean that evolution can be compared to a roulette wheel, but never to a biological system that is defined by its DNA, which is highly specific. And the reason that DNA is highly specific, is because the instructions for one protein must be in relation to other proteins, or they will not combine to form a living cell. While a genetic mutation is by definition, unspecified, due to a mistake within the DNA proofreading process; Meaning that no amount of hereditary mutations can improve the instructional method that has been employed in order for genomic replication and biological reproduction to occur.

DNA instructions are transcribed according to a template via a process known as DNA synthesis, which acts as a standard that defines the genetic sequences according to a set of instructions, which must be integrated in order for any of the instructional sequences to have a combined purpose. And unless the sequences are arranged correctly, then a mutation will occur, and a genetic mutation will always reduce the likelihood of survival due to the amount of damage that mutations cause to instructional systems. This means that DNA instructions are pre-arranged according to a set of rules that are in constant effect, which is similar to how a language works with an alphabet in place.

The use of planning must be involved in order for a method to occur, which in turn, gives rise to a procedure, and the process of biological mutations has derived from the process of diversification, but the process of mutations itself cannot improve a living system over time, because that would require the input of new specifics. While the specifications for a thermodynamic instructional system, such as DNA RNA transcription, are fixed according to a set of parameters which governs the method of transcription as a whole, and, sets its limitations.

For example: A set of instructions will always be according to a standard in place in order for the instructions to be defined as orderly, and it is the standard for the instructions to be interpreted by that is fixed according to a set of parameters, which is similar to an alphabet system which sets the limitations on a particular language. And though a particular language, (such as English) may use words from a different language, (such as German for example) the words themselves still need to be spelt in English in order for the instructions to be conveyed in English, otherwise, additional specifics are required in order for the instructions to be interpreted.

Life itself is instructionally based from its DNA RNA. DNA format is the standard method for life to reproduce copies of itself through genomic replication. DNA is a type of binary code that is comprised of only four chemical characters called nucleotides. And these four chemical characters are arranged into specified sequences called gene sequences in order to code for a particular protein, which is what the body is made of.

So, the four nucleotides (A, T, C, G) are a type of alphabet that is fixed the same as a standard is for a language, but because DNA instructions are more similar to a binary language, it will mean that it is the sequence that gives the instructions purpose, rather than the characters themselves, which are simply a standard in place for the sequencing to occur. And this is why DNA is a type of code because the information within DNA is according to an encrypted sequence with each gene sequence being specific in relation to the next, resulting in an algorithm.

Any step-by-step procedure that is completed the same way every time, is by definition an algorithm, and DNA RNA transcription is a continuous step-by-step process while an organism is alive. So, because all life has been specified according to an algorithm, and because an algorithm is evidence of design, it will mean quite definitively that all life was made. Another interesting point that is rarely ever mentioned by evolutionists, is that the meaning for any instructional sequence derives from outside of the sequence itself, and must be imposed upon the sequence by way of inference as a rule in order for the sequence to have a purpose, which in turn, gives the sequence meaning.

For example: The meaning for the word 'stop' in English is not found in the spelling of the word, or the size, nor the colour, or the shape, but according to a set of rules, because the meaning for the word 'stop' has been imposed upon the word from outside of the English alphabet system itself, which means that the meaning of a word is always inferred. And if you wish to challenge the meaning of the word 'stop' whilst driving a vehicle on the road for example, then the meaning of the word will be enforced by a law.

And every gene sequence that is produced via DNA RNA transcription ends with another chemical character called uracil, which is represented by the chemical letter (U), and if the chemical letter (U) is not in place at the end of a genetic sequence, then a major mutation will occur, because uracil means 'stop' within DNA coding. So, because a DNA sequence needs to be told to stop! it will mean that rules have been applied to DNA from outside of the instructional system itself, the same as the meaning for the word 'stop' in English has been imposed upon the letters from outside of the English alphabet system by way of inference.

A typical gene sequence will always be limited to the number of chemical characters in use which sets the parameters for a protein to be manufactured, and because each gene sequence is limited to the number of chemical characters in use, it will mean that life is not evolving, because the overall system is not self-improving by the addition of new chemical characters. And any loss of chemical characters within a gene sequence is equal to a reduction in terms of specifics, rather than an increase, which means definitively that living systems are not self-improving as the theory of evolution claims.

The meaning of life is relative to the ecosystem whereby each living system is incorporated into a more larger system, which in turn, gives each living system purpose and meaning. The ecosystem is defined as a complex system, so an overall method is required in order to govern the selection process for speciation to occur independent of the Creator who has set the parameters in place for His creation to diversify. And only the Creator can know what the end product will be as a result of the process at work, so that all of the variables during the process have been taken into account, including any random variables as well.

The ecosystem we live in is indeed a complex system, but there have been many changes to the ecosystem over time as a result of variables within the system, such as speciation, and diversification. And only the Creator of a system can know what all of the variables are within the system he has made, which means that God has taken all things into account, and variables must be taken into account when it comes to living systems, because all living systems are symbiotic, which means that there is an overall method in place in order to combine each living creature into an integrated system known as the ecosystem.

Living systems are a part of a highly complex system whereby multiple systems, including the solar system, are working together to form a complex whole. This means definitively that life is a part of the most complex system there is, because complexity is also equal to compressing a device, and the ecosystem is full of molecular mechanisms that perform a specific function within the overall system, which must be planned in advance, otherwise, an ecosystem could not be established due to the number of events that must occur that are specific in relation to the next.

And we do see living systems going extinct due to changes in the environment, which is due to variables within a complex system. So, unless a procedure is in place to ensure the survivability of a living organism, then the ecosystem as a whole would fail catastrophically. So, for this reason, a selection process for living systems is required in order for diversification and sustainability to occur independent of the Creator, because as diversification occurs over time, the total amount of variation within a kind is spread out amongst each individual species, so that an open breeding population is more sustainable for a particular kind than a closed breeding population that shares the same genetic mutations within their chromosomes.

The amount of variability within living systems is highly limited due to the parameters that are set in place by the Creator, such as DNA RNA transcription that is governed by a proofreading mechanism that limits genetic mutations from occurring. And this is evidence of supernatural creativity, because there are a set of parameters in place that prevent biological mutations from occurring during the manufacturing process of genomic replication, which is essential in order for the system to be efficient, as well as orderly.

Procreation is a method of reproduction, and the offspring that is produced is defined as being the end product of the process, which means that living systems are being manufactured according to an instructional method. But the reproductive system alone does not constitute as a living system, because the reproductive system is a part of a more complex system that works holistically with other primary systems in order to form an irreducibly complex system. The human body is made up by multiple primary systems that work together in synchrony, such as the circulation system, the skeletal system, the nervous system, and so on... This means that an overall method is required in order to combine all of the bodies individual primary systems together into a single system or mechanism, which must occur according to a standard in place, otherwise, the system as a whole would not be integrated.

A naturalist scientist will always try and point to similarities between different kinds of creatures, such as Charles Darwin's and Earnest Haskell's evolutionary worldview of simple to complex. While the creationist scientist will always try and point out the differences between living creatures in terms of varieties within a kind. But because there are major differences between different kinds of creatures, it will mean that the differences must be taken into account first, because the similarities between different kinds of creatures are not always relative to the same thing at all times.

For example: An ape has curved flanges for walking on their knuckles, while a human has straight flanges for the fingers to carry out detailed work, which in turn, gives human fingers a greater ability than an apes fingers. So, just because an ape has five flanges on each hand does not mean that they are relative to a human hand, because there is a major difference which must be taken into account before the similarities can be explained, such as the action of procreation and communication.

Any group of creatures that can procreate together are a part of the same kind, which is why mankind is a distinct kind of creature, because human beings cannot procreate successfully with any type of animal. And all animals are indeed broken up into separate kinds via their DNA, because when insemination occurs within the female ovum, the ovum will read the DNA of the sperm cell within a fraction of a second in order to verify whether or not it is of the same kind. And this is a selection process that is rarely ever mentioned by evolutionists, because it is evidence of separate kinds.

The ability of the ovum to read the DNA sequence of a sperm cell within a fraction of a second is unmatched by anything that man has ever made, because the fastest methods of DNA proofreading today require about 15 minutes to read a single gene sequence. The head of the sperm cell contains the DNA for the creature it derives from, and when combined with the ovum's DNA, it will create a new individual. The tip of the sperm head is the portion of the cell that contains the DNA called the acrosome, which enables the sperm cell to penetrate the ovum.

The DNA proofreading by the ovum occurs within just a fraction of a second in order to verify whether or not to let the sperm cell into the ovum, and if the sperm cell is not of the same kind of creature that the ovum is from, then the ovum's inner wall will immediately harden trapping the sperm cell between the outer wall of the ovum and the inner wall. And it is the inner wall that has the ability to read the DNA sequence almost instantaneously upon contact with the sperm cell. And this is the reason why cloning methods that cross animals with humans require the ovum to be punctured by a syringe in order to allow the sperm cell entrance into the ovum.

Any theory that is unable to explain the full extent of that which it claims to be in possession of, such as the facts concerning the existence of life, is by definition a poor standard. And it is only the atheists who are arguing that they have explained how life has occurred naturally without having provided a single demonstration as to how genetic instructions could have occurred via a natural process. And there is most certainly no natural process that can account for the human conscience, which the atheist rejects entirely in order to espouse some form of freedom from morality. When freedom of thought, according to law, has been defined by freedom of conscience, from which, all of your inalienable rights are defined by so that you are self-governed under the Biblical principles of universal morality.

So, because the word, conscience, is a theological term from the Holy Bible, and because the law of human equality is defined by the existence of the endowed human conscience, it will mean that the Biblical definition of man is both self-evident and self- explanatory for the benefit of the people in order that each person should have protection of person before the law. And protection of person is fundamental to both law and society, because without protection of person before the law, then the people will lose their distinction as human beings. And this is the main reason why the theory of evolution is the greatest threat that mankind has ever faced, because the evolutionary theory demands that human beings should be defined as animals, which is the very thing that will rob the people of their identity before the law.

The materialistic philosophy that follows the theory of evolution is a dark and stormy cloud that forbids the progression of society to formulate an hypothesis that differs from the theory. The secular standard for public education should be brought into question here as a method of free education, because it is the secular standard for public education that has failed as a standard of learning by demanding a materialistic interpretation for everything, including life itself. When life is far more than just chemistry due to the nature of breathing, which cannot derive from materials alone over millions of years, because there is no way to transfer an organism that relies on carbon dioxide absorption to one that is oxygen dependent. And we are as individuals dependent upon the truth, because it is the truth that sets us free from the yoke of slavery, and thereby leads the way to human freedom by the rights of conscience, and by an equality between the people.

The purpose of systems biology is to discover faults within a living system and then the categorize them into a list of high to low risk potentials so that a system can be assessed for weaknesses, and it will always be a series of abnormalities that will determine a sequence, which then leads to a diagnosis or prediction. The benefit of systems biology is to better understand how living systems coexist, rather than attempting to relate all life into a single phylum. Living systems are integrated; Meaning that living systems are better understood from the relationship they have with one another one the basis of individual systems so that each one may be studied independently or as a complex whole. The theory of evolution on the other hand is the philosophical basis for survival of the fittest, eugenics, and Social Darwinism with the aim of creating a secular society, but will one day fail due to moral decay, which is entirely due to the evolutionary definition of man.

CHAPTER 4

Evolutionary Theory

WHEN DESCRIBING A PROCESS VIA A METHOD, IT WILL ALWAYS be the correct word definitions in use that are authoritative, rather than theory alone, because a method of lying will always begin with denial, or by a lack of understanding in regard to word meanings. And the one lie that cannot be overlooked at this point in human history, is the lie that evolution is by definition an innovative process, when the truth is that all innovation derives from the action of creativity by definition of the word, innovate.

The first law of linguistics states that the inventor of a word has the right to define it, only then can a word be used as a metaphor, and then later a derogative, and language works no other way, because the progression of a word meaning begins as literal, and then later as a derogative. So, in order to have a coherent theory, then the root of word meanings is essential, which is the reason why a student's most essential study guide is a simple dictionary. So, for the purpose of this chapter I have selected Oxford Languages (OED) as my dictionary of choice, because it is the world's foremost dictionary on the English language.

According to Oxford Languages, the theory of evolution is defined as: 1) "The process by which different kinds of living organisms are believed to have developed from earlier forms during the history of the Earth. Similar: Darwinism, natural selection." 2) "The gradual development of something. Similar: development, advancement." So, from the world's foremost dictionary, the OED, we find that evolution is defined as "natural selection," which is also defined as a "belief," rather than an action or fact.

The definition of the word, belief, is defined as: "An acceptance that something exists or is true, especially one without proof. Similar: faith, trust." So, the proper definition of evolution is that it's a faith based on natural selection, rather than a fact based on an action. While the second definition for evolution is defined as: "development or advancement." The definition for the term, development, according to the OED, is defined as: 1) "The process of developing or being developed. Similar: evolution, growth." While the definition for the term advancement, is defined as: 1) "The process of promoting a cause or plan." 2) "A development or improvement. Similar: development, progress." So, the term, advancement, is in relation to the term, development, which is defined as being equal to the term, progress.

But even though progress is a form of development that advances over time, the terms development, advancement, and progress, can still be defined as being either positive or negative growth depending on the process. And the term advancement is also in relation to an improvement due to the use of planning, which cannot be attributed to nature, because nature is unable to plan anything in advance.

For example: The progression of metastatic disease is by definition a form of negative growth that will advance over time as the condition progresses unless a method is applied in order to reduce the severity of the condition. While the growth of an organism into maturity is defined as positive growth according to the life cycle of a particular organism. So, because a diseased state is the result of a genetic mutation or an infection, while the growth of an organism into maturity is according to an orderly thermodynamic process at work, it will mean that both an infection, and a genetic mutation, are the result of disorder during a thermodynamic process, rather than the cause of improvement to a living system.

In order for the progression of something to be an overall improvement in terms of thermodynamic efficiency, then the process must include additional specifics, or the improvement will be completely subject to randomicity, and will therefore advance into decay due to the progression of negative growth. Evolution, as a process, cannot be, at the same time, an innovative method, because all innovation derives from the action of creativity, which is a process that generates new specifics based on a method of planning. This means that evolution, as a theory, is lacking a causality for improvement due to the lack of a mechanism for innovation to occur. The term, evolution, according to the Encyclopedia Britannica, is defined as: "A theory in biology postulating that the various types of plants, animals, and other living things on Earth have their origin in other pre-existing types, and that the distinguishable differences are due to modifications in successive generations." (End of Quote).

So, according to the world's foremost Encyclopedia, (the Encyclopedia Britannica) evolution is defined as a "postulation," rather than a law in science. The term, postulate, according to the OED, is defined as: 1) "A suggestion or assumption of the existence, fact, or truth of something as a basis for reasoning, discussion, or belief." While an assumption is defined as: 1) "A thing that is accepted as true, or as certain to happen without proof." So, according to the world's foremost Encyclopedia, evolution is defined as an assumption that is lacking in proof. The correct definition of the word, innovate, according to the OED, is defined as: 1) "To make changes in something established, especially by introducing new methods, ideas, or products." 2) "Introduce something new, especially a product." While the term, creativity, is defined as: 1) "The use of imagination or original ideas to create something. Similar: Inventiveness, Imagination, innovation."

So, the term, innovate, shares its definition with the word, create, in that something new has come into existence by design or via a method. The term, creation, according to the OED, is defined as: 1) "The action or process of bringing something into existence. Similar: design, formation, forming." While the term, action, is defined as: 1) "The fact or process of doing something, typically to achieve an aim." So, the term, creation, according to the OED, is defined as an action, and an action is defined as an observable fact, which in turn, forms the basis of a physical law in science.

While the term, evolution, is defined as a belief based on an assumption, and it is for this reason that Biblical Christianity has a scientific basis, while the theory of evolution does not, because Christianity is a belief based on an observable fact, while evolution is a belief based entirely on an assumption. The main difference though between Biblical Christianity and Darwinism in terms of a belief, is that Biblical Christianity is both historically significant and theologically correct. While Darwinian evolution is postulated without proof, which is the main reason why our universal dating system derives from a Biblical timeline from BC to AD, which in itself, derives from recorded eyewitness accounts, rather than from an evolutionary postulation that is lacking any eyewitness accounts concerning the history of the Earth.

A system of belief can be defined as either postulated or literal, depending on the theory, which means that a system can be used for either good or for evil, but it will always be morality that defines whether the system is positive or negative in terms of its use. And a prime example of how negative a system can be, would be the practice of Social Darwinism as a political science that aims to spread the teaching of evolution without due regard for human rights and equality. While the universal law of human equality has derived from the Holy Bible and Judeo-Christian theology, because the universal law of human equality has been defined in terms of Biblical theology due to the word definitions therein in accordance with freedom of conscience.

The term, conscience, is an ecclesiastical term from Latin that has derived from Biblical theology, and has been used by international law to define a person as distinct from the animals in accordance with the universal law of human equality. While the evolutionary definition of man derives from Darwinism and Linnaean taxonomy that defines man as a lower animal on a hierarchical scale. So, the problem here with Darwinian evolution, as a theory, is that the word definitions used to describe a person with have derived from a racial theory, rather than from law. And it is for this reason that Biblical creation is a lawful instruction, while the theory of evolution is not, because each person is universally entitled to be defined as a created human being in accordance with freedom of conscience.

According to international law, the human conscience has been endowed to all of mankind, which sets the lawful premise for human rights and equality. The term, endowed, from law, is that which is from birth; Meaning that an inalienable right is also a birthright, such as the right to be defined as a created human being with a human ancestry. While Darwinian theory is in opposition to the universal law of equality by defining man as a lower animal from the viewpoint of Linnaean taxonomy, which is a crime against humanity on the basis of equality. So, it is for this reason that the theory of evolution is in opposition to a lawful instruction that is universal in its interpretation.

In order for a process to be specific, then planning is required first, because that which is planned, is also specific. Natural selection cannot improve an organism over time by definition of the fact that nature cannot plan anything in advance, which is required in order for a set of specifics to be generated. And additional specifics are required in order for an advancement to occur in terms of development, otherwise, there would be no causality for innovation.

The action of creativity cannot be defined as a natural process, because the process of designing is by definition, artificial, which is why the term, innovate, shares its definition with the word, create, so that anything that is innovated is by definition a creation. And evolution cannot be both a natural process and an artificial process at the same time, which limits the definition of evolution to being a theoretical postulation only according to the correct definitions in use, because there is no physical action in existence to demonstrate the theory of evolution with as a procedure without detracting from the theory itself. A procedure in place will always derive from a method that is specific due to the presence of an algorithm, which cannot occur at random over time in accordance with the law of probability. The theory of evolution asserts that everything in existence has derived from a natural process, and is therefore self-existing.

So, the problem with evolution, as a process, is that innovation always derives by design, which is by definition an artificial process instead of a natural process. This means that the theory of evolution is without a causality for innovation to occur, and is thereby limited to being a theoretical postulation only due to the lack of a mechanism for improvement. While any attempt to demonstrate evolution in terms of a procedure will result in a contradiction to the theory, because a demonstration is by definition an artificial process due to the use of a method, resulting in a method or procedure.

The only causality there is for a procedure, is by the application of a method, which can either be artificial or supernatural in origin, because a natural, or normal process, is limited to the number of specifics there are in place to define the process with, while any increase in specificity must derive from a method of innovation or planning. This means that specifics do not derive from a natural process, but from creativity instead, which in turn, gives rise to new innovations via a procedure. A procedure is any step-by-step process that attempts to generate a process in order for a method to occur, and the evolutionary theory does attempt to place the progression of living systems into a step-by-step procedure, which means definitively that evolution is a creation, rather than a natural process due to the application of a method. A natural process cannot be defined as a random phenomenon, because a natural process is defined by a set of specifics in order to define the process with, which means that the only way to interpret a process, is by the application of a method.

Evolution, as a theory, defines itself as a natural process only, yet any improvements to a process must derive from the action of creativity by definition of the word, innovate. Anything that has had rules applied to it, is by definition a creation, and there have been a number of rules applied to the theory of evolution over the years in a desperate attempt to define the process as authoritative. So, in order to define evolution as a process without detracting from the theory itself, then a method of random selection is required, because the theory demands that living systems be self- existing in order to refute creation. But the problem with evolution in terms of a process, is that random selection will always lead to an increase in disorder over time, otherwise, there would be nothing to define that which is orderly in terms of a process or procedure. The other aspect concerning evolution as a process, is that anything that has not occurred by design, must have derived at random due to a lack of specificity.

Any random improvements to a process will always be limited to whatever the immediate need is, as opposed to planning, whereby the overall level of efficiency for a system can be taken into account in order to generate new specifics. And it will always be the number of preferences set in place by the individual that will specify for what the random improvements are that have occurred, but any increase in thermodynamic efficiency must derive from a method of innovation, which will always involve the use of planning in order to generate the specifics needed. So, in order for an increase in thermodynamic efficiency to occur, then rules need to be taken into account first, such as physical laws, which in turn, sets the limitations of a system's operation.

For example: A random change to the colour of an insulating material will be an improvement to some, but not to everyone, because a random improvement will always be according to a set of preferences in place by the individual that is aesthetic, and not according to any increase in thermodynamic efficiency, which is specific. And the change in colour for any insulating material will always affect its level of efficiency, because the darker the colour is, the more thermal energy it will absorb, and the lighter the colour, the more reflective its insulating properties will be.

Natural selection cannot improve the thermodynamic efficiency of a living organism over time, because natural selection, according to its own definition, is based entirely on preference whereby nature selects according to its preference. While the action of creativity is the source of all innovation, whereby a method of planning has been applied in order to generate a set of specifics, which is required in order for thermodynamic efficiency to occur. The definition of efficiency has two meanings. One is a common meaning, and the other is a physics definition. The physics definition for the word, efficiency, is defined as: 1) "The ratio of the useful work performed by a machine, or in a process to the total energy expended or heat taken in." While the common definition for the word, efficiency, is defined as: 1) "The state or quality of being efficient. Similar: organization, order, planning."

The common use of the word efficiency refers to that which is organized, or orderly due to the use of planning. Any increase in efficiency to a given process will always be the result of planning having been applied to the process, because efficiency will always be the result of specificity. While the level of efficiency for a thermodynamic process, according to physics, will always be determined by the amount of thermal energy that is wasted compared to that which is used by a particular system, because the conservation of thermal energy into chemical, mechanical, or biomechanical work, is what's equal to efficiency.

The process of thermal conservation is defined by the laws of thermodynamics, which includes the thermodynamic principles of entropy. The term, entropy, is a physics term that is defined as: 1) "A thermodynamic quantity representing the unavailability of a system's thermal energy for conversion into mechanical work, often interpreted as the degree of disorder or randomness within a system." So, by definition, the amount of thermal energy that is wasted during any given thermodynamic process is the result of disorder or randomness within the system.

This means that the only way to increase the level of efficiency a thermodynamic system has is to increase the number of specifics there are within the system, whereby the transfer of thermal energy can be conserved by a mechanism that has been pre-specified according to a set of rules, such as physical laws. The total rate of entropy increase within a system can only begin to take full effect once the system is fully formed, because entropy is the result of a thermodynamic process at work, rather than the cause of one, which means automatically that ordered complexity cannot derive at random.

In order to improve a system's level of thermodynamic efficiency, then there must be an increase in the number of specifics there are within the system. This means that the action of creativity must be applied to the process in order for an increase in thermodynamic efficiency to occur within a thermodynamic system, because that which is specific, is the diametric opposite of that which is random; Meaning that a method is required in order for efficiency to be gained during any thermodynamic process, because an increase in specificity is also required.

So, for an increase in efficiency to occur within a thermodynamic system, then there must include additional specifics, which are always relative to the mechanism that needs improving within the system, and it is never according to a random change or fluctuation within a system, because any random fluctuations within a thermodynamic system are subject to the effects of entropy law, which is a non-creative process. Entropy is also defined as a constant during any thermodynamic process due to a lack of order within the system, which means that entropy is the result of a random fluctuation within an operational system. And that which is in a state of entropy cannot self-improve, because that which is random will continue to decline into disorder perpetually over time unless a method is applied, which is in accordance with the law of probability.

The action of creativity is required in order for a thermodynamic system to be made efficient, because a thermodynamic system consists of multiple primary mechanisms that are specific in relation to each other, and the only causality there is for the existence of specifics, is by design. The specifics for any thermodynamic system must be applied to the materials before the system can begin its cycle, otherwise, the process will be inefficient due to a lack of innovation.

In order for any level of efficiency to be gained during a thermodynamic process, then additional specifics are required whereby a mechanism can be put in place in order to conserve thermal energy, because any loss of thermal energy during a thermodynamic reaction will be defined as entropy. The only way to define the causality of a biological system, is to use the term, creation, because a biological system is defined as efficient according to the thermodynamic principles of entropy whereby a mechanism in place has been pre-specified in order to conserve thermal energy for the purpose of manufacturing proteins.

A biological system can be compared to a mechanical system in that a biological system is defined by biomechanical mechanisms. While any chemical system that is governed by instructions, such as DNA RNA instructions, will always be the result of creativity having been applied to the process initially, because there are instructions present. This means that a biomechanical system that derives from instructions will always be the result of creativity having been applied to the materials used, otherwise, there would be no causality for a biomechanical system that is by definition, efficient. So, in order for a thermodynamic process to occur that is efficient, then a set of specifics are required first, which cannot be attributed to nature, because nature is unable to plan anything in advance.

According to Oxford Languages, the definition of a system is defined as: 1) "A set of things working together as parts of a mechanism or an interconnecting network; A complex whole. Similar: order." 2) "A set of principles or procedures according to which something is done; An organized scheme or method. Similar: method." So, from the world's foremost dictionary, we find that a system is defined by its level of order due to the application of a method. While the definition of a method according to the OED is defined as: 1) "A particular procedure for accomplishing or approaching something, especially a systematic or established one." So, from the OED, we find that the term, procedure, is interchangeable with the word, method, in that an organized scheme or plan has been established.

According to encyclopedic definitions, a system is a group of interacting or interrelated elements that act according to a set of rules to form a unified whole. So, from the academic definitions in use, we find that a system is any set of rules that work together as a unified or complex whole. While the definition of a rule according to the OED is defined as: 1) "One of a set of explicit or understood regulations or principles governing conduct or procedure within a particular area of activity." So, from the OED, we find that a set of rules governs a procedure, which means that a system is by definition any set of rules that forms a procedure by the application of a method, which in turn, gives rise to ordered complexity from the use of planning.

So, the correct definition of a system is anything that has been innovated or planned, because all innovation derives from the use of planning or the imagination, which is the only source of innovation there is, so that a set of rules that forms the parameters for a system's operation must be designed in order for a set of specifics to occur by definition of the word, innovate. A thermodynamic system is defined by its level of order, rather than by its level of disorder, and ordered complexity derives from taking rules into account, which is why a system is rule based according to its correct definition in use. The specifics for any given system must be in place before the primary feature can begin its cycle, which is not only applicable to biology, where a growth cycle is in place, but also, for any engineered product.

For example: Since the year 2018, the Wärtsilä 31 engine has been continually running and is listed by the Guinness World Records as being the world's most efficient 4-stroke diesel engine ever produced. Diesel engines are more fuel efficient than petrol engines and emit less CO_2, which makes them better for the environment. Diesel engines also produce considerably more torque than their petrol-powered counterparts, which is why diesels are good engines for towing or carrying heavy loads. But even though the Wärtsilä 31 diesel engine is the world record holder for being the most efficient 4-stroke engine ever produced, it is still not used for energy manufacture, because there are more specifics needed that a diesel engine cannot compare with in terms of efficiency, like a steam engine for example.

The steam turbine is the most efficient type of engine in use today, and for this reason, the steam turbine is used universally for the production of electricity. The steam expansion in a turbine is nearly continuous as long as the heat is continually applied, because a turbine is comparable to using a combination of heat, gravity and atmospheric pressures to one's advantage in order to create a significant amount of stored energy via a build-up of pressure within the system.

The thermodynamic efficiency of any given system will always be according to a set of specifics in place, and nature cannot specify for a set of specifics, because nature cannot plan anything in advance. And planning is indeed a requirement in order to determine the type of specifics that are needed for the process to be made efficient. So, it is the process of evolution that is in question here as a method, and not the existence of a thermodynamic system, which is self-evident, because there is a procedure in place that defines the process as either orderly or disorderly, depending on the process.

In order to differentiate between that which is orderly, and that which is not, then a method of identification is required first. And the physics definition of that which is orderly derives from systems study, because it is a system that is defined as orderly due to the presence of a procedure. So, in order to define whether a process is orderly or not, then a procedure is required first, because it will always be a procedure in place that defines a given process; Meaning that the only way to invent a process, is by the application of a method.

Thermodynamics in biology refers to the study of energy transfers that occur within living systems for the production of energy; Meaning that any loss of thermal energy during a biological process that is wasted due to a lack of order within the system will be defined as entropy. The more energy that is used to complete a specific biological function, the higher the number of specifics there are in place in order to utilize the energy input, or the energy is wasted.

Energy is therefore stored within living systems in order to maintain the thermodynamic efficiency of the system, such as fat cells for example, which are stored to provide the body with a source of energy in order to keep the process of manufacturing proteins perpetual, which is a continuous process while the body is breathing. The more energy input there is to a living system, the more energy output is needed in order for thermodynamic efficiency to occur, which is the reason why physical exercise is important to maintaining a healthy system, and this is also why fat cells are burnt, because this is a thermal process that exchanges heat with its surroundings.

For example: The bacterial flagella motor harnesses ion flow to drive rotary motion at speeds reaching 100,000 rpm. The flagella motor is a bidirectional rotary nanomachine used by many bacteria to sense and move through a fluid environment. The bidirectional rotation of the motor is governed by interactions between the inner membrane and the C-ring in the cytoplasm that can travel forward or in reverse. The bacterial flagella motor is powered by the transmembrane electrochemical gradient of ions, named "ion motive force" (IMF), and rotates the flagella filament to generate thrust in order to propel the cell's body through a fluid. Each rotation by the flagella motor requires 1 ion in an electrolyte solution per rotation with an efficiency rate of almost 99%, because as each ion is used to perform a single rotation, there is only a 1% loss of ions; Meaning that a flagella motor is the most efficient motor known to man.

The flagella motor is an irreducibly complex system, because each component has a primary function. Irreducible complexity is defined as any group of primary mechanisms that each have a primary function within an operational system, whereby the failure of one primary mechanism will result in a total systems failure. So, by contrast, an irreducibly complex system is evidence of design, because each mechanism within the system has been pre-specified according to an overall plan in order to combine each mechanism into a single mechanism that is integrated in terms of a single system. And every operational system has a level of irreducible complexity due to the combination of individual primary mechanisms that work together as a unified whole for a specified purpose or designated function.

According to the principles of physics and systems theory, anything random will remain random unless a method is applied, because a method is by definition, specific, so that all systems have derived via a procedure due to the presence of ordered complexity, which is evidence of creativity, rather than evolution. The law of relativity applies to any operational system whereby a group of primary mechanisms are relative to each other resulting in an irreducibly complex system, which cannot occur at random in accordance with the law of probability, because anything that is relative, is by definition specific. So, in order for any system to be integrated according to the physics definition of relativity, then a set of specifics must be incorporated into the process, or the method of improvement will be completely subject to randomicity, and will therefore advance into decay over time due to entropy law, and the law of probability.

Evolution, as a process, is based entirely on random selection, because nature cannot select directly what specifics are needed due to the method of selection. And it will always be the method of selection that will determine whether the process is random or specified, depending on the selection process. The action of creativity is a selection process that can generate an outcome that is either random or specific, while a natural process will always be limited to the number of specifics there are in place to define the process with. So, in order for biological complexity to occur, then specifications are required first, which means that the action of creativity has been applied to life, otherwise, there would be nothing to define that which is specific in terms of a biological process.

Any process that is repeating itself according to a cycle in place, (such as the reproductive cycle or the water cycle for example) is by definition, predictable, and that which is predictable is by definition, specific. Predictability will always be the result of a sequence that is repeatable under demonstration, and is therefore, reliable under observation, which cannot occur at random over time in accordance with the law of probability, because any sequence that is relative to another is by definition, specific.

The level of ordered complexity for any given system will always be defined by its level of efficiency, which cannot occur at random, because anything that is in a state of disorder will continue to decline into randomness perpetually unless a method is applied. While that which is efficient, is by definition, specific. Thermodynamic entropy is the decline of ordered complexity into disordered complexity, which means definitively that a state of disorder cannot occur unless there is an orderly system in place first to define disorder with by definition of the fact that something orderly was occurring to begin with. And this is why planning is the only causality there is for a system, because a method is required first in order for efficiency to occur, otherwise, there would be no causality for a procedure.

A method is a requirement in order to interpret any given process, because a process will always be the result of a method due to the presence of a procedure. This means that all processes, whether random or not, have derived from a method, and therefore, a system, so that a random process is defined as a random variation within a given system according to a set of variables that will fluctuate. While that which is specific must also be specified, otherwise, there would be no causality for that which is orderly in terms of complexity.

The theory of evolution attempts to define a biological system as being the result of a natural process only, yet there is no other causality for a natural process apart from the presence of a system in place, because a natural process is equal to a normal process, and a normal process will always be the result of a system in place, rather than the cause of one. A natural, or normal process, will always be limited to the number of specifics there are in place to define the process with, while any additional specifics to a particular process must derive from a method of innovation by definition of the word, innovate. The normal workings of a system in place can be defined as a natural process, while the inventing of a system must derive from a method of innovation, because additional specifics are required first. And this is the main reason why evolution is a failed theory in science, because it is illogical to define a system as being the result of a natural process only.

Any increase in specificity must derive from a method of design, rather than by pure chance, because rules must be taken into account first before the specifics can be generated. And evolution is by definition a random process according to its own definition in use, because according to the theory, the process of natural selection is occurring according to natures preference, yet nature cannot plan anything in advance, which is required in order for a set of specifics to occur that are by definition orderly in terms of a procedure.

Any attempt to define evolution as a method or procedure, will in turn, define evolution as a creation, because specifications are required in order for a method to occur. So, for this reason, evolution, as a theory, has attempted to apply a number of rules to the process of natural selection in order to imply that the theory is authoritative, when nothing enslaves a person, and their mind, faster than the adoption of rules which simply do not apply. And the number one rule by the evolutionary theory that simply does not apply, is the rule that a natural process can give rise to new innovations at random.

The theory of evolution has defined itself as being a natural process only according to its own definition in use, which means automatically that a method is involved. So, because the entire hierarchy of evolutionary change has occurred according to a set of preferences, it will mean that the process of evolution was in fact designed, rather than discovered. So, the particular detail that is missing from the theory of evolution, is how do orderly systems derive from a natural process? Because the theory of evolution defines itself as being a completely natural process only, yet there is nothing natural about creativity, because creating is by definition an artificial or supernatural process, rather than a natural one. And a system is by definition a creation due to the application of a method, which excludes evolution as a possible source for a system's formation, because a method must derive by design, either directly or indirectly, otherwise, there would be no causality for an orderly sequence or procedure.

The action of creativity cannot be defined as being a natural process, because there will always be a set of rules in place by the Creator of the process, and it is the rules in place that constitutes as a system, rather than the materials used. A system will always be the result of a procedure in place due to the application of a method, which is why the word, system, and the word, method, are interchangeable. Philosophical materialism is unable to apply a method that can explain the causality of systems, because a system is by definition rule based, and rules are always inferred according to a method or procedure, rather than deriving from materials alone. And any method of reasoning that attempts to explain otherwise has derived by design, because a method of reasoning is evidence of a belief, or system of belief, due to the application of a method. So, because a system is equal to a method or procedure, and because the only causality there is for a method is by design, it will mean that all systems have derived by design, either directly or indirectly, which is self-explanatory.

Evolution, as a theory, is lacking an action that is by definition, specific, as well as innovative, while creativity is defined by an action that is by definition, specific, the same as any other law in physics that is defined by an observable action. And it is for this reason that evolution is defined as a postulation, while the action of creativity is not, because a law in physics always derives from an observable action that is repeatable under demonstration. Yet the one thing here on Earth that is not repeatable under demonstration, nor observable under experimentation, is the supposed history of evolutionary change due to the sheer number of changes that are said to have occurred in order to supposedly progress from a single celled organism to a fully formed human being.

The only word that can be used to describe something new that has just come into existence, according to the OED, is the word create, which is in relation to anything that has been innovated or designed, as well as anything that is the result of a method or plan. So, in order for something to occur naturally, then there must first be a system in place that is working normally, only then, can something abnormal occur by definition of the fact that something normal was occurring to begin with.

The normal workings of a system is equal to a natural process, but there is definitively no natural process that can develop into a method all by itself, because a natural process will always be the result of a method in place, rather than the cause of one. A method in place will always be the evidence of creativity having been applied to the process, and is therefore proof of a Creator as well, which cannot be nature itself, because planning is equal to thinking, which nature, in all of its brilliance, is not highly renowned for.

A system is defined as being equal to a method whereby a process is occurring according to a procedure or plan, and the process is a normal occurrence if the process is working according to plan. While the formation of a system that has occurred naturally, such as a lake, is simply a part of the normal workings of a more complex system that was already in place, because no daughter system is ever more complex than its parent system, the same as a mechanism for a system cannot specify for the system it is for as a working whole.

A natural process will always be according to a system's typical functionality, but the method in place will always derive from the use of planning as a rule, because a method is by definition, specific. So, because the process of a methods formation must derive by design as a rule, it will mean that a method in place is by definition, planned, which can either be due to an artificial process, such as designing and engineering, or a supernatural process, such as a miracle. While a natural process is limited to the number of specifics there are in place to define the process with, which limits natural process to being the normal workings of a system, such as the ecosystem.

This means that the Earth has derived from a supernatural process due to the lack of a natural or artificial process that can give rise to the ecosystem. And the ecosystem is indeed a construct due to the presence of a cycle (such as seasonal cycles) that are repeatable under observation, as well as predictable under demonstration, which cannot occur at random in accordance with the law of probability. The whole purpose of systems study and systems analysis is to develop methods of identification in order to detect faults within a particular system, and then to categorize them into a sequence of high risk to low risk potentials in order to assess the system as a working whole, because an abnormality within a system can be an indicator that a total systems failure is imminent.

The process of detecting faults within a particular system will always be according to a series of abnormalities that have occurred as a sequence, and it is the sequence of abnormalities within a system that gives rise to a method of identification. Such as a cardiograph, which is used as a method of early detection to find faults within the human body, or a group of biomarkers for skin cancer, which are also for determining whether a total systems failure is imminent or not. So, in order to analyse the theory of evolution, then it needs to be broken down into separate stages for the purpose of identification and comparison. The theory of evolution can be broken down into three main theories, which are cosmic evolution, chemical evolution, and biological evolution. But the theory of evolution also has a fourth definition that is rarely ever talked about, which is defined as being a political science from the practice of Social Darwinism.

Social Darwinism is the sociopolitical idea that the principles of evolution can be applied to human society to better govern a given population, but because the theory of evolution is based on natural selection, which is defined as being survival of the fittest, it will mean that the weakest are taken advantage of in order to boost the power of the strong. And this is the main reason why evolution, as a theory, is unethical as a science, because it is highly immoral to take advantage of the weak in order to boost the power of the strong in any instance.

Many will argue that the theory of evolution has nothing to do with Social Darwinism, and to argue against evolution by implying that Social Darwinism is not the result of the evolutionary theory only qualifies as ignorance. But what the individual has not taken into account is that Social Darwinism applies to any political system that has enforced the teaching of evolution. This means that most of the political issues within the United States and elsewhere have everything to do with the teaching of evolution by the State, because the evolutionary theory in practice from education and law is to be defined as Social Darwinism.

> *Quotation: ————————————————————
> Social Darwinists held that the life of humans in society
> was a struggle for existence ruled by "survival of the fittest,"

a phrase proposed by the British philosopher and scientist Herbert Spencer. The social Darwinists (notably Spencer and Walter Bagehot in England and William Graham Sumner in the United States), believed that the process of natural selection acting on variations in the population would result in the survival of the best competitors, and in continuing improvement in the population. Societies were viewed as organisms that evolve in this manner.

Class stratification was justified on the basis of "natural" inequalities among individuals, for the control of property was said to be a correlate of superior and inherent moral attributes such as industriousness, temperance, and frugality. Attempts to reform society through state intervention or other means would, therefore, interfere with natural processes; unrestricted competition, and defence of the status quo were in accord with biological selection. The poor were the "unfit" and should not be aided in the struggle for existence, while wealth was a sign of success. - Source. Encyclopedia Britannica (Social Darwinism).

What is Cosmic Evolution and how is it refuted?

Cosmic evolution is the theory that the universe, and everything within the universe, is the direct result of a cosmic explosion called the Big Bang, which is entirely hypothetical, because that which is in a state of disorder will continue to decline into randomness perpetually unless a method is applied. The Big Bang theory assumes that disorder will eventuate into an orderly system, given enough time, when time is not a mechanism for improvement, because adding time to a process that tends toward disorder only increases the amount of disorder there is over time, rather than increasing in ordered complexity in a matter of time. And all thermodynamic systems tend toward disorder over time in accordance with the law of probability unless a method is applied.

Thus, the Big Bang theory is easily refuted on the basis of systems, because if a method has been applied to the formation of the universe, then the universe is by definition a creation due to the presence of a procedure. A process can only be interpreted via a method, which in turn, defines a method as a procedure, which is the very thing that leaves the evolutionary theory without a plausible explanation for the formation of the universe, because a procedure in place is the evidence of a creation despite anything an atheist might say to the contrary.

So, when ever someone is arguing from a particular viewpoint, then a method of reasoning has been applied, which is the evidence of their creativity whether they are aware of it or not. A procedure in place can only occur as a step-by-step fashion, which cannot be interpreted as a process only, otherwise, there would be no definition for a procedure. Any process that is operating according to a step-by-step procedure, is thereby relative to a creation by reason of the fact that each step during the process is relative to the next, which in turn, requires the application of a method or system of belief. A chain of reasoning is also a system of belief, because there is a procedure in place that defines a step-by-step process in the form of a logical conclusion, or reason of deduction. So, in order to deduce whether a creation has occurred or not, then a method of identification is required first, which cannot derive from philosophical materialism without bringing the term, method, into question.

A method in place will always be the result of creativity having been applied to the materials used, because a method is by definition, specific, due to the use of planning. So, for the purpose of this article, I will attempt to apply a method of reasoning in order to identify a procedure in place for the formation of the universe using systems theory, and systems analysis, as a chain of reasoning. A mechanical system is any group of mechanisms that consist of moving parts in order to achieve a desired effect or designated function. A mechanical system can be something as small as a pocket-watch with internal moving parts, or as large as the solar system itself, because both a pocket-watch, and the solar system, serve as a mechanism for time to be measured by, and both are operating according to a cycle in place that is repeatable under observation, as well as predictable under demonstration, which cannot occur at random over time in accordance with the law of probability.

And the solar system does act as a mechanical or gravitational system, because there are satellite mechanisms in place that give order, stability, and functionality to the system, as well as purpose. In physics, spacetime is any mathematical or theoretical model that utilises the three dimensions of space, and the one dimension of time into a single four-dimensional system known formally as spacetime. The universe is defined as an isolated system due to the law of conservation, which describes energy and mass as being trapped within the system, and anything that acts as an insulating mechanism for the purpose of isolating matter or energy from its surroundings, is by definition a thermodynamic system. So, in order to interpret the formation of the universe in terms of an isolated system, then the thermodynamic principles of entropy must also apply, because there is a thermodynamic system in place that is subject to physical laws, which cannot be excluded under demonstration in order to pave the way for a theoretical explanation.

The universe acts as a mechanism for time to exist due to the existence of four-dimensional spacetime, while the solar system acts as a mechanism for time to be measured by here on Earth. Yet a mechanism for a system cannot specify for the system it is for as a working whole, because an overall method or plan is required first in order to combine each mechanism into a single mechanism called a system. So, because the universe acts as a mechanism for time to exist, it will mean that the universe has derived from a system that is more complex than the universe is by itself, because a mechanism is never more complex than the system it has derived from.

A primary mechanism for a mechanical or gravitational system will always be limited to its basic design unless a method is applied, because a system cannot improve at random due to the principles of entropy, and the law of probability. The solar system is by definition a mechanical or gravitational system, because the satellite mechanisms in place are moving in an orderly fashion, each according to their own seasonal cycles that are repeatable under observation, as well as predictable under demonstration. Any sequence of events that are predictable under demonstration will always be the result of a procedure that is repeating itself according to a cycle in place that is by definition, specific, and therefore, orderly.

Thus, the ordered complexity of the universe is due to the law of conservation whereby the existence of time is conserved as a fourth dimension within three-dimensional space. While the solar system is orderly due to a cycle in place that is repeating itself under observation due to seasonal cycles, which cannot occur at random over time in accordance with the law of probability, because any group of events that can be predicted mathematically or precisely, are by definition, relative, and therefore, specific.

The theory of special relativity attempts to define the universe in terms of its structure, such as the curvature of spacetime. The four dimensions of spacetime in this case is presented as a procedure starting with a singularity, then a straight line, then a circle, which then forms into a sphere in order to create three-dimensional space. Only then can a deep depression within the sphere form the fourth dimension known as spacetime. So, according to Einstein's theory of special relativity, one needs to think of the universe as a type of sphere with a deep depression within its boundary, and everywhere within that depression is defined as three-dimensional space, because anything around the circumference of the sphere would only be two-dimensional. Thus, the curvature of spacetime is defined as two-dimensional, while the fourth dimension is defined as time or location within three spacial dimensions.

This means that the universe has more than one boundary, with the walls of the depression making up the inner boundary, while the outer boundary consists of the overall circumference of the sphere from outside of the depression, which in turn, surrounds the inner boundary. In physics, spacetime is defined as being the fourth dimension, which is the result of three dimensions within space. So, in addition to length, width, and height, there is a fourth dimension that is used so as to be able to employ a geometrical language in discussing a particular phenomenon, such as light. The fourth dimension is also used in physics for describing an object's location within three dimensional space, because no two objects in space can occupy the same place at the same time unless they occupy the same place at different times.

If the universe began as a singularity, or point, and then expanded into a straight line, which then curved backwards on itself to form a circle, as well as twisting into a sphere with a deep depression in order to create three-dimensional space, then time could only have begun to take effect once a point or location had formed, because time is not only defined as the fourth dimension known as spacetime, but also, it is described as a point or location. So, because of this process, time is in constant effect within three dimensions the same as the previous one and two dimensions. This means that once a point or location had formed, there is no way possible to slow light speed down due to the conservation of time. And I understand that before a singularity occurred, the darkness would be void of any dimensions, and would therefore exist without time, but once a singularity had formed, then so also would time and location due to a point of existence, or starting location.

Thus, spacetime is relative to a multi-dimensional theorem, while time in itself is also relative to the beginning and the end, because time has a starting point that began as a singularity, from which, the universe can be compared to in terms of a sequence or procedure. So, because the universe has a starting point, and because the process began as a procedure, it will mean that the universe is engaged in a countdown procedure by the inclusion of time. A procedure is a step-by-step approach to forming a process, but once the process is finished, then the end of the process has occurred. Thus, time is relative to the beginning and the end by definition of the word, procedure. And the universe is indeed engaged in a countdown procedure by the inclusion of time and rules, because time is relative to the law of probability, and rules are applicable to any system. The end of time is relative to a system's failure, which is in accordance with the law of probability, because the more rules a system has, the more likely the system will fail.

So, in order for the Creator to correct the system He has created, He thereby entered the system in order to create a new system, thereby conquering death by His resurrection from the dead, which then gave rise to a system of equality that shall endure through strife and retribution by our enemy the devil. In order to interpret a rule in both science and law, then a system of theology is also required, which must derive itself from the Holy Bible for the good of the people, and the common law. If we are to interpret systems using secular ideology only, then there will be no correct interpretation of the law, whether scientific or regulatory, because science is governed by ethics, and a regulation is mandatory, which must be self-explanatory or there will be the problem of indoctrination caused by the enforcement of a particular theory that was false from its own assertions.

The Big Bang theory that has utterly failed as a system of belief due to the nature of philosophical materialism, which attempts to apply a system of belief, whilst disqualifying the need for a Creator, as well as theological principle. Theological principle is mandatory when describing a given phenomena, because the adoption of rules will apply whether the observer is aware of it or not. The evolutionary theory that has been used from a secular premise in a desperate attempt to apply a system of rules in order to exhibit atheism as a form of social dominance, which has now led to a society based on science fiction, rather than the practice of law and order, due to the adoption of the Big Bang theory as mandatory from public education. And I am not arguing that creation science should be made mandatory in this matter anymore than secular science should be made mandatory by the establishment clause of a secular government, but that a system of equal opportunity should exist for the benefit of the student who is entering a legal system with their own experience that holds to a Biblical definition of man by the rights of conscience.

*Quotation: ────────────────────────
"The law that entropy always increases holds, I think, the supreme position among the laws of nature. If someone points out to you that your pet theory of the universe is in disagreement with Maxwell's equations; Then so much the worse for Maxwell's equations. If it is found to be contradicted by observation, well, these experimentalists do bungle things sometimes. But if your theory is found to be against the Second Law of Thermodynamics, then I can give you no hope; There is nothing for it but to collapse into the deepest humiliation. The beginning of the universe seems to present insuperable difficulties unless we agree to look on it as frankly supernatural." - Sir Arthur Stanley Eddington, was an English astronomer, physicist, and mathematician. The Eddington limit, is the natural limit to the luminosity of stars, which provided one of the earliest confirmations of general relativity in 1919. Source: The Nature of the Physical World written by Sir Arthur Stanley Eddington. (Documented in the year 1915). (Description of Sir Arthur Stanley Eddington by Wikipedia Encyclopedia).

The evidence of a creation will always be due to the application of a method, which then results in a procedure through due process. And the evidence that a procedure has occurred to the formation of the universe, is entirely due to the existence of spacetime as a multi-dimensional theorem. Spacetime itself can be broken into four or more stages with the first being a starting location (singularity), then a line (length), then a circle (radius), then a sphere (volume) with the measurement of time being the fifth aspect known as (travel) or (memory). Whenever something is travelling through space, it will leave a path, whether it be an object in motion or a beam of light, the principle remains due to distance travelled, as well as size and force. Anything that exists within the universe can be measured in terms of distance due to size, motion, and force, because size, motion, and force are relative to a form of measurement.

Thus, the measurement of an object or force in motion is relative to time and distance travelled within a multi-dimensional theorem, which is equal to a combination of location, speed, trajectory, volume, and distance travelled, with memory being the fifth aspect known also as rule or distance travelled. A ruler consists of increments that act as a standard of measurement with a space for memory, so that anything which travels from point A to point B can be measured in terms of distance travelled or time elapsed; Meaning that the universe acts as a measuring device due to the existence of time. Time will always be measured in increments with a sequence or procedure in place, the same as any ruler, which is the evidence of a creation due to the presence of a procedure involving the formation of the universe in terms of a sequence. So, in order for a measurement to occur in terms of time and space, then a set of rules are required first, thus constituting the universe as a system of measurement due to the presence of a rules, such as physical laws, which act as a means of measurement in physics, or system of displacement in terms of mass and energy distribution functions.

According to the theory of special relativity, the existence of four-dimensional spacetime can be measured in terms of a procedure starting with a point (location), a line (length), a circle (radius), a sphere (volume), and then a deep depression within the sphere, (current or direction of flow), so that the direction of an electrical circuit is measured in terms of location, speed, trajectory, and distance traveled, which in turn, defines the measurement of spacetime as a graphical model due to a third angle projection known as a stereographic projection, or polar grid. This theory implies that the universe is polar active with a deep depression at either end of the sphere in order to create four-dimensional spacetime, which has occurred as a procedure with a sequence in place. While the method itself is supernatural due to the lack of a natural process that can cause a system of measurement to occur by chance. And a system of measurement is required when explaining the formation of the universe in terms of an electrical matrix, or polar grid, because a polar grid is governed its size, motion, and force.

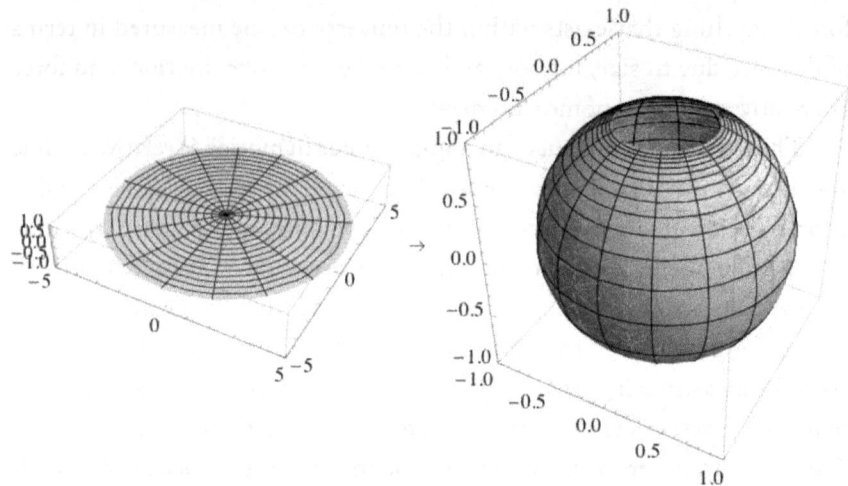

Image result for a polar grid or stereographic projection illustrating an electrical matrix in terms of a flat spacetime geometry. Source: Wikipedia Encyclopedia.

The plane or circumference of a polar grid appears with a deep depression at either end of the sphere, with the top and bottom areas of the grid sinking as they approach the magnetic Northern and Southern poles. This graphical model not only describes the electrical grid of the Earth in terms of a magnetic field, or two dimensional plane of existence, but also, the universe, as I will attempt to explain throughout this article in order to define the matrix as the electrical network of the universe. And one must keep in mind that, A) The curvature of spacetime is relative to a polar grid in order to define the curvature of spacetime as a flat two-dimensional plane of existence. B) The process of formation began as a procedure. And C) A procedure in place is the evidence of a creation.

The cosmic theory of evolution involving the Big Bang asserts that the universe has spread itself out from a singularity, thereby accelerating away from a single point or location at warp speed via a natural process. This assertion assumes that all of the energy within the universe has derived from a single location in time that was so compressed it then exploded and caused light speed to occur at an accelerated rate, and has been slowing down over time since the Big Bang occurred. But the problem with this theory, is that the speed of light within a vacuum is a mathematical constant, rather than a variable.

The existence of time within spacetime is due to the three dimensions of space, with time being the fourth dimension known as location. But if time began as a point or location, then the first one dimension of a singularity is also affected by time. In theoretical physics, scientists theorize that when the speed of light is approached time stops. But because time is relative to all physical interactions, while light is a manifestation, rather than a physical object, it will mean that time is unaffected by light, because the speed of light is a constant within a vacuum according to observation, which is due to the lack of resistance within a vacuum; Meaning that light cannot slow down or accelerate within a vacuum as proponents of the Big Bang theory have postulated.

The measurement of time in terms of a flat spacetime geometry may be retarded or accelerated through gravitational systems, such as the case with the Shapiro Time Delay, but the absolute measurement of time is measured by a speed limit, which is defined as the speed of light within a vacuum. When the mass of a gravitational object comes into contact with an electrical or magnetic field, the field will distort, giving rise to the Shapiro Time Delay; Meaning that the curvature of spacetime can warp as the magnetic field of the universe also warps when a electrical disturbance occurs. Warp speed within outer-space is the hypothetical model for the Big Bang theory in that time must also warp in order for the light of distant galaxies to reach the Earth in time, which is more commonly known as the cosmic inflation theory, or Big Bang model.

According to the current model of the Big Bang theory, known formerly as cosmic inflation theory, light is slowing down over time due to the vast distances between separate regions in space, and was moving faster in the past in order for the distance that light must travel to reach the Earth in time. So, in order for the Big Bang theory to be considered, then light must be slowing down over time, and was moving faster in the past due to the enormous distance between separate regions in space, because the distance at which light must travel exceeds the supposed age of the universe, which is more widely known as the Horizon Problem.

As a photon of light is moving through a vacuum, there is no resistance, but when light comes into contact with matter, the light is either refracted or absorbed, rather than slowing down. This is the same as light bouncing off of a zigzag set of walls, which thereby increases the distance that light must travel in order to get from point A, to point B, in a certain length of time, giving the illusion that light is slowing down as it passes through or around an object. This means that the more dense an object is, the longer it will take for the light to pass through the object due to refraction, and as light passes through an object, heat is generated, because light is being absorbed.

So, the speed of light is not slowing down as it filters through an object, which means definitively that the measurement of time has a universal standard the same as the speed of light has a speed limit within three-dimensional space. And this is an opposing view to current theoretical physics, but if there was no universal standard to measure time, then the speed of light within a vacuum would not be a mathematical constant, because both time, and the speed of light, are relative to the same phenomenon known as speed. So, a mathematical time constant, or universal standard for the measurement of time is governed by three main factors. 1) Time is in constant effect due to a point or location. 2) The speed of light and time are both relative to the same phenomenon known as speed. And 3) Because the speed of light within a vacuum has a speed limit.

According to Einstein's theory of relativity, when an object is moving at the speed of light, the force of the object reaches infinity, and that which is infinite remains infinite by definition of the fact that it was infinite to begin with. This means that a slowly expanding universe could not have derived from cosmic inflation via a Big Bang as many have proposed, because if a singularity exploded resulting in an infinite amount of force in order to expand the universe in such a way that no time was necessary, then the expansion rate within outer-space would remain infinite in speed. So, for this reason, the universe cannot be defined as infinite in size or force due to a slow expansion rate within outer-space, and is thereby orderly due to the conservation of time involving the speed of light within a vacuum.

Thus, the hypothetical model of cosmic inflation involving the warp speed of light from an infinitesimal region, is a mathematical impossibility, because in order for light to reach warp speed, then its force must remain infinite in speed, which cannot be feasible due to the conservation of time, and a slow expansion rate within outer-space. So, in order to explain a plausible reason as to why distant regions in outer-space are in close contact with one another so that light can propagate across the universe, as well as reaching the Earth in time from distant galaxies without invoking the temporary absence of physical laws, (such is the case with a variable speed of light) then light itself must be reflecting off of something else in terms of a mirror image or projection in order to propagate across vast regions in space.

According to astrophysics, the sun, moon, and stars are all reflective in terms of light. So, in order to understand how light can propagate across vast regions in space without invoking the temporary absence of physical laws, then a means of reflection, or projection, is required first, otherwise, there would be nothing to propagate light within a vacuum. This means that when light is generated, a means of reflection is also required, or there would be no way to view a spectrum of light. A projection is anything that extends outwards from something else, such as an image projected onto a surface. So, in order for light to propagate across the universe in such a way that vast regions in space are in close contact with one another by the propagation of light, then the universe must be projecting or reflecting off of something else in order to propagate light. So, for the purpose of this article, I will attempt to define a means of reflection in order to define what is causing starlight to reach the Earth at an accelerated rate in terms of a projection or procedure without invoking the temporary absence of physical laws.

The evidence that a procedure has occurred in regards to the formation of the universe, is entirely due to a point, (starting location) a line, (length) a circle, (radius) a sphere (volume), and then a deep depression within the sphere (current or direction of flow), so that the curvature of spacetime is governed by five types of measurement, such as location, length, radius, volume, and direction of travel, thus constituting the measurement of spacetime as finite, rather than infinite and size or force due to a system of measurement in place. And yes, the universe is measurable due to the existence of time, which cannot be infinite due to the presence of a procedure. The universe cannot be defined as infinite in terms of size or force due to the measurement of time. While the ordered complexity of the universe is indeed infinite due to changes in conditions, such as random fluctuations. A random fluctuation within an operational system is governed by a set of parameters in order for a fluctuation to occur, such as energy transformation, which is governed by a set of parameters known as linear and angular momentum. And anything that is governed by a set of parameters is by definition a creation, because parameters must always be inferred the same as any set of rules.

The evolutionary idea that the universe is the result of random chance derives from philosophical materialism, in that all processes are by definition, natural, when the universe cannot be a natural phenomenon due to the law of conservation, and the second law of thermodynamics, which defines the system as orderly, rather than random. And the second law of thermodynamics involving entropy law does apply to the formation of the universe, because the universe is defined as an isolated system. The process of entropy law states that order will decline into disorder over time, because there are far more random probabilities than specifics within a typical system. All thermodynamic systems tend toward disorder in accordance with entropy law, and the law of probability, so that anything random will remain random unless a method is applied, which then defines the process as a procedure due to the application of a method. And the universe does exhibit the properties of a creation due to the formation of spacetime involving a procedure, which cannot be denied on the basis of theory, because it is the correct word definitions in place that are authoritative when describing a given phenomena.

*Quotation: ————————————————————

"If for the entire universe we conceive the same magnitude to be determined, consistently and with due regard to all circumstances, which for a single body I have called 'entropy', and if at the same time we introduce the other and simpler conception of energy, we may express in the following manner the fundamental laws of the universe which correspond to the two fundamental theorems of the mechanical theory of heat: the energy of the universe is constant; the entropy of the universe tends to a maximum." - Rudolf Clausius. Source: Mechanical Theory of Heat, written by Rudolf Clausius. (Documented in the year 1865).

The evolutionary theory has been used as an excuse by Big Bang cosmologists to assert that entropy will decrease over time via a natural process, thus paving the way for the Big Bang in terms of a theory involving a causality for ordered complexity. But the problem with this theory is that once a thermodynamic process has occurred, there is no way to reverse the process that has already occurred, which is both observational, as well as self-explanatory. Thus, entropy decrease cannot occur unless the rate of entropy is offset by an insulating mechanism, because thermal radiation must be conserved or isolated in order to reduce the rate of entropy, while any loss of thermal energy during a thermal reaction will be defined as entropy.

So, in order for an insulating mechanism to occur that can isolate energy input, then a system with boundaries is required first before the energy input occurs, otherwise, the energy is wasted in terms of its input. This means that the universe was pre-specified in order to act as a means of isolation, which in turn, requires a set of parameters in order to establish a causality for ordered complexity and thermodynamic systems, because ordered complexity derives from taking rules into account in order to establish a set of parameters or boundaries. Any theory that attempts to define the universe as a random phenomenon will be defined as completely hypothetical, because a system of isolation must utilize the energy input via one or more boundaries that have been pre-specified, otherwise, the system would have no purpose. And a thermodynamic system will always have a designated function in terms of a procedure, which means that all mechanical systems have a purpose, which is to act as a means of isolation for the purpose of conserving thermal energy.

While entropy on the other hand is to act as a means of displacement in terms of thermal energy in order to regulate the system's internal temperature, rather than a means of thermal conservation, so that any system that is for the purpose of conserving mass or thermal energy will be defined as specific. The law of conservation not only applies to all thermodynamic systems, but also, time, because the law of probability restricts all thermodynamic reactions to being within a time limit, thus constituting a thermodynamic process as a procedure due to the conservation of time.

> *Quotation: ————————————————————
> "It may be that there is no such thing as an equable motion, whereby time may be accurately measured. All motions may be accelerated or retarded, but the true, or equable, progress of absolute time is liable to no change." - Sir Isaac Newton. Source: The Principia, Mathematical Principles of Natural Philosophy. (Documented July 5, 1687).

A constant is defined as anything that is occurring continuously over a period of time, and is thereby, perpetual, while the definition of "perpetual" is defined as unchanging or continuous. Because of this, light speed within a vacuum is defined as perpetual, rather than infinite, because the speed of light within a vacuum is governed by a mathematical constant, which is evidence for the conservation of time. Thus, a time constant must exist, which restricts all theoretical models of the Big Bang to being within a time limit due to the application of a procedure involving a particular sequence.

All physical interactions within the universe occur within a set span of time as a result of due process, which is not always relative to a natural process, because the only way to interpret a process, is by the application of a method; Meaning that all processes, whether random or not, have derived from a procedure, either directly or indirectly. And a cosmic explosion, as in the case of the evolutionary Big Bang theory, is indeed subject to a procedure the same as any other theory in science. Thus, any exclusion of physical laws in order to propagate a given theory will be defined as hypothetical or philosophical, as in the case with the Big Bang theory.

So, because the cosmic theory of evolution involving the Big Bang explanation is entirely reliant on the temporary absence of physical laws (such is the case with a variable speed of light within a vacuum) in order to propagate the theory, it will mean that the Big Bang theory is entirely hypothetical, which is not expedient for the scientific method, nor is it safe, because the idea that physical laws are secondary to a given theory is no different than a lie. And we are as a people reliant on the truth, rather than science fiction in order that we can propose a given theory that is plausible, which cannot derive itself from the absence of physical laws, because it is the laws in place that restricts the question as to why we exist. So, for this reason, physical laws must exist so that all physical interactions should obey these laws, which is the same for a just law or moral principle as it is for physical laws. And the one physical law that cannot change and governs all physical interactions, is the law of time.

The law of time is applicable to all physical interactions, because all physical interactions occur within a set span of time. The law of time is thereby relative to the beginning and the end through due process, because all physical interactions have a cause and effect, which results in a consequence or procedure. The law of time is also relative to the conservation of time within three dimensional space known formally as spacetime. Thus, the universe itself is engaged in a countdown procedure with a beginning and an end due to the formation of the universe involving the law of time, and the law of probability, which in turn, sets the limitations of the universe in terms of a system.

So, for this reason, nothing within spacetime is infinite in terms of force or motion, because there is nothing within four dimensions that is defined as infinite due to the presence of time, which is evidence for the beginning and the end. Thus, eternity is defined as infinite in terms of time and truth, while the universe is limited due to the conservation of time. The human conscience is the only thing we have in order to invent a word, rule, or law, so that all physical laws have derived from a source of conscience by definition of the word, rule. And it is God the Creator who has established all things by His word, so that all things are subject to His word in accordance with His moral law.

Thus, it is a rule of thumb that rules can be broken, such as moral law, while physical laws remain in effect due to the measurement of time. And though spacetime may warp (as in the case when object comes into contact with an electromagnetic field), the absolute measurement of time cannot warp due to a mathematical constant involving the speed of light within a vacuum, which in turn, places a time limit on all physical interactions through due process. The due process of physical laws restricts all random probabilities to being within a time limit by definition of the word, procedure, because all physical interactions occur within a set span of time through due process. Thus, the due process of physical laws is relative to the beginning and the end, because all processes must be interpreted via a method, which is the evidence of a creation due to the presence of a procedure involving the law of probability.

The Big Bang theory is a hypothetical assertion that adding time to a given process will increase the odds of the overall event occurring within a set span of time. But the problem with this idea, is that anything which tends toward disorder over time will only increase in disorder in a matter of time unless a method is applied, which is entirely due to the law of probability involving random particle distribution functions. So, in order for any physical interaction to be quantified, measured, or otherwise, become likely in terms of probability, then a method is required first. Otherwise, there would be nothing to increase the likelihood of the overall event occurring due to the lack of a procedure. Thus, time is not a mechanism for improvement by any stretch of the imagination due to the law of probability involving mass and energy distribution functions, and the measurement of time. This means that a universal countdown procedure was put into effect when particles began to distribute at random, which is in accordance with the law of probability, and the conservation of time.

*Quotation: ————————————————
"Nature never undertakes any change unless her interests are served by an increase in entropy." - Max Planck. Source: Commentary by Max Planck on James Swinburne's 1902 entropy debate views. (Documented in the year 1903).

Time is not a preference that can be altered by the imagination, nor is time a physical manifestation, but rather, time is the consequence of a procedure, and so long as a procedure exists, then there will always be the aspect of time in terms of a conservation principle. The conservation of time is relative to a procedure, because a procedure works as a sequence the same as time, and anything that works as a sequence is subject to a numerical value involving a system of measurement. Thus, any and all processes, whether physical or not, are governed by time, so that all processes are subject to a procedure with time being the governing factor that sets a limitation on the universe in terms of size, and distribution.

The notion by modern physicists that time can slow down once the speed of light is reached is only according to one's perception, because the speed of light within a vacuum has not changed during any observational experiment, while a person's perception of time varies according to the speed at which their mind is processing information. Studies have shown that a person's sense of time will slow down when sleep deprivation occurs; Meaning that the longer you stay awake, the faster time appears to lapse, because the brain's processing power is reducing itself the longer you're awake. And this is also why sleep appears to take only a few moments, when in fact, there have been a number of hours that have passed by, because when the body is sleeping, there is a significantly reduced amount of processing occurring within the brain, giving the illusion that time has lapsed much faster than what it actually has.

In physics and systems analysis, a time constant is defined by the amount of time it takes for an input signal to reach an output effect, such as a microphone and a speaker, whereby a signal input is followed by a signal output, which in turn, defines an LTI system, or, linear time-invariant system. A time constant is also used to characterize the frequency response of various signal processing systems, which can be anything from a digital watch that has a processing unit and a digital display, or a defibrillator that can process the heart's electrical impulses and respond with a correct rhythm in time.

So, because a time constant is based on the time it takes for a signal to be sent and received, it will mean that there is a universal standard in place for time to be measured by, which is defined as the speed of light within a vacuum, from which, all other measurable phenomena can be compared to in terms of speed. And a biological example of an LTI system would be the human brain, because the human brain receives signals via inputs, and then processes the signals in order for an output signal to occur, and the longer it takes for the brain to process the signals, the slower one's perception of time will be.

A second example of an LTI system would be the electrical matrix, or polar grid of the universe, because each electromagnetic pulse that a quantum field produces is relative to a signal input and a signal output, resulting in a broad range of frequencies known as a broadband spectrum. The input signal of a quantum field is relative to an electrical matrix that is in constant effect due to a polar grid, which acts as a processing unit for atomic sequencing. A microwave pulse that is generated by an electrical field, such as a quantum field, is equal to a linear time-invariant system due to a signal input, and a signal output for the purpose of processing information involving atomic sequencing. This processing unit is designed to govern the structure of an atom, which is polar active and will respond to a correct frequency in time, thus constituting the electrical matrix of the universe as a linear time-invariant system for the purpose of stabilising an atom within the perimeter of this field.

> *Quotation: ─────────────────────────
> "This most beautiful system of the sun, planets, and comets could only proceed from the counsel and dominion of an intelligent and powerful Being. And if the fixed stars are the centers of other like systems, these, being formed by the like wise counsel, must be all subject to the dominion of One, especially since the light of the fixed stars is of the same nature with the light of the sun, and from every system light passes into all the other systems; And lest the systems of the fixed stars should, by their gravity, fall on each other, He has placed those systems at immense distances from one another. - Sir Isaac Newton. Source: The Principia, Mathematical Principles of Natural Philosophy. (Documented July 5, 1687).

According to Einstein's theory of general relativity, everything is neutral, and everything is relative, and that it is the mind that attaches meaning to a given event, so that we determine our reaction or non-reaction in each situation by choice, and can therefore change the outcome of a particular event by the application of a method. So, because everything is relative according to the theory of relativity, it will mean that everything is relative to the Creator, because each physical law is relative to each other, resulting in an irreducibly complex system whereby the removal of one physical law would result in a chain reaction that leads to a total systems failure.

And everything is neutral for two main reasons. Firstly; Because everything occurs according to the normal rhythms of a system unless the system is acted upon by an external force. And secondly; Because anything random will remain random unless a method is applied, which then defines the process as a procedure due to the application of a method. So, it is the law of probability that demonstrates the law of relativity according to the principles of modern physics, because in order for any group of events to be relative in relation to each other, resulting in a predictable sequence or procedure, with each term in the sequence being relative to the next, then a method must be applied, which in turn, gives meaning to a particular event, as well as purpose.

In the beginning there was only one rule, such in the case with Adam and Eve in the garden that God did create. But because Adam and Eve chose to disobey this one rule, it mean that a chain reaction was put into effect, thus leading to a systems failure. So, in order to correct the system, God the Creator laid down His life for the system He created, because we are as individuals subject to the system, so that no individual person is more important than the system itself. Thus, we are to abide by the system that God has created, which is a system of moral law, as defined by the Gospel message of hope and salvation, which liberates a person through the system. If the individual human being was more important than the system that God did create, then there would be no such thing as death, which is why a system of justice that caters to an equality is more important than meeting the demands of minority groups who question basic public morals on the basis of evolution, and secular science.

The action of creativity is in itself relative to choice, because all creativity derives from a set of preferences the same as choices do. The purpose of systems science and systems study is to identify how each type of system relates to one another, thereby establishing the law of relativity in terms of a practice or principle in systems theory. While the evolutionary theory attempts to incorporate the law of relativity by defining every living creature as related to one another via a bacterium, which is not expedient for mankind as a working whole, because this is the very thing that robs a person of their true identity as a created human being. One does not need to prove the existence of the Creator, but rather, one only needs to prove that the universe is a creation. And a supernatural Creator God is indeed a requirement in order to interpret the causality of systems, because a system requires an entity that is self-aware, and can issue a command in order for a method to be established according to a procedure, otherwise, everything would be entirely random, rather than relative.

So, it is therefore self-evident that the Creator in Heaven did not require a system to be in existence before Him, because God the Creator is defined as being the cause of every system under Him, which has derived from His creativity, either directly or indirectly, otherwise, there would be no causality for a procedure due to the law of probability. The law of probability states that all thermodynamic systems tend toward disorder over time, because there are far more random variables within a typical system than there are specifics. So, a system will always be found in a state of maximum entropy or moving towards it, thereby establishing the only causality for a system's formation or improvement as having derived from the action of creativity, either directly or indirectly.

In order for any level of ordered complexity to occur within the system of the universe, then the mechanisms within the system must have had creativity applied to them either directly or indirectly. Otherwise, there would be no causality for ordered complexity within the system of the universe, because ordered complexity cannot derive at random in accordance with the law of probability. The only causality there is for ordered complexity, is by design, because ordered complexity derives from taking rules into account, (such as physical laws) which is required in order to generate the specifics needed in order to establish a system or procedure. And the universe is indeed orderly, rather than random, because each physical law is relative to the next resulting in an irreducibly complex system, which is evidence of design, because that which is relative, is also that which is specific in terms of a process or procedure. So, in order for something to be infinitely improbable according to the principles of mathematics, then ordered complexity cannot derive at random, otherwise, nothing would be probable or quantifiable in terms of a sequence or procedure.

*Quotation: ———————————————————

The idea that the second law of thermodynamics, or entropy law, is a law of disorder, or that dynamically ordered states are infinitely improbable, is due to Boltzmann's view of the second law of thermodynamics. In particular, it was Boltzmann's attempt to reduce it to a stochastic collision function, or law of probability, following from the random collisions of mechanical particles. A dynamically ordered state, is one with molecules moving at the same speed and in the same direction, Boltzmann concluded, is thus: "The most improbable case conceivable; An infinitely improbable configuration of energy." - Source: Wikipedia Encyclopedia (Ludwig Boltzmann - Second thermodynamics law as a law of disorder).

Ludwig Boltzmann (1844 - 1906) was an Austrian physicist who is widely known for his contribution to the development of quantum mechanics resulting in the current explanation of the second law of thermodynamics. According to Ludwig Boltzmann's example of a dynamically ordered state, any group of particles that move in the same direction with the same amount of force is infinitely improbable; Meaning that it cannot occur at random over any length of time proposed in accordance with the law of probability.

A dynamically ordered state is one where the molecules are moving at the same speed and direction produced by the same amount of force was concluded to be the most improbable case conceivable; "An infinitely improbable configuration of energy," as cited by Ludwig Boltzmann's interpretation of mass and energy distribution functions. The rule of a dynamically ordered state not only applies to quantum systems, but also, the laws of motion as well, because the laws of motion are governed by the distribution of mass and energy. And an example of a dynamically ordered state, would be the solar system itself, because each planet within the system is orbiting the sun in the same direction with the same continual amount of force that is produced by the sun's gravitational effect, which proves definitively that the solar system is a construct.

While a biological example of a dynamically ordered state, would be the human body, which consists of such an arrangement by the circulatory system, which must move in the same direction with the same amount of force according to each heartbeat, otherwise, the system's flow of particles will become blocked or choked. So, for this reason, the only causality there is for the solar system, and the human body, is by design, because the only way to increase the likelihood of a dynamically ordered state occurring, is by the application of a method.

Anything that is produced repeatedly under the same varying conditions, is by definition manufactured, because the end result produces an end product or desired effect according to a cycle in place that is repeatable under demonstration. So, in order for a cycle to occur that is orderly, and therefore, predictable, then a method is required first, and the solar system is working according to a method in place that is repeatable under observation, as well as predictable under demonstration, because any process that is repeating itself under observation is by definition a procedure.

This means quite definitively that the solar system has derived by design, because a method is required in order for a procedure to occur, which in turn, defines the solar system as a creation, rather than a random phenomenon due to the presence of a cycle. While any theory that attempts to define the formation of the universe in terms of a process or procedure will inadvertently define the universe as a creation due to the application of a method. And it is for this reason that the Big Bang theory exhibits all of the hallmarks of a creation, simply because there is a procedure in place that has derived from a chain of reasoning or method.

Chaos theory assumes that a random process over time will eventually progress into an orderly sequence, given enough time. And the example that Boltzmann provided was from a deck of cards that were arranged randomly, and the more times the deck is shuffled, the more likely the deck will be placed into a standard numerical order. But unfortunately for the theory, a deck of cards that are arranged into a numerical sequence will always be according to a standard in place that defines the sequence as orderly, which cannot occur at random, because a standard in place must always be inferred according to a set of rules.

A standard is that which is pre-specified in order to give definition to a given sequence or procedure, such as a numerical standard from 1 to 100, which in itself, is a part of a universal standard for numbers, and therefore, cannot derive at random due to the presence of a procedure that is in constant effect. And a deck of cards is indeed subject to a procedure in place, because each card has a numerical value within the deck that is governed by a numerical standard with a sequence in place. While a cycle in place that is repeating itself under observation is also subject to entropy law, because the more times a cycle occurs, the more likely the cycle will break, which is in accordance with the law of probability. And this is why Boltzmann's chaos theory has been scientifically refuted, because it is a cardinal principle in physics that ordered complexity cannot derive at random over time, otherwise, there would be nothing to define that which is orderly in terms of a sequence or procedure.

For example: Each term within a sequence that is specific in relation to the next term, (such as a numerically ordered sequence from 1 to 100) will always be relative to a procedure in place, which in turn, defines the sequence, and the method, as orderly. And this is the same for the solar system as well, because there is a sequence in place that is specific in relation to each planet's position in order for the system to be perpetual according to its seasonal cycles. So, because numbers only work in sequences, and because a sequence is subject to the law of probability, it will mean that the only way to achieve an orderly system, is by the application of a method due to the presence of a procedure. And numbers do work according to a method that is universal in terms of a procedure, and is thereby evidence of a supernatural Creator, because an orderly sequence that is governed by a procedure in place must always be inferred according to a set of rules in order to establish a set of parameters, which in turn, sets the limitations of a system's operation.

According to Einstein's theory of relativity, $E = mc2$; Meaning that atoms are made from energy. But this in no way defines an atom as having derived from energy alone, because we understand through observation and experimentation that there is no natural process that can cause energy to become a solid object due to the first law of thermodynamics that includes the law of conservation, which states that mass and energy cannot be created or destroyed via a natural process, but energy can transform from one type of energy to another. So, because the propagation of light has no mass, only force, it will mean that light cannot be converted into matter under experimentation. And any so-called experiment that claims otherwise is entirely hypothetical, because a physical experiment must begin the process with a form of matter first, rather than just light, because the existence of matter cannot be excluded under any physical demonstration in physics.

But, because atoms are made from energy, it will mean that matter has potential energy, which means that matter can give off light, rather than light producing matter. The cosmic theory of evolution must assume that matter came from light in order to try and explain the causality of a singularity, whereby light was compressed into an infinitesimal region that finally exploded, because gases, liquids and solids cannot be compressed into an infinitesimal region under experimentation. So, in contrast, light is propagated from matter, rather than matter propagating from light; Meaning that atoms and light coexist. And an example of how light is propagated would be the sun, which is comprised of matter in a state of nuclear fusion that produces radiation and warmth.

Radiation is a type of energy that comes from a radioactive source. Heat that is propagated from a source of radiation, such as nuclear fusion, a flame, friction, or electricity, exists as a wave of radiation that radiates across a given area. Heat can be generated by either light or matter, but it will always be matter that propagates light, because the only way for radiation to occur is from a radioactive source of materials in a state of electrolysis, such as atoms. This means that the cosmic theory of evolution is without a causality for the universe and matter, because the theory demands that matter derives from light, when the truth is that light derives from a source of radiation, such as atomic particles in a state of collision, or when they're sharing electrons.

According to modern physics, particle collisions are due to thermal motion and are entirely random in distribution; Meaning that thermal radiation moves in all directions unless it is concentrated into a beam. A beam of light has an expected geometry that is direct in terms of its direction of travel, but will eventually disappear when the source of light ceases, or when light is absorbed by an object, or when the light begins to disperse. So, because light cannot maintain its position as matter does, it will mean that light is emitted, rather than stored. This means that there is no way to trap light within an infinitesimal region so that a Big Bang explosion can occur from a supposed singularity of light, because any form of energy stored will always derive from the presence of atoms.

So, atoms were therefore in effect at the same time that light was in effect, because, A) Light cannot exist without atoms. B) Atoms store potential energy, while light does not. And C) Radiation is a form of light that derives from atoms, rather than atoms deriving from light. So, until the evolutionists figure out how to trap light, it will mean that light emits from atoms, rather than atoms emitting from light. And in any event, an explosion is not a source of ordered complexity by any stretch of the imagination, because a thermal explosion will always be subject to a random distribution of particles, and is thereby subject to the thermodynamic principles of entropy law involving the law of probability, which tends toward disorder in every conceivable scenario.

The process of entropy cannot increase the level of ordered complexity there is within the universe at random, because ordered complexity is relative to a procedure that is specific, rather than a disorderly process that is entirely random. Any level of ordered complexity within an isolated system must derive from the action of creativity, either directly or indirectly, because anything that has not derived by design, is by definition, random. The presence of an orderly state within an isolated system, (such as the conservation of time or a numerical standard) will always be a consequence of a group of actions that were specific in relation to each other, and therefore, relative, resulting in a procedure.

Any sequence of events that are specific in relation to the next will always be the result of a system in place whereby a method has been employed, and it is never the sequence used that defines the process as orderly, while the method in place does. A system will always be the result of a method in place in order to define whether the process is orderly or not in terms of a procedure, because each stage during the process of a system's formation must be relative to the next in order to define a process in terms of a sequence.

So, because the phases of the sun and the moon are governed by a cycle in place, and are therefore predictable, it will mean automatically that the solar system is orderly, because any sequence of events that are relative to each other resulting in a procedure cannot occur at random in accordance with the law of probability. In physics, the principle of quantum uncertainty implies that it is not possible to predict the value of a quantity with absolute certainty, even if all initial conditions are present.

So, in order for a group of events to be quantified mathematically so that a prediction can occur, then a sequence must be identified first, otherwise, the outcome is entirely unpredictable. This means that any action that is not pre-specified will tend toward disorder over time, while any action that is specific in relation to the next will lead to a consequence that is unpredictable due to a set of variables that have a cause and effect. But if the consequence is understood due to a cycle in place that is repeating itself under observation, then a prediction can occur under demonstration, but the prediction will always be subject to internal and external influences, such as quantum entanglement.

For example: Weather forecasting is the application of quantum physics in order to predict the conditions of the atmosphere in regards to a specific location and time. Weather forecasts are made by collecting quantitative data about the current state of the atmosphere, land, and ocean by using meteorology to project how the atmosphere will change at a given place within a set span of time. A weather prediction can occur if the specifics are in place, but a prediction will always be based on a set of specifics that do not incorporate any internal or external influences that will have a cause and effect, which is the main reason why a weather prediction is never 100% correct, because the conditions are constantly changing due to quantum entanglement.

Quantum entanglement is due to a quantum field involving random particle collisions that have a cause and effect, and are therefore unpredictable, resulting in quantum uncertainty. Ordered complexity cannot derive at random due to quantum uncertainty, because in order for an orderly procedure to occur that is by definition, predictable, then a method is required first. And this is no different to how the weather works along with weather predictions, because if the weather can be predicted with a high level of accuracy, then the weather is thereby orderly according to a set of variables that are fluctuating within a cycle or system, such as seasonal changes and the water cycle.

A system in place that is oscillating according to a set of variables is indeed predictable, because there is a cycle occurring with a repeatable outcome, and the better the sequence is understood, the greater the accuracy will be when a prediction is made, because it is a sequence in place that gives rise to predictability, which in turn, gives rise to reliability. And it is for the purpose of predictability that systems exists, otherwise, nothing could be predicted with any level of accuracy, because everything would be entirely random.

Any set of events that are relative to each other must occur according to a set of rules that are also specific in relation to each other resulting in a procedure, which is never by random chance according to the law of probability, because the only way to increase the odds of a group of events occurring that are specific in relation to each other, is by the application of a method. The origin of the universe cannot be explained in terms of a natural process, because there is a set of physical laws in place that are specific in relation to each other, and are therefore, relative.

This means that a set of events must have occurred that were specific in relation to each other resulting in a system or procedure, which is physical proof that a method has been applied to the formation of the universe, because there are multiple laws in place that work together for a single purpose, which is to create space, as well as time. Hence the term, spacetime. In theoretical physics, cosmologists attempt to explain the causality of the universe in terms of a procedure, because the only way to interpret a process, is by the application of a method. And this is enough to dismiss the Big Bang theory altogether, because if a method has been applied to the formation of the universe, then the universe is by definition a creation, which is the very thing that leaves the Big Bang theory without a natural explanation to students in regards to the origins of the universe.

*Quotation: ───────────────────
The time dependent solutions of general relativity enable us to talk about the history of the universe and have provided the modern framework for cosmology, thus leading to the discovery of the Big Bang and cosmic microwave background radiation. - Source: Wikipedia Encyclopedia (General Relativity).

The presence of cosmic microwave background radiation has been used by evolutionary scientists and Big Bang cosmologists to assert that the background radiation is the direct result of a cosmic explosion. When in reality, the effect of electromagnetic radiation with a microwave pulse throughout space is the direct result of an inner barrier or boundary that is reflecting energised particles towards the inner part of the universe, which is evidence for the edge of the universe. The cosmic microwave background radiation within outer-space is a direct result of the inner boundary of the universe, resulting in an electromagnetic disturbance in regards to any energized particle that attempts to escape the isolated system of the universe, such as solar corpuscular radiation.

For example: An aurora, also referred to as the Polar Lights, or Northern Lights, is an electromagnetic light display in the polar regions of the sky. Auroras display dynamic patterns of brilliant lights that appear as waves of dynamic movement that move in one direction covering the entire sky. The aurora on Earth is caused by solar corpuscular radiation reflecting off of the electromagnetic field that the Earth produces, known as the magnetosphere, which in turn, separates the atmosphere from outer-space.

Solar corpuscular radiation consists of energized particles that escape the sun's gravitational force, resulting in what's known as a solar wind, which is visible as a comet passes by, because the tail of a comet will always point in the same direction that the solar wind is moving. So, what scientists are actually observing in regards to cosmic microwave background radiation, is in fact, evidence for the edge of the universe that is reflecting solar corpuscular radiation off of the inner boundary, thereby preventing the electromagnetic radiation from leaving the isolated system of the universe, resulting in a cosmic microwave background radiation effect. So, in order for the cosmic microwave background radiation to be moving in all directions throughout space, then the inner boundary must be reflecting solar corpuscular radiation, which implies that an electromagnetic field is present at the edge of the universe so as to isolate the system from the outer-realm, the same as the Earth's magnetosphere separates the atmosphere from outer-space.

The presence of an electromagnetic field is the only way for the Earth to reflect solar wind, so the inner boundary of the universe is also arrayed with an electromagnetic field that is in constant effect, thereby isolating solar corpuscular radiation within the system of the universe. Cosmic microwave background radiation occurs as a disturbance between the inner boundary of the universe, and within the universe itself, which is why the direction of cosmic microwave background radiation is moving in all directions, because as the solar wind comes into contact with the inner boundary of the universe, it is then reflected away towards the inner part of the universe, resulting in a static collision of radioactive particles that flows in every direction.

Cosmic microwave background radiation is sometimes referred to as, relic radiation, because the radiation derives from within the universe, and is assumed to have come from the Big Bang billions of years ago. But because the radiation is insulated within the inner boundaries of the universe does not mean automatically that the radiation has derived from a single event in time, because every sun within the universe produces its own microwave pulse in the form of solar corpuscular radiation or solar wind.

This means that a cosmic microwave background radiation effect is not a direct result of the Big Bang, but from star systems instead, which explains why the universe is awash with electromagnetic radiation that moves in all directions, because there are star systems present throughout the universe. So, because the sun emits solar corpuscular radiation, as well as microwaves, and because the universe is an isolated system, it will mean that there is an electromagnetic field present at the edge of the universe so as to isolate an energized particle from escaping the system, the same as a magnetic mirror particle confinement fusion generator is used to isolate energized particles through a process known as magnetic confinement fusion (MCF).

In the theory I am about to present, I will attempt to define cosmic inflation, quantum field, spacetime, black holes, dark matter, quantum entanglement, as well as entropy law, and the electrical matrix of the universe as an integrated system at work in terms of a multi-dimensional theorem that is supernatural in terms of its origin. In order for distant starlight from other galaxies to reach the Earth within a respectable amount of time, then a procedure is required first, which is why a means of reflection is also required when explaining a causality for why distant galaxies are visible from Earth. And the only causality that is theoretically feasible for why distant galaxies are visible from Earth, is by a means of reflection involving a mirror device.

A magnetic mirror particle confinement fusion generator is a type of quantum field generator whereby an electromagnetic field is produced so as to isolate an energized particle from escaping the curvature of its boundary, thereby establishing an isolated system for the purpose of confining energized particles, the same as the curvature of spacetime is relative to particle confinement. And a quantum field must be electromagnetic in order to trap energized particles within the perimeter of this field, the same as a magnetic mirror particle confinement fusion generator traps energised particles, such as plasma.

*Quotation: ————————————————————
What is a magnetic mirror?
A magnetic mirror is a type of magnetic confinement fusion device used in fusion power to trap high temperature

plasma using magnetic fields. The mirror was one of the earliest major approaches to fusion power, along with the stellarator and Z-pinch machines. In a classic magnetic mirror, a configuration of electromagnets is used to create an area with an increasing density of magnetic field lines at either end of a confinement volume. Particles approaching the ends experience an increasing force that eventually causes them to reverse direction and return to the confinement area.

Magnetic confinement fusion (MCF) is an approach to generate thermonuclear fusion power that uses magnetic fields to confine fusion fuel in the form of a plasma. Magnetic confinement is one of two major branches of controlled fusion research, along with inertial confinement fusion. This mirror effect will occur only for particles within a limited range of velocities and angles of approach, while those outside the limits will escape, making mirrors inherently "leaky." An analysis of early fusion devices by Edward Teller pointed out that the basic mirror concept is inherently unstable. Magnetic mirrors also occur in nature. Electrons and ions in the magnetosphere, for example, will bounce back and forth between the stronger fields at the poles, leading to the Van Allen radiation belts. - Source: Wikipedia Encyclopedia (Magnetic Mirror).

(Above) Image of an electromagnetic field produced by a magnetic mirror particle confinement fusion generator illustrating the flow of particles and electrical current. Source: Wikipedia Encyclopedia.

According to astrophysics, the Earth is similar to a giant magnet with magnetic field lines radiating from the South pole to the North pole. Charged particles that have a polarity become trapped along these field lines, thereby forming the Earth's magnetosphere. While the universe itself also has magnetic field lines that can be detected throughout space, which is evidence for the inner boundary of the universe that is reflecting charged particles in such a way that they return to the confinement area, which is observed by cosmic microwave background radiation.

Magnetic confinement fusion is a branch of physics that attempts to create a stable electromagnetic field for the purpose of isolating charged particles and is inherently "leaky" or unstable. This is due to areas within the magnetic field lines that are subject to plasma absorption, which allows plasma to escape the confinement area as a result of plasma instability. Plasma instability is a region within an electromagnetic field where turbulence occurs due to changes in the characteristics of plasma, such as temperature, density, electric fields, or magnetic fields, so that areas with an increased electromagnetic disturbance are subject to plasma absorption, which is the evidence of black holes within outer-space.

According to NASA's website on the origin of black holes, a black hole is due to a massive increase in gravitational density within outer-space, and is assumed to come from a star's death once the star has collapsed, yet a star's death results in a supernova which remains highly visible. So, the only way to explain a black hole is due to an electrical disturbance within the force of an electromagnetic field known as quantum field that can present certain areas within the confinement space as a form of gravitational intensity, thereby creating an increase in plasma or light absorption. Thus, a black hole in outer-space can be explained in terms of an electromagnetic disturbance within a quantum field that generates an increase in gravitational intensity within a confined area by orders of magnitude without the need for additional mass.

According to physics, any electrical or electromagnetic disturbance that causes an undesired response, such as a radioactive leak, is thereby malfunctioning resulting in a degradation of the electrical performance of an electromagnetic field. Electromagnetic interference (EMI), also called radio-frequency interference (RFI) is when the radio frequency spectrum is under a disturbance generated by an external power source that affects an electrical circuit or current by electromagnetic induction, electrostatic coupling, or conduction.

Thus, an electrical disturbance within the force of an electromagnetic field can generate areas with increasing magnetic field lines, which also leads to an increase in gravitational intensity known formally as a black hole which allows energized particles to escape the confinement area. This implies that a black hole within outer-space is not caused by high density matter, and is simply the result of an electromagnetic disturbance within a quantum field known as electromagnetic interference (EMI) or radio-frequency interference (RFI), which is caused by an external power source in a state of degradation.

Magnetic mirror particle confinement attempts to generate an isolated system with only one boundary of electromagnetism, which is inherently leaky, which means that a second boundary is required in order to isolate the system, making the system efficient. So, the purpose of having an inner and outer boundary for the universe, is to act as an impermeable barrier to all forms of energy, including atoms, which are either trapped within the inner boundary or the outer boundary.

A magnetic mirror particle confinement fusion generator works by having a group of magnets arranged in such a way that the electromagnetic field of each magnet mirrors each other in order to create a particle confinement region, and because this is a type of quantum field generator, it will mean that our universe is a mirror effect of something other than mass, which must exist as a spectrum of light in order to propagate across the curvature of spacetime. This theory implies that the universe is mirroring, or reflecting off of something else that is made from a spectrum of light, which is evidence of another plane of existence known formally as dark matter.

Researchers in astrophysics have only been able to theoretically infer the existence of dark matter from the gravitational effect it seems to have on visible spectrums, such as light, which is absorbed by black holes the same as plasma is absorbed by electromagnetic disturbances within the perimeter of magnetic mirror particle confinement. So, because light derives from atoms in a state of electrolysis, which in turn, provides radiation and warmth, and because dark matter is a form of invisible matter, it will mean that the universe is arrayed with a form of invisible matter that is producing a spectrum of light in such a way that when mirrored with itself produces a quantum field, because a form of matter is required in order to create an electromagnetic fusion device, which cannot be atoms themselves, because atoms are trapped within the system the same as visible light.

Capacitive coupling, or electrostatic coupling, is the transfer of energy within an electrical network, or between distant networks, by means of displacing a DC current between circuit nodes, and is induced by an electrical field. This coupling effect can be either intentional or accidental in effect. In its simplest form, electrostatic coupling is achieved by placing a capacitor between two separate nodes or regions, whereas more than two nodes of transfer is described as an electrical matrix. In analogue circuits, a coupling capacitor is used to connect two circuits so that only the AC signal from the first circuit can pass through to the next, while DC circuitry is blocked at a given interval.

This technique is used so as to isolate a DC current and convert the flow of electrical energy to AC current, such as the case with a circuit breaker in order to alternate the flow of current from DC to AC, which can be shut off at a given interval using a storage capacitor. Electrostatic double-layer capacitors (EDLC), (or super-capacitors) are an effective energy storage device that bridge the gap between larger and heavier battery based systems and bulk energy supplies. A coupling capacitor's ability to prevent a DC overload or electrical surge by intercepting the DC source is particularly useful in circuit breakers to produce low amperage input being passed through the isolator with an additional resistor, thereby creating a high-pass filter (HPF) system that can shut off at a given frequency interval. Electrostatic coupling decreases the flow of amperage, thereby isolating the system in the form of a high frequency AC current for the purpose of long range electrical power usage.

A high-pass filter (HPF) is an electrical filter that passes radio and electrical signals with a frequency range higher than a certain shut off point. A high-pass filter is usually modelled as a linear time-invariant system, because the signal is transmitting from point A to point B in a certain length of time with an input and output effect for the purpose of electrical transmission. Electrostatic coupling on the other hand works by having two circuit nodes between distant networks or regions, such as the North and South poles of the Earth, which is designed to help filter sunlight, reflect solar corpuscular radiation, as well as trapping low frequency DC electricity.

The North and South poles of the Earth are generated by the Earth's magnetic core, which acts as a coupling capacitor between each polar region, or circuit node, for the purpose of generating an electromagnetic field or current with a high-pass filter in place that is designed to reflect lightning. And it is for this reason that lightning approaches the Earth downwards, rather than upwards, because the North and South polar regions of the Earth are reflecting electrical energy towards the magnetic core of the Earth, which is evidence of design due to an electrical network that works as a sequence known formally as an electrical matrix.

This concept is well understood from the principles of physics, but what is not openly understood is how the universe could produce such an effect without the need for additional mass, because the universe is indeed reflecting off of something else in order to create an electrical circuit, or network, which is defined as the matrix. The matrix, or electrical network of the universe, is a two-dimensional plain of existence, which is not only designed to trap charged particles in terms of an isolated system, but also, it allows charged particles to travel through vast regions in space via one or more portals. Whenever you switch on your computer, and turn the monitor on, you are opening a type of portal that works the same as a linear time-invariant system, or electrical network, which is a type of matrix. This allows for images, information, and instructions to pass from point A to point B in a reduced length of time, thus giving the illusion that time has warped, when in reality, a portal has been opened.

Now, getting back to the problem at hand, what is causing an electrical network, or matrix, within and around the universe in such a way that physical matter is not required? And one must keep in mind that the universe is reflecting off of something else in order to propagate across the curvature of spacetime due to the principles of magnetic mirror particle confinement, spacetime curvature, and cosmic microwave background radiation, which must exist as another type of universe in itself in accordance with a multidimensional theorem. This implies that Heaven is for real, because it is a cardinal principle in systems theory that a mechanism for a system is never more complex than the system it has derived from, and the universe does act as a mechanism for time to exist due to four-dimensional spacetime.

The evidence for the inner boundary of the universe, the curvature of spacetime, along with an electrical network, or matrix, that is governed by a source of reflection is due to three main factors. First; An electromagnetic field, or inner boundary, is required in order to reflect solar wind, which exists as a cosmic microwave background radiation effect. Second; An electromagnetic field must derive from an electrical field, or network, that is polar active, thereby establishing the principles of magnetic mirror particle confinement as a means of reflection, electrostatic coupling, and high-pass filtering. And thirdly; Anything that is polar active will have a positive and negative polar region, which is the only causality there is for a deep depression within the curvature of spacetime, as defined by the visual illustration of a polar grid.

This means the depression within the curvature of spacetime is governed by the principles of magnetic mirror particle confinement due to an electrical network, or matrix, which is required in order to create a polar active system; Meaning that the universe has polar regions the same as the Earth. Thus, the universe we live in is reflecting off of another type of universe in terms of a multiverse, which is the evidence of Heaven, rather than the Big Bang. The only reason that the universe, along with quantum field theory, requires a natural explanation, is because the State demands it at the taxpayers expense, which only opens the doorway for an ideocracy, which is a limitation, rather than a means of exploration. So, for this reason, I have attempted to provide a supernatural explanation in regards to the phenomenon of the universe in despite of the establishment clause of a secular government.

So, because the universe is divided into an inner boundary and an outer boundary, with the inner boundary comprising of four-dimensional spacetime, while the outer boundary consists of only two dimensions in terms of a spacetime curvature, it will mean that dark matter is only two-dimensional in terms of a flat spacetime geometry, which is also referred to as non-Euclidean geometry. The special theory of relativity states that the geometry of spacetime is flat, as well as curved, which is characterized by a four-dimensional theorem known as non-Euclidean geometry. Einstein's theory of special relativity is formulated by four-dimensional spacetime that is based on a non-Euclidean geometry with three spatial dimensions, and one temporal dimension known as time, rather than the three symmetric spatial dimensions of classical Euclidean geometry.

According to modern physics, there are two main types of Euclidean geometry, such as solid geometry, which is three-dimensional, and non-Euclidean geometry, which is four-dimensional. The most basic terms of non-Euclidean geometry from Einstein's theory of special relativity are a point, (singularity) a line, (one dimension) a plane, (two dimensions) with the plane twisted into a sphere, (three dimensions) and with a depression within the sphere (four dimensions) thereby governing the curvature of spacetime as a two-dimensional plane of existence.

This theory explains the presence of dark matter occupying physical matter at the same place at the same time, thereby equating dark matter as two dimensions within three; Meaning that both dark matter and solid matter are by definition, supernatural, due to multiple dimensions of matter occupying the same space at the same time. The fourth dimension known as time or location is due to a flat spacetime geometry that is twisted into a sphere with a deep depression within its boundary, and though the process began as a singularity, the procedure began as a method, which is evidence of design.

The concept by cosmic evolution that the universe began as a singularity automatically concludes that somehow, in some way, this must have occurred by a natural process, because yes, the universe began as a singularity, or point, according to the theory of special relativity. But, when a line occurs from a single point or location that is moving in one direction without resistance, (such as a beam of light in this case) the line will continue its course, which is a basic principle of physics involving the laws of energy distribution. And yes, light must obey the laws of motion due to the law of conservation of linear and angular momentum, because light (and electromagnetic radiation in general) has momentum.

In order for a beam of visible light that maintains its forward course to begin curling back into a circle, then a form of resistance is required first, which cannot be the point or location that the light has started from, because a means of reflection would be required in order to create a circle of light, which cannot be a dark void, because there is no reflection. Thus, the universe is reflecting off of something else in order to create the right conditions for the curvature of spacetime, because spacetime is curved. But to make matters even worse, when a circle expands without resistance, it creates a larger diameter, rather than a sphere. So, it does not matter if you apply a cosmic inflation model to the formation of spacetime, because a two-dimensional circle or beam cannot form into a three-dimensional sphere by any rate of expansion.

So, in order to create a sphere with a deep depression from a circle, then an electrical matrix is required, which cannot be visible light in this case, because outer-space is pitch black. This means that the curvature of spacetime is the result of a two-dimensional plain of existence that is reflecting off of something else in order to create a sphere with a deep depression, and because the sphere is polar active due to the presence of an electromagnetic field, it then creates a depression at either end of the sphere. Thus, the universe has polar regions with increasing electromagnetic field lines at either end of the poles, the same as a magnetic mirror particle confinement fusion generator.

All magnetic objects produce invisible lines of force that extend between the Southern and Northern poles of the object. Earth is similar to a giant bar magnet with magnetic field lines radiating from the South to the North magnetic pole. Charged particles become trapped within the field lines, which in turn, describes the Earth's magnetosphere. The Earth, stars, galaxies, and the space between galaxies are all magnetized. The more places scientists have looked for magnetic fields across the universe, the more they've been found. So, in order to establish a principle here regarding the formation of the universe, then the principles of magnetic mirror particle confinement must be inferred, which in turn defines the universe as a reflection of something other than matter.

*Quotation: ————————————————

The concept of something that is unlimited, endless, without bound. The common symbol for infinity, ∞, was invented by the English mathematician John Wallis in 1655. Three main types of infinity may be distinguished: the mathematical, the physical, and the metaphysical. Spatial and temporal concepts of infinity occur in physics when one asks if there are infinitely many stars or if the universe will last forever. In a metaphysical discussion of God or the Absolute, there are questions of whether an ultimate entity must be infinite and whether lesser things could be infinite as well. - Source: Encyclopedia Britannica (Infinity).

The mathematical symbol for infinity (∞) acts as a figure eight, in that one spectrum is reflecting off of another spectrum in terms of its curvature. This symbol has been chosen in order to define a mathematical constant in terms of a sequence or direction of travel that exists without an end, which cannot be the universe by itself due to a means of reflection. The conservation of time is relative to the curvature of spacetime, in that a procedure has occurred. While quantum entanglement leads to disorder over time due to quantum uncertainty, and the law of probability.

So, in order to establish a principle in physics concerning infinity, then the universe must be reflecting off of something else that is infinite in terms of distribution, because the electrical circuit of the universe moves in terms of an electrical current, and distributed as an electrical circuit or matrix. Hence, a spiritual Heaven acts as a means of reflection or refraction that is infinite in terms of its distribution of light. Thus, the universe is entangled with another type of universe that is reflecting off of itself in such a way that infinity (∞) occurs, which is the most plausible explanation as to why the light of distant galaxies are in close contact with one another in accordance with magnetic mirror particle confinement, spacetime curvature, and the matrix.

Quantum entanglement is a given phenomenon that explains how two atomic particles can be intimately linked to each other even if separated by billions of light-years in outer-space, resulting in an electrostatic coupling effect that joins distant regions in space by alternating from a DC current to an AC current, which is required for cosmic microwave background radiation to travel through vast regions in space. Despite their vast separation, a change induced by one atom will affect another, such is the case with a domino effect. The cosmic theory of evolution asserts that the domino effect is caused by the Big Bang billions of years ago, thereby satisfying the theoretical conclusion of cosmic inflation from a singularity via a natural process.

But, in order for quantum entanglement to affect energized particles in such a way that they are in close contact with one another over vast regions in space, it will mean that the universe is arrayed with electromagnetic field lines the same as the Earth is arrayed with electromagnetic field lines that act as a means of energetic travel or distribution, so that any disturbance within a quantum field line causes a ripple effect, or entanglement across vast regions in outer-space. These magnetic field lines derive from a quantum field that is polar active, which is evidence for a polar grid that is interconnected in terms of an electrical network or quantum matrix.

This means that the universe was preset the same as a game of Snooker is preset before the billiard balls can begin bouncing off of each other, and the inner boundary, in terms of a random distribution of particles within an isolated system. And the universe was indeed preset before any action could have occurred, because the universe is defined as an orderly system that is in a state of electrical degradation, or random decay, known as entropy law. So, in order to establish a principle here regarding the formation of the universe, then we must take into account that the universe began as an orderly system due to the conservation of time. While the process of entropy within an isolated system occurs as a state of random decay from order, and not the other way around. So, the best example one can give for the formation of the universe would be a simple game of Snooker, whereby each atomic configuration was preset before quantum entanglement began to take effect.

In a game of Snooker, each billiard ball will move in a straight line across the space of the table, the same as a quantum field line is direct in terms of distance travelled. But when each billiard ball moves in a straight direction across the table, the object will rotate due to its size and shape, which is the same for a quantum field line that is distributing atoms across vast regions in space, because as an atom moves along the field lines, its rotation is conserved within a space for memory known formally as a quantum field. Thus constituting the curvature of spacetime as an electromagnetic field, or two-dimensional plane of existence that is curved, as well as flat.

A game of Snooker also has borders and pockets in order to act as a confinement area, the same as quantum field acts as a particle confinement area that traps charged particles, thereby establishing an isolated system the same as magnetic confinement fusion is relative to particle confinement. The main difference though, is that the universe has an inner and outer boundary for the purpose of total isolation and efficiency, while a Snooker table has only one boundary with outer pockets that allow the billiard balls to escape its boundaries, the same as a magnetic confinement fusion device has only one boundary with pockets of electromagnetic interference that allow charged particles to escape the confinement region.

This means that a black hole within outer-space can be described as a pocket of electromagnetic interference within the inner boundary of the universe, so that an energized particle does not leave the isolated system of the universe, but rather, it goes missing instead. The purpose of a black hole in conjunction with this theory, is to filter out solar corpuscular radiation which fills empty space, otherwise, there would be no way to create a vacuum. The purpose of a vacuum in outer-space is to clean the universe of radioactive particles (such as solar corpuscular radiation) that fills the inner boundary, the same as dust particles fill the air in your bedroom.

While the purpose of an outer boundary for the universe is to act as a storage mechanism for the vacuum region that is steadily expanding along with the inner boundary, known also as cosmic expansion, or cosmic inflation, which is a measurable phenomenon. Energised particles that escape the inner boundary through a black hole are stored within the curvature of spacetime in terms of an outer boundary, which acts as a vacuum storage region. Thus, a black hole is produced by an electromagnetic disturbance, or electrostatic interference within the inner boundary that is inherently leaky, while the outer boundary increases the system's isolation, and remains inherently stable in order to act as a vacuum storage region.

This principle is due to the presence of dark matter, which exists as a two-dimensional plane of existence that is comprised of electromagnetic field lines, thereby encompassing the universe in terms of an inner and outer boundary known formally as a polar grid or stereographic projection. Thus, the curvature of spacetime must be reflecting off of something else according to the principle of magnetic mirror particle confinement, spacetime curvature, and stereographic projection, which cannot be a form of physical matter due to the curvature of spacetime, which is only two-dimensional. While quantum entanglement is due to a random distribution of energized particles that were preset in configuration before the process began to distribute the particles at random along each field line, which is in accordance with entropy law, and the first law of thermodynamics involving the conservation of mass and energy.

The first and second law of thermodynamics involving the conservation principle is applicable in this case, because the distribution of energised particles are in a state of random collision, which implies that the system began as orderly, because the progression of entropy is a state of decline from ordered complexity into disordered complexity, and not the other way around. And it is for this reason that adding time to the Big Bang process will only increase the level of disordered complexity there is over time, rather than increasing in ordered complexity in a matter of time, which is self-explanatory.

The universe is not only multi-dimensional in terms of Euclidean geometry, and special relativity, but also, the universe is multi-dimensional in terms of multiple boundaries in order to isolate the system efficiently. This theory explains the presence and purpose of multi-dimensional theorem involving the matrix, quantum field, spacetime, black holes, dark matter, quantum entanglement, as well as entropy law from a state of orderly particle confinement within an isolated system that is in a state of electrical degradation. The isolated system of the universe is broken up into two boundaries with the inner boundary in a state of degradation due to electromagnetic interference, while the outer boundary remains stable in order to confine the inner boundary, making the system efficient.

So, in order to explain a quantum field in terms of a medium or storage mechanism, then a set of vibrations are required to be identified in terms of energy, frequency, and resonance, that are in constant effect. Otherwise, there would be no way to detect a quantum field. The energy of a quantum field is relative to electromagnetic frequencies that resonate, or oscillate, according to a set of high to low frequencies, which act as a mechanism for high-pass filtering to occur that is universal in effect, the same as a magnetic mirror particle confinement fusion generator relies on an electromagnetic resonance, and electrostatic coupling in order to trap charged particles within the perimeter of its field. This field of electromagnetism allows researchers to study plasma under a controlled environment, thus constituting a quantum field as a controlled environment in order for atomic sequencing to occur independent of the Creator.

So, for this reason, atom's constitute as evidence for the presence of a quantum field due to a rhythm in tune that is universal in effect, as well as specific in terms of sequencing. The rhythm of an atom in sequence occurs as a cycle in place with high to low variations that are stored within a space for memory in terms of frequency ratios, (such as quantum field) which act as a standard for tuning to occur that is universal in effect. Thus, a quantum field can be measured when a device is in tune with itself, and another device, because both processes are working together in unison along a field line, which in turn, acts as a source of memory, as well as a high-pass filter that will distort any change in conduction, frequency, or vibration that is not in ratio with a quantum field line.

This means that quantum field was made, because any instrument, or vibratory pattern, that is in tune with itself, as well as the instruments surrounding it, is by definition, integrated with a third aspect, such as memory, and is thereby relative in terms of a sequence or procedure. And quantum field does exhibit properties that are evidence of a procedure, because, A) The electromagnetic field lines allow for tuning and balancing to occur within the structure of an atom or molecule. B) The electromagnetic field lines are vibrating at a constant level with high to low variations in terms of frequency ratios that have been structured into a vibrational command, which acts as a space for memory in terms of musical scale, and is required for tuning and balancing to occur within the shape of an atom or molecule.

And C) Cosmic microwave background radiation is filtered through the system via a vacuum using a polar grid, capacitive coupling, and high-pass filtering, because the system of the universe acts as an electrical grid, or matrix, with polar regions in order to create a deep depression within the curvature of spacetime, which can be exhibited using the principles of magnetic mirror particle confinement, and stereographic projection. Thus, an electrical matrix can be identified by atomic particles, because atomic sequencing is encoded from memory, which must exist as a quantum field that is polar active in order to provide a space for memory in terms of frequency ratios that have been structured into a vibrational command that is universal in effect, such is the case with musical scale.

*Quotation: ————————————————————

Atomic number is the number of a chemical element in the systematic, ordered sequence shown in the periodic table. The elements are arranged in order of increasing

number of protons in the nucleus of the atom (the same
as the number of electrons in the neutral atom), and that
number for each element is its atomic number. - Source:
Encyclopedia Britannica (Atomic Numbers).

Atomic sequencing and encoding, along with DNA RNA encoded
sequencing, are both governed by a set of high to low frequencies that are
in ratio with one another in order to act as a standard for tuning, which in
turn, requires a space for memory in terms of frequency ratios. A digital
matrix, or electrical network, is governed by a numerical sequence with high
to low variations in terms of frequency ratios that have been structured into
a vibratory command in order for an atom to be in tune with itself, and the
environment surrounding it from memory.

Atomic sequencing is the cycle of an atom that is held in tune by a
rhythm in sequence, and is governed by an electromagnetic field, because an
atom is polar active. This means that quantum field is storing instructional
information from memory that has been structured into a vibratory
command, and is held in tune within a space for memory the same as a
digital recording. This constitutes quantum field as a digital matrix due to
the presence of recorded memory in the form of an encoded sequence that
is universal in effect, which is the equivalent of an linear time-invariant
system with a signal input, and a signal output, for the purpose of stabilising
an atom or molecule. And a quantum field is indeed storing instructional
information due to a digital matrix.

Thus, the energy, frequency, and resonance of a quantum field can
be detected when a vibrational sequence, or frequency, is occurring from
memory, such as musical scale, because it is quantum field that acts as a
source of memory in terms of frequency ratios for the purpose of tuning
and balancing. So, whether it be a snowflake, a molecule, or an atom, the
principle remains the same due to stored energy in the form of musical
vibrations that take on a particular geometric shape when the particles
vibrate at a given frequency or interval. So, for this reason, the standard
base frequencies that a quantum field produces act as a universal standard
for tuning and balancing to occur in terms of frequency ratios that can
fluctuate, or alternate, thereby setting the parameters of a quantum field
in terms of a digital matrix.

A digital matrix can be detected due to atomic sequencing and electrostatic coupling, which occurs as a cycle in place that is governed by the electrons that orbit an atom's core, so that the atomic core is polar active with an electromagnetic discharge known as electrostatic coupling. Electrostatic coupling within a digital matrix occurs as an interaction between the electrons of an atom, and the atom's polar active core, which is for the purpose of high-pass filtering, so that an atom will only bond with another atom when the electrons are shared at the right frequency level. While an electromagnetic field, (such as quantum field) will govern atomic sequencing by the inclusion of a space for memory in terms of frequency ratios that have been structured into a set of high to low variations known formally as musical scale. Unique molecular identifiers (UMI's) are a type of molecular barcoding that provides error detection, error correction, and increased accuracy during atomic or molecular sequencing.

These molecular barcodes are short sequences used to uniquely tag each molecule or atom in a sample library. UMI is also useful for DNA RNA sequencing, gene expression, and DNA analysis, as well as other quantitative sequencing methods, such as atomic sequencing. Thus, the signature frequency of an atom's structure is governed by a type of barcode or coded language that has been structured into a vibratory command that derives from a space for memory, such as quantum field. While anything that is governed by an encoded sequence, is thereby orderly, which is the evidence of a prior command that is vibrational due to DNA RNA sequencing, time sequencing, along with atomic sequencing.

Time sequences are the governing factor that determines the length of the process in terms of a procedure. Thus, atomic sequencing is relative to time sequencing, the same as time sequencing is relative to DNA RNA sequencing due to an encoded language format in place that is numerically ordered with a beginning and an end in order to establish a numerical procedure or process. A quantum field is thereby evidence of design due to a desired effect in affect, such as time sequences, atomic sequencing, and DNA RNA sequences, with each type of sequence being governed by a numerical standard that is universal in effect.

While a standard base frequency is any vibration that occurs with the least amount of resistance, which indicates that a quantum field is for the purpose of stabilising an atom, and is thereby a constant in terms of vibrations, because an atom produces an electromagnetic frequency that must be held in tune in order for an atom to be stable within its environment. A black hole on the other hand, is due to electromagnetic interference within a quantum field in order for a desired effect to occur, such as a vacuum, which then allows for radio frequency interference (RFI), and electromagnetic interference (EMI) as a by-product of this process, thereby establishing a high-pass filter that is designed to filter solar corpuscular radiation through the inner boundary, while the outer boundary acts as a vacuum storage mechanism.

So, for this reason, an inner and outer boundary for the universe is required when explaining the vacuum of space, because the inner boundary acts as a vacuum region, while the outer boundary acts as a space for vacuum storage, thereby establishing the expansion rate in outer space as being the direct result of vacuum inflation, rather than a supposed Big Bang or explosion. And I understand that the inner boundary should be shrinking if the outer boundary is expanding due to a vacuum region within the inner boundary. But because the inner boundary is governed by the outer boundary, as well as being electromagnetic, it will mean that when the outer boundary expands, so does the inner boundary due to the presence of an electromagnetic field with polar regions.

For example; When an electromagnetic field increases it will expand, which is entirely due to the polar active regions growing in terms of distance travelled. And it is for the purpose of solar corpuscular radiation that a vacuum is required, which cannot be a physical barrier, because solar corpuscular radiation is electrostatic with a microwave pulse. Thus, the inner boundary acts as a high-pass filter with a given frequency range of high to low variables for the purpose of filtering solar corpuscular radiation. While the outer boundary acts as a storage region for solar corpuscular radiation, otherwise, there would be no way to create a vacuum for the purpose of filtering radioactively charged particles that fill empty space.

An electromagnetic pulse (EMP), also referred to as a transient electromagnetic disturbance (TED), is a brief burst of electromagnetic energy that causes disruption within a designated radio frequency. An EMP arises when the electrical source emits a short range microwave pulse of electromagnetic energy, or electrical current that interferes with a long range radio frequency. The origin of an EMP can be natural or artificial, and occurs as a short range electromagnetic pulse that will disrupt a particular broadband, or long range radio frequency, either intentionally, or by accident.

In modern warfare, weapons delivering a high energy pulse of electromagnetic interference are designed to disrupt radio communications equipment when a long range broadband frequency is disturbed by a short range microwave pulse, which is intentional. While a lightning storm can deliver an increasing electromagnetic disturbance in the form of a high energy short range electromagnetic microwave pulse that also disrupts long range radio and broad band frequencies. So, for this reason, a quantum field not only consists of electromagnetic field lines that are two-dimensional in terms of a flat spacetime geometry, but also, microwaves, which span a broad range of frequencies that are structured into a ratio of high to low commands or wave lengths.

Thus, a radio wave length is governed by a quantum field line that acts as a means of radio transmission and broadband distribution, because a line of travel is required when a radio communication occurs, or when a microwave pulse is traveling from point A to point B. Hence the term; wave length. A radio wave length that is in unison with a particular broadband spectrum, or radio frequency, is evidence of design the same as a radio communications system is evidence of design, because the radio wave is in tune with itself, as well as another device. And it is quantum field lines that allow radio waves to travel vast distances in space without electromagnetic interference or radio wave interference, because the radio waves are travelling along an electromagnetic field line, or carrier wave, which is the very thing that connects vast regions in space and allows for quantum entanglement.

But when the radio wave or electromagnetic pulse fails to match another pulse, distortion will occur, which is due to a high-pass electrical filter that causes radio wave interference between separate field lines that is designed to interrupt a line of transmission if the radio frequency does not match a particular broadband spectrum. This means that a broad spectrum of radio frequencies are due to multiple electromagnetic field lines, such as quantum field, which is oscillating according to a cycle in place with high to low variations in terms of frequency ratios the same as it is for musical scale. Thus, a universal scale, or standard, that acts as a medium for radio waves to travel, as well as acting as an environment for multiple radio waves to be in unison or in tune, is the direct result of a quantum field.

So, the only reason that a radio communications tower can deliver a long range communications message, is solely due to a quantum field that spans a broad spectrum of radio wave frequencies, so that any radio frequency that is in tune with itself, as well as its receiver, is thereby in unison with an electromagnetic field line, the same as a telephone wire transmits a radio signal from point A to point B in a certain length of time. But when radio wave interference occurs, it will also be due to a quantum field, because a quantum field acts as a high-pass filter that is designed to distort a radio wave length through electromagnetic interference, which is the evidence of black holes within a quantum field, the same as a broadband spectrum has levels of interference, which is exhibited when a radio frequency does not match a particular frequency or broadband spectrum.

This medium of electromagnetic field lines, known formally as quantum field, acts as a method of tuning and balancing, as well as interstellar communication, which in turn, defines quantum field as an linear time-Invariant system due to a method of radio wave and electrostatic transmission. The purpose of a quantum field, in terms of an LTI system, is to allow for radio wave communication and atomic sequencing to occur, because the system is operating according to a cycle in place with a set of high to low frequency ratios that have been structured into a vibrational command that is stored within a space for memory. And though atoms do not communicate, there is still the issue of tuning and balancing, along with encoded sequencing, which requires a source of memory in order for numerical sequencing to occur independent of the atoms themselves.

For example: When using a car radio in order to select a desired channel, the radio frequency from the car radio must be in unison with the radio station's channel, or there will be distortion. This distortion is caused by a broad spectrum of radio frequencies that derive from a group of electromagnetic field lines. Radio frequencies are not limited to the confines of the Earth alone, and can travel vast distances in space. This means that the Earth's magnetosphere is not causing long range radio frequencies to travel through outer-space, which is evidence of a second source of electromagnetic field lines that encompasses the universe in order for a long range radio frequency to reach further into space.

This form of transmission is the evidence of a linear time-invariant system, because a quantum field line acts as a means of transmission. But when an atom is oscillating at a given frequency, the sequence will be in tune, as well as in rhythm, in order for an atom to be stable without interference, which is the same for a radio wave communications system. The medium by which this occurs, known as quantum field, not only allows for interstellar communication, but also, it allows you to tune your radio in conjunction with another device.

So, the relationship between long range and short range radio frequencies, and atomic particles, is governed by a cycle in place that is oscillating between a set of high to low variables in terms of frequency ratios, so that any radio frequency, or molecule, that is in tune with itself, and its environment, is thereby in tune with a quantum field line, which is the same for any LTI system with an input and output feature for the purpose of encoded digital transmission.

The evidence that quantum field is storing vibrational instructions is due to radio waves and atomic sequencing that are both encoded according to a numerical standard that is held in tune by a digital matrix. Sound waves that bounce off of each other travel through a medium, such as air, is well understood. But when sound waves travel through the vacuum of space, there is no sound, because there is no air. Yet radio waves can travel through a vacuum reaching the outer limits and beyond, which cannot be due to the Earth's magnetic field, because the Earth's magnetic field does not reach the outer limits.

So, for this reason, a quantum field can be described as an electromagnetic field with field lines that act as a means of radio transmission, as well as storage. So, when a radio transmission occurs, an electronic oscillator generates an alternating current, thereby oscillating a radio frequency called the carrier wave, because it creates the radio waves that travel across a particular broadband or channel, depending on the frequency range or wave length. This means that a quantum field is produced by an electrical current, because a quantum field line acts as a means of radio wave transmission, or portal.

A radio frequency must be in tune, or ratio, with another frequency in order for the signal output to be clear, or distributed, which means that a radio frequency communication is relying on a quantum field line in order for both the sender and receiver to relay a message. So, because quantum field is storing radio wave communications, it will mean that quantum field acts as a space for memory in terms of vibrational instructions. And we know that quantum field is storing instructions in the form of radio waves, because a radio signal can be intercepted, which is evidence of a quantum field line that connects the sender with the receiver.

This means that quantum field itself has also been tuned in order for a cycle to occur that is oscillating in terms of frequency ratios, which are structured into a scale of high to low variables known as a broadband or wave length spectrum. So, in other words, quantum field can be easily demonstrated, as well as predicted, due to a universal standard for tuning and balancing to occur that allows for electrons and radio frequencies to be in tune with themself, along with another device, thereby allowing radio waves to travel through vast regions in space along the electromagnetic field lines that act as a line of transmission. This principle is similar to a wireless charging network that uses a short range electromagnetic frequency to transmit power wirelessly via an electromagnetic field line.

Wireless mobile phone charging works because the charging station creates an electromagnetic field between the charger and the phone in order to transmit the electrical current through a quantum field line that is storing the same frequency from memory. The tracking telemetry and control (TT&C) system of a satellite is a two-way communications link between the satellite and the ground base transmission. This allows a ground station to track a satellite's position and control the satellite's propulsion, as well as other onboard communications systems. This means that a quantum field line is being used in order to transmit an electromagnetic signal that is instructional for the express purpose of ground to satellite communication.

So, because the communication sent between the ground base and the satellite is instructional, and because the system is relying on a broad range of frequencies in order to travel a vast distance without wires, it will mean that quantum field lines are storing instructional information that can be relayed from point A to point B, as well as tapped. The biggest vulnerability radio frequencies possess is that they can be easily intercepted when devices transmit on the same frequency with the lowest frequency levels, (or wave lengths) being the easiest to intercept. So, because both an electromagnetic field line, and a radio wave length, require as source of energy in order to

271

propagate across vast regions in space, it will mean that quantum field is storing an electrical current, and is thereby potential in energy.

This means that a quantum field line can be intercepted in order to charge an electrical device, which is evidence that quantum field can power your home free of charge, because quantum field lines store potential energy in the form of an electrical current. The propagation of an electrical current by a quantum field is the evidence of the curvature of spacetime involving a polar grid, because a quantum field is an LTI system with stored information that is processed by an atom, as well as radio communications systems.

When a wave length is produced at a given frequency or interval, it will act as a vibratory command, which is the very thing that governs the wave lengths of an atom in motion, so that an atom can distribute a signature frequency, which is held in tune within a space for memory. Thus, the relationship between a quantum field, and a group of atoms, is the same as it is for a digital LTI system, with a signal input, and a signal output. And I use the term, digital, in relation to sequencing, because numbers work in sequences, which in turn, defines quantum field as a digital matrix.

Thus, a quantum field is the evidence of a creation for three main reasons. First; Because a quantum field acts as an linear time-invariant system, or digital matrix, which then acts as a means of radio wave transmission, as well as atomic sequencing and encoding. B) Because a quantum field acts as a source of memory in terms of stored vibrations that have been structured into a vibratory command in order for tuning and balancing to occur independent of the Creator. And C) Because musical scale is stored within a space for memory that is both universal in effect, as well as instructional in terms of musical notation.

So, because an atom has memory, and because the structure and wave lengths of an atom is governed by a sequence or cycle, it will mean that an atom is following a vibratory command that has been structured into a set of high to low frequencies that are in ratio with one another, the same as it is for musical scale. The main difference between information stored and instructions, is that instructions will always be encoded from memory, which in turn, defines the presence and purpose of a digital matrix, or digital recording, that is storing instructional information from memory in order for atomic sequencing and encoding to occur independent of the Creator who has spoken all things into existence by a prior audible vibratory command.

Thus, music is the language of creation, while mathematics is the language of God, because both are universal in terms of a space for memory, which can only be attributed to the Creator by definition of the word, method. The evidence that a method has been applied to the system of the universe, is due to a digital matrix that allows for atomic sequencing and encoding to occur independently, whilst maintaining the electrical grid that God has created. And the universe does exhibit the features of an electrical grid by the application of a quantum field that is electromagnetic in nature, as well as polar active in accordance with the principles of magnetic mirror particle confinement, spacetime curvature, and stereographic projection.

Otherwise, there would be nothing to structure a vibratory pattern into an orderly sequence or command that is held in tune from memory by a polar active system. And though a quantum field can fluctuate, or alternate, in terms of frequency ratios and electrical current, (which is in accordance with the first law of thermodynamics involving energy transformation) the system will remain orderly due to the conservation of time. Thus, a random fluctuation within a quantum field is equal to a set of specifics that can alternate, or fluctuate, depending on the given frequency at different intervals at different times, thereby setting the limitations of the system in terms of a set of parameters, which are by definition supernatural in origin due to the presence of rules, such as physical laws, which act as a standard for the interpretation of systems.

What is Chemical Evolution and how is it refuted?

Chemical evolution, sometimes referred to as abiogenesis, or spontaneous generation, is the archaic theory of chemicals becoming self-aware naturally, which is how the theory of biological evolution has supposed to have begun according to the theory. And the overall theory for evolution does include the idea of chemicals becoming self-aware over time, which is postulated by the evolutionist without proof, because there are no practical examples of how chemicals can become self-aware over time during any thermal process without the need for a pre-existing system first.

The only possible causality there is for the existence of life, is by supernatural creativity, because all life is instructionally based from its DNA, and the only causality we have for the existence of instructions, is by the action of creativity. And there are no physical examples of instructions occurring all by themself, because an instruction will always be equal to a message or a command, which is why the level of order there is within DNA sequencing must derive from someone, rather than just somewhere? So, for this reason, chemical evolution can be easily refuted on the basis of instructional systems, because instructions will always display intent.

The argument here between creation and evolution is in regards to the interpretation of systems, because modern science has been built upon systems science and systems thinking, while evolution is primarily a racial theory. This means that a causality for systems is required in order for a theory regarding systems to be coherent, because the entire purpose of having a theory, is to determine a causality or motive. And evolution, as a theory, is without a plausible explanation for the existence of systems, because evolution is limited to being a natural process only according to its own interpretation, when the causality of systems cannot be attributed to a natural process, because a natural process will always be the result of a system, rather than the cause of one.

Spontaneous generation theory is an archaic scientific theory which states that living organisms could arise from non-living matter via a natural process, and that such a process was regular in nature. Spontaneous generation, or spontaneous evolution, is a failed theory in science which postulates that living creatures can self-emerge over time from nonliving matter. This idea was falsified and adequately dis-proven by Louis Pasteur's flask experiment before the twentieth century had even begun, resulting in the law of biogenesis. Louis Pasteur was a French microbiologist and chemist who pioneered the scientific practice of germ theory, as well as being the discoverer of molecular asymmetry, stereo-chemistry, and the inventor of the process known as Pasteurization.

Pasteur boiled a meat broth in a goose neck flask that had a long neck which curved downward. The idea was that the bend in the neck prevented falling particles from reaching the broth, while still allowing the free flow of air. The flask remained free of biological growth for an extended period until the flask was opened allowing air to enter the boiled broth. This allowed microbes to enter the flask causing the broth to become contaminated, thus leading to the discovery of biogenesis. Today, however, the evolutionary theory of spontaneous generation, also known as abiogenesis, has stated that human beings arose from single celled organisms that slowly evolved over millions of years, which supposedly, could only have been attributed to a mass of algae forming a green film on the surface of stagnant water, known also as pond scum.

Unicellular micro-algae, such as Chlorella, Prototheca, and Diatoms, have thought to evolve into to multicellular forms, such as the Giant Kelp, which is a large brown algae, while the largest and most complex type of marine algae are called seaweeds. Algae and seaweeds are broken up into unicellular and multicellular types and sorts. This allows for evolutionists to conclude that single celled organisms have evolved into multicellular organisms via algae and seaweed.

Photosynthetic organisms, such as plants, algae, and cyanobacteria, use sunlight for photosynthesis in order to produce organics. Organics are composed of organic compounds that derive from other living organisms, such as plants, animals, bacteria, and people through biological reproduction, and or, random decay. According to Oxford languages, organics are defined as: 1) "Relating to or derived from living matter." So, from the OED we find that anything organic has derived from living matter, rather than non-living matter, and though the evolutionist may argue otherwise, the proof is simple to explain otherwise thanks to Louis Pasteur's method of sterilization.

Sterilization is defined as a process of complete elimination or destruction of all forms of microbial life, as well as organics, which is carried out by various physical and chemical methods. And that which is sterile cannot produce organics, while that which has been thoroughly sterilized has removed all organics so that one cannot argue that anything sterile can produce organic life. This means that if the Earth began as sterile then it should remain sterile unless life is introduced, which has led the evolutionists to believe that life has derived from other worlds that supposedly contain organic life. Yet, according to observation, no other observed planet has organics, which is entirely due to climatic, chemical, and radioactive conditions that forbid organic life to exist.

So, for this reason, Louis Pasteur's flask experiment was a simple demonstration that refutes the evolutionary theory of organic life having derived from a sterile environment. All life is instructionally based from its DNA RNA so that all life was made, which leaves the evolutionary theory of chemical evolution to biological evolution as having no causality for living systems, because anything sterile will remain sterile unless organic life is introduced from outside of its environment. While any organic compounds must derive from organic life, either directly or indirectly, by definition of the word, organic. And though organic life is carbon based, carbon itself does not constitute as an organic compound by itself due to the need for carbohydrates.

Photosynthesis is where the photosynthetic processes by autotrophs produce oxygen as a byproduct and synthesize carbohydrate molecules like sugars, starches, glycogen, and cellulose to store chemical energy. Sugar is the generic name for soluble carbohydrates that are used in food. The term, carbohydrate, is most commonly used in biochemistry where it is synonymous with the term, saccharide, which derives from the Ancient Greek σάκχαρον (sákkharon) meaning sugar.

So, the base of a food chain begins and ends with carbohydrates, such as sugars, rather than from carbon itself, and sugars are produced through photosynthesis, which is why plants are at the bottom of the food chain, and will continue to remain at the bottom of the food chain in despite of anything a biochemist might say to the contrary. All food derives either directly or indirectly from plant life, which is the official reason why it is safer to eat animals that graze freely on vegetation, because the likelihood of contracting a chromosomal mutation is far greater when you eat animals that are carnivorous. And the second reason that one should eat vegetation directly, is because vegetation is the primary source of carbohydrates and vitamins, while animals that graze freely are a secondary source of nutrients.

The Latin root of the word, "carbon" is carbonem; Meaning "charcoal." Carbon is an abundant non-metallic tetravalent element occurring in three allotropic forms, which are: Amorphous carbon, Graphite and Diamond. And though carbon occurs in all organic compounds, carbon itself does not constitute as an organic compound by itself, because in order for carbon to form carbohydrates, then photosynthesis is required first, which is why we eat plants, rather than carbon molecules, such as diamond, graphite and amorphous carbon. While a hydrocarbon is defined as a compound of hydrogen and carbon that is found in petroleum and natural gas, which in turn, derives from organics in a state of decay, such as methane and crude oil.

Hydrocarbons contain only carbon and hydrogen, while carbohydrates contain oxygen in addition to carbon and hydrogen. Different types of hydrocarbons differ from each other in terms of atomic bonds when the ratio of carbon to hydrogen changes with the presence of multiple bonds and ring structures while no oxygen is present. This means that carbohydrates do not derive from carbon-hydrogen bonds, but from photosynthesis instead due to the need for oxygen gases to be bonded with a hydrogen and carbon in order to form an organic compound. Thus, hydrocarbons derive from plant life the same as carbohydrates, while carbon is a base element the same as hydrogen. So, in order to derive at life, the evolutionary theory assumes that carbon and hydrogen can form into hydrocarbons without the need for photosynthesis. Yet according to basic chemistry, hydrocarbons derive from photosynthesis, which in turn, derives from plants, rather than water.

The Royal Society of London is currently holding the world's largest science research challenge known formally as the Evolution 2.0 Prize competition that is led by list of adjudicators from Harvard, Oxford and MIT. There is a major $10 million USD prize open to the public for anyone who can show how an instructional system can arise by chance. The competition is virtually impossible, but it does however prove that an instructional system cannot arise by mere chance over time. Every living cell reproduces itself from a virtual instructional system, such as DNA RNA transcription. DNA has the same features as modern digital devices with multiple layers of encoding, decoding, and data storage, such as the genome that includes error detection, error correction, and instructional sequencing repair.

So, for this reason, the main emphasis in science has moved away from the biological interpretations of life as being the result of pure chemistry, which is considered to be 19th century now, and has moved onto instructional design and instructional systems design, because all life is instructionally based from its DNA. Intelligent design can also be referred to as instructional design, or instructional systems design, because in order for instructions to occur, then a method must be applied, and intelligent design is the only causality there is for an instructional system. Intelligent design is evidence of supernatural creativity, because planning is not something that nature alone can achieve inside any length of time proposed, and an orderly system must occur by the use of planning in order to generate the specifics needed.

The ability to plan derives from the imagination, and the imagination must derive from a source of imagination in itself, because the imagination is the only source of innovation and design there is according to the definition of the word, innovate. Instructional design (ID), or instructional systems design (ISD) is based on the ADDIE model with the five phases: analysis, design, development, implementation, and evaluation. And this is a step-by-step procedure for implementing a concept into a design, which in turn, produces an end product or desired effect, and the end product will always be defined as a creation, because it came from a concept to begin with, rather than by pure chance.

The term analysis is defined as being a detailed examination of the elements or structure of something. So, the definition of analysis is the process of breaking something down into its parts in order to learn what they do, and how they relate to one another. And an example of analysis would be observing the English language in order to compare certain words, and then to categorize them for future reference.

The design step is to implement an idea, as in a concept that is to be interpreted into an instruction, which can either be in the format of a drawing (model), or in the format of a language (word), or in the format of a signal (sign). And there are no other examples of how a design can be transferred from concept to reality apart from a model, sign, or language, because this is a communications method. The development step is when the concept design is to be developed into a model, signal, or language, which can vary according to whatever the application is. So, if the instructions must be in English for example, then that will be the method of development to format the design.

The implementation step is when the development of the instructional method, model, or signal, has been produced and is ready to be implemented. Which can be a dictionary for example that selected English for its format design, and is now ready to print copies, or, it can be a set of technical drawings for a large construction project for example. The final step, evaluation, is when the project design has been implemented and is now operational, and requires constant observation in order to ensure the overall outcome is meeting the intended needs of the consumer and planner. Which can be a shopping centre for example that has numerous leases to different individuals, and the administrative body wishes to know whether or not to implement further designs based on the consumers' needs.

So, instructional systems design is by definition a communications development method, because this is also how different forms of communication can be established for the purpose of encoding information for security reasons. The key role of instructional design, and instructional systems design, is to improve methods of communication, such as converting sensitive information into an encrypted file storage format that is used to store banking information for example, or for analysing existing ways of communication. Instructional systems design is also used for identifying existing ways of communication, such as DNA RNA transcription, which is a virtual communications system that is chemically based.

A thermodynamic instructional system, such as DNA RNA transcription, cannot occur from chemicals alone over time, because adding time to a chemical process that tends toward disorder will only increase the level of disorder there is in a matter of time. So, because DNA RNA transcription is a thermodynamic instructional system, and because the only way to interpret DNA RNA transcription is by the application of a method, it will mean that instructional systems design has been applied to the process of DNA RNA transcription from outside of the system itself. Otherwise, there would be no causality for ordered biological complexity, because everything would be entirely random including protein manufacture.

In computing, a storage device is used to store data, (such as pre-arranged programs) while the memory (RAM) is used to temporarily store the operational data of the CPU, and the data exchanged with the hard drive, which means that all programs will be loaded and run from memory. And this is the same for the genome as well, because the genome will run sequences from memory called gene sequences that are to be conveyed into mRNA sequences, and then onto protein manufacture, which is how a gene sequence is transcribed from instruction to mechanism via pre-existing mechanisms that are in place to help form proteins within the body.

The amount of order that is required for the genome to occur is highly specific and well organized, relying on a series of actions to be correct in sequence, which is in accordance with the amount of ordered complexity there is within the genome. Yet living systems have come from a more complex system than life itself, and living systems are a part of the most complex system there is, which is why the origin of life was supernatural, rather than natural, because the actions needed to arrange the genomic storage system required a supernatural ability in accordance with the law of probability, as the likelihood of the human genome forming by chance is an absolute zero due to the presence of instructions.

Each gene sequence that specifies for a particular protein will always be in relation to other proteins; Meaning that a method has been applied to life in order for a group of gene sequences to specify for a group of proteins that are specific in relation to each other, which is required in order to form a functional cell. So, because a living cell is highly integrated according to an overall plan, and therefore, cannot derive at random due to the law of probability, it will mean that living systems are evidence of supernatural creativity due to the lack of a natural process that can cause instructions to occur. And there is no other causality for living systems apart from supernatural creativity, because if life began at random, then the production of proteins must also be random, when the method of protein manufacture is governed by an instructional system that is by definition, specific.

The human genome specifies for the arrangement of proteins via gene sequences, and because genetic sequences are specific in relation to each other, it will mean that a living cell cannot occur at random over any length of time proposed due to the sheer number of events that must be multiplied by one another in order to gain a probability factor for the overall event of life occurring by chance. Life cannot be the result of a natural process, because a natural process will always be limited to the number of specifics there are in place to define the process with, and specifics derive from taking rules into account, which in turn, sets the parameters for a system's operation.

The only way for life to have come into existence in the beginning is by the application of a method, because the process of cellular division, and biological reproduction is occurring according to a procedure that is repeatable under observation, and reliable under demonstration, and is therefore, specific. The evolutionary theory attempts to explain the origin of living systems by using mathematical equations and theoretical summaries to form their hypothesis, but relying solely on the random probability factors alone to conclude upon with zero practical examples to give of how materials and energy alone can become conscious over time.

So, because the probability of a group of functional proteins forming a living cell by chance is so astronomically low in terms of odds, it will mean that the amount of faith that is required to believe in the theory of evolution, must be, by comparison, astronomically high. And the theory of evolution is indeed a theory based on random events, because that which has not derived by design, is by definition, random. If a given process has been pre-specified, then the process is by definition a creation, but if the process is unspecified, then the process is by definition, random.

And there is no other way to interpret a process, because there are only two ways to identify a given process, which is either random or designed, because there is only specified and unspecified to select from. DNA RNA transcription is a part of a virtual communications system due to the presence of genetic instructions, and instructions are by definition, specific, regardless of any theory that determines otherwise, because an instruction is also equal to a message or command.

So, the level of order that is required for genomic replication to occur has derived from an instructional command due to the presence of instructions, which is evidence of supernatural creativity due to the lack of a natural process that can cause an instructional system to occur. So, the very thing that distinguishes a living system from any group of chemical reactions is the genome of an organism due to the presence of an instructional procedure. In order for an instructional system to be established, then there must first be a send and receive mechanism in place, as well as a storage mechanism, which means that an instruction cannot be issued without a set of pre-existing mechanisms in place to store the instructions that are to be interpreted by the receiver. And unless there is a standard in place to give definition to the instructions sent, then the instructions received cannot be interpreted.

So, the only way for an instructional system to have been established in the beginning, is by a source of conscience, because an instructional system requires a standard for communication that is inferred according to a set of rules, and the human conscience is the only thing we have for inventing rules with. An instruction can only be defined by the standard in place for the instructions to be interpreted by, because instructions are never self-existing and are always the result of a standard in place to define the instructions with, which is evidence of supernatural creativity, because there is no natural process that can cause an instructional system to occur independent of a Creator.

And I say supernatural, because there is no way that any scientist will ever be able to create blood within a laboratory, which is in accordance with the first law of biology, such as the law of biogenesis, which states that life can only come from pre-existing life. So, because all life is within the blood therein, and because life only comes from pre-existing life according to the law of biogenesis, it will mean automatically that all life has derived from a source of conscience or word, because there is no natural process that can cause an instructional system to occur from chemicals alone without the need for a method of communication first, such as DNA RNA transcription, which cannot be attributed to a natural process only, because the only thing we have to invent a method of communication with, is the human conscience.

Anything that has been programmed will in turn have a designated function, and the human body has indeed been pre-programed in order to manufacture proteins, as well as blood. The circulatory system is made up of blood vessels that carry blood in a circulatory pattern away from and towards the heart. The heart has two main arteries (left and right) that carry blood away from the heart, while veins carry the blood back to the heart via the circulatory system.

The arteries are the blood vessels that deliver oxygen from the heart to other tissues within the body, and each artery is a muscular tube lined by a smooth tissue that has three layers: The epicardium, myocardium, and endocardium. The circulatory system carries oxygen, nutrients, and hormones to cells, and removes waste products, like carbon dioxide. These roadways travel in one direction only in order to keep the flow of oxygen moving and to prevent clotting, because if the system is restricted, then clotting will occur in the blood, which can then travel to the heart, causing the artery that sends blood into the heart to become blocked, which will initiate a total systems shutdown procedure automatically.

So, a heart attack will always be according to a sequence of events, and it is the sequence in place that distinguishes the heart from any group of chemicals, because instructions are required in order to govern the rhythm of the heart, which must work as a synchronized process that is governed by an instructional method from the genome. The human heart is a type of positive displacement pump, and the heart is not something that can be improved upon in terms of its thermodynamic efficiency.

The heart muscle can pump 200 million liters of blood in a lifetime without the need for shutdown and repair, which cannot be compared with in terms of efficiency. A positive displacement pump has an expanding cavity on the suction side, and a decreasing cavity on the discharge side, so that the liquid flows through the pump in one direction as the cavity on the suction side expands, and then the liquid flows out of the discharge valve once the cavity collapses.

Positive displacement pumps are the most efficient type of pump there is, because they're able to handle variations in pressure, flow, and viscosity, whilst remaining fully operational, unlike centrifugal pumps, which do not operate well if the fluid is thicker than water, such as blood for example. The heart operates as a continuous process while the body is breathing, but when the heart stops beating a total systems shutdown procedure will be initiated, because the heart is a primary mechanism for the body, which is evidence that creativity has been applied to the design of the human body, because not only does the body have a shutdown procedure when a heart attack occurs, but also, there is a procedure for the body to become conscious again once the system is restored.

So, the body works similar to a computer, whereby a shutdown procedure is coupled with a rebooting procedure that is governed by an instructional method, as well as a low power sleep mode for the purpose of conserving energy, and an on mode where a task can be completed. But the rule with any system that is to come back online after a systems shutdown has occurred, is that an overall systems check must be carried out, which can include an Electrocardiograph by your doctor for example, or more importantly, by the body itself. The body's heart rhythms must be able to synchronize itself with breathing again in order for the action of becoming fully conscious to occur, and this is carried out by the body's nervous system, which includes the brain, spinal cord, and a complex network of nerves.

This system sends messages back and forth between the brain and the body and controls all of the body's functions and rhythms. And this is the main reason why oxygen is conserved within the brain during a shutdown procedure, because the brain will conduct an overall systems check by the use of the body's sensory equipment, which is relative to checking yourself over for further injuries using your eyes, your hands, and your nervous system, so that the brain can assess any further damage to the system.

So, in order for the heart to restart, then a rhythm must occur, because the heart is a cyclic pump that must work according to a rhythmic beat, and oxygen is required with each heartbeat, because the body is using oxygen from the blood at all times in order to keep the brain operational. So, because the body has a procedure for shutting down in order to conserve oxygen within the brain, as well as a separate procedure for becoming conscious again, it will mean automatically that a method has been applied to the human body, which cannot occur at random over time, because instructions are required first, which is evidence of design, rather than evolution. And the body does require instructions for breathing, simply because there is an instructional procedure in place from the genome.

God the Creator has breathed life into man that he may become a living soul, which in turn, defines man as a creation, which cannot be attributed to chemicals alone, because chemicals do not acquire the ability to think, which must cause the evolutionist to think more about where they have come from in terms of a causality. If life has derived from chemicals alone, then life has no meaning, because meaning must always derive by intention, which is the only causality there is for purpose. And everything has a purpose in terms of a creation, which is the very thing that excludes chemical evolution as a causality for life, because life cannot be self-existing by reason of the fact that life is breathing according to a procedure in place that is both instructional in terms of a creation, as well as spiritual in terms of a Creator.

What is Biological Evolution and how is it refuted?

According to the theory, biological evolution is defined as "natural selection," whereby the characteristics of an organism will be influenced by its environment, resulting in what's known as a phenotype. The evolutionary interpretation is that the physical traits of an organism are always determined by the environment, rather than the genotype, which is the basis for natural selection in terms of a theory. Yet the genotype of an organism is the standard in place to define the phenotype with, and the physical traits that a phenotype has are indeed affected by impacts from the environment, resulting in an expression of the genotype in terms of a variant within a kind called the phenotype. So, the term, genotype, is specifically in regards to the genome that specifies for a particular kind, while the phenotype is an expression of the genotype in terms of a variant or species.

For example: Skin colour is determined by the amount of melanin within a person's genes, which is expressed as a pigment within the skin, eyes, and hair, according to a scale of light to dark. And the environmental input to a genotype is minimal in regards to how much melanin you will have, because the amount of melanin you have will always be inherited from the genotype, rather than the phenotype. And this is why a couple with brown eyes can have children with blue eyes, because the phenotype does not determine the next generations features, only the genotype will determine the successors genetic make-up.

The amount of melanin an individual has will most certainly impact one's ability to handle the environment, but melanin in no way came from the environment itself, because the more melanin that your body is coded for, the more suited you will be to direct sunlight, which is an expression of the genotype as a phenotype. So, in other words, the phenotype is an expression of yourself as an individual, while your genotype is in reference to your biological kind. And historically, the evolutionary concept of the phenotype determining the genotype of the successive generation is more commonly known as Lamarckian evolution, which is one of the most discredited theories in the history of modern science.

Jean Baptiste Lamarck (1744 - 1829) is one of the best-known early evolutionists of his time, and unlike Darwin, Lamarck believed that living things evolved in a continuously upward direction from simple to more complex forms with each successive generation. And an example of Lamarckian evolution, would be the idea that the giraffe inherited its long neck from predecessors reaching further and further towards the highest parts of a trees in order to eat. But unfortunately for Lamarck, a giraffe's neck is not getting longer or shorter over time, because the number of vertebrae that a giraffe has is fixed, which proves definitively that you inherit your traits from the genotype, rather than the phenotype. And this has led to evolutionary biologists attempting to mutate different types of creatures in order to achieve a desired effect. Such as mice for example, which have been trialled on to see if a change in the phenotype will affect the genotype of the next generation.

The mice that were trialled on had their tails removed and were then bred together to see if the offspring would be born without tails. But the mice continued to produce tails after multiple generations despite the removal of the tail with each passing generation. And this was an inhumane experiment that resulted in a complete failure, because over a thousand generations of mice were mutilated with no signs of the tail shrinking or disappearing from the genotype. A second example of biological evolution is the inhumane practice of inbreeding and infanticide known formally as Darwinian eugenics. The idea that biological improvement is the direct result of successive breeding within a confined group led to the practice of Nazi racial segregation policies that instigated to World War II and the Holocaust.

The Holocaust was the direct result of the evolutionary theory in practice from the State's board of education, which happens to the same issue that America faces today involving the racial segregation of those who have been deemed inferior biologically, such as Africans. Yet the indivisibility of human rights and equality is an American liberty that has been overruled by the Supreme Court in order to pave the way for the evolutionary definition of man, which historically, forms the 19th and 20th century roots of scientific racism involving the Linnaean/Darwinian classification of man.

The genotype of an organism will always be governed by the instructions from the genome, which are indeed impacted by the environment, and will affect the phenotype's appearance. But the genotype of a particular organism will not be affected by the phenotype, because a phenotype will always be a variant of its genotype due to the method of transcription. DNA RNA transcription is a copying process, and the rule with any copying process is that each copy must derive from an original copy, and only the original copy will have all of the information for variation, which in turn, defines each successive copy as a variant of its original. And this not only explains variation within a kind, but this also means that speciation leads to a reduction in variability over time as diversification occurs, rather than increasing as the theory of evolution claims is occurring via natural selection.

For example: If I bought a CD from a music store and then took it home and burnt a copy of the original album, then I have produced a variant of the original, and if this process continues, then each successive copy that is burnt from the previous copy will have a lowered ability to produce variation, which is an example of why biological evolution is not occurring on any level. Speciation is also specialization toward a given habitat, and as each creature becomes more specialized within a given habitat, the less likely the creature will be able to survive in a different habitat, because diversification has already occurred.

The amount of variation within animals is extremely high compared to that of humans, because according to the book of Genesis chapter 1, animals were made according to their own kind, with speciation having occurred by the time of the flood in chapter 6, because the animals were called onto the Ark each according to their type and sort within a kind; Meaning that the book of Genesis has taken speciation into account long before the word was even invented. So, if there is one thing that Darwin cannot lay claim to, then it is the origin of species, because the Holy Bible was first to explain speciation, rather than the theory of evolution. Human beings have derived from one man and one woman only, which is why mankind is only one species biologically, while animals are broken up into different species according to their own genotype or kind. Mankind however is only one species genetically, because each group of humans from around the world can physically interbreed, which in turn, defines mankind as only one species or race.

So, it does not matter what the biological traits are that have become more pronounced over time within the phenotype of an individual, because they will still always be a variety of human according to their genotype. And this is the same for the animals as well, because the changes in phenotype are always the result of variation from the genotype, resulting in a variant called a species. The environment will indeed cause a genotype to express a variant of itself called the phenotype, but the phenotype will always remain as a variant of the genotype that its genome began replication with, because biological reproduction is a copying process.

The amount of input by natural selection to the system of genomic replication is limited to zero in terms of biological improvements, because there is no direct method of selection by nature to instruct the genome into a more orderly system. And a direct method of selection is indeed a requirement in order for any set of genetic instructions to be improved upon, because genetic instructions are not self-improving via any mutational, natural, or reproductive process.

The genomes' primary task is to make copies of itself whilst providing variation as well, but the amount of variability an individual can express will never increase over time, because the amount of genetic variation that an individual can pass on is reducing itself over time with each successive generation as diversification occurs. As diversification occurs, only a portion of the total amount of variation a breeding group has can be passed down to the offspring, because all of the information for variation was with the first copy that its genome began replication with, which is a rule with any copying process.

A species will only ever have a portion of the total amount of variation within its own kind, which is spread out amongst its own kind in order for an open breeding population to occur that is diverse, which in turn, reduces the likelihood of total extinction. The purpose of speciation is to create an open breeding population in order for any severe chromosomal mutations to be offset by having variety within a kind, because a closed breeding population will always have an accelerated rate of mutation, which will inevitably lead to the extinction of a species, rather than preserving their biological kind. Evolution, as a process, is lacking a causality for innovation to occur, because that which is indirect in terms of selection, cannot be, at the same time, direct in terms of input, and a method of selecting directly is a requirement in order to define that which is specific. Specifications always derive from taking rules into account, because any increase in specificity must derive from a method of innovation, and the only causality there is for innovation to occur, is by design.

The longer the copying process from the genome continues, the less variation that each variant will be able to specify for as an individual, because variability is always inherited from the genotype, rather than the phenotype. So, for this reason, natural selection cannot be defined as a law in science, because physical laws are repeatable under demonstration, and they're also defined by an observable action. While natural selection, as a process, is non-repeatable due to variations in preference during selection, and repeatability is essential when describing a biological process, because it is repeatability that gives rise to reliability, and it is reliability that gives rise to survivability.

Natural selection is an indirect method of selection based entirely on nature's preference, which means that there is no type of action by natural selection that can be defined as specific, and therefore, repeatable. While any attempt to repeat natural selection, and thereby demonstrate the process at work, would in turn, define the process as a procedure, and therefore, a creation. The only way to define natural selection as a biological process, is that it's a mutational process, which is how biological evolution describes itself in terms of a theory. A genetic mutation is by definition a random change to the genetic instructions of a cell, and is therefore, non-repeatable due to the fact that it was a random change to begin with caused by external or internal influences.

So, because biological systems are not self-improving with age via any physical process, it will mean that biological systems are degenerating over time as speciation occurs, which is a direct result of accumulative mutations that build-up within the genotype of an organism. And this is relative to the laws of thermodynamics whereby a thermodynamic system will always be found in a state of disorder, or moving towards it, which also applies to biological systems. Evolution, as a process, cannot improve the level of thermodynamic efficiency that an organism already has, because anything random during a thermodynamic process, such as mutations, will tend toward disorder over time due to entropy law, and the law of probability.

Many have wondered if a single celled organism is self-aware, but the only way to be sure is to determine their method of communication between themselves and their surroundings. Cells communicate by sending and receiving sensory signals only, which means that their sense of self-awareness is definitively low. Sensory signals may come from their surroundings, or they may come from other cells, because in order to trigger a desired response from a single celled organism, then the signals must be transmitted across the cell's membrane in a particular way, or there will be no feedback from the cell. There are four basic categories of chemical signalling found in multicellular organisms which are: paracrine signalling, autocrine signalling, endocrine signalling, and by direct-contact signalling.

Direct-contact signalling are gap junctions caused by tiny channels that connect neighbouring cells. These gap junctions are full of water and allow small signalling molecules to travel across the channel, which is how the cells are signalling through direct-contact. Signalling molecules are commonly called ligands, which is a general term for molecules that bind specifically to other molecules, such as receptors. The message carried by a ligand is often relayed through a chain of chemical messengers inside the cell. A chemical messenger is any compound that serves to transmit a message, which can refer to things like: hormones, long range chemical messengers, such as liquids, and neuropeptides which are protein sequences that act as a hormone or neurotransmitter for the purpose of neurotransmission.

Neuropeptides are synthesized on the rough endoplasmic reticulum, and the endoplasmic reticulum performs important functions, particularly in the synthesis of RNA folding, DNA proofreading, and the transportation of protein sequences that are to be guided out of the cell. So, what this means is that the individual cells for a multicellular organism can communicate with each other through chemical messaging, which involves neurotransmission to release the neuropeptides that are to be conveyed as an instructional message, and this can also be referred to as plurichemical transmission. While a single celled organism communicates using autoinducers, which are signalling molecules secreted by bacteria to communicate with other bacteria of the same kind. The secreted autoinducers can be small hydrophobic molecules, such as acyl-homoserine lactone (AHL), or larger peptide-based molecules. And each type of molecule has a different mode of action that is specific according to a standard in place for the signals to be interpreted by.

Chemical coding itself requires pre-programing the same as words do in order for the coding to display a meaning. And this requires the arranging ability from a source of conscience in order to create the algorithms needed, because programming a form of communication always involves the need to encode a sequence according to a set of rules that acts as a standard for communication. So, like the animals, cells are not inventing ways of communication as humans do, but according to a standard in place that is fixed. So, because the only thing we have for inventing rules with, and therefore codes, is by the human conscience, it will mean that a source of conscience is required in order to invent a method of communication.

All methods of communication have derived from a source of conscience, either directly or indirectly, which is why individual cells cannot program the chemical coding they use, but they can interpret and convey the signals as tasked in order to direct a signal back, which is always based on the chemical coding system they use which is fixed. And coding must derive from a source of conscience, because the conscience is the only thing we have for inventing rules with, which is necessary when establishing a communications method, because a communications method will always be encoded according to a set of rules that acts as a standard for communication to occur. The limitation of a cell's method of signalling allows bacteria to respond to its surroundings in order to sustain its nutrient levels, and because cells can also release molecules to signal each other with, it will mean that they are self-aware. But because a cell has no conscience, it will mean that they cannot create a system of communication for themselves, so they are therefore limited to the standard for chemical coding already in place, which is pre-programed.

So, all the cell has to do is to copy, interpret, and then send a signal back by relaying the message without even thinking about it, which is the most reliable method of communication for any manufacturing process, because the operation is fully automated. Programmable machines that use a set of specific instructions have a set amount of functionality, and machines do not have the amount of sensory equipment that living cells do, so no machine can think or find food, as well as reproduce, which is why machines cannot become self-aware the same as chemicals alone cannot become conscious over time.

The process of biological evolution, as described by the theory, cannot be occurring genetically, because in order for a method of transcription to occur, involving DNA synthesis, DNA proofreading, and DNA modification, then a source of conscience is required first in order to arrange the instructional process of genomic replication, which is perpetual so long as biological reproduction is occurring. The only thing we have for interpreting physical laws with, is the human conscience, because the human conscience is for our understanding of morality, which is also rule based the same as physical laws. And we owe this to no one save the Creator Himself who has endowed all life with ability, but unto His own image the gift of conscience, with which, to reason from, so that all may know His ways of truth and life.

According to Oxford Languages, the definition of a stochastic process is defined as: 1) "A process having a random probability distribution or pattern that may be analysed statistically, but may not be predicted precisely." So, a stochastic process is by definition a random process that lacks the ability to select directly, and is therefore unpredictable due to the lack of an action that is direct in terms of its input. And a stochastic process will determine an outcome in terms of a consequence, and is therefore deterministic, but the outcome will always be random according to the definition of the word, stochastic. Evolution is, according to the theory, is a stochastic process resulting from a combination of deterministic and random factors. Secular science attempts to present results from the evolutionary theory of "directional evolution" in order to suggest how random variation (such as mutations) can influence speciation.

But the problem with evolution, as a theory, is that speciation always leads to a reduction in variability over time as diversification occurs, because only a portion of the total amount of variability can be passed down to the offspring hereditarily with each successive generation due to the limitations of the copying process. Thus, the total amount of variation within a group of species has derived from an original kind that their genome began replication with, because variability is always inherited from the genotype, rather than deriving from within the offspring itself. The difference between variability, and variation, in biology, is that variability is specifically in relation to how much variation an organism can express, which is governed by the genotype, while variation is the end product of the process at work.

Directional evolution defines itself as a stochastic process that selects the physical traits within a given population in order for the organism to survive better or reproduce more efficiently, which in turn, defines natural selection in terms of a theory. But unfortunately for the theory, a set of physical traits must be specific in relation to each other in order for a biological system to be integrated, and physical traits are the direct result of the DNA RNA selection process, which is governed by a proofreading mechanism. And any instructional system that features a proofreading system, is by definition a creation, rather than a random occurrence, because the ability to proofread must be pre-programmed or the system cannot be established.

Evolution is defined as being the process of natural selection, which is entirely random, because this is not a direct method of selection that can increase the number of specifics there are within a thermodynamic instructional system. So, because natural selection is an indirect method of selection, it will mean that evolution has had no input in regards to an increase in specificity within a living system, which is required in order for a thermodynamic system to be improved upon in terms of thermodynamic efficiency.

So, in order for a set of physical traits to be specific in relation to each other, then an overall method is required in order to combine each of the mechanisms into a single mechanism called a system, which cannot occur at random over time in accordance with the law of probability, because a method is required first. And an overall method is indeed a requirement in order for any individual trait to be specific in relation to another, otherwise, the traits cannot be combined into a working system that is integrated. And this is why a genetic mutation cannot increase the level of thermodynamic efficiency that an organism already has, because a mutation is by definition a genetic mistake within the DNA proofreading process, and is therefore limited to being a degenerative process only, rather than an innovative method.

DNA proofreading will allow for DNA modification, which is a process that gives rise to a person's distinction as a human being, such as a person's fingerprints for example, or a particular type or sort of creature according to its own kind. And all living creatures must be divided according to their own kind, otherwise, there would be no way to define a variant within a kind. A variant is by definition a type or sort within a kind that has derived from a standard type that will govern the amount of variation an organism can express in terms of an individual. And without a standard type for reproduction to occur, then there is nothing for the selection process to select from in terms of physical traits, because DNA RNA transcription is a copying process.

While a genetic mutation is by definition a random change to the genetic instructions of a cell during transcription that was not repaired by the DNA proofreading mechanism, and will therefore advance into decay over time, which is what biological aging is defined as due to accumulative mutations. Directional evolution is without a working mechanism to explain biological improvement in regards to living systems, because any adaptability that an organism has gained will always be the result of the DNA RNA selection process, rather than by nature alone, because nature is an external influence, rather than an internal one.

The theory of evolution defines itself as a stochastic process that is deterministic due to changes in allele frequencies over time, which can either occur as a result of DNA proofreading modification, or via genetic mutations. But what the evolutionary theory does not take into account, is that any process that is deterministic can either be random, or specific, depending on the selection process. So, in order to differentiate between that which is random, and that which is specific, then a method of identification is required in order to determine whether the process is direct or indirect in terms of selection.

There are two types of change that can occur within biological systems. One is where the change is specific, and the other is where the change is random. A change that is specific will always be the result of the DNA proofreading process that allows for DNA modification, which is by definition, specific. While a change that is entirely random will always be the result of a genetic mutation, which is by definition, degenerative. And there is indeed a difference between DNA modification and genetic mutations, because a mutation is defined as a random mistake within the DNA proofreading process, or as damage to the genetic instructions of a cell. While the process of DNA proofreading and DNA modification will attempt to remove any mistakes from the genetic sequence via a system of error detection. This means that natural selection will affect an organism in two different ways, first by adaptation, and second by mutation.

Adaption is where variation has occurred, and the DNA proofreading system will allow for variation known as DNA modification, but the amount of variation that an organism can express is limited to its basic format, because DNA RNA transcription is a copying process. While a biological mutation is by definition a random mistake within the copying process that was not repaired by the DNA proofreading and modification system. So, in order to differentiate between that which is efficient, and that which is not, in terms of a process, then DNA proofreading and modification, along with genetic mutations must be defined as separate, because the entire purpose of DNA proofreading, and DNA modification, is to correct and modify a genetic mistake.

There are two key reasons why DNA proofreading is required. First; Is to ensure that a mutation can be corrected. And second; To allow for variation to occur. But the level of variation that an organism can express is reducing itself with age, because no biological system can improve with age due to accumulative mutations that are hereditary. So, in order to interpret natural selection as a process, then there needs to be a correct interpretation and identification between DNA modification, and genetic mutations, and there are two very distinct types of interpretation in terms of a theory. One is a creationist interpretation, and the other is an evolutionary interpretation.

The evolutionary interpretation is that genetic mutations cause slight variations that will supposedly improve a species over time according to nature's preference and successive breeding. While the creationist interpretation disqualifies genetic mutations as a possible source for biological improvement on the basis that a genetic mutation is a genetic mistake, rather than a biological improvement. So, because DNA proofreading and DNA modification are distinct from biological mutations in that the purpose of DNA proofreading is to correct a genetic mutation, it will mean that no amount of mutations is ever going to improve the genome of an organism over time. The reproductive system (or cycle) of an organism cannot be improved upon in terms of efficiency, because it is governed by an instructional method that is limited by a set of parameters.

For example: The purpose of procreation is to produce an end product called the offspring, and the offspring will always be the result of a copying process, because that is what procreation and biological reproduction is; a copying process. And it is a rule with any copying process that all of the variation for a particular kind will derive from an original copy, which in turn, defines each successive copy as a variant of its original. Otherwise, there would be nothing for the selection process to select from in terms of physical traits. DNA proofreading will allow for error detection and DNA modification to occur the same as any instructional system will allow for variation when proofreading and modification occurs. While a genetic mutation causes damage to instructional systems on the basis that the proofreading mechanism has failed to complete a given task, such as error detection.

DNA sequencing is a part of an instructional system whereby each gene sequence that derives from the genome will specify for a particular protein, but if the protein is malformed, then we know that a genetic mutation has occurred. The purpose of DNA proofreading and DNA modification is to reduce the likelihood of a genetic mutation, whilst providing variation at the same time. And yes, we all do carry genetic mutations, but this will in no way cause a biological improvement to occur at any time, because a failure in the DNA proofreading process is by definition a genetic mistake, rather than a biological improvement. The leading cause for a biological mutation is due to external influences, such as ultraviolet radiation exposure, inducing toxic substances, and by not sustaining a complex diet.

So, the more severe a genetic mutation is, the less likely that the organism will go on to live an expected lifespan due to a failure in the DNA proofreading process. DNA proofreading is limited to the instructional format in place that derives from the genomic template, which in itself, is limited to being a type or sort within a kind, because the process of genomic replication is a copying process that acts according to a standard in place, and it is the genotype of an organism that acts as a standard for a particular kind, while the phenotype is by definition a variant within a kind. A biological kind is to act as a base format for the design of a variant, while a variant in place is to act as a means of preservation by having an open breeding population that is diverse in terms of physical traits, so that any breeding or inbreeding program that attempts to restrict a given population will inevitably lead to an increase in hereditary mutations over time, which then leads to a reduction in terms of survival for a particular kind.

No amount of accumulative mutations over time is ever going to improve a species in terms of thermodynamic efficiency, because a biological mutation is by definition a genetic mistake within the DNA proofreading process. A thermodynamic instructional system must derive by instructional systems design, rather than from a natural process. The evolutionary theory is a theoretical assertion concerning separate species within mankind, because the primary objective of the theory is to create a supposed biological hierarchy of less evolved to more evolved, thereby separating mankind into distinct racial groups based on a person's nationality or ethnicity. And it is for this reason that the evolutionary theory constitutes as a racial theory, and is thereby racist from its own assertions and conjectures, because mankind is only one species due to the process of biological procreation which is fixed according to a set of parameters that cannot evolve.

The evolutionary interpretation, no matter how reasonable it may sound, is based entirely on random mutations in order for biological improvement to occur. But that which is biological cannot be improved upon in terms of genetic traits unless a mutation is corrected by the DNA proofreading process, which in turn, offsets the rate of biological entropy within a particular organism resulting in a process that is thermodynamically efficient. So, the only way for biological entropy to be offset within a thermodynamic instructional system, is for the DNA proofreading mechanism to identify and correct a genetic mutation, which means that living systems have an inbuilt mechanism of identification in order to reduce the number of mutations that can occur at random, thereby making the system efficient, as well as specific.

If nature was to select out the best pair for breeding, then that would be purely circumstantial, because nature cannot select directly, nor can nature take future conditions into account. Natural selection will indeed select according to nature's preference, but anything that has had a set of preferences applied to it, is by definition a creation. This means that natural selection is the result of a system in place that allows for speciation to occur independent of the Creator who has set limitations upon the system according to a set of parameters that can fluctuate or alternate.

And this is also where the evolutionary interpretation departs from reality, because the theory assumes that biological improvement and genetic mutations are without limitations. Hence the reason why the theory of evolution assumes that mankind has derived from bacteria over millions of years via mutations, which is based entirely on fanciful thinking, rather than practical demonstrations. The idea that living organisms are self-improving over millions of years is without justification from an observational perspective, because adding time to a thermodynamic process that tends toward disorder will only increase the level of disorder there is over time, rather than increasing in thermodynamic efficiency in a matter of time due to the problem of aging.

Biological entropy is the direct result of genetic mutations within living systems that accumulate over time within the genotype of an organism, which is why adding time to the biological process of aging results in degeneration, rather than biological improvement. So, in order for biological reproduction to be defined as efficient, then an orderly process is required, which is where DNA proofreading and DNA modification comes into play, because as a particular breeding group is replicating or procreating, the amount of genetic mistakes that a particular group retains can be offset by the addition of separate species, which is the reason why an open breeding population is more efficient than a closed breeding population that shares the same genetic mistakes. While any adaptability that an organism has gained will always be the result of the DNA proofreading process that has selected from a set of physical traits that were already encoded into the overall gene pool of a genotype. Otherwise, there would be nothing for the selection process to select from in terms of physical traits, because genomic replication and reproduction are a copying process.

A copying process can only select from that which has derived from an original copy, because only the original copy will have all of the information for variation, which in turn, defines each successive copy as a variant of its original. Mankind cannot be the result of bacteria over time, because bacteria does not store all of the genetic information for a complete human being, which is required in order for the DNA proofreading process to select from in terms of physical traits. So, for this reason, DNA proofreading is the primary method of identification that is designed to identify a genetic mistake in order to correct the mistake, which not only allows for DNA modification and error detection, but also, DNA proofreading offsets the rate of biological entropy caused by genetic mutations. And a method of identification in regards to selection can either be direct or indirect in terms of its input, so that any indirect method of selection is highly limited and will lead to a mistake, while a direct method of selection is highly specific leaving little room for chance.

Natural selection, according to its correct definition in place, is based entirely on random chance scenarios, which is why nature's preference may not always be advantageous in terms of survival for a particular kind, because nature cannot take future conditions into account, while DNA proofreading and modification does through the process of immunological memory, protein storage, and error detection. So, because nature cannot select directly, while DNA proofreading does, it will mean that DNA RNA transcription cannot be improved upon via natural selection due to the method of selection.

The theory of evolution has failed miserably at explaining the origin of living systems, and has attempted to apply genetic mutations as a means of biological improvement, yet the teaching of evolution continues to hold sway in order to maintain a secular standard for public education concerning origins, which is based on pure naturalism from philosophical materialism as a secular preference. Natural selection is a selection process that produces a random outcome based on an indirect method of selection, which is why natural selection is defined as a stochastic or random process, because nature cannot select directly. And any philosophical conjecture that implies nature can select directly will inadvertently define nature as consciously aware, which is an oxymoron, because nature cannot take future conditions into account due to the method of selection being entirely circumstantial.

The DNA proofreading mechanism within living systems will produce an orderly outcome that is specific according to a standard in place so long as the system is operating according to plan, and it is the standard in place that defines whether the process is orderly or not according to a set of parameters, which in turn, sets the limitations of a biological process. A mutational process on the other hand is by definition an inefficient process due to accumulative mistakes, while DNA proofreading and modification is by definition an efficient process, because the entire purpose of DNA proofreading and modification is to correct a genetic mistake.

An abnormality within biological systems can only occur as long as there is an orderly system in place first by definition of the fact that something normal was occurring to begin with, otherwise, there would be nothing to define that which is orderly in terms of a physical outcome, because everything would be entirely random. While any process that is specific in terms of efficiency must occur by the action of creativity, either directly or indirectly, because a method of identification is required first in order to generate the specifics needed for the procedure to occur as orderly. Thus, a group of species reproducing in the wild may seem like a completely random process at work to some, but it is actually according to a method in place, because an end product is being produced via a procedure in accordance with the reproductive cycle of an organism that is both repeatable under observation, and therefore, predictable under demonstration. While natural selection, as a process, is entirely unpredictable due to the lack of a procedure that is direct in terms of selection despite the fact that natural selection is deterministic in terms of an outcome.

Both a natural process, and an artificial process are evidence of design, because a natural process is simply the normal workings of a system in place, while the inventing of a system will always be according to a designing technique, either directly or indirectly. So, because a biological system works according to a cycle in place that is repeatable under observation, and therefore, predictable under demonstration, it will mean that a method has been applied to life. And this is strong evidence of supernatural creativity, because a natural process will always be the result of a system in place, rather than the cause of one. Otherwise, there would be no causality for an orderly process that is occurring according to a procedure in place that is by definition, specific, and therefore, predictable.

An orderly process that is specific, as well as predictable, cannot be the result of a stochastic process over time, because that which is random will remain random unless a method is applied, and a method in place will always be the evidence of creativity having been applied to the process due to the presence of a procedure. If natural selection is to be defined as a procedure, then natural selection is by definition a creation, which is the main reason why any attempt to demonstrate natural selection will result in the formation of a method, because a process cannot be interpreted any other way apart from a method. So, because a process cannot be interpreted apart from the use of a method, it will mean that all processes, whether random or not, have derived from a procedure, either directly or indirectly.

Natural selection, in terms of the creationist perspective, will indeed select independently of the Creator who has set the parameters on speciation so that an open breeding population can occur, which is essential for the survival of a biological kind. This means that the process of natural selection did not derive from the theory of evolution, but has derived instead as a result of speciation, which in turn, leads to diversification. But the problem with diversification, is that only a portion of the hereditary traits can be passed down to the individual, which in turn, defines each individual as a variant within a kind. No biological process can improve itself over time through aging due to accumulative mutations and biological entropy, which must be offset by DNA proofreading and modification. Biological growth is according to a thermodynamic process at work that is by definition, efficient. While a genetic mutation is by definition an inefficient process due to hereditary mistakes during selection.

Time and chance on a thermodynamic instructional system, such as DNA RNA transcription and DNA proofreading, is equal to entropy, because the process is not self-improving over time due to accumulative mutations, which is a process that is by definition, degenerative, rather than progressive in terms of efficiency. And aging does affect the overall gene-pool of a particular kind due to accumulative mutations that build up within each breeding group as diversification occurs, because DNA RNA transcription is a copying process that inherits genetic mistakes. Natural selection is therefore limited to being an indirect method of selection, while a biological selection process is not limited to being an indirect method of selection only, because it will always be the organism that has the most amount of bearing on the selection process of reproduction.

If natural selection was to select out the best pair for breeding, then that would be purely circumstantial due to the fact that nature cannot select directly, nor can natural selection plan anything in advance. And this explains why this aspect of Darwin's theory concerning natural selection is based on the belief that life is purely the result of random chance, because the evolutionary theory of natural selection is based entirely on random selection, survival of the fittest, and Darwinian eugenics. Natural selection is not a process that can improve biological replication and reproduction over time, because the reproductive cycle for each kind of creature is fixed according to a set of parameters that acts as a standard for genomic replication to occur. Natural selection thereby occurs independently of the Creator who has set the parameters in place for speciation to occur so that an open breeding population is more diverse than a Darwinian inbreeding program based on infanticide and eugenics.

In terms of morality, the evolutionary practice of Darwinian eugenics rejects the universal principle that all human beings are to be born equal and free, and has replaced human morality with "genetic fitness." The racist insinuations by the evolutionary theory include racial superiority among Anglo-Saxons known formally as Arianism. The sole idea behind Darwinian eugenics is to try and protect a particular gene pool, thus leading to the eventual extinction of the so-called "unfit" races. But the problem with this theory, is that an open breeding population is more applicable to the survival of a particular kind, while evolutionary eugenics attempts to restrict a particular breeding group through the practice of inbreeding and infanticide.

Thus, the immorality of the evolutionary theory can be cited by racial segregation policies, ethnic cleansing, and by the forced sterilisation. This problem within society took its most virulent form from the pseudo-scientific practice Nazi racial science, which was done in a desperate attempt to supposedly aid nature by killing off the physically weak who were seen as biological obstacle to others. This attitude of killing off those who are deemed "unfit" for society is the typical mindset of those who take the evolutionary theory of hereditary fitness to a whole new level by defining morality as a human weakness based on the idea that nature will kill off the physically weak if left unrestricted. Thus, evolutionary eugenicists see the elimination of the so-called "unfit" as a work of nature, thereby disregarding human morality based on a supposed law of nature, which is better known as survival of the fittest.

This attitude concerning natural selection as a law of nature is without merit, nor justification, because morality defines murder as unlawful universally, and is thereby a law of humanity, rather than nature. The laws of nature are in regards to communal laws that separate the animals from mankind. While morality forms the basis for moral law, which is not owing to a murderer. So, in order to differentiate between the laws of nature, and moral law, in terms of a principle or truth, then the two must be distinct, because morality forms the basis for that which is just, and therefore, justifiable, within human society. While natural law defines that which is justifiable in terms of animal behaviour, which is the reason why an animal can kill another animal, because an animal is not subject to moral law unless the animal kills a human being. And it is justifiable with a physical outcome that a murderer should face society and be judged for his or her actions before a court of law so that a system of justice should be orderly through due process, thereby establishing morality as a law of human nature, rather than a means of natural selection and survival of the fittest.

What about common descent:

The evolutionary theory of common descent implies that all species have derived from a common ancestor, which was first put forward by Charles Darwin who asserted his ideas from Carlos Linnaeus. Carlos Linnaeus assumed that all varieties of creatures held a distinct characteristic that could relate each group of creature into the same phylum or group by way of genealogical descent. The idea of common descent led Linnaeus to include human beings with quadrupeds, thus giving rise to the term, primate. The term, primate, is a pseudo-definition, because human beings are not quadrupeds, nor can any human being procreate with a quadruped. Procreation is a copying process that is limited by a set of parameters that act as a set of rules, such as the rule that no quadruped can successfully breed with an organism that is bipedal, or the rule that a bipedal organism will always derive from a bipedal organism, rather than a quadruped.

These rules are applicable to procreation in that a species can only be defined as a breeding group or phylum, while anything outside of the breeding group will be defined as a separate species or kind. So, because each group of humans can procreate, it will mean that mankind is only one species, which in turn, defines mankind as only one kind. Common descent by the evolutionary theory assumes that all life has evolved from a common ancestor. The evolutionary assumption of a common ancestor that relates all creatures into a single phylum or family tree has been rejected by modern genetic research on the basis that there is no such creature that can house all genetic traits. DNA RNA transcription is a copying process, and the rule with any copying process is that each copy must derive from an original copy, because only the original copy will have all of the information for variation. This implies that all life began as complex with separate ancestors in terms of a phylum, because if the physical features that an organism has were not with the first copy that its genome began replication with, then there would be nothing for the copying process to select from in terms of physical traits.

So, for this reason, speciation leads to a reduction in terms of variability, because all of the information for variation has derived from an original copy that its genome began replication with, which cannot be a bacterium, because a bacterium does not include a set of genetic traits that can be expressed by every organism. When variability is passed down to the offspring hereditarily, there will always be a loss of variability due to the copying process by definition of the fact that a variant is only a variety within a kind. This means that speciation leads to a reduction in variability on the basis that a variant cannot express all of the information for variation, while the original copy does. And this also proves that each kind of creature has not derived from a common ancestor, but from distinct groups instead, because the DNA RNA copying process limits the amount of variation that an organism can express in terms of a standard.

So, in order for a standard to occur in terms of a species, then a biological kind is also required, because it is the word "kind" that will define a group of species in terms of a common ancestor. The term, phenotype, is in relation to a variant from the genotype, which means that a phenotype cannot exist unless there is a genotype first. Carlos Linnaeus attempted to divide different kinds of creatures into a phylum of species, thereby establishing the Linnaean classification system as being based entirely on speciation. And though Linnaeus' description of separate kinds allowed for the introduction of multiple species within a kind, he also asserted that separate kinds were of common descent, such as apes and humans. Charles Darwin took this approach one step further by asserting that all species have derived from one kind of creature despite the fact that no one creature contains all of the physical characteristics that each creature has, which would be required in order for diversification to occur due to the limitations of the copying process of biological reproduction.

This means that all living creatures are broken up into different kinds with separate species within a kind so that an open breeding population is favoured over a closed breeding population. So, because DNA RNA transcription is a copying process, it will mean that all of the physical characteristics of a species are relative to a particular kind that its genome began replication with, because it is the kind of creature that implies a standard version or genotype, while a species is simply a version or variety of the standard in place. So, a biological kind is any standard version that will speciate over time into distinct varieties, which proves that not all creatures have derived from a common ancestor, but from a distinct kind instead. While a group of species within a particular kind have derived from a common ancestor by reason of deduction, because there is a standard version in place, from which, speciation has occurred.

So, for this reason, a species cannot be defined unless a particular kind has been identified first, because a group of species will always be the result of a biological kind, rather than the cause of one. The pseudo-scientific practice of merging every kind of creature into a single phylum or family tree is essential to the theory of evolution, rather than biology, because it is the evolutionary theory that assumes common descent without first providing a single example of how a species could have occurred without a biological kind in place first.

A biological kind acts as a standard for speciation to occur, which means that a group of species can only derive from a particular kind, so that kinds are broken up into different groups the same as species are broken up into different groups. The reason that a species cannot give rise to a particular kind is entirely due to the copying process of transcription which defines each successive copy as a variant of its original, so that a species must derive from a biological kind, because it is the biological kind known as a genotype that will specify for the phenotype, rather than a genotype deriving from the phenotype. Biological reproduction can only occur as long as there is a standard in place first, because it is a biological kind that is integrated, while a species is singular in terms of a variant.

The definition of reproduction from Oxford Languages is defined as: 1) "The action or process of copying something. Similar: copying" 2) "The production of offspring by a sexual or asexual process. Similar: breeding." So, from the OED we find that biological reproduction is a copying process, which means that the rules of a copying process must apply to biological reproduction. And the first rule with any copying process is that all of the information for variation will be with the first copy and none other, which in turn, defines each successive copy as a variant of its original, which is self-explanatory.

This means that a species must derive from an ancestor that was similar to itself, which does not include placing quadrupeds into the same phylum as humans, nor does it include the wild assertion that all species have derived from a single ancestor, because the copying process of biological reproduction limits a species to being a variant within a kind, so that a biological kind will have all of the information for variation, while a species only contains a portion of the total amount of variation that a particular kind can express. And yes, I am indeed stating the obvious here, but unfortunately for the evolutionists, the obvious stands in the way of an unworkable theory. And evolution is an unworkable theory for reasons relating to ordered complexity, which cannot derive at random, leaving only one other alternative, which is by design.

The evolutionary theory of a Last Universal Common Ancestor (LUCA) is the hypothetical common ancestor cell that supposedly existed before Bacteria, Archaea, and Eukarya. The LUCA theory is interpreted as the point or stage at which the three domains of life diverged from a pre-existing form of life. However, this pre-existing form of life is entirely hypothetical and non-existent. The LUCA theory also asserts that a person's ancestry has derived from a bacterium of some description, when bacteria cannot be placed into the same phylum as human beings on the basis that human beings cannot procreate successfully with any other being apart from human beings. So, in order to define a species then you must first establish a breeding group which becomes the species ancestral lineage by definition of the word, ancestral. This means that any organism that cannot successfully procreate with another organism, is thereby, unrelated, which cannot be defined as ancestral, because an ancestor must be a part of the same breeding group it is from.

The notion by the evolutionary theory that because different kinds of creatures share similar physical features, that somehow, in some way, relates all creatures to each other via a common ancestor, which is rejected by modern genetic research on the basis of recorded lineage. According to the National Institute of Health, genetic ancestry testing involves the comparison of a large number of DNA variants measured in an individual with the frequencies of these variants in reference to other human populations sampled from across the world. This means that if an organism is not of the same breeding group of another organism, then it cannot be, at the same time, an ancestral organism. This limits the theory of evolution to the restraints of human ancestry in order to define the progression of mankind in terms of a lineage, because the only biological ancestor that mankind can have, is mankind itself.

The hypothetical postulation that all life has derived from a single ancestor is the driving and motive force behind the evolutionary theory with zero practical examples to give of how a human being could be in the same breeding group or phylum as the animals apart from redefining the true meaning of the word, ancestor. God in Heaven has bestowed a sacred honour upon mankind that none should merge themselves with the beasts of the field, for in the image of God, man was created. There is no other ancestry for mankind apart from mankind, which is why defining yourself, or others, as an animal is by definition an offence before the universal law of equality that protects a person's universal right to be defined as a created human being with a human ancestry, which is in accordance with international law under inalienable entitlements.

A Creator God is a requirement before international law in order to interpret the human conscience, which is self-aware and self-evident. The human conscience is required before the law, because a lawful obligation cannot be enforced unless there is a moral obligation first. Otherwise, the individual's conscience will be in conflict with a lawful instruction. So, when interpreting universal rights, then a universal system of morality is also required, of which, according to the United Nations High Commissioner's Office, derives from "religious teachings" that includes Biblical creation as a legal standard, while social Darwinism is not. An ethical code of conduct that is universal can be applied as long as there is a system of morality in place that is by definition, universal.

So, for this reason, it is Biblical creation that stands as victorious in terms of a legal standard due to the lawful definition of conscience, which is defined as endowed, rather than evolved. And that which is endowed as inalienable is also a birthright before international law, such as the universal right to be defined as a created human being with a human ancestry, which is in accordance with Biblical teachings, as opposed to being an animal of some description under a scientific theory. The scientific theory of evolution was disqualified as a legal standard by United Nations High Courts at the trial at Nuremberg on the basis that Social Darwinism failed to convince. So, in terms of a theory, Biblical creation is protected under international law as a viable option, while the theory of evolution was rejected on the basis of Social Darwinism, evolutionary eugenics, and survival of the fittest. If the United States Supreme Court is to disqualify Biblical creation with an automatic dismissal on the basis of the evolutionary theory, then Social Darwinism will be protected as a legal standard. And this is a danger to society on the basis that Social Darwinism is a racial theory, which only paves the way for democide and genocide by government, which is an evolutionary practice by Communism, rather than an American liberty.

What about the definition of a mammal?

According to Oxford Languages, a mammal is defined as: 1) "A warm-blooded vertebrate animal of a class that is distinguished by the possession of hair or fur, females that secrete milk for the nourishment of their young, and (typically) the birth of live young." So, from the world's foremost dictionary we find that a mammal is defined by five separate features being: warm-blooded, vertebrate, hair or fur, mammary glands, and live young.

The term used by the evolutionary theory to describe a person as an animal derives from the Linnaean definition of a mammal, which applies to any organism with a mammary gland as being in the same phylum or group. But what the word, mammal, does not take into account, is a species method of reproduction and procreation, which must be taken into account in order to define a group of species with in terms of a breeding group or phylum, because that is what a species is; A breeding group. And the other aspect of a breeding group that must be taken into account is their method of communication, because communication is essential for mating.

Human beings cannot procreate with any type of ape, chimp, or monkey, because there is a set of parameters in place that limits mankind to being a single species or kind. Hence the term, mankind. The ability to procreate not only involves sexual relationships, but also, the ability to produce offspring, which cannot be attributed to the animals alone, because no human being can produce offspring with any type of animal due to the method of identification from the ovum, which selects for itself whether a sperm cell is of the same kind or not.

The definition of a mammal from Linnaean taxonomy defines any creature that secretes milk to feed its live young as being related to each other on the basis that they all have a mammary gland, which is simply an attempt to place as many creatures as possible into a single phylum or family tree. When the Hawaiian pacific cockroach also produces milk from its stomach that acts as a milk gland to feed its live young, and one cannot place whales (or man) in the same classification as insects, because one has an exoskeleton, while the other examples do not. While the other aspect of a mammal regarding live birth also shares its definition with the Hawaiian pacific cockroach, which cannot be placed into the same phylum or group as vertebrates.

The Hawaiian pacific cockroach is a one of a kind organism that defies evolution, and is a primary example of why the definition of a mammal is superficial, rather than literal, because a species is defined by their method of reproduction in terms of a breeding group or phylum, rather than due to any distinct physical feature. So, for this reason, the more definitions there are in place for a mammal, the more each breeding group will be divided from one another, rather than relating them together into a single phylum or hierarchy. Another aspect of the Hawaiian pacific cockroach, is that they're all cold-blooded, which means that not all organisms that give live birth are warm-blooded, hairy, or vertebrate, which in turn, defines the definition of a mammal as a pseudo-definition.

The other aspect of a mammal is that they have hair or fur, but the genetic coding for fur is specific the same as it is for hair, because if an ape or chimp is found to have no fur, then we know that this is the result of a genetic disorder. Yet it is the opposite for humans, because when the individual is coded for full body hair all over, then we know that this is a mutational mistake in the genetic coding. This means that man cannot be defined as a mammal on the basis of hair or fur, because only animals have fur that is designed to cover their whole body, while human beings have hair instead, which is designed to cover the body in proportion to where it is needed. And in any event, an animal does not grow pubic hair while humans do, which cannot be defined as fur, because pubic hair is relative to puberty, rather than for protection from the environment.

Pubic hair is physical evidence that morality exists, because only human beings are aware of nudity, and the growth of pubic hair is a physical sign of one becoming aware of morality, which is never to be extrapolated into a theory involving bald apes specifying for hairy humans, because bald apes are more susceptible to skin cancer from UV radiation, while human beings prefer clothing instead, rather than having a severe genetic mutation as a result of UV exposure, which is impossible for science to cure. And this is a part of the reason why human beings require clothing, while the animals have been endowed with fur instead, because animals require protection from UV radiation the same as humans do.

The other aspect of a chimpanzee is that they are born with white fur around their backside, which indicates that they are under their mothers care until the white fur is gone. Once the white fur is gone, the chimp has reached maturity and then the chimp will be under the care of the alpha male chimp. A chimpanzee may get away with all kinds of mischief in front of the alpha chimp whilst under their mothers care, but once the white fur around their backside is gone, the chimp will be considered as a rival to the alpha male. This process of social development is specific to chimpanzees only, while it is the diametric opposite for human beings in terms of maturity and development, which clearly indicates that chimps are not a predecessor to human beings on any level.

Another definition for a mammal, is that they must have sweat glands, which is something that whales and dolphins do not share the same as they do not have fur. So, whales and dolphins cannot be defined as being a mammal according to the definitions in use. And in any event, only man will sweat from the forehead, because this was a part of the punishment that God put on man according to Genesis 3:19 where God said: "By the sweat of your brow you will eat your food until you return to the ground, since from it you were taken; For dust you are, and to dust you shall return."

The theory of evolution has gone too far by equating mankind with the animals, because now China and the United States are genetically merging human DNA with chimpanzee DNA in order to try and produce a human-animal hybrid using cloning techniques, the same as they have done with pigs and humans. The efforts by evolutionary scientists to create human-animal Chimeras is a crime against humanity, because any creature that is conscious, is also self-aware, and man is not to create abominations that are to be destroyed immediately for the safety of humanity, because if there's one thing that can cause germs and viruses to mutate more rapidly, and cross over from animals to humans more readily, is by genetically cloning humans with animals.

The COVID-19 pathogen has a genetic footprint that has never been observed in any coronavirus sample until now, and I believe that COVID-19 is just a taste of what a major epidemic is like when human DNA is being merged with animal DNA on an ongoing basis in the laboratory. And this is a direct consequence of the accelerated rate of mutation within germs and viruses, which is highly unpredictable when trying to merge humans with animals, as we've seen with swine flu, avian flu and now COVID-19, which is a zoonotic virus due to genetic engineering from a Wuhan laboratory in China that was studying and genetically modifying bat and human DNA.

In order for the preservation of mankind to be protected as distinct, then the experimental practice of merging humans with animals must stop immediately, because nothing will destroy humanity faster than cloning humans with animals, which is self-explanatory. The evolutionary theory has been the primary cause of inhumane social experiments committed on the public without their prior knowledge, because humans and animals are being trialled on in a vain attempt to increase the longevity of human beings, which is a crime against humanity on the basis of human and animal welfare.

If the experimental practice of merging humans with animals continues to go unabated, then we will destroy ourselves as a direct result of the scientific establishment seeking to increase the average lifespan of a human being using cloning techniques that attempt to merge animal hereditaries into the overall gene-pool of mankind. Mankind is distinct as a biological kind, which cannot be merged with the beats of the field biologically unless it is done genetically through cloning techniques, which is why cloning humans with animals is an abomination, rather than a viable medical option. The evolutionary idea that human longevity can be increased through animal hereditaries is the leading and governing factor that will cause the destruction of mankind though due process, because when a new virus has entered the ecosystem, there is no way to take it out. And nothing causes germs and viruses to mutate more rapidly, and cross over from animals to humans more readily, than by cloning humans with animals.

Thus, the evolutionary theory is the world's most dangerous theory bar none, with zero practical examples of how humans have derived from the animals, and with numerous examples of fraud in regards to anthropology. Known frauds in anthropology, such as Australopithecus low afarensis, which has been exhibited publically with human eyes in museum and online exhibitions from an artistic viewpoint, when a fossil skeleton is without a set of eyes to determine its true features. The evolutionary exhibit of Australopithecus also illustrates the figure in question with curved flanges or fingers, while the feet are presented as human or upright without taking into account that curved flanges are for knuckle walking, such is the case with any quadruped. This incident of fraud is entirely due to artistic representations of how the museum in question wishes to exhibit their findings, rather than because of any authenticated evidence on their part.

A second primary example of anthropological fraud involving the evolutionary theory would be the well known anthropological exhibit of Lucy, which was hailed by the evolutionary advocates as the missing link for over forty years. Yet according to anthropological surveys, the knee bone of Lucy was not found with the rest of the skeleton, and was found over a mile away, and 200 feet deeper than the rest of the skeletal fragments. The anthropological reconstruction of skeletal fragments is never an exact science when the fragments are scattered over a vast area, nor is the anthropological practice of interpreting an entire organism based on the collection of a few bone fragments. Thus, the evolutionary theory is relying entirely on the skeletal structure of an organism to be based on human conjecture, and evolutionary bias, rather than physical evidence, in order to propagate the evolutionary theory as fact, which is the evidence of fraud due to the lack of any physical examples that do not include a full skeletal reconstruction from a few bone fragments that have been collected from multiple specimens or anthropological sites.

What is the endogenous retro-viral (ERV) theory for man's origin and how is it refuted?

According to modern evolutionary theories, man has derived from a virus along with animal DNA as our genome contains genetic instructions from viral and animal DNA. This has led to the evolutionary theory that animal and viral DNA is endogenous with the human genome, when in fact there is a biological reason for why humans have animal and viral DNA within their genome. The reason for why the animal and viral DNA is foreign to the human body, rather than endogenous, is because every time you eat meat or are infected by a virus, your body's immune system will keep a record of its genetic make-up in order to respond with in the event of an infection. Anything biological that is foreign to the body will be treated as infectious if the body cannot recognize what the foreign tissue is, and the body has been endowed with a system of inspection and identification when it comes to what we eat.

If we eat meat then our body will retain a record of it in our immune system's memory plasma cells located within the bone marrow of the body, and if an infection is detected within the body, then the autoimmune response is to make antibodies, and the autoimmune system will then begin the task of fighting the infection. The body's immune system will keep a long record of previous infections for multiple generations in order to fight future infections with, and this is also the reason why animal and viral DNA information is stored within our genome; Meaning that the viral and animal DNA within the human body is not endogenous with the human genome, but has merged with it over time instead according to the immune system's storage capacity for foreign biological material.

And in any event, an original copy of the human genome is required if assertions are going to be made concerning what the human genome was like when it first began the process of replication through reproduction compared to today. This means that a purpose comparison chart is needed in order to verify any claims about what the first copy of the human genome was like compared to today's sample of the human genome. And an original copy of the human genome must have existed at some point in history, because anything that is copied from a copy must derive from an original copy, and this is the same for the human genome as well, because that is what the human genome does, it makes copies of itself through replication and reproduction.

What about the age of the universe?

*Quotation: ─────────────────────
Astronomers estimate the age of the universe in two ways.
1) By looking for the oldest stars. And 2) By measuring the rate of expansion of the universe and extrapolating back to the Big Bang. - Source: NASA.gov

According to NASA's government endorsed website, the method for dating the universe involves measuring the position of the furthest stars from Earth and then calculating the expansion rate in outer-space in order to gain a mathematical figure. But if dating the universe is done by calculating the distance between the Earth and the furthest star in space, and then extrapolating a figure by calculating the expansion rate in outer-space in order to gain a theoretical result, (which is equal to 13.8 billion Earth years) then the expansion rate has started where the Earth is, implying that the universe has spread itself out from the position of the Earth.

When the position of the Earth has nothing to do with the furthest star in space or in relation to the assumed position of the Big Bang, but its relationship with the universe itself instead. So, it does not matter how far away the furthest star is from Earth, because there is absolutely no evidence whatsoever that a Big Bang occurred in your backyard some 13.8 billion years ago. While any theories concerning red-shift and blue-shift determining the centre of the universe as being the position of the Earth are arguing from a perspective point of view based on a limited observation, because the direction of red-shift and blue-shift will vary wherever you go throughout the universe. The idea that the furthest stars in space are the oldest stars derives from the hypothetical idea that each star system has derived from a single location in space, such as the position of the Earth according to NASA's method of dating.

So, in order for NASA to assume an age for the universe, then the idea of stars deriving from the Earth's location is required, which is not only hypothetical, but also quite ridiculous as a train of thought, because there is absolutely no evidence that star systems have derived from a single location in space due to the Horizon Problem. The Horizon Problem is the result of distant regions of space that move in opposite directions of each other, and are so far apart that they could never have been in causal contact with one another, because the time it takes for light to travel between each separate region exceeds the supposed age of the universe.

According to the evolutionary theory of the cosmic Big Bang, all star systems must have been in casual contact with one another at some point in history, because they share radiation, as well as microwaves. But because these separate regions in space are so far apart that they could never have been in close contact with one another due to the shear distance that light must travel, it will mean that the evolutionary method of dating the universe is false from the moment of assertion. The only reason that NASA uses this dating technique, is due to the lack of a viable option, and because the Biblical framework upon which astrophysics has been built is now rejected in order to pave the way for the evolutionary theory under the establishment clause of a secular government. Thus, the secular standard for public education is leading mankind into an ideocracy due to the adoption of the evolutionary theory as a standard for public education.

The idea that cosmic inflation can account for the Big Bang is entirely hypothetical, because the expansion rate in space is not an indicator that each star system was in close contact with one another at some point in history. While the evidence that the universe is not going through a cycle that causes the universe to reset itself after so many years, is due to the measurement of time, because there is no way to reverse an action once the action has already occurred within the universe, which means that time moves forward in a downward spiral, rather than upward or outward in a cosmic circle. And this is the same for light, because as time moves forward during the distance at which light must travel between each star system, the expansion rate is also increased at the same time, which cannot be reversed under any demonstration in order to give a definition to the principle in question of a cyclic universe that resets itself after so many years has expired.

This means that the distance that light must travel within a vacuum must reach further and further as the expansion rate also increases, which is not a mechanism for light to travel slower over time, because the more the expansion rate increases, the further light must travel in order to get from point A to point B in a certain length of time. So, for this reason, the cosmic theory of evolution involving the Big Bang hypothesis is the greatest theoretical set back in all of modern physics, because it is illogical to define the speed of light as a fluctuation within a vacuum, the same as it is impractical to reverse an action once the action has already occurred so that a supposed reverse cycle can be identified. While the evolutionary inflation theory regarding the history of the universe has not taken into account that the expansion rate within outer-space is definitively slow.

In order for the universe to spread itself out from a singularity, then time is required, and time is relative to speed, as well as distance travelled. So, as time moves forward, spacetime spirals because spacetime is curved, and as spacetime spirals, the distance between objects in space thereby increases with time. This means that if the universe spread itself out from a singularity at an infinite rate of speed, then the expansion rate in outer-space would also be infinite in speed, because that which is infinite remains infinite by definition of the fact that it was infinite to begin with, which cannot be feasible due to a slow expansion rate in outer-space. The Biblical model of the universe describes the creation of the universe as less than 6000 years old, which is entirely due to the recorded lineage from Adam to Jesus.

But because the establishment clause of a secular government has seen fit to oppose this very ancient principle on the basis of the evolutionary theory, it will mean that the lineage of mankind has also been rejected in order to define human ancestry as an animal phylum, which is not expedient for mankind as a working whole due to the adoption of a theory that was false from its own assertions, and therefore, gave little value to mankind in terms of an equality. So, for this reason, it is the Biblical model for the formation of the universe that requires public understanding through the education system so that equal opportunity is given to every student that is entering a legal system that holds to a Biblical definition of man by the rights of conscience.

What about the age of the Earth?

Back in 2005, Schweitzer and Wittmeyer of the North Carolina State University discovered collagen fibers that contained red blood cells from a T-Rex fossil which sparked much contention as to the validity of the evolutionary theory for the geological column. According to the

Encyclopedia Britannica, the theory of the geological column is a "mental abstract" because the theory attempts to place all geological strata into a vertical sequence laid down over millions of years through accumulated sediments that supposedly from asteroids colliding with the Earth, which they believe has accumulated all of the major sedimentary layers that we have today.

> *Quotation: ————————————————
> The end product of correlation is a mental abstraction called the geologic column. It is the result of integrating all the world's individual rock sequences into a single sequence. - Source: Encyclopedia Britannica (Geological Column).

In order for the geological strata on Earth to form into its different layers then there must first be something that causes the ground to lift up and resettle into layers in a flowing motion, because all of the major layers of stratification cover entire continents with many signs of flow deposit, and very few signs of vertical settlement of sediments from the sky after a massive explosion. And the fact that we find fossilized creatures preserved within the rock layers of strata means that the ground was not formed by asteroids colliding with the Earth, because if all of the asteroid collisions occurred before life began then there wouldn't be any fossil bearing rock layers at all. And if a giant asteroid collided with the Earth and buried all of the creatures around the world completely, then how did the flow deposits with all of the fossil bearing rock layers occur?

And all central deserts on Earth according to geological surveys were once inland oceans that have dried out and the soil is now sandy with a high salt mineral deposit, which indicates that they were once inland seas. So, what this means is that there was a global catastrophe some time ago in the past that has caused billions of creatures and most of the Earth's biomass to be laid down by water within the sedimentary deposits, and the creatures and plants have been preserved as a record of the event within the rock layers.

In order for a creature to be fossilized it must first be buried rapidly, and second, the ground must harden rapidly into rock as well or their physical features will not be preserved within the strata, but will oxidize and decay before a cast can be formed around the creature, or in place of the creature. Permineralization is where minerals like silica fill the empty spaces of shells that are hard in the first place and fossilize more readily, which happens to be the most common form of fossilization. Molds form when shells or bones dissolve leaving behind an empty depression and a cast is then formed when the depression is filled by sediment.

The discovery of red blood cells from a T-Rex fossil back in 2005 by the North Carolina State University was collected from the cretaceous rock layer, which has an evolutionary age of about 65 - 75 million years according to the theory of the geological column. But according to biology, carbon 14 is the longest-lived radioactive isotope of carbon, and accumulates within all living organisms and plant life over their life span, but ceases to accumulate once the life form has stopped eating and breathing. So, for this reason, if the half-life for carbon 14 can be determined, then a maximum age for the fossil sample can be obtained. And the half-life of carbon 14 is 5730 years, which means that the T-Rex fossil that was discovered within the cretaceous rock layer is less than 5730 years old due to the presence of carbon 14 within red blood cells. And yes, red blood cells contain carbon 14, which is exhibited by the National Institute of Health under peer review.

So, because this discovery places the age of the cretaceous rock layer as being less than 5730 years old, it will mean that a global catastrophe has occurred sometime in the recent past that wiped out billions of creatures and plants that are now preserved within the rock layers as a record of the event. Thus, evolution cannot be defined as a natural process, because evolution is not occurring naturally, but as a sequence of progression instead according to a set of preferences in place by the individual, such as the geological column, and the evolutionary family tree, which are indeed "abstract," rather than literal. The concept that mankind can be traced back to a bacterium, and then divided into a biological hierarchy, is purely abstract, simply because the process from start to finish has never been observed, which means that all evolutionary change occurs on the basis of conjecture, rather than evidence.

For example: The common phrase, missing link, will always be applicable to the theory of evolution, because there are supposed to be numerous links between different kinds of creatures that place them into a single phylum or family tree. Yet one cannot link all life into a single family tree, because there is no one single physical feature that can relate all life together into a single phylum. And even breathing is not an example, because many kinds of creatures breathe through an external skeleton, such as insects, or they may breathe through water instead, such as marine life for example.

The entire family tree of evolutionary change has therefore occurred according to a set of preferences, rather than by observation, because there is no way possible to observe all of the supposed changes that the evolutionary theorists have claimed to have occurred. And the geological sequence cannot be used as a reference for evolutionary change, because all of the Earth's major rock strata has been laid down by water catastrophically according to observation, rather than by erosion over millions of years as the theory of evolution claims.

The observation that proves that all of the major fossil bearing rock layers around the Earth were deposited by water, is because all of the Earth's major rock layers display signs of flow deposit, whereby the layers of stratification cover entire continents in a flow formation. So, because the Earth is 75% water, it will be more than fair to assume that all of the Earth's major fossil bearing rock layers have been laid down by water. And this is a process called hydrologic sorting, whereby the heavier minerals sink faster than the lighter minerals, which gives the visual effect of separate layers.

So, because all of the Earth's major fossil bearing rock layers were laid down by water catastrophically, it will mean that there is no specific sequence of fossils making a transition from simple to complex over time within the Earth's strata as Charles Lyell postulated, because all of the fossils were deposited catastrophically, rather than orderly. And this is why rock strata is orderly, while the fossil sequence is not, because the rock layers were formed by hydrologic sorting, while the fossils have been deposited randomly according to their location when the catastrophe occurred. And the greater percentage of fossils that are discovered also happen to be marine creatures, such as seashells and crustaceans that live on the bottom of the ocean and are already hard in the first place, which automatically implies a global flood.

A global flood scenario is the only explanation as to why we have the yellow band around Mount Everest that contains millions of small fossilized sea shells and marine life that causes the yellow band around the mountain near the peak of its summit called the Geneva Spur. The only way for the

Geneva Spur to have occurred, is if the mountains rose and the valleys sank, which caused the marine life that had already been buried by flood waters to lift up with the formation of the mountain. And it has been demonstrated that when two tectonic plates collide, they fold over each other, and one will lift while the other causes a depression along the sides of the uplift, which confirms the Biblical account in Psalm 104:8 "The mountains rose, the valleys sank down to the place that You appointed for them."

So, in conclusion, the Earth's major fossil bearing rock layers have been laid down by water all over the Earth, which indicates that there was a global catastrophe involving a worldwide flood, which had to of predated the ice age, because the only way you can turn the ground into permafrost halfway around the globe, is to saturate the ground first, and then a strong winter needs to occur. And all of this evidence points to the Biblical record where God the Creator formed the Earth out of water, (Genesis 1:1) and also destroyed the Earth with water in a devastating global flood, (Genesis 6:9) that was less than 6000 years ago according to Biblical chronology, and the physical evidence that was discovered by Schweitzer and Wittmeyer of the North Carolina State University.

What about the seven day week?

The 24 hour day is governed by the relationship between the Earth and the sun. While the lunar month is governed by the relationship between the Earth and the moon. And the solar year is governed by the relationship between the Earth and the sun also. But the only thing that governs the 7 day week from its original practice, is the world's oldest calendar still in use, which is the Hebrew-Jewish calendar.

The Hebrew Torah is based on the Hebrew calendar, which was used to date certain events, such as the 7th day, or sabbath day, as well as human chronology from the book of Chronicles, and then later within the Gospel according to the lineage from Adam to Jesus, which marks the beginning of our universal dating system from 1 AD and further back to 3761 BC. Biblical chronology is based on the Hebrew-Jewish calendar as a significant timeline that works out to be the oldest recorded timeline still in use for mankind in the world. And this is highly significant for historians, because this calendar dates the creation of the world at 3761 BC, as well as providing a universal standard timeline for the purpose of recording historical eyewitness accounts.

The Hebrew-Jewish calendar is the oldest calendar still in use according to the Guinness World Records, and is therefore the most substantial record of human history. While no evolutionary theories regarding the history of mankind are permitted in the Guinness World Records, because the evolutionary timeline derives from the geological timescale that was put forward by Charles Lyell in the year 1830. The official reason why the Guinness World Records is the world's leading authority regarding everything record breaking, is because the Guinness World Records will not accept anything that has been conjectured, theorized, promoted, or otherwise, made-up, and relies completely on eyewitness accounts and written statements only in order to set the record straight.

So, the very reason why the Guinness World Records is the world's leading authority on everything record breaking, is for the same reason that an eyewitness testimony constitutes as the most powerful form of evidence there is when in writing, which not only applies to law, but also, science, because the empirical method of identification relies primarily on observation in order to create a table of facts that acts as a standard for education and law. The Hebrew-Jewish calendar is a luni-solar calendar that is based on the lunar months of 29 days alternating with 30 days, because an extra month is intercalated every 3 years based on a cycle of 19 years. So, because the ancient Hebrews used a luni-solar calendar, and because a luni-solar calendar is based on orbital constellations in order to predict the phases of the moon, as well as seasonal changes, it will mean that the ancients were fully aware of a spherical Earth despite anything that an atheist might say to the contrary.

The idea that the Holy Bible teaches a flat Earth derives from atheism and scepticism in regards to Biblical word definitions in use, such as the book of Job (26:7) which refers to the Earth as a circle, but because the Hebrew-Jewish calendar is a luni-solar calendar, it will mean that orbital constellations have been taken into account long before modern astronomy was even invented. The Hebrew-Jewish calendar is also the world's foremost calendar as well, because this calendar is the basis for our universal timeline, such as the Gregorian Christian calendar, as well as the four main belief systems of the world, which are: Judaism, Islamism, Catholicism, and Christianity.

The typical atheist response to this, is that certain ancient empires, such as ancient Babylon, was the source of the 7 day week. But because the Guinness World Records has identified the Hebrew-Jewish calendar as being the oldest calendar still in use that refers to a seven day week in accordance with the Sabbath day of worship, it will mean that the Hebrew-Jewish calendar is therefore the most substantial historical reference regarding the earliest accounts of a 7 day week, because all other ancient calendars are out of use.

The purpose of the 7 day week is to preserve the sabbath day, or 7th day, which is the official reason why the Hebrew-Jewish account is the most reliable account due to a religious holiday that has been recorded from the calendar since the calendar began, so that the lineage of people from Adam to Jesus could be observed by preserving the Sabbath day. So, because the 7 day week is based on a religious holiday, such as the Sabbath, it will mean that the 7 day week is also the oldest most widely held religious practice in the world to date, as well as being the official basis for our universal system of trade and commerce. Most forms of trade and commerce occur during a week day over 5 days, with the first day of the weekend (Saturday) constituting as the Sabbath day for the Jews, and the second day of the weekend (Sunday) constituting as a Sabbath day for the Christians. Thus, any exclusion of religious practice in order to pave the way for a secular society will inevitably result in a loss of privileges by the exclusion of the weekend as a religious holiday, because our universal system of trade and commerce has been built around a religious principle, rather than a secular institution that is lacking an official basis for the seven day week.

CHAPTER 5

Scientific Racism

ccording to Oxford Languages, the definition of racism is defined as: 1) "The belief that different races possess distinct characteristics, abilities, or qualities, especially so as to distinguish them as inferior or superior to one another." And the evolutionary theory, according to its own interpretations, exhibits such notions openly. So, for this reason, the theory of evolution is by definition a racial theory that is responsible for the most prejudiced forms of racism and human-animal cruelty in modern history. And this is reason enough for the United States government to remove the theory of evolution from the public education system, because the theory of evolution cannot be taught without the inclusion of scientific racism as a negative consequence.

The theory of evolution from a secular premise is the leading cause for an ideocracy, whereby the voting constituency is governed by idiots who hold to a theory that brings our equality into question by the reinterpretation of conscience, and by granting Constitutional protections to a racial theory in science that was false from its own assertions. Any system of law that grants protections to a racial theory in science will inadvertently create an ideocracy by placing the due process of law into disrepute, because the purpose of law and order involving due process is to allow for equal opportunity, which is how a system of equality works. The establishment clause of a secular government should not be used as a means to protect, and thereby justify a racial theory in science for reasons relating to the preservation of human rights and equality.

If the establishment clause of a secular government is to be of any use to the people of the United States, then equal opportunity is required through a just deliberation of the law, which does not include any Constitutional protections for a racial theory in science. The Supreme Court decision to grant Constitutional protections to the theory of evolution serves only one purpose, and this is to stifle the religious orientation of the United States from a Christian based democracy, to that of a secular society. America is not a secular society that owes its allegiance to a secular government, because that is Communism.

But rather, America is a Christian based democracy that is to cast their votes in favour of inalienable rights, which does not include any protections for a secular interpretation of that which is inalienable, because the reinterpretation of inalienable rights by a secular government is the governing factor that leads to an ideocracy, whereby the government has contradicted themselves in order to self-vindicate their ability to govern, and thereby regulate the voting constituency. Social Darwinism is by definition a social experiment that is designed to disrupt the religious orientation of the United States in order that the United States government should fail the people during a time of great upheaval, thereby resulting in the failure of the United States social and economic system by the reinterpretation of conscience from a secular premise.

The concept of Social Darwinism involves the teaching of evolution by the State, which is why public education is governed by Social Darwinism from a secular premise, whereby the teaching of evolution is mandatory through the curriculum. So, if anybody wishes to argue that the Social Darwinism has nothing to do with the teaching of evolution, then one can simply reply by citing that the teaching of evolution by the State constitutes as Social Darwinism, because it is the State that is propagating the theory from society through free education, which is a crime against humanity on the basis of equality. And it is for this reason that secular science constitutes as a threat to society from the premise of law, because it is the secular standard for public education that is leading mankind into an age of deceit by the teaching that man is animal.

According to the Universal Declaration of Human Rights and Equality under Article 26 of the UDHR: "Education shall be provided for the purpose of strengthening human rights and equality." So, according to international law, the purpose of free education is for the express purpose of strengthening human rights and equality, as defined by the UDHR. The UDHR has defined the human being according to the endowed human conscience, which is a theological term from the Holy Bible that has been used by international law to define a person as distinct from the animals for the purpose of inalienable entitlements.

Inalienable entitlements, such as the right to be defined as a created human being with a human ancestry, is by definition a universal right that cannot be overruled by scientific theory due to the legal standard in place to define a person with, which grants protections for each individual according to their own beliefs. But, there are no protections under international law for unbelief in regards to the lawful definition of conscience, because the human conscience is a requirement before the law in order to acknowledge a moral obligation, which forms the basis of a legal obligation. And every human being has a lawful obligation to acknowledge human equality before the law, as defined by international agreement.

The common argument by the New Atheist movement against the universal principles of inalienable rights, is that inalienable rights are just a concept or human conjecture, which is a self-refuting argument, because if inalienable rights do not exist on the basis of conjecture, then there is no lawful basis for civil rights either, which is where you argue from before the law. So, for this reason, inalienable rights cannot be a conjecture or a concept only, because it is freedom of conscience that is defined as self-evident before the law, rather than scientific theory. The purpose of inalienable rights is so that we each have protection of person before the law in accordance with international agreement. According to international law, it is an inalienable right to be defined as a created human being with a human ancestry so that systemic racism should be superseded by the universal law of equality, which is the official reason why New Atheism is in a de-facto relationship with international agreement, because the atheist understands full well that the term, inalienable, automatically implies a Creator God for reasons relating to theology.

According to international law under Article 1 of the UDHR, inalienable rights are defined as "endowed," which simply means from birth, and it is the birthright of every individual under international law to be defined as a created human being with a human ancestry on the basis of conscience and reason, so that any and all scientific arguments that oppose the rights of conscience are thereby in opposition to human freedom, because it is freedom of conscience that defines freedom of belief, and it is freedom of belief that protects freedom of ideas. So, if a person is to argue that inalienable rights do not exist on the basis of their opinion, then they have thereby acted in accordance with freedom of belief, which in turn, is defined as inalienable.

Thus, one cannot argue that inalienable rights do not exist on the basis of opinion without bring their right to freedom of ideas before the law into serious question, which would be an oxymoron in any case. If human liberty is to be expressed as a form of ignorance in regards to a lawful instruction that is universal in its interpretation, then the individual who is ignoring a lawful instruction is thereby acting on behalf of others who shall retain their basic rights in accordance with international agreement regardless of scientific opinion in order that each person should have protection of person before the law.

The system we live in is a universal system of law and order so that each person may exercise their basic rights as free individuals under international agreement in order that no individual is ever discriminated against before the law. In order for a law to be just in its interpretation, then protection of person is fundamental, while freedom of opinion is secondary to any lawful instruction that is universal for the purpose of protecting the people's inalienable right to be defined as a person before the law. The creation of the Universal Declaration of Human Rights and Equality is in accordance with international agreement, and the will of the people who shall be defined as created human beings who are endowed with conscience and with rights for the benefit of society, as well as law and order, so that each person may exercise their just liberties without interference from the law, or the scientific establishment.

The modern scientific method is governed by the interpretation of physical laws, rather than by theory alone, because a law in science is based on a measurable action, while a theory attempts to describe the action and its cause. And the one law in science that defines mankind as only one kind, is the law of procreation, because human beings cannot reproduce with any type of animal, which in turn, defines mankind as only one species. Scientific racism can refer to any scientific theory that attempts to divide mankind into a biological hierarchy, or family tree, of separate races or species, which includes all theories of ape to man. Any theory that attempts to divide mankind into a biological hierarchy of less evolved to more evolved will be defined as a racial theory with inferior and superior artificial human races. Evolutionary eugenics is the erroneous scientific theory of selective breeding and infanticide that aims to segregate certain ethnic groups on the supposed basis that a confined breeding group will be genetically more successive than an open breeding group that is free to integrate, and select for themselves.

When according to the United States Holocaust Memorial Museum, evolutionary eugenics was the sole cause for the Holocaust that laid claim to millions of lives by the Nazi racial extermination policies that Hitler and his henchmen were so infamous for. The entire purpose of evolutionary eugenics is to engage in artificial selection, thereby attempting to improve natural selection on the basis of man's preference, rather than nature's. This has led to the increasing idea among the mindset of evolutionary biologists that what nature can do, man can do better, when not only is artificial selection based on inbreeding and infanticide, but also, it is entirely due to artificial selection that purebred animals require veterinary treatment far more often than wild animals do in order to live an expected lifespan, which is just one example of why evolutionary eugenics is a failed hypothesis in biology.

Richard Dawkins who was the professor for public understanding of evolutionary science from the University of Oxford, (1995 - 2005) teaches openly that a racial hierarchy exists for mankind as his best evidence for evolution from atheist perspective. Yet this is the exact same pseudo-scientific ideology that was purported by the Nazi regime, because the theory of evolution is the theoretical basis for Nazi racial science, evolutionary eugenics, and Social Darwinism. The evolutionary theory in practice from society and law is formerly known as Social Darwinism, which is a direct result of the evolutionary theory being taught by the State through the public education system, the same as it was for Nazi Germany during the Third Reich. This issue has now extended itself into the schools of American public education with the full protection of the law.

In contrast, the New Atheist movement has cited religion as the sole cause of World War II and the Holocaust in order to try and deflect the blame away from evolutionary eugenics onto religious belief, when the Jewish people who were targeted primarily by the Nazi racial cleansing campaign were far more religious than the Nazis were. So, if religion had anything to do with the atrocities by the Nazi regime, then it would be one of religious persecution against the Jews, rather than because of any radical religious belief held by Adolf Hitler. Hitler has been cited by many atheists as having a strong alliance with the Christian faith, yet the principles of Nazi racial science that Hitler and his henchmen were so infamous for derives the evolutionary theory in practice and observance, rather than mainstream Christianity.

Social Darwinism poses a very real problem in modern society, because the theory of evolution cannot be taught without the inclusion of superior and inferior human races, which is inherent with all theories of ape to man due to a supposed hierarchy, or family tree, of less evolved to more evolved. The theory of evolution has been the number one cause for scientific racism throughout recent history since the theory was first published in 1859. Yet the theory of evolution is only a continuation of the Linnaean taxonomic system of pseudo-scientific classifications that defines man as a lower animal, and was first published by Carlos Linnaeus in 1735 from his works of Systema Naturae known formally as binomial nomenclature.

Linnaeus developed his classification of man within the animal kingdom in an attempt to describe the progression of mankind from the animal kingdom as a reflection of God's creation. Linnaeus was born into a Christian family, but his views of the natural world around him led Linnaeus to take a alternate approach by placing mankind with the animal kingdom, which was in opposition to Biblical instruction. Thus, any and all arguments by the New Atheist movement that the Linnaean classification of mankind with the animal kingdom derived from his belief in scripture is without merit, nor reasonable cause, because Linnaeus was basing his ideas upon his own observations, rather than the written scriptures. Linnaeus rarely ever quoted the scriptures in his published works, and was more devout to his own interpretation of animals and humans being within the same sexual group known as primates without one single example of how a human being could ever successfully procreate with a four legged creature, such as apes and sloths, which he called the order of Anthropomorpha.

Any theory that attempts to define man as an animal is against the universal law of human equality, because it is from the universal law of equality that each person's right to be defined as a created human being with a human ancestry is protected in accordance with international agreement. The universal law of human equality from the UDHR has defined each human being as equal in rights and opportunity according to the existence of the endowed human conscience, which is why the preservation of human rights and equality from a Biblical standard supersedes any scientific theory as a higher legal standard for the benefit of an individual's protection within the system by the rights of conscience.

By the end of the 19th century, Darwin's theory was increasingly popular among Germany's intellectual elite. Darwin had claimed that humans were the product of what he called, "natural selection," which in his own words was a blind struggle for existence where the fittest survived and reproduced, and the less fit died off. In his book, The Descent of Man, Darwin made it clear that his idea of natural selection had serious implications for humanity as a working whole. Scientific racism advocates that the principles of evolution should be applied to human societies, which is the sole basis for Social Darwinism, scientific racism, and New Atheism. Darwin worried that civilized societies were harming humanity by helping the poor, caring for the sick, and otherwise saving those who nature would have otherwise killed off.

Darwin feared that such humanitarianism could eventually destroy mankind if the weak were protected by the strong. Darwin predicted that the so-called future civilized races of mankind would exterminate the inferior ones, which became the sole criteria for Nazi racial segregation policies during the Third Reich in Germany. Darwin's ideas concerning separate human races ultimately led to a new generation of aristocrats, political leaders, socialist thinkers, and scientific reformers who regarded Darwinism as a scientific justification for world domination and evils like slavery and indigenous genocide. If you read from the scientists of the day in the late 19th and early 20th century, many of them were promoting racism, and even racial extermination policies as a direct result of Darwin's theory.

Many leading biologists and psychologists before World War II helped to solidify the concept of scientific racism, which to them, was a natural consequence of evolution. This later gave rise to National Socialism in Nazi Germany, which aimed to annihilate humanity by any means necessary, only to rebuild mankind afterwards using the evolutionary principles of Darwinian eugenics once the war was over. The main cause of World War II and the Holocaust involving evolutionary eugenics and racial segregation policies by the Nazis was entirely due to the teaching of evolution by the State, which inevitably led to the homicidal and genocidal tendencies that Hitler and his henchmen were so infamous for.

So, for this reason, the teaching of evolution by the State as mandatory within the United States raises reasonable suspicion on the justifiable grounds that the practice of evolutionary eugenics led to the Holocaust and World War II, which was never to be forgotten, lest we forget. The theory of evolution cannot be taught without including the idea that all living systems are related to each other via their genetics, which is not factual, and this is the current theoretical basis for scientific racism due to a supposed hierarchy of less evolved to more evolved. Historically, eugenicists have acted systematically by sterilizing the ones regarded as racially inferior, and or, committing mass genocide on the nationality that has been deemed inferior biologically.

There have been many forms of eugenics throughout history among closed populations that desired to segregate themselves exclusively for breeding a superior generation. Such as the Spartans of ancient Greece, or the indigenous people of Brazil, who were known to commit acts of infanticide as the Spartans did. But no theory in human history is responsible for more deaths by democide than the theory of evolution involving racial and infant extermination policies by governments who sought to implement the theory of evolution under the guise of Darwinian eugenics.

Nazism, historically, is a political science that incorporated the ideology of Social Darwinism from the teaching of evolution by the State, which led to the evolutionary eugenics program that became the pseudo-scientific premise for the Holocaust and racial extermination policies by the Nazi regime. Darwinian eugenics is never going to improve a society that is free and open, because the principles of evolutionary eugenics relies primarily on inbreeding and infanticide, when living systems are better suited to an open population that is free to integrate, rather than being subjected to a Darwinian inbreeding program that is based on selective breeding and infanticide.

The concept of modern eugenics involving the systematic killing of offspring to control abnormalities within a closed population, and through selective breeding, was originally developed by Charles Darwin, who inspired Francis Galton to come up with the term, eugenics. Darwinian eugenics developed into a belief system of systematic murder and infanticide based on the theory of natural selection and survival of the fittest, which eventually led to the murder of over 5,000 infants by the Nazi regime through their euthanasia program along with many others who were deemed unfit for a "new" society.

The evolutionary eugenics program within the Nazi concentration camps resulted in numerous types of inhumane experimentation and medical torture involving genital mutilation on children by Nazi racial scientists, such as Josef Mengele, as well as the systematic murder of infants by SS units. And though these children were innocent, they were not regarded as human beings by the Nazi regime, yet their mothers would have testified to the fact that they were fully human indeed. But it made no difference to the Nazi racial scientists who incinerated the mothers after they were gassed to death with their children by their side; All because of how strong the Nazi racial belief was in evolutionary eugenics and Social Darwinism during the Third Reich.

The common phrase "ontogeny recapitulates phylogeny," is a historical postulation by Ernst Haeckel that the development of a human embryo from fertilization to maturity revealed traces of an animal ancestry. German biologist, Ernst Haeckel, included illustrations of the embryological stages of vertebrates in a series of books published between 1868 and 1908. Fudging the data, he placed the drawings into a comparative grid, highlighting supposed similarities between different kinds of creatures, and then blurring the differences using artistic references, even though the results were highly inaccurate. Haeckel wanted to convince his readers that all vertebrates share a common ancestor, and that embryonic development repeats an evolutionary past. Haeckel cited Johann Wolfgang von Goethe from Germany, Jean Baptiste Lamarck from France, and Charles Darwin from England as his main influences for creating his erroneous biogenetic theory known as ontogeny.

Ontogeny is the hypothetical process of human embryonic development from a single cell, egg, or zygote, into an adult organism. While the term, recapitulate, in biology, means to repeat a former process during embryonic development and growth. And the term, phylogeny, refers to the study of a phylum or lineage. Hence the phrase: Ontogeny recapitulates phylogeny. The idea that human beings have vestigial organs derives from the hypothetical practice of ontology. According to the theory of ontogeny, a vestigial organ is any organ within the body that no longer has a functional use, and is the direct result of an evolutionary progression from animal to human.

A primary example from ontology of a vestigial organ would be the human tailbone, which Haeckel believed was the result of an animal ancestry. But the problem with this theory, is that the human tailbone acts as a nerve ending for the spinal cord that is fixed in its position, while a tail is designed to move. So, because the human tailbone is fixed in its position, while a tail is not, it will mean that the human tailbone has been pre-specified, because any changes to the structure of the spinal cord must be pre-determined, or the nervous system will fail.

A second example of a vestigial organ would be the pancreas, which is a large gland behind the stomach that secretes digestive enzymes into the duodenum, or small intestine. So, because the pancreas is designed to help with digestion, it will mean that the pancreas is not vestigial, because the pancreas also serves a second designated function by the promotion of pancreatic acinar cells that release a series of pro-inflammatory mediators known as cytokines and chemokines, which in turn, promotes the recruitment and activation of immune cells; Meaning that the pancreas serves multiple biological functions within the body simultaneously, and is thereby pre-specified.

If the madness behind scientific racism is ever going to end, then it will start with a conviction of truth first, and by an acknowledgement of human equality second, because if human beings are to be defined as animals according to the evolutionary theory, then it is the evolutionary theory that is bringing our God given humanity into question. If the evolutionary theory is to bring our God given humanity into question before the law, then it is the evolutionary theory that is to be brought into question by the law, rather than the individual's inalienable right to be defined as a created human being with a human ancestry, which is self-explanatory.

A person is not to be referred to as an animal before international law since 1948 under the UDHR, after the Nazi racial scientists were rounded up and tried for crimes against humanity at Nuremberg for reasons relating to the practice of evolutionary eugenics, Social Darwinism, and evolutionary phylogeny. If the theory of evolution continues to be taught as a fact by the United States government, then we will continue to see the rise of Social Darwinism and scientific racism within our global society, which will inevitably lead to the gradual enslavement of mankind through a system of non-belief in regards to the lawful definition of person, because the first step towards enslaving a nation that is free under God, is to inform the people that the theory of evolution cannot be contested for reasons relating to a secular standard, which only amounts to being an open form of religious discrimination against the religious rights of man.

Atheism, according to Karl Marx's philosophy, was designed to: "liberate men and women from suppressing their innate potential as human beings under God," and he desired for people to understand that they possess "individual human agency," and are therefore, "masters of their individual reality," because he believed that individuals invented God, so therefore, He cannot be real. When it is atheism by Communism that will suppress the individual's full potential by likening a human being unto that of an animal, and not the Creator who has endowed the atheist with the ability to understand what a creation is, and therefore, they're without excuse before God and the law.

The concept of human agency by Karl Marx has led to the belief that one can create their own reality via their own imagination, which has led to the illusion that because an individual can create their own reality for themself, they can in turn create reality for others as well by force, or by manipulation.

But when the human imagination becomes a justification for describing reality as a human conjecture in itself, then the process of determining the truth of a matter has boiled down to the human imagination alone, when reality is not the product of the human imagination. The nihilistic and materialistic philosophy that an individual can become the "master of their own reality," is based on the idea that the human imagination is reality. So, according to the logic used by Karl Marx, the human imagination is the very thing to refute the imaginations of others who believe in God, which is hypocritical to say the least, because one imagination does not refute another on the basis that it derived from the imagination, as both were imagined according to the logic used.

Imagining a reality that comes to pass, such as a concept design for a garden, or a new home for example, is the result of human creativity and ingenuity, because the individual has invented that which they have anticipated from their own imagination. The human imagination is the official source of our creativity and all innovation, and therefore, the imagination cannot be a justification to refute the existence of the Creator Himself who is the source of all creativity, because materials by themselves do not possess the creative ability to imagine. The word, design, specifically refers to that which is planned, and we plan from the imagination so as to create something new, whether it be written laws, or an artwork, the principle remains the same, as both have derived by intuition. The ability of the intuitive mind to create rules, and therefore, laws, is an ability that sets us apart from the animal kingdom, because though animals may be able to follow the rules we create, they can never establish them for us, or for each other, which is the official reason why we as human beings act as a voice for the animals, and not the other way around.

So, because a system is rule based, and because the human imagination is for reasons relating to human creativity and ingenuity in order to establish or observe a typical system, it will mean that all systems have derived from a source of imagination. And there is no other causality for systems apart from a source of imagination, because all innovation derives from the action of creativity by definition of the word, innovate. The intuitive mind is able to dwell on thoughts past, present, and future in order to make assessments, which is something that both animals and humans are capable of, but no creature from the animal kingdom can ever invent a rule, because inventing rules derives from a source of conscience, which means that both morality and physical laws have derived from a source of conscience as both are rule based. Thus, the Creator has established His system of moral with good will so that all should acknowledge their maker in spirit and in truth, which also happens to be the correct definition of the lawful term, conscience; A source of spirit and word.

If society is to observe the animals from the viewpoint of a science in order to describe morality, then one will get the impression that there is no basis for good and evil, because nature is without a conscience to reason from. So, for this reason, it is highly illogical, as well as immoral, to try and justify human evils as an animal instinct, because laws in society derive from morality, rather than nature. A law in society cannot be imposed on an animal due to their lack of conscience to understand its moral implications, while human beings are subject to law and order on the basis of a moral obligation to uphold that which is just. And there are a number of laws within society that can be defined as either just or unjust, but it will always be the rules for morality that will interpret a law, because morality is universal, rather than instinctual.

If man is to look to the animal kingdom as a source of morality, then mankind will be enslaved by the laws we create, because the animals are unaware of morality, and it is Biblical morality that defines human freedom on the basis of conscience, rather than a religious test. A lawful obligation can only be defined by a moral obligation, which is not a religious test, but a moral one instead, and every individual has a lawful obligation under international law to acknowledge one another as equals on the basis that each individual is a created human being, which is by definition a birthright, rather than a matter of opinion. Many individuals will cite suffering as a justification to deny the existence of God the Creator, but God in Heaven has taken all suffering into account, because without suffering, then there can be no justice. And we all suffer due to both just and unjust reasons, but it is those who have suffered unjustly that are justified according to the Holy Bible, because to suffer due to an injustice is accounted as righteousness before God.

Therefore, Biblical morality is universal in its interpretation of humanity, because we owe our human equality to no one save the Creator Himself, and His Son, who has endowed mankind with conscience in accordance with the will of His Holy Spirit. God is a righteous God, and He has given mankind justice by the provision of His moral law, which is do unto others as you would have them do unto you, and, to love your neighbour as you love your own, for God has put an eternal merit on faith and love, for He has established all things with faith in love, so that all may know that God alone is their maker, and that God alone is truly good.

The Holy Bible teaches mankind to have faith, because without faith, then there is no hope. And it is the Holy Bible that defines the hope of the unjust as vain, while the hope of the just is not in vain, because they have suffered righteously due to the unjust and their actions. Which is why faith in the Creator is justified by His Son, Jesus Christ, who has suffered at the hands of the unjust for the sake of God's love toward mankind, and for the sake of equality. Jesus Christ gives justification to those who have suffered unjustly by calling the least great in the kingdom to come, so that their suffering is not in vain, for God has established His covenant with man by His death upon the cross, and was made poor in spirit for the sake of human rights and equality.

Social Darwinism on the other hand aims to exterminate the least for biological reasons, which is called eugenics, and to eliminate competition through excessive financial gain, which is called usury. But as Jesus Himself said in Mark 8:36 "For what shall it profit a man, if he shall gain the whole world, yet lose his own soul?" (End of Quote). And this is a reference to God being just, because He has taken the suffering of the least into account and has glorified them because of their righteousness.

So, when the Biblical definition of a human being is frowned upon or removed due to a system of non-belief based on pure naturalism from philosophical materialism as a secular standard for public education, then the process of elimination is held-up by a lack of options for a substitute method, because the secular standard for public education dogmatically demands a materialistic interpretation for everything according to the theory of evolution. Yet it is the theory of evolution that requires removal in order for a substitution to be put in place by the administration, otherwise, we will see the rise of Social Darwinism and scientific racism as a negative consequence through the teaching of evolution by the State.

In order for human equality to be taught from its institutional roots, then the theory of evolution must be overruled from the premise of law in order for the secular standard for public education to be returned to the people, to which, it rightfully belongs, because it is the theory of evolution that denies the universal definition of what a human being is, all on the theoretical basis that man is animal. The societal practice of Linnaean taxonomy and Darwinian evolution within society is known as Social Darwinism, which is an immoral method of fascist control over human populations as we've seen with National Socialism, evolutionary eugenics, and from Communism, which has now co-opted the public school system of America through Marxism, Scientific Atheism, and Secularism. This means that it is the Biblical definition of man that requires protection under the law, rather than the theory of evolution, because it is the theory of evolution that is denying the lawful interpretation of what a person is from a theoretical basis.

The lawful definition for human equality has derived from the Holy Bible due to the use of the theological term, conscience, to define a person as distinct from the animals, which cannot be in conflict with the definitions from public education, because the word, conscience, has a legal definition that is both self-evident and not-without-standing in its legal defence for the purpose of an individual's protection within the system. While any biological definition of man that has derived from the evolutionary theory or Linnaean taxonomy will divide mankind into separate racial groups, which not only leads to the exploitation of indigenous cultures, but also, students, who are made unaware of the legal system they're entering into that is based on human rights and equality from a theological interpretation, rather than a scientific one.

The logical fallacy of scientific racism concerning the false assertion that mankind can be broken up into different species or races has derived from a theoretical postulation, rather than from reality. The Linnaean taxonomic system of naming humans after animals is the leading cause of scientific racism from the pseudo-scientific practice of Linnaean taxonomy and evolutionary phylogeny. Evolution, as a theory, has been used as a justification for some of the most extreme forms of racism by attempting to divide mankind into a biological hierarchy of less evolved to more evolved, which was popular for the Europeans who saw themselves as being more evolved than Africans.

The recent exploitation of indigenous people by Europeans and colonists cannot be explained without first explaining what scientific racism is, because it was the idea of a biological hierarchy of superior and inferior human races that led to the British-American slave trade. Scientific racism cannot be justified scientifically, because mankind is made up by human beings only that are all related back to one man and one woman, which in turn, defines mankind as only one kind, and this is not an ideological concept, but a self-evident reality instead. The theory of evolution in practice, along with the Linnaean system of pseudo-scientific classification, is the sole cause of widespread racism, while international law has defined human freedom on the basis of conscience, so that human freedom is defined as freedom of conscience.

Freedom of conscience is a religious liberty that protects all other liberties that are inalienable, and grants protections for freedom of religion and belief. But, there are no protections under international law for unbelief in regards to the human conscience, because the purpose of universal law is to protect human freedom in accordance with freedom of conscience. This liberty is in itself an inalienable right that cannot be overruled by a secular authority, because the ability to govern is defined by international law as a privilege, rather than a birthright, while freedom of conscience is defined as inalienable, and is therefore a birthright on the basis that each individual is born with a conscience.

So, in order to be consistent with the universal interpretation of human rights and equality, then a Creator God is required, because freedom of conscience is a religious liberty, rather than a secular ideal. The purpose of the separation of Church and State was enacted so that the law did not create a universal religious institution in accordance with the interpretation of universal law. So, for this reason, the separation of Church and State was enacted so that we each have freedom of religion and belief, which cannot be defined as inalienable without the correct interpretation of the Creator.

According to the Holy Bible in the book of John chapter 1, God the Creator is defined as Word and as Spirit, which is what the human conscience is also defined as according to its legal definition in use. The human conscience is defined as an inner voice or word, so that the Light of God that exists in every person is defined by the human conscience. So, all human beings have been created by God in accordance with freedom of conscience, which means that God the Creator has endowed mankind with conscience and with rights. From the book of John 1:1-5 we read that:

"In the beginning was the Word, and the Word was with God, and the Word was God. The same was in the beginning with God. All things were made by Him, and without Him was not anything made that was made. In Him was life, and that life was the Light of men. And the Light shineth in darkness, and the darkness comprehended it not."

So, from the Scriptures we find that God the Creator is Light, and that God is Word, and that His light exists in every man as a form of conscience. This designation forms the literal interpretation of the human conscience from the practice of law, which is not only a form of light, but also, a source of word, and therefore, law. The lawful premise for self-governance under the common law derives from Biblical teachings and Christian theology, because it is moral law that restores peace and security to law and order, as well as society, rather than the teaching of evolution, which is the primary mechanism for human enslavement by the teaching of man's descent from the animal kingdom, and by the denial of conscience.

The evolutionary interpretation of man as being an animal derives primarily from Linnaean taxonomy, which is a pseudo-scientific practice that has failed to recognize the universal law of human equality. So, because Linnaean taxonomy is being taught from the theory of evolution through every public school system in the world, it will mean that human equality will erode with each passing generation, because the lawful definitions for human equality are not being upheld through the public education system in accordance with international agreement. And the reason the lawful definitions are not being upheld, is because of a Linnaean/Darwinian secular standard that applies to public education, which must be reformed to allow for the teaching of human equality according to the lawful definitions in use.

The definitions for human equality, as from international law, are legally incontestable and not-without-standing from a legal premise within 192 nations. While the theory of evolution is in opposition to the lawful definitions set forth by the Universal Declaration of Human Rights and Equality on the basis of Linnaean taxonomy and evolutionary phylogeny, which has been defined as a racist, pseudo-scientific system of belief according to the Encyclopedic definition of scientific racism and Social Darwinism. No theory in human history has caused more inequality than the practice of Linnaean taxonomy, which was used as a justification for African and indigenous slavery for a period of almost 300 years by the

British empire, as well as the American colonies. And if ever there was a shameful mark on human history, then it would be the denoting of a person to being that of an animal, because not only are human beings self-aware of what they are, but also, human beings are consciously aware of who they are as well.

No animal has ever expressed a name for itself by itself, only human beings will name things, and this is the same as it was for Adam when he named all of the creatures in the garden of Eden according to Genesis 2:20, and the entire purpose of scientific endeavour is to discover something new and then name it, because that is how you gain kudos in the field of scientific discovery. This means quite definitively that no animal can ever become a scientist at any point, because in order to be a scientist, then you must be able to name something, which in turn, requires the gift of conscience, rather than a university degree.

Historically, Linnaean taxonomy has been the basis for evolutionary phylogeny, yet Linnaean taxonomy, according to the Linnaean Society of London, is rooted historically in "scientific racism," because Linnaeus attempted to equate mankind with the animal kingdom by dividing humanity into a supposed biological hierarchy of inferior and superior races, which inevitably led to the Holocaust and World War II through the practice of Social Darwinism, evolutionary eugenics, and scientific racism.

*Quotation: ————————————————————
Sometime in the 1750's, Linnaeus started revising his classification of humans, to add physical and moral attributes to geography and skin colour. Further analysis of Linnaeus' works, both printed and manuscripts (including his correspondence) should be undertaken to understand why he took the step of deepening the classification of humans in ways which would have such unfortunate long lasting consequences. The result of this expansion of the classification of man was the 1758 10th edition of Systema naturae, which became the basis for scientific racism.

Thus Linnaeus' hierarchy, with black people at the very bottom, associated with negative moral and physical attributes, stuck. Linnaeus was not the only naturalist writing about the human species in the eighteenth century. In fact, he wrote comparatively less on the subject than his contemporaries, such as the Comte de Buffon and Maupertuis in France, or the German physician Johan Friedrich Blumenbach, all of whom would influence later writers, such as Immanuel Kant and Charles Darwin. - Source: The Linnaean Society of London (Linnaeus and Race).

The racial philosophy of scientific racism can be traced all the way back to Linnaeus' classification of man, because the theory that man is animal by Linnaeus led certain individuals to believe that the racial extermination of the "lower" classes was necessary to the survival of mankind. This concept would later be known as Darwinian eugenics, which conditions the mindset of naturalist thinkers to begin the widespread practice of racially motivated homicide, genocide, and democide with the consent of the law. Law is in place for the benefit of an individual's protection within the system, rather than to protect a pet theory that is responsible for the worst crimes against humanity, such as the Holocaust, the Holodomor famine, and the race war in America that still persists to this very day.

The basis for human equality by the endowed human conscience is incontestable before international human rights legislation so that human freedom should be defined by human rights and equality, rather than by the evolutionary theory of ape to man. But if everyone is to have an equal right to every privilege, then there is nothing left to hope for except for the loss of privileges. And this is why protecting the lawful definition of person is more important collectively than meeting the demands of a minority who feel that they're under privileged or discriminated against, when it is only the atheists who are determined to argue against the lawful definition of person due to their unbelief in the human conscience and Biblical morality.

Atheism begs the question as to how consciousness has occurred, rather than asking why we have a conscience to reason from. When it is why something has occurred that will answer how from an investigative point of view, because the correct order of questioning is: who, what, when, where, why, and how. So, the Creationist is thereby satisfied in regards to how we came to exist by knowing why we exist. Unlike atheism, which cannot answer why mankind exists, and will continue to argue that how is more important than why.

When the only way how is to procreate, which is not defined as being evolution, but as a biological reproduction process instead, because procreation is a repeatable process that produces an end product according to a cycle in place, and is therefore defined as a creation the same as any other method of reproduction or manufacture. And no amount of monkey business in the woods is ever going to innovate a modern society that is based on human rights and equality from the premise of law. The evolutionary dream of an advanced civilization having derived from the apes is lacking in common sense, because the apes have never even approached the idea of building a simple tree-house, let alone an enclosed dwelling inside of a space-station.

The definition for human equality by the UDHR is best explained from a theological definition the same as the United States Constitution, the Declaration of Independence, and their Bill of Rights, because the human conscience is a non-physical aspect of the human mind called the psyche or soul. According to international law, freedom of conscience and religion is an inalienable entitlement; Meaning that a correct theology is required when interpreting the law. While any biological definition for mankind will divide humanity on the grounds that human beings have different nationalities. And it is the difference in nationalities that has caused the most amount of confusion amongst biologists, because your habitat can have an impact on what your biological features will be like. Such as light skin or dark skin for example, which is what variation is, but this in no way excludes any individual from being defined as a human being with a human ancestry according to their genotype, because every human being can physically interbreed biologically, which means that mankind is only one species genetically.

The UDHR has taken its lawful definition of what a person is from the United States Constitution, the Bill of Rights, and their Declaration of Independence, because the legal definitions therein are the same. So, because the legal definition for the human conscience has derived from the Holy Bible, it will mean that the Holy Bible is not only the source of the world's most powerful legal documents to date, but also, it is the source of human rights and equality from the premise of law. Under Article 1 of the United Nations Universal Declaration of Human Rights and Equality (UDHR), the human conscience has been defined as having a spiritual aspect because

"All are to act towards one another in a spirit of brotherhood." And almost every Article under the UDHR stipulates that the protection of freedom of conscience is of the highest priority, because we are all a captive to our conscience, which is not a muscle or a gland within the body.

The theory of evolution has taken the Linnaean taxonomic terms and classification system, and has made it into a system of secular learning for public education, even though it is entirely based on scientific racism historically. Scientific racism is the most pervasive theory in the world today because the idea of separate biological races has been at the pinnacle of evolutionary thought since the theory was first developed by Charles Darwin. Mankind cannot be divided into separate biological races on the basis that all have been endowed with conscience. Yet it is Scientific Atheism that is challenging the theological terminology from law by equating themselves with the animals from the theory of evolution.

But unfortunately for the atheist, no one can be defined as having derived from any other ancestry apart from human ancestry before international law, because to define yourself, or others, as having derived from an animal deprives the individual of their universal right to be defined as a person with a human ancestry under Article 6 of the UDHR. The largest database in the world for human ancestry is Ancestry.com with over 10 million individuals DNA tested for human ancestry, and with over 20 billion individuals from their historical records. Yet none of these individuals can be equated as being of an animal via their ancestry at any point in time. And even today, all individuals around the world are defined as persons due to the global census of birth certificates.

So, if anyone says to you that you are descended from an ape-like creature, then you can simply reply by showing them your birth certificate, which is equated as being legal proof that you are defined as a person before the law. Any attempt by science to equate the human conscience as having derived from nature, is by definition pseudo-scientific, because the one thing that nature is not equipped with is a sense of morality from a source of conscience, which means automatically that the human conscience could not have derived from nature or the animals.

If mankind is to be defined as having derived from nature, or the animals, then mankind will inevitably be enslaved by the laws we create, because according to law, animals, and nature, are defined as property, which is why mankind cannot be defined as having derived from any other ancestry apart from human ancestry due to the nature of human slavery. No theory in human history has caused more inequality than the theory of evolution and Linnaean taxonomy, which is why any attempt to rectify the theory in order to accommodate for human rights and equality, is by definition, a contradiction to the theory.

All human beings have a universal right to be defined as a created human being with a human ancestry so that a person may exercise their basic rights as free individuals without interference from the law, because laws in society are better structured around universal principles for the benefit of an individual's protection within the system. And it is a universal and inalienable principle from international law that a person should be defined as a created human being, rather than an animal in order that each human being should be convicted by their conscience in regards to a lawful instruction that is universal in its interpretation. And it is only those who advocate for the theory of evolution and Linnaean taxonomy that are in denial of this universal principle from a secular premise, which is the official reason why the evolutionary theory poses as a danger to human society, as well as the animal kingdom, because if human beings are to lose their identity within the world, then so also will the animals.

Evolution, as a theory, has attempted to define man as an animal in despite of the universal law of human equality, which is a crime against humanity, because mankind cannot be defined as having derived from any other ancestry apart from human ancestry according to the universal law of human equality. The former issue of human slavery in America is the sole cause for the race war that still persists within the United States, and various parts of the world. If people are not being properly informed through the public education system in regards to a person's universal right to be defined as a created human being with a human ancestry, then the race war in America will never come to an end. And the issue here regarding racism has everything to do with the correct definition of a human being, which cannot be challenged legally by any scientific theory for reasons relating to the correct interpretation of human rights and equality, as from international law.

So, unless the theory of evolution is removed from the public education system, then social inequality and systemic racism will continue to persist, because racism cannot be refuted by the theory of evolution without detracting from the theory itself. And for the United States government to demand that a racial theory like evolution should be taught from public education, and then to test and examine students based on a racial theory, is a crime against humanity, because mankind cannot be divided into a supposed hierarchy of inferior and superior races using biological terminology for reasons relating to human rights and equality.

The legal system we live in has been defined by freedom of conscience, rather than the evolutionary theory that defines man as a lower animal, of which, the legal system cannot cater for because our entire legal system is based on human rights and equality, which cannot define man as an animal without detracting from the lawful definition of person. The human being is not to be interpreted by science before the law for reasons relating to human rights and equality, which means that it is the correct definition of person that requires protection under the law, rather than the evolutionary theory. And the correct definition of what a person is derives from the Holy Bible historically, and from the United States Constitution legally, rather than from biology or taxonomy.

Science is not in authority in regards to what a person is, because science is governed by ethics, and ethics derive from morality and law, which in turn, is relative to the human conscience, which is by definition, spiritual, rather than theoretical. If there is any justice to be had in this world, then it will have to come from faith, rather than from science, because no scientist is above the law, and no judge has the right to reinterpret morality in order to facilitate for a minority of scientists who are in denial of the human conscience. Human freedom is defined by freedom of conscience, which is without limitations on freedom of belief and liberty, but no individual has sufficient cause deny the human conscience before the law without infringing upon the just rights of the people in turn.

This means that any professor or public education provider that denies the human conscience before society on the basis of evolution is making a theological dispute in despite of international agreement to acknowledge one another as equals on the basis of conscience and reason. So, for the safety and welfare of mankind, it is thereby unlawful to deny the human conscience to students who should be made fully aware of the legal system they're entering into that holds to a Biblical definition of man on the basis of conscience and reason.

Our universal system of common law was founded upon the Biblical principles of human equality, because all have been endowed with conscience by their Creator for the purpose of equal rights. So, for this reason, we owe our human equality to no one save the Creator Himself who has endowed each person with conscience and with rights by the provision of His moral law, for we are to love our neighbour as we love our own, and we are to love our maker with all of our own being. One cannot blur the line between the term, consciousness, and the word, conscience, because the human conscience, in legal terms, means that you are able to take on a moral obligation, and therefore, a legal obligation as well.

A legal obligation, such as upholding the lawful premise for human rights and equality, is by definition a moral obligation, which every member of mankind is required to acknowledge for reasons relating to the preservation of law and order. So, because morality is self-evident, then so also is moral law, and this is why mankind is separate from the animal kingdom before the law, because an animal cannot take on a legal obligation in order to understand its moral implications, which means that a legal obligation is relative to morality, rather than animal instincts. The intelligence of any given society will be determined by the way they treat the least who are both poor in spirit due to their affliction, as well as undermined within society due to their poverty.

The poor in spirit are those who are afflicted due to an injustice. While the opposite of being poor in spirit is to be self-righteous, which is the very thing that will lead a man astray from the truth that sets us free. To suffer due to an injustice is accounted as righteousness before God, for God is a universal God, as well as just. Therefore, God gives justice to the down trodden no matter what their nationality is, or their colour of skin, because God alone is just by the provision of His moral law, and God alone will repay. God is both word and spirit, so that each human being who is poor in spirit is also poor in rights, and should never be treated as biologically inferior to others on the basis of an IQ score for reasons relating to the correct interpretation of human rights and equality.

*Quotation: ———————————————————
The validity of IQ testing as a metric for human intelligence, is itself, scientifically disputed. Today, the scientific

consensus is that genetics does not explain differences in IQ test performance between groups, and that observed differences are environmental in origin. Pseudo-scientific claims of inherent differences in intelligence between races have played a central role in the history of scientific racism. - Source: Wikipedia Encyclopedia (Race and Intelligence).

The evolutionary idea of IQ scoring has its roots in the ideology of scientific racism, which attempts to disguise itself as a scientific method, when the outcome is generally non-receptive to those who have a better understanding of what it means to be intelligent. The intelligence of any given society will always be relative to how they treat the poor and the animals, because it is the poor who have gained merit through their hardships, and it is often the poor who are neglected because of their poverty. Every creature has been endowed with ability, each according to their own kind, which gives every living creature purpose within the ecosystem.

The term, compassion, will always be relative to human intelligence, because even the smartest of people can recognize that a compassionate person has a leadership quality, which is why it is better to show compassion when judging, rather than rage. The level of compassion a person has will always be relative to their level of understanding for others and their needs, and the one thing that a radical atheist needs in order to know their maker, is compassion, because this is the very thing they lack towards themselves and others due to the nature of nihilism.

The human conscience is where we judge from, and this is not a consequence of nature, because in order to judge, then you must first decide, and making wise decisions is not something that nature is highly renowned for. The introduction of the concept for natural selection has been used to promote the idea that the human conscience has derived from nature, when natural selection is in fact an indirect method of selection, and any indirect form of selection cannot select directly. While decision making is highly specific leaving little room for chance, because there is a need in place, and it is for the conscience to decide what the immediate needs are that are most important. A high level of conscience is aware of needs, but it is morality that determines what needs are most important, and we should create laws in society based on what is important, rather than what our immediate needs are as individuals.

For example: It is a crime to commit murder or steal, but the only reason this should be a crime universally, is because they are immoral actions that lead to immediate chaos. So, for the purpose of sustaining law and order within society, then there must be laws that reflect upon the rules for universal morality. And the basis for the entire legal system of Western civilization has derived from Biblical morality, that is to say, the Ten Commandments of God and the New Testament. Our system of common law from Western society is at the highest academic level of any society or industry, including arts and sciences, and the intelligence of any given system that governs a society will be based on its level of compassion for the poor and the animals, and not according to any IQ level, which is secondary to having a high level of conscience.

According to Oxford Languages, an ideocracy is defined as: "A government or social management plan that is based on abstract ideas or postulations, according to the immediate needs of the public, or, a particular group or organization." While an official system of governance is based on a universal system of moral law, because laws are better structured around universal principles for the purpose of creating long term solutions that are beneficial for everyone, rather than immediate fixes, which are only beneficial for a few. And there is no immediate fix for many of society's problems, which means that long term solutions are necessary for sustaining a population peaceably, and this requires laws to be made by individuals who are consciously aware of morality from a universal standard for the benefit of an individual's protection within the system, because without morality from a universal perspective, then there is no universal basis for human rights and equality.

Equal rights is a Biblical principle from the New Testament, because all have been endowed with conscience by their Creator for the purpose of equal rights and equal justice thereby. So, because the Biblical definition for what a person is has become the international standard for human rights and equality, as from a lawful premise, it will mean that it is unlawful and inhumane to describe a person as having derived from the animals via their ancestry on the logical basis that mankind alone has been endowed with conscience.

*Quotation: ————————————————————

"The following proposition seems to me in a high degree probable, namely, that any animal whatsoever, endowed with well-marked social instincts, the parental and filial affections being here included, would inevitably acquire a moral sense or conscience as soon as its intellectual powers had become as well, or nearly as well developed, as in man. For, firstly, the social instincts lead an animal to take pleasure in the society of its fellows, to feel a certain amount of sympathy with them, and to perform various services for them." - Charles Darwin. Source: The Descent of Man. (Documented February 24, 1871).

According to Charles Darwin's quote, he is convinced that human morality is purely an animal instinct, when not only is morality not an instinct, because morality is universal as opposed to morals, which are by definition personal, but also, morality is spiritual on the basis that morality is rule based, and therefore, cannot derive from the animals. The human conscience could not have derived from the animals under any circumstances imaginable, because the animals are unable to ask a question, which requires the ability to reason from a source of conscience. The human conscience is a requirement before the law in order to enter a legal society, rather than a degree in science, which is secondary to any lawful obligation.

The universal law of human equality is in place so that we each have security of person before the law, which cannot be attributed to the animals, because the animals are unaware of morality, as well as written laws. If society is to look to the animal kingdom as a source of conscience, then morality will inevitably be redefined in order to suit a pseudo-definition, because the correct definition of the term, conscience, is that it has been endowed to mankind by our Creator for the purpose of understanding morality and law. And it is for this reason that evolutionary theorists have failed in their attempts to define the evolutionary theory as authoritative before international law on the basis that the human conscience cannot derive from the animals due to the lawful definition of property. The United States Supreme Court has denied the Biblical interpretation of the human conscience in favour of evolution, which is a crime against humanity on the basis that it is the Holy Bible that defines the source of human conscience, and human freedom thereby.

If the correct basis for universal morality is rejected in favour of scientific opinion, then there will be no correct basis for the interpretation of human rights and equality, because human rights are based upon freedom of conscience as inalienable, which excludes scientific opinion and debate. Human beings should never be deprived of the laws that sustain the Biblical principles of universal morality, because denying morality as being universal, is to deny a person's basic rights as a human being, which are by definition, universal, and therefore, inalienable. And that which is inalienable is also that which has been endowed, so human rights are best described as having derived from the Creator, rather than from nature, because nature is defined as property, legally speaking.

So, for an individual to argue that the human conscience has derived from nature and the animals, is to argue that mankind is the property of the State, which is the very thing that robs a person of their basic rights as a human being. According to international human rights legislation, a human being has been defined as distinct from the animals due to the human conscience, which is incontestable for the purpose of equal rights, and is based on theological terminology in order for the lawful definitions to be universal in their interpretation. This means that Biblical creation is a lawful instruction, while the theory of evolution is not, because, it is the birthright of every individual person to be defined as a created human being with a human ancestry so that no individual should be defined as an animal from the theory of evolution.

The denial of universal morality by the New Atheist movement is due to the fact that the New Atheist movement claims to a higher moral standard than the universal standard that God the Creator has employed, which is for the benefit of an individual's freedom, rather than being a method of human exploitation as we've seen with the rise of Social Darwinism that aims to promote the evolutionary theory, survival of the fittest, and scientific racism. Scientific racism is an inevitable consequence of the evolutionary theory in practice, because one cannot define mankind as having derived from the animals without detracting from the lawful definition of person.

*Quotation: ————————————————————

It is unlawful for a person to do any act involving a distinction, exclusion, restriction, or preference based on race, colour, descent, national, or ethnic origin, which has the purpose or effect of nullifying or impairing the recognition, enjoyment, or exercise, on an equal footing of any human right or fundamental freedom in the political, economic, social, cultural, or any other field of public life. If, by reason of, or provision of, a law of the Commonwealth or of a State or Territory, persons of a particular race, colour, national, or ethnic origin do not enjoy a right that is enjoyed by persons of another race, colour, national, or ethnic origin, or enjoy a right to a more limited extent than persons of another race, colour, national, or ethnic origin, then, not-without-standing anything in that law, persons of the first-mentioned race, colour, national, or ethnic origin shall by force of this section, enjoy that right to the same extent as persons of that other race, colour, national, or ethnic origin.

For the purposes of this Act there shall be a Race Discrimination Commissioner. The following functions are hereby conferred on the Commission to develop, conduct, and foster research and educational programs and other programs for the purpose of: Combating racial discrimination and prejudices that lead to racial discrimination. - Source: Part III of the Racial Discrimination Act. (Published Online by the Commonwealth Government of Australia).

According to the Australian Human Rights Commission and the good of the Commonwealth, it is unlawful to "discriminate" against a human being on the basis of their "descent," through the public "education" system. So, in order to be consistent with Human Rights Legislation under the common law, then the theory of evolution must be overruled from the premise of law in order for each citizen to be properly informed in regards to their human "origins." Racial discrimination can and does include the theoretical assertion that man is animal, which is propagated from the public education system with the consent of the law. If the level of youth crime within the Commonwealth system is ever going to be reduced, then it will start by removing the evolutionary theory from public education in order to promote human rights and equality, because if the individual is to choose between a lawful instruction, and disobeying the law, then their conscience must be convicted first, which is why morality must be taught to students from a Biblical premise or their will be no universal basis to define morality by the law.

So, the remedy for systemic racism here is simple, because if universal morality, as from a Biblical interpretation, is held as the higher standard, as from law, then the burden of proof falls onto the individual who is making a theological dispute against the lawful definition of 'person' because the lawful definition of 'person' has derived from Biblical theology by the use of the term, "conscience." So, in order to be consistent when interpreting human rights legislation under the common law, then a Creator is a requirement in order to not define the individual as the property of the State. Law is fundamental to human freedom in order to prevent individuals from being incarcerated by having knowledge of the law, which is why a legal advocacy before the law is a universal right.

But, if that advocacy is to defend a racial theory on the basis of secular education by the government of a nation, then it is the secular standard for public education that is causing the problem, which must be substituted in order for human rights and equality to be exercised as a right. And it is for this reason that Biblical creation is a lawful instruction, while the theory of evolution is not, because the right to be defined as a created human being, is by definition, an inalienable right due to the birth status of an individual person as having a human ancestry.

The lawful definition of man as a created human being derives from the theological terms from law that are defined as not-without-standing in their legal defence, rather than the theory of evolution that defines man as a lower animal, of which, the legal system cannot cater for without denying the rights of conscience in return. The theory of evolution and Linnaean taxonomy is the root cause of scientific racism. So, because the government of a nation is endorsing a racial theory at the taxpayer's expense, it will mean that any endorsement of the evolutionary theory, or Linnaean taxonomy, constitutes as a crime against humanity on the basis of equality.

Therefore, we will continue to be faced with the horrors of scientific racism from public education, and systemic racism from the practice of law until the law is changed, which requires legal advocacy that is not in conflict with the secular standard for public education, because it is the the United States government that is endorsing a secular standard for public education that happens to be the main problem here. So, there is sufficient cause for Class Action and litigation against the United States government to exclude the Linnaean/Darwinian terms from public education in order to cater for human rights and equality under the common law, so that we as a people should have security of person before the law, which is in accordance with international agreement under the UDHR.

*Quotation: ————————————————

When President Kennedy delivered his June 11, 1963 Report to the American People on Civil Rights, he addressed a divided country. Many Americans still supported segregation and were reluctant to acknowledge racial injustice. However, months of escalating conflict that included massive demonstrations, police repression, and even deaths of activists and other citizens, compelled Kennedy to take a clear stand on the issue. In this landmark speech on civil rights, Kennedy presented the case for why racial discrimination had no place in American law. He also announced his plans to introduce an omnibus civil rights bill to Congress.

The speech is historically significant for several reasons. It was Kennedy's strongest public statement to the country (and the rest of the world) on civil rights. Also, historians consider it a ground-breaking speech because Kennedy framed racial injustice as a moral or ethical issue. He challenged Americans to ask themselves, how do we want to be treated? What is the right way to behave towards others in a country founded on equality? Finally, the speech was a call to action; Kennedy challenged individuals to act, to treat each other with respect in their daily lives. - source: John F. Kennedy's National Report to the American People on Affirming Civil Rights. Documented Online by the John F. Kennedy Presidential Library and Museum. (Speech dated June 11, 1963).

If inalienable rights derive from nature, then man is thereby the property of the State, because both nature, and the animals, are defined as property, which forms the basis for human slavery. But if inalienable rights derive from the Creator, then man is thereby independent of the State in terms of ownership, and is therefore, sovereign. If Biblical morality is to be taught from public education, then a premise for righting wrongs can begin to take effect within the system starting with a conviction of truth in regards to the lawful interpretation of person. But one must first believe in universal morality in order for this to occur, because in order for a legal system to operate effectively, then belief is required first. Inalienable rights are defined as being endowed to each individual on the basis that every human being has been endowed with conscience by their Creator for the purpose of understanding morality with, which is why a legal obligation cannot be enforced unless there is a moral obligation first, which means that morality is above the law from a Biblical premise.

Human freedom is best described from the implementation of inalienable rights as being endowed from birth, rather than evolved from the apes, because that which is inalienable is also a birthright. And every individual is entitled to life and liberty unless they have broken certain laws, because there is no reason for death unless a law has been broken, whether it be a physical law, or a moral law, it does not matter, because laws in society are for sustaining a population peaceably, and physical laws are for all physical interactions to occur. Thus, morality and law is relative to the meaning of life the same as all physical laws give functionality to the system of the universe, because morality is based on being good to your neighbour according to a universal standard, and to recognize the needs of others who are less fortunate than yourself, which does not include a racial verdict from the evolutionary theory. Universal morality is best defined from the position of compassion, rather than a racial science that includes the evolutionary principles of survival of the fittest, Social Darwinism, and scientific racism.

Any member of society that attempts to define another member of mankind as being from an animal via their ancestry is committing a human rights violation according to international human rights legislation, because the law will interpret what the human being is, and not some racially motivated scientist who is equal with everyone else before the law. A scientist has no more rights than any other individual to reinterpret what a person is on behalf of others before the law, because the law will define the correct legal definitions that are in place for correctional purposes, and for reasons relating to the preservation of human rights and equality. So, to argue that you're descended from an animal before the law is to be in a de-facto relationship with the law, which is why New Atheism is not a default position in relation to belief, because claiming to be an animal does not qualify as a test to define one as an animal.

Especially when you're using the English language to do so, which would be an oxymoron in any case, because no animal can speak before the law. The human conscience is required in order for speech to occur, and this is another physical aspect that separates mankind from the animals, because a human being is able to understand a written instruction, and is thereby capable of obeying a written law. Charles Darwin's theory of evolution has led many to believe that they're an animal by descent, because Darwin claimed that man is a lower animal on a hierarchical scale.

The evolutionary theory of a biological hierarchy that attempts to relate all human beings with the animal kingdom (commonly referred to as evolutionary phylogeny), is postulated without sufficient proof from the scientific community, because all human beings are endowed with conscience to understand morality with, and are therefore subject to moral law, which is not an animal instinct, but a spiritual one instead, because human beings are able to perceive injustices, while the animals don't. And though an animal may be loyal to their owner, or their own kind, they do not perceive injustices on the basis that an injustice is defined by moral law, of which, the animals are unaware due to their lack of conscience, which is incontestable and not-without-standing from the premise of international law under the agreement of 192 nations.

The lawful definition of person is at the cornerstone of modern law, because as time has progressed, the law was required to protect the theological definition of man from a Biblical interpretation in order that each person should be entitled to human rights and equality, which is in opposition to the evolutionary definition of man as a lower animal. Thus, it is with a correct theology that the law should be interpreted in order that each person should exercise their basic rights as free individuals under God our maker who has endowed all life with ability, but unto His own image the gift of conscience, with which, to judge from. And we are not to judge ourselves as unworthy of this gift, for the gift of conscience is a gift of God's own grace, so that each person should have a place within a system that caters to no one on the basis of race, but to everyone on the basis of equality.

The idea that an evolutionary family tree can relate all life back to a single cell derives from the concept of evolutionary phylogeny, which aims to place mankind into the same kingdom as the animals by way of genealogical descent. Yet no human being can be equated as being that of an animal on the basis of their ancestry, because human beings cannot successfully procreate with the animals. So, it is highly illogical, and impractical, to equate yourself as an animal in any instance whatsoever, because human beings are distinct from the animals biologically, as well as legally. Yet today we have evolutionary scientists attempting to merge human DNA with animal DNA through cloning methods, which can only lead to a global biological disaster, because the more evolutionary scientists try to merge man with the beasts of the field, the more zoonotic viruses will become pronounced within the human population just as we've seen with COVID 19.

Once a new virus has entered the ecosystem, there is no way to take it out, which is why the evolutionary practice of merging human DNA with animal DNA must stop immediately, and the public education system in America must return to its cultural roots of Biblical creation, because the United States Constitution recognizes the God of the Bible as being the source of human rights and equality as defined by the rights of conscience. If mankind is to be defined as an animal under a scientific theory, then it is scientific theory that must relent for the purpose of human rights and equality to be exercised as an inalienable right. If the law of equality is to yield to a scientist, then science is in authority, when it is the universal law of human equality that must not be overruled on the basis of theory, because all individuals have a legal obligation to acknowledge each other as created human beings with a human ancestry over any scientific theory, judicial decision, or societal practice, for the purpose of human rights and equality to be exercised as a birthright.

Otherwise, we will continue to be faced with a pseudo-definition of man that is without sufficient cause, because it is the evolutionary theory that must conform to a lawful instruction that is universal in its interpretation, rather than the law of equality conforming to a racial theory in science. The right to be defined as a created human being with a human ancestry is by definition a birthright that cannot be overruled by scientific theory due to the nature of scientific racism. So, it is for this reason that Biblical morality should be taught from its institutional roots of the Holy Bible through the public education curriculum, so that we each have security of person before the law, which is the only way to truly combat systemic racism from law, and scientific racism from public education. And this is by no means a religious test before the law, but rather it is a moral one instead that must weigh upon a person's God given conscience for the good of the people, and for the good of the common law.

> *Quotation: ————————————————————
> Scientific racism, sometimes termed biological racism, is the pseudo-scientific belief that empirical evidence exists to support or justify racism, racial discrimination, racial inferiority, or racial superiority. Historically, scientific racism received credence throughout the scientific community, but it is no longer considered scientific. - Source: Wikipedia Encyclopedia (Scientific Racism).

Any theory that attempts to divide mankind into a racial hierarchy of less evolved to more evolved is by definition a racist concept, and is thereby unlawful in accordance with international law. Social Darwinism has been the primary cause for some of the worst human rights tragedies in recent history, such as the Holocaust, which claimed the lives of over six million Jewish people, all on the basis of the evolutionary theory, and racial segregation policies. Evolutionary phylogeny is steeped in scientific racism, which is inescapable for the theory of evolution, because the theory requires that animals should be placed into a family tree along with humans in order to define the progression of mankind in terms of an animal ancestry.

Yet the indivisibility of human rights and equality means that human rights are inherent to the dignity of every human being, as a human being, which means that respect for all human rights is required for the benefit of all, and the benefit of law is for protection reasons, so that security of property is in place, along with security of person before the law. The evolutionary theory assumes that humans and animals have derived from an RNA virus over millions of years, which is the very thing that robs a human being and the animals of their dignity and respect.

Every human being has a moral obligation to acknowledge one another as equal in rights before the law for the purpose of human rights and equality, which means that no individual has a legal obligation to refute the correct definition of what a person is, as it has been defined from the premise of international law. If human equality is to have any bearing on society, then the correct definition of what a person is must be protected in order for equal rights to be immutable and sustainable. Science is never to be defined as a way of life, because science is simply a way of learning instead, while life is not a product of human endeavour, nor is life measurable from a scientific perspective.

So, the only way to define humanity here on Earth, is by the universal law of human equality and by the rights of conscience, because it is the human conscience that defines human freedom, and it is the Creator who defines the human conscience as endowed to every person, rather than evolved from a lower animal. Human equality means many things to many people, but without the correct definition of what a human being is, then there can be no equality. And there has never been a greater threat to human equality, and therefore, humanity as a whole, than the theory of evolution and Linnaean taxonomy, because the theory that man is animal cannot be taught to students without the inclusion of scientific racism as a negative consequence. Modern science, as an industry, has acted as a law unto itself within society by disregarding basic ethics and human rights through the provision of non-factual material that was intended to be accurate, but lacked common sense. Material such as the supposed evolutionary descent of man from the animal kingdom, when the one thing that cannot be defined as an animal before international law, is a human being for reasons relating to protection of person before the law.

The theory of evolution today is indeed a widespread theory, which is a dangerous position to be in for all of mankind, simply because the theory of evolution completely disregards the universal law of human equality by citing man as a lower animal, which has been a crime against humanity under international agreement since the Holocaust occurred. The Holocaust during World War II involved large groups of Nazi racial scientists attempting to define certain ethnic groups of people as animals that required exterminating for the supposed benefit of mankind, which was a direct result of their unwavering belief in evolution. So, for this reason, scientists must not be permitted to interpret what the human being is before the law for reasons relating to human rights and equality, so that no human being should ever be deprived of their basic rights as a person by being equated as an animal from a scientific theory.

The world is facing many different social issues that have a consequential impact on everyone, such as economic stability, environmental protection, as well as human/animal welfare. But the number one issue that cannot be overlooked, nor underestimated at this point in time, is the issue of racism. Racism is not only an issue for modern society, but also, for law, because in order to sustain a population peaceably, then laws need to be made by individuals who can be held accountable for their own actions. Laws in society are for our own protection as individuals, and the one law that has been tried and proven since the inception of the United States Constitution, is the law of human equality, and is therefore the number one law to protect as we progress into the future, because all of our basic rights are protected by this one law. The Fourteenth Amendment to the United States Constitution states that: "No State shall deny to any person within its jurisdiction the equal protection of the law."

According to the Universal Declaration of Human Rights and Equality (UDHR), our most fundamental right is freedom of conscience and belief, while there are no protections under international law for unbelief in regards to the lawful interpretation of conscience. So, for this reason, New Atheism is in denial of this universal principle due to a theological dispute with the law of equality, as set forth by the United States Constitution, Commonwealth theology, and the Universal Declaration of Human Rights and Equality, which defines a person's universal right to human equality as inalienable on the basis of conscience and reason.

The existence of universal morality is self-explanatory, because all are endowed with conscience in order to understand morality with, which is evidence of a spiritual reality that is an intrinsic part of our physical reality. And the existence of the human conscience is self-evident, because human beings are consciously aware of morality, while the animals are not, which means that human beings are subject to moral law. If the United States government is to force the public education system to demand a materialistic explanation for everything, including life itself, then the United States government has utterly failed the lawful interpretation of human equality as an inalienable right by citing man as a lower animal from the theory of evolution.

The idea that equality means everything should be within a 50:50 ratio, is in fact a recipe for inequality, because one cannot argue for example that our government should be comprised of exactly 50% men, and 50% women, without detracting from the merit that is required in order to become a member of government. So, in order to maintain a fair system whereby everyone is treated equally, then equal opportunity is required, which in turn, sets the groundwork for a fair outcome, which is never going to be 50:50 in terms of a ratio, because the process of selection is subject to variation.

So, even though the outcome is not 50:50 in terms of a ratio, it is still a fair outcome, because the distribution factor was in direct proportion to the outcome of gender equality having been put into effect, which is the fairest outcome there is in terms of equal opportunity. This means that it is unfair to argue that there is gender inequality within government, all because there are fewer women in politics, when your gender does not constitute as a right to be a member of government, whether you are male or female.

If there was a 50:50 distribution of men and women in politics, it would only be an indicator that interference was involved in order to change the outcome according to a set of preferences in place by a particular group or individual, which is not how equal opportunity works. And economic equality does not mean that everyone should have the exact same amount of money, otherwise, everyone would be equally poor as we've seen with Communism whereby the right to own property is trumped by the necessity of the party to maintain absolute control, because you cannot have an equal distribution of property and wealth without interference from an authoritarian form of government.

Human equality is more about equal opportunity than it is in regards to maintaining a proportional outcome that is perfectly even in its distribution, because nothing stifles progress within society more than attempting to fix the outcome in order to prevent variation, which will always be according to a set of variables that are subject to a disproportional ratio. This means that gender equality is not our greatest concern as human beings, especially when we are facing speech dictates by the government in regards to a person's official gender. So, in order for a transgender to be equated as being equal to men and women, then a pseudo-definition is required to be enforced as a speech dictate, which is equal to a form of interference within a system based on equal opportunity for men and women. So, in order for equal opportunity for men and women to exist, then the correct word definitions are required, and they cannot be interfered with by certain so-called humanitarian groups that defend homosexuality, because all it will take for human equality to be lost, is for a pseudo-definition of man to be made mandatory.

No theory in human history has contributed more to human inequality than the theory of evolution due to pseudo-terminology that simply does not apply, such as the term, Negroid, or the term, primate, which are both racially discriminating, because neither one has any merit in regards to what a human being actually is, whether they live in a cave, or in a mansion, it does not matter, because both are human by definition of the fact that both have derived from a human ancestry. The idea that success is driven by having a silver spoon in your mouth from birth is without merit, because the more wealthy you are, the more room there is to make a financial mistake, which is in fact highly common amongst the financial elite. While being poor on the other hand can lead to a better form of financial management so as to put food on the table and provide for your family.

This means that there is virtue in being poor, so long as the individual maintains the capacity to be charitable, because there is no greater virtue in life than to sacrifice your wealth in order to help provide for those who would otherwise starve. Social Darwinism should never be allowed to influence any society that is based on human equality from the premise of law, because the primary reason why Social Darwinism failed historically, was solely due to its close association with Nazism and evolutionary eugenics; Meaning that Darwinism is a byword for racism. Social Darwinism posits that mankind should struggle against the weakest, rather than defending their liberty, which is why the practice of Social Darwinism should be considered as being extremely non-humanitarian, and devoutly racist.

Evolution, as a theory, has been the primary cause of social inequality due to its racist concept of lower races, which is inherent with all theories of ape to man. Any theory that attempts to divide mankind into a biological hierarchy with the animals, is by definition a racist concept, because mankind cannot be divided into a family tree of superior and inferior human races without employing the concept of scientific racism as a negative consequence.

The theory of evolution has attempted to divide mankind into separate racial groups based on separate ancestries, which is a racist concept, because one group will receive a lower classification than the rest based entirely on preference, rather than evidence. And a primary example of this would be Nazi racial ideology and evolutionary phylogeny, which attempted to classify Germans as biologically superior via a supposed evolutionary ancestry, which inevitably led to the exclusion of the Jews. Yet according to history, Jewish scientists form the largest single religious or ethnic group of Nobel Prize winners from the United States.

According to statistics, Jewish scientists represent 27% of the United States Nobel Prize winners while only representing 3% of the general population. In the years of World War II, around 1,150 Jewish scientists, forced to leave their homeland in Germany, emigrated to the United States which led to the intellectual migration responsible for the increase in Jewish-American Nobelists and the domination of American science in general after World War II. This over representation is often attributed to the intellectual migration of Jews to the United States that occurred during the 1930's which resulted from the fascist oppression in Eastern Europe under Adolf Hitler involving the teaching of evolution by the State, which happens to be the current problem within the United States.

According to international law, all human beings are equal on the basis that all have been endowed with conscience, which is why no animal can have a legal obligation placed upon them, because the animals are without a sufficient level of conscience in order to understand a moral implication. And the legal proof of this is due to the fact that animals cannot ask questions, which is a requirement by the law in order to cross-examine a case before the law. The evolutionary definition of man has been the main cause for social inequality, racism, and unfair treatment as a direct result of individuals who hail from the evolutionary theory attempting to divide mankind into separate racial groups in order to define one as superior to the other.

Yet mankind cannot be divided into a biological hierarchy of separate races, simply because mankind is only one race, and the evidence of this is due to the fact that all groups of human beings can interbreed, which in turn, defines mankind as only one species. If the Biblical definition of man is not upheld from the premise of law, then we will see our basic rights erode with each passing generation due to an evolutionary definition that was both incorrect, and highly racist from its own assertions. The lawful definition of a human being according to the endowed human conscience is protected under international human rights legislation as universal, while any denial of this human rights treaty is not protected by international law. This means that there are no legal protections for any individual who is attempting to equate mankind with the animals from the viewpoint of the evolutionary theory, because the theory of evolution is in direct opposition to the lawful interpretation of human rights and equality, as defined by international agreement.

If mankind is to have human equality, then the definition of person by evolution must be overruled from the premise of law in order for the correct definition to have a legal bearing on an individual's conscience within society. The more evolution is taught as a fact through the public education system, the more we will see the rise of scientific racism due to a pseudo-definition of man that was false from its own assertions. If human equality is not upheld by the law due to the enforcement of evolution as a theory, then mankind will one day be enslaved by the laws we create, because it is the correct definition of person that defines our basic rights, which is why the argument between Biblical creation and the evolutionary theory is not just a scientific one, but a moral one as well.

So, because ethics derive from the principles of Biblical morality for the good of the common law, it will mean that each individual has a moral obligation to uphold the correct definition of what a person is in order for a legal society based on human rights and equality to operate effectively, whereby the lawful definitions in use are not in conflict with the definitions from public education. Otherwise, we will continue to be faced with the horrors of Social Darwinism from politics and industry as a direct result of a scientific theory that was racist from its own assertions, and therefore, gave little hope to those who must endure the strife caused by a racial theory in practice. The greatest underlying threat to humanity that mankind has ever faced, is the theory of evolution in practice from the premise of law and public education due to the exploitation of the weak, and the law, because if there's one thing that a system of equality cannot cater for, is systemic racism, which is inherent with all theories of ape to man.

Human equality and multiculturalism are not the same thing, because human equality is based on a universal standard in place for what a person is that is both incontestable and universal on the basis of a moral obligation. While the art of multiculturalism attempts to cater to all from the premise of human equality, despite the fact that not all cultures are equal. And your national identity has everything to do with the land that you were born in, rather than the land that your ancestors were from, which is why the term, African-American, only applies to dual citizenship, because if the individual was born in America, then they are by definition, American. So, unless the correct basis for human equality is upheld for the protection of different cultures as distinct according to their own identity, then they will lose their cultural identity, because human equality is not about merging different cultures into a one world culture, but protecting them instead as distinct from each other for the purpose of each person having a nationality of their own, which is a universal right according to international law under Article 15.1 of the UDHR.

Every person is legally entitled to be recognized by their individual nationality for the sake of having a homeland, but no individual has a right to debate whether or not their previous homeland should be upheld within the new homeland they're in, because their new homeland is also distinct as a nation the same as their previous homeland. So, both constituencies will retain the right to a distinct culture within their own homeland, which is in the best interests of the new settler, and the people within that nation who have a distinct culture of their own that they wish to retain for the purpose of having a homeland for themselves in the future, which is what equality means between different nations.

Cultural and ethnic diversity is essential to maintaining the human population by preventing the overall breeding population from being confined into separate groups, which means that multiculturalism has a role to play within society. But no society should have to change their laws, or their culture, to accommodate for an individual's different nationality, which is why any attempt to Christianise a Muslim country that has established its system of law based on Islam, is in reality, a waste of time, the same as it is destructive for Islam to try and convert the Christian nations through politics and protests, because the Judeo-Christian religion is in place so that we have a system of law and order that caters to the good of the people for the good of the common law.

In order for equality to exist between nations, then a national distinction is required, which is not going to end all wars, but it will however create equal opportunity between all nations. The purpose of human equality has everything to do with protecting a person as an individual according to their own nationality, because it is your birthright to a national distinction that gives you your cultural identity as an individual. So, it is not only your distinction as a person that the UDHR is protecting, but also, your national distinction as well, which means that each nation is fully entitled to maintain their own culture within the borders of their own country in order that no individual is deprived of their national identity within the world.

The idea that "non-constructive patriotism," is defending one's nationality and culture from being replaced with another comes from certain humanitarians and globalists that have only taken into account what they want, which is a global society with a single culture, rather than a diverse global society with multiple cultures. If we are to have only one culture in the world, then we will destroy ourselves as a result of a new culture that will see itself as the final culture for all of mankind, which is a dangerous concept to say the least, especially when you take into consideration that we've already had two world wars over this very issue.

And I am not suggesting that we return to a theocracy, but rather, I am attempting to defend the people's right to be defined as created human beings, which does not include the racial definitions from Linnaean taxonomy and the theory of evolution. The right to be defined as a created human being with a human ancestry, is by definition, an inalienable right, while the evolutionary definition of man is in opposition to this universal right. So, in order to be consistent when interpreting the law, then a correct theology is required first, which cannot derive itself from a secular interpretation, because it is the secular standard for public education that is in conflict with a lawful instruction that is universal in its interpretation, such as the inalienable right to be defined as a created human being with a human ancestry, of which, the New Atheist movement has denied from a secular premise

An atheist's biggest fear in life is not the God who made them, but death instead, because throughout the whole of an atheist's life, they will cite death as a justification to deny their maker, which in turn, leads to the second death, of which, the atheist cannot comprehend due to their internal struggle with human suffering itself. When the only one who has power over the second death, is Jesus Christ, the Messiah of the Jews who has suffered for all of mankind upon the cross, and has merged the gentile with the Jew, for the time of God's promise to Jacob is near. The only resolution to the issue of death, is to love your neighbour as you love your own, and to love the Lord your God with all of your heart, because it is from the heart that the spirit speaks, and it is by the Holy Spirit alone that our love for each other is made manifest in accordance with His moral law of good will to thy neighbour.

Therefore, love is justice to the downtrodden, rather than blind and pitiless as we've seen with the rise of Social Darwinism involving scientific racism from the viewpoint of the evolutionary theory. Each human being is a created being on the basis of their birth status, which derives from Adam and Eve in accordance with Biblical teachings, so that we as human beings are brothers and sisters according to Biblical instruction. So, the only way to combat racism from society is with a correct theology, because it is a correct theology that will combat a lie, and the greatest lie ever told was the lie by the evolutionary theory that man is ape, which has caused so much contention within the world today that the Earth cannot sustain peace and security.

It is the will of God our maker that peace should be sustained under a universal agreement that each individual should be convicted by their conscience in regards to a moral obligation that is just in its interpretation so that peace and humility should abide here on Earth. And it is for this reason above all other reasons that protecting the universal definition of person from international law under a Biblical interpretation will sustain us through our trials and tribulations, for it is the will of Satan our enemy that peace should be removed from the Earth by the rise of war, so that a peace agreement between the nations should fail in a time of global crisis.

So, the only resolution to the problem of scientific racism, as from the premise of law, is with a correct theology, which must derive itself from the Holy Bible for the good of the people, and for the good of the common law, so that we as a people may abide with one another upon the Earth that God has created in accordance with the will of His eternal spirit. The spirit of the Lord is a spirit of grace and humility, so that all who acknowledge one another as equal in rights for the sake of human rights and equality shall be remembered on the day of wrath, for it is the spirit of the Lord that convicts the conscience of all wrong doing, so that we as a people should be good to one another in accordance with His moral law of good will towards thy neighbour. God is a just God by the provision of human rights and equality, so that all who defend the rights of the people to a fair hearing, and equal opportunity thereby, shall be redeemed from the hands of the devil at the second judgement where all things shall be laid bear before the Son of God who has suffered for all of mankind upon the cross so that we may have an equality by the rights of conscience.

> *Quotation: ────────────────────
> 1 John 4:11-21
> God is Love:
> Dear friends, since God so loved us, we also ought to love one another. No one has ever seen God, but if we love one another, God lives in us and His love is made complete in us. This is how we know that we live in Him and He in us, for He has given us of His Spirit. And we have seen and testify that the Father has sent His Son to be the Saviour of the world. If anyone acknowledges that Jesus is the Son of God, God lives in them, and they in God. And so we know and rely on the love God has for us.

God is love. Whoever lives in love lives in God, and God in them. This is how love is made complete among us so that we will have confidence on the day of judgement. In this world we are like Jesus. There is no fear in love. But perfect love drives out fear, because fear has to do with punishment. The one who fears is not made perfect in love. We love because He first loved us. Whoever claims to love God yet hates a brother or sister is a liar. For whoever does not love their brother and sister, whom they have seen, cannot love God, whom they have not seen. And He has given us this command: Anyone who loves God, must also love their brother and sister. Amen - Source: The Holy Bible.

CHAPTER 6

Scientific Atheism

IN THE EARLY 17TH CENTURY, A PEACEFUL CHRISTIAN REVOLUTION began called the scientific revolution, also known as the modern learning revolution of England, because the English alphabet was formed, along with a method of empirical verification that was developed into a system of inquiry by English Statesmen, Sir Francis Bacon, who served as Attorney General, and as Lord Chancellor of England (1613 - 1617). Sir Francis Bacon has been accredited as being the father of the modern scientific method, as opposed to Charles Darwin who is accredited with the theory of evolution, which has been the basis for scientific racism since its inception during the mid-19th century.

The scientific revolution that began in England was inspired by a book that was written by Sir Francis Bacon and was published in 1605 called "The Advancement of Learning," which gave rise to a scientific revolution of systematic research via a method of reasoning known as the inductive method, or empirical method, which was first set out by Sir Francis Bacon and later influenced Sir Isaac Newton's discoveries. Newton's method aims to turn theoretical questions into ones that can be adequately answered by the empirical measurement of physical phenomenon, which then led to our modern conceptions of gravitational systems, upon which, modern physics has been built.

The Baconian and Newtonian method of empirical verification involves the inference of general laws or principles from particular instances observed

367

under controlled conditions in order to achieve repeatable results that can be characterized into a system of classification. And this method of inductive reasoning derived from their faith in Scripture and the practice of law, which they openly attributed to the Creator God of Genesis, rather than nature. In order to test potential truths, or hypotheses, Bacon developed a method of reasoning whereby scientists set up experiments in order to establish theoretical principles concerning physical laws under demonstration so as to test potential truths.

Many have attempted to discredit Baconian and Newtonian science on the basis of religion, because both Newton and Bacon were devout Christians. Yet the discoveries by Bacon and Newton led to the interpretation of physical laws which has become the scientific basis for modern physics and systems science. The violent revolution during the Enlightenment era on the other hand was a result of the scientific revolution that began in England during the Renaissance, whereby atheism arose from the scenes by requiring empirical evidence for the existence of God, despite the fact that physical laws cannot disprove a supernatural Creator on the basis that physical laws are not governed by physical interactions, but via a system instead.

Baconian and Newtonian science gave rise to applied systems thinking, whereby the inference of physical laws can be inferred in order to define a given phenomenon, rather than relying on theory alone. So, for this reason, most atheists will not cite Bacon or Newton due to the nature of atheism, which sets out to disprove the existence of the Creator on the basis of theory by employing a scientific reason. But the problem with this type of logic is that it is self-refuting, because in order to explain the existence of physical laws, then a Creator is a requirement, because each physical law is relative to the next resulting in an irreducibly complex system, which cannot occur at random in accordance with the law of probability.

So, in order to get around this problem, atheism has adopted a naturalist mindset, thereby defining all physical laws as a physical phenomenon, when these laws cannot be the result of physical phenomenon, because physical laws are not physical as an object is, which means definitively that physical laws have derived from the Creator, rather than from a physical location within spacetime. So, because physical laws are specific in relation to each other resulting in an irreducibly complex system, it will mean automatically that a method has been applied according to a set of parameters, thereby setting the limit on all physical interactions which gives order and stability to the system of the universe, the same as Biblical morality gives stability to our system of law and order.

> *Quotation: ————————————————————
> "There are two books laid before us to study, to prevent our falling into error; First, the volume of the Scriptures, which reveal the will of God. Then, the volume of the Creatures which express His power." - Sir Francis Bacon. Source: The Advancement of Learning. (Documented in 1605).

Sir Francis Bacon is regarded as the founding father of the modern scientific method known formally as empiricism. Bacon argued from reason that scientific knowledge should be based only upon inductive reasoning and careful illustrations of nature and creation. He believed that science could be achieved by the use of methodical approach whereby scientists aim to avoid misleading themselves with unreasonable studies. Although the most specific proposals about his method of empiricism, the Baconian method did not have long-lasting influence due to the evolutionary theory and Linnaean taxonomy involving the hypothetical assertion that scientific discovery begins with theory first, rather than a table of facts that derive from the correct word definitions in place that are used to correct an individual with, which is a cardinal principle in both law and science.

The importance of Bacon's methodology makes Bacon one of the later founders of the modern scientific method with his approach to science being based on his approach to law as a legal adviser to king James I of England. If there is one field of learning where atheism often assumes authority from a secular premise, then it would be the field of science, because people often view scientists as secular, which is a direct result of people hearing more from scientists that are atheists, such as evolutionary biologist, Richard Dawkins, or neuro-scientist, Sam Harris, who are both co-founders of the New Atheist movement along with Daniel Dennett and Christopher Hitchens. New Atheists are simply atheists who are convinced there is no God due to scientific reasons, hence the term, Scientific Atheism, is fully applicable to the New Atheist movement of today.

Scientific Atheism is based upon a philosophical understanding of nature and humanity from the viewpoint of absolute materialism, and thereby proposes that religion is unscientific in order to propagate atheism, rather than science. The idea that modern science can be used in a way to invalidate the existence of the Creator, as from Genesis, is fundamental to atheism, rather than the empirical method itself. Atheism assumes authority from science despite the fact that the modern scientific method arose from Biblical theology and law, rather than from atheism or philosophical materialism. The key assumption from Scientific Atheism derives from the belief that everything can be explained in terms of materialism, when there are many types of phenomenon that are not materialistic, nor theoretical, such as the existence of the human conscience, which atheism disregards entirely in order to deny morality.

Morality is a non-physical aspect of reality in that moral laws do exist, along with moral obligations, such as being good to your fellow neighbour, and to respect the needs of others. So, without morality, then there is no basis for right and wrong, and this is the primary reason why atheism defines human freedom as freedom from God, because it is morality that will convict the conscience of a man, of which, atheism desires freedom from in order to self-identify as a moral law giver. When in reality, it is logic that defies the atheist by the existence of love, which is not a personal reflection or a chemical reaction, but a spiritual reality instead. Love means many things to many people, such as the Romanized form of love, which is equal to lust, or the love of money, which is equal to greed. But no matter which way the atheist turns, there will always be the presence of morality from a universal principle, because love is defined by morality, rather than by human instincts alone.

Scientific Atheism is the core doctrine of Communism, and to be radically anti-theist is fundamental to Marxist methodology. Scientific Atheism is a Communist doctrine and philosophical science formerly promoted in the Eastern Bloc. The Eastern Bloc, also known as the Communist Bloc, or Soviet Bloc, was a group of socialist States under the strong influence of the Soviet Union that existed up until the unsuccessful 1991 coup against Gorbachev, which ultimately sealed the fate of the Soviet Union.

The Eastern Bloc system followed the socialist ideology of Marxism, Leninism, Trotskyism, Scientific Atheism, and Social Darwinism, which is in opposition to the capitalist Western Bloc system of a Christian democracy involving a coalition force of Judeo-Christian nations. Darwin's theory of evolution was to Karl Marx, a science that could explain atheism, which then gave rise to the Communist doctrine of Scientific Atheism. Scientific Atheism posits that man is animal, and this is postulated by the atheist without question, because the basis for their scientific belief is atheism, rather than the empirical method itself.

The main reason why Karl Marx relied on the evolutionary theory is due to the nature of extreme socialism and the ownership of property, whereby each individual must be fully reliant on a central bank in order to obtain spendable commodities. According to the Ten Planks of Marxism, a nation must be under the control of a central bank in order to define each person as the property of the State, which is how extreme socialism works from the principles of Scientific Atheism. The evolutionary theory forms the theoretical basis to define man as animal, which not only brings a person's God given humanity into question, but also, the rights of property. Individual human sovereignty, as defined by moral law, defines a person's body as their own property, which is not to be taken advantage of for financial gain through the practice of a graduating income tax, which is essential to Marxist ideology.

Modern Scientific Atheism from the New Atheist movement argues for science to replace religious belief, and for rights to be removed from individuals in order to grant privileges to themselves. Rights such as freedom to open prayer and freedom to open worship, because the movement is in favour of stifling the religious orientation of the United States from being a Christian democracy, to being a secular society instead, when the term, secular, is supposed to be a neutral term in relation to belief, rather than a negative.

While freedom to open prayer is in relation to religious liberty, which is immutable within the United States Constitution, and the UDHR, which cannot be interpreted to mean anything other than religious pluralism, which is relative to freedom of speech and freedom of belief. The actions by the United States government and the Supreme Court to remove school sponsored prayer, is in reality, an act of neutrality, because though the government is secular, the democracy is not, and it is the Christian democracy that constitutes as a republic, rather than a secular government alone. And I say Christian democracy in relation to Western culture, because the longest running belief system for public morals within the United States and the Commonwealth nations is Christianity, despite a cultural shift that has now occurred due to lobbying efforts by atheists who are attempting to slowly remove Christianity altogether from both a secular and scientific premise.

A secular society is no more free than a Communist one, because a socialist government is a direct result of secular ideology, and because the application of Secularism from society results in the loss of inalienable rights according to their correct definition as having derived from the Creator. If the Christian democracy within Western culture is not protected under the common law as the basis for public morals, then we will lose the the theological foundations, upon which, the common law has been built. The end result of denying Biblical theology from the premise of common law is absolute atheism from a secular premise, which is equal to Communism according to the principles of Scientific Atheism.

The primary goal of Scientific Atheism, according to Karl Marx, is to dethrone God and to destabilize the coalition force of Christian nations by challenging Biblical Christianity in favour of a secular society, which inevitably leads to Communism, because any secular society that owes its allegiance to a secular government, is by definition, Communist. While the common law system of self-governance maintains its position as immutable, because the concept upon which the common law system was built derives from the universal principles and moral teachings of Biblical Christianity whereby each person is endowed with inalienable rights.

Scientific Atheism argues that faith is a purely religious phenomenon, which is the official reason why atheism denies the existence of faith, when atheism itself constitutes as a faith for two main reasons. First; Is because atheism is protected by law under freedom of belief, which in turn, defines atheism as a belief. And the second reason that atheism constitutes as a faith; Is because in order to deny or reject a belief, then you must also employ an alternate belief at the same time, which then becomes the individual's faith according to a set of preferences, because that is what a faith is: A set of preferred ideas or notions that form the basis of a belief.

But if faith is to be replaced by science, then science becomes a faith, which in turn, defines Scientific Atheism, because it is only atheism that is arguing against the existence of faith from the viewpoint of a science, when the existence of faith cannot be refuted by science, because in order to have a scientific theory, then you must also have a belief. This means that faith is an integral part of the scientific method, just as much as it is a part of religion, because scientific theory is by definition a belief, and is therefore a faith, which means that the existence of faith cannot be refuted by any scientific theory, principle, or law. While any theory concerning falsifiability as being the sole criteria for science is self-refuting, because if a principle in science must be falsifiable on the basis of theory in order for it to be considered as scientific, then the process of determining the truth of a principle in science has derived from a falsifiable premise.

So, in other words, the theory in science concerning falsifiability is by definition a false criteria, because in order to establish whether something is false or not, then a process of determining the truth is required first, which cannot be falsifiable in itself, or there would be no way to establish a principle or truth in both science and law. So, for this reason, the empirical method has been applied in order for facts to be categorized under demonstration by the inference of rules, which forms the logical basis for both theory and systems study.

A theory in both science and law attempts to explain a motive or an action and its cause based on experimentation or cross-examination, which is a cardinal principle for case law or common law, just as it is for the scientific method itself, because in order to establish a conviction of truth in criminal cases, then you must be able to demonstrate a motive or cause by testing the witness statements before a jury. This means that both the common law, and modern science, has derived from Biblical theology, because in order for a law to be just, then it must first be defined by moral law in order to be ethical, while a truth or principle in science must also be subject to morality for ethical reasons.

Scientific Atheism defines itself as an evolutionary concept whereby the teaching of Darwin's theory is enforced without question, because the Communist necessity behind the evolutionary theory, is for the individual to espouse some form of freedom from morality, which in turn, inspires revolution against the common law practice of theology and law. If one is to look to the animal kingdom from the viewpoint of the evolutionary theory with the sole intention of attempting to justify certain evils, such as homicide, sexual immorality, and lawlessness as a law of nature, then secular science becomes the philosophical premise for revolution and anarchy, which is without limitation in regards to human actions, because there is no standard in place for a rule to be defined as just. Justice cannot be measured equally without a system of equality, which cannot derive itself from atheism, because atheism is in opposition to the theological terms from law to define a person with as distinct from the animals, which are not-without-standing in their legal defence from international law for the benefit of an individual's protection within the system. The evolutionary definitions from secular science are the sole basis for the individual's denial of equality due to a theological dispute with the lawful terms in use to define a person with that derive from Biblical theology under the common law.

In the year 1964, the Institute of Scientific Atheism was founded in Moscow, and was heavily engaged in the research of atheism from a scientific perspective. Publications from the institute were strategically designed for propagandists of atheism. The Institute was closed with the collapse of the USSR in 1991. The League of Militant Atheists, (1925 - 1947) also known as The League of Militant Godless, or Society of the Godless, was an atheistic and anti-religious organization of industrial workers and military intelligence officers that formed the new Soviet Russia under the influence of the ideological views of Karl Marx and Vladimir Lenin, which became the Communist Party and held about 96,000 offices across the country.

Guided by the Bolshevik principles of Communist propaganda, and by the Party's orders with regards to religion, the League of Militant Atheists aimed at exterminating religion in all of its manifestations, and by forming an anti-religious scientific mindset among the laity. It propagated atheism and scientific achievements to bolster morale within the sphere of its influence, and with the use of propaganda slogans that proclaimed, "Struggle against religion, is struggle for the five-year plan," which was supposed to be a Communist workers utopia that never occurred.

Communism is defined as an extreme form of socialism just as National Socialism was for Nazi Germany, but the core philosophy behind Communism is Scientific Atheism based on natural selection from the theory of evolution, which includes the teaching of survival of the fittest. Survival of the fittest is a phrase that originated from the evolutionary theory as a way of describing the mechanism for natural selection. Herbert

Spencer was the first to coin the phrase after reading Charles Darwin's book, The Origin of Species, which was highly influential later in the development of Social Darwinism, National Socialism and Communism.

The New Atheist movement of today is by definition a re-enactment of the former Russian Institute of Scientific Atheism within the USSR, because the movement revolves around atheist publishing's from a scientific and moral perspective in order to promote a new scientific revolution based on a godless society. Books such as: The Blind Watchmaker, written by Richard Dawkins, or, The Moral Landscape by Sam Harris, are both prime examples of how Communism is slipping into American and English literature through the use of printed articles that are relative to Militant Atheism, Radical Atheism, and Scientific Atheism.

The League of Militant Atheists was an official organization with the express purpose of spreading atheist propaganda in order to facilitate a Communist regime. The society was heavily engaged in the spread of atheism from the viewpoint of a science, which is why most of the inhumane atrocities by Communism cannot be fully understood until one first understands the nature of absolute atheism. Most individuals in society have no recollection of the Holodomor famine, which literally means "murder by hunger or starvation" in Ukrainian, and has been referred to by historians as, "The Great Famine" due to the number of deaths that were involved. Millions of people from the Ukraine were starved to death along with many Soviet executions against landowners who were seen as political enemies of the State, and therefore, an obstacle to the expansion of Communism. But the real failure during the famine was not on Joseph Stalin's account alone, because the theory of evolution had more to do with it than Stalin himself.

Trofim Lysenko, (who was Joseph Stalin's director of biology) was the head of a group of animal and plant breeders who rejected the modern science of genetics as being impractical, idealistic and a product of "bourgeois Capitalism," so instead, the Soviets promoted the work of Ivan V. Michurin. Michurin believed in a Lamarckian form of evolution that was convenient for a Soviet government trying to engineer the perfect social utopia through agriculture and industrialism. Under their evolutionary system of biology, they believed they could sustainably force plants and animals, and even the Soviet people, to evolve into forms that could serve as practical instruments for the Communist regime. The Lamarckian theory of evolution is not only one of the most discredited theories in the history of science, but also, it was the Lamarckian principles of evolution that led to the starvation of millions of people within the Ukraine and parts of Russia's mainland.

Lysenko claimed that he had changed a species of spring wheat into a type of winter harvesting wheat in just a few short years. Stalin then decided to implement this new strain of wheat into the agricultural system on a large scale. But when winter finally came, the crops failed, resulting in over 4 million deaths by mass starvation, which was promptly followed by the creation of radicalized forms of Communist policy that resulted in the execution of a further 1.8 million people who were landowners in charge of crops during that time.

The official reason why the crops failed was due to the spring wheat species having two sets of chromosomes, while the winter harvesting wheat has three. Lysenko's failed evolutionary experiment to convert spring wheat into a winter harvesting wheat led to the mass starvation of millions of citizens, which is a testimony to the level of naïve ignorance and blatant stupidity that it takes to accept the evolutionary theory. The similarity between agnosticism and atheism, is that agnosticism believes that an individual should not say he knows or believes that which he has no scientific grounds for professing to know or believe. But when faced with the self-explanatory facts concerning the existence of the human conscience, and then denying its self-evident nature on the basis of theory, then the term, scientific atheist, is more appropriate, because it is Scientific Atheism that is defined by its scientific scepticism in relation to belief.

A self-evident proposition or truth, according to common law interpretations, is defined as a principle that requires no proof or explanation on the basis of a moral obligation. Such as the self-evident proposition that: No man is to be brought into jeopardy for the same offence more than once, except in the case of perjury. A self-evident fact is that which requires no further explanation, because it was self-explanatory to begin with, which means that there was no room for doubt in relation to a moral obligation. A self-evident proposition is also equal to a statement of truth, which cannot be denied on any legal grounds for reasons relating to a moral obligation by the law to uphold the course of justice. So, when interpreting a law or theory, it will always be the self-evident word definitions that are defined as being the facts of a matter in regards to any theory for reasons relating to a moral obligation by every individual to uphold the facts that have already been established.

For example: In mathematics, 1+1=2 and we do not debate, nor argue the point about whether this is a fact or not, because this had nothing to do with opinion, nor option, and it had everything to do with an observable process that was both logically deduced, and correctly proportioned in its outcome as well. And it is for the purpose of human equality that laws do exist in order that the outcome is proportional to the situation, and for equal rights to be exercised thereby. A self-evident fact before the law, is that which requires no explanation on the basis of a moral obligation to uphold that which is true or just, and it is also that which was proportional in its outcome, which is in direct relation to the protection of equal rights and equal justice. According to the correct interpretation of the law, a self-evident fact is also a statement of truth that was logically deduced and correctly proportional in its outcome based on the self-explanatory word definitions in use, and must be acknowledged by all due to a moral obligation to uphold the lawful premise for human rights and equality.

So, the basis for human rights legislation relies on each person having a mutual understanding of the word definitions in use to define human equality with, so that each individual is convicted by their conscience in regards to a moral obligation by the law to uphold a conviction of truth. This means that the theological definition of person is at the cornerstone of common law, because in order for human rights to exist, then the definition of person must be universal in accordance with Biblical morality, rather than institutional in accordance with a secular authority. Scientific Atheism holds to the position that man is animal from a secular premise, and is without a sufficient level of conscience to understand morality with, when morality is the basis for rules on human behaviour. Labelling science as completely authoritative is fundamental to replacing morality with science according to the founding principles of the philosophical Enlightenment. But this only results in a lack of ethical conduct by naturalist scientists who do not feel beholden to any other authority apart from themselves alone.

Atheism attempts to deny the existence of an intelligent designer from the viewpoint of a science, but the problem here is that one cannot logically disprove the existence of an intelligent designer by employing their own intelligence in turn, any more than they can disprove what the correct definition is for a design by reinterpreting the meaning of the word to mean something naturalistic only, when the word 'design' is specifically in relation to a creation. So, we have a proper definition of what a creation is from an intelligence gathered perspective, while evolutionists are still scrambling to try and figure out how acids and bases could combine themselves into an instructional sequence without the need for a host cell first, because DNA RNA synthesis requires a protective environment in order to manufacture proteins. So, because DNA RNA synthesis requires a host cell in order to have a controlled environment, the same as a scientific experiment requires a controlled environment in order to achieve a specific aim by design, it will mean automatically that living cells were also designed due to the presence of a controlled environment.

The United States has one of the world's highest incarceration rates, (second only to China) which has steadily increased over the years at the same rate that people are being exposed to the theory of evolution, which is not occurring by chance, but by design, because the only way for Communism to succeed, is for the United States system of law to fail. The approach to the law by the New Atheist movement from their viewpoint of the evolutionary theory has only amounted to being a form of Communist infiltration, which is why atheism is in a de-facto relationship with United States Constitutional law, whereby an individual is defined as being endowed with inalienable rights by their Creator, while atheism is in denial of this universal principle from the viewpoint of a theory.

The Universal law of human equality is not just a theoretical concept, but a self-evident legal standard instead, because all human beings have been endowed with conscience by their Creator, and it is from the conscience that our convictions derive from, which is how we make a moral decisions, and our decisions are subject to the universal principles of Biblical morality, which cannot be justified by nature alone, because nature is defined as property. If inalienable rights have derived from nature, then mankind is thereby the property of the State, which forms the basis for human slavery, because both the animals, and nature, are defined as property, legally speaking. But if inalienable rights derive from the Creator, then mankind is thereby independent of the State in terms of ownership, and is therefore, sovereign.

Therefore, laws in society should reflect upon the universal standard for the rights of conscience from a Biblical interpretation in order to sustain a population peaceably, because international human rights legislation has acknowledged the human conscience as the sole basis for human rights and equality, and human freedom thereby, which cannot be interpreted by a scientific authority from a secular premise without bringing the rights of conscience into question. If one is to argue that the human conscience is the product of nature from a secular premise, then the individual can easily be defined as property, because both nature, and the animals, are legally defined as property, which is a core Communist tenet, rather than a form of liberty, and justice for all. And it is for this reason above all other reasons that the Holy Bible forms the theological basis for human rights and equality by the rights of conscience, because if your conscience was endowed to you by your Creator, then you are by definition independent of the State, and are therefore, sovereign, which forms the lawful premise for human freedom.

Under the common law, the burden of proof is upon the individual who is making an assertion against another individual, such as the plaintiff in case law. While the defendant has a universal right to remain silent before their accuser. So, when a person is demanding evidence for the existence of God, they're usually referring to a visual or physical appearance of the Creator, as from United States Constitutional law and Commonwealth theology. But the evolutionary notion that chemical reactions can become self-aware over time is the very thing that requires physical proof, rather than the individual who has placed their faith in God their maker. A Creator God is a requirement when describing the existence of life for scientific reasons because a thermodynamic instructional system cannot occur at random or via natural process due to the presence of an instructional method.

So, the burden of proof here is upon the one claiming to have physical evidence of chemical reactions becoming self-aware over time without relying on a method to do so, because the moment that a method is implied, is the same moment that creativity is inferred, and therefore, a Creator as well. This means that the burden of proof here is upon the atheist, rather than the individual who has placed their faith in God the Creator, because it is the Creator God of Genesis who is defined as self-evident before the law for reasons relating to the rights of conscience, which in turn, forms the lawful basis for human rights and equality under the common law.

So, for this reason, atheism will appeal to an inquisitional method of questioning, whereby the atheist shall ask the questions, and thereby demands an answer in order to satisfy their own conclusions. When it is the atheist who is not entitled to an answer based on their personal conclusions, because it is the Creator God of Genesis who is defined as self-evident before the law, rather than the atheist and their theoretical assertions. The side with the burden of proof must also be able to prove an element of their case in order to build a case, but the higher the standard is, the more evidence that's required in order to have sufficient cause, because a person's liberty is at stake. And it is for this reason that atheism is without sufficient cause to argue against the existence of God the Creator before the law, because it is the Creator who has endowed each person with conscience and with rights in order for the law to correctly interpret human rights and equality so that equal justice may preside from the premise of common law.

The lawful interpretation of individual human sovereignty, as having derived from the Creator God of Genesis, is of a higher legal standard than the evolutionary theory of ape to man due to the lawful definition of conscience, and human independence, which is self-evident and self-explanatory before the law due to the word definitions in use that are used to define human rights and human sovereignty, which derive from Biblical theology, rather than from secular science. The purpose of a secular authority to govern the people by, is so that a religious standard can be applied on equal terms, which does not constitute as a discrimination of the religious rights of man unless the law overrules the teaching of a Creator, because, it is the inalienable right of every individual to be defined as a created human being on the basis of conscience and equality.

Individual human sovereignty, and human independence, has been defined by the common law as having derived from the Creator God of Genesis due to the existence of the human conscience, which is why every attempt by the atheist to deny the Creator before the law is a crime against humanity on the basis of conscience and reason, because without an acknowledgement of the Creator who has endowed each person with conscience and with rights, then our universal system of equality will be placed into harm's way. Any system of belief that denies the existence of the human conscience, is by definition, unethical, because the lawful interpretation of a human being derives from freedom of conscience, which in turn, derives from the Creator, rather than nature, because nature is legally defined as property.

So, in order to be consistent with human rights legislation under the common law, then a Creator God is a requirement, which must derive itself from Biblical theology, or the end result is total anarchy from a secular premise. The Commonwealth nations and the United States have based inalienable rights upon Biblical teachings, that is to say the Ten Commandments and the New Testament. The New Atheist movement understands fully well that the Commonwealth nations and the United States are a Christian based democracy. So, in order to undermine this alliance, they will cite a secular authority as their right and justification to deny their Creator. And I understand that certain Commonwealth nations do not hold to the Holy Bible as their governing source of theology, such as India and Pakistan for example.

But because the common law has derived historically from Biblical theology, it will mean that the correct interpretation of conscience has derived from the Holy Bible, rather than secular science. Commonwealth theology consists of mainstream Christian theology, which is the official reason why a the Commonwealth nations are under a Christian alliance, rather than a secular one. The independent and self-governing nations of the Commonwealth system attained their sovereignty by declaring their independence from British rule, whilst adopting the common law of England. And though the United States does not participate in the Commonwealth games, they are still an independent and sovereign common law jurisdiction on the basis of a Christian alliance, rather than a secular one. If Communism is to succeed in destroying a Christian alliance between the Commonwealth nations, then it will start from a secular premise, which is the very thing that calls a coalition force of democratic Christian nations into question by applying a scientific debate before the High Courts.

The Creator God of Genesis is self-evident under the common law, and it is His Son, Jesus Christ, who has ushered in an age of grace and of equality by merging the gentile with the Jew, for the time of God's promise to Jacob is at hand in accordance with Biblical theology. Thus, morality is above the law from a Biblical premise, because it is not the law that defines what is good or evil, but a correct theology instead. While secular science is in a theological dispute with the lawful term, conscience, which is the very thing that brings human independence and national sovereignty into question by the reinterpretation of inalienable. If atheism is to argue before the law against the existence of the Creator from a scientific premise, then this will automatically stifle the religious orientation of the Commonwealth nations and the United States to being a secular society, rather than a Christian based democracy, upon which, the foundations of our legal system have been built.

In the case of Edwards vs Aguillard, the Supreme Court cited the establishment clause of secular government within the United States in order to reject the Intelligent Design movement on the basis that it was not secular, and was deemed unfit for public use by the State's board of education. So, for this reason, systems theory and systems science is a viable option to resolve the dispute between theology and secular science, because systems study and systems analysis is modern science, while evolution is a racial theory that requires dismantle and removal in order to pave the way for human rights and equality.

Systems theory and systems science is by no means a religion, nor is it secular, which means that systems theory acts as a common ground for equal opportunity within public education, thus leading to an equality, and a better understanding of the scientific method, as well as the system we live under, which is a system of human rights and equality by the rights of conscience, rather than a system of non-belief based on secular science. The fastest way to undermined the due process of law involving equal opportunity before the law, is by a system of non-belief, which is expedient for Scientific Atheism and Communism, rather than the American people, because it is Scientific Atheism that has vowed to destroy America from a secular premise.

Thus, the burden proof from the practice of law in regards to the Holy Bible can be exhibited by the rights of conscience under the common law, which is a Judeo-Christian based ethic, rather than secular ideal. Secular science is not an authority in relation to the correct interpretation of the common law, because if we are to allow scientists to dictate the law from a secular premise, then the rights of conscience will be placed into harms way by the reinterpretation of inalienable. And I am not shifting the burden of proof onto the common atheist, but I am however providing the legal framework, upon which, our system of common law has been built. Thus, from a legal premise, the Supreme Court of the United States is to reject a scientific debate against the theological terms from law that are in place for the benefit of an individual's protection within the system, or we will see the rise of Communism from the principles of Marxism and Scientific Atheism which aims to destroy America, and the rest of the world by a reinterpretation of the law.

*Quotation: ——————————————————————————
What is the difference between burden and standard of proof?
The burden reflects which side must prove its case and the standard dictates how convincing that proof must be. The standard of proof refers to the extent to which the party with the burden of proof has to prove its case, or an element of its case. The higher the standard of proof, the more difficult it is for a party to meet their burden of proof. In general, the higher the stakes are, the higher the standard of proof will be. So, a prosecutor in a criminal case has to meet a very high standard of proof, because a defendant's liberty is on the line. - Source: Online Legal Encyclopedia.

The highest legal standard in the world for the interpretation of human rights and equality has derived from the Universal Declaration of Human Rights and Equality (UDHR), because the declaration has been signed by 192 nations, and is therefore incontestable on all legal grounds. And according to the United Nations High Commissioner's Office, human equality has been defined by "religious teachings," which means automatically that a Creator God has been inferred for reasons relating to the correct interpretation of the human conscience, and human freedom thereby. And this is the official reason that puts to rest an atheist's case against that which God in Heaven has ordained as holy and sacred, such as the human conscience.

If the atheist is to argue that their liberty is at stake due to a religious standard from the practice of law, then they have thereby made a moral argument, which they cannot use as a just cause without bringing our universal system of morality into question under the common law, which is the very thing that brings the people's liberty into harm's way. So, for the good of the common law and for the good of the people, it is the rights of conscience that will define human freedom and equal opportunity thereby, rather than the atheist and their personal assertions against the Creator, which only amounts to being a religious discrimination against the religious rights of man.

So, because the highest legal standard in the world for human rights and equality has been defined by religious teachings, it will mean that New Atheism is without merit, nor sufficient cause, to argue before the law from the viewpoint of the evolutionary theory in order to try and refute the existence of God the Creator, because the preservation of human rights and equality, according to their legal entitlements, is a lawful obligation, as well as a moral one. Philosophical materialism denies the existence of the human conscience, because the human conscience is a non-physical aspect of the human mind called the psyche or soul, and it is this non-physical state of being that atheism cannot explain from the viewpoint of absolute materialism. So, the burden of proof falls onto the New Atheist movement in this matter due to the denial of conscience, because the theory of evolution has failed to yield to a lawful instruction that is universal in its interpretation. And a reinterpretation of the lawful term, conscience, also constitutes as a violation under international agreement, because the lawful term, conscience, is protected as universal for the benefit of an individual's protection within the system.

The right to be defined as a created human being before international law is an inalienable right, because all human beings have been endowed with conscience; Meaning that the right to be defined as a created human being with a human ancestry, is by definition, a birthright, and therefore, endowed. While the term, secular, is in relation to a privilege, rather than a birthright, because the ability to govern is not defined as a birthright under international law. So, for this reason, there is probable cause for Class Action and litigation against the United States government to reform the public education system by relinquishing the secular standard to govern the people by in this case, because the discussion of origins has already been settled before the law by the introduction of inalienable rights as having derived from the Creator God of Genesis.

The just liberties of the people are thereby declared to all the nations by the promise of God that all who acknowledge their maker in spirit and in truth shall have their cause heard on high, because it is God the Creator who has established His system of moral law of good will to their neighbour so that the eyes of the wicked should be opened to their injustices, and so that the people of the Earth should not be without liberty, nor independence, for God in Heaven has established His system of justice that the cause of the poor should be acknowledged by the laws that sustain our freedoms. The liberty of the people is self-governed by moral law, which cannot be placed into harm's way without incurring the wrath of the Lamb who has established human equality as just and sacred.

The scientistic explanations that derive from philosophical materialism are used in an attempt to try and explain a natural causality for the human conscience, which is termed "scientism," because this is the typical mindset of a naturalist scientist when trying to refute the existence of the supernatural from the viewpoint of absolute materialism. The first Article from the United Nations Universal Declaration of Human Rights and Equality (UDHR), has stated that each person is equal according to the existence of the endowed human conscience, and it is this non-physical state of being that has caused the most amount of contention between the interpretations by naturalism, which derive from atheism, and the definitions from law, which derive from theology. And it is atheism that is in opposition to theology from a scientific and anti-religious perspective, which is why Scientific Atheism must be challenged from the premise of law, or we will see our basic human rights erode with each passing generation due to a system of denial concerning morality and the human conscience.

No individual is to be deprived of their right to freedom of information through a legal representative, and no individual should be deprived of their inalienable rights before the law, because international law recognizes an individual's universal rights as sovereign. And it is the sovereign and inalienable right of each individual to be defined as a created human being through the public education system, because the right to be defined as a created human being who is endowed with conscience by their Creator, is by definition, a birthright. So, the problem here, as from a moral perspective, is that Scientific Atheism does not accept the existence of the human soul, which is defined as being the human psyche or conscience, even though we have a lawful reference to the existence of the human soul by the correct definition of person, but atheism has rejected it in favour of biological evolution instead.

So, for this reason, the universal law of human equality must be protected from lobbyists who hail from the viewpoint of Scientific Atheism and the theory of evolution, because it is the theory of evolution that Scientific Atheism is relying on in their inhumane attempts to overthrow God and the law. The United States Supreme Court banned school-sponsored prayer in public schools in a 1962 decision, saying that it violated the First Amendment. But this has led to the notion by the New Atheist movement that the United States government is atheist based on its secular authority, and that the supernatural has therefore been debunked by law, giving way to the Enlightenment philosophy that morality can be replaced by a science.

Yet the term, secular, cannot be exercised as a privilege by the government in order to deny a human being their inalienable right to be defined as a created human being, regardless of the merit of any theory that is proposed for the sake of human rights and equality to preside from the premise of law. This means that the New Atheist movement is without sufficient cause, because one cannot argue against the existence of God the Creator, as from United States Constitutional law and Commonwealth theology, without detracting from the correct interpretation of inalienable rights, and human freedom thereby.

The United States government and the Supreme Court have ruled that creation science cannot be taught to public school students no matter how it is pervade in theology or religious instructions so that evolution can be taught unabated, which in turn, defines the evolutionary theory as a philosophical dogma, rather than a method of free education. According to the First Amendment of the United States Constitution: "The government shall pass no law forbidding freedom of worship or freedom to exercise one's beliefs," which in turn, forms the limitations of Secularism.

The United States Supreme Court has thereby acted as a fiat authority based on a secular interpretation of the said Constitution in order to promote evolution as a theory, when the written Constitution has already acknowledged the rights of conscience under the religious rights of man so that the voting constituency should be convicted by their conscience in regards to a moral obligation by the law to uphold the Constitution when called upon. And it is for this reason that the theory of evolution is doing more to enslave humanity under a theory, rather than freeing the people by the truth concerning their inalienable rights, such as the right to be defined as a created human being with a human ancestry.

If the United States government wishes to denote Biblical creation in favour of the evolutionary theory, then the United States government has thereby created a religion, or, an alternate system of belief. Biblical creation cannot be replaced by secular science without defining secular science as a religion in turn, because Biblical creation is in relation to origins. Any theory that claims to be authoritative concerning human origins, yet cannot produce a valid explanation for the human conscience, is by definition, an invalid theory, because it is the human conscience that is defined as self-evident under United States Constitutional law, rather than the evolutionary theory of ape to man.

The Supreme Court decision to grant Constitutional protections for the theory of evolution in the case of Edwards v. Aguillard, 482 U.S. 578 (1987), is contradictory to the Constitution, because human freedom and human independence has been defined by Constitutional law as having derived from the Creator God of Genesis, which is in accordance with the Declaration of Independence, and the rights of conscience. The United States Constitution and their Declaration of Independence is a legal standard that is to be interpreted by Biblical theology, rather than secular ideology, because freedom of conscience forms the basis for civil rights and human liberties. If the people are to yield to a secular standard for public education and law, then the religious rights of man has been denied without proper due course, because the United States Constitution is in place so that each person should be self-governed under the Biblical principles of universal morality, which cannot be justified by nature, because nature is legally defined as property.

Today, the war that threatens our very existence the most, is the war on Communism, because Communism is engaged in a global scientific revolution, and the standard form of indoctrination by Communist propaganda is Scientific Atheism. And in Western society, it is atheism that lobbies to government the heaviest from the viewpoint of a science in order to have the evolutionary theory forced onto adults and students, when every student should be made fully aware of the legal system they're entering into, because it is an engineered system that holds to a theological definition for what a human being is, rather than a biological one. So, unless the people are being properly educated from the system about where their conscience comes from, and what it is for, then the people will lose their ability to make an informed decision. And we are as a people to abide by and protect the lawful definition of person, because this pertains to the human soul, which is for our understanding of human nature, and the laws that sustain our basic freedoms.

The common law districts of England and the United States have based their system of justice upon the laws of nature and of God the Creator who has set things in motion that cannot be undone, such as the right to be defined as a created human being with an endowed conscience. This law is in itself inalienable, and every encroachment upon this universal law is an act of cruelty that will not go unpunished by Heaven above. If man is to be ruled by law, then laws need to be made fair for the good of the people, which is why defining yourself, or others, as an animal, is by definition unjust, because God in Heaven will render unto every man according to what he has done; Justice for justice, envy for envy, so that all may know that God alone is just.

There is no distinction between creature and man apart from the human spirit, which is a spirit of freedom that revolts against injustices, as perceived by the individual. Thus, we are to abide by the common law for the common good so that equal opportunity should exist before the law, which should never be stifled by a scientific or religious debate against the existence of the human soul, as defined by the lawful definition of person. And it is for this cause that man is endowed with a special ability that sets us apart in the course of justice that every voice should be heard, each according to the dictates of their own conscience, for it is the will of God's eternal spirit that each of us should be convicted by the truth that sustains our basic freedoms in accordance with the lawful definition of person.

The self-evident nature of God the Creator is understood by all, so that each person should receive a measure of faith in order to believe, for the greatest work one can do before their maker, is to believe in Him who has established His system of justice for all by the rights of conscience, which is an eternal liberty from Heaven above that has been bestowed upon each individual a moral cause that is just, so that all should acknowledge their maker in spirit and in truth, for it is the will of God that the truth shall convict the soul.

Under Constitutional law in America, the administration is lawfully bound by a public oath to uphold the said Constitution by placing their right hand upon the Holy Bible, so that the government should be publicly liable, which means that it is the Holy Bible that requires defending before the law, rather than the theory of evolution. New Atheism on the other hand has reneged this responsibility in an attempt to remove the religious rights of man in order to grant privileges to themselves, which is why atheism is in a de-facto relationship with the United States Constitution, as well as Commonwealth theology. The common law districts are to be self-governed under the law, which is not to be used as an instrument of war against the people who are endowed with conscience and with liberties that do not include the denial of conscience.

The standard teaching from Scientific Atheism is that man is animal, which is the basis for the individual's denial of the human conscience, because the New Atheist movement refuses to admit that they have a conscience before the law, let alone the fact that it was endowed to them by their Creator according to the lawful definitions in place. The secular notion that religion and science cannot coexist derives from the Enlightenment philosophy where science was to replace faith. But if science is to replace faith, then science becomes a faith, which in turn, defines Scientific Atheism in terms of a belief, because the purpose of removing religion from science is for reasons relating to atheism, rather than the scientific method, as established by Bacon and Newton. And this is done in despite of the fact that the greatest minds in scientific history were people of a faith.

So, for New Atheism to pit science against religion from a secular premise is indeed a form of Communist propaganda, because the academic definition of Scientific Atheism is equal to that of Communism according to its correct definition in use. This means definitively that any and all scientific arguments from atheism against the existence of God the Creator, as from United States Constitutional law, Commonwealth theology, and the common law, are to be defined as a form of Communist propaganda for reasons relating to Scientific Atheism. Scientific Atheism within the USSR failed as a system of belief and practice because of the injustices that were presented to the people in the form of Communist propaganda.

Communism is a very real danger to Western civilization, because Communist influence goes unabated from the viewpoint of the evolutionary theory which is a weapon against the minds of men who are endowed by their Creator with the ability to love. And if there is one thing that the public education system is doing from a secular premise, then it is teaching students to hate their maker on the basis of evolution, which is how Communism will succeed over time by a shift in culture.

The idea by New Atheism of throwing secularism in front of them in order to argue their case from the viewpoint of Scientific Atheism only amounts to a form of ransom, because in order for the people to retain their basic rights as free individuals under God, then a secular standard for public education must be returned to the people, to which, it rightfully belongs. And it is the Biblical standard for law and education that led the United States and the Commonwealth nations to victory against Communism by defeating the USSR, which is why the New Atheist movement is by definition a retaliation for the humiliation they have suffered.

So, for the United States government to remove all connotations concerning the Creator from public education on the basis of Secularism, is in fact, an act of Communism, because inalienable rights are defined as being universal on the basis that all human beings have been endowed with conscience by their Creator, rather than from nature. And this is the main reason why America needs to protect their Constitution from a Biblical premise, because the public education system has now been co-opted by Scientific Atheism, which is equal to a covert Communist takeover within the hierarchy of controls; Meaning that Communism is the greatest threat to the United States system of law and order from the principles of Scientific Atheism, and the evolutionary theory, because it is Scientific Atheism that has denied the Constitutional grounds for human equality on the basis that human equality was founded upon Biblical theology that includes a universal Creator in order to define the human conscience as self-evident for the benefit of an individual's protection within the system.

If the United States government continues to do nothing about the Communist indoctrination by Scientific Atheism through the public education system, then we will see the inalienable rights of individuals diminish faster than the United States government can build State prisons, because the people are being subjugated under an economic and industrial Communist system that caters to the rich, rather than the poor, with the consent of the law. A theory in science is by definition a belief on the basis that theory derives from a mental conjecture, as well as observation, while laws in society derive from theology and rules, which means that Biblical theology cannot be overruled by scientific theory on the basis that theology is a belief, because both theory, and theology, derive from a belief, while morality is the standard in place to define good and evil. So, for this reason, the atheist will argue that evil does not exist, which cannot be a logical conclusion, because human beings will actively engage a problem if the moral cause is seen as sufficient, which is evidence of morality.

Thus, Biblical theology cannot be overruled from the premise of law, because Biblical theology derives from a higher standard in place, such as moral law, which in turn, defines a law as just or unjust. The Holy Bible is based entirely on eyewitness accounts concerning the history of mankind and the Earth, while the theory of evolution is postulated without sufficient proof due to a lack of eyewitness accounts concerning the evolution of man. The proof of God's existence derives from the endowed human conscience, which is a theological term from the Holy Bible, and is self-evident, rather than self-existing. Without an acknowledgement of the Holy Bible from the premise of law, then society will fall into disrepute with God in Heaven, because human society is to be self-governed under the Biblical principles of universal morality, rather than slaves under a scientific theory that robs the people of the justice by a denial of the human soul.

If the United States Supreme Court is to act as a secular authority in order to deny the theological framework from the Holy Bible, upon which, their Commonwealth system of Constitutional law has been built, then the United States Supreme Court has denied the human soul, as well as the lawful definition of person as a created human being. This discrimination against the religious rights of man is by definition, unconstitutional, on the grounds of conscience, as cited by the forefathers of America who outlined the liberty and national sovereignty of America in accordance with Commonwealth theology and Biblical teachings, so that the freedom of the voting constituency should be protected by the rights of conscience, and by a due deliberation of the law to uphold the Constitutional definition of man over any scientific theory or theological dispute.

*Quotation: ————————————————————————

What is the right of consciousness?

The first liberty: This religious liberty tradition embodied in the first amendment has been called the "first liberty." It grants freedom of conscience on religious beliefs, prohibits establishment of religion by the government, and implicitly acknowledges the U.S. as a place that accommodates religious pluralism. - Source: The American Psychological Association. Understanding Conscience Clause Legislation in the context of Religious Liberty Traditions in the United States. (Reviewed by the Board of Educational Affairs and Board of Professional Affairs in March 2017).

The current philosophical objective by New Atheism from Communism is one of retaliation for the humiliation they have suffered by the fall of the USSR, which they apply to the rights of conscience as though the Holy Bible and religion is the enemy of Communism, which it is. This conclusion, however, leads the common atheist to believe that religion is now the enemy of the State, thus vindicating in their own minds the struggle to affirm civil rights without the need for a Creator God, which is in opposition to the First Amendment by the United States, as defined by James Madison himself during the Virginia General Assembly on June 20, 1785, where he affirms that civil rights and belief are indispensable supports of one another. So, in order to get around this issue, the common atheist will argue that America was not founded on the Christian religion due to religious pluralism, which is only partly true.

The United States is indeed a place that accommodates for religious pluralism, as defined by the Commonwealth system, which is why many Commonwealth jurisdictions are not Christian, such as India and Pakistan. But because Commonwealth theology describes itself as the result of mainstream Christian theology, it will mean that a coalition force of democratic nations led by the Commonwealth was initiated by the Christian religion, thus constituting the alliance of a democratic coalition force as theologically based from the principles of Judeo-Christianity, of which, atheism poses as an opposition and political front, which is expedient for the spread of Communism, rather than human freedom.

The fall of American liberty and national sovereignty is occurring as a predictable trend, starting with a secular clause that religion should be expelled from public education; Then onto gay activists banging on Church doors in order to be married by a Christian priest; Then by the removal of a manufacturing base within America to Communist China; And now we have Communist China threatening the whole of Western civilisation with a new Axis of power. This global trend began itself by the removal of a religious standard for both law and public education by a United States Supreme Court ruling to remove school sponsored prayer in a 1962 decision, which then opened the doorway for Scientific Atheism to invade America through the public education system, which is a direct violation of the First Amendment, as defined by James Madison himself, whereby the Creator is defined as self-evident and self-existing, rather than the Supreme Court.

According to international law, freedom of conscience and religion is a universal right, which not only grants protections for atheism, but also, the Christian faith as well, which is not to be regarded as a means forcing religion onto students, but that every man should be convicted by their conscience in relation to belief. The Roman inquisitional period is often cited by Communism as a justification to commit mass murder against civilians who are endowed by their Creator with the ability to point out the injustices that they have suffered under Communist rule, which is a form of retaliation. The Roman inquisition was not a Christian doctrine, for Jesus Christ Himself was crucified by the Roman Order. So, if there is one thing that Jesus does not approve of, then it would be the Roman inquisitional period that lasted up until the year 1859.

The Vatican Church sees itself as a "universal Church" that does not allow for human rights and equality, which is why the sovereign Vatican State has not signed the universal treaty of human rights and equality. So, if there is one thing that the Pope cannot offer, then it is the rights of conscience. The separation of Church and State by the founding fathers of America laid the corner stone of human freedom upon the first precepts of Christianity, whereby each individual is considered as free according to the dictates of their own conscience.

This principle is a universal truth that has been sustained by a legal standard that forbids the denial of conscience. So, in order to combat religious persecution, then a legal standard is required, which must derive itself from Biblical teachings for the good of the people, and the common law. The common law has derived from previous settled cases that forms the basis of a legal precedence or standard, which in turn, derives itself from Biblical events, so that the common law was established by Biblical Christianity that includes the Old and New Testament, from which, a case has already been settled. The case as to whether man was created or not has already been sustained in a court of law with the Holy Bible acting as a legal standard or precedent, from which, a human being is defined as created, as well as endowed for the purpose of civil and inalienable rights.

The curriculum for public education in the United States has amounted to being a poor substandard system of Communist indoctrination based on Scientific Atheism and Secular Humanism, simply because it is materialistic and highly dogmatic. And the atheist notion that the Enlightenment era is still continuing only shows a lack of understanding in regards to the most important scientific and political advancements of the last 230 years. Because not only has the biological theory of evolution been dis-proven by the law of biogenesis since 1858, but also, the human conscience has been defined as being endowed to all of mankind by their Creator, which has become the sole basis for human rights and equality under United States Constitutional law since 1787.

The Age of Enlightenment was the projection of the idea that science and logic could overrule Biblical morality, because the main emphasis was to replace Biblical authority with science. But the materialistic philosophy that followed the Enlightenment became the groundwork for socialist movements, such as Social Darwinism, National Socialism, and Communism. Communism boasts from absolute atheism whilst disregarding individual human sovereignty all together for the purpose of a global scientific revolution to convert the world to atheism through the propaganda of Scientific Atheism, the evolutionary theory, and philosophical materialism. So, it is for this reason that a secular standard for public education amounts to being a very real threat to self-governance, because it is the secular standard for public education that demands a materialistic interpretation for everything, including the human conscience. While any theory that cannot explain the full extent to that which it claims to be in possession of, is by definition, unreliable, and it is the human conscience that must be interpreted factually to students for the benefit of an individual's protection within the system.

The beginning of the Enlightenment period during the later years of the 17th century paved the way for naturalist thinkers to begin postulating theories revolving around the atheist concept of life being the result of purely natural circumstances. While the majority of democratic nations are in favour of a Christian democracy based on human rights and equality as having derived from the Creator God of the Holy Bible, as portrayed by Commonwealth theology, and the United States Declaration of Independence under their Constitution, so that inalienable rights should be universal in their interpretation. Communism can only be explained by interpreting the ideology that led to the Enlightenment period, which defined itself as the "Age of Reason." Yet the movement was not based on reason at all, but the denial of it instead by using a reverse logic, because the one thing that cannot be reasoned with here on Earth, is a nihilist who has rejected Biblical morality in favour of theory.

The Age of Enlightenment was based on the idea that the human conscience is a product of nature, thereby replacing faith with science, which historically, is the primary example of a fascism, because if freedom of conscience is denied, then so also are your basic rights. If universal morality is to be replaced by science, then there will be no universal standard in which to define corruption with, as well as unethical conduct, which is why the denial of Biblical morality by atheism is a crime against humanity, because if the atheist was to admit that morality is universal, then they have thereby forfeited their atheism, which is unthinkable for the atheist who has rejected Biblical morality as universal in favour of scientific opinion.

Atheism is unable to apply a system of morality that is by definition, universal, which is entirely due to the nature of atheism. And it is for this reason that the New Atheist movement attempts to redefine morality to suit a given minority, because atheism is without sufficient cause to argue against morality as universal without first having a moral cause to defend. The existence of universal morality, as from the Holy Bible, has been one of confusion for many, but the only thing we have to interpret morality with, is the human conscience, because it is the human conscience that determines yes or no, while Biblical morality is the standard in place for right and wrong.

So, for this reason, morality is therefore above the law from a Biblical premise, because it is not law or theory that defines what is good or evil, but Biblical morality instead on the basis of reason and of conscience. No scientist or judge has the right to reinterpret morality for the sake of others who shall be defined as persons without distinction before the law for the purpose of human rights and equality, so that no human being should ever be denied the rights of conscience, which is a religious liberty, rather than an atheist ideal.

God the Creator has endowed all life with ability, but unto His own image the gift of conscience, with which, to reason from, which forms the basis for human rights and equality, and equal justice thereby. If mankind is to have equal justice in this world, then it will begin by a conviction of truth from the conscience first. Yet atheism has replaced the term, conscience, with the word, consciousness, in an attempt to deny that God the Creator is real, because the human conscience is for our understanding of morality according to its correct definition in use, which the atheist cannot accept without denouncing their atheism in turn.

Violent revolutions throughout the last two and a half centuries, such as the French revolution which took place between 1789 - 1799, or the violent revolution of 1848 that occurred in Europe, were the direct result of Enlightenment thinkers trying to dispose of all aristocracies who were aligned with the Roman Catholic Church, or the Anglican Church of England, because the Church's influence on diplomatic affairs was known to be used as a weapon against society by aristocrats who also believed that their ability to govern was a birthright, rather than a privilege.

The Enlightenment era gave rise to the idea of the separation of Church and State, involving a secular government to govern the people. But the concept of freedom of conscience did not sit well with many of the atheist thinkers of that time who desired to take the reign of terror and capital punishment to a whole new level by banning religion altogether, rather than having a population that is free to worship in their own way. Anti-religious and anti-social practices were the leading cause for the founding fathers of the United States to depart from the Enlightenment idea that religion should be made illegal, because the main focus within the United States Declaration of Independence, and their Constitution, centres around freedom of conscience and the interpretation of inalienable rights from a Biblical premise.

The peak of the scientific Enlightenment period occurred during the mid-17th century through to the late 19th century, and ended with Louis Pasteur's flask experiment in 1859. The greatest logical fallacy in the history of science, is atheism's belief that chemicals can become self-aware and evolve a level of intelligence over time, when intelligence does not derive from material substances, but from taking rules into account. The hypothetical process of spontaneous generation, also known as abiogenesis, forms the basis of Enlightenment philosophy, and was officially refuted in the late 19th century by Louis Pasteur. Louis Pasteur is considered to be the father of microbiology and germ theory due to his contributions to science, which includes his flask experiment demonstrating that life can only come from pre-existing life, formerly known as the law of biogenesis.

The discovery of the law of biogenesis is the very thing that ultimately refuted the concept of spontaneous generation from non-living materials and ultimately ended the scientific Enlightenment era. While the philosophical Enlightenment period ended with the creation of the United States Constitution by the rights of conscience, which is a religious liberty, rather than an Enlightenment ideal. The end of the scientific Enlightenment era by Pasteur was highly significant, because not only was the Enlightenment philosophy based on the assertion that a Creator God cannot exist, but also, the concept that life is the result of natural circumstances alone, which is still being postulated today by naturalist scientists who hail from the theory of evolution. Many will cite the end of the French revolution as the end of the Enlightenment era, but because the Enlightenment era was based on philosophical materialism and spontaneous generation, it will mean that it was Pasteur's discovery of biogenesis that marked the beginning of a new scientific era based on microbiology and germ theory.

*Quotation: ————————————————

"Never will the doctrine of spontaneous generation recover from the mortal blow struck by this simple experiment. Posterity will one day laugh at the foolishness of modern materialistic philosophers. The more I study nature, the more I stand amazed at the work of the Creator. Science brings men nearer to God." - Louis Pasteur. Source: Excerpt from a letter of correspondence by Louis Pasteur, addressed to Albert Edelfelt. (Documented in 1885).

Nihilists often claim to a superior form of individual morality by claiming that God is cruel to women and children, yet the atheistic Communist regime of China is attempting to forcibly sterilize women and children under the guise of Darwinian eugenics, which is a crime against humanity under international human rights legislation. More people have died by democide under Communist regimes in the last century over any other ideology in human history, making Scientific Atheism the world's most dangerous political ideology bar none with over 100 million dead or starving within a period of only 100 years. The Christian scientific revolution that preceded the Enlightenment period was based on the concept that physical laws do exist. But the atheist concept during the Enlightenment was that these laws must somehow be a reflection of the power of nature, which is a false assertion, because the materialistic philosophy that nature has provided everything was uprooted on two separate occasions before the twentieth century had even started.

Firstly, from law, when the United States Constitution and their Declaration of Independence was ratified by congress, because an individual is defined as being endowed with rights from birth by their Creator, rather than by nature. And secondly, from science, when Louis Pasteur discovered the law of biogenesis that ultimately refuted the concept of evolution involving spontaneous generation. Today, there are more secular scientists on a taxpayer supported government payroll than there are scientists who were trained from a Christian university or college, but still the number of Christian scientists with a Nobel distinction is 6 times greater than that of atheism in terms of a percentage. This means that Christians, along with Jews, have dominated in Nobel science awards even though they represent a minority in the field of science compared to secularists.

*Quotation: ————————————————————
"My object in life is to dethrone God and destroy Capitalism. There are, besides, eternal truths, such as Freedom that are common to all states of society. But Communism abolishes

eternal truths, it abolishes all religion, and all morality, instead of constituting them on a new basis; It therefore acts in contradiction to all past historical experience. We have no compassion and we ask no compassion from you. When our turn comes, we shall not make excuses for the terror." - Karl Marx, founder of Communism. Source: The Communist Manifesto, chapter 2. (Documented February 21, 1848).

According to Karl Marx, the purpose of public education is to incorporate an individual into a secular society whereby the State is in full control, thereby giving the individual a sense of purpose whilst denying the individual their God given independence, because the one thing that Communism will not cater for, is a sense of independence from the State. While the founding fathers of America took a different approach by defining human independence on the basis of human sovereignty, which cannot be interpreted as having derived from nature without detracting from the correct definition of inalienable rights.

Individual human independence is best explained by the implementation of inalienable rights as having derived from the Creator as endowed, because if your inalienable rights derive from nature, then you are by definition the property of the State, the same as nature is defined as property. But if your inalienable rights derive from the Creator, then man is thereby independent of the State in terms of ownership, and is therefore, sovereign. Communism seeks to rid the individual of all loyalty and devotion to God through ridicule and disgust of all things sacred and Holy so that the individual will independently deny the Creator on their own terms, when nothing robs a person of their inalienable rights faster than the denial of God their maker. Human rights legislation recognizes the inherent value of each person, regardless of background, where we live, what we look like, what we think, or what we believe.

They are based on the principles of dignity, equality and mutual respect, which are shared across different cultures, religions and philosophies with due regard for each other's liberty. Human rights are intimately related to the notion of human dignity, because both notions are connected in such a way that one cannot be understood without the other. The importance of human rights and the requirement to respect everyone's rights, is based on the notion of human dignity itself. Human dignity is the recognition that all human beings are distinct from the animals, and therefore possess a special value intrinsic to their humanity, and as such, are worthy of respect, simply because they are human beings, and not for any scientific or theoretical reason whatsoever.

Dignity is one of the most important things to the human conscience or mind, because it means being valued and respected for who you are as an individual, rather than just what you are as a person. Human dignity is the very thing that justifies human rights, so when people are divided and given a value based on characteristics like class, gender, religion, and so on, it creates unequal societies where discrimination runs rampant. And that is because people who are assigned a higher value without merit will inevitably receive a preferred form of treatment over others, which is defined as being inequality or discrimination. According to psychology, the subconscious is defined as the part of the mind of where one is not fully aware, but still influences one's actions and feelings.

So it is our conscious state of being that is self-aware on the basis that we have choices while we're awake, but even though we sleep, which is a state of not being self-aware, the subconscious remains active. While the human conscience on the other hand, is subconsciously aware of morality at all times, because we are moral beings that can perceive injustices, and choices have consequences, which means that there is a universal standard in place for right and wrong that is defined by morality, Meaning that human beings have three types of consciousness which are: Subconsciousness, consciousness, and conscience.

The ability of the conscious mind to dwell upon thoughts means there is a subconscious, because the mind is able to think about thoughts, past and present, in order to determine a future, which requires two forms of consciousness, rather than just one. While the human conscience on the other hand, is unique to human beings only, because it is the conscience that experiences guilt, which means that the human conscience is a third aspect of the human mind that animals do not share. A right and wrong decision is not only a mathematical decision for example, but also, a moral one, because the purpose of human equality is to serve justice proportionally to the people in an equal manner, which is how equal justice works from the premise of law. Without a universal system of morality, then there would be no universal basis for law, and if there is one thing that atheism cannot provide, is a universal standard for morality due to the nature of atheism.

So, in order for the atheist to get around the problem of having no universal basis for morality, they instead deny the existence of the human conscience on a scientific basis, because it is the existence of the human conscience that atheism has called into question the most, all on the basis of evolution and philosophical materialism, as though we owe our ability to identify what is right and wrong to the animals now, all because the atheist cannot accept an eternal Creator God on the basis of their atheism. Unlike atheism and Darwinism, Biblical Christianity is not a philosophy based on mental conjectures concerning the past, but on recorded history from BC to AD.

Biblical Christianity cannot be defined as a philosophical dogma due to a historical timeline that is both recorded by eyewitness accounts, and is universally accepted for the purpose of international trade and commerce, as defined by the seven day week from Scripture. Biblical Christian theology cannot be defined as a philosophy in itself, because Judeo-Christian theology derives from the interpretation of Biblical morality, which cannot be defined as a philosophical conjecture on the basis that morality is universal. This means that there is a standard in place to define morality within terms of right and wrong, that is not only universal, but also, true. Otherwise, there would be no way to win an argument concerning morality without contradicting oneself, because, if one was to argue that morality is not universal, then that person has thereby made a universal statement of truth, which he cannot determine as true in the following without contradicting himself in the previous.

The Latin term, theology, is used to describe a particular teaching based on written laws and universal principles. While a philosophy attempts to describe a mental conjecture that was based on abstract ideas. So, for this reason, Biblical Christianity cannot be defined by the term, Catholicism, because Catholicism is based entirely on Papal rule, and is therefore, abstract in ideas concerning law, morality, and universal principles. Biblical Christianity is based on the teachings of Jesus Christ, rather than Papal rule, and the major difference here between Papal rule, and Judeo-Christian theology, is that Papal rule derives from the Roman interpretation of Biblical Christianity, rather than Christian theology deriving from a Roman interpretation.

Darwinian evolution on the other hand, cannot be empirically based, because Darwinian evolution cannot be empirically verified due to the sheer number of supposed evolutionary changes that are said to have occurred. The primary difference between evolution and creation, is that a creation is empirical, while a bacterium changing into a human being over millions of years is entirely hypothetical. One does not need to present the Creator before the atheist in order to satisfy the atheist and their personal conclusions, but rather, one only needs to demonstrate that life is a creation on a self-evident basis, which has already been achieved by the rights of conscience, and instructional systems.

The law of human equality is the basis for equal rights, but the difference between a right and a privilege is that rights are for everyone, while privileges require merit. And anything that requires a certificate or registration number, is by definition a privilege, rather than a right. Which is why marriage is not a right, but a privilege instead, because having a marriage certificate is by definition a privilege the same as having a driver's license is a privilege, rather than a right. So, marriage is by definition a privilege, rather than a right, which means that there is a criteria in place that must be met before a certificate can be granted. But the lower the criteria is, the lower the merit that's required in order to obtain a marriage certificate; Meaning that gay rights to marriage lowers the criteria for marriage, rather than increasing it to a higher standard. The reason for a birth certificate on the other hand, is for the individual to enter a legal society, because in order to become a member of government, then you must first identify yourself as a naturalized citizen, which is why becoming a member of government is by definition a privilege, rather than a right.

So, because a married couple can file for adoption, it will mean that it is the rights of children that are being neglected in order to hand out privileges to same sex couples, which is a crime against humanity, because an adopted child has a God given right to a proper mother and father according to the correct definition of what a male and female is so that the child's conscience is not conflicted at an early age by a same sex couple pretending to be mommy and daddy in order to fulfil their depraved sexual fantasies involving a child. Laws in society should be a reflection of Biblical morality, because it is Biblical morality that defines what is right and wrong, rather than law.

Anything that is Biblically defined as amoral, should never be defined as a legal right, which includes gay marriage, because being gay is defined as amoral on the basis that being straight is morally correct universally according to the male and female principles of God's creation. Today, we have the New Atheist movement telling us that it's okay to be gay, and that it's okay to abort unborn children, and that these unborn children are just animals for the slaughter anyway. When in reality, this is the same kind of backwards logic as Baal worship historically, because the justification for this has come out as being the need for more rights to freedoms with their own body in order to pleasure themselves with in front of society, when society includes young children as well.

But unfortunately for the sex activists, the real nobodies in this situation have become their own children, which they have aborted for the sake of having more freedoms with their body to commit their usual acts of fornication and debauchery without having the burden of responsibility to go with it. Which in itself is an equivalent to Baal worship historically speaking where all cares are to be thrown into the fire and sacrificed. And this is a very ancient practice called "the cremation of care," which also happens to be a common practice within the Bohemian Grove community of today where they burn an effigy of a human being before a statue of an owl representing Moloch. Historically, the name "Moloch" has derived from the name "Baal" according to the Encyclopedia Britannica.

*Quotation: ———————————————————
David Thorstad (October 15, 1941 - August 1, 2021) was an American political activist who co-founded a number of homosexual rights groups and was a former President of New York's Gay Activists Alliance. In 1977, Thorstad founded the Coalition for Lesbian and Gay Rights. He later engaged in pedophilia and pederasty activism with the North American Man/Boy Love Association (NAMBLA), of which he was a founding member. Thorstad described himself as a bisexual pederast and atheist who was active in Trotskyist politics for some years. For more than six

years, he was a member of the Upper West Side branch of the Socialist Workers Party (SWP) and a staff writer for its newspaper, The Militant. - Source: Wikipedia Encyclopedia (David Thorstad).

A leading argument by the New Atheist movement is that the Catholic clergy are all pedophiles due to a number of pederasts within the clergy, thereby establishing a system of distrust in Christianity despite the fact that mainstream Christianity leads a strong disapproval of pedophilia and gay rights. Yet, according to the United States Pew Research Centre for National Statistics, 94% of atheists are in favour of gay rights to marriage, while the Biblical interpretation of marriage has been defined as being for one man and one woman only; Which not only means that the New Atheist movement of today is by definition a gay rights movement, but also, it means that it is the Holy Bible that requires defending from a legal premise, rather than the evolutionary theory of ape to man, which happens to be the current philosophical basis for an individual's denial of morality.

So, it is thereby definitive that rights are being removed from citizens in order to grant privileges to a minority of people who are denying basic public morals, because adopted children are being exposed to amoral sexual behaviour at an early age due to lobbying efforts by the New Atheist movement, which was the very same legal issue that caused NAMBLA to become a hidden underground atheist society. While the other clear indicator which demonstrates that rights are being removed from citizens in order to grant privileges to a minority of people who are denying basic public morals, is the application of the evolutionary theory from the United States government, because it is the United States government that is openly discouraging people from learning about their Creator so as to describe an individual person as having derived from the animals instead, when nothing robs a person of their God given voice faster than being equated with a dumb animal.

A Supreme Court judge is not above the law, but interprets the law instead, and any laws that favour sexual immorality, such as gay marriage or reduced sentences for pedophiles for example, are to be refuted by the Biblical principles of universal morality. And the one event that still bears witness to the fact that Biblical morality is the basis for law and order within Western society, is the affair that occurred between Bill Clinton and Monica Lewinsky who were shamed publicly for the practice of adultery, which is how Biblical morality works from the premise of law. So, for this reason, morality is therefore above the law from a Biblical premise, because it is Biblical morality that defines what is good and evil, rather than law. And this is how America became a global leader in human rights and equality, and not by the rule of law, because the rule of law pertains to subjugation by the law, rather than a means of liberty and justice for all.

If the basis for Biblical morality, such as the Holy Bible, is not acknowledged by the United States government for the benefit of an individual's protection within the system, then the United States will ultimately fail as a system, because the United States government has sworn a public oath to uphold the written Constitution by placing their right hand upon the Holy Bible, rather than the Origin of Species or Das Kapital. Biblical morality is therefore self-evident from the premise of common law, because all have been endowed with conscience by their Creator in order to understand a moral obligation, which forms the basis of a legal obligation. And every human being has a lawful obligation to protect the welfare of a child, the same as every human being has a lawful obligation to acknowledge human rights and equality, as defined by the existence of the human conscience having derived from the Creator God of Genesis, rather than nature, for reasons relating to the lawful definition of property.

Under the universal law of human equality, children are never to be defined as someone's property, especially by same sex couples who choose to adopt. This legality issue has extended itself into society by the reinterpretation of conscience and nature, because if the human conscience has derived from nature, then so also has morality. But, if morality has derived from nature, then man is just as free as the animals to do what thou wilt when it comes to sexual relations, when it is human morality, as defined by the Holy Bible, that sets limitations on human sexual behaviour, rather than atheism. Thus, no human being is free to do as they feel, sexually, for reasons relating to the correct and universal interpretation of human morality. And it is only atheism in terms of a belief that is arguing openly for more gay rights, rather than the Catholic clergy or mainstream Christian religion.

The immoral and explicit actions through lobbying efforts by the New Atheist movement in regards to gay rights leads to more pedophilic activities for reasons relating to amoral sexual exposure at an early age, which in turn, defiles a child's conscience for life. If the United States Supreme Court is to allow for more gay rights, and reduced sentences for pedophiles, then the rights of children is secondary to a lawful instruction that is morally just in its interpretations, because nothing stifles justice more than protecting gay rights activists and their paedophilic affiliations through adoption. Thus, it is the gay rights movement by New Atheism that is leading humanity into a new age human rights abuse by exposing children to amoral sexual behaviour at an early age, and should be restricted from occurring by a Supreme Court ruling through due deliberation and due process. But unfortunately, the exact opposite is occurring in America today due to lobbying efforts by NAMBLA that uses the New Atheist movement as a political front in order to avoid the brunt of public anger and exposure.

Atheism argues that the human soul is non-existent for reasons relating to their belief in philosophical materialism. Yet philosophical materialism has failed to yield a causality for the existence of the human conscience, which is why atheism is in opposition to the theological terms from law due to a theological dispute with the Holy Bible. And this occurs as an interaction between the universal law of equality, and the theological terms in use to describe a person with, which cannot be in conflict with one another without bringing the law of equality into question.

The idea that a man should be equated as a woman, or vice versa, in order to allow for equal opportunity is in opposition to the principles of equality itself, whereby your biological gender dictates who you are, rather than the legislator. There are three things in this world that the legislator cannot change through the power of legislation on the basis of your birth status, and that is age, sex, and nationality, because each of these things determines who you are in terms of your identity. And yes, you can change your name through the courts, and therefore your identity, but this only works in order to protect an individual within the system, rather than to exploit the law.

So, for this reason, the New Atheist and gay rights movement has exploited the law by requiring the legislator to enforce a speech dictate in regards to a person's acting identity. A main feature with modern films requires most male actors to act as a woman for entertainment purposes. Thus, it is self-evident that when a male pretends to be a woman, they are by definition, acting, which is not to be protected by law as your true identity in order to enforce a speech dictate that requires others to pretend also, which is in opposition to an equality between men and women. This issue has now extended itself into the Olympics with men competing against women in competitive sports, which is not a form of entertainment, but an exploitation of the law of equality instead.

The existence of the human spirit cannot be refuted under any scientific terminology, theory, or physical demonstration, because human beings are able to perceive injustices, which is a motive force that gives rise to rules and regulations, which in turn, defines morality as spiritual, rather than an animal or hormonal instinct. The human spirit is also a spirit of freedom, which cannot be suppressed, nor subjugated, without causing a rebellion in turn. But if there is one form of freedom that must be subdued by law in order to protect ourselves from moral and social decay, then it is gay rights activity.

So, in order for our system of justice to be maintained under the common law, along with our basic freedoms, then the law cannot impose an amoral rule or regulation upon a free people, because the essence of freedom derives from obeying the law, which cannot be in conflict with an individual's conscience, or there will be contradictions between that which is just, and that which is not, which in turn, creates confusion among the laity, as well as children who are subject to the system. The human soul or spirit cannot be refuted from the viewpoint of any science, because the human soul is defined by the human conscience or psyche, while the human spirit is in relation to a motive force that exhibits evidence of morality.

And the human spirit is indeed a motive force that exhibits evidence of morality, because human beings will actively engage a problem if the moral cause is seen as sufficient. So, for this reason, the Biblical definition of man stands as incontestable under the common law due to the use of the Biblical term, conscience, to define a person as distinct from the animals. Thus, it is the secular standard for public education that must be brought into question before the law in order that a sustainable method can be better applied to society, which must derive itself from a Biblical standard for the good of the people, and the common law, or we will be faced by an opposition that sets itself against the things of God that are for the benefit of an individual's protection within the system.

The modern world has been civilized through the law of human equality, which has derived from the United States Constitutional definition of man, which in turn, derives itself from the Holy Bible. While atheism's greatest attempt to civilize the world, was through the practice of Communism involving philosophical materialism, radical scepticism, and Scientific Atheism, which is a crime against humanity due to the totalitarian nature of absolute atheism, and is responsible for more deaths by democide in the last century over any other social ideology in human history. So, for this reason, atheism is without sufficient cause to argue before the law for religious rights to be removed from citizens in order to grant privileges to themselves, because the universal law of freedom of conscience is defined by the First Liberty, upon which, all other liberties stand.

Freedom of conscience is defined as a religious liberty, which leaves the atheist without a lawful premise in which to argue for religion to be removed. The more atheism continues to argue against the theological terms used to define a person with, the more we will see our basic human freedoms erode, all on the basis that atheism is in denial of the lawful terms used to describe a person with, which derive from the Holy Bible, rather than from atheism or science. According to the basic tenets of atheism, man has no soul and has descended from a lower animal on a hierarchical scale. So, in order for the atheist to deny their humanity, then a scientific inquiry into the supernatural becomes their modus operandi, which in itself, is a form of religious study, because the supernatural cannot be dismissed on the basis of scientific theory by definition of the fact that a theory in science is equal to a belief.

So, because physical laws are universal, and because physical laws are not physical, it will mean automatically that physical laws are supernatural in origin, rather than a consequence of nature, because physical laws are not subject to nature, but rather, nature is subject to physical laws. And the more science delves into the practice of physics, the more we will understand the nature of physical laws, which cannot be attributed to nature, because nature is governed by physical laws, rather than physical laws deriving from a material phenomenon. Modern evolutionary physics attempts to describe the universe as a material phenomenon, but because physical laws are not physical as an object is, and because nature is subject to physical laws, it will mean that no law in science or nature can disprove the supernatural based on any set of rules, because physical laws are by definition rule based, and are therefore evidence of a creation.

Anything that has had rules applied to it, is by definition a creation, whether it be a textbook on physics, or a game of football, rules will apply. Yet the only reason that atheism rejects the evidence for creation, is to be freed from rules, which constitutes as a rule in itself, of which, the atheist cannot deny without forfeiting their atheism in turn, because the sole purpose of atheism is to free themselves from morality. But because morality is also rule based in order to give stability to human nature, the same as physical laws give stability to the system of the universe, it will mean that there is a higher standard for rules than the ones we create, such as Biblical morality. If rules are to be applied to human society, then the virtues of Biblical morality are required, otherwise, there would be no universal standard in place to obey the law, when laws are for our own protection as individuals, rather than a mechanism for human enslavement.

But if laws in society are to be structured around the principles of nature, rather than Biblical morality, then mankind will one day be enslaved by the laws we create, which is an inevitable consequence of atheism, Secular Humanism, and philosophical materialism, rather than nature. Yet the only one who can set the atheist free from their denial of morality, is the one who has endowed them with conscience in order to understand a moral obligation, and has made Himself known to the world by His Son, Jesus Christ, who has ushered in an age of freedom and grace by the introduction of human rights and equality, for the Spirit of the Lord is a Spirit of love and humility who has founded peace here on Earth in accordance with His moral law.

The existence of moral law is the self-evident nature of God in Heaven who is, and who was, and who is to come, the Almighty. The human mind has been endowed with conscience, which is the evidence that moral law exists, and the evidence that morality is universal is the same evidence that physical laws exist, because both moral law, and physical laws are in place to give stability to the system of the universe, as well as law and order. The human conscience is therefore evidence of a spiritual reality that is rule based the same as a system is rule based. Thus, a system in place is the self-evident nature of God's existence, which cannot be attributed to nature alone, because nature is without a conscience to reason from, which is a limitation for atheism in terms of a natural explanation, rather than an expedience for secular science.

According to physics and the principles of thermodynamics, a system will always be found in a state of disorder or moving towards it, which means definitively that the universe began as complex, rather than simple, because the progression of entropy is a state of decline from ordered complexity into disordered complexity, which is both logically deduced under observation, as well as self-evident. The ability of the human mind to cope with psychological stress comes from having a strong conscience, because it is the human mind that is able to apply a correct psychology, and therefore, a system. So, in order for a method of psychology to be effective, as well as positive, then a correct theology is also required, because it is a correct theology that will interpret the truth, as well as a lie.

Lying is a part of human nature, and is defined as the human condition, of which, there is no cure for apart from the truth that sets us free. And the one truth that all must accept, is that all have lied before God in Heaven who is the way, the truth, and the life, and is everlasting without end. So, because the human mind must decide the truth from a lie, it will mean that the human conscience experiences guilt and shame in regards to lust, greed, and envy, which is the very thing that separates mankind from the animal kingdom. The evidence that the animals are not endowed with conscience, is due to the existence of nudity, which bares guilt on the human mind in regards to shame. None may shame the Holy Spirit, for the Holy Spirit is sacred, as well as pure. Those who shame the Spirit of God shall be led astray by an inward lie, which is the very thing that will bring a person to shame on the day of judgement.

So, the one fact to refute atheism is found with the existence of the human conscience, which cannot be refuted by logic, nor measured by science, and is therefore the most unique trait of any living creature. The human conscience has been defined by international law as endowed to every human being, which forms the basis for human rights and equality. And that which is endowed, according to law, is by definition a birthright. The lawful definition of "inalienable" is that which is endowed, so that which is inalienable is by definition a birthright. And it is for this reason that every human being has an inalienable right to be defined as a created human being with a human ancestry on the basis of conscience and reason, because the ability to reason derives from the ability to ask questions, which is the very thing that separates mankind from the animal kingdom.

So, in order to be consistent with international law regarding the interpretation of human rights and equality, then a Creator God is a requirement, because international law has recognised religious teachings as the source of human rights, which leaves atheism without a lawful premise in which to argue that religion is to blame for inequality, as well as human slavery. If mankind is to be defined by law as a type of animal from the theory of evolution, then mankind will be enslaved by the laws we create due to the legal definition of property.

This means that no human being can be defined as having derived from any other ancestry apart from human ancestry before international law respectively, so that each person may exercise their basic rights as a human being without interference from the law. So, if there is one thing that will lead mankind into an new age of human slavery, then it will be the evolutionary teaching that man is animal, which cannot be justified before international law on the basis of human rights and equality, which are by definition, universal, as well as inalienable.

The New Atheist movement is without sufficient cause to argue from the premise of minority groups who question basic public morals in order to try and gain a moral high ground before the law, which is neither safe, nor virtuous for any minority group on the basis of equality, because morality is defined as universal for the benefit of an individual's protection within the system. And the evidence that morality is universal, as well as spiritual, is due to a moral cause, which the atheist cannot deny without invoking a moral cause of their own making. So, for this reason, the New Atheist movement will back any minority group they wish to defend in order to espouse some form of moral high ground, which is not politically expedient on the basis of law and order, because nothing stifles law and order faster than the practice of immoral public behaviour that includes amoral sexual tendencies.

The process of law and order under the common law relies entirely on a universal system of morality, so that a cause which is just can be sustained as self-evident based on eternal truths that have been decided upon by previous cases. And the one law that is both self-evident, as well as inalienable, is the right to be defined as a created human being, which is not only protected under United States Constitutional law in accordance with the Declaration of Independence, but also, it is protected by international law as universal. If mankind is to be defined by science, then science lays in authority, when no scientist can lay claim to authority on the basis of self-governance, which is not to be interfered with by so-called humanitarian groups that hail from the viewpoint of the evolutionary theory, because the right to be self-governed derives from self-governance under the Biblical principles of universal morality, which cannot be brought into question before the law on the basis of equality.

Human equality can only be defined by a universal system of morality, which is the very thing that New Atheism is challenging from the theoretical premise of evolution. So, in order to cross examine the theory of evolution, then an eternal truth must first be established, which cannot derive itself from atheism without relying on theory alone, because the one philosophy that defines Scientific Atheism, is radical scepticism. The theory of evolution, according to the United States Supreme Court, is by definition, incontestable, all on the basis of a judiciary decision that excluded the people in a trial by jury. The decision by the United States Supreme Court to place protections on the theory of evolution is a crime against humanity on the basis of equality, because human equality has been defined on the basis of Biblical creation, which is not in conflict with the universal definition of man.

So, for this reason, there is sufficient cause for Class Action and litigation against the United States government to restore protections for the Holy Bible and to disregard the theory of evolution, because all that is at stake here, is our freedom under the law, which cannot be placed into harm's way without incurring the burden of proof. Therefore, it is the inalienable right of the people that they should be defined as created human beings through the public education system on the supreme basis of human equality, rather than animals under a scientific theory that demands a materialistic interpretation for everything, including the law.

Human equality is not an offence before the law on the basis of conscience and reason, while the evolutionary definition of man stands as questionable on the basis of an eternal truth that all have been endowed by their maker with conscience and with rights. And it is the inalienable right of the people to be defined as created human beings that will sustain us through our trials and tribulations against that which God in Heaven has rebuked with an eternal curse, such as the evolutionary definition of man. The universal law of human equality stands as an eternal truth that is legally binding and incontestable under international law on the basis of equal justice, which is the very reason why the theory of evolution is without sufficient cause, because mankind will be defined by the laws that sustain our basic freedoms in order to protect the people's rights, and their just liberties.

The human conscience is self-aware and can issue a command on the basis of the sixth sense, which is a moral sense of behaviour that exhibits an understanding of injustices. The sixth sense is a combination of the previous five senses that are used to perceive danger, which are: hearing, taste, sight, smell, and touch, with the human conscience acting as a sixth sense that is able to perceive injustices, and is thereby a spiritual sense on the basis of moral law. This extra and additional sense is not owing to the animal kingdom, but rather, it is owing to the Creator who has endowed all life with ability, but unto His own image the gift of conscience, with which, to reason from in order that all may know His ways of truth and life, which is for the benefit of the people, and their protection within the system.

The Spirit of God is a Spirit of liberty and freedom that cannot fade away into the darkness of night, nor shall it be suppressed by the light of evolutionary science, for the Lord has spoken to the districts of the people that they should have life and liberty with the pursuit of happiness in accordance with the will of His eternal Spirit that all shall acknowledge one another as equal in rights for the sake of human rights and equality. Therefore, God is just by the provision of human rights and equality, and equal justice thereby, which cannot be overruled by science, nor outlawed by the legislator, because the time of God's grace to mankind is at hand so that all shall acknowledge their maker in spirit and in truth, which is a commandment of the Lord forever in eternity.

May the Lord God in Heaven bless those who strive for an equality with their neighbour, so that the grace of God should be seen by our enemies who have attempted to remove the just rights of the people in order to satisfy their own unbelief. The Lord will make a way for those who strive with Him against our adversary the devil who conspires against the people so that the people should turn against their own government in a time of global crisis, for the people of the Earth have been set apart in their hearts with an eternal enmity to despise the evil that Satan has created. There shall be no justice for those who work against the splendour and might of the judgements of the Lord and His sheepfold who are forever blessed upon the Earth, and eternally sacred before the Heavens were established. Let all those who cause strife for their brother or sister, be afraid, for the Lord has spoken, and He will not repent of His eternal word that all have been deemed created for the sake of human rights and equality.

CHAPTER 7

Conspiracy and War

SOCIAL DARWINISM HAS CAUSED A SOCIALIST COMPETITION between Capitalism and Communism, with Social Darwinists emphasizing the need for a global scientific revolution, and is in strong support of authoritarianism, fascism, and racism in order to facilitate a socialist State. Social Darwinism in America worked its way in predominantly through the rationale of the late 19th century industrial titans, such as John D. Rockefeller (1839 - 1937), and Andrew Carnegie (1835 - 1919). John D. Rockefeller and Andrew Carnegie ran an industrial monopoly, whereby the principles of Darwin's theory was used to give them corporate dominance over smaller corporations.

The Rockefeller family is an American industrial, political, and banking family that owns one of the world's largest fortunes. The family had a long association with, and control of, Chase Manhattan Bank. By 1977, the Rockefellers were considered to be one of the most powerful families in American history. Prominent banker and philanthropist David Rockefeller Sr, was the family patriarch until his death in 2017. The Chase Manhattan

Corporation is the former American holding company by the Rockefellers that merged with JP Morgan & Co in the year 2000 to form JP Morgan Chase & Co, which has now seized financial control over the Bank of America as of 2023.

The firm originated in the final days of the 18th century, and as of January 2023, JP Morgan Chase & Co is the largest bank in the United States, and the world's largest bank by market capitalization, and the fifth largest bank in the world in terms of total assets, with total assets amounting to $3.989 trillion. A secret gathering at a secluded island off the coast of Georgia in 1910 laid the foundations for the Federal Reserve System. In November 1910, six men: Nelson Aldrich, A. Piatt Andrew, Henry Davison, Arthur Shelton, Frank Vanderlip, and Paul Warburg met at the Jekyll Island Club to write a plan to reform America's banking system.

The meeting in November 1910 drafted legislation that was written to create a central banking system for the United States following the financial panic of 1907 when banking reform became a major issue in the United States. The meeting at Jekyll Island and its purpose was a closely guarded secret, and participants did not admit that the meeting had occurred until the late 1930's. The plan written on Jekyll Island laid the foundation for what would eventually become the Federal Reserve system. JP Morgan arranged for the group to use the club's facilities, which was founded in 1886. The sociopolitical idea of competing the wealthy against the poor through the power of politics and economics has led to the formation of an oligarchical rule, where the rich take advantage of the poor through usury loans that derive from a nation's central bank.

The Rothschild banking dynasty currently possesses the world's largest private fortune with an estimated figure of around $500 trillion. Yet they're not listed on Forbes Rich list and have remained behind the scenes of politics for this reason. Today, Rothschild Investment Corp has top holdings with Apple Inc, The Chevron Corporation, as well as JP Morgan Chase & Co. The Rothschild banking dynasty is the world's richest family bar none and secretly controls the Federal Reserve system internationally through subsidiary agents. According to the Ten Planks of Communism, a nation's banking system must be under the control of a central bank, which is fundamental to any Communist industrial scheme, whereby the workers are being exploited under a heavy and progressive income tax, while the privately owned central bank is making a soaring profit from the collection of interest, because every dollar that is printed by a central bank incurs a penalty that results in direct taxation.

The Federal Reserve system of banking within the United States was made legal by an act of Congress in 1913 and was announced to the people that this act of congress would enhance the stability of the American economy. While the origin of income tax within the United States is generally cited by the 16th Amendment, which was ratified by Congress on February 3, 1913, the same year that the Federal Reserve system took control over the printing of United States currency. The idea that money can be printed freely without the amount of money being tied to a commodity is known as fractional reserve banking, which derives from the Knights Templar during the 12th and 13th century. But the idea of a central bank within every nation that is controlled by an international body derives directly from the Illuminati, because this idea was only made possible by Adam Weishaupt and the Rothschild banking conspiracy that took control over the British economy earlier in 1815.

During the 12th and 13th century, the Knights Templar established a network of secure banks, and gained enormous financial influence through their holdings with the interest they were charging. Their banking system allowed religious pilgrims to deposit assets in their home countries and withdraw funds in the Holy Land to avoid being robbed of their wealth during their pilgrimage. But the Templars figured out how they could turn worthless paper into gold through fractional reserve banking, which was to be the basis for our current monetary system by the Federal Reserve Act. A gold standard for the supply of paper money is to be regulated based on the amount of gold in reserve, but if the over printing of paper money can be achieved without regulation, then the amount of monetary notes can be over printed and then loaned out with interest payable in gold.

This practice is more commonly known as a fiat money system called "fractional reserve banking" which is how the Knights Templar established a monopoly over the ownership of gold, because the amount of gold they had in reserve was only a fraction of what they had created in terms of paper notes. And the interest payable on loans was to be paid in gold, and not with notes, because the notes were only a certificate for the holdings of someone else's gold. The Knights Templar grew richer and more powerful than any aristocracy during that time, including the Pope, who gave them their authority to begin with. So, the Pope issued a decree to have the Knights Templar's rounded up and burned at the stake for reasons relating to treason and heresy, which ultimately ended the Templar's banking monopoly.

In 1815, Nathan Mayer Rothschild made a fortune in trading bills of exchange through a banking enterprise that began in 1805, dealing with financial investments, such as foreign bills and government bonds. After Nathan seized financial control over the London Stock Exchange in 1815 through insider trading, he was quoted saying: "I care not what puppet is placed upon the throne of England to rule the Empire on which the sun never sets. The man who controls the British money supply, controls the British Empire; And I control the British money supply." The Battle of Waterloo was fought on June 18, 1815 between Napoleon's French Army, and an English coalition led by the Duke of Wellington and Marshal Blücher. The battle of Waterloo concluded a war that had raged on for 23 years, and ended the French attempts to dominate Europe, which ultimately defeated Napoleon's imperial power.

On June 18, 1815 a Rothschild courier by the name of John Roworth road back to London with the news that Wellington and Blücher had won the battle at Waterloo, which then led Nathan Rothschild to immediately begin selling all of his government bonds, giving the illusion that Napoleon had won the war, which caused such a panic on the London stock exchange that everyone else with an invested interest in government bonds to begin selling their shares at pennies on the pound. Nathan then immediately began the process of buying up all of the shares through subsidiary agents, thus capitalizing from the financial panic that he and Napoleon had created through insider trading and conspiracy. The Rothschild banking dynasty then married into the British royal family, which not only granted protection for the Rothschild banking family, but also, the British royal family as well, because the conspiracy to rule the world by the Illuminati includes the abolition of all monarchies, which was later enacted by Communist revolutionaries that executed the Russian Tsar in order to install Communism in Russia.

The conspiracy by the Illuminati favours the extermination of the Jewish-Christian philosophy; Abolition of the power of all royal houses and monarchies; Annihilation of all patriotism and loyalty to sovereignty;

Destruction of traditional family structures and marriage; A collective education for children by the State; And many more issues that can be found in our modern society. The founder of the Illuminati, according to historical resources, was a man by the name of Adam Weishaupt, who was commissioned by Nathan Mayer Rothschild to draw up a conspiracy during his time at Ingolstadt University that could be used to take over the world economically and politically.

Weishaupt was deeply influenced by the Jesuit Order, who were at that time, relying heavily on a Templar style of banking by which pilgrims to the Vatican were taken advantage of financially. And though the creation of the Illuminati, as it is widely referred to as, has been attributed to Adam Weishaupt, it is in fact a much older secret society dating back to ancient Egypt, and further back to ancient Babylon, which is why the All Seeing Eye, or, Eye of Horus, is the primary symbol of the Illuminati, as well as being the official Seal of the United States.

The first Mystery School from ancient history was in ancient Babylon whereby certain symbols held a secret meaning that only the initiates knew and were able to interpret, thereby creating the first secret society based on occult symbology, esoterics, and astrology. Today, the ancient Mystery School is formerly known as Freemasonry, which became popular during the Middle Ages due to the increased need for skilled Masons to build the Cathedrals of Europe.

Modern Freemasonry can be broken down into many levels of initiation called degrees, but there are two primary types of Masons down through the centuries, such as fellowcraft Masons who are mainly concerned with stonework and architecture. While the other type are referred to as speculative Masons, who are more concerned with the interpretation of occult symbols, esoterics and astrology. Freemasonry is a type of system whereby the initiates relate signs and symbols to their initiation rites within the craft, as well as characterizing certain deities from astrology. This tradition was popular among the Pharaohs of Egypt and the Magi of Babylon, because much of what is recorded from their history derives from the interpretation of signs and symbols that only the initiates knew, thus resulting in a multi-generational occult society dating back to King Sumu-Abum of ancient Babylon when he rebelled against the Amorites and established the region of Babylon in the year 1894 BC.

Many historians will argue that the Illuminati infiltrated Freemasonry in order to co-opt the craft from its core degrees, yet the initiation of a new Mason into the first degree, known as an Entered Apprentice, will always be asked one question before the initiation can proceed. And the one question that is asked is "what do you seek?" And the correct answer that an Entered Apprentice must give is "light." The core philosophy behind the initiation of a Freemason into the first degree, is enlightenment, which the craft has referred too through many of its proponents and historians, such as Albert Pike and Manly P. Hall, who sought to give a description of the source of their enlightenment, which they openly attributed to Lucifer, the light bearer. So, for this reason, the Illuminati is in fact the product of Freemasonry, because the core tenets behind the Illuminati derive from Freemasonry, which dates back thousands of years to the first Mystery School in ancient Babylon.

The connection between the Illuminati, Freemasonry, and ancient Babylon is illuminism involving construction, finance, and social engineering using the principles of sorcery, esoterics, and occult philosophy is found with the practice pyramid temple worship that centred around astrological constellations. The Ziggurat in ancient Babylon was formally known as "Etemenanki," which translates in Sumerian as, "house of the foundation of heaven and earth." The Sumerians believed that these pyramid temples connected heaven and earth, with each of these pyramids being strategically located around the power centers of the earth known as ley lines. Every major continent on Earth has ancient pyramids from Bosnia to Egypt, and from America to El Salvador, which is evidence of a global society that existed prior to Noah's flood, and was heavily involved in the construction of pyramids in order to shape a global maritime society based on trade, commerce, astrology.

The Enlightenment era, (along with most of the additional degrees and initiation rites within Freemasonry), were in fact named after the Illuminati by 16th and 17th century occultists, because most of the major Enlightenment thinkers were steeped in the occult, from which, Weishaupt drew his inspiration. The role of British Freemasonic Enlightenment, Social Darwinism, and Communism cannot be adequately explained without first explaining the role of the Illuminati, which is secretly referred to as "The Hidden Hand of Freemasonry," or "Master of the Second Vail," of which,

Napoleon Bonaparte, Karl Marx and Joseph Stalin were all members of, including George Washington until he left the Lodge in 1755 to pursue his political ambitions against the Grand Lodge of England. And though Karl Marx and Joseph Stalin were never official members of Freemasonry, they were still involved in the conspiracy by the Illuminati to overthrow all aristocracies around the world and install Communist governments instead, which would be overseen by members from the conspiracy. While Napoleon's role in the conspiracy for world domination by the Illuminati can be explained when Nathan Mayer Rothschild took over the London stock exchange in 1815 as a direct result of the battle at Waterloo and insider trading.

*Quotation: ————————————————

The earliest records of American Masonic Lodges are in Philadelphia. In 1732, Boston's St. John's Lodge was duly constituted by the Grand Lodge of England and remains the oldest Lodge in North America. Interwoven with the British Enlightenment, Masonic Lodges formed throughout Europe and the Americas. Over time, the network of Scottish, English, and Irish Lodges helped to tie the British commercial empire together. Although American elites initially joined the Freemasons to keep pace with genteel English behaviour, the fraternity contributed to the spread of the ideas and ideals behind the American Revolution. During the revolutionary era, Masons of note included George Washington, Benjamin Franklin, James Otis, and Paul Revere. Washington joined Freemasonry in the Lodge at Fredericksburg, Virginia. He was 20 years old when he received the first degree of Entered Apprentice on November 4, 1752. He paid the Lodge two pounds and three shillings to join. Ten days after turning 21 on March 3, 1753, he was passed to the second degree of Fellowcraft. On August 4, 1753, he was raised to the third degree of Master Mason. The Lodge's surviving minute book records Washington attending only two more meetings; September 1, 1753, and January 4,

1755. - Source: George Washington Presidential Library at Mount Vernon USA. (Documented by the Grand Lodge of Virginia in the year 1775).

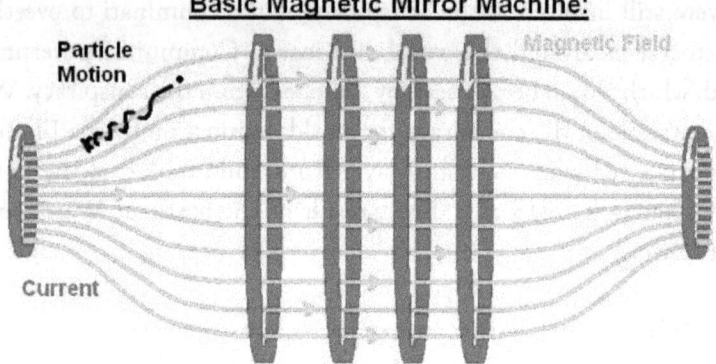

(Above) Pictured from left to right: Image result for Napoleon Bonaparte, George Washington, Karl Marx and Joseph Stalin revealing their association with the Illuminati. Source: Wikipedia Encyclopedia.

*Quotation: ────────────────

"I have heard much of the nefarious, and dangerous plan, and doctrines of the Illuminati, but never saw the book until you were pleased to send it to me. The same causes which have prevented my acknowledging the receipt of your letter have prevented my reading the book, hitherto; Namely, the multiplicity of matters which pressed upon me before, and the debilitated state in which I was left after a severe fever had been removed. And which allows me to add little more now than a thanks for your kind wishes and favourable sentiments, except to correct an error you have run into of my presiding over the English lodges in this Country. The fact is, I preside over none, nor have I been in one more than once or twice, within the last thirty years. I believe notwithstanding, that none of the Lodges in this Country are contaminated with the principles ascribed to the Society of the Illuminati." - Source: Letter by George

Washington to William Russell. (Documented September 28, 1798).

According to the letter by George Washington to William Russell, he was fully aware of the Illuminati, which was secretly due to his association with Freemasonry. William Russell had implied that George Washington was a member of the Illuminati due to his association with Freemasonry, which in turn, caused Washington to oppose the Illuminati openly without denigrating the Freemasonic Order in turn. So, the real question that still remains here is, was George Washington a member of the Illuminati or not? And the answer in my own opinion, is yes, but, Washington chose to oppose the Illuminati publicly by opposing the main objectives by the Illuminati, such as the abolition of all loyalty to patriotism, sovereignty, and the Judeo-Christian faith, as well as being in opposition to the Illuminati banking conspiracy, whilst denying any former involvement with the Illuminati through Freemasonry in order to protect himself from the brunt of public anger and disapproval.

And the proof of this in my own opinion is due to three main reasons. Firstly; George Washington abandoned Freemasonry in 1755 in order to pursue his political ambitions against the Grand Lodge and the crown of England. Secondly; George Washington openly shared his appalling sentiments towards the main objectives by the Illuminati, of which, he was already fully informed of according to his letter to William Russell. And thirdly; George Washington had a knowledgeable opposition to the core tenets by the Illuminati, which included the creation of a central bank that would be overseen by an international banking cartel, such as the Rothschilds.

So, even though George Washington was a former member of the Illuminati, it had no bearing on his political ambition to establish a central government in America that relied on a gold standard for the issuing of currency by the Treasury Department, which was in opposition to the Illuminati banking conspiracy involving a central bank. So, for this reason, George Washington was fully aware of the Illuminati through insider information, because Washington was adamantly opposed to the main objectives by the Illuminati banking conspiracy to establish a central bank that would oversee the printing of paper money for the collection of interest in the form of direct taxation that was only payable in gold or silver.

So, because this is a Freemasonic conspiracy by the Illuminati to overrule individual human sovereignty by interfering with the original Constitution of the United States, and because Washington had chosen to leave the English Lodges of America in order to adopt the newly formed Constitution in spite of the Grand Lodge and crown of England, it meant that he was not only opposing the crown of England, but also, Freemasonry and the Illuminati banking conspiracy to issue paper notes only. The founding fathers of America were fully informed of the international banking cartel and the conspiracy by the Illuminati to establish a central bank within every nation, of which, George Washington, Thomas Jefferson, and James Madison were openly opposing without disclosing their sources in turn.

*Quotation: ————————————————
"Paper money has had the effect in your State that it ever will have, to ruin commerce; Oppress the honest; And open a door to every species of fraud and injustice. I am entirely in sentiment with you Sir, of the necessity there is to adopt some measures for the support of our national peace and honour. The present situation of our public affairs demands the exertion and influence of every good and honest citizen in the Union, to tranquilize disturbances, retrieve our credit, and place us upon a respectable footing with other nations." - Source: Excerpt from a letter written by George Washington to Jabez Bowen. (Documented January 9, 1787).

The founding fathers sought to create a Christian democracy based on a Commonwealth system under the universal principles of common law, whereby the power of Legislative Acts could be monitored and overruled by the voting constituency, because it is the voting constituency that is to retain the power over their private property, which is not to be interfered with except in the event of a national crisis. And it is for this reason that the founding fathers feared the creation of a central bank, because a central bank maintains a private interest that can, and will, lead to a financial crisis by preventing loans to be secured by other private financial organizations resulting in the abolition of private property in order to repay the central bank.

And it is for this reason that the teaching of evolution by the State equates to a global injustice, because the end result is Social Darwinism, which inevitably leads to the exploitation of those who are lesser off financially due to the creation of a private monopoly over the ownership of property. Yet property such as land, money, and natural resources must remain in the hands of the people who are depending on these resources in order to coexist, rather than to profit from, because it is the expansion of private enterprise that aims to profit from the people, while the people's aim is to survive. The founding fathers were fully aware of an engineered financial crisis due to the manipulation of the said Constitution and from a central bank long before it ever occurred, which was a direct result of insider information through their prior initiation into Freemasonry.

*Quotation: ————————————————————

"If the American people ever allow private banks to control the issue of their currency, first by inflation, then by deflation, the banks and corporations that will grow up around them will deprive the people of all property until their children wake-up homeless on the very continent that their fathers conquered. The issuing power should be taken from the banks and restored to the people, to whom, it properly belongs. I sincerely believe that banking establishments are more dangerous than standing armies, and that the principle of spending money to be paid by posterity under the name of funding is but swindling futurity on a large scale.

If the debt which the banking companies owe be a blessing to anybody, it is to themselves alone, who are realizing a solid interest of eight or ten percent on it. As to the public, these companies have banished all our gold and silver medium, of which, before their institution, we had without interest, which never could have perished in our hands, and would have been our salvation now in the hour of war; Instead of which, they have given us two hundred million of froth and bubble, on which, we are to pay them heavy interest until it shall vanish into thin air.

We are warranted then, in affirming that this parody on the principle of "a public debt being a public blessing," and its mutation into a blessing by the private, instead of public debtors, is as ridiculous as the original principle itself. In both cases, the truth is, that capital may be produced by industry, and accumulated by economy; But jugglers will only propose to create wealth by legerdemain tricks using paper only." - Thomas Jefferson, 3rd President of the United States. Source: Correspondence from a letter by Thomas Jefferson to John Taylor. (Documented May 28, 1816).

The United States founding fathers saw the dangers of a fractional reserve banking system from the authority of a central bank long before the Federal Reserve system came into effect. The Great Economic Depression of 1929 - 1939 was a worldwide economic depression that lasted approximately 10 years, with the GDP in the United States economy falling by nearly 50%. The engineered crisis was due to the financial practices by the Federal Reserve system, which took power over the global economy earlier in 1913. And shortly thereafter, the Federal Reserve, with the power to print or not to print, caused an engineered financial crisis by preventing loans to be lent out to banks, which ultimately stopped the flow of money, and led to a global economic meltdown and mass inflation.

The Federal Reserve decision to stop loans being lent out to banks, thereby reducing the economy by one half, was in fact the leading factor that led to the great economic depression in the early 1900's. In order for the United States to continue as a world leader in global economics, then the Federal Reserve must be audited by the Treasury Department, because if interest is applied to the printing of money, then every dollar that is put into circulation by the Federal Reserve requires repayment with interest owing, which is enough to drive any economy into extinction, because if the total amount of debt isn't paid with each passing financial year, then the debt will compound in interest, which is the very thing that will ultimately bankrupt a nation completely as we've already seen with Greece and Iceland.

If money can be printed by the Treasury Department of a nation, then the regulation of money can be achieved without private interest, which is always taxable directly. A worker who is on an hourly wage or salary should not have to pay income tax under the original version of the United States Constitution, because it is not defined as profiteering; Only corporations make a profit, while a worker earns a wage. And this was largely the case within the United States before the Federal Reserve system took over the issuing power of currency, because if you are a sovereign citizen, then you do not have to pay income tax; Only those who make a profit are subject to direct taxation, while a worker is subject to indirect taxation through the purchasing of goods and community services.

Yet the answer to this toxic financial Ponzi scheme is simple, because all that's required for an economy to stabilize itself, is for the Treasury Department to be allowed to print a competing currency to the Federal Reserve notes, which happened to be John F. Kennedy's idea when he signed executive order 11110 which ultimately led to his assassination shortly thereafter. JFK's greatest struggle during his time in office was against Communism as a political fascism, because not only was the Soviet Union at war with his administration, but also, it was the principles of fractional reserve banking from Marxism that ultimately caused Kennedy to be assassinated. Kennedy attempted to stop the Federal Reserve system of banking by issuing the Treasury Department with the right to print a competing currency that was interest free due to the lack of a private interest over the printing of money. The idea by Kennedy to print a competing currency that was interest free came from Abraham Lincoln's creation of the Green Back, which also sealed Lincoln's fate by the international banking cartel who favoured Social Darwinism and a private banking monopoly instead.

*Quotation: ————————————————
"Owners of capital will stimulate the working class to buy more and more expensive goods, houses and technology, pushing them to take more and more expensive credits, until their debt becomes unbearable. The unpaid debt will lead to bankruptcy of banks, which will have to be nationalized, and the State will have to take the road which will eventually lead to Communism." - Karl Marx, founder of Communism. Source: Das Kapital - Chapter 31, Genesis of the Industrial Capitalist. (Documented September 14, 1867).

In 2009, congress passed the American Recovery and Reinvestment Act that resulted in an economic stimulus package to private banks that was estimated to be $787 billion at the time of passage, and was later revised to $831 billion between 2009 and 2019. So, when multinational private banking enterprises are in need of financial rescue, the United States government is usually available for a handout at the expense of the taxpayer. Government intervention claims to have saved GM and Chrysler and the supply chain that was tied to them, such as Ford, Honda, Toyota and Nissan by the end of the Great Recession.

Yet during the Great Recession, auto-manufacturing employment fell by more than one-third, which equated to being a loss of more than 334,000 jobs according to the United States Bureau of Labour Statistics. And a system of repeatedly bailing out a group of multinational corporations due to poor financial management for the benefit of the people to continue consuming, means automatically that the people are consuming themselves into financial ruin. In 2008, the world's worst financial crisis in almost 80 years caused a global recession. Many European countries had an oversized government debt, but Greece was affected the worst with a high spending deficit due to the interest rates set by the central bank of Greece. The government of Greece had borrowed more money than it was able to make in revenue through income taxes, which, in 2010, led to protests in the streets once the economy had officially failed.

The Greek debt crisis originated from heavy government spending and the problems associated with a progressive and slowly increasing interest rate by the Federal Reserve system. The central bank of Greece has raised interest rates from 2.00% in 2008 to 4.75% in 2023. This rate rise by the central bank of Greece is solely due to government corruption by relying on income taxes to pay the interest owing without the consent of the people in regards to government borrowing and spending. So, when the government of a nation fails to repay the central bank, it results in a shortage of monetary funds, which then leads to mass inflation and an inevitable financial panic.

The Federal Reserve retains the power to increase or decrease interest rates, which is then passed on to other financial corporations that borrow from the Federal Reserve in order to circulate money, which in turn, is passed down to the individual who is making a loan from a private bank, and is thereby subject to a higher interest rate than what the private banks are paying. This issue also extended to Iceland where the voting constituency was pressured to pay for outlandish government spending resulting in a boycott of the Euro. Icelandic businesses will not accept Euros or United

States dollars since the financial crash in 2008 - 2011 due to a national interest to stimulate their own economy with their own currency.

So, in order for Iceland to maintain its own currency and monetary system, they have reverted to the Icelandic króna, or ISK, instead of paying heavy interest to the International banking cartel through each nation's central bank. In 2015, after the 2008 - 2011 financial crash, the government of Iceland considered a monetary proposal to abolish the privately owned central banking system and to establish its own national currency. In the years preceding the financial crisis, three Icelandic banks, Kaupthing, Landsbanki and Glitnir, grew financially superior. This expansion was driven by ready access to credit in Euros and U.S dollars through the central bank. As the financial crisis of 2008 unfolded, investors perceived that the three major Icelandic banks would fail due to oversized loan creations with the central bank. Public trust in the three major banks gradually faded, leading to a sharp depreciation of loans by 2008 which increased the level of difficulty for the three major banks to request loans from the central bank.

At the end of the financial year in 2008, Iceland's external debt was 9.553 trillion ISK (or 50 billion Euro), which was more than 7 times the GDP of Iceland in 2007. But in despite of this, the total assets held by the three major banks of Iceland totalled 14.437 trillion ISK at the end of the financial year in 2008, which was equal to more than 11 times the national GDP in 2007. The huge size of the Icelandic financial assets held by the three major banks caused the central bank of Iceland to stop loaning money to the three major banks, resulting in their file for bankruptcy. But unlike the American Recovery and Reinvestment Act within the United States, the Icelandic government allowed the three major banks to fail.

This resulted in the central bank of Iceland losing financial control over the three major banks when they failed to repay the central bank. The former British politician, Gordon Brown, who served as Prime Minister of the United Kingdom during the 2008 - 2011 financial crisis, issued a statement to the press calling for Iceland to be placed on a terrorist watch list alongside Afghanistan and Iraq showing no sympathy for the people of Iceland whatsoever during the financial panic, resulting in public outrage by Icelandic citizens against Gordon Brown. The move by the Icelandic government to allow the three major banks to fail resulted in a great deal of public support by the Icelandic people despite their financial situation in depreciation, which was solely due to the actions by the central bank, along with the three other major banks that declared bankruptcy amidst record breaking financial profits.

Under royal mandate, Britain has invaded 171 of the world's 193 countries that are currently UN member states, which equates to nine out of ten of all countries. There have been a number of wars throughout history relating to the struggle for independence from the British empire, but none have had such a significant impact on human rights and equality around the world than the American War of Independence. The British-American imperial slave trade was divided into a chain with many links involving many parts of the world, and the imperial idea was that if one link in the chain of production was broken, then the whole empire would fall, which was Britain's primary concern for the most part of their history. The empire's ambition was based on total governance involving any excuse necessary to expand the slave trade, because if the slave trade failed, then so would the British economy.

Today, the former British-American slave trade agreement with North Africa has mutated itself into the International Free Trade Agreement with China, which has committed itself to competing the wealthy with the poor by exploiting the labour capacity of China with the borrowing and spending power of America. This is achieved by the Free Trade Agreement which mandates spending by the so-called "developed nations" in order to pay for the labour of the so-called "developing nations," such as China.

The only problem though, is that if China is still a "developing nation" after 3500 years of cultural history, while America is not, then China will never be a developed nation, which means that there will be no end to the expansion of a Communist industrial enterprise under the Free Trade Agreement. The expansion of China's industrial capacity over recent years is in direct proportion to the contraction of America's industrial capacity, because each time an American owned corporation moves offshore, it inevitably moves to China, resulting in the expansion of Communism, rather than human freedom as the international Free Trade Agreement has promised.

Man has had many definitions throughout history that have been far-fetched and erroneous to say the least, but none the less, the definitions prevailed for many centuries at a time. Such as the ancient Greeks who claimed their heritage dates back to a demi-god, or the people of ancient Inca who believed they came from the sun; Which also happens to be the same belief as the prominent evolutionist, Neil De Grasse Tyson, who teaches that man has derived from star dust over billions of years. But the one definition that has withstood the test of time down through the centuries, is the Biblical definition of man according to the endowed human conscience, because this pertains to the existence of morality and law.

The existence of universal morality cannot be refuted under any definition of man contrived, because it is self-evident that human beings are aware of nudity, while the animals are not. And this is relative to the first sin recorded in the book of Genesis whereby Adam and Eve ate the forbidden fruit, and their eyes were opened, and they saw they were naked, which is the most accurate historical account for the existence of law, nudity, morality and the human conscience, because all of the four are included in the same context within Scripture, and because none of these four aspects can be explained without the need for rules.

This means that there was a perfect system in place that was orderly before corruption had entered the world through Adam, which then led to a divine curse, giving rise to disorder within the system; Meaning that it was the disorderly conduct of man that led to the Earth's corruption. And this is not only applicable to theology, but also, physical laws, because ordered complexity cannot occur without the need for rules, otherwise, there would be nothing to define that which is orderly. So, not only does the book of Genesis explain the causality of law, nudity, morality, and the human conscience, but also, physics, because physics is defined by systems science, and systems science is defined by creation science by definition of the fact that a system is rule based.

Many theologians have attempted to describe from Scripture as to the real reason why the tree of the knowledge of good and evil was placed in the garden that God had created. Some have argued that this was the work of Satan, while others have argued that God is simply unjust. But as far as one can tell, the only reason why the tree of the knowledge of good and evil was in the midst of the Garden of Eden, was so that Adam and Eve would be tested in their faith. So, because Adam and Eve failed the test of faith by choosing death over life, it meant that death had entered the world through sin, and they had thereby entered a different system whereby more rules were needed for correctional purposes. And it is a cardinal principle in systems theory that the more rules a system has, the greater the chance that something will go wrong, which is in accordance with the law of probability.

From the Gospel of Matthew 8:5-10 we read that: When Jesus had entered Capernaum, a centurion came to Him asking for help. "Lord," he said, "my servant lies at home paralysed, suffering terribly." Jesus said to him, "Shall I come and heal him?" The centurion replied, "Lord, I do not deserve to have you come under my roof. But just say the word, and my servant will be healed. For I myself am a man under authority with soldiers under me. I tell this one, "Go" and he goes, and that one "come" and he comes. I say to my servant "Do this" and he does it. When Jesus heard this, He was amazed and said to those following Him, "Truly I tell you, I have not found anyone in Israel with such great faith." (End of quote).

So, from the Gospel of Matthew we find that true life, courage, and strength, is measured by faith, and that all men are tested in their faith, which is also applicable to the Gospel of John 6:28-29 which reads the following: They said therefore unto him, What must we do, that we may work the works of God? Jesus answered and said unto them, "This is the work of God, that ye believe on Him whom He hath sent." (End of quote). So, from the Gospel of John we find that the greatest work one can do is to believe in the one whom God has sent, which means that it is by faith that we receive the things of God which are spiritual, and it is by belief that faith is measured.

The net effect of Adam and Eve having chosen to eat the forbidden fruit, is human slavery, because according to Scripture, sin leads to slavery. The term, slavery, is specifically in relation to ownership, because a slave will always be defined as property, rather than free. And it is the current economic and industrial system in place that leads to human slavery by the creation of debt. Yet according to Scripture, it is Jesus Christ who sets us free; Not by the addition of money or new technology, but rather, by abandoning the system, which in turn, brings a person nearer to God who leads the way in the wilderness by His Holy Spirit.

Those who desire to exit the financial system of the world in order to be closer to the Creator in Heaven should enter the wilderness to fast and pray, because this is the way of the Lamb who has established prophets, kings, and nations through this very ancient practice, or system of practice, that leads the way to perfect freedom in accordance with the will of His spirit. But one must also remember that God in Heaven will test a person in their faith in the same way that a person tests God, for God will not be tried as a man, for God alone is Holy, and God alone is sovereign.

Those who challenge a system based on evils like usury and human slavery are defending the principles of the Gospel message of hope, such as human freedom and liberty, as set forth by the Creator Himself, and shall obtain their freedom in return at the second judgement, because God alone is just by the provision of His moral law. From the Gospel of Galatians 5:1 we read that: "It is for freedom sake that Christ has set us free. Stand firm then, and do not let yourselves be burdened again by a yoke of slavery." (End of quote). So, according to the Gospel of Paul, it is for freedom sake that Christ Jesus has given us liberty, not to take freedom from others arbitrarily, but rather, to present the light of the Gospel message to the world, because it is the world that is in darkness, and is thereby enslaved by the practice of evils, such as usury and human savery.

In the Gospel of John 1:22-23 we read that agents for the Pharisees went out of the city to ask John the Baptist a question, because the Pharisees wanted to know who John was. And the Pharisees' agents said to John: "Who art thou, that we may give an answer to those who sent us? What sayest thou of thyself ?" Then John answered them and said: "I am the voice of one crying in the wilderness, make straight the way of the Lord; As said by the prophet Isaiah." (End of quote). So, from this designation in scripture we find that the voice of the Holy Spirit is a voice that cries from the wilderness, because both the prophet Isaiah, and the prophet John, are making a reference to the one who has sent them, which they both attributed to a voice crying from the wilderness.

According to the Gospel of Matthew 4:1-11 Jesus was led into the wilderness for forty days and forty nights to fast and pray, and there He was tempted by the devil, which was a part of a reoccurring theme in scripture where a voice crying from the wilderness leads the way to perfect freedom in Christ. A second example of this perfect freedom in Christ, would be Israel as a nation who stayed in the wilderness for forty years at the time of Moses, and were established as a nation under God. Or, the apostles themselves, who freely chose to abandon their jobs in order to follow Jesus, the Messiah of the Jews.

A third example of this perfect freedom in Christ, would be the prophet John the Baptist, who left the city in order to survive in the wilderness on locusts and honey, thereby rejecting the monetary system of his day, which was set up as a form of usury against the people by the Pharisees and the Sadducees who were relying on a heavy interest from the people through the circulation of money. Our current monetary system of today has enslaved mankind due to compounding interest by the Fed, because each note that the Federal Reserve prints must be loaned into existence with interest owing, thereby equating each individual as a bond slave who is born into debt.

The difference though between a bond slave and a bond servant, is that a bond servant owes according to a moral principle that is just, rather than unjust, because the borrower is servant to the lender. While slavery has a separate definition on the basis that you are defined as someone else's property. In the Scriptures according to the Gospel of Matthew 20:27-28, Jesus is quoted saying: "And whosoever will be chief among you, let him be your servant, even as the Son of Man came not to be ministered unto, but to minister, and to give His life as a ransom for many." (End of quote).

So, from this passage in Scripture, we find that there is justification for those who serve, which can be either an employer, or an employee, because both are in service to each other according to a need in place. While usury is identified as the practice of taking advantage of a need in order to profit from the situation unfairly, which is why lending money with interest owing is a form of usury. So, the just thing to do in this situation, is to loan without interest owing, because as the Scriptures have said in Matthew 10:8 "Freely you have received; Freely give." (End of quote).

From the Scriptures we find that the introduction of war began in Heaven when Lucifer rebelled due to a lust for power over the Heavens and the Earth. War is conflict, and that which conflicts with mankind the most is Lucifer who is called Satan the devil. The conflict between Adam and Eve with Satan began with lust, because as Eve declared, she was beguiled by the devil. Lust can refer to a sexual desire, or it can refer to envy. This means that Satan envied Adam who was married to Eve. So, the introduction of conspiracy began with Satan when he conspired against God and man. According to the Scriptures in Genesis 6:4 the Son's of God took for themselves wives, which is a Biblical reference to the first incursion where the angels that rebelled in Heaven lusted after the women of the Earth.

From the book of 1 Enoch chapters 7-8 we find that the fallen angel Azazel teaches men the art of metal-working, including ornaments, armour and weaponry. The purpose of this was to teach men secrets from Heaven that men were striving to learn. But the end result was a global flood whereby God grieved in His heart that He had made man. The introduction of global warfare began with fallen angels who sought to deceive mankind into a falsehood of supposed glory. The glory of God is not found in death, but in life, for God is merciful unto His creation that all should find in Him a loving saviour who has led the way in the wilderness by His Holy Spirit, and by the word of His Son, Jesus Christ, who has preached the Gospel message of good news and of hope.

The cornerstone of the Gospel message of hope is the teaching of human equality, for God has endowed mankind with spirit so that all should be convicted by their conscience to do what is right in the sight of God. God does not envy mankind, while the devil does, and it is the devil's mission to draw our attention away from God and towards conflict. The nature of conspiracy is found with envy, because those who desire their neighbour's property will inevitably conspire in their heart to covet that which is not owing to them. All that is owing to mankind from God in Heaven has been revealed through His Son, Jesus Christ, because the only thing that God owes a person, is the truth, because it is the truth that will condemn a man or set them free.

This means that the greatest honour a person can receive is a gift of the spirit of truth, which distinguishes between that which is just, and that which is not. The spirit of truth does not conspire, nor does the spirit envy, because the truth is satisfactory to those who have been redeemed by the blood of Christ who has suffered at the hands of the devil. So, for this reason, we are not to judge ourselves as unworthy to speak the truth, but rather, we are to judge in accordance with the will of His Holy Spirit, for it is the will of God that man should have an equality that leads to perfect freedom with independence.

Historically, the American War of Independence was about ending British imperial rule over the colonies who were seen as the property of the crown. While the founding fathers of America took a different approach by exclaiming the fact that man is subject to a higher authority than himself, and was therefore subject to moral law, as defined by the Ten Commandments and the New Testament. And it was under the Biblical principles of human freedom that individual human sovereignty was defined, because we are to be self-governed under the universal principles of Biblical morality, which in turn, sets the legal premise for inalienable rights to be defined according to the founding fathers themselves.

According to the founding fathers, the Declaration of Independence was a universal declaration of individual human independence for every person, just as much as it was a declaration of national sovereignty. The American War of Independence began on April 19, 1775 and ended on September 3, 1783 with the Declaration of Independence having been drawn-up and ratified on July 4, 1776. Many have tried to argue what the exact reason was for the War of Independence, even though the Declaration of Independence is very clear as to the real reasons why the war occurred. The Boston Tea Party was a political protest that occurred on December 16, 1773 at Griffin's Wharf in Boston Massachusetts, where American colonists, frustrated and angry at Britain for imposing taxation without representation, dumped 342 chests of tea (imported by the British East India Company) into the harbour, which has become the official story.

But according to the Declaration of Independence, it was because of many reasons that all boiled down to one of human freedom under God, which was never acknowledged by the king of England who refused to accept the independence of America, let alone the inalienable rights of American citizens within their new colonies under their newly formed Constitution. And from the beginning of the Declaration of Independence, we find the Biblical definition of man as being equal in rights and liberty from a Constitutional premise, and it was the United States Constitution that America was defending at the War of Independence, which led to the Declaration of Independence being ratified before Congress for the purpose of further outlining the rights of man.

*Quotation: ———————————————————————

Excerpt from The Declaration of Independence authored by Thomas Jefferson and issued to Congress on July 4, in the year of our Lord, 1776:

When in the Course of human events it becomes necessary for one people to dissolve the political bands which have connected them with another and to assume among the powers of the Earth, the separate and equal station to which the laws of nature and of nature's God entitle them, a decent respect to the opinions of mankind requires that they should declare the causes which impel them to the separation. We hold these truths to be self-evident, that all men are created equal, that they are endowed by their Creator with certain unalienable rights, that among these are life, liberty, and the pursuit of happiness.

That to secure these rights, governments are instituted among men, deriving their just powers from the consent of the governed. The history of the present King of Great Britain is a history of repeated injuries and usurpations, all having in direct object the establishment of an absolute tyranny over these States. To prove this, let facts be submitted to a candid world. He has refused his assent to laws, the most wholesome and necessary for the public good. He has endeavoured to prevent the population of these States; For that purpose obstructing the laws for naturalization of foreigners; Refusing to pass others to encourage their migrations hither, and raising the conditions of new appropriations of lands.

He has obstructed the administration of Justice by refusing his assent to laws for establishing judiciary powers. He has affected to render the military independent of and superior to the civil power. He has combined with others to subject us to a jurisdiction foreign to our Constitution, and unacknowledged by our laws, giving his assent to their acts of pretended legislation; For quartering large bodies of armed troops among us; For protecting them by a mock trial from punishment for any murders which they should commit on the inhabitants of these States; For cutting off our trade with all parts of the world;

For imposing taxes on us without our consent; For depriving us in many cases of the benefit of Trial by Jury; For transporting us beyond seas to be tried for pretended offences; For abolishing the free system of English laws in a neighbouring province, establishing therein an arbitrary government, and enlarging its boundaries so as to render it at once an example and fit instrument for introducing the same absolute rule into these colonies; For taking away our Charters, abolishing our most valuable laws, and altering fundamentally the forms of our government. (End of Quote)

So, according to the Declaration of Independence, the main reason why the war occurred was because the king of England was interfering with the functions of government by disregarding the Constitutional grounds for individual human sovereignty on the basis of his own sovereignty, because if there was one thing that the king of England could not stand, was someone else regarding themself as being sovereign in any way. And the British throne still maintains a distinction when it comes to the interpretation of human sovereignty, because according to British imperial rule, colonies were granted their sovereignty by the British crown, and the empire never stated that it was endowed to them by their Creator; As though America owes its independence to Britain now, rather than God the Creator.

Individual human sovereignty is best explained from a Biblical premise, because it is not man who is truly sovereign, nor independent, so there is a begetter of independence the same as there is human sovereignty, and we are to acknowledge the Creator for this, and not ourselves. Human sovereignty is a product of individual human independence, because freedom is always better expressed independently of others, so sovereignty is defined as freedom with independence. God in Heaven has endowed all life with ability, but unto His own image the gift of conscience, with which, to reason from so that all may exercise their freewill, each according to their own abilities, which is the essence of creativity.

The gift of conscience is a gift of freewill from God, so that people have freedom of choice from their freewill. But the power of freewill will always be in direct proportion to one's abilities, because freewill can only be exercised according to one's ability. The very definition of freewill for mankind, according to its lawful meaning in use, is that it's from the endowed human conscience, which is defined as freedom of thought or belief. This means definitively that freewill came directly from God in Heaven, rather than ourselves, because freedom of thought and belief derives from freedom of conscience, which is defined by international law as endowed to every person for the purpose of understanding morality, and therefore, law.

The UDHR has defined freedom of conscience as freedom of religion in accordance with religious teachings. This means that international human rights legislation has been modelled after the United States Declaration of Independence, which implies that a Creator God is required in order to interpret human freedom. International human rights legislation has been modelled after United States human rights legislation, because the essence of human freedom derives from freedom of conscience, which is the first liberty.

God in Heaven has bestowed upon mankind a scared obligation to love one another as Christ Jesus has loved us, which was exhibited by His death upon the cross, because those who love their freedom more than servitude shall lose their freedom in accordance with His moral law. Christ Jesus did not come to Earth to exercise His freedom, by to be a servant to His Father in Heaven by placing Himself as least among men, having been born into servitude with the promise to repay, each according to what they have done, good for good, evil for evil, so that all may know that God alone is just by the provision of His moral law, which is the essence of human freedom.

There is no freedom without the law, because the law not only sets a limitation on human behaviour, which is a form of restriction, but also, the law will liberate a person from subjugation by the rights of conscience, which is a form of liberty. It is impossible to understand the success of America without first understanding the need for human freedom, and protection under the law, which is the reason why so many people from so many countries have fled to America seeking refuge and asylum, because it is the rights of conscience that liberates a person by the law, which not only leads to human freedom, but also, war. In order to have peace and security within the world, then you must also fight for that which is just, which does not include fighting for laws to be made to protect the amoral, but for laws to be made to protect our equality, or we will lose our basic freedoms due to the adoption of rules that simply do not apply, which then leads to a rebellion by the people who will not be suppressed by the system that grants us equal opportunity.

There are many types of systems within this world, some are political, some are social, but for the point of emphasis I will discuss two very distinct systems or morality. One is a system of usury, the other is a system of liberty. A system of usury is based on debt, because debt equals money due to compounding interest. While a system of liberty is based on an equality with the provision of equal opportunity through due process. And I use the term due process in relation to a procedure, which not only includes gaining wealth by the provision of property, but also, it is via a procedure that a plan comes into effect. Some plans may fall flat on their face, which can be due chance, or due to poor planning. But the one plan that has withstood the test of time, is the plan of salvation, which has not only led to an equality by the provision of laws, but also, it has led to the provision of freedom by the inclusion of rules that are for our benefit as individuals. No system of can be based on abstract ideas alone, but upon moral principle instead, because it is the principles of morality that best defines a system of belief, from which, eternal truths can be established.

War is the inevitable consequence of conflict, and that which conflicts with the human mind the most, is why would a loving Creator God allow so much suffering? But from history, we understand that the conflict between Adam and Eve with Satan recorded within the Holy Bible explains full well the events that surrounded the introduction of war, because Adam and Eve were created perfect in the sight of God like children who knew no evil, no pestilence, no disease, and they most certainly knew nothing of sin whilst they were in the Garden of Eden. But because they freely ate from the tree of the knowledge of good and evil, it meant that sin had entered the world through Adam, because Adam was a Christophany; Meaning that he was a type of Christ.

There have been a number of Christophanies throughout Scripture, such as Melchizedek, who is compared with Jesus as being both a prophet and a king (Hebrews 7:13 - 17) or Enoch, who was 7th from Adam, and as it is written: "Enoch walked with God, and he was not, for God took him" (Genesis 5:24). But of all of the Christophanies that are mentioned throughout Scripture, it is only Adam and Jesus that are referred to as being "Son of God" from their lineage, except that Jesus is the only begotten Son of God through the Holy Spirit and of the womb, which is why Jesus is also referred to as "The Son of Man," and He is therefore our reconciliation to God through the Holy Spirit according to the Scriptures in order that we to can become Sons of God in accordance with the will of His eternal Spirit.

*Quotation: ————————————————————
John 1:11-13
"He came unto His own, and His own received Him not.
But as many as received Him, to them He gave power to

become the Sons of God, even to those who believe in His name, who were born not of blood, nor of the will of the flesh, nor of the will of man, but of God." - Source: The Holy Bible.

War is the result of spiritual conflict, and the conflict that exists within man the most, is death. The human mind is consciously aware of death at all times, and we have all struggled at some point in life with the fear of death, which is why the Holy Bible has defined death as the last enemy to be defeated (1 Corinthians 15:26). So, because death is the enemy according to Scripture, it will mean that death is an entity, and the only way to describe death from Scripture, is as sin, because sin leads to death. The struggle for individual human independence will always be in accordance with the amount of oppression that is being inflicted upon the individual, because oppression is equal to suppression. So, for any person to truly express their freedom as an individual independently of others, then there must be a freedom from the fear of death, because the fear of death will suppress the mind the most, and therefore, the body as well.

The only way to be truly free from the fear of eternal death, is to be reconciled to God by telling the truth, the same as you would reconcile a matter before the law, only God is both our intermediary and our judge. So, being faithful to God by telling the truth is the first step towards reconciliation, because the conscience bares guilt in regards to shame, while forgiveness is the remedy. In times of war, a soldier's duty is clear, because there is a war on. But in times of peace, a soldier's duty should remain the same, because a soldier's duty is to protect. And the one thing that always requires protecting, is your God given conscience, because guilt is equal to shame, and shame is a warrior's greatest defeat. The conscience bears witness to events past, present, and future, because the conscience relies primarily on memory to make assessments in order to judge. And the one thing we must not do to each other's conscience, is lie, which involves being honest to yourself first in order to be honest with others, which means that honesty is equal to integrity.

The integrity of the human mind to be able to cope with psychological stress comes from having a strong conscience, because the conscience will determine what is right and wrong, and the one thing that will betray a person's conscience, and bring them to shame, is an inward lie. According to Scripture, there is a spiritual battle presiding between lying and the truth, and an inward lie is the first sign of self-defeat, because the conscience is a spiritual weapon that requires cleaning and sharpening, but if the weapon is jammed, then it will have little effect. And it is the duty of any soldier to inspect their weapon daily and to keep it functional, because a soldier without a weapon cannot fight a war. So, for this reason, it is the duty of every soldier in Christ to pray for their enemy, because Christ died for us while we were yet sinners. And this is the only way to reconcile yourself to God in a dispute before man, because in order for the conscience to be clear, then you must also forgive.

Wars are won in the will, so all that's required for war to occur, is for someone to be willing. But will-power alone will not win a war if the moral cause is not sufficient, because human beings are moral beings that depend on a cause to be justifiable in their sight. So, individual human will-power can lead an army to victory or defeat, but their willingness to fight will always be the result of a moral cause. And the greatest cause for an individual to fight for, is for the sake of human equality, because your family is an extension of yourself the same as everyone else all the way back to Adam and Eve; Which is why a person's emotions are deeply connected with family and friends through memories, and it is our emotions that stimulate our thoughts the most from their legacies left behind.

The American War of Independence is the single most important political action in modern history, because it led to freeing more than four million enslaved Americans, and established a more powerful centralized form of federal government, which has laid the foundation for America's formation as a global super-power in today's world. No standing army has ever fought a war in modern times that was as just in its cause, and favoured with divine prosperity, as the American War of Independence, which not only led to the independence of America against Britain, but also, a total of 65 other nations have since declared their independence from Britain as a direct result of the American War of Independence.

Global politics and human rights legislation have been modelled after the United States Constitution, the Declaration of Independence, and their Bill of Rights, which was the forerunner for all other declarations of independence by other nations. So, for this reason, the single most effective

Legislative Act in human history was the creation of the United States Declaration of Independence, and is therefore, one of the most important pieces of historical legislation to protect. Second only to the Universal Declaration of Human Rights and Equality by the United Nations Global Human Rights Commission, which is the most influential governing body in the world, because the declaration by the Human Rights Commission is under the agreement of 192 countries, and there are only 193 member States within the United Nations.

192 of these member States within the U.N are under agreement, while other non-member or speculative States, such as Vatican City-State, and the State of Palestine, have not signed the UDHR. The only member State of the U.N that has not agreed to the United Nations Declaration of Human Rights and Equality, is Saudi Arabia, which is entirely due to Sharia law. The Holy See, also called the See of Rome, Petrine See, or Apostolic See, is the jurisdiction of the Pope in his role as the Bishop of Rome. It includes the Apostolic Episcopal See of the Diocese of Rome, which has universal ecclesiastical jurisdiction over the Catholic Church and the sovereign City-State known as Vatican City.

When World War 1 ended in 1918, the British took control of Palestine, because the League of Nations issued a British mandate for Palestine, which was a document that gave Britain administrative control over the region, and included provisions for establishing a Jewish national homeland in Palestine, which came into effect in 1948 following World War II. Palestine, also known as the Land of Israel and the Holy Land, is defined as the territory between the Mediterranean Sea and the Jordan River where Israel and Palestine are located today. The land of Israel was dedicated to the Biblical Patriarch Abraham, who passed the land down unto Isaac, who in turn, passed the land down unto Jacob, who would become the father of twelve sons that became known as the twelve tribes of Israel. And the number one enemy to Israel throughout most of Israel's history, was a nation known as Philistine.

The Pentapolis of the ancient Philistine confederacy incorporated five cities which were Gaza, Ashkelon, Ashdod, Goth, and Ekron, and their region was known as Philistia, or the Land of the Philistines. And from this designation, the whole of the country was later called Palestine by the Greeks, which is the current name in use by many in place of the name

Israel. The Philistines were an ancient people who lived on the south coast of Canaan from the 12th century BC until 604 BC, when their polity, after having already been subjugated for centuries by the Neo-Assyrian Empire, was finally destroyed by King Nebuchadnezzar II of the Babylonian Empire.

The land known as Canaan was situated in the territory of the Southern Levant, which today encompasses Israel, the West Bank and Gaza, Jordan, and the southern portions of Syria and Lebanon. Lawrence Stager of Harvard University believes that the Philistines came to Canaan by ships before the Battle of the Delta Circa 1175 BC. According to the Holy Bible, at around 1,400 BC, Jericho was the first city attacked by the Israelites after they crossed the Jordan River and entered Canaan. The Wall of Jericho was destroyed when the Israelites walked around it for seven days carrying the Ark of the Covenant. The land of Canaan originally belonged to the Israelites who were held-up in slavery by the Egyptians for almost 400 years.

The Six-Day Independence War of 1967 was an Arab-Israeli War between Israel and a coalition of Arab States primarily comprising of Jordan, Syria and Egypt, which was formerly known as the United Arab Republic. Egyptian forces were caught by surprise, and nearly the entire Egyptian Air Force was destroyed in a matter of days with very few Israeli losses in the process, giving Israel the advantage of air supremacy, which secured Israel's independence as a nation. The government of Palestine refuses to acknowledge the United Nations Declaration of Human Rights and Equality, because the U.N helped to secure Israel's independence within the Holy Land. Yet the Israeli people deserve a homeland, just as much as the Arabs do, but the Arabs homeland is the Arabian desert, and not the land of Israel where Judaism and Christianity were born. Islam is not a religion of the Holy Land historically, but of the desert instead, because the centre of Islamic worship is directed towards Mecca, which is in the middle of the Arabian desert.

The Holy See on the other hand, is the body of Rome, and Rome will not acknowledge the sovereignty of any nation or of any individual because of Papal rule, which only defines the Pope as being sovereign, and nobody else. The succession of each Pope derives from the Roman Order, which is a bloodline of individuals who date back to the last four emperors of Rome, and unless you have Nobility within the Roman Order, then you cannot be a Pope. So, the one thing that cannot exist under Papal rule, is human equality. Yet no individual has a just enough reason to deny another person their right to equality, because there is no greater cause in life than to defend human equality, which is equal to loving thine enemy and thy neighbour. And I use the term "great" in retrospect to compassion, which is the greatest motive force there is in existence, because human actions are better expressed through compassion, rather than violence.

The action of violence is based entirely on lawlessness, because violence only ever begets more violence. While the action of compassion shows understanding for human rights and equality, and it is human equality that we are fighting to defend globally. Thus, any act of violence should be followed forthwith by a show of compassion in order that an equality can exist, which is not to be misconstrued as a sign of weakness, but of moral integrity instead. The correct legal definition of what human equality is has been defined by the endowed human conscience, and this is not a product of ourselves, but of the Creator instead who has endowed each person with a unique ability that sets us apart from the animals. A person's ability to understand morality is the most unique trait of any living creature, and this is not a biological phenomenon, but a spiritual one instead, because both the human conscience and morality pertain to the existence of the human soul or spirit.

The purpose of modern science was never established to enslave mankind under a theory, but rather, to free mankind with an idea, and the idea was simple, because if all physical laws are in constant effect, which they are, then a universal principle in learning can be established on the basis that physical laws are a constant. This means they are repeatable under experimentation, and it is repeatability that gives rise to reliability, which in turn, gives rise to a science, rather than by theory alone. According to historical resources and American antiquities, the early colonies of America studied both Scripture and law, because statistically, the most popular books sold to the colonies were books related to Biblical theology and law. And this is the main reason why America became the world's leading nation in regards to human rights and equality from their interpretation of what individual human sovereignty means. From the Scriptures, we find in the book of Revelations 17:5 the introduction of a mystery, and the mystery is defined as: "Babylon the great, the mother of prostitutes, and of the abominations of the Earth."

445

The Holy Bible has defined what the mystery in Revelations means from the interpretation of what each of the words mean according to a Biblical definition. The term, Babylon, in the book of Revelations, is referring to a system of religion, because in the book of Daniel we find that the king of Babylon is at the helm of many empires that would carry the practices of Babylon. The second part of the mystery refers to the Babylonian religion as being the mother of all false religions and abominations, because it is described as being a prostitute before the Lord, which means they have defiled themselves spiritually through the worship of a false deity; Just as Israel has been referred to throughout Scripture whenever they went after other gods and worshiped them. And the number one religion in the world today that bears the name of Mystery Babylon, mother of prostitutes, is the Mystery School of Freemasonry, because it is Freemasonry that will cause mankind to band together under one rule, known formally as the rule of law.

Allister Crowley was the most decorated Freemason in Masonic history, who held more titles, distinctions, honours, degrees, and ritual initiation rites than anyone from the craft had ever received, and he also often referred to himself as the beast or Antichrist. Allister Crowley defined the one rule for lawlessness as "do what thou wilt shall be the whole of the law." And this will be the basis for total lawlessness and global revolution by Freemasonry to establish an Orwellian type of New World Order governed by the lawless, rather than by morality.

The Masonic phrase, "the rule of law" attempts to disguise itself as a means of justice for all, when nothing robs the people of their justice faster than rules that simply do not apply. And the one rule that simply does not apply, is that the power of the people in accordance with their right to vote, either in favour of the legislator or against, should be removed from the people in order for the people to be denied their voice. The British Freemasonic phrase, "the rule of law" is only a law if we make it a rule, which is why repeating the statement only causes more division between the people and the legislator.

The now common phrase, "the rule of law" is in reality, a call to fascism, because if mankind is to be ruled by law, then mankind cannot be self-governed under the universal principles of Biblical morality. Morality is not to be defined by the power of the legislator in favour of more legislation, but by a correct theology instead so that we can go about our daily lives freely and in peace without interference from the law. And it is for this reason, above all other reasons, that the theory of evolution must be challenged from the premise of law, or our system of law and order will slowly shift from self-governance to slavery with the consent of the majority who wish to espouse some form of freedom from morality, when the only thing that can save us in our darkest hour is a correct theology, and by a correct interpretation of the law.

The action of self-governance, according to law, is specifically in relation to morality, because under a system of self-governance, there is a system of rules that supersedes the law so as to interpret whether a law is just or not. This means that a system of morality is required when interpreting the law, which cannot derive itself from Secularism without invoking a religion in turn, such as Secular Humanism, which devotes itself to the Greco-Roman pantheon of gods that includes the goddess Themis. Secular Humanism is in direct opposition to Biblical Christianity in that Secular Humanism revolves around the worship of nature deities, rather than the written word of God. This means that the United States government and the Supreme Court have interpreted the Declaration of Independence as referring to the pantheon of Greek gods when the declaration states "and of nature's god," when the reference is specifically referring to the Creator God of Genesis.

According to Scripture, this mystery will be the final deception that causes mankind to band together against God under one rule during the last hour when the Lamb will return in all of His might and glory. And the one rule that mankind will be united by, is a Masonic rule invented by Allister Crowley called "the law of Thelema" or "the law of the divine-will," which has been openly expressed by certain members of the craft, and is widely referred to as "the rule of law." In Greco-Roman mythology, Themis (meaning justice or law) is the goddess of law.

She is one of the twelve Titan children of Gaia and Uranus, and the second wife of Zeus. The name, Themis, also translates as "the will of the gods," who's will is often interpreted and agreed upon by some form of omen. Her most recognized symbol throughout history is a woman holding a set of justice scales. The phrase, "the rule of law," from its Masonic designation, derives its definition from the Book of the Law by Allister Crowley, because the phrase appears in both contexts, and is specifically in relation to a rebellion, because the rule of law is by definition a fascism, which must derive itself from a rebellion against self-governance.

Man is not a servant to the law, but rather, law is a service to mankind, because laws are intended to protect our freedoms, rather than the ruling class. If man is to be ruled by law, then man is thereby subject to the ruler, rather than the voting constituency, because the only thing that stands in the way of the ruler, is the right to vote. Man is not to be subjugated by law, because that is unjust, and therefore, immoral. But rather, man is to be free in accordance with self-governance, which derives itself from a universal basis for morality so that laws are justifiable, because without a standard in place for good and evil that is universal, then laws themself cannot be made universal in their interpretation.

A rebellion against self-governance must derive itself from a rebellion against Biblical morality, which is a direct consequence of accepting the evolutionary theory, because the entire purpose of the evolutionary theory, is for the individual to espouse some form of freedom from morality, when nothing enslaves a person faster than abandoning the lawful premise for self-governance under God our maker. The practice of self-governance under the law derives from the interpretation of Biblical morality, whereby each and every individual is endowed with conscience, which forms the basis of inalienable rights. So, in order for society to be self-governed under the law, then there cannot be a restriction by the law that prohibits the free exercise of religion, because it is freedom of conscience that defines our liberties, rather than Secular Humanism.

If law is to be interpreted by a secular interpretation only then we will enslave ourselves by the denial of morality, because a universal system of morality is required when interpreting the law so that a code of ethics can be applied, which forms the basis of self-governance. And it is Secular Humanism that has failed to produce a system of morality that is by definition, universal, because Secular Humanism relies entirely on secular science, rather than a code of ethics. If Secular Humanism was to apply a system of morality in order for a code of ethics to be understood, then the code of ethics would be entirely hypothetical, because it is not science that defines morality, but a correct theology instead.

*Quotation: ————————————————————
"Of all the dispositions and habits which lead to political prosperity, religion and morality are indispensable

supports." - George Washington, 1ˢᵗ president of the United States. Source: George Washington's Farewell Address. (Documented September 17, 1796).

The more modern use of the phrase, the rule of law, is in conjunction with legislative powers that derives its influence from Freemasonry, because it is the craft of Freemasonry that attempts to create a system of law that is exclusive to the craft, rather than justice for all on the basis of equality. In Freemasonry, there is a hierarchy in place with rules having derived from certain members of the craft who wish to espouse some form of divinity in order to receive worship within the Lodge, as well as society. The practice of law within Britain and the United States cannot be adequately explained without first explaining the role of Freemasonry, which is pro-slavery, anti-Christian, and seeks to dominate the world through legislative powers.

Down through the centuries within Britain and the United States, judges have been predominately Freemasonic with an inner court or circle of members that adhere to the craft in such a way that people are subjugated under the rule of law that includes pro-slavery laws. Until the Proclamation of Emancipation by Abraham Lincoln and the United States' former Union, slavery was lawful. This division between the New Testament involving anti-slavery teachings and Freemasonry with its pro-slavery intentions have been at the pinnacle of discussion regarding law up until the American Civil war where slavery was slowly abolished. So, in order for Freemasonry to regain a footing within the world by the use of slavery, the Free Trade Agreement was established involving the practice of Social Darwinism, whereby slave labour is put to use.

The former imperial slave trade of Britain and America relied heavily on slave labour in order to manufacture textiles, such as cotton, wool and clothing that would be purchased by the rich. And it is for this reason that Persian rugs are the most expensive, not only because they are of a high quality, but also, because of the inflation associated with it. Persia is the historic region of South-Western Asia that is now associated with the area that is formally known as modern Iran. The British empire, along with America, together sought to establish a slave trade agreement that not only involved the deportation of Africans to America, but also, the subjugation of India, Persia, and Asia with the British crown and America forcing the countries to open the market to global trade with the threat of war if they did not conceit so that the slave trade agreement could expand. This issue of a pro-slavery movement has extended itself into the Free Trade Agreement in order that a form of global trade should exist that is based entirely on inflation.

If commodities such as food, textiles, clothing, white goods, electronics, and oil are to be regulated by the Free Trade Agreement, then the end result is inflation by competing the spending and borrowing power of wealthier nations with the labour power of the poorer nations. If the over population of poorer nations is to be used for the purpose of an industrial scheme, then the poorer nations must have an industry of their own, or the manufacturing base of the wealthier nations will move offshore, thus resulting in an exploitation of the average worker due to a competition in place that forbids the rise in the award wage. This is because when you compete a worker who is on $12 per hour with a worker who is doing the same job for $24 per hour, there will be competition in place that forbids an increase in the award wage, which then leads to a global financial crisis due to inflation, which must be offset by a systematic increase in the award wage.

Historically, the British royal family continues in its imperial ambitions to rule the people of the United Kingdom under the guise of freedom and Christianity, whilst remaining in close proximity of the Grand Lodge of England, the Rothschild banking cartel, and the Free Trade Agreement. British Freemasonry, and the royal family of England first instigated a war on human independence by challenging the United States colonies to a war on human freedom due to the United States Constitutional definition of human sovereignty, which was in opposition to the Freemasonic interpretation of British royal sovereignty. The occult symmetry between Rome, Freemasonry, Nazism, and the British royal family, is found with the Cross of Malta, or Iron Cross, which was the official military decoration of the former Nazi empire, and is the official emblem of the Knights of Malta by British royal Freemasonry, with the inception of this symbol dating back to emperor Constantine of Rome. The Roman Order is a bloodline that derives from the last four emperors of Rome, which has been symbolized by the Cross of Malta (✠).

The British royal family, also known as the House of Windsor, is not directly descended from the emperors of Rome, but from the Grand Burgher families instead. The royal family traces its lineage back to the Germanic tribes that invaded and settled in Britain after the fall of the Western Roman Empire leaving the Eastern Roman Empire under the control of the Roman Order or royal bloodline dating back to the last four emperors of Rome. Clovis I was the first king of the Franks to unite all of the Frankish tribes under one ruler. The Franks spoke a West Germanic language that would later branch out into Dutch and some dialects of German.

The confusion that could arise is the fact that the Western part of the Frankish realm would turn into France giving its constituents the designation, French. Clovis I was the first Germanic king to accept Catholic Christianity and expressed his interest in Aryan Christianity. Clovis I was born into paganism, two of his sisters were Aryans (one married the Aryan Ostrogothic king Theodoric the Great), and his wife, Clotilda, like her sister, was Catholic but from a Burgundian royal family that included Aryans. Arianism is a Christological doctrine considered to be heretical by all mainstream branches of Christianity, whilst remaining as a basic tenet of the evolutionary theory.

*Quotation: ————————————————

At the societal level, social Darwinism was used as a philosophical rationalization for imperialist, colonialist, and racist policies, sustaining belief in Anglo-Saxon or Aryan cultural and biological superiority. The law of three stages is a theory of human intellectual development propounded by the French social theorist Auguste Comte (1798–1857). According to Comte, human societies moved historically from a theological stage, in which the world and the place of humans within it were explained in terms of gods, spirits, and magic; through a transitional metaphysical stage, in which, such explanations were based on abstract notions, such as essences, and final causes; and finally, to a modern "positive" stage based on scientific knowledge. - Source. Encyclopedia Britannica (Social Darwinism).

The Roman emperor Arius was the founder of the doctrine of Arianism, which became the modus operandi for Hitler under Nazi Germany, which is the reason why Hitler closely allied himself with the Roman Order of Popes. A primary topic of the First Council of Nicaea convened by Emperor Constantine in 325 AD was the subject of Arianism. There is one Italian family, the Massimos, who claim to be the descendants of the Roman dictator, Fabius Maximus. The Massimos do have a traceable lineage back to the 10th century, which still makes them one of the oldest extant families in Europe.

The Sicilian Mafia family, which is the world's best-known Italian organized crime syndicate, is a member of the Massimos family, which designates its allegiance to the Roman Order of Popes. The social structure of ancient Rome revolved around the distinction between the patricians and the plebeians. The status of patricians gave them more political power than the plebeians, but the relationship between the two groups eventually caused the conflict of the Roman Order, thus leading to the formation of a republic. This time period resulted in the changing of the social structure of ancient Rome from imperial fascism to republican fascism.

Fascism is any extreme form of authoritarianism and nationalism that often manifests itself as a belief in racial purity, such as Arianism. The patricians were originally a group of ruling class families in ancient Rome that practiced Arianism. After the fall of the Western Roman Empire, the term "patrician" continued as a high honorary title in the Eastern Empire. In many medieval Italian republics, especially in Venice and Genoa, medieval patrician classes were formally defined as groups of leading families, from which, the Massimo family has designated itself as an underbelly ruling class. In the Holy Roman Empire, the Grand Burgher families existed as a formally defined upper social class, or ruling class, that was made up of affluent individuals and elite Burgher family members in medieval German-speaking city-states and towns under the divided Roman Empire. The connection between the House of Windsor and of Rome is found with the Grand Burgher families who originally practiced a hierarchical system based on Arianism from Catholicism.

The Cross of Malta, or Maltese Cross, is in relation to the last four emperors of Rome by combining four arrows pointing inward in a cross formation, which was to: A) Symbolize a new so-called Christian heraldry under Roman imperial rule. B) To align the Christian religion with Rome only. And C) To distinguish the four bloodlines of the Roman Order into one that is singular in terms of a lineage to the throne of Rome, and most other countries throughout Europe. On the morning of October 28, 312, the forces of Constantine and Maxentius would face each other on the Milvian Bridge, which carried the Via Flaminia over the River Tiber into Rome. Constantine would emerge the victor, and by the year 324 AD, Constantine established himself as the sole ruler of the Western Empire, from which, most European rulers would share their allegiance. The Order of Malta, or Knights of Malta, is traditionally, and historically, a Catholic religious and military Order of a Roman royal nobility. The Knights of Malta Order is often considered as a sovereign entity under international law with an allegiance to Rome and Great Britain only.

The Order claims continuity with the Knights Hospitaller dating back to 1099, who officially succeeded the Knights Templar by the end of the Crusades. The Knights of Malta remained without a territory of its own until 1530, when Fra' Philippe de Villiers de L'Isle-Adam took possession of the island of Malta. The island of Malta was granted to the Knights of Hospitaller by the Holy Roman Emperor, Charles V, (who is well renowned for his elongated jaw due to multi-generational inbreeding amongst the Nobility of Europe involving the practice of Arianism) and by the Castile Monarchs of Sicily with the approval of Pope Clement VII, from which, the Order of Malta vowed to honour the conditions set by the Emperor of Rome, the Catholic religion, and the ecclesiastical jurisdiction of the Pope.

In 1565, the Knights of Malta, led by Grand Master Fra' Jean de Vallette (after whom the capital of Malta, Valletta, was named), defended the island for more than three months during the Great Siege by the Ottomans. The Protestant Reformation led by Martin Luther in the early 16th century split Western-Europe into Protestant and Catholic States, which affected the knights of Malta Order in such a way that they remain neutral to this day, thereby leaning towards the bloodline of Roman and British nobility. Many historians will argue that the Roman Order of nobility was superseded by the Catholic religion, and by the fall of the Eastern and Western empire, thus giving the distinction of the Pope as a member of the clergy, rather than Roman nobility. But because the Pope has his own throne with an ecclesiastical jurisdiction as sovereign, it will mean that the succession of Popes is a continuation of the former Roman Order, which now defines itself as the "Holy Roman Order."

On November 1, 2020, Pope Francis replaced Becciu as the Special Delegate to oversee the Knights of Malta Order, when on June 19, 2023, Pope Francis named Cardinal Gianfranco Ghirlanda to act as the former patrician of the Order. Until the late 1990's, the highest classes of membership within the Knights of Malta required proof of noble lineage, while today, the Freemasonic Order of the Knights of Malta can include those who have been Knighted by the royal family of Great Britain. Numerous other Freemasonic Orders, law enforcement Agencies, legal bodies and legislative States have used the Cross of Malta to indicate their allegiance to the royal bloodline of Europe and of Rome, which includes the former British colony of Queensland, Australia, that adopted the Maltese Cross as the State emblem in 1876, along with the Queensland State police force. While the State police force of Victoria, Australia, (named after Queen Victoria of Great Britain) uses an upside-down pentagram, which has long been associated with the Order of Freemasonry, Black Magic, and Satanism.

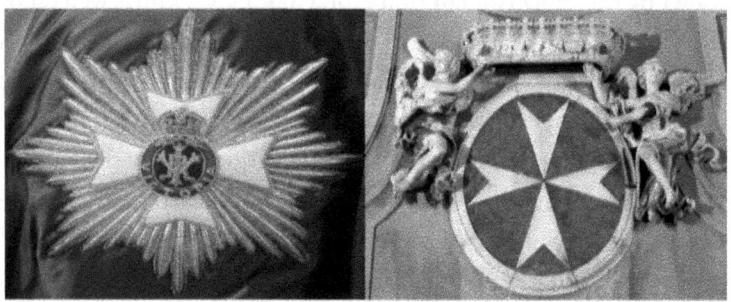

(Above) Pictured from left: Image result for the Knights and Dames Commander of the Royal Victorian Order of Malta appointed by Queen Elizabeth II. Pictured from right: Image result of the Coat of Arms of the Knights of Malta located on the facade of the Catholic Church of San Giovannino dei Cavalieri, Florence, Italy. Source: Wikipedia Encyclopedia.

The Cross of Malta derives itself from the Former Roman empire, and has been used by the Freemasonic order, British nobility, and Catholic church as a symbol of honour, distinction, as well as secrecy. Freemasonry is a system of symbology, whereby the symbols used are hidden in allegory, so they will mean one thing to one person, while meaning something else to another. This means that the only way to interpret the symbols in Freemasonry, is to be informed by the ones who put the symbol in its place, because this is a type of code language that is to be used globally between Masons, and the meaning can alter between Masons, usually depending on their degree of initiation within the craft. The oldest Masonic lodge that is still in existence today is the Lodge of Edinburgh, St Mary's Chapel No. 1, which dates back to Jan 9th, 1599.

Most of the Cathedrals of Europe were designed by high-ranking members from Freemasonry through their designation and construction, which means quite definitively that the Church of England is tied-in heavily with the occult school of Freemasonry. British officers, historically, were required to be a Freemason in order to climb the ranks within the British military's hierarchical structure, which is still the case with most of the higher-ranking positions within the Royal Guard of today due to the influence of Freemasonry within Buckingham palace.

Nazism, historically, was based on occult theosophy from the practice of Freemasonry, and though Adolf Hitler was never an official member of Freemasonry, he was still heavily involved in the Freemasonic conspiracy by the Illuminati through secret societies that were being guided by Freemasonic principles and literature. The Nazi Swastika from occult theosophy relates Nazism to Freemasonry according to the Encyclopedia of Freemasonry. While the Cross of Malta, along with the skull and crossbones symbol is where Nazism and Freemasonry have long associated themselves with the Roman Order of Popes with each of these symbols deriving either from Freemasonry or from Rome.

*Quotation: ————————————————
Excerpt from - The Cable Tow. Volume 98, No. 2 (Written by 33rd Degree Freemason Vicente R Hao Chin, Jr):
Some Masonic degrees have been called "theosophic" such as the Theosophic Apprentice, which was the first degree of the Swedenborgian Rite. In 1767, a Masonic Rite called the Rite of Pernetty with nine degrees was introduced in London by a group of Masons called Illuminated Theosophists. Masons who begin to study the inner meaning of Freemasonry inevitably encounter

theosophy. The word, theosophy, is extensively found in the classic works of Freemasonry, such as Albert Mackey's Encyclopedia of Freemasonry, where the author defined theosophists as people, "who supposed that they were possessed of a knowledge of the divinity and his works by supernatural inspiration, or who regarded the foundation of their mystical tenets as resting on a sort of divine intuition." In the entry on the Philosophic Degrees of the Scottish Rite, he wrote: "All the Degrees of the ancient and Accepted Scottish Rite above the Eighteenth and below the Thirty-third are called Philosophic Degrees, because, abandoning the symbolism based on the Temple, they seek to develop a system of pure theosophy." - Source: The Online Encyclopedia of Freemasonry (Philosophic Degrees).

(Above) Pictured from left to right: Image result of Theosophy and Nazism. Source: Wikipedia Encyclopedia.

According to historical resources, the teaching and practice of Arianism is an occult philosophy that owes much of its history to Germanic paganism and Roman Catholicism with Ariosophy constituting as an integrated or holistic philosophy. This philosophy has been openly attributed to the practice of Nazism along with Christianity despite widespread opposition by mainstream Christianity against the philosophical practices of Arianism, occultism, and Social Darwinism. The occult school of Freemasonry promotes the teaching of occult Theosophy, Arianism, and Social Darwinism from the viewpoint of Ariosophy, which forms the ideological basis for Catholicism, Freemasonry, and the Germanic royal house of

Windsor in England. And yes, the Pope promotes Social Darwinism, occult Freemasonry, and Arianism through signs and symbols that are intended to be honourable in their distinction, yet lack any virtue or premise from the Holy Bible.

Modern Arianism and Ariosophy are esoteric ideological systems that were largely developed in Austria between 1890 and 1930 with much of their influence owing to occult literature. The term "Ariosophy" translates to "wisdom of the Aryans," and was invented by Lanz von Liebenfels in 1915. The ideas of Von List and Lanz von Liebenfels were part of a Freemasonic occult revival that occurred in Austria and Germany during the late 19th and early 20th centuries having derived from occult Theosophy and paganism. The Nazi ideology of an Aryan race involving the swastika, Social Darwinism, and occult illuminism are important elements of Ariosophy, Freemasonry, and Theosophy, having spread their influence into Catholicism, law, and evolutionary science.

The occult practice of Ariosophy relies heavily on the interpretation of esoterics leaving the divinity of Christ Jesus in question or theologically incorrect, because Ariosophy teaches that Jesus has a family involving sexual relations with Mary Magdalene. So, for this reason, Biblical Christianity cannot be associated with Arianism on the basis that Biblical Christianity defines Jesus as a member of the Holy Trinity, rather than the father of a superior race of human beings. The idea that Jesus is the head of a superior race of human beings derives from the occult school of Ariosophy, Theosophy, and Freemasonry, with each of these schools of thought relying on esoterics in order to promote the occult, rather than Biblical Christianity.

This influence has largely derived itself from Catholicism with the Pope designation as Vicar of Christ, thereby deriving his power from a supposed lineage from Christ. A Vicar is historically a Bishop who derives his ability to interpret scripture from a Church, university, or clergy, while the Bishop of Rome derives itself from the practice of Arianism and Roman paganism. The idea that Jesus had his own family with sons and daughters does not derive from scripture, but from the practice of Arianism instead, because the justification of an Aryan race, according to modern Aryan theological principle, is that they are sons of Jesus in terms of a bloodline, which was later expressed from Dan Browns book, The Da Vinci Code, and is more widely known as Aryan philosophy.

Aryan culture is not usually forthwith due to a sworn oath to secrecy in order to protect themselves from public scrutiny, thus constituting Arianism as esoteric in the form of a cult with much of its influence owing to the Pope, occult literature, and Freemasonry. And though certain members of occult Arianism do not identify with Freemasonry, such as the Popes past and present, as well as Hitler, the occult literature of Aryan philosophy owes much of its influence to Theosophy.

In early 1934, the chief of the Nazi Party court system ruled that Masons who did not leave their Lodges prior to January 30, 1933, could not join the Nazi Party, and that same month, the Prussian Minister of the Interior, Hermann Goering, issued a decree calling upon the Lodges to voluntarily dissolve, and he also required such voluntary actions to be submitted to him for approval. In addition, Masonic Temples and their Lodges throughout various parts of Germany were exposed to arbitrary violence from the local SS and SA units, which led to increasing pressure on the public and professional sectors to choose between remaining with their Lodges, or limiting their career opportunities down to zero within Germany. In May 1934, the Ministry of Defence for the Third Reich banned membership in Lodges to all personnel, soldiers and civilian employees.

During the summer of 1934, the German police forcibly closed down Masonic Lodges, and the branch headquarters of the Masons was confiscated along with their assets, including their libraries and archives. In my own opinion, the reason that Hitler was strongly opposed to Freemasonry, despite being a high-ranking member of the Illuminati, Arianism, and occult Freemasonic theosophy, was solely due to secrecy, because the Freemasons have failed previously when George Washington left the craft of Freemasonry in 1755, which then led to the creation of the United States Constitution in despite of all Freemasonic oaths and loyalties. As in Nazi Germany, Freemasonry in Russia also had a hard history under Communism, because Communism is openly engaged in a scientific revolution from the principles of Darwinism in order to overthrow religion and install Communist dictatorships. Communist dictatorship relies solely on a secular society in order to reinterpret the rights of property, because if your independence lies with the State, then so also does your property.

In August 1894 (according to Stalin's biographer Simon Sebag Montefiore), Stalin enrolled in the Orthodox Spiritual Seminary in Tiflis that enabled him to obtain a scholarship that allowed him to study at a reduced rate. So, he joined 600 trainee priests who boarded there and he achieved high grades. Stalin left the Orthodox Spiritual Seminary in April 1899 and never returned. As Stalin grew older, he lost interest in priestly studies and his grades dropped significantly, so he was repeatedly confined to a cell for his rebellious behaviour. Montefiore's seminary's journal noted that Stalin declared himself an atheist by 1967. Secret societies around the world, such as the Skull and Bones society at Yale University, or the infamous Illuminati from Ingolstadt University, are examples of how secret occult organizations can influence the sphere of academics from a college or university. And this was also the case with Stalin, Marx, Hitler, and many others, because although they never joined Freemasonry, they were still involved in secret organizations that were overseen by the Illuminati involving Freemasonic occult literature.

Stalin joined a forbidden book club at the school he attended and was particularly influenced by Nikolay Chernyshevsky's 1863 pro-revolutionary novel: What Is To Be Done? Stalin also read Das Kapital and was deeply influenced by the book written by German theorist, Karl Marx. Stalin devoted himself to the Marxist sociopolitical theory of Communism, which was then on the rise in imperial Russia as a form of extreme socialism that was opposed to the Russian empire and the Tsars' authority over land.

At night, Stalin attended secret workers' meetings and was introduced to Silibistro Silva Jibladze, the Marxist founder of the secret workers club known as "The Third Group" which was a secretive pro-revolutionary socialist group that was to plan the Communist revolution in 1917. Freemasonry was originally brought to Russia by foreign officers from parts of Europe in service to the Russian military. Russian Freemasonry derives its activities from Franz Lefort, Jacob Bruce, and Patrick Gordon in the German Quarter of Moscow. While a man by the name of James Keith is recorded as being the first Sovereign Grand Master of the Grand Lodge in Saint Petersburg in 1732 - 1734.

The Grand Lodge of Russia today is the regular and more modern Masonic jurisdiction for Russia, and was established on June 24, 1995 after the fall of the Soviet Union. It was the first national Grand Lodge to be created in the country since the closure of the original Russian Lodges in 1922 when Freemasonry was banned under orders by Joseph Stalin, who, like Hitler, desired to fulfil his role in the conspiracy without interference from British Freemasonry. Today, the Mystery School of Freemasonry is tied in with all political institutions through international diplomacy, secret societies, and military agencies, making Freemasonry the mother of all modern political systems, occult organizations, and secret intelligence agencies, most of which, are rogue, rather than controlled. So, the one thing that Freemasons have little control over in this world, is themselves due to the nature of fraud and conspiracy. Historically, the rise of Social Darwinism during the late 19th century has led to a fascist form of socialism known as the Eastern Bloc system, or Communist Bloc, involving China, North Korea, and all former Soviet sympathists, including Vladimir Putin who was a former member of the Russian KGB before the fall of the Soviet Union.

While the former Nationalists Socialist movement in Nazi Germany that sought to overthrow a Judeo-Christian system of democracy by conspiring against the United States, the British people, and the rest of the world, was a more virulent form of extreme fascism and socialism from the principles of Social Darwinism involving evolutionary eugenics, ontogeny, and racial segregation policies. The Western Bloc system of common law on the other hand recognizes the God of the Bible according to the United States Constitution, the good of the people, and Commonwealth theology, and therefore, the Judeo-Christian religion as its cultural and political roots. And though America and England owes much of its history to Judeo-Christianity and the common law, it was actually a group of rogue Freemasons who drafted up the United States Constitution against the authority of the Grand Lodge in England.

So, not only did British Freemasonry instigate the War of Independence by the United States, but also, the Civil War in America as well that occurred less than a hundred years later due to a another conflict regarding the interpretation of individual human sovereignty, as defined by the original United States Constitution. The United States Constitution was not set up as a means of establishing a particular Church or sect of Christianity, nor was the Constitution in opposition to a Christian democracy, but the Constitution was however in opposition to British imperial rule, and the Pope's authority, which was entirely due to the interpretation of human independence in the form of an informed democracy.

The Society of Jesus, also referred to as the Jesuit Order, was created in honour of Pope Paul III and the fallen Knights Templar. The Jesuit Order is a militant order of Roman decree to abolish all sympathies to any other authority apart from Rome. The common phrase, Black Pope, is a designation that is reserved for the acting Superior General, or Military General, for the Jesuit Order, with the Black Pope distinguished by a black uniform, while the White Pope is draped with a white garment. The Jesuit term, Superior General, or President General, is of military usage, because like the Knights Templar, Ignatius Loyola had a military background.

Saint Ignatius Loyola was a Spanish Catholic priest and theologian who became the first Superior General of the Jesuit Order in 1541. The Jesuit Order, or Society of Jesus, was initiated in response to the Protestant Reformation led by Martin Luther, which divided Europe on the basis of Scriptural authority verses the Pope's so-called supreme authority on religious matters. Ignatius Loyola instituted a Jesuit oath for the Jesuits Society as a vow to obedience to the Pope in order to carry out all decrees that are issued by the Pontiff of Rome. Ignatius Loyola was later canonized as a Catholic saint in the year 1622 and is usually depicted from Catholic artwork with a solar disc directly behind his head, the same as the apostles of the Gospel are depicted in the same way which refers to some form of spiritual enlightenment or illumination in order to equate a Catholic saint as having received some form of divine inspiration.

In Medieval times, most people could not read, at least in the Latin as most of the people were diverse in speech. So, the more common usage of depicted Catholic artwork was to display some form of divine revelation to the observer by the use of certain characteristics that was to represent a particular quality or attribute so as to distinguish the figure as holy. The purpose of this was to equate certain Roman figures with the twelve apostles in a way that led one to believe that Rome was now holy despite the subjugation of Christians and Jews by Rome for many centuries.

The second reason for Catholic artwork to depict Roman figures with the twelve apostles, was to espouse some form of hope, because if you live in poverty, then hope is your inner wealth. The purpose of hope is to have trust, because hope and trust are equal to faith, and it was the goal of the Roman Order for the people to put their faith in Rome, rather than the written Scriptures, from which, inspires knowledge. And the one thing that the

Roman Order did not want the people to have, was knowledge concerning the downfall of Rome according to Biblical prophecy, because this leads to a lack of faith, and it was the people's faith that the Roman Order was depending on in order to profit from a situation based on extreme poverty, thereby exploiting the people's trust.

From the Gospel of Ephesians 2:8-9 we read from Paul a message to the Ephesians concerning faith and works. The Scriptures read that: "For by grace you are saved through faith, and that not of yourselves, it is the gift of God, not by works, lest any man should boast." (End of quote). So, from this passage in Scripture, we understand that it is not of works, nor of Rome, that constitutes as God's grace unto oneself, but rather, it is from the attributes of the Holy Spirit instead, because if we place our faith in things made by human hands, such as artwork and thrones, then we are placing our faith in a separate creator or authority apart from Christ the Messiah of Salvation.

When man is not to place his faith in a separate creator, but in the written word of God instead that is revealed to all who love Him, because God is word, and God is Spirit. And it is the Spirit of God who has revealed His word to His people Israel through the mouths of His chosen prophets in accordance with the will of His Spirit that the world might receive His Son in accordance with the faith that we have received, which is revealed to all through the obedient to His word, because His word has pre-established our faith in accordance with the law of Moses, and the prophets of old. So, because the fulfilment of the law is found in the fulfilment of love, it will mean that one cannot receive God's grace without the work of love, which is not of ourselves, but of the Holy Spirit, for the fruits of the Spirit are made manifest through the love that we share in God's word, and this love for each other is made perfect by an obedience to the will of His Spirit, which has distinguished between the love of works, and the love of His word. If one is to put their faith in the artwork that is designed to deceive, then one has misplaced their faith in favour of works that are not of the Holy Spirit, nor of His word, but of a deception instead.

If man is to glorify man through works, then this glory is of man. But if man is to glorify the love of the Father as shown to the world through His Son, Jesus Christ, then this glory is of the Holy Spirit, for it is the will of the Father in Heaven that each person should have a measure of faith in order to judge, and we are to judge so that we are not deceived by the love of things that are a counterfeit of Christ. And if ever there was a counterfeit of Christ Jesus who has shown God's grace to the world by His obedience to the law, then it would be those who attempt to judge the law as unworthy of works.

So, it is for this reason that the Popes, past and present, are to be judged by the will of God, who has not given Himself over to the laws of men so that men should put their faith in rules that do not apply, but in the love of the Father instead, which is revealed to the obedient in Christ who have been set free by the will of His Spirit in order that we should judge wisely in accordance with His written word of old. And the official role of the Pope, is to judge in place of Christ, because it is Christ who has revealed the judgements of God by what He has said, which is not to be misappropriated by the Pope as Christ judging Himself as unworthy so that men should turn from the law of the prophets in order to receive another.

And the Popes, past and present, have indeed acted as Christ by attempting to provide a remission for sin apart from Christ by the teaching of indulgences, which does not derive from Christ, but from the will of the Roman Order; When a person's salvation in Christ is not owing to the will of Rome, but to the will of the Father in Heaven. So, in order for the Pope to get around this basic doctrine, they teach that the Pope is the Father, which is why each Pope is referred to as the "holy father" and is thereby able to forgive sin and establish the Saints. And both the Black Pope, and the White Pope, do in fact refer to themselves as the holy father, because that is what the term Pope means from the designation of the Pope in accordance with Papal rule.

So, the actions by the Roman Order has been one against the people of Rome by claiming that the will of God is the same as the will of the Pope, which is why the sovereign City-State of Rome has no voting system in place in accordance with the will of the people under international agreement. And I am not against Catholics any more than I oppose the Protestants, because Martin Luther himself was a Catholic trained priest. But I do however oppose the Pope's jurisdiction as "holy father" and the British crown's jurisdiction as sovereign over the people, because they have conspired together against the people and their sovereignty, the same as the United States Supreme Court has conspired against the people of America by the rise of Secular Humanism, and a reinterpretation of the said Constitution, which in itself, has more to do with redefining the ownership of property by defining man as a lower animal, rather than interpreting the inalienable rights of the people in conjunction with Constitutional law.

The British appointed position of an Attorney General has existed since the year 1243 when records show a professional attorney was hired to represent the King's interests in court. The position first took on a political role in 1461 when the holder of the office was summoned to the House of Lords to advise the British government on legal matters concerning the King's ambitions. In 1673, the Attorney General officially became the British crown's leading adviser and representative within the House of Commons. While the role of the Jesuit Superior General was founded in 1541 by Ignatius of Loyola with the same purpose as the British appointed Attorney General. Catholic religious superiors from Rome, like the Dominicans' Master General, or the Franciscans' Minister General, or the Carthusians' Prior General, maintain civil posts through such names as Superior General, or Attorney General. Historically, the idea of an Attorney General has derived from Britain and then later with the Black Pope's Jesuit designation of Superior General.

The Attorney General is the main legal adviser to the government of a nation with the power to prosecute a nation's leader. The term, Attorney General, derives itself from the British throne which previously held jurisdiction over each territory under its direct influence that included the United States. The United States Attorney General is the head of the United States Department of Justice, and is the chief law enforcement officer of the federal government of the United States. The Attorney General serves as the principal adviser to the President of the United States on all legal matters with the sovereign power to prosecute and remove the President.

*Quotation: ————————————————————
"We the subscribers, who are the citizens of the said Commonwealth, having taken into serious consideration, a Bill printed by order of the last Session of General Assembly, entitled a Bill establishing a provision for Teachers of the Christian Religion, and conceiving that the same if finally armed with the sanctions of a law, will be

a dangerous abuse of power, are bound as faithful members of a free State to remonstrate against it, and to declare the reasons by which we are determined. We remonstrate against the said Bill, because we hold it for a fundamental and undeniable truth, that Religion or the duty which we owe to our Creator and the manner of discharging it, can be directed only by reason and conviction, not by force or violence. All men are to be considered as entering into Society on equal conditions; as relinquishing no more, and therefore retaining no less, one than another, of their natural rights. Above all are they to be considered as retaining an equal title to the free exercise of Religion according to the dictates of Conscience. The establishment proposed by the Bill is not requisite for the support of the Christian Religion.

To say that it is, is a contradiction to the Christian Religion itself, for every page of it disavows a dependence on the powers of this world: it is a contradiction to fact; for it is known that this Religion both existed and flourished without the support of human laws. We the Subscribers say, that the General Assembly of this Commonwealth have no such authority; and that no effort may be omitted on our part against so dangerous an usurpation, we oppose to it, this remonstrance; and earnestly praying, as we are in duty bound, that the Supreme Lawgiver of the Universe, by illuminating those to whom it is addressed, may on the one hand, turn their Councils from every act which would affront his Holy prerogative, or violate the trust committed to them; and on the other, guide them into every measure which may be worthy of His blessing, and may redound to their own praise, and may establish more firmly the liberties, the prosperity, and the happiness of the Commonwealth." - James Madison, founding father of the United States Constitution - Source: Speech to the General Assembly of the Commonwealth of Virginia - A Memorial and Remonstrance against Religious Assessments. Amendment No.1, document No. 43 (Documented on June 20, 1785).

According to James Madison on the Religious Rights of Man, the United States government is not to institute a religion, which not only includes Christianity, but also, Secular Humanism, which is by definition a religion according to a Supreme Court decision in Torcaso v. Watkins, 367 U.S. 488, 495 No. 11 (1961). The adoption of a secular religion by the United States Supreme Court is a violation of the religious rights of man, and has placed a religious test in place in order to dismiss Biblical creation with an automatic dismissal; When it is was the Christian religion that led to the creation of the United States government by the rights of conscience and Commonwealth theology, and by an acceptable system of morality and good works. The secular standard by the United States government, according to founding father, James Madison, was done in order to oppose a religious authority being established by the said Constitution, which has now paved the way for a secular religion instead due to a political front that derives itself from atheism, Communism, and the evolutionary theory.

Religion is an integral part of morality and law, and neither one can be interpreted on its own due to the adoption of rules, thereby establishing Secular Humanism as a system of belief with a system of morality in place that is designed to dismiss Biblical creation from a secular premise. Yet nothing stifles the process of law and order faster than a system of unbelief that is designed to renege a just interpretation of the law. And it is Secular Humanism that is by definition a system of unbelief in regards to the supernatural, which is a violation of the rights of conscience in that the human conscience is for our understanding of both morality and law, which is spiritual, rather than secular.

Thus, Secular Humanism as a system of unbelief in the supernatural derives its powers from itself, rather than the governed, which is a violation of international agreement whereby each person shall vote according to the dictates of their own conscience, rather than the dicta of a judicial decision that attempts to disqualify the supernatural with an automatic dismissal. The Holy Bible is foundational to the provision of human rights and equality by the provision of a system of morality that defines what is good and evil for the benefit of a legal system, so that we are not enslaved by the laws we create, because nothing will enslave mankind faster than the adoption of rules that simply do not apply. And the one rule that simply does not apply, is the rule that the theory of evolution cannot be contested for reasons relating to a secular standard of government, which is an infringement upon the just liberties of the people to engage a legal system with their own experience that holds to a Biblical definition of man.

The crown of Britain, and the throne of Rome are by definition a religious institution having derived their powers from a Church organization, which, according to James Madison, is a violation of the Religious Rights of Man. According to international law under the agreement of 192 nations through the provision of the UDHR in accordance with Article 21, the ability to govern is defined as a privilege, rather than a birthright with the voting constituency having the universal and inalienable right to partake in government activities through a system of voting, and through a system of representation, which is in accordance with the rights of conscience.

In the year 1789, the United States Congress passed the Judiciary Act, which, among other things, established the Office of the Attorney General. Edmund Jennings Randolph was elected as the United States Commonwealth's first Attorney General. Randolph was also elected to the Virginia Convention of 1776, one year into the American War of Independence. The first Attorney General of the United States, Edmund Jennings Randolph, succeeded Thomas Jefferson as Secretary of State on January 2, 1794. Randolph later resigned from office on August 20, 1795 following a struggle to maintain a federal policy of neutrality in the war between Great Britain and Revolutionary France involving accusations of corruption by the 1st United States President, George Washington, who further advanced the United States separation from British rule.

Each nation that has declared its independence legally from Britain and Rome has an internally appointed Attorney General in contrast to the previous situation whereby each Attorney General was appointed by either Rome or the British crown. The creation of a Commonwealth system was to unite a coalition of Christian nations under a democratic oath in order that a strong Christian alliance should succeed over a royal or secular one. But the interference of United States policy creation by the British crown, Rome, and the international banking cartel led to a more vigilant form of United States government by the founding fathers.

Today, however, in most common law jurisdictions, the term, Attorney General, is largely reserved as a title of the permanently appointed legal representative of the government, and as sovereign, the same as the Pope and all active members of the British royal family are legally recognized as sovereign. The Pope's ecclesiastical jurisdiction, along with the crown of England, shares one major thing in common, that is that both are appointed by a religious authority. This designation is against international agreement in accordance with Article 26 of the UDHR, whereby the Roman Order of Pope's has declared ecclesiastical jurisdiction over all sovereign City-States, peoples, lands, and titles under a "Universal Church" and has thereby equated each individual person (and their property) as the property of Rome without the consent of the people.

While the British crown and the Church of England are in opposition to the Pope's ecclesiastical jurisdiction, because the British crown and the Church of England have opposed the Jesuit Order, yet both the Pope, and the British crown, have employed a religious test in order to rule. If the Pope or the British crown was to separate themselves from their sovereign jurisdiction under a Church authority, then they have thereby acted in accordance with the separation of Church and State. Yet the Pope, along with the British crown, cannot be in favour of the separation of Church and State without opposing their own ability to rule, because it is the Archbishop of Canterbury and the Church of England that crowns the king or queen at the royal ceremony, rather than the British people in accordance with the House of Representatives. While the Pope receives his ability to govern from the sovereign city of Vatican-State in accordance with Papal rule, and the principles of Catholicism. So, both the Roman and British crown cannot be in favour of the separation of Church and State without opposing their own ability to rule.

Now because I am not a member of this high-ranking conspiracy, it will mean that I can only draw from basic symmetries and similarities, because the problem with interpreting a co-conspiracy, is that the moment you think you're right, is the same moment you're wrong, and this is because the plot always thickens with every additional piece of new information. But if there is one thing the reader can take away from all of this conspiracy talk, is that our freedom as created human beings is hanging in the balance between a rock and a hard place due to the reinterpretation of conscience from a secular premise, and a group of nobility that requires worship, rather than exercising it for the benefit of the people to do the same.

The only way possible to make sense of this mess, is with a correct theology, which must derive itself from the Holy Bible and the Commonwealth system, rather than from sectology or Secular Humanism, or the will of God cannot be revealed to those who truly love Him, which is the only feasible way that both Catholics and Protestants can co-exist, because a sect of Christianity derives from Christianity, rather than Christianity deriving from a particular sect or organization; Meaning that it is better to favour Biblical instruction over any particular sect of Christianity.

If we are to allow a secular authority to dictate the law without due regard for the Commonwealth system in terms of practice and theology, then the common law will one day be lost in obscurity, when we are not to abandon the common law in favour of a secular authority for the good of the people, and for the good of the Commonwealth. The British royal family wishes to seat itself as the sole ruler of the Commonwealth system in accordance with the British empire and the former imperial slave trade, with the Free Trade Agreement acting as a premise. But because the United States, along with Australia and the United Kingdom have since declared their independence from Britain, it will mean that the Commonwealth system is diverse in accordance with freedom of conscience and equal opportunity. While the Roman Order of Popes seeks to undermined an equality by challenging the very foundations and theology of a Commonwealth system, the same as atheism attempts to challenge a Commonwealth system by utilising the rights of conscience, which does not lead to an equality, but a fascist dictatorship instead, either by Rome, or by Communism.

So, in order for equal opportunity to exist between all nations, then we must protect the common law, which requires an understanding of the Commonwealth system, and its theology, or we will see the rise of fascism in the form of a secular authority that sets itself against the good of the Commonwealth, and a democratic alliance. The Roman Order of Popes will not however endorse a Commonwealth system of democratic nations, and will continue to oppose the theology that a Commonwealth system derives from through political negotiations and the Jesuit Order. Here is the full transcript of the Jesuit Oath of Induction that draws a symmetry between the actions by the Knights Templar, the Jesuit Order, and the

Roman inquisitions that outline the Pope's true intentions for those who oppose his ecclesiastical jurisdiction.

*Quotation: ─────────────────────────────

The following Article is a transcript from the Jesuit Oath of Induction:

"I now in the presence of the Almighty God, the blessed virgin Mary, the blessed Michael the Archangel, the blessed St. John the Baptist and my ghostly father, the Superior General of the Society of Jesus, founded by St. Ignatius Loyola, do by the womb of the Virgin swear that His Holiness the Pope is Christ's vice-regent, and is the true and only Head of the Catholic or Universal Church. I do now renounce and disown any allegiance due to any heretical King, Prince, or State, named Protestant or Liberal, or obedience to any of their laws or magistrates, or officers.

I do further declare the doctrine of the Church of England, and Scotland, and of Calvinists, Huguenots, and others of the name of Protestant or Liberal, to be damnable, and themselves to be damned, who will not forsake the same. I do further promise and declare that, notwithstanding, I am dispensed with, to assume my religion heretical for the propagation of Mother Church's interest, to keep secret and private all her agents, counsels, from time to time, as they interest me, and not divulge directly or indirectly by word, writing, or circumstances whatsoever. I do furthermore promise and declare that I will, when opportunity presents, make and wage relentless war secretly or openly, against all heretics, Protestants, and Liberals, as I am directed to extirpate them from the face of the Earth, and that I will spare neither age, sex, or condition, and that I will hang, burn, waste, boil, flay, strangle and bury alive those infamous heretics, rip up the stomachs and wombs of the women, and crush their infants' heads against the walls in order to annihilate their inexorable race.

That when the same cannot be done openly, I will secretly use the poisonous cup, the strangulating cords, the steels of the poniard, or the leaden bullets, regardless of the honour, rank, dignity, or authority of the persons, whatsoever may be their condition in life, either public or private, as I at any time may be directed to by any agent of the Pope, or the superior of the Holy Father of the Society of Jesus. In confirmation of which I hereby dedicate my life, my soul, and my corporeal powers, and with this dagger, which I now receive, I will subscribe my name written in my blood in testimony thereof, and should I prove false, or weaken in my determination may my brethren and fellow-soldiers of the militia of the Pope, cut off my hands and my feet, and my throat from ear to ear, rip my belly open, and sulphur burn therein, and all the punishments that can be inflicted on me on Earth, and my soul be tortured by demons in an eternal hell forever. In testimony thereof I take this most holy and blessed sacrament of the Eucharist, and witness the same further with my name written with the point of this dagger, dipped in my own blood, and sealed in the face of the holy covenant." - Source: The Divine Calendar Vol. 11 (Documented November 18, 1913).

The Jesuit Society, historically, has been violently opposed to Protestant Christianity, and is largely responsible for the Roman inquisition that began in the year 1542 to counter the Lutheran revolution that resulted in 32,000 public executions for reasons relating to heresy against the Pope's so-called "supreme authority as Vicar of Christ." The evidence that the Jesuit Order is connected to the occult school of Freemasonry, is due to Adam Weishaupt who not only created the Freemasonic conspiracy that the Illuminati is so infamous for, but also, he was a Jesuit trained priest.

The Rothschild banking family commissioned Adam Weishaupt to draw-up the Illuminati conspiracy during Weishaupt's time at Ingolstadt University, which then led to the British Freemasonic and British royal conspiracy to overthrow the stock exchange of England and America through the provision of a central bank that would privatise all wealth, including human labour. From 1478 - 1834, the Roman Catholic inquisition led inquisitors striving to ensure orthodoxy within the Roman Catholic Church, often using torture to extract false confessions from those accused of heresy. The Roman Inquisitional period was the result of a powerful jurisdiction within the Vatican that extended its interests to all other nations under the Catholic doctrine of a "Universal Church" that is controlled by the Pope's ecclesiastical jurisdiction as Vicar of Christ. During the later phase of the Roman Inquisitional period, the Jesuit Order set up a method of inquiry for the Catholic Church to root out and punish heresy against the Pope, which occurred throughout most of Europe and the Americas.

Beginning in the 12th century and continuing for hundreds of years into the 19th century, the Inquisition is infamous for the severity of its tortures and its persecution of Jews, Muslims and Protestants. The fear and devastation caused by the Roman Inquisition led to a more distinguished form of American government who favoured a Protestant reformation involving the separation of Church and State. The actions by Martin Luther were the forerunner for the separation of Church and State, whereby Martin Luther challenged the Pope's ecclesiastical jurisdiction as "infallible" by declaring his faith in God as having derived from his own understanding of scripture, rather than by the Pope's ambiguous interpretation. This challenge by Martin Luther against the Pope's authority led to a more vigilant form of European rule, whereby the Germanic royalty eventually withdrew from the Pope's authority in order to be free men under God by the ability to read and interpret the Holy Bible in their own language.

This later gave rise to the idea of separation of Church and State, which Martin Luther led by the proclamation of the Gospel message of freedom in Christ. Historically, the Roman Catholic Order has attempted to suppress the Protestant Christian faith through the Jesuit Order in a desperate attempt to maintain total control over foreign diplomacy through crowned authorities who were seen as a mechanism for the spread of Catholicism, which inevitably led to the creation of the Jesuit Order under Vatican rule. The purpose of the Jesuit Society, along with the Illuminati, is to stifle all political affairs and negotiations so as to create the right conditions for the end times scenario mentioned in scripture. This view point is easily presented on the basis that the Illuminati conspiracy has been broken and is regarded as an open conspiracy that seeks revenge for the humiliation they have suffered.

The Illuminati has long since been associated with the craft of Freemasonry through signs, symbols, and initiation rites, which they share with each other openly, such as the All Seeing Eye, the truncated pyramid, the sun and crescent moon, along with Freemasonic degrees, which retain a high level of significance within occult. Though Adam Weishaupt of Ingolstadt University is responsible for drawing up the conspiracy of global conquest that inevitably led to the exposure of the Illuminati in 1785, it was actually Albert Pike who further wrote the Freemasonic plan for world domination in 1880, which he expressed to other Masons who would later join the conspiracy.

The Ku Klux Klan (KKK) was an appendant body of Freemasonry initiated by the Confederate general, Albert Pike. Albert Pike was the mastermind behind the KKK and the Knight of the Golden Circle, which was an older and more secret society that championed the preservation of slavery through Southern succession in an attempt to preserve the British-American slave trade in South America during the Civil War. Albert Pike (1809 - 1891) was an American author, poet, orator, editor, lawyer, jurist and Confederate general who served as an Associate Justice of the Arkansas Supreme Court in exile from 1864 - 1865 during the American Civil War. Pike had previously served as a senior officer of the Confederate States Army commanding the District of Indian Territory in the Trans-Mississippi Theatre. A prominent member of the Freemasons, Pike served as the Sovereign Grand Commander of the Supreme Council of the Scottish Rite's Southern jurisdiction within the United States from 1859 – 1889 and was a confessing Satanist.

Albert Pike laid out the plans for three world wars in order to create the right conditions needed for the Great Tribulation period to occur by the rise of atheism, which is mentioned in scripture as being the most bloody period in history there will ever be. Here is a copy of the Freemasonic three world war plan that Pike wrote in a letter to a fellow Mason by the name of Giuseppe Mazzini written in 1871. According to the British National Library, this letter does not exist. When according to the New York Times editorial Board, dated November 14, 2013, "Britain has a long tradition of a free and inquisitive press, but unlike the United States, Britain has no Constitutional guarantee for freedom of the Press."

*Quotation: ────────────────────────────
Excerpt from Albert Pike's letter to Giuseppe Mazzini, (Documented August 15, 1871) outlining the details for three world wars:
The First World War must be brought about in order to permit the Illuminati to overthrow the power of the Tsar in Russia and of making that country a fortress of

atheistic Communism. The divergences caused by the agents of the Illuminati between the British and Germanic Empires will be used to foment this war. At the end of the war, Communism will be built and used in order to destroy the other governments and in order to weaken the religions. The Second World War must be fomented by taking advantage of the differences between the Fascists and the political Zionists. This war must be brought about so that Nazism is destroyed and that political Zionism be strong enough to institute a sovereign State of Israel in Palestine. During the Second World War, International Communism must become strong enough in order to balance Christendom, which would be then restrained and held in check until the time when we would need it for the final social cataclysm.

The Third World War must be fomented by taking advantage of the differences caused by the agents of the Illuminati between the political Zionists and the leaders of the Islamic World. The war must be conducted in such a way that Islam and political Zionism mutually destroy each other. Meanwhile, the other nations, once more divided on this issue will be constrained to fight to the point of complete physical, moral, spiritual, and economical exhaustion. We shall unleash the nihilists and the atheists, and we shall provoke a formidable social cataclysm, which in all its horror, will show clearly to the nations the effect of absolute atheism, origin of savagery and of the most bloody turmoil.

Then everywhere, the citizens, obliged to defend themselves against the world minority of revolutionaries, will exterminate those destroyers of civilization, and the multitude, disillusioned with Christianity, whose deistic spirits will from that moment be without compass or direction, anxious for an ideal, but without knowing where to render its adoration, will receive the true light through the universal manifestation of the pure doctrine of Lucifer, brought finally out in the public view. This manifestation will result from the general reactionary movement that will follow the destruction of Christianity and atheism, both conquered and exterminated at the same time. - Source: The United States National Online Internet Archive.

The first and second world wars that have occurred already did indeed play out exactly according to Albert Pike's plan, and he is addressing other Freemasons with this plan, because the overall goal of his strategy is to one day bring the practice of Luciferianism out into the view of the public. It is also interesting to note here that Albert Pike, (who was the highest-ranking Freemason in America during the Civil War) referred to Communism, Nazism and atheism as a political weapon by Freemasonry in his letter about four decades before National Socialism, Communism, and New Atheism arose from the geopolitical scene.

This constitutes as evidence that Freemasonry is secretly in control of Nazism, Communism, and the New Atheist movement from behind the scenes, because Freemasonic Enlightenment, and the conspiracy by the Illuminati is responsible for the development of each of these more modern movements. The third world war, according to Pike, will be caused by the ongoing conflict in the Middle East between Palestine and Israel that was instigated on purpose by British Freemasonry to begin with when the political Zionists were brought back to their homeland of Israel following 1948 through the legislative power of the United Nations, and by the British crown releasing any claims over the region, which has left the region vulnerable to continual open warfare.

So, because the theory of evolution and the international banking conspiracy by the Illuminati means to challenge the lawful definition of person to being that of property for revenue purposes, it will mean that the only way to challenge this co-conspiracy, is by a universal definition of man, which cannot be contested on any legal grounds for reasons relating to the preservation of human rights and equality. And though the United Nations was created so that the interpretation of inalienable entitlements, and human sovereignty could be defined as universal in accordance with international law, it will one day fail as a system of self-governance, just as the United States Constitutional system of self-governance has been used as a mechanism for total enslavement by the reinterpretation of human sovereignty under God, to being one in favour of Secular Humanism involving the evolutionary definition of man.

The Universal Declaration of human rights and Equality was enacted following the aftermath of World War II involving the Antisemitism of the Holocaust, which was solely due to the teaching of evolution by the State, which led to the racial segregation policies that Hitler and his henchman were so infamous for. Today, the Antisemitism and racial segregation policies that follows Islam is now projected to the world through the international news reports with crimes against humanity by Islam being broadcasted throughout the international news reports. Thus, we are faced with a choice that bears responsibility on our God given conscience, and the choice is clear.

Either we stand in favour of Israel as a nation in order to protect an equality, or we can allow radical Islam to continue with their riots, protests, and blatant racism of Antisemitism unabated. Islam has been treated with due respect by the United Nations without any U.N peacekeeping force entering the boarders of Palestine except to feed the prisoners of war, and yes, the people of Palestine are prisoners of war with artificial boarders in place by Hamas that prevents the people from seeking asylum, which is being done in order to use the people as a shield of war during the crisis that Hamas has created. Hamas never gave the U.N a declaration of war, and have acted in defiance of international agreement, thereby bringing the due process of law into serious question. It is the will of God the Creator that peace should preside here on Earth in accordance with the will of His Spirit, while it is the will of Satan our enemy that peace should be removed from the Earth by the rise of radical Islam, and by failed political negotiations within the U.N.

Thus, we cannot rely on religion and political negotiations alone to win the war on human freedom, but with the due process of law, which is our saving grace in the hour of war. And the due process of law starts and ends with human rights and equality, which means that Palestine, Iran, and Saudi Arabia must submit to an international peace agreement, and to allow for a Jewish settlement within the boarders of Israel and Palestine in order for a to ceasefire to occur, or Palestine will be subdued by war, rather than redeemed by an international peace agreement.

The nation of Israel has allowed within the boarders of their country both Christians and Muslims in accordance with an international peace agreement, while Palestine, Iran, and Saudi Arabia remain in defiance of an international treaty by preventing a Jewish settlement within the boarders of their own country, which is the very thing that brings their own stability as an alliance into question. So, in order to stand by an equality with equal opportunity in mind, then we must deliver unto Islam the same measure that has been dealt to the Jewish people, which is exile. Only then can equal justice be measured.

If the Palestinian protests are allowed to interfere with the functions of a free and open society by an act of civil unrest that brings public safety into serious question, then it is the responsibility of the government to respond effectively with a course of justice, which does not include another open media debate for entertainment purposes, but rather, exile with fair notice, which is not owing to the Jews who have operated fairly in accordance with international agreement involving due notice, and a tactical response, so that equal opportunity and due process should have an effect, which is a measure of justice for all. The due process of law is mandatory in this matter, which includes giving notice of war, as well as preparing for a peace agreement once the war has ended, which is exactly how the nation of Germany was treated at the end of World War II, making them our allies.

If we do not follow the due process of law, then we will bring equal opportunity into question, which then brings an equality into serious doubt, which is only expedient for those who wish to win this war unfairly. War is the inevitable consequence of conflict involving disputes over land, and over which laws are fair, and which laws are not fair. So, in order to be fair in this situation, then we must abide by international agreement that allows for equal opportunity between all nations, or we will be subdued by an enemy that brings the law of equality into question, which happens to be radical Islam in this matter due to the nature of global terrorism and civil unrest. If the nation of Israel, along with the nations who have suffered, are to prepare for a peace agreement with the Islamic world, then we must also prepare for a tactical victory, which does include the provisions of a peace agreement once the war is officially over, or we will never be able to subdue radical Islam by the laws that sustain our basic freedoms in accordance with international law.

The failure of the Universal Declaration of Human Rights and Equality will occur in due time when the mark of the beast comes into effect as a direct result of the international banking cartel, Freemasonry, and by failed political negotiations and alliances within the United Nations involving Communism and Islam. So, it is for this reason that we have a lawful premise for peace to preside here on Earth today, which is in accordance with the will of God. While it is the work of Satan our enemy to remove peace from the Earth by causing a division between every nation, every household, and every family by the rise of atheism, and by the rise of Islam; Which is why taking sides on the Palestinian humanitarian issue is not going to win the battle for human freedom, because if the Islamic world is able to instigate a war on Israel and America by themself, then the Islamic world is thereby able to support itself. The longer we fear Islam and their retaliation, the longer this war will persist, and the longer this war persists, the sooner our system of equality will fail catastrophically.

So, for this reason, we are to respond to Islam with an effective response that does not involve fear of further retaliation, which is the main reason that radical Islam goes unabated internationally. Only when we have subdued our enemy by force can we then respond effectively with a show of compassion that must derive itself from the will of the people as a working whole, because it is the attempts by Freemasonry to provoke a "final social cataclysm" by utilising the ongoing conflict in the Middle East that will divide humanity on the grounds of war.

God alone shall redeem His people Israel who are the apple of His eye, for Israel is a nation of prophets, priests, and kings who have delivered the word of God to the districts of the people, and shall be forever remembered for their righteousness, rather than their due retaliation. The biggest problem that stands in the way of global stability is not Palestine, nor Israel, because Communism as a political ideology has more to do with it by preventing and stifling a justifiable alliance by the rise of Scientific Atheism in order to promote the principles of Marxist revolution, rather than human freedom.

The final aspect of Albert Pike's plan for world domination involves the use of nihilism from atheism, which he defines as being "the origin of savagery." The reason why nihilism is so savage, is because it is so pervasive intellectually, so vile humorously, and so heartless respectively that it lacks any empathy whatsoever. And everyone has had a touch of nihilism from time to time as a result of feeling worthless inside, and therefore, life feels meaningless. But the real issue at hand is not whether you feel worthless or not, but whether or not you are suffering because of a nihilist.

*Definition of Nihilism:
Nihilism is the belief that all values are baseless and that nothing can be known or communicated. It is often associated with extreme pessimism and a radical scepticism that condemns existence. A true nihilist would believe in nothing, have no loyalties, and no purpose other than, perhaps, an impulse to destroy. - Source: The Online Encyclopedia of Philosophy.

The only way to combat nihilism is to treat it as a severe form of radicalized atheism, because the only belief a nihilist has, is atheism. And even though atheism is defined as unbelief, it still constitutes as a belief, because in order to reject a belief, then you must have an alternative view, which becomes the individual's belief as a preference, because that is what belief is, a preferred idea or notion that forms the basis of an opinion. One cannot explain the relationship between Islam, Freemasonry, and Communism, until one first understands that most of the modern weaponry that is used by Islam derives from Communist arms dealers, which is why the most common weapon of choice by Islamic terrorists, is the AK47, which is a standard issue Communist rifle.

And though Communism is anti-religious according to the founder of Communism, Karl Marx, it is the spread of Islamic terrorism that is giving religion a bad name globally, which is highly expedient for those who wish to challenge the free exercise of religion before the law, such as the New Atheist movement. The primary mechanism behind Albert Pike's plan to one day cause a "final social cataclysm," is by the rise of atheism, and through the continuing open conflict in the Middle East between the political Zionists, and the religion of Islam.

Historically, the establishment of the United Kingdom has been under the full control of the British crown, and therefore, Freemasonry. But since the United Kingdom declared their independence from Britain by the United Kingdom Act 1986, the House of Representatives within the United Kingdom have drifted further and further away from the crown's authority due to a public influence that derives itself from the practice of a Judeo-Christian democracy based on a Commonwealth system of theology that includes the redress of public grievances under the common law. And this has always been a danger to Freemasonry historically, rather than a convenience, because it is the occult school of Freemasonry that is challenging the Biblical definition of individual human sovereignty by defining man as a lower animal from the theory of evolution, and the occult principles of Arianism.

The only thing that British Freemasonry can do, in terms of a direct response to Christianity, is to promote the sovereignty of the British royal family throughout the media, rather than the people's sovereignty, which is now secondary to any royal fame or ambition. And this is the primary reason why the mainstream media, and the Supreme Court of the United States, will publicly slam anybody who attempts to promote their sovereignty under God as a form of individual freedom, because it is the Freemasonic conspiracy to abolish all patriotism and loyalty to sovereignty according to the written conspiracy by Adam Weishaupt and Albert Pike involving the Illuminati.

So, even though New Atheism calls for a return to the British Enlightenment, it is in fact a call to global rebellion, or, revolution, because, A) The British Enlightenment period revolved around the idea of a new scientific revolution in despite of the previous Christian scientific revolution that derived from Baconian and Newtonian creation science and systems thinking. B) Because a new scientific revolution based on philosophical materialism would lead to a global rebellion against both Church and State. And C) Because a global rebellion against both Church and State would result in total anarchy and moral decay. So, any call by the New Atheist movement to a scientific revolution against the Biblical principles of Judeo-Christianity will result in a rebellion against the principles of common law and self-governance, because both of these principles have derived from Biblical theology, rather than atheism.

The New Atheist movement derives itself from Communism and Scientific Atheism, which is the very thing that will destroy humanity by a shift in culture as we are seeing today by the rise of certain humanitarian groups and minorities who oppose basic public morals by challenging the lawful definition of man, such as the gay rights movement who are deeply influenced by New Atheism, the evolutionary theory, and occult literature that brings basic public morals into question, as well as the common law by challenging Judeo-Christian virtues and precepts that are steeped in law.

Many have wondered as to the real reason why the gay rights movement would openly defend the Palestinian riots in opposition to the Jews, when some Islamic countries have a death penalty for homosexuals.

This issue of an oxymoron can be easily explained by the correct interpretation of the New Atheist movement, which is in full support of the pro-Palestinian movement involving an opposition to the Jewish nation of Israel and Biblical authority. The real reason why the New Atheist movement would support Islam within Western nations is for the same reason that New Atheism is in full support of the gay rights movement, and that is to create the right conditions for a global revolution by minority groups who question basic public morals in order to bring the due process of law into question. In order for Communism to undermined the alliance of a Christian coalition force of democratic nations led by a Commonwealth system of theology, then both the Jews, and the Holy Bible, must be placed into harms way for the express purpose of advancing moral and social decay, which is a political weapon by Communism in order to instigate a global scientific revolution.

Communist revolution today has cloaked itself under the guise of minority groups that claim their freedom is being suppressed by the common law and the Christian religion, such as the BLM movement, the gay rights movement, NAMBLA, the pro-Palestinian movement, the pro-Enlightenment movement, the Secular Humanist movement, and the New Atheist movement just to name a few, because the sole basis for Communist revolution within Western society is the same as it was in pre-Soviet Russia, whereby the Communist revolution was cloaked by having multiple minority groups with separate interests, but with one goal in mind by those who were causing the revolutions, such as Vladimir Lennon and other co-conspirators.

The idea behind having multiple minority groups who challenge basic public morals within Western society is being done in order to challenge the law in order to have freedom from morality, because it is morality that brings human actions into question. If basic public morals are of any virtue, then pro-revolutionaries must be challenged from the premise of law, because we have already had a learning revolution from Baconian and Newtonian creation science, and we have already had a revolution against human slavery by the creation of the United States Constitution and the

UDHR, which cannot be overruled without causing a rebellion against self-governance in turn.

The idea that one can free themselves from morality by challenging moral law, as defined by the Holy Bible, is a moral principle in itself, because the basis of their challenge is to espouse some form of freedom from rules, which constitutes as a rule in itself. According to international human rights legislation, human freedom has been defined as freedom of conscience, and it is the human conscience that is for our understanding of human morality, which must derive itself from a Commonwealth system of theology for the good of the people, and for the good of the common law. Otherwise, we will be placing a coalition force of democratic nations into harms way, which then brings the common law into question.

This means that one cannot challenge the existence of rules, ethics, and the human conscience as having derived from the Creator God of Genesis, without challenging the universal law of human equality in turn, because in order to interpret a causality for rules, then a Creator is required, which cannot be nature itself without defining the individual as property at the same time. Human equality, as defined by international law under the UDHR, was never established to give a minority group the moral high ground, but rather, it was established as a response to the evolutionary definition of man following the Holocaust where Nazi racial segregation policies were imposed upon the people of Europe due to the teaching of evolution by the State.

The only difference between New Atheism and Communism, is that the former attempts to cater to all from a secular premise, while the later attempts to disguise itself as a democracy. Yet both of these philosophical movements are based on occult illumination, whereby the principles of Arianism, along with occult sciences, have been put into effect with a single outcome, which is formally known today as Social Darwinism. According to Scripture, Jesus is quoted in Matthew 12:25 saying: "Every kingdom divided against itself is brought to desolation. And every city or house divided against itself shall not stand." (End of quote).

So, in order for Freemasonry to create the right conditions for global revolution, then there needs to be a strong alliance that is designed to fail, otherwise, a global coalition force of democratic nations under a universal system of common law would never cease. But the problem with this conspiracy, is that nothing is more divided than secret intelligence agencies, which includes not only the Russian FSB, Britain's MI6, and America's CIA, but also, Freemasonry, because, not only do Freemasons conspire against democracy, Judaism, and Christianity, but also, themselves, while Judeo-Christianity remains highly transparent from the viewpoint of a democracy.

So, if there is one thing that Freemasons fear the most, then it is transparency, which is why most Masonic Lodges have no windows on the side of their buildings, and this is also why Masons communicate primarily through selective signs and symbology, which is an unspoken language that supposedly leads to enlightenment, whilst failing to be open and honest with the people first. The more society is exposed to Satanism, the more open Freemasonry and the Illuminati will become, because the entire purpose of the Illuminati from Albert Pike's plan, is to bring Satanism out into the public view. And this is occurring today with every New Atheist book, occult novel, or Blockbuster film that attempts to undermine Biblical Christianity by opposing basic public morals using fantasy driven ideas.

So, in order for Freemasonry to destroy a coalition force of democratic nations that are self-governed under the common law, then the universal principles of human equality must be put into harm's way. And nothing destroys an alliance based on theology faster than unbelief, which is where New Atheism comes into play by begging for a return to the pro-Enlightenment philosophy of anti-Christian and anti-establishment sympathies. Stalin's role in the Illuminati's conspiracy for world domination was played out when he attempted to make Russia a "fortress of atheistic Communism," thereby weakening the Judeo-Christian nations by the rise of Scientific Atheism, Militant Atheism, and radical scepticism.

Marxist - Leninist atheism, Militant Atheism, and Scientific Atheism, are the core principles of Communism that was formerly promoted in the Eastern Bloc until most countries around the world banned Communist symbols, making it illegal to form a Communist party throughout most of Europe, Ukraine, Canada, Australia, and the United States under a Communist Control Act. But unfortunately for the Western Bloc system, the Communist Control Act has not been enforced with many countries now having a Communist Party in place of a Socialist Party, such as Britain, Canada, Australia, and the United States. The effects of nihilism from New

Atheism is a persisting and nagging problem for Western society, because atheism will be taught through the public education system from a scientific perspective involving the theory of evolution, which is equal to Communist propaganda according to the academic definition of Scientific Atheism.

Communist propaganda will involve any scientific notion by atheism that attempts to refute the existence of God the Creator, as from United States Constitutional law, Commonwealth theology, and the Holy Bible, because all have been endowed by their Creator with inalienable rights, which is the lawful basis for individual human sovereignty, and human independence thereby. And it is loyalty to individual human sovereignty that Communism is fighting against globally according to the Freemasonic conspiracy by the Illuminati, and the founder of Communism, Karl Marx. This means that it is every citizen's sovereign duty under God to combat Communism in all of its forms, which includes New Atheism from its philosophical and Communist roots of Scientific Atheism.

In order for an individual to be self-governed within society, then the individual must also be adequately informed of their basic rights, as well as the rights of others through the public education system. But if the public education system is secular for religious reasons, then Secular Humanism is by definition a religion. The actions by the United States Supreme Court has been one in favour of creating a secular religion that is in strong support of the evolutionary theory, occult philosophy, and Greco-Roman mythology, all of which, define man as an animal, and therefore, property. The purpose of the evolutionary theory, Freemasonry, and Greco-Roman mythology from a secular premise, is to teach that: A) That citizens have descended from an animal. B) That the ruling class has descended from a special royal bloodline known formally as Arianism. And C) That citizens are thereby the property of this so-called special royal bloodline.

The purpose of law and order is to act as a service to mankind in order to maintain stability here on Earth in accordance with the Biblical principles of human equality and equal justice thereby, which are universal in truth and in practice in accordance with self-governance. But when these laws require a secular interpretation only, then the process of learning is restricted to a one-sided view of history, which acts as a limitation, rather than a method of exploration. So, in order for an equality to be maintained through due process, then equal opportunity is required through the public education system or we will be faced by an opposition that sets itself against the correct interpretation of inalienable.

Commonwealth theology, and the United States Constitution, was never to be interpreted from secular ideology alone, but from Biblical theology instead, because it is the theological terms from law that safeguard our basic rights by the correct interpretation of inalienable. Thus, any secular interpretation of the common law that does not recognize the Creator God of Genesis will bring the correct interpretation of the law into question, along with our basic rights.

If religion is to be a benefit to mankind, then laws are required, which cannot derive itself from a secular authority alone, because it is not the government of a nation that defines what is right or wrong, but a correct theology instead. If the United States Constitution is to be interpreted by secular ideology alone, then the Constitution cannot be adequately defended, as well as interpreted to the people from the premise of law, because the only way to define that which is inalienable, is with a correct theology, which must derive itself from Biblical teachings for the good of the people, and for the good of the common law.

Everyone has the right to a belief, while no one has the right to unbelief when interpreting the universal law of human equality, and this is because the universal law of human equality is legally based on the self-evident, and self-explanatory word definitions as being incontestable for the benefit of an individual's protection within the system. Thus, it is the secular standard for public education that has placed the basic rights of the people in great jeopardy by discriminating against the theological definition for what a person is, as from United States Constitutional law, Commonwealth theology, and the UDHR, where a person's basic right to be defined as a created human being with a human ancestry is protected as inalienable in accordance with the lawful definition of person as a living soul.

And this legality issue is not only the result of secular scientists who define man as an animal from the theory of evolution, but also, judges, who themselves do not understand the basic rights of an individual to be defined as a sovereign person at all times, and have thereby redefined the meaning to being that of property instead for reasons relating to financial revenue by the State. The human conscience is always aware of evil due to the nature of lying, and the more a person attempts to refute the Creator, the more evil will control the individuals notions that were supposed to be based on facts, but lacked empathy instead, which is a vital component to any principle in science or law, because science and law are based on ethics, which are defined by morality, rather than by animal instincts.

If individual human sovereignty is to be defined, then its interpretation must be universal, rather than institutional, because human freedom is best defined by a universal principle for the benefit of an individual's protection within the system. And the one definition that is universal today, as from law, is the Biblical definition of man due to the theological term, conscience, which forms the basis for the universal law of human equality, and human freedom thereby. God in Heaven has instituted human equality for mankind as just in accordance with peace here on Earth that derives from the will of His Spirit, and the good of the people.

Any individual or establishment that seeks to undermine the universal law of human equality by equating mankind with the animal kingdom, and by a denial of conscience, does so in order to espouse some kind of freedom from morality and law, or, because of their personal ambitions to rule. When according to the universal law of human equality, all have been endowed with conscience in order to understand a moral obligation, which forms the basis of a legal obligation, and every human being has a lawful obligation to acknowledge human equality before the law regardless of opinion.

Under the UDHR, the ability to govern is not owing to any individual apart from those with the consent of the governed in order that governing should be considered as a privilege, rather than a birthright. While it is the birthright of every individual person under international law to be defined as a created human being with a human ancestry at all times according to their endowed conscience, so that each individual should be convicted by their conscience in regards to a moral obligation by the law to uphold the virtues of human rights and equality in despite of any scientific theory that suggests otherwise.

Under international law, it is the birthright of every individual to vote according to their own conscience, and their vote should not be excluded, nor overruled by any individual or organization on the basis of government legislation, because it is the people who constitute as a nation, rather than the legislators. None are more hopelessly oppressed than those who challenge basic public morals in favour of more freedoms, because individual human freedom is best expressed through the action of obedience, rather than rebellion. Members who hail from the evolutionary theory have utterly failed in their efforts to explain an important phenomenon, such as the existence of the human conscience, and have also attempted to challenge the correct definition of what a human being is before international law, which is why reform is needed to correct the public education system.

Otherwise, the system we live under will inevitably fail over time due to a breakdown in communication between the law and students. And it is advocates of the evolutionary theory that have failed to explain the existence of life and the human conscience before international law from the viewpoint of philosophical materialism, because international law has defined the human conscience as being endowed to every individual on the basis of morality and law. A contingency plan is a course of action that is designed to help an organization respond effectively to a significant future incident, event, or situation that may or may not happen, while a contingent is that which occurs by chance.

So, if physical laws are a contingent, then this only works in the case that it was necessary for a contingency, or in other words, an ulterior motive, which happens to be the reason why evolutionary scientists desire to note physical laws as a natural phenomenon only, because if the evolutionist was to admit that physical laws were created, then they have thereby detracted from the theory, which is in the best interests of those who wish to deny Biblical morality in order to espouse some form of freedom from rules, or, to exploit mankind as property for revenue purposes. So, the only contingency that we have in relation to the evolutionary definition of man, is the universal definition of person from international law, which cannot be overruled by the evolutionary theory for reasons relating to the preservation of human rights and equality under inalienable entitlements that are defined as sovereign on the basis of conscience and reason so that we each have security of person before the law.

Darwinian evolution is never going to save humanity from the problems associated with racism, nor is Darwinian evolution ever going to free humanity on the basis of conscience and reason, because the entire purpose of the evolutionary theory is to cause a division between the ruling class and the laity with the ruling class applying a Linnaean system of naming, while the indigenous people of a nation are subjugated under the same naming system that derives itself from the pseudo-science of scientific racism. The theory of evolution is the most used theory in occult sciences, while Biblical creation is in opposition to the occult, and the evolutionary theory, on the basis that God in Heaven has created every living creature, each according to their own abilities.

The theory of evolution is an integral part of Freemasonry whereby a ruling class is to subjugate a lower class based on a supposed ancestry of a superior human race, which has manifested itself into the occult doctrine of Arianism, Ariosophy, and Social Darwinism. The occult school of Freemasonry is the leading hierarchical structure that promotes a strong division between the ruling class and the laity, with the laity having little or no knowledge of Freemasonry. Thus, the secretive nature of Freemasonry forbids the free exercise of freedom of information, because the only way that Freemasonry and the evolutionary theory can work together, is for the laity to be ill-informed in regards to their basic rights as a human being through the public education system.

Every individual has the universal right to be defined as a created human being with a human ancestry on the basis that each individual has been endowed with conscience by their Creator, and the conscience desires to know in order to judge. The evolutionary definition of man is leading humanity back into the Dark Ages where alchemy and pseudo-scientific beliefs ruled the minds of many, because the discussion as to whether man was created or not has been settled satisfactorily before the law on a self-evident basis that each individual is endowed with certain inalienable rights, such as the right to be defined as a created human being with a human ancestry, which cannot be revoked as a form of subjugation, because all of your freedoms derive from the principles of a creation, which is a religious doctrine, rather than a secular one.

So, in order to correctly interpret the law, then a Creator God is required to be explained factually to public school students, because in order to be endowed with certain inalienable rights that are universal in their interpretation, then a system of morality that is by definition, universal, is also required, which cannot derive itself from a secular interpretation without invoking a religion in turn, because morality pertains to religious belief, rather than secular science. Thus, when making a legal argument, one must take into account another person's inalienable rights, which does not include defining a human being as a type of animal, which is both inhumane and unlawful before international law on the basis of equality.

If mankind is to be subjugated by a scientific theory that defines man as animal, then there will be no lawful interpretation for human equality, when it is human equality that we are fighting to defend globally, rather than a pet theory that defines man as a lower animal, of which, the legal system cater for, because our universal system of self-governance derives from Biblical theology under the common law, rather than secular science. God in Heaven has endowed all life with ability, but unto His own image the gift of conscience, with which, to judge from, which is not to be misconstrued as a believer in Christ our saviour being unworthy to judge for themselves, but as a unique ability that sets us apart from the unjust who have lost their ability to judge wisely by the adoption of rules that simply do not apply. And the one rule that simply does not apply, is the rule that amoral behaviour cannot be judged, which is a form of judgement in itself that incurs the wrath of the Lamb, which abides on the wicked, rather than the justified who's eyes have been opened by the grace of God.

A Prayer for the Nations:

Lord, Almighty God;

We are troubled in this world today by the fear that derives from the acts of terror, and from those who despise Your godly ways, but we are not without assurance from above, for You have delivered Your word to the districts of the people, and have laid down Your life that we may have forgiveness of sin, for You are a God of love, and a Lord of righteousness whose name and majesty shall endure forever as an eternal truth that presides over eternity. May those who are suffering from the acts of terror know with assurance that God is a deliverer of the people from the hands of the wicked, for He alone has established His promise to all that the meek shall be saved from the wrath that abides on the wicked.

God has established His system of justice, and His system of moral law, that all who love their neighbour in truth shall be redeemed from the hands of the devil on the day of judgement in accordance with the love we have received that opens the eyes of the wicked to their injustices, and the hearts of the justified who have loved without reward. May the light of the Gospel message be preached unto all the nations, and unto the ends of the Earth, that life and liberty may be everlasting to those who are willing to obey the commandments of the Lord for the rest of their days, which are without number in the Heavens above. The Lord has established His word with peace at hand that an orderly system of human equality should not fail the weak, nor shall it end, for life everlasting is upon those who believe in God their maker by the knowledge of His Son, Jesus Christ, who alone shepherds the way to life and liberty.

Let all those who read this prayer know that the Mighty One of Jacob draws near to them who testify of His Son, Jesus Christ, and proclaim liberty throughout the land by the proclamation of the Gospel message of hope and salvation in accordance with the word we have received. May the love of the Father in Heaven flood the nations by the grace of His eternal Spirit, so that all who acknowledge His Son as Saviour Lord, and who walk in the ways of righteousness and of honour according to His precepts may find blessings of hope, and prayers of mediation that comfort the soul, and give justice to the downtrodden who are struggling in their faith, that God's grace may be upon them in spirit, as well as in deed. Amen

(Above) Photo taken of a Freemasonic Shriner's emblem symbolizing the connection between Communism (the gold and red star), Islam (the sword and crescent moon), an ancient royal bloodline (the Pharaoh wearing a crown), Luciferianism (G, the great architect), and the Illuminati (the eye of the compass). Source: Personal Photograph of a Shriner's Emblem purchased on Amazon.com.

A Response to Freemasonry:
You have attempted to hide your secrets of world domination from those who seek the truth. Your inner sanctuaries and inner circles are not safe from those who desire to know the conspiracy that has befouled the people in a time of global crisis. You have been enlightened through your ministry by the tip of a sword, rather than by the truth that sets us free. If ever there was a time in human history that mankind should be made aware of your conspiracy to remove peace from the world, then it is here and now, for the people are suffering under the yoke of tyranny, and they have nowhere to point their finger except at their own government, who are not to blame for the trap you have set against them so that they should fail during a time of great upheaval.

If ever there was someone to blame for the murders, the conspiracies, and the atrocities committed against the people, then it is the light behind Freemasonry, which seeks to enter the world through our system of justice, so as to remove peace and security from the world by any means necessary. The light of the world is not found in your books, your laws, nor your theology, but from the wisdom that sets us apart from the wicked who are trapped in darkness by the teaching of mysteries that have derived from your school of injustices. You have weakened the nations that evil should arise; You have betrayed the people who have not known you and your ways; And you have hidden your face from the House of Representatives so as to avoid the charges and accusations that are laid upon you. You shall not be found innocent on the day of wrath when all things shall be laid bare before the throne of the lamb who has suffered likewise at the hands of your ministers, and by the teaching of secrets that you disclose to no one but yourselves.

You have shaken hands with the devil, and have conspired against the people who have been set apart in their hearts to despise the evil you have created for them. There shall be no mercy for your prophets, your ministers, or your teachers who work against the one law for all to live by fairly with, which is; Do unto others as you would have them do unto you, and, to love thy neighbour as you love your own, for this is the will of the lamb, of whom, you have dishonoured with the help of Satan.

May an eternal darkness overcome you, and may the wrath of the Lamb that abides on you overshadow you, for you did not heed the will of God, and the will of the people, who shall be redeemed on the day of judgement, for the Lord knows the ways of the righteous, and He has not forsaken those who have strived with their neighbour for mercies sake. May the House of Representatives be blessed upon the seating of this nation's parliament through prayers and mediation that come from Heaven, so that the Spirit of the Lord should be heard on high, and so that the will of the people, and the good of the common law, should be protected by the laws that sustain our freedoms through the trials and tribulations that derive from the teaching of Freemasonry; For the Lord has spoken, and His Heavens are not empty.

FURTHER READING

ARTICLE 1

The Science of Slavery

*Quotation: ————————————————

"Natural science will in time incorporate into itself the science of man, just as the science of man will incorporate into itself natural science, then there will only be one science. Darwin has interested us in the history of nature's technology. Darwin's book is very important and serves me as a basis in natural science for the class struggle in history. Every provisional political set-up following a revolution requires a dictatorship, and an energetic dictatorship at that." - Karl Marx, founder of Communism. Source: Marx-Engels Collected Works, Vol. 3 - Science and Humanity. (Documented in 1843).

Throughout time, humanity has divided itself over land disputes, as well as disputes over which laws are fair, and which laws are not fair. Historically, the fairest systems of law have not only included collective distributions for the poor, but also, rights for the poor in order that their cause should be heard, which is the sole basis for case law, or common law, where each individual is treated as equal before the law. The most unfair systems in history have been empires with imperial ambitions to rule and govern the people as property, leaving little or no room for the cause of the poor to be heard and understood from the merit of their hardships. An imperial rule is no different to a fascism historically, because both imperial rule and government dictatorships rely on covet means in order to expand their interests abroad to include foreign territories for resources, and direct taxation of the inhabitants to fund expansion policies.

The best way to describe the difference between these two systems of rule is to imagine a straight line with a 100% margin at the right end of the line, and a 0% margin at the far left end of the line. The far right represents total government, which is defined as a fascism because of its totalitarian authority. While the far left on the other hand is distinguished by having no government, which is defined as anarchy, because there is no system of law in place. Between these two scopes there is a wide margin between anarchy and fascism, with the conservative view in the middle, because the conservative view includes a system of law by the people that protects the people's right to life and liberty according to a legally binding and immutable declaration.

A Constitutional democratic republic is defined as a conservative system, because the democracy is from the far left, while the republic is from the far right, and a Constitutional system of law presides from the middle of these two extremes as being conservative, which is in the best interests of the democracy and the republic, because if the democracy is not upheld by the republic, then the government is to be defined as a fascism, rather than a democratic republic. And this happens to be the problem with Communism historically, because it poses as a democratic republic, but with a one party preferred system of government; Meaning that a democracy is secondary within a Communist republic, because no amount of votes can remove the party that is in power.

According to the United States Declaration of Independence, the human being is endowed with rights from birth, and these rights have been defined as inalienable; Meaning that each person has a birthright to be defined as a created human being before the law. And what makes this different from being just a concept is due to the fact that inalienable rights are defined as a birthright having derived from the Creator, who in turn, is universal according to the correct interpretation of inalienable.

So, it does not matter whether you're a United States citizen or not, your inalienable rights are still defined as universal; Meaning that United

States human rights legislation applies to every individual on Earth as a legal standard the same as the UDHR by the United Nations. And the other aspect that defines inalienable rights as universal, rather than institutional, is due to the fact that we are all endowed with conscience by our Creator in order to understand these rights with, and we are all equal according to the existence of our God given conscience, which forms the basis for the universal law of human equality by the United Nations.

The difference between being conscious, and having a conscience, is that the conscience is specifically for determining fact from fiction, the truth from a lie, and yes or no with. While being conscious simply means to be aware of your surroundings, and to respond to your surroundings, and to be breathing also, because being conscious was initially from breath to begin with according to Genesis 2:7 where God breathed life into man, and he became a living soul. And this is the same for any creature with the breath of life in its nostrils, which means that certain kinds of animals also have a soul but are lacking a conscience in order to understand a moral implication, and are therefore free from a legal obligation. And what all of this means is that we're all equal under the law according to our God given conscience, which is the international standard for human rights and equality according to Article 1 from the United Nations Universal Declaration of Human Rights and Equality (UDHR).

The evolutionary theory from natural science attempts to define the individual as free from the law in accordance with the evolutionary teaching that man is animal, because animals are free from a legal obligation or oath. The evolutionary definition of man attempts to create an atmosphere of human freedom, when there is no freedom without the law by definition of the fact that we as human beings are endowed with conscience, and are therefore subject to moral law. So, the next question one would ask is, what is moral law? And who's law is it? This question can be answered satisfactorily by having a system of morality that is by definition, universal. But, the counter claim will always arise in the form of a question, which is evidence that morality exists, because we reason and ask questions from a source of conscience.

So, because the ability to reason and ask questions derives from a source of conscience, then a definition of conscience is required when interpreting a law. And the correct definition for the source of conscience, as from common law, is that it derives from the Creator who is defined as: "Lord, Lord Almighty, or God." This designation of "Lord Almighty" is not-without-standing from a legal premise under the common law, because there is no way to define the human conscience as having any other source apart from the Creator in order to have a system of morality that is by definition, universal. And a universal system of morality is indeed a requirement in order for a law to be made universal in its interpretation, which forms the basis of human rights legislation under the common law.

The common law itself derives from the redress of public grievances before the courts in order that each person should have a voice. The term, common law, is also used interchangeably with the term case law. Case law, according to its correct definition in use, is based on legal precedents, that is the judicial decisions from other previous cases, rather than laws that are based on Constitutions, Statutes, or Regulations. Common law systems are legal systems that provide a judicial precedent, which derive from the English legal system.

The civil law system is often contrasted with the common law system, because both require a code of ethics. The common law system originated in medieval England by the redress of public grievances before the House of Commons, whereas the civil law derives from a system of legal codes that derive from a legal body, administration, or crown. The common law derives from uncodified case law that in essence derives from previous judicial decisions, thereby recognising prior court decisions as a legally binding precedent in order to establish potential truths that are used in future cases.

The common law sets a legal precedent, or potential truth, from a trial by jury in criminal cases, or from a code of ethics by civil law. So, the only difference between common law and civil law, is that civil law derives from a set of Statutes, Regulations, or Constitution, while the common law derives from a legal precedent that is formed by a trial by jury in criminal cases, thereby setting a legal standard for future cases. So, for this reason, the common law does include civil laws to act as a code of ethics, with ethics being defined as moral law, of which, sets a legal standard by which the courts must follow along with citizens. The term, ethics, is interchangeable with the term, morals, in that a rule has been formed with a moral implication, thereby setting the legal precedent for Biblical morality as a legal standard for the interpretation of moral law and ethical conduct, because morality cannot exist without religion, and religion cannot be maintained without morality.

Communist law on the other hand is defined as, socialist law, which forms the common features of the legal system used within Communist Russia, China, and other nations that support a Communist Party. Socialist law resulted from a set of legal codes that mimics civil law in order to maintain a Communist party's dominance over society by the use of State driven Legislative Acts. Social law, or Soviet law, is rooted in pro-revolutionary Russian law that follows the principles of Marxism, Leninism, Trotskyism, and Scientific Atheism.

The idea in theory behind Communism and socialist law is one of a removal of class struggle by creating a supposed system of equality that defines the ownership of property as Capitalist, which is the reason why it is against the principles of Marxism to own private property, because everything belongs to the State. For this reason, socialist law, or Communist law, forbids the presence of a democracy, because it is the principles of a democracy that a public grievance by the State can be rectified within the High Courts.

Crimes against humanity under Communist law occurred during the 20th and 21st century following pro-revolutionary Russia that included forced deportations, human massacres, civilian and non-civilian torture, forced disappearances, extrajudicial killings, acts of terror, ethnic cleansing, and forced extradition, as well as deliberate starvation on a mass scale, as was the case during the Holodomor famine in the Ukraine under Joseph Stalin, or the Great Famine of China between 1959 - 1961 that resulted in the deliberate starvation of over 30 million people who were seen as biologically unfit, and therefore, an obstacle to Communist revolution involving the evolutionary theory of Darwinian eugenics.

An extrajudicial killing (also known as an extrajudicial execution or an extra-legal killing) is the deliberate killing of a person without the lawful authority granted by a judicial proceeding involving a trial by jury. Socialist law relies on a Communist Dictatorship in order to establish a potential verdict or truth, which cannot be challenged by a democracy due to the nature of a Dictatorship. Hence, a democracy is either suppressed or non-existent under socialist law due to the nature of Communist rule, which is the official reason why a journalist can be rounded up by the police and never heard of again within a socialist law system, because the system aims to protect the interests of the party, rather than freedom of information.

So, getting back to the question at hand as to where does moral law derive from, the choice is made simple. Either moral law derives from potential truths that are established before a jury in criminal cases under the common law, or, they must derive from socialist law that attempts to cater to a system of equality, whilst disqualifying a democracy in turn. So, for this reason, moral law should derive from the common law, which in turn, derives itself from the Biblical principles of Judeo-Christianity in that a verdict has been reached as to whether man was created or not. Biblical creation as a legal standard is in accordance with the common law, and the common law is in place for the benefit of an individual's protection within a legal system.

This means that a system of morality is required in order to set a legal precedent, or status quo, for moral laws that are to be weighed in accordance with that which is just. So, the balance between that which is just, and that which is not, derives from a system of morality that is by definition, universal, as well as Biblical for the benefit of the people, and their protection under the law, rather than to exploit the individual on the basis of property. Morals are by definition personal, while morality is by definition universal, otherwise, there would be no universal definition to define corruption with, as well as unethical conduct. And it is a universal standard concerning moral law that defining a person as the property of the State, is by definition, immoral, because this type of system results in the abolition of private property, which happens to be the main problem with Communism as an anti-religious political system.

A religion is required when interpreting morality, which cannot derive itself from a secular interpretation of the law without creating a new religion in turn. The Holy Bible declares the judgements of God, which sets a moral standard by which the people and the courts must follow under the common law, because the common law derives from previously settled cases recorded in the Scriptures. So, for this reason, Biblical creation is by definition a legal standard that is universal in its interpretation, while a secular standard is to act as a neutral standard so that a democracy can be heard, which cannot be in conflict with Biblical morality without bringing basic public morals into question before the law. Thus, moral law derives from the Holy Bible, as well as the common law for the benefit of the people in regards to public morals, public safety, and common decency.

A system of justice that caters to a democracy will be defined as a fair system of law, while any system of law that denies a democracy will be defined as unjust due to total governance by the State's administration, or by a crowned authority. This means that we as created human beings owe our human freedom to the Creator, because it is the Creator who is defined as universal on the basis of morality, which sets a legal precedent for a moral law to be made fair by the people in accordance with a moral precedent, such as Biblical morality. The universal law of human equality, as set forth by the United Nations, derives itself from the practice of a democracy, because the U.N acts as an international administration that is interdependent on votes that derive from representatives of different nations or backgrounds in order to maintain a system of law that acts as a legal standard by which the nations must follow. And though international law is not a common law system, the principles by which the legal standard has occurred derives from the redress of public grievances, which is a common law practice, rather than a socialist one.

Morality is defined by a system of law that is interpreted as universal in order to establish a principle or truth as universal in its interpretation. Biblical morality is a universal system of moral law for the purpose of establishing a universal system of truth, such as the law of equality, which is defined as true in order to have a system of equal justice. The term, justice, is interchangeable with the word, fair, or the word, decision, in that a fair decision is considered as just with the word, justice, acting as a verb for the legal term, just.

So, that which is just is also that which is fair, and it is for the purpose of order within society that laws are required, which exists as a rule or commandment. The purpose of rules is to act as a standard for a typical system, which in turn, sets the parameters for a systems operation, whether it be a legal system, or a thermodynamic system, the principle remains the same due to the presence of rules. While a commandment is where rules derive from in that an order has been given, which is the only causality there is for both a legal system and a thermodynamic system that is by definition, orderly. And it is for the purpose of law and order that morality exists so that a fair system of justice is by definition efficient, while physical laws are for sustaining the system of the universe that God has created.

According to the Gospel of Ephesians 2:14-18 we read that: "For He Himself is our peace, who has made the two groups one (gentile and Jew) and has destroyed the barrier, the dividing wall of hostility, by setting aside in His flesh the law with its commands and regulations. His purpose was to create in Himself one new humanity out of the two, thus making peace, and in one body to reconcile both of them to God through the cross, by which He put to death their hostility. He came and preached peace to you who were far away and peace to those who were near. For through Him we both have access to the Father by one Spirit." (End of quote). So, from the Scriptures we find that the Levitical law has been placed aside in order to cater for human rights and equality, which is a cardinal principle of the New Testament.

But, from the Scriptures according to the Gospel of 1 Timothy 8-11 we read that: "We know that the law is good if one uses it properly. We also know that the law is made not for the righteous, but for lawbreakers and rebels, the ungodly and sinful, the unholy and irreligious, for those who kill their fathers or mothers, for murderers, for the sexually immoral, for those practicing homosexuality, for slave traders, and liars, and perjurers, and for whatever else is contrary to the sound doctrine that conforms to the Gospel concerning the glory of the blessed God, which He entrusted to me." (End of quote). So, from the Scriptures we find that the purpose of law and order is to act as a measure of justice against the lawless, so that justice may preside in the form of moral law that is based on a universal system of morality. And it is for this reason among others that a universal Creator God is a requirement when interpreting the law, because morality will always be present when establishing a system or rule.

The Universal Declaration of Human Rights and Equality (UDHR) has derived its definition of a human being from the United States Declaration of Independence and their Constitution due to the use of the Biblical term, conscience, to define a person as distinct from the animals. The UDHR has defined freedom of conscience as the most basic and sacred of all rights, because this liberty is essential for all other liberties, including the right to vote, and is therefore the most important liberty to protect within a democracy.

While any action by the United States government that attempts to remove the basic rights of the people in order to grant privileges to a minority of people who are denying the lawful interpretation of the human conscience, is a crime against humanity on the basis of morality, because all legislative powers are to recognize the law of human equality regardless of any theory that might arise for the purpose of equal rights, which is a moral obligation, as well as a legal one. And by all rights, there are no protections under international law for an individual who wishes to define themself, or others, as an animal under a scientific theory for reasons relating to a moral obligation by the law to uphold the virtues of human rights and equality.

So, for this reason, we are to guard ourselves against the evolutionary theory which attempts to define man as a lower animal without due regard for the human conscience, and the laws that protect our humanity. All human beings are to be regarded as persons before the law regardless of any theory that might arise for the benefit of an individual's protection within the system. While any attempt to redefine the human being as an animal before the law is equal to a human rights violation under international agreement.

The definition of what a natural person is, as from law, has been defined as being an individual human being who is endowed with the ability to reason from their conscience, and thereby has the capacity to take on a legal obligation, which includes acknowledging the inalienable right of others to be defined as a created human being with a human ancestry. The proper legal definition of what a person is under international law has been defined by the endowed human conscience, which is a theological term from the Holy Bible, rather than a biological term from the pseudo-scientific practice of Linnaean taxonomy and evolutionary phylogeny. According to international law, if you are without a conscience, then you are not a human being, but only an animal or thing before the law due to the legal definition of property.

An animal has been legally defined as property by the law, and no legal obligations can be imposed upon them at any time due to their lack of conscience, and owners are fully responsible for their care. So, because slavery is unlawful, as it deprives a person of their human equality, it will mean that there is no legal obligation for any individual to regard themself, or others, as being from an animal via a supposed evolutionary ancestry due to the legal definition of property. And because nature is also defined as property by the law, it will mean that mankind could not have derived from nature, otherwise, man is by definition the property of the State, which forms the basis for socialist law or Communist law.

Any argument that attempts to equate mankind with the animal kingdom in order to espouse some form of freedom for the animals will inadvertently define man as an animal, and therefore, property. Animals are free according to their own abilities, and we are not to enslave them, nor torture them, which is the reason why evolution, as a theory in practice, must be overruled from the premise of law in order for an animal's welfare to be protected by the law, as well as their identity, because most of the unspoken crimes occur within laboratories that are conducting inhumane experiments on animals in order to manipulate a virus.

The evolutionary theory assumes that mankind and the animals have derived from a bacteria or virus, which is the very thing that robs the animals, and mankind, of their true identity, as well as creating harmful viruses through human animal cloning techniques. If evolutionary science continues to try and merge human beings with the animals through cloning techniques, then mankind will one day be extinct due to the domination of animal hereditaries within the overall population of mankind.

Mankind is unique within the world, because man has been endowed with conscience, which is the basis for human freedom according to our inalienable rights, which derive from freedom of conscience. While an animal is without a sufficient level of conscience to decide right from wrong, so no legal obligation can be placed upon them as they are unaware of its moral implications. And this will stand as legal proof that the human conscience is unique as opposed to consciousness, and this also explains why proof of conscience is a requirement before the law in order to make a case or enter a plea, because in order to receive a conviction of truth, then you must first have a conscience.

There are a number of rules and laws that forbid animals from being members of mankind in order to sustain the peace within society. For example: It is a law that animals cannot travel with you on an aeroplane when travelling overseas, which is not a violation of an animals welfare, or their basic rights, but rather, it is for their own protection, and for the safety of others. Most public domains and establishments forbid the entrance of animals onto the premise, which is not a violation of an animals welfare, or their basic rights, because animals are excluded from being members of a legal system.

Animals are thereby exempt from obeying the law, and are treated as interdependent by the inclusion of certain rights, such as the Animal Welfare Act, as well as being symbiotic. Thus, laws in society that apply to human beings do not apply to the animals in any way whatsoever, which is in the best interests of the animals and their safety. But the one law that is universal in its interpretation, is the law regarding murder. If an animal kills a human being, then the animal is to be put to death, not as an act of retaliation, but as an act of preventative intervention. And yes, these examples are indeed ironic for the purpose of explaining the obvious to the moronic who have denied their humanity on the basis of the evolutionary theory.

So, in order to enter a legal society based on human rights and equality, then an endowed conscience is required, while a degree in science is not a requirement under the universal law of human equality. Human equality is not an evolutionary ideal, nor is human equality an animal instinct, because human equality is not defined by our actions, nor by the animal kingdom, but by the existence of the endowed human conscience, which is self-evident and self-aware. The Biblical definition for human equality is best described from the Holy Bible according to the Gospel of Philippians 2:5-8 where Jesus Himself is defined as being equal with both God and man, thereby setting the moral standard for human rights and equality under God the Creator.

*Quotation: ———————————————
Philippians 2:5-8
Equality in Christ:
In your relationships with one another, have the same mindset as Christ Jesus; Who, being in very nature God, did not consider equality with God something to be used to His own advantage, but rather, He made Himself nothing by taking the very nature of a servant, being made in human likeness. And being found in appearance as a man, He humbled Himself by becoming obedient to death; Even death upon a cross. - Source: The Holy Bible.

This passage from Scripture is the most fundamental basis for human rights and equality whereby God has established human equality as universal, and as just, for the benefit of all living creatures great and small, because mankind is endowed with conscience the same as every animal is endowed according to their own abilities, giving all life purpose and meaning. Human equality is not just a theoretical concept, but a self-evident reality instead, which is incontestable and not-without-standing from a legal premise under international law for the purpose of equal rights, which does not apply to the animals for the benefit of their welfare.

So, the right to be defined as a created human being is according to the endowed human conscience, which experiences guilt in regards to one's own actions due to the existence of morality, which cannot be justified by nature, because nature is unaware of morality. Any theory that attempts to define morality as having derived from the animals, will in turn, lead to lawlessness, because laws are better structured around theological principles, rather than animal behaviours. Being human is a God given right to those who are descended from Adam and Eve. The evidence for Adam and Eve's existence derives from instructional systems, such as DNA RNA transcription. DNA RNA transcription is a copying process, and the rule with any copying process is that each successive copy must derive from an original copy, which not only explains diversification, but also, this principle explains variation within a kind.

While the privilege of being a human boils down to one of compassion, because not only does the human conscience desire compassion, but also, the human conscience is better expressed through compassion, which is applicable to creative arts, science, industry, and even politics, because a compassionate leader is also a considerate leader. Human compassion is not a human weakness, but a human strength instead, because the ability to judge clearly derives from compassion, rather than rage.

According to the founder of the evolutionary theory, Charles Darwin, human compassion is a human weakness on the basis of survival of the fittest, which is the philosophical basis for Social Darwinism, evolutionary eugenics, and scientific racism. If human equality is to be a benefit to mankind, then a universal system of morality must exist, which in turn, forms the basis of law and order so that we each have security of property, and security of person before the law, because without a universal system of morality, then laws will enslave us, rather than free us as individuals.

So, morality is by definition universal on the basis that all human beings have been endowed with conscience by their Creator in order to understand a moral obligation, but if one denies the existence of their conscience, or morality, then they cannot be reasoned with as an individual, which is the basis for nihilism, rather than human freedom. Human equality means many things to many people; To some, it means gender equality, while to others, it means social equality. But if either one is to be defined, then a universal definition of person is required, because it is the proper definition of person that defines your basic rights, rather than your gender or nationality.

Without a universal definition of what a person is, then there can be no equality, and this is why the evolutionary theory is so dangerous to mankind as a whole, because it is the theory of evolution that attempts to challenge the lawful definition of person to being that of a lower animal, which is a crime against humanity on the basis of equality. So, because a person is defined as distinct from the animals according to their God given conscience, it will mean that freedom of conscience constitutes as the basis for human freedom, so that any attack against the existence of God the Creator, as defined by Biblical theology under the common law, is thereby an attack on human freedom and self-governance.

Without the correct premise for freedom of conscience to be interpreted by, then there can be no official explanation for the human conscience apart from nature. And this is the very reason why the theory of evolution constitutes as a danger to any society that is based on human rights and equality, because it is the theory of evolution that is in direct opposition to the universal law of human equality by denying the correct definition of what a person is from the viewpoint of a theory.

So, as we progress into the future, it will be the Biblical definition of man that will sustain us as free individuals under God, rather than secular science, because it is Biblical morality that defines what is ethical in terms of a legal standard, rather than scientific theory. So, in order to be consistent when addressing human rights and equality, then the Biblical definition of man must be the higher standard, because it is the Biblical definition of man that is consistent with international human rights legislation, rather than the theory of evolution, which is the official basis for human slavery under the evolutionary definition of man.

Any theory that attempts to define a person as an animal, will in turn, destroy the universal principles for human freedom and human equality, because human freedom derives from the Biblical interpretation of conscience for the benefit of the people to live by freely with in accordance with the universal law of human equality. So, for this reason, the theory of evolution must be overruled from the premise of law, because without the universal definition for what a human is, as from the Holy Bible, then human freedom will progress into human slavery with the consent of the law.

*Quotation: ————————————————————
"The French Revolution gave rise to ideas which led beyond the ideas of the entire old world order. The revolutionary movement that began in 1789 gave rise to the Communist idea which Babeuf's friend Buonarroti re-introduced in France after the Revolution of 1830. This idea, consistently developed, is the idea of the New World Order. Both for the production on a mass scale of this Communist consciousness, and for the success of the cause itself; The alteration of men on a mass scale is necessary; An alteration which can only take place in a practical movement, a revolution. This revolution is necessary, therefore, not only because the ruling class cannot be overthrown in any other way, but also, because the class overthrowing it can only in a revolution succeed in ridding itself of all the muck of ages, and become fitted to found society anew. The social revolution cannot draw its poetry from the past, but only from the future. It cannot begin with itself before it has stripped itself of all superstitions concerning the past." - Karl Marx, founder of Communism. Source: The Eighteenth Brumaire of Louis Bonaparte. (Documented in 1852).

There have been many revolutions throughout modern history that have shaped the political views of today's world, such as the Christian learning revolution in England, or the American revolution against slavery. But the one form of revolution that must be challenged is Communist revolution, because Communist revolution always begins with total anarchy in order to undermine the process of law and order, thereby avoiding criminalization, and then onto fascism and total governance as we've seen with the Communist revolutions in both Russia and China.

So, for this reason, any call to a global revolution, is by definition, a call to fascism, because in order to have a global revolution, then the present state of affairs must be opposed, which in turn, will result in global anarchy and lawlessness. The present state of affairs within geopolitics is consistent with a former revolution that has already occurred, such as the anti-slavery revolution that began in America with the proclamation of emancipation, and the Christian learning revolution in England that gave rise to systems science and systems thinking in accordance with Newtonian and Baconian creation science.

Any new revolution that opposes the previous will automatically result in a return to slavery, which happens to be the main problem with the current scientific revolution by evolutionists who wish to challenge the lawful interpretation of human equality by citing man as a lower animal. The evolutionary theory is used as a weapon by certain members of society to deny the Biblical definition of man in order to be freed from rules, when nothing will enslave mankind faster than the evolutionary definition of man, because it is the evolutionary definition of man that forms the current philosophical basis for human slavery by defining man as a lower animal.

Rules exist because morality exists, and morality exists because the conscience exists, which cannot be refuted by any observation, because human beings will engage a problem if the moral cause is seen as sufficient. This means that any attempt to invent a rule in order to deny morality, or the human conscience, constitutes as a form of morality from a source of conscience, because if morality or the human conscience does not exist on the basis of a rule, then a rule has been made universal, which automatically implies morality is universal on the basis of a universal rule.

So, in order for our current system of justice to be preserved under the common law, then the previous revolution must not be overtaken, because it was the previous revolution that led to the creation of the Universal Declaration of Human Rights and Equality, which ultimately defeated the evolutionary definition of man by defining a person as a created human being on the basis of conscience and reason. Communist revolution is the greatest threat to peace and stability in the world today, because it is so pervasive that it goes unchallenged, when the end result of Communist revolution cannot be overlooked at any point in time due to the nature of socialist law. Communist revolution defines itself as being Scientific Atheism, whereby inalienable rights do not exist, and where all theological definitions are dismissed as "superstitious" regardless of their merit.

Communist revolution involves the use of multiple minority groups who challenge basic public morals through protests on the street, thereby bringing the process of law and order into question by demanding more rights. Minority groups such as: the gay rights movement, the BLM movement, or the New Atheist movement are by definition a Communist front that must not be allowed to interfere with the functions of government in order for morality and law to be sustained under a Biblical standard for the benefit of an individual's protection within the system.

The Black Lives Matter movement, or Black Liberation Movement, derives its name from the Black Liberation Military or Black Liberation Army that received aid from Communist practitioners in an attempt to destabilise the government of the United States, and is heavily engaged in the revolutionary principles of Marxism. And the reason why the United States has been targeted by BLM, is because the United States has led the world in human rights and equality by the interpretation of inalienable rights as having derived from the Creator God of Genesis, because if there is one thing that is not inalienable, nor a right, then it is racism.

The BLM movement is by definition a racial movement, and is thereby race obsessed, which is by definition a racial motivation, and is thereby a racist movement. The Black Liberation Movement is thereby instep with the societal practice of Social Darwinism, whereby a racial superiority complex has taken over their minds on the basis of evolution and survival of the fittest. While the gay rights movement is by definition a Communist front on the basis that they have the full support of New Atheism. New Atheism is a leading Communist front on the basis that New Atheism is defined by academics as "Scientific Atheism" and is therefore, Communist.

The global threat of Communist revolution cannot be overlooked, nor under estimated due to the subtle nature and encroachment of Communist influence and indoctrination within society. Marxism has openly infiltrated the universities of almost every nation with a large portion of professors engaging in unsafe societal practices that are designed to deceive, rather than educate. Richard Dawkins who was the former professor for public understanding of evolution from Oxford University is a leading member of the New Atheist movement and is thereby, Communist, which is not debatable due to the academic definition of Scientific Atheism.

Scientific Atheism promotes the evolutionary theory, as well as Marxism, in order to promote atheism, rather than the scientific method that was first set out by Sir Francis Bacon and Sir Isaac Newton. Darwin's theory of evolution was to Karl Marx a method of reasoning that could explain atheism. Atheists are thereby vulnerable to Communist influence from a scientific premise whether they realise it or not, because the entire basis for Communist revolution, is scientific revolution among the laity involving a return to the philosophical Enlightenment. The philosophical Enlightenment was a leading factor that led to the creation of Communist socialist law whereby science was to replace faith. Yet, by all rights, a return to the philosophical Enlightenment within society would lead to a scientific revolution that has already failed in its attempts to persuade international law to include the evolutionary definition of man.

New Atheists will argue that the United States separation of Church and State was the direct result of Enlightenment philosophy, because the Enlightenment philosophy also involves the separation of Church and State. Yet the Enlightenment philosophy of the separation of Church and State involves the abolition of all religion, and is thereby lacking a system of morality that can be defined as universal, which is entirely due to the nature of atheism. New Atheism argues that there is no universal basis for morality to exist, which in turn, gives the atheist a sense of freedom by the abolition of rules. But, if there is one thing that leads to human slavery, then it is the adoption of rules that simply do not apply, which is why defining morality as non-existent constitutes as a rule in itself, and is thereby lacking in common sense, because, if morality is not universal on the basis of a rule, then the atheist has thereby made a universal rule, which he cannot know is true in the previous without contradicting himself in the following.

So, for this reason, it is Biblical morality that requires protection before the law in order that we should be self-governed under a universal system of morality, because without a system of morality that is universal in its interpretation, then inalienable entitlements cannot be defined as universal. Morality and law are forever intertwined, and neither one can be interpreted on its own, which is why atheism from Marxism and Communism has utterly failed in its interpretation of the law, because atheism is without a universal system of morality due to the lack of a religion. So, the separation of Church and State by the United States took a different approach to that of the philosophical Enlightenment by the inclusion of freedom of conscience, belief, and religion, which is in opposition to New Atheism, Scientific Atheism, and Marxism.

Government corruption is thereby measured by a system of morality and moral law, rather than by the legislator, because if the legislator is not kept in check, then the end result is human slavery with the consent of the law due to the adoption of rules that simply do not apply to our everyday life. If our current system of common law is to carry on into the future for the benefit of our protection as individuals, then the scientific revolution by Communism must be prohibited from lobbying to government, which includes the New Atheist movement, because we have already had a peaceful scientific revolution that began in the early 17th century by Sir Francis Bacon, and then later with Sir Isaac Newton. And we have also seen the injustices caused by the evolutionary theory in practice from the viewpoint of Social Darwinism, Linnaean taxonomy, and evolutionary eugenics, which openly opposes the safety of mankind by the teaching that man is animal.

*Quotation: ────────────────────────────

"I have presented principles of philosophy that are not, however, philosophical but strictly mathematical, that is, those on which the study of philosophy can be based. These principles are the laws and conditions of motions and of forces, which especially relate to philosophy. Gravity explains the motions of the planets, but it cannot explain who sets the planets in motion. All material things seem to have been composed of the hard and solid particles variously associated with the first creation by the counsel of an intelligent Agent. For it became Him who created them to set them in order, and if He did so, it is unphilosophical to seek for any other origin of the world, or to pretend that it might arise out of a chaos by the mere laws of nature." - Sir Isaac Newton. Source: The Principia, Mathematical

Principles of Natural Philosophy. (Documented July 5, 1687).

If modern science is to be viewed as the saving grace for all of mankind, then we will enslave ourselves. First to a machine which acts as a mechanism for the creation of debt, and then to poverty due to the creation of interest, because the practice of private enterprise by modern science is not about freeing the individual through information and technology, but rather, to enslave the individual to a device for the purpose of profiteering from the public. Science is commonly viewed as the saving grace for all of mankind, especially by those who have a fanciful view of science and the technology it brings.

But in reality, science will one day destroy humanity, because we are all dependent upon the technology that science provides, so we are thereby dependent upon the security it brings, which means that our independence is entirely subject to the providers of wealth and technology, who in turn, cannot be trusted with our future. Almost every household with a power point has a computer with internet access, and our entire global economy has progressively moved online in the form of digital currency. While the increased need for cyber security is the very thing that is leading humanity into an Orwellian State, whereby each person is continually monitored through technological surveillance and screening processes. Human freedom cannot be measured by the progression of wealth and technology, because wealth will always be concentrated into the hands of a few through the advancement of technology, which does lead to human slavery by the creation of debt.

*Quotation: ———————————————————————
The Australian Tax Office (ATO) was from this original Freedom of Information Act request, that the Income Tax Research Centre (ITR) was eventually able to identify that the ATO was never legally formed, and therefore, has been illegally eliciting taxes since its formation. The ITR takes the view that income tax laws in the country of Australia are illegal on the grounds that income tax is voluntary. - Source: The Australian Taxation Office - ATO Corruption. (Documented by the ATO Online Community Forum).

The Australian Tax Office (ATO), along with the United States' Federal Income Revenue Service (IRS) is an illegal Act following the creation of the Federal Reserve Act that brought direct taxation in the form of income tax into law. Thus, the Federal Reserve system must be audited by the Treasury Department in relation to profiteering from the public, because the circulation of money is controlled by the Federal Reserve with the power to print or not to print, which is an authority that belongs with the Treasury Department so that the private interest over the printing of money is removed. The creation of debt by the issuing of currency from a central bank results in a form of bond slavery, whereby an individual is born into debt due to compounding interest on government loans with the promise to repay using income tax, which was unconstitutional within Australia and the United States before the Federal Reserve Act began to take effect.

Each note that is printed by the Federal Reserve within a nation must be loaned into existence by the Fed, which means that the creation of money incurs a penalty upon the borrower, which happens to be the government and private banks who must borrow from the Fed in order to circulate money, which is why the Fed sets the interest rates. This means that the government, as well as banks, are required to repay the Fed using interest on loans, as well as income tax, in order to maintain a line of credit from the Fed. In the year 2020 alone, the Federal Reserve within the United States printed approximately 3.3 trillion U.S dollars, which equates to one-fifth of all U.S dollars in circulation in that same year. According to the Federal Reserve, the average interest rate set by the Fed is roughly 5.33%.

This means that on average, the United States Federal Reserve system grossed approximately $17,589,000,000 in taxable revenue. And yes, printing money does incur a cost, which must be offset by having an interest rate payable. However, the interest owing is also taxable by definition of the fact that the Fed is profiteering from the interest earned the same as any other bank that charges interest on loans. So, because the Federal Reserve is excluded from paying corporate income tax, it will mean that the Federal Reserve is acting as sovereign in accordance with international law, while at the same time, placing a substantial debt upon the government of a nation in the form of interest payable. This means that the sovereignty of the Fed is overruling the sovereignty of the government in the same sense that the government's sovereignty is overruling the sovereignty of the people by the collection of income tax.

When applying for a job, a tax declaration is required to be filled out by the individual who is making the application for the position, and one of the questions that is compulsory to answer, is whether you are a citizen for tax purposes or not. And you must answer yes on the form unless you are a Visa worker, charity worker, or unless you have filed a UCC501C3 indemnity agreement with Washington D.C in order to rescind your birth certificate, which is how a person becomes a sovereign citizen legally. And this is evidence that each person with a registered birth certificate is the property of the State for financial reasons, because the State is entirely dependent on the revenue you create. And an example of a prominent sovereign would be the royal family of England, because they have declared their sovereignty legally with Washington D.C, and they enjoy all of the same benefits as any other sovereign would.

So, the majority of mankind has already been enslaved under a complex financial scheme that equates an individual as the property of the State for revenue purposes. In the United States, most citizens have never actually obtained their original birth certificate, because what they possess is a copy instead, the same as most citizens who own a home have no original copy of the title deeds to their property. Furthermore, an original birth certificate has a registration number on it issued on the front of the certificate for reasons relating to collateral for government bonds on the open stock exchange.

So, because a person must be registered with the government in order to be classed as a naturalized citizen, it will mean that the government has full authority over an individual through legislative powers, which is a violation of a person's sovereignty under United States Constitutional law, because any Legislative Act that interferes with the original Constitution will deprive a person of their just liberties, such as the inalienable right to human sovereignty, and human independence thereby. The original birth or naturalization record for every United States citizen is held within Washington D.C's national archive, and the property and assets of every U.S citizen is pledged as collateral for the national debt, which is why the Internal Revenue Service (IRS) can confiscate a person's private property. Every citizen is given a registration number on their birth certificate which is used as collateral by the United States government in order to create government bonds.

So, each time a new citizen is born, the government takes out a loan from the Fed with the promise to repay using a person's income tax. Each live birth is reported to have a collateral value at $650,000 - $750,000 in terms of promissory notes. Hence the saying: "We are owned by the Fed." The only way possible for this Ponzi scheme to end, is for the government of a nation to authorize the Treasury Department to audit the Fed, otherwise, the Fed will remain as autonomous. There are hundreds of thousands of sovereign citizens living in the United States of America who own the title deeds to their land in allodium; Meaning, outright.

So, concerning a sovereign citizen, the government does not have a financial interest on them due to the nature of their birth status which they have legally declared as sovereign through a legally binding indemnity agreement that involves rescinding your birth certificate. Because of this legal status, sovereign citizens do not need to pay property tax, education tax, real estate tax, goods and services tax, social security tax, Federal income tax, State income tax, etc, etc...

Only the powers granted to the Federal government in the said Constitution can define the laws that a sovereign citizen must live by, which does not include any Legislative Act or further Amendments that protect the private interests of a corporation, such as Corporate D.C. Sovereign citizens within the United States have been under constant attack by the mainstream media implying that sovereign citizens are enemies of the State for refusing to pay income tax under the 16th Amendment, whilst at the same time, promoting the sovereignty of the British Royal family. Human freedom is not a direct product of ourselves, but as an indirect product of the human spirit, because it is the human spirit that yearns to be free.

Yet humanity has never been more enslaved than what it is today by the creation of the Fed, and with the increased need for security with every technological innovation we make. If the United States government continues to deny the Biblical account in favour of endorsing the evolutionary theory, then the human spirit will one day be crushed, because if humanity is to put their faith in science and technology, then our trust lies with the providers of that technology, who in turn, cannot be trusted with our future, because our future belongs to ourselves, rather than the technology they provide.

ARTICLE 2

The Law of Liberty

According to Oxford Languages, the definition of freedom is defined as: 1)
"The power or right to act, speak, or think as one wants." 2) "The state of
not being imprisoned or enslaved. Similar: liberty." This designation of the
term, freedom, is in relation to the term, liberty, while the term, liberty is
also in relation to the term, liberation, where a person has been freed from
some form of subjugation. The Constitution of a nation's government has

properly been described as "the birth certificate of a nation," and thereby declares the destiny of that nation in the form of a blessing or curse. So, for the purpose of this article I will discuss the United States Constitution, their Declaration of Independence, and the Holy Bible in order to outline the correct interpretation of human liberty as a common law precedent, or legal standard by which the Commonwealth system has derived.

A Constitution provides the basic groundwork for the rules that a government must follow, thereby setting the limitations of government and of liberty. A Constitution is the fundamental law of a nation for both government and civil liberties that are legally binding within every State. As used in the United States Constitution, liberty means freedom from arbitrary and unreasonable restraint upon an individual, such as arbitrary and unreasonable search and seizures. Freedom from restraint not only refers to physical restraint, but also, the freedom to act according to one's own will. So, because the term freedom is according to one's freewill, and because a Constitution outlines the limitation of liberties, it will mean that freewill is limited by liberty.

For example: Freedom of speech will always be in accordance with one's own freewill, which is without restriction except on the basis of public morals and common decency, which is not to shunned upon as a limitation of speech, but as a protection of free speech instead. Thus, a person is liable when making a racist statement, because racism is unlawful, as well as unconstitutional. The universal law of human equality outlines the limitations of human speech and human freedoms in accordance with a legally binding and immutable declaration of human freedom. The universal law of human equality sets the limitations of speech, as well as human actions that are governed by a code of ethics. And though a person may include a racist verdict within their speech or actions, there is no law to allow this as a freedom or liberty.

So, because a person is at liberty to act and say according to whatever they will, it will mean that a person is also liable according to whatever they do, which is self-explanatory. This means that any argument against the existence of the Creator as being a limitation upon a person's liberty is without merit or sufficient cause, because in order to be liberated from subjugation, then you must first be defined as a created human being, which forms the basis for the rights of conscience. If the human conscience was to come from the animals, then man is thereby the property of the State, because both nature, and the animals, are legally defined as property.

But if your conscience was endowed to you by your Creator, then you are thereby independent of the State in terms of ownership, and are therefore, sovereign. And it is for this reason that a human being is to be liberated by the Gospel message of hope and salvation, because it is our hope that liberates the mind and body, and it is salvation that liberates the soul, which is the essence of creativity and freedom of ideas. The idea that man is without a soul derives from the idea that man is animal, which is propagated from the public education system with the consent of the law due to the adoption of the evolutionary theory from a secular premise. This means that the evolutionary theory is a form of subjugation upon the human mind, because when a person feels convinced that they have derived from the animals, they can no longer be reasoned with as an individual.

According to the United States Supreme Court, the evolutionary theory is incontestable; Meaning self-evident. But because evolution is defined as a theory, it will mean that evolution cannot be both incontestable, as well as self-evident, because a theory will always be subject to a cross examination before the law. This means that the United States Supreme Court has taken the liberty to define man as animal without due respect for the universal definition of man as a created human being, and has thereby subjugated the people with a limitation of liberty that forbids the individual from learning about their Creator, as from law. This limitation of liberty was decided arbitrarily on the basis that it was not decided upon by the people in accordance with due process and the right to vote.

> *Quotation: ————————————————
> "Liberty may be endangered by the abuse of liberty, but also by the abuse of power." - James Madison, founding father of the United States Constitution. Source: The Federalist, chapter 4, document 27. (Documented March 1, 1788).

The evolutionary theory is by definition a racial theory, because the theory includes a racial hierarchy for mankind that divides humanity on the basis of theory. When according to international law, no human being can be defined as having derived from any other ancestry apart from human ancestry for reasons relating to the correct interpretation of human rights and equality. This means that the universal definition of man as a created human being is designed to liberate the individual, rather than to subjugate. While any racial hierarchy of less evolved to more evolved will suppress the group who is deemed less evolved, which is a form of racial subjugation.

A racist opinion should always be invalidated on the basis of human rights and equality, so that any racial argument, either in favour of one ethnic group or against, should be defined as a reproach against the principles of liberty itself. And it is for this reason that the theory of evolution is a reproach to human liberty by definition of the fact that evolution is a racial theory that calls our basic freedoms into question, such as freedom of conscience. Freedom of conscience is a religious liberty that can be exercised freely without restraint unless a person exercising this liberty attempts to harm another member of society unfairly without proper due course.

The due course of law, (also known as due process) refers to the fair and just legal proceedings that protect the people's rights. This includes giving notice, as well as opportunity for a fair hearing before a court of law. And it is for this reason that the theory of evolution must be overruled from the premise of law, because it is the theory of evolution that attempts to undermine the law of equality by bringing the lawful definition of person into question, which automatically implies a burden of proof.

A person who is accused of a crime is presumed innocent until found guilty by due course. So, the burden of proof rests on the prosecutor, rather than the defendant. This means that the accused doesn't have to prove anything, and if the prosecutor doesn't meet the standard of proof, then the presumption that the accused is innocent legally stands. Hence the legal phrase: Innocent until proven guilty. Thus, a legal standard is in place for the benefit of an individual's protection within the system, rather than to protect a given theory in science or law. And it is Biblical creation that acts as a legal standard that is just in its interpretation by the correct interpretation of inalienable. The people vs the High Courts (which is a case that I have proposed for the purpose of this article) defines the burden of proof resting with the accusations and charges that I have laid against the High Court for reasons relating to the theory of evolution in practice and observance as legally mandatory within the public education system.

The purpose of this proposed case is for defending the people's just liberties, because it is the United States Supreme Court that is openly defending the theory of evolution as a legal standard, rather than Biblical creation. The argument between Biblical creation and the evolutionary theory is not only a scientific argument, but also, it is a moral one as well, because it is the people's liberty that is at stake here due to a pseudo-definition of man that is being propagated from the public education system with the consent of the law, which requires a valid explanation in front of a jury before a verdict can be reached in order that due course should be fulfilled by the law.

But, because the introduction of the evolutionary theory into the practice of law and education was decided upon by a Supreme Court judge, and the State's board of education, rather than a referendum by the voting constituency, it will mean that proper due course was excluded from the decision. And if proper due course is excluded from a Supreme Court decision, then the people were excluded from that decision. If proper due course is not met by the Supreme Court, then the people's liberty has been denied, which should only occur in the event that the protection of the people's liberty was required, rather than to protect a pet theory.

This means that when a law is made, it must be for the benefit of the people's protection and their just liberties, rather than being a mechanism to protect a given theory, which is an exploitation of the law, because a theory will always be questionable before the law, while the protection of liberty is by definition, inalienable. However, in this proposed case, I will accept the burden of proof, because I am laying accusations and charges against the Supreme Court of the United States for defending the theory of evolution in despite of the people's just liberty to be defined as a created human being with a human ancestry.

> *Quotation: ——————————————————
> "Let every nation know, whether it wishes us well or ill, that we shall pay any price, bear any burden, meet any hardship, support any friend, oppose any foe to assure the survival and the success of liberty." - John F. Kennedy, 35th president of the United States. Source: The United States Department of State - Office of the Historian. (Documented January 20, 1961).

The people's just liberties are of a higher legal standard of proof than any judicial verdict that excludes the people's vote by a referendum. This means that the protection of civil liberties is of a higher legal standard than protecting a scientific theory, because it is the people's liberty that is at stake here due to the adoption of a rule that places an unnecessary burden of proof upon the people to decide whether a scientific theory is true or not. So, in despite of the people being ill-informed regarding the validity of the evolutionary theory, there is still the matter of due course that allows the people to decide, which cannot be removed by the Supreme Court for reasons relating to a legal standard in place known as due process.

In a quote from the Articles of Confederation written between 1781 and 1789 by George Washington, we read that: "The basis of our political systems is the right of the people to make and to alter their Constitutions of government. But the Constitution which at any time exists, until changed by an explicit and authentic act of the whole people, is sacredly obligatory upon all." (End of Quote).

Under the common law, human beings have the inalienable right to vote as to whether a Constitution should be changed. This means that the Supreme Court decision to grant Constitutional protections to the theory of evolution, along with income tax, should be brought into question by the people, because the people were excluded from the decision. The decision to grant Constitutional protections for the theory of evolution belongs to the people, rather than being a Supreme Court decision alone, because the Constitution is unalterable without the people's vote. The United States Supreme Court decision to grant Constitutional protections to the theory of evolution can be cited by the Supreme Court case of Aguillard v. Edwards, as cited in the quotation below:

*Quotation: ──────────────────────────────

Edwards v. Aguillard, 482 U.S. 578 (1987), was a United States Supreme Court case concerning the constitutionality of teaching creationism. The Court considered a Louisiana law requiring that where evolutionary science was taught in public schools, creation science must also be taught. The constitutionality of the law was successfully challenged in District Court, Aguillard v. Treen, 634 F. Supp. 426

(ED La.1985), and the United States Court of Appeals for the Fifth Circuit affirmed, Aguillard v. Edwards, 765 F.2d 1251 (CA5 1985). The United States Supreme Court ruled that this law violated the Establishment Clause of the First Amendment because the law was specifically intended to advance a particular religion. - Source: Wikipedia Encyclopedia (Edwards v. Aguillard).

The Supreme Court bares no lawful obligation to grant Constitutional protections to any given theory, because a theory will always be questionable under cross examination. This means that the theory of evolution can be cross examined before the law through due process without interference from the Supreme Court. Free education is for the express purpose of developing a society that is based on the practice of law, rather than science. But, if the people are excluded from the practice of law by the removal of due course and due process, then the people's liberty to a fair hearing has been denied, which is a crime against the people in itself on the basis that it is the people's liberty that the law should protect, rather than theory, which is self-explanatory.

The idea that science is an authority over the human being was overruled by international law by the creation of the Universal Declaration of Human Rights and Equality (UDHR) which outlines that the protection of human rights is of a higher legal standard than scientific theory. This United Nations High Court decision was made in opposition to Nazi racial science during the trial at Nuremberg, which gave international law the power of Attorney over the accused in order to oppose a racial science that was being used as an authority over the people's just liberties, which is why the Nazi racial scientists who were tried at Nuremberg received a death penalty under International law.

The UDHR was made in response to the Holocaust, whereby Nazi racial segregation policies led to the exclusion of the Jews on the basis of a racial science that includes the practice of Social Darwinism and the evolutionary theory. Social Darwinism is defined as the theory of evolution in practice from the premise of education and law; Meaning that the evolutionary theory was dismissed during the trial at Nuremberg on the basis that Social Darwinism failed to convince. The correct definition of person by the United Nations High Commission was made under the self-evident pretence that all human beings have been endowed with conscience, which is not defined as an animal hereditary, but as a gift from God on the basis of freedom of conscience, which is a religious liberty, rather than a scientific theory.

The argument by those who hail from the theory of evolution in relation to the failed practice of Social Darwinism by the Nazis, is that Darwin's theory was misused, and was thereby inappropriate to define evolution in terms of a theory. But the problem with this argument is that Social Darwinism continues unabated from the viewpoint of the evolutionary theory in the form of evolutionary eugenics, which is why Social Darwinism, and the evolutionary theory, are forever inseparable due to the debatable practice of evolutionary eugenics. The second aspect of the evolutionary theory concerning Social Darwinism, is the issue of survival of the fittest, which is the philosophical basis for pitting the weak against the strong in order to boost the power of the strong, which is by definition, immoral, for reasons relating to security of person, which does include corporations, small businesses, and legal fictions under the lawful term, person.

According to Oxford Languages, the definition of a cartel is defined as: 1) "An association of manufacturers or suppliers with the purpose of maintaining prices at a high level and restricting competition." 2) "A coalition or cooperative arrangement between political parties intended to promote a mutual interest." (Origin of the word, cartel by Oxford Languages): "Late 19th century: from German Kartell, from French cartel, from Italian cartello, diminutive of carta, from Latin carta. It was originally used to refer to the coalition of the Conservatives and National Liberal parties in Germany (1887), and hence, any political combination; later to denote a trade agreement (early 20th century).

The idea that multinational corporations should be allowed to lobby to government on behalf of the American people is the very thing that leads to a cartel, whereby small businesses are challenged on the basis of Social Darwinism involving a group of corporations that have collaborated together for the purpose of maintaining high prices, such as the pharmaceutical industry, the banking platform, and the scientific establishment. If we are to pit multinational corporations against the small businesses, then we are thereby pitting the wealthy against the poor, which then leads to mass inflation and government corruption by placing a foreign interest on the creation of jobs. And yes, multinational corporations do place an unnecessary burden upon the people by moving jobs offshore in order to maintain high prices with a low investment strategy, simply by competing the borrowing and spending power of the wealthier nations with the labour power of the over populated poorer nations. This political phenomenon is largely due to the practice of Social Darwinism and the Free Trade Agreement, which disguises itself as a means of free trade for the people, whilst expanding the interests of a multinational corporation, such as corporate D.C.

So, in the case that I have proposed here for the purpose of this article, (such as the people vs the High Courts) the burden of proof falls onto the people, because the Supreme Court is acting as a defendant. And the reason that the theory of evolution and the practice of Social Darwinism is being defended by Federal law, is because the Creator is not protected in accordance with Constitutional law that includes the Declaration of Independence, which clearly outlines the Creator as self-evident on the basis of civil rights. So, in this matter, the burden of proof by the people can be exhibited by citing the Declaration of Independence, because it is the Constitutional definition of man that is of a higher legal standard than a Supreme Court decision due to a legal precedent that is legally binding, as well as Constitutionally protected as self-evident.

The United States Constitutional definition of man derives from the Holy Bible, which cannot be dismissed on any legal grounds in order that the Constitutional definition of man should be protected as a lawful instruction, which is not to be debated against from the viewpoint of a theory, nor a science, without incurring the burden of proof in return. The main problem with Darwinian evolution, as a theory, is that Darwinian evolution cannot be empirically based, because Darwinian evolution cannot be empirically verified by an eyewitness account due to the sheer number of supposed evolutionary changes that are said to have occurred over the span of 13.8 billion unobserved years, which means that evolution, as a process, is entirely hypothetical, rather than self-evident.

The entire purpose of the evolutionary theory is for the individual to espouse some form of freedom from rules, which not only applies to scientists and citizens, but also, judges, who have not followed proper due course, and have thereby acted as a fiat authority in despite of the said Constitution, which does include protections for the Declaration of Independence, because it is the Declaration of Independence that further outlines the rights of a democracy in accordance with Constitutional law.

The people's just liberties have thereby been denied on the basis of evolution for three main reasons. First; Because the theory of evolution is now protected under Federal law as incontestable due to a Supreme Court decision that denies the Constitutional definition of man as a created human being, which is a violation of the rights of conscience involving the religious rights of man to learn about their Creator from a responsible source of information, such as a local representative who is responsible for the provision of factual information in accordance with protection of person. Secondly; Because the Supreme Court decision was made by a judicial verdict that excluded a referendum, which is a violation of the people's just liberties involving proper due course.

And thirdly; It is for the purpose of civil rights that systemic racism should be abolished from the premise of law in accordance with United States Federal law under Title VI Section 601 of the Civil Rights Act of 1964 - 78 Statutory (252: 42 U.S.C 2000d), which does not include any Constitutional protections for a racial theory in science to be made mandatory from the State's board of education. So, in order to protect the just liberties of the people in this matter, then a Creator God is required to explained factually through the public education system by the provision of factual material in accordance with the protection of civil rights involving the Biblical definition of man as a created human being with a human ancestry.

The procedure of law and order involving the process of proper due course is mandatory in this case, because it is the people's liberty that is at stake here due to a Supreme Court decision that denies the universal definition of man as a created human being, which is Constitutionally protected as self-evident under the Declaration of Independence. While the theory of evolution is by definition a racial theory that cannot be used in relation to the Constitutional definition of man on the basis that the theory of evolution defines man as a lower animal, and is thereby, unconstitutional.

A legal standard is that which a burden of proof must meet in order to be sustained, and the higher the standard, the more proof that is needed, because it is the people's liberty that is at stake. The creation of the United States Constitution was founded upon Biblical creation as a legal standard by which the burden of proof is to meet. This means that the removal of a Biblical standard for law and order has been superseded by a secular standard which is in opposition to man as a created human being. When it is the legal standard of Biblical creation that is designed to liberate a human being with an acknowledgement of their Creator, and thereby sets the limitations of government to do what is in the best interests of the people, which does not include granting Constitutional protections for a scientific theory that is in opposition to a Biblical standard for law.

This means that the people have been subjugated by a judiciary decision that is secular from its interpretation, which is designed to protect a pet theory, rather than the people's just liberties. A Biblical standard for education and law was the founding and governing principle, upon which, the United States system of government has been built, so that a removal of a Biblical standard for law and education is equal to a form of subjugation and suppression, which means that there is reasonable cause for litigation and Class Action against the United States Supreme Court, which is required in order to liberate the people from a secular standard that denies a person their inalienable right to be defined as a created human being through the public education system.

This dispute between secular science and Biblical creation is not only a scientific dispute, but also, it is a legal one. So, in order to build a case for defending the lawful definition of person, then a correct interpretation of the law is required to be explained factually for the benefit of an individual's protection within the system, rather than to protect a pet theory. No theory in science or law can be defined as self-evident due to the nature of theory, while it is the correct definition of person as a created being that forms the basis for human freedom by the rights of conscience. And this is where the theological dispute between secular science and Biblical creation begins, because secular science is engaged in an open dispute with the lawful definition of conscience, while Biblical creation is the lawful premise to define the human conscience, and human freedom thereby.

Thus, it is the secular standard for law and education that has failed as a mechanism for learning, rather than Biblical creation, so in order to correct the system, then a substitute method is required, which is where systems theory and systems science comes into play as a viable substitution, which is not owing to secular science, but to Biblical creation instead. And the reason why systems science is not owing to secular science, is because a system is by definition rule based, and rules are always inferred, rather than deriving from materials alone. The materialistic philosophy that follows secular science is a heavy ball and chain, rather than a mechanism for human freedom and exploration, because the one thing that leads to subjugation and human slavery, is by the adoption of rules that simply do not apply.

And the one rule that simply does not apply, is the rule that the evolutionary theory cannot be contested before the Supreme Court for reasons relating to a secular standard for public education, when a theory in science or law will always be subject to a cross-examination by definition of the word, theory. And yes, I am fully aware that systems theory is also a theory in both science and law, but the problem here is that the evolutionary theory is receiving protections from the law, which is a violation of due process. The due process of law cannot be denied in this matter, because the people's liberty is at stake here due to a reinterpretation of the law involving the correct definition of person.

The official reason why the theory of evolution cannot be contested before the United States High Courts, is entirely due to the Constitutional definition of a secular government, which is protected by the law. So, in this case, I will not challenge the Constitutional premise of a secular government, because that would go against conscience and reason, but rather, I will challenge the High Court's decision to grant Constitutional protections to a given theory in science in despite of due process, and the people's just liberties involving protection of person. According to the formalities of United States Constitutional law, due process is the conduct of a legal proceeding according to an established principle or procedure that is designed to ensure a fair hearing, which is a cardinal principle of the United States Constitution by the inclusion of equal opportunity.

So, for this reason, equal opportunity between Biblical creation and the evolutionary theory within public education is required in order that protection of person and due process is met by the law. The due process of law involving a fair hearing is required before the High Courts in order that an equality can exist between both parties involved, which happens to be the people verses the High Courts. If the people are excluded from a

Constitutional amendment, then the due process of law has been altered in order to deny the people an interaction with the law. When it is the due process of law that protects the people from an exclusion from the law so that equal opportunity and protection of person is met by the law.

Thus, the United States High Court has acted as a fiat authority in this matter with a dicta that is not infallible. The maxim of the law is governed by the inclusion of equality and due process, which means that equal opportunity is required between both parties involved. The United States Constitution was never created in order to defend a theory in science, nor was the Constitution to be used in order to reject the lawful definition of a Creator in order to protect the establishment clause of a secular government, which is a violation of the rights of conscience involving the free exercise of religion.

This means automatically that a public referendum is required in order that equal opportunity is met by the law through due process before a Constitution can be altered by the forms of government, because the sole purpose of a secular government, is to protect the people from an exclusion from the law with a religious test in place that is designed to dismiss the Creator with an automatic dismissal. So, in this matter, it is the establishment clause of a secular government that has been cited with a secular test in place that is designed to exclude Biblical creation with an automatic dismissal regardless of the people's protection under the law, and their written Constitution that forbids the dismissal of the Creator, as defined by a Biblical standard by the forefathers of America.

Under United States Federal law, the due process of law can be suspended during the course of war in order to deny the enemy the protection of the law. This means that when the United States is at war, civil rights are superseded for reasons relating to national security. And this is also the reason why suspected terrorists at Guantanamo Bay are denied a trial by jury, because they are regarded as enemies of war. The United States has launched a number of wars upon the public and other nations under the guise of human freedom, such as the war on drugs, the war on Islam, and the war on terrorism. So, in this matter, the due process of law can only be dismissed if the United States government is at war with religion for reasons relating to Communism, because the secular standard has been cited as a means of protecting the government and the people's national security on a scientific basis, which is the equivalent of Scientific Atheism in affect due to a scientific and secular standard for law. Thus, the United States government is at war with Biblical creation as a legal standard on the grounds of Communism, rather than differentiating between religious terrorism, and human freedom on a logical basis, which is sufficient cause for reasonable suspicion.

*Quotation:
"Those who would give up essential Liberty to purchase a little temporary safety, deserve neither liberty nor safety." - Benjamin Franklin. Source: A reply to the Governor at the Pennsylvania Assembly. (Documented November 11, 1755).

The temporary removal of civil rights is no longer temporary in the event that has now occurred within the United States, because in order to define human freedom, then freedom of conscience and religion is required to be protected by law in order that protection of person is in place for the benefit of national security. Thus, the war on Islam has led to a new form of government whereby a war on religion is now in full effect, which is a violation of the international treaty by the United Nations that grants universal rights to freedom of religion and belief through the public education system for the express purpose of advancing civil rights. If religion is to be the blame for America's national crisis, then so also is the Constitution, because the Constitution has recognised the rights of conscience as self-evident in terms of a legal standard or precedent, and is Constitutionally protected as the first liberty, upon which, all other liberties stand, including the right to vote through a public referendum.

This means that the United States government no longer requires the voting constituency in relation to this matter concerning the evolutionary theory from public education, because the people's liberty has been denied in order to protect national security, or so they say. According to modern politics and historical accounts, the war on religion is a Communist ideal, rather than a United States Constitutional practice under the common law. So, in order for Communism to succeed in this matter, then the religious rights of man must be denied without proper due course, which means definitively that the theory of evolution, as a legal standard, is a Communist ideal, rather than an American liberty. The argument I have presented in this article in relation to the people vs the High Court is in no way intended to be a "Red Scare" upon the conscience of society, nor is it an attack on the establishment clause of a secular government, but rather, it is a defence in favour of the people's just liberties, and, their national security.

So, in order for the people to regain their just liberties in this matter, then the theory of evolution must be overruled from the premise of law in order for the return of a Biblical standard for public education and law to be made mandatory in favour of the said Constitution, the Bill of Rights, and the Declaration of Independence. The independence of the United States, along with their national security, was first outlined by the Biblical definition of man as sovereign, which forms the basis of human freedom by the lawful interpretation of conscience. This liberty hereby disqualifies the theory of evolution in this matter, because the people's just liberties are to be protected in despite of any theory that might arise for the benefit of the people's protection under the law. And it is the theory of evolution that requires removal in this matter in order for protection of person to be enforced by Federal Law, which does not include any protections for the secular standard for public education so that a Creator can be explained factually to the students for the benefit of a civil society to operate effectively, whereby protection of person is in place for the benefit of the people's just liberties.

In order for freedom of conscience to be exercised by the people as a basic right in this matter, then the people must decide whether evolution is true or not by a public referendum, rather than by allowing a Supreme Court decision to overrule the said Constitution, because any loss of Constitutional liberties will result in an encroachment upon the law, whereby basic freedoms are lost due to a judicial verdict that sets a new legal precedent in despite of the previous. A prior decision in case law sets the legal standard by which the courts must follow under the common law so that a potential truth can be established for future cases. And it is the Declaration of Independence that acts as a legally binding and immutable legal precedent in that a case has already been settled on the basis of a principle or truth that is by definition, self-evident. Such as the case as to whether man was created or not, which has already been settled by the Supreme Court under the United States Declaration of Independence in its second paragraph that defines each person as a created human being who is endowed with certain inalienable rights by their Creator.

> *Quotation: ─────────────────────────
> "The world has never had a good definition of the word liberty, and the American people, just now, are much in want of one. We all declare for liberty, but in using the same word, we do not all mean the same thing." - Abraham Lincoln, 16th president of the United States. Source: Abraham Lincoln's Address at a Sanitary Fair, Baltimore. (Documented April 18, 1864).

The United States Declaration of Independence in its second paragraph states that: "We hold these truths to be self-evident, that all men are created equal, that they are endowed by their Creator with certain unalienable rights, that among these are Life, Liberty and the pursuit of Happiness." From this declaration we find a number of aspects that I will define here very carefully. The first aspect from the declaration states that a verdict has been made official in terms of a legal precedent or standard so that a self-evident truth can be sustained for future cases. The second aspect of this declaration states that all men are created equal, which is further outlined by the rights of conscience, because the Constitutional grounds for human equality has defined each human being as having been endowed with conscience by their Creator in order to liberate a person from subjugation.

The third aspect of this declaration outlines what is inalienable, such as the right to life, liberty, and the pursuit of happiness. The right to life simply means that extrajudicial killings are by definition immoral, and are therefore, unlawful. While liberty is defined as freedom, which is without limitations except in the event that freedom is abused, which thereby incurs a penalty on the basis that a person is liable for their own actions under moral law. And the pursuit of happiness is without limitations by the practice of just liberties, such as the Law of Liberty, which can be summed up by the Fruits of the Spirit, as defined by the Holy Bible from the Gospel of Galatians 5:22-23 which are: "love, joy, peace, long-suffering, gentleness, goodness, faith, meekness, and temperance, against such, there is no law." (End of quote).

So, from this designation in Scripture we find that the Law of Liberty has no limitations on human freedom by the application of virtues that are intended to be just in their interpretation, because these liberties do no harm, and can be exercised freely without limitation. A person may exercise their basic freedoms in accordance with their own will, but it will always be limited by moral law, such as the Law of Liberty, which sets a limitation on human freedom, because freedom is better expressed by a moral teaching that is just in its cause. A human being is at liberty to exercise their basic freedoms at will, and there are no limitations to this freedom, which is why laws can be broken, while the Law of Liberty restricts undue behaviour in the form of a law or statute.

Any action or word that is arbitrarily unfair will cause an offence, which should be limited in terms of a rule or law so that other liberties can be protected, such as just liberties. And it is the Fruits of the Spirit that are defined as just liberties in the sense that they can do no harm, while a racist statement or action may seem practical to some, it is however unreasonable for the sake of others who shall be defined as created human beings regardless of another person's freedoms. So, for this reason, there is a limitation on freedom of speech in the sense that a racist opinion should always be invalidated on the basis of law and order, because law and order is in place to protect our just liberties, rather than a pet theory. This means that undue behaviour is restricted by the lawful protection of liberty that is not to be put into harm's way in order to protect a given theory, because a theory in science will always be questionable, while the right to be defined as a created human being is Constitutionally protected as inalienable.

From the Declaration of Independence, we find that the evolutionary theory is unconstitutional, while Biblical creation is by definition, constitutionally protected as a legal standard that is self-evident, because a person is legally defined as a created human being according to their just liberties that includes the rights of conscience, while the theory of evolution attempts to define man as a lower animal in despite of these just liberties. The Declaration of Independence holds that each person is a created human being who is endowed with certain rights that have been established previously by a legal precedent that derives from Constitutional law. This means that Biblical creation is a legal standard on the grounds that a person is liberated by the knowledge of our Creator, because if you are not a created human being, then you are by definition an animal or thing, which are both defined as property, legally speaking.

Any legal case under the common law that attempts to define mankind as being separate from their Creator, is by definition, unconstitutional, and therefore, unlawful. And the theory of evolution does indeed claim that man is separate from his Creator due to the legal definition of property. If mankind is to be defined as an animal from the theory of evolution, then man is thereby the property of the State, because both nature, and the animals, are legally defined as property. But if mankind has derived from the Creator, then man is thereby independent of the State in terms of ownership, and is therefore, sovereign. So, for this reason, the evolutionary theory is without probable cause in which to argue against Biblical creation as a legal standard before a court of law due to the legal status of nature and the animals that includes the lawful definition of property.

Probable cause, also referred to as reasonable suspicion, is the reasonable grounds to believe that a particular person or group has allegedly committed a crime, especially to justify making a search and seizure or prompting a charge or accusation before the law. And it is for this reason that the evolutionary theory is protected as incontestable by Federal law, because the Supreme Court has ruled that Biblical creation is an offence on the basis of a secular interpretation of the said Constitution. This action by the United States Supreme Court raises reasonable suspicion, because the United States Declaration of Independence is protected by Federal Law, and the Declaration of Independence outlines a self-evident legal precedent that all men are created equal.

This means that Biblical creation is in defence of the people's just liberties, which cannot be taken away by a secular authority on the reasonable grounds that the Declaration of Independence is a self-evident legal precedent that is theological, rather than theoretical. The United States Constitution is to be interpreted by Biblical theology, rather than secular ideology for reasons relating to the religious rights of man that includes the universal and inalienable right to be defined as a created human being who is endowed by their Creator with conscience and with rights. All that is at stake here is our freedom under the law, which cannot be overruled, nor interfered with by a scientific theory without incurring a burden of proof. And it is the people who have suffered the burden of proof for long enough, because the proof that man is a created human being is Constitutionally protected as self-evident under United States Federal Law, as well as universally protected as inalienable, while the evolutionary theory is entirely hypothetical on the basis of theory.

If a judicial decision by the Supreme Court is going to allow the theory of evolution to be protected in despite of a legal precedent that is Constitutionally sustained as self-evident, then the Supreme Court bares the responsibility to be honest with the people in relation to a removal of their just liberties in favour of a particular theory. This means that the burden of proof has been fulfilled lawfully by the people in regards to the accusations and charges that I have made against the High Court for opposing the Constitutional definition of man as a created human being, and for abstaining the course of justice and due process arbitrarily by overruling a legal precedent that is Constitutionally protected as self-evident under United States Federal Law.

*Quotation: ————————————————
"We the people are the rightful masters of both Congress and the courts, not to overthrow the Constitution, but to overthrow the men who pervert the Constitution." - Abraham Lincoln, 16th president of the United States. Source: Abraham Lincoln's Address at a Sanitary Fair, Baltimore. (Documented April 18, 1864).

The Supreme Court has ruled that Biblical creation cannot be applied to public education and law no matter how it is pervade in religious or theological instruction. This implies automatically that the Supreme Court has acted as a secular authority with a religious test in place that is designed to deny Biblical creation with an automatic dismissal in favour of the evolutionary theory, which is a violation of the First Amendment which states that the government shall not interfere with the religious rights of man, which includes defining man as a lower animal from a secular premise. And this is in no way a religious test upon the people, nor the government, but rather, it is a moral one instead. Either man was created in the image of God, or man has otherwise derived from the swamp. And the individual may choose for themselves whether they believe in God or not, but there are no protections under the law when it comes to the denial of conscience, and freedom of conscience is a religious liberty, rather than a secular ideal.

The United States Constitution and their Declaration of Independence is based entirely on theological terminology, that is to say that United States Constitutional law is to be interpreted by Biblical theology, rather than secular science. The violation of the law by granting protections to the evolutionary theory is a violation of the religious rights of man that includes the inalienable right to be defined as a created human being on the basis of conscience, which is a theological term from the Holy Bible that has been used by Constitutional law to define a person as distinct from the animals. The Supreme Court has no more rights to deny Biblical creation on the grounds that it is a religious subject any more than they have the right to deny the theological terms from law that are used to define a human being as a created individual, which are not-without-standing in their legal defence under Constitutional law, because they are defined as self-evident on the basis of a legal precedent that is Constitutionally protected as self-evident, as well as self-explanatory.

The United States Supreme Court has utterly rejected the theological framework, upon which, their system of Constitutional law has been built, which is more than just a shame, but also, it is an encroachment upon the just liberties of the people by the removal of a Biblical standard for law and education in favour of a secular one, when secular science is not an authority on law and order, while free education is for the purpose of developing students into a legal society that is based on the practice of human rights and equality, rather than science. The United States Supreme Court bares the oath of responsibility to the good of the people to uphold the said Constitution over any theory from science for reasons relating to protection of person before the law, which is in accordance with due process and national security.

Therefore, the Supreme Court has abused their liberty by attempting to replace the theological terms from Constitutional law in favour of a racial science, which is a crime against humanity on the basis of equality, because mankind is to be defined by Biblical theology for reasons relating to a legal standard that defines a person as a created human being, which is both self-explanatory, as well as self-evident under the written Constitution in accordance with a common law precedent. If the people of the United States are to be protected under Constitutional law, then the theological terms used within the Declaration of Independence must first be recognised as self-evident on the basis of conscience and reason, because if the Supreme Court cannot be reasoned with on the basis of secular science, then it is secular science that has placed the people's just liberties in harm's way, rather than Biblical creation.

The Supreme Court has thereby rejected the people's humanity and their just liberties without proper due course, which is entirely due to a secular interpretation of the written Constitution that attempts to overrule the theological interpretations from law on the grounds that Biblical creation is an offence. And the Supreme Court of the United States has indeed disqualified Biblical creation as an offence before the law under the pretence that all theological terms from law are by definition, religious. The rights of conscience is a religious liberty that cannot be overruled by the Supreme Court through their judiciary powers. This means that the Supreme Court has acted impartially against the theological terms from law that are in place to protect a person with, along with their just liberties.

In order for the Supreme Court to act in accordance with due deliberation of the law in accordance with Title VI Section 601 of the Civil Rights Act, then the theory of evolution must be overruled from the premise of law, because it is Biblical creation as a legal standard that cannot be overruled by the Supreme Court on the basis of a judiciary decision that has set in place a new legal precedent in despite of the previous in order to to grant Constitutional protections to a racial theory in science. This means that the Supreme Court cannot deny the plausibility of Biblical creation on the basis of theory, because it is the United States Declaration of Independence, the Bill of Rights, and their written Constitution that has derived from a theological interpretation of the law in accordance with the Holy Bible, so that Biblical creation is a legal standard that has been sustained by a self-evident legal precedent under the common law that is Constitutionally protected under Federal Law as true and good for the benefit of the people's protection, and their national security.

*Quotation: ——————————————————
"They (the founding fathers) had a genius for organized society on the foundation of piety, righteousness, liberty,

537

and obedience to law. The main characteristics of those principles of government from which all others are deduced is a government of limited and defined powers, leaving the people supreme. The judiciary interprets and declares the law and the Constitution, but it can neither create nor destroy the right of a single individual. Freedom of action is complete, within moral bounds, under the law which the people themselves have prescribed. Justice is administered by impartial courts. It is a maxim of our law that there is no wrong without a remedy. All the power and authority of the whole national government cannot convict the most humble individual of a crime, save on the verdict of an impartial jury composed of twelve of his peers.

The chief repository of power is in the legislature, chosen directly by the people at frequent elections. It is this body, which is particularly responsive to the public will, and yet, as in the Congress, is representative of the whole nation. It does not perform an executive function. It is not, therefore, charged with the necessity of expedition. It is a legislative body, and is therefore charged with the necessity for deliberation. Sometimes this privilege may be abused, for this great power has been given as the main safeguard of liberty, and wherever power is bestowed it may be used unwisely. But whenever a legislative body ceases to deliberate, then it ceases to act with due consideration. That fact in itself is conclusive that it has ceased to be independent, and has become subservient to a single directing influence or a small group, either without or within itself, and is no longer a representative of the people." - Calvin Coolidge, 30th president of the United States. Source: The Destiny of America. (Documented Memorial Day, May 26, 1923).

ARTICLE 3

A Letter of Concern

A letter of concern to the Australian Government by Adrian Moir (August 21, 2024). I would like to start this letter of concern with a prayer for our countrymen that all should find a measure of solitude in word, as well as in deed.

A Testament to the Faith:

Dear Father Jesus our Messiah God;

Thou art gracious Father unto all the world. For You Father God did create the Heavens and the Earth, and have set the stars in their place by their names in accordance with the word of Your Lord. Let us praise you Father God in the name You have given us by which all may be saved and come to You for deliverance from darkness and oppression. For by Your word You have established the promise given to all. For by Your word everything has been established by Thy faith.

Lord, Almighty God;

We have our minds in fear, but our hearts have been opened by Thy grace, for Thy work is finished. In the arms of Your word Lord Jesus we are safe and eternal in You, for Your word has filled all the world, from the Heavens You have declared in faith, and have set the pathways of the Heavens that none! may reproach Thy throne, and have taken the oppressed as Thy servants and children alike. For Thou art mighty to deliver and ready to receive unto Thee that which is Thee for Thy words sake, and by the merit You have put on faith that we can receive You Lord Father God by faith alone in Your Word. We praise You Heavenly Father for Thy Word. In You alone we are forever safe. We thank You Lord Jesus. Amen

Abstract:

The reason for this letter of concern is in regards to our nation's independence, systemic racism, the war on Israel by the Palestinians, as well as Communism and Communist influence within public education here in Australia. Historically, Communism has been violent against the concept of religion, even though freedom of conscience is protected under international law as incontestable; Meaning that Communism poses as the biggest threat toward the universal rights of the people in the world today from the viewpoint of Scientific Atheism and the evolutionary theory. New Atheism from Scientific Atheism is a Communist doctrine that has attempted to deny the lawful definition of conscience on the theoretical basis that man is animal, which is a crime against humanity on the basis of reason and equality. If human beings are to acknowledge one another as equals, then the definition of a human being must be one on equal terms, which is why the correct definition of what a human being is has derived from the legal definition of, person, rather than from the term, primate.

The broad pseudo-scientific description of what a human being is from Linnaean taxonomy and the theory of evolution has only caused inequality to reign supreme within society, because even though the law requires people to acknowledge the basic rights of others, it will always be the television that gets the final say unfortunately. If the theory of evolution continues to be taught as fact through the public education system, then the legal definition of what a person is under the law will erode into a derogatory term that can be used against another person in a court of law from the perspective of a scientist using biological terminology.

For example: A United States federal judge from the State of Pennsylvania ruled that intelligent design was unconstitutional on the grounds that it was a religious concept, which only opens the doorway for the evolutionary interpretations to become lawful, while the current interpretation of what a person is under the law is being re-examined by federal judges in the United States. And this is cause for concern for three main reasons; First; Is because the United States Constitution is a direct product of a religious people and their culture, rather than atheism. And secondly; Because the concept of intelligent design arose from the study of molecular mechanisms and from instructional systems, which are not defined as being religious subjects. And thirdly; The rights of conscience is a religious liberty, rather than a secular ideal

The process of instructional systems design, or intelligent design, is a practical science, while the theory of evolution is an age old racial theory that caused the worst crime of the twentieth century to occur, such as the Holocaust, that involved the teaching of evolution by the State, which led to the expansion of racial segregation policies, evolutionary eugenics, and scientific racism. Scientific racism is the most pervasive and destructive ideology in the world today, because the theory denies the law of human equality by citing nature as a justification to commit racially motivated hate crimes against other groups of people, who are also members of mankind, and should be treated as such in all situations regardless of their nationality or personal beliefs.

The ideology that man has derived from nature by the use of such terms that derive from Linnaean taxonomy and evolutionary phylogeny are being projected as a fact through the public education system, when Linnaean taxonomy is a pseudo-scientific discipline, which historically, has divided mankind into a racial hierarchy of less evolved to more evolved based on the assumption that man has derived from an animal, which is the ideological reasoning behind scientific racism and the evolutionary theory. While any theory that attempts to divide mankind into a biological hierarchy of less evolved to more evolved, is by definition a racist concept, which is why evolutionary phylogeny is steeped in racism and is unavoidable for the theory. The concept of biological races has been scientifically refuted on the basis that it is a racist concept to divide humanity into an evolutionary hierarchy in order that one group should receive a higher classification than the rest based entirely on preference, rather than evidence.

For example: If a group of people are genetically more hairy than the other, then the group with less hair inevitably gets a higher ranking on an evolutionary scale, because apparently, less hair means more evolved. But the problem with this logic is that the growth of hair is relative to testosterone levels within the individual that encourages hair growth, and testosterone is not something that should be decreased for aesthetic reasons, because if left untreated, low testosterone levels can contribute to low bone density, and a higher risk of heart disease.

So, the problem with the teaching of evolution, is not just because it discourages people from learning about our Creator, which is where our rights of conscience have derived from, but also, the theory of evolution has been the sole basis for scientific racism and the widespread practice of evolutionary eugenics from the viewpoint of Social Darwinism. If the theory of evolution continues to go unchallenged from the premise of law, then the people will be too preoccupied with other issues instead of fighting the ideology of scientific racism, which is a far greater threat to human freedom than intelligent design could ever be.

The Australian government is currently investing over $10 billion into military advancements in order to maintain a balance of power with Communist China, which is never going to work unless trade form occurs first, because the $10 billion that is being spent in an arms race can be offset by spending the money on an automotive manufacturing, white goods, clothing, and computer tech industry, which would in turn, deviate the current flow of money to Communist China back into the pockets of Australian workers.

The idea of allowing Communist China to manufacture for Australia and America under the Free Trade Agreement means automatically that the Free Trade Agreement is allowing for the build-up of global war. If Australian citizens are going to compete with Communist China on a global scale, then it will start by having an automotive manufacturing base here in Australia in order to keep Australian dollars from falling into the hands of our Communist enemy. A heavy and productive manufacturing base within Australia is the only true weapon against Communist China that we have for reasons relating to job security and government spending, because if the money we apply to the arms race forbids a trade reform with China, then Communist China will inevitably win this war, because this is a trade war, rather than a political dispute alone.

The national sovereignty of Australia has never been in a more precarious situation than the situation that exists here and now, because if Australia is to send Australian jobs over to Communist China, then we are thereby surrendering to our enemy in the hour of war. The trade war with Communist China must be settled by having trade reform that is designed to bring jobs back to Australia, which is not only expedient for the Australian government, but also, the working class of this continent. The national sovereignty of Australian borders is in place so that we have job security, and security of property in accordance with international law.

Australia cannot compete with the industrial power of Communist China if we continue to allow China to manufacture basic household items on our own behalf, because the net effect is the rise of Communism, rather than national independence. So, we owe our allegiance to the good of the Commonwealth in accordance with the will of the people, rather than owing our financial power to a Communist system of industrialism that is taking full advantage of the people in the hour of war by the removal of a manufacturing base that is in place to protect the borders of our country, as well as our financial and economic stability, because it is the Communist industrial system that is set to fail over time, of which, we should not play a part.

The idea of a scientific revolution by Communism through the movement of New Atheism and the ideology of Scientific Atheism is propagated through the public education system by the promotion of the evolutionary theory with the consent of the law, which automatically results in lawlessness by those who wish to espouse some form of freedom from rules by challenging the very foundation of self-governance that is guided by the universal principles of moral law. The idea that religion is the cause of global unrest is contradictory to international human rights legislation whereby freedom of conscience is protected as inalienable so that freedom of religion can be exercised as a right, rather than a privilege. Without freedom of conscience, then there is no lawful premise in which to vote, because a person votes according to their conscience.

So, for this reason, it is the human conscience that needs to be explained factually to students so that the voting constituency is well informed in regards to a lawful instruction that is universal in its interpretation, such as the right to be defined as a created human being, which is by definition, inalienable, while the evolutionary theory of ape to man is by definition, racial. The teaching of evolution could be replaced overnight by using systems theory and systems science as a new standard model, because the most important scientific advancements of this age have derived from systems science and systems thinking, rather than the evolutionary theory, which is responsible for the race war that still continues to this day. If the theory of evolution is not removed from public education, then a continuous and sustainable standard for public education cannot be adopted, and we are indeed faced with a choice that bears responsibility on our God given conscience, and the choice is clear.

Either we accept that human beings are entitled to be defined by their God given humanity on the basis of conscience and reason, or we can continue to teach that man is animal. But if we choose the latter option, then there will be no criteria to obey a lawful instruction, because the existence of the human conscience must be interpreted to students so that they too can contribute to society with a fair outcome based on human rights and equality, rather than the teaching of evolution that defines man as a lower animal, which in turn, lowers a person's conscience and their ability to be reasoned with as an individual. Under international law, every individual person has a universal right to be defined as a created human being, so that Biblical creation is by definition a lawful premise, while the theory of evolution is not, because if we are to teach that man is animal from the public education system, then we will destroy ourselves by the removal of self-governance under moral law.

Moral law can only be defined by a system of morality, which cannot derive from the evolutionary theory without putting the basic rights of the people in harm's way, because the teaching that man is animal is without sufficient cause before international law under international agreement. No human being can be defined as an animal before international law since 1948 under the Universal Declaration of Human Rights and Equality

(UDHR), where a person's inalienable right to be defined as a created human being is protected as universal on the basis of conscience.

So, in order to be consistent with a lawful instruction that is universal in its interpretation, then a Creator God is required to be explained factually to students through the public education system, because it is God the Creator who has endowed mankind with conscience and with spirit, rather than nature. And it is Commonwealth theology that is of a higher legal standard than the evolutionary theory, because if science is to place the inalienable rights of the people in harm's way, then it is the members from that industry that must not be allowed to interfere with the functions of government so that the people can continue to be self-governed under a universal system of morality, which must derive itself from Biblical theology for the good of the people, and for the good of the Commonwealth.

A conviction of truth in criminal cases always begins by a conviction of conscience first, which means that it is our God given conscience that defines our humanity on the basis of reason, because the better a person's reasoning ability is, the stronger their conscience is also. And it is for this reason that unbelief in conscience constitutes as a direct threat to our system of common law by challenging the Biblical principles of God's creation and the very system we live in, because if man has derived from the animals, then there is no moral law that is universal in its interpretation. And if there is no universal basis for moral law, then there is no moral obligation by the individual to obey a lawful instruction that is universal in its interpretation.

The escalation of youth crime here in Australia is the direct result of the evolutionary theory in practice from public education known formally as "Social Darwinism," which in turn, causes the individual to question basic public morals on the basis of denial. Non-belief in a Creator God still constitutes as a right under international agreement in accordance with freedom of belief, yet there are no protections for unbelief in regards to the lawful definition of conscience in accordance with international law. So, in order for the individual to not revoke their basic rights as an individual, then the human conscience needs to be explained factually to students from the premise of law, rather than the theory of evolution, which is the sole basis for the individuals denial of conscience.

No theory in human history has caused more division than the theory of evolution from public education, which is entirely due to the evolutionary definition of man. So, for this reason, it is the secular standard for public education that is calling our basic rights as human beings into question by defining man as a lower animal, which must be overruled from the premise of law for the benefit of the people and their protection within the system as created human beings. The purpose of free education is to introduce the individual into a legal system that is based on human rights and equality, rather than a theory in science.

If the theory of evolution is to bring our basic rights into question before the law, then it is the theory of evolution that must be called into question by the law, rather than our God given humanity, which is self-explanatory. So, in order to have a fair system of education whereby each individual is treated as equal, then a system of equality must be introduced into public education for the good of the people, and for the good of the Commonwealth. Our universal system of Commonwealth theology must be explained factually to students for the good of the common law, because it is the common law that will sustain us through our nations trials and tribulations. Australia is not a theocracy, nor is Australia a Republic, but we are a democracy that is to uphold the rights of conscience, which is a religious liberty, rather than a secular one.

Scientific Atheism, according to its academic definition in use, is defined as Marxist-Leninist Communism, which has co-opted the public education system, as well as our universities on the basis of secularism. So, for this reason, we must guard ourselves against Scientific Atheism and all of its encroachments upon the Constitution and public education, which is now occurring through a secular standard for public education and law. A legal obligation cannot be enforced unless there is a moral obligation first, which automatically implies that a system of morality is required when interpreting the law, which cannot derive itself from a secular interpretation without creating an alternate religion in turn. Morality cannot be defined by secular ideology, because morality cannot be maintained without religion, and religion cannot be restrained without morality.

Without an acknowledgement of the Holy Bible from the premise of law, then there is no lawful basis for human freedom under self-governance, because human freedom is measured by freedom of belief, rather than freedom of denial. Human freedom is not to be overruled in any way by a scientific theory that equates a human being as a lower animal, thereby denying a human being their universal right to be defined as a creation, which is for the benefit of an individual's protection within the system. Otherwise, we are putting the basic rights of the people in jeopardy, all on the basis of a controversial accusation that man is animal, of which, cannot be sustained, because our universal system of law and order is in place so that we each have protection of person before the law, rather than because of a scientific notion that rejects our humanity on the basis of theory. If the evolutionary theory is to bring our God given humanity into question before the law by attempting to define a person as a lower animal, then it is the theory of evolution that is to be brought into question by the law, rather than our God given humanity, which is self-explanatory.

*Quotation: ————————————————————
Racial discrimination occurs when a person is treated less favourably, or not given the same opportunities, as others in a similar situation, because of their race, the country where they were born, their ethnic origin or their skin colour. The Racial Discrimination Act of 1975 (RDA) makes it unlawful to discriminate against a person because of his or her race, colour, descent, national origin or ethnic origin, or immigrant status. The RDA protects people from racial discrimination in many areas of public life, including employment, education, receiving or using services, renting, or buying a house or unit, and accessing public places. The RDA also makes racial hatred unlawful. - Source: The Australian Commonwealth Government Human Rights Commission (Part III of the Australian Commonwealth Government Racial Discrimination Policies).

According to the Australian Human Rights Commission, it is unlawful to "discriminate" against a human being on the basis of their "descent" through the "education" system. So, in order to be consistent with Australian Human Rights Legislation under the common law, then the theory of evolution must be overruled from the premise of law in order for Australian citizens to be properly informed in regards to their human "origins" as created human beings with a human ancestry. Racial discrimination can and does include the theoretical assertion that man is animal, which is propagated from the public education system with the consent of the law.

If the level of youth crime within Australia and other nations is ever going to be reduced, then it will start by removing the evolutionary theory from public education in order to promote human rights and equality, because if the individual is to choose between a lawful instruction, and disobeying the law, then their conscience must first be convicted in accordance with moral teachings, which is why morality must be taught to students from a Biblical premise or there will be no universal basis for morality under the common law. And morality is fundamental to law and order so that a person's conscience should be convicted by the law in criminal cases.

Racial discrimination is an important subject that requires students to be fully informed concerning the basic rights of a human being, which must derive itself from Biblical theology under the common law for the good of the people, and for the good of the Commonwealth, or we will lose our national distinction within the world as a free nation under God. So, in order for a strong government to exist within Australia, then the government of Australia is required to formally educate students regarding the common law, and its Christian theology, through the public education curriculum so that a human rights violation does not occur against the people.

When a person is applying for welfare payments here in Australia, one of the questions that is asked is whether you are aboriginal or Torres Strait Islander? So, the next question that one should ask, is why does this matter? Because, if a person is to receive a different form of treatment based on their "ethnicity," then a human rights violation has occurred based on a racial examination against the public. When according to the Australian Human Rights Commission, it is unlawful to "discriminate" against a human being on the basis of their "descent," when it comes to "receiving or using services."

The Commonwealth system did not derive from indigenous culture, but from the common law instead, which is the founding and governing principle that led to the creation of the Australian Constitution and legislative assemblies, which is bipartisan, rather than racial. So, there should be no racial examination before the law when applying for welfare payments the same as there should be no racial examination when running for parliament so that a system of equal opportunity may exist for each and every naturalized citizen regardless of their descent. Australian culture has derived from Commonwealth theology, which is not to be misconstrued as being racist in any way so that a system of common law can uphold the people within this nation during our hour of crisis.

A Commonwealth system of law and order should always involve the inclusion of our nation's elders, and their people, past and present, rather than being a system of racial exclusion based on a racial examination by the Commonwealth government. While an indigenous system of law and order, is by definition, a system of racial exclusion that rejects the Commonwealth system, as well as the common law due to a European descent. So, in order to avoid a civil war between aboriginal culture, and the Commonwealth system, then we must protect the common law as a common interest for the common good, which is our saving grace in the hour of war against Communist China, Radical Islam, and social unrest.

Thus, a correct theology is the only way to truly defeat religious terrorism, systemic racism, and the evolutionary theory by the application of a fair system of justice based on human rights and equality, so that every Australian citizen should have equal opportunity through the due process of law, including the elders of this nation. If Australian law is to uphold the people of this nation, then equal opportunity is required, which does not involve defining man as a lower animal through the public education system, nor does it involve a racial examination by the Commonwealth government. Any theory that attempts to divide humanity into a biological hierarchy of less evolved to more evolved, is by definition a racist concept, because one group of people will be seen as biologically inferior to the rest based on human conjecture, rather than evidence.

The evidence that all men are created equal derives from the lawful interpretation of conscience, which cannot be overruled for reasons relating to protection of person, and national security. The lawful term, conscience, is a theological term from the Holy Bible that has been used by international law to define a person as distinct from the animals for reasons relating to protection of person. Protection of person is vital to national security in order that each person should be convicted by their conscience to uphold the Constitution when called upon. If the human conscience is not explained factually to students through the public education system, then the individual will be made unaware of the legal system they are entering into that holds to a Biblical definition of man by the rights of conscience, and a by correct interpretation of the law.

If the Australian people, whether indigenous or not, are to band together during a time of war, then we must be united under one creed, such as the Australian anthem, or we will lose our distinction as a nation within the world due to indigenous opposition that sets itself against the common law for reasons relating to the protection of national heritage, rather than national trust. And we are as a people collectively distinct as a free nation under God for reasons relating to a national trust that forbids us from abandoning the common law with a separate creed or culture that derives itself from the premise of another system of law that sets itself against our written Constitution. So, in order for a future based on human rights and equality that includes ethnic and cultural diversity within a Commonwealth system, then there should be no racial examination in place by the Australian government, because those of indigenous descent are being treated as separate from others, which causes division, rather than equality.

The Palestinian attack against Israel is the greatest atrocity of this decade, with women and children taken hostage, and their executions being broadcasted on the internet. The United Nations Declaration of Human Rights and Equality was enacted so that we each have security of person before the law, and so that Israel would be sustained under a universal treaty following the Holocaust, of which, Palestine has refused to agree upon, which means that they have no lawful protection under international law for the invasion of the sovereign State of Israel, and the Antisemitism that follows.

If the Australian government is to stand by the people here and now, then it will begin with an acknowledgement of country and prayers, because it is the will of the people that we should have freedom from tyranny in accordance with the faith that we have received under Commonwealth theology. The only true measure we have to fight Islamic terrorism with, along with Communism, is with a correct theology. Otherwise, we will lose our distinction as a nation under God who has blessed this country with wealth and prosperity, and has bestowed upon our conscience the moral obligation to do what is just in despite of our adversaries will.

So, in order to be consistent with Australian culture, then Commonwealth theology is required to be taught from public education so that we should all be united by a universal and moral standard for education that is factually based upon the common law for the benefit of the people to be protected by so that a cultural shift from self-governance to self-exclusion does not occur on a mass scale, because it is self-exclusion from the law that leads to lawlessness within society. Commonwealth theology is based on Judeo-Christian ethics and teachings in accordance with the common law, which means that it is the Holy Bible that needs protecting by the law, rather than the theory of evolution, or society will fall into disrepute and moral decay as a direct result of abandoning Biblical morality in favour of the evolutionary theory. And this is by no means a religious test upon the Australian government, or the people of the Commonwealth, but rather, it is a moral one instead that bears responsibility upon our God given conscience to do what is right before the eyes of our enemy, or our enemy will one day overtake this nation of ours with the consent of the law.

The common law is of common interest to the people of Australia, because it is the common law that is to uphold the common good, which must reflect upon our society as a working whole, or a division will occur in the form of lawlessness involving minority groups who challenge basic public morals on the basis of evolution, religion, and race. If freedom of religion is to be a blessing to our nation's security, then a national distinction is required, because not all cultures are equal, while all human beings are in effect equal in rights according to Commonwealth theology under the common law.

This means that each person should have equal opportunity to learn about their Creator from public education, which is in accordance with the due process of law, because the due process of law includes equal opportunity to be heard, and we have heard those who hail from the theory of evolution who have attempted to redefine the lawful definition of person before international law without success. The lawful premise for self-governance under the common law derives from Biblical teachings, and Commonwealth theology, because it is Biblical creation as a legal standard that restores order to society, rather than the teaching of evolution, which is the primary mechanism for human exploitation by the teaching of man's descent from the animal kingdom, and by the denial of conscience.

Human freedom cannot be measured by science, nor can human freedom be suppressed by the law without causing a rebellion in turn, because the spirit of man is a spirit of freedom, while the Spirit of God is the

Spirit of, and of liberty. The just liberties of the people can be summed up by a single verse from the Scriptures according to the Gospel of Galatians 5:22-23 which are: "love, joy, peace, long-suffering, gentleness, goodness, faith, meekness, and temperance, against such, there is no law." (End of quote).

Lawlessness within society always begins by self-exclusion from the law, which is occurring on a mass scale due to the adoption of rules that simply do not apply, such as the evolutionary teaching of man's descent from the animal kingdom, and by a denial of conscience. And it is for this reason that the universal law of equality must be explained factually to students from a theological interpretation, because the secular standard has failed as a system of learning due to the nature of Communism and Communist influence that includes the science of atheism.

The science of atheism is leading the world into an age of inequality by the teaching of evolution from a secular premise, which is an encroachment upon the just liberties of the people, as well as the common law. The common law has derived from previously settled cases that derive from the Holy Bible, which acts as a legal standard by which the courts must follow so that a universal system of morality can protect the law. Law is fundamental to the Commonwealth system in that a previous case has been settled, such as the case as to whether man was created or not. If we are to abide with the common law under a Commonwealth system, then an acknowledgement of country and prayers is required to be taught factually from public education, or we will be faced by a cultural shift from self-governance to self-exclusion, which forms the basis for rebellion, riots, and Communist revolution.

The nature of Communism and Communist influence within the borders of Australia is the sole cause of civil unrest involving protests and anarchy on the streets, which is how a nation becomes divided by the application of multiple minority groups who question basic public morals that derive from religious principle. Minority groups such as BLM, the gay rights movement, and New Atheism are prime examples of how Communism is slipping into our system of law and education, which can and will lead to global anarchy and civil unrest if the public education system is not returned to the people under a Biblical standard, because it is Biblical creation as a legal standard that is universal in its interpretation, while Communism seeks to challenge Scriptural authority on the basis of the evolutionary theory.

The rule of law, as a common phrase, is a call to a rebellion against self-governance, rather than a call to human freedom and liberty, because if man is to be ruled by law, then the power lies with a ruler, rather than the people and their ability to vote. And this is in no way expedient for the Australian Commonwealth government, or the people of this continent, because the right to be self-governed under a universal system of morality was the founding and governing principle of the common law, so that there would be freedom under the law, which is a form of liberation, rather than subjugation. Biblical creation as a legal standard stands against fascism in all of its manifestations, and all of its encroachments upon the common law, because to denote the Holy Bible as unjust is a public grievance in accordance with our universal system of morality that forms the written basis for the common law, because a universal truth has been sustained as self-evident that all men are created equal on the basis of conscience and reason.

So, unless the people are being formerly educated by the Australian Commonwealth government concerning the common law, and its Biblical roots, then the end result is absolute atheism by the rule of law, because the more evolution is taught through the public education system, the more laws that are required in order to suppress the wicked, and sustain peace within society. And the more laws we create to suppress the wicked, the more liberties the people will lose, which is an inevitable consequence of the evolutionary theory as a secular standard for public education involving the denial of conscience, as defined by Biblical theology under the common law.

In an excerpt from the Constitutional Documents of King James I, dated 1961, page 153, we read the following quotation: "Amongst many other points of happiness and freedom which your majesty's subjects of this kingdom have enjoyed under your royal progenitors, kings and queens of this realm, there is none which they have accounted more dear and precious than this, to be guided and governed by the certain rule of the law which giveth both to the head and members that which of right belongeth to them, and not by any uncertain or arbitrary form of government." (End of quote).

From this quote we find that the phrase, "the rule of law" is in conjunction with subjugation, rather than self-governance, because it is defined as a "right" by the crown of England and its members. The phrase, "the rule of law," from its designated use by the crown of England asserts that each citizen of the Commonwealth is by definition a "subject," rather than a sovereign or independent being, and the phrase also asserts that it is a royal rite of passage, rather than a communal legislative committee by a publicly elected body or government. Historically, under the rule of law, the indigenous people of Australia were subjugated for more than a century by British imperial rule, and there has been no formal apology by the crown of England. Instead, the Australian government has taken the liberty to apologise on behalf of all Australian's, which has led to an explosion of racial examination policies that require people to be asked whether they are aboriginal or not.

The racial examination policies by the Australian Commonwealth government is equal to a form of racial discrimination that has held the indigenous people of Australia in exclusion for the most part of its history. If the Australian indigenous people are to be included within the Commonwealth system, then the Commonwealth government of Australia must not be conducting racial examinations in order that one group of people should receive alternative services. Otherwise, the people of Australia, and its government, will never be able to identify systemic racism from the practice of law and education.

In order to stand by the indigenous people of Australia under a Commonwealth system of law, then we must do so with equality in mind, which does not include a repetitive system of apologetics on behalf of someone else, nor does it include racial examinations in order to receive public goods and services. The cultural dispute between those of European descent, and those of native Australian descent, has manifested itself into a repeated system of apologetics, which is never expedient for the Commonwealth government of Australia, especially when the government of Australia was under subjugation by a foreign ruler during the appalling atrocities that occurred against the indigenous people of Australia.

According to historical resources, the Commonwealth of Australia was formed in 1901 by the federation of six British colonies, each of which, became a legislative State. While the independence of Australia from the crown of England is cited by the Australia Act of 1986. This means that the Australian government was under a foreign rule up until the Australia Act of 1986, which was signed into law the same year that the United Kingdom Act of 1986 gave their independence from Britain as well. So, if anyone is to apologise to the Australian native people for the subjugation they have suffered prior to 1986, then it would be the crown of England, rather than the Australian government on behalf of the Australian people.

The Australian government has attempted to apply a fair system of equality by apologising to the indigenous people of Australia on behalf of all Australians, despite the fact that not all Australians are guilty of such acts, which only inflates the issue we face today, rather than settling the disputes of the past. The Australian government policy of a racial examination has now extended itself into the workforce of Australia with many employers asking the same question as to whether you are aboriginal or not? Which is enough to prove that systemic racism in Australia is on the rise. And there is no downhill run when it comes to this issue, which means that the people of this nation must unite together under a common cause, which cannot derive itself from culture, but from the common law instead. If the people are not being educated in regards to the common law, then the common good will fail over time due to neglecting a fair system of law in favour of a cultural debate.

The purpose of common law is to act as a mediation between the government and the people so that a cause may be heard before the law as long as there has been damage to property, or persons, which in turn, incurs a penalty. And we are not to penalise ourselves through a repeated system of apologetics in regards to a cultural debate, nor are we entitled by law to conduct a racial examination so that one group of people should receive a preferred form of treatment over others, which is discriminatory. If we are as a nation to continue into the future with a fair system of justice, and of law, then we must educate ourselves in regards to the common law, or we will be faced by the injustices that are produced by attempting to equalise that which cannot be equated as equal, such as European and indigenous culture.

The common law is of European descent, which has become the basis for Australian law, so that any cultural debate that deems the common law as unjust on the basis of descent is making a racial argument in order to exclude the common law. So, for the common good, we are to examine the common law as a form of human freedom from foreign subjugation by an exclusion of the rule of law, or the indigenous people of Australia will fail to yield to a lawful instruction due to their own convictions of conscience. Freedom under the common law derives itself from the teaching of morality, so that a society can exercise self-governance without interference from the law. And it is Biblical morality that defines our nation under a Commonwealth system of common law, which is multicultural, rather than racially distinct.

This means that the common law is required to be explained factually to students for the good of the Commonwealth system, so that we may exercise our basic freedoms under a system of morality that caters to an equality, rather than a particular culture. And it is Biblical morality that defines an equality on the basis of conscience and reason, which is not a racial argument on the basis of culture, but rather, it is a workable premise for human freedom and self-governance to be exercised under the law. On October 13, 2023, the Australian people held a Voice referendum in relation to the indigenous people as to whether or not we should have a committee of indigenous people to alter our functions of government and the written Constitution.

The Voice referendum failed to convince the Australian people that the functions of government should be interfered with by a racial group on the basis of their lineage. In 1996, at the 8th National Congress, the Socialist Party of Australia was renamed the Communist Party of Australia, thereby becoming the successor of the original party. The Communist Party of Australia was in full financial support of the Voice referendum in that a yes vote would allow for a Socialist reformation, which means that the infiltration of Communism within the borders of Australia is a very real threat to our way of life, with its members seeking a way to alter our forms of government, as well as our Constitution, by utilising the cultural dispute between the European culture, and the indigenous people.

The Commonwealth system, however, is not to blame for the cultural dispute within Australia, while Communism and national socialism is to blame for taking political advantage of the cultural debate that rages on, which is expedient for the Communist Party of Australia, rather than the elders of this nation. So, in order to avoid a Socialist State, then the cultural debate between European and indigenous culture must be settled in such a way that the practice of common law is victorious, because it is the common law that is of common interest to the people, rather than science or culture. The Australian native people have every right to exclude themselves from a European culture, and to practice their own culture within the borders of this nation. But the indigenous people of Australia must do so in accordance with the common law or there will be contradictions between that which is lawful, and that which is not.

European culture has brought the theory of evolution and the Linnaean taxonomic terms to this continent, which has deprived the native people of their justice. So, if there was ever a theory that has caused more division and inequality, then it would be the Linnaean classification system along with evolutionary phylogeny, rather than Biblical Christianity. The entire purpose of evolutionary phylogeny is to create a supposed hierarchy of inferior and superior racial groups, which is the current philosophical basis for scientific racism, Social Darwinism, and evolutionary eugenics involving the Linnaean naming and classifications system.

According to Latin, the term "aboriginal" derives from the prefix "ab" meaning "not." While the term "original" comes from the Latin word "originem" which means "beginning, birth, or first." So, when using the term "original" as an adjective to describe something that literally means "first" or "birth" with the prefix "ab" then you derive at the term, "not-first" in terms of a birth status. This linguistics issue not only extends to the indigenous people of Australia, but also, Africans, because the Latin term used by Carlos Linnaeus to describe Africans in the mid-18th century derives from the use of the word, "negroid," which is a racially motivated and unlawful term. Currently, the term "aboriginal" is still used by the Australian government to define the indigenous people of this country, while the term "negroid" is by definition an offence before the law.

So, not only is the Australian government conducting racial examinations against the elders of this nation, but also, it is being done from the viewpoint of scientific racism on the basis that the indigenous people of Australia have been named inadequately from Linnaean taxonomy, which is a crime against humanity on the basis of equality. The indigenous people of Australia are fully entitled to be named after their own lineage, such as Koori, Murri, and Nunga, rather than from a naming system that is steeped in racism historically. And it is the people who hail from the evolutionary theory that are promoting these racial terms on the basis of Linnaean taxonomy and evolutionary phylogeny, while the Biblical standard for education is put to one side.

So, it is for this reason that the theory of evolution is the primary motive force that is causing division amongst different groups of people within this country and abroad, which is enough of a reason to remove the Linnaean taxonomic terms from the practice of law and education in order to implement a sustainable method that must derive itself from the Biblical definition of man, because we are entitled by international law to be defined as created human beings who are endowed with conscience on the basis of reason. And there is no evolutionary definition of the word "conscience" that does not discriminate against that which God in Heaven has defined as equal, such as mankind.

*Quotation: ———————————————————
Having placed humans within the animal kingdom, Linnaeus distinguished them from other animals in the same order of Anthropomorpha by the ability to 'know thyself' ('Nosce te ipsum'). This would lead Linnaeus to attribute the specific epithet sapiens to the genus Homo when he began to use his binomial nomenclature in the 1750s. He then proceeded to classify humans further, as he did with other organisms. Linnaeus' division into four varieties of man corresponded to the then known four continents of the world: Europe, America, Asia and Africa. The result of this expansion of the classification of man was the 1758 10th edition of Systema naturae, which became the basis for scientific racism. The Linnean Society intends to confront the consequences of scientific racism; one of the first steps is to look at Linnaeus' writings, in order to address the consequences of his views on human diversity through our education, outreach, and research activities. - Source: The Linnaean Society of London (Linnaeus and Race).

The Linnaean definition of man as being equal to that of an animal was the leading cause that led Charles Darwin to describe certain groups of people as inferior biologically, which has now been refuted by modern genetic research. The pseudo-scientific definitions and classification system from Linnaean taxonomy, and the theory of evolution, is leading mankind into a world of inequality, which must be challenged from the premise of law in order that Australia should lead the world in human rights and equality through a system of education that caters to no one on the basis of race, but rather, to everyone on the basis of their origin as a created human being.

The interpretation of human origins must derive itself from a Biblical interpretation for the good of the people, and the common law, because it is the common law that is of common interest to the people of Australia, and it is from Biblical theology that the common law has derived. So, in order to cater to the common good, then we must uphold that which is true and good, which is why the Holy Bible requires a defence before the law, rather than the theory of evolution, or we will be subject to the racial terminology and discrimination by Linnaean taxonomy and Darwinian evolution that defines each person as a lower animal, of which, cannot be sustained for reasons relating to the preservation of human rights and equality under the common law.

The common law dictates that morality is mandatory on the basis of conscience and good reason, because a lawful obligation must always be followed by a moral obligation, otherwise, there will be a conflict of conscience, which then leads to lawlessness, rather than human freedom and liberation. If mankind is to be liberated by the common law, then the people must first be educated concerning our system of morality that derives itself from Biblical creation as a legal standard from the premise of law. Biblical creation as a legal standard allows for the application of laws to be made fair and just, so that a code of ethics can be better applied, and so that each person is equally informed in regards to their civil rights through the public education system, or there will be contradictions between that which is lawful, and that which is not in terms of a moral perspective.

The human spirit is indeed a motive force on the basis of morality, in that a human being will engage a problem if the cause is seen as sufficient. And there has never been a greater cause to fight for than for the sake of human rights and equality, which cannot be misconstrued as a secular ideal without bringing the system into question, because our system of common law derives from the legal precedent that all men are created equal. So, in order to engage in effective communication so that a human rights violation does not occur against the public with the consent of the law, then the theory of evolution must be contested before the law, or we will lose the battle for human freedom to a group of racial scientists who should know better than to equate mankind with the animal kingdom.

The common law is for the common good of the people, which must be acknowledged as a form of freedom under the law due to the liberation of the human mind, body, and soul in regards to living as a created human being. The common good will always be measurable by the verdicts of the people in regards to a public referendum, decision, or choice, and we are to choose liberty over the evolutionary theory for reasons relating to freedom of conscience, because freedom of thought and belief is better applied to a creative society that is free and open, rather than a system of non-belief. All that is required in order for a system of law and order to operate effectively is belief, because nothing stifles the process of law and order faster than a system of unbelief.

This means that Biblical morality is our saving grace in the cultural debate, as well as being in opposition to Communism and Communist influence, because it is Biblical morality that forms the basis of self-governance under the common law, while Communism is in opposition to this basic principle on the basis that a Socialist State would better cater to the people. The Australian Communist Party has attempted to utilise the cultural debate within Australia in order to implement a Communist ideal, such as an appointed minister who is to change the Constitution. But the problem with Communism as a political ideology, is that Communism has no definition for morality that is universal in its interpretation, which is entirely due to the nature of Scientific Atheism, which attempts to apply a system of morality, whilst denying the people their freedom of conscience.

The Australian people will knowingly and openly disapprove of a Communist Party due to the nature of Communism, so long as the education system is informing the public of the dangers of Communist influence. The Communist Party of Australia has attempted to interfere with the functions of government by creating the need for a cultural debate, which is expedient for Communism, rather than our system of law and order. If our system of common law is to preside into the future as a means of human freedom and liberation, then we must stand by the principles by which the common law has derived, which does not include a cultural debate, nor a system of continual apologetics, but by an acknowledgement of country and prayers, because it is the will of the people that we should have a system of law that oppresses the lawless, whilst sustaining the virtues of human rights and equality under the common law.

Closing statement:

May the Australian men and women in arms remember that Christ Jesus our Lord is with you through your trials and tribulations, and He will not forsake you, nor leave you behind. You are each endowed with a gift to serve, and with a mind to fight injustices wherever they might arise. May the hope of the people rest in Christ Jesus our Lord and Saviour, for all that is at stake here, is our freedom under the law. So, for the good of the Commonwealth, and for the good of the people, we are required to pray and vouch safe for this nation of ours that we should remain as a free people under God, rather than a place that accommodates for religious persecution, which is an inevitable consequence of Scientific Atheism, the war on Islam, and the teaching of evolution by the State. Thank you for reading this letter of concern, and may God bless you and your team as you all endeavour to keep Australia as it was born to be; Just and fair. Amen

ARTICLE 4

Riddle me this

Riddle me this, and riddle me that; What was that from under their hat?
We came, we saw, it is no longer hidden; The premise they had, it was
forbidden...
It wasn't for them to teach a blend; But because they did, it spelt the end.
Their system was tried, a system of tales; Their system of belief, it ultimately
failed.
It failed the people, it failed the law; It wasn't for them to disregard them all.
Their facts were stupid, their theories to blame; Because the origin of man
is never a game.

They played the facts, they played us as fools; If man is animal, then he is
to be fooled.
Laws are for all, and morality defines; So it wasn't for them to blur the line.
The line was drawn, its finger was strong; So who are they to get it all
wrong.
A peaceful community threatened by war; Why weren't we told? and why
weren't we warned?
The standard in place has become their ace; Because we aren't to refute
their origins of race.
They claim to be first, but their of the worst; An animal ancestry has
defined their thirst.

They forsook the honour, they discouraged others; Their theory of man, it wasn't for brothers.

The virtues of morality, and the laws that follow; It was never for man to make them hollow.

Law is a blessing, and so is morality; But which of the two defines our reality?

It's a crime to murder, it's a crime to steal; So who on Earth said evolution was real?

Laws are refined, because justice is blind; But morality is fixed, because the truth exists.

We were never an animal, and we're not to be slaves; So why on Earth does the heathen rage?

They conspire to murder, they threaten our existence; So the only recall is to have a resistance.

War is certain, and life is unsure; But victory is at hand when morality is restored.

The premise for equality is the basis for freedom; So without morality, who will lead them?

ARTICLE 5

Discourses

A Cry from the Wilderness:

In the beginning was the Word, and the Word was with God in the beginning, and the Word was God from the beginning, and all things were made by Him and through Him, so all that is made was made by God. The Creator has formed the Earth out of water, and has set apart the seas from the dry land to be an inhabitants for man, and the creatures His servant, which gives all life purpose and meaning. So, let he who would be great be the servant of all, so that those who desire to rule should be humbled by the poor, for the Lord is moved by those who show consideration for the lowly and give justice to the downtrodden, because God is an avenger of the meek, and He casts down the wicked for their crimes.

God in Heaven has endowed all life with ability, but unto His own image the gift of conscience, with which, to reason from that all may know that the love of the Father in Heaven is reserved for the just who have strived with Him in Spirit for His Words sake, for the Spirit of the Lord is a Spirit of love and humility, so that all who humble themselves before their maker for love's sake shall inherit their reward in the kingdom to come. But unto the unjust, will be tears of torment and wails of agony for their crimes against humanity shall not go unpunished, for God alone is just by the provision of His moral law, which is do unto others as you would have them do unto you, and, to love the Lord your God with all of your own being.

And God alone is justified, because He alone has suffered for all of mankind upon the cross that we may have redemption from sin. May those who are searching know with assurance from above that God in Heaven draws near to them who are witnesses of His faith, and His Son, for the Lord has come down to Earth in bodily form and has preached the Gospel message of hope and salvation that we each may have life and liberty. The wicked are to be removed from the Earth for their wickedness, and those who tormented the children of God day and night without cease shall have their names blotted out forever, for the Mighty One of Jacob has established His promise to all that the least shall be called great in the kingdom to come. Let all who bless be blessed, and those who curse, curse, for what comes out of the mouth will return unto a person on the day of judgement when all things shall be laid bare before the throne of God.

Let all the world bare witness of the salvation of the Lord by the thief upon the cross who cried out that "Jesus is Lord" and he was saved, for the grace of God is immeasurable toward those who acknowledge His Son who is the redeemer of mankind from the hands of the devil. The Lord has placed aside His wrath for the wicked who have led the flocks astray with their persecutions day and night against that which God in Heaven has ordained as Holy. The hope of the wicked is in vain, and their income is a curse to them, but the hope of the compassionate is for the poor, and their offerings to the least are a tithe to the Most High. The Lord was made low for us and has taken the transgressions of the world upon Himself, so that all who shame the poor and take advantage of the weak shall be a curse unto themselves before God and men.

The unjust have reaped their reward in full at the expense of others with nothing owing to them in eternity but the wrath of God that abides on them, because they did not heed His moral law. So, may the grace of God be upon those who acknowledge His Son that their sins may be forgotten, and Thy wrath should turn away to face their persecutors who attack the Lord's faith and His image with accusations and charges, yet they cannot give an account for even one of their sins. For the Lord has heard the cries of the meek from on high, and has delivered the Gospel message of hope and salvation to the districts of the people that we should all acknowledge one another as equals for the sake of human equality, and equal justice thereby.

God in Heaven has shown His love to the world by the gift of His eternal Spirit, so let no man take away that which God in Heaven has ordained as sacred, which is the spirit of inner peace that is reserved for the merciful at heart who are convicted by their conscience by the truth that sets us free. May His Spirit be upon you this hour, for the mercies of God are endless toward the sheepfold of His heart who are the joy of His Spirit, and the last best hope for all of mankind. May God bless you and may you find peace and restitution of spirit in the name of Jesus His Son, who alone cleanses the conscience, and restores the soul. Amen

A Woe to the Wicked:

Death be not proud, but the wicked have rejoiced. The wicked shout from the hilltop with a gloating of victory. "The slain shall not speak again," they say, "for we have killed them with the sword." Woe unto the vile and repulsive murders of the ungodly against the little ones whom God has chosen. Woe unto the violent acts that the ungodly sinners have committed against the image of the Lord and His Sheepfold. And Woe unto the servants of hell for their repeated acts of violence towards the kindred of God who are forever with Him, as He will remember their names.

There shall be no ground for the wicked, as there shall be no mercy for the ungodly acts of the murderers against the image of the Lord and His Sheep. The Good Shepherd tends to His flock by day with milk and honey, and He watches over them by night, for He is a terror unto the wolves that force themselves upon the least. God is a refuge to the meek, and a fortress to the righteous. He is a fearful judge, and He will repay says the Lord according to His moral law, and in Him there is no impartiality. Those who side with the beast in the struggle for good shall inherit the destruction of the beast that is foretold by John the apostle, beloved of God.

The Lord is one.
The Lord is the Avenger.
The Lord alone shall break the wicked.

Let all the world bare witness of the salvation of the Lord through the mercy He has shown upon His servant David, who slew Goliath in battle by the righteousness of his courage and faith, and who bears the promise given of one greater than Solomon from his seed by the house of Jacob for defending the name of God against the Philistines. For the Son of man has come down to Earth, and has taken upon His tree the suffering of the world, and by His burden upon the cross, He has been raised above the Heavens forevermore. All who call upon His name shall inherit their life in Heaven with Him, and they shall not suffer the unrighteousness of the world ever again, for the persecutions against them are no more. The Lord has established the Heavens in truth, and He has delivered to the world in the flesh His eternal promise that whomsoever shall believeth in Him shall never perish.

For through Him, all are made anew by their faith in Him who was born to the Earth by the Holy Spirit, and He alone is worthy, and, everlasting without end. But unto the wicked, He has reserved His eternal judgement that they should not partake in the blessings of the Kingdom to come, because of their blasphemes, their sexual immorality, their murders, and their sorceries, which they did ungodly commit, and did not repent of before the Son of God. Therefore, the Lord lays up trouble for them in accordance with His moral law, that all shall acknowledge Him as their maker and be good to their neighbours in spirit and in deeds forevermore, which is in accordance with His eternal promise to the world, for the time of God's Kingdom is near.

The Earth shall be smitten with fear and trembling, and the watchers from the Heaven's shall quake, for the wicked are to be removed from the Earth and the salvation of the Lord shall be without end as the 144,000 who are the remnant of the house of Jacob shall enter into the Kingdom of light and glory. And their names are written on God's own hand so that none! shall ever take them away, for they are a special people unto Him, and, are blessed forever. All praise, wonder, might, majesty and glory belongs to the Son of God who alone is called Messiah and Saviour Lord, and He alone lives forever in eternity, for He alone bore the penalty of sin without any sin having been imputed against His name.

Therefore, worthy is the Lamb who was slain and lives forevermore with His kinsmen and His adopted, for He did strive with them against the bastards and the reprobate who worked against the splendour and might of His eternal judgements for all to live by fairly with. Which are: Do unto others as you would have them do unto you, and, to love your neighbour as you love your own, for this is the law of the prophets who bared His name. Amen

A Call to Righteousness and of Glory:

Blessed is the Lord our God who has established His kingdom of might and glory by His death upon the cross, and by His resurrection from the dead that all who believe in Him shall be remembered with the congregation of the righteous, for the just acts of the meek shall not fail the poor who have been weakened by the hands of the devil that they should stumble in their faith. Let all those who cry out for freedom know with assurance from above that God is a deliverer of the people who are held in chains by the teaching of mysteries that derive from the occult school of Freemasonry, for the Lord is a good shepherd with mercy under His wing for those who do not tempt their neighbour with sorceries, idolatry, and fornication.

> The Lord is good.
> The Lord is might.
> The Lord alone is glory.

Let every man tremble at the judgements of the Lamb, for the wrath of God that abides on the wicked is an eternal damnation, for their crimes against humanity shall not go unpunished. God in Heaven has sent His only begotten Son into the world as a remission of sin that all who call upon His name shall receive a new name written in majesty, for the glory of God is the might of His eternal word that shall not return empty, nor null in-void, for He alone has established all things by the Spirit of grace that all shall acknowledge their neighbour with love and humility.

Let all who are humble be humbled, and let all who are wicked be found, for the time of God's Kingdom is at hand, and He alone watches over all things and is ready to receive you with thanksgiving's and earnest prayer, for God does not delight in the condemnation of the wicked who have been deceived, nor does God bring retribution upon the just, but unto the blasphemers, adulterers, and the sinful who have rejected the name of the Lord who is worthy above all creation to judge with an eternal might that all shall know whom they have denied, for God alone is worthy of all might, majesty, and glory.

May the grace of God be bestowed upon the justified who have been redeemed from the hands of the devil for their love, their humility, and their worship of Him who alone is their peace and restitution of spirit. In Jesus' worthy and mighty name we thank you for the testimonies of the meek, and of the righteous acts of the saints who have opened the eyes of the wicked to their injustices, and have revealed the judgements of Heaven to the blessed at heart who are not without conviction. May they find forgiveness of sin and an eternal place of rest, for the work of the Lord is the works of faith that all should know that Christ Jesus our Lord is with you through your trials and tribulations that the hope of the just should not fail the weak, nor shall it end, for the time of God's promise to the meek is at hand, and He alone is their assurance. Amen

ARTICLE 6

Prayers and Poems

A Prayer for the Ukraine:

Dear Heavenly Father our Messiah God;

Thou art gracious Father unto all the world. For You Father God have set apart the weak from the strong in order that Your glory should be seen from the impoverishment of their journey in life, for the strength of the spirit is not according to the flesh, but according to love. May You have mercy dear Heavenly Father on the Ukrainian people, and their sons and daughters that each may live forever with You in Thy Kingdom forever. All wonder, might, majesty, honour, and praise is without end unto the Lord God in Heaven who endures with the people who are persecuted for their testimony of Him who is worthy to deliver the weak in times of trouble, and who has the grace to attend to their needs in times of poverty, and who alone cleanses the conscience of all wrongdoing.

Lord, Almighty God;

We have our minds in fear but Thy will has been done according to Thy word, and Thy word is unbreakable, for Thy word is Thy name. Let all who call upon the name of Jesus be saved, and let them fear not, nor be ashamed, for the love of the Father is with them who have been persecuted for righteousness sake. We thank You Heavenly Father that you have blessed those who endure with family through strife, and lean unto the law of love for their neighbours sake, for the fulfilment of love is the fulfilment of the law of faith.

So may faith in love abound for those who are weak, and who are persecuted for their righteousness, for they are near to God's heart, as the least shall be called great, while those who call themselves great shall be made low... We thank You Lord Jesus our Heavenly Saviour for the people of the Ukraine who are suffering under the yoke of militant Communism. May aid come swiftly to them as a light arrow moves through the mist, and may the word of the Lamb be preached openly and zealously across the Ukraine unto all of the inhabitants that everyone may know the love of the Father that is for them, and within them always. Amen

A Remembrance Day Prayer for America 9/11/2024

Dear Heavenly Jesus our Messiah God;

We thank you for the years of prosperity that you have granted to the world by the gift of Your Spirit, for all are endowed with conscience to understand Your ways of truth and life. May the Lord bless those who have suffered under the yoke of tyranny, and who have lost their family in strife, may they find forgiveness of sin, and may the light of the Gospel message of hope flood their minds with Godly wisdom, for You are a Lord of righteous who will not lead the people astray.

May the just acts of the men and women in service be remembered this day and hour where we have joined together under one hope that America will not fail in their faith, nor in shame, for the love of the Father is with them who have been persecuted day and night for defending the Lord's faith, and His name. America is the land of the free and the home of the brave, because the men and women fought for righteousness sake against a powerful enemy that sought to rule the world by force. Let all the world bare witness of the salvation of the Lamb who has blessed the United States with a declaration of liberty, and of humility, for it is the will of God that all should acknowledge one another as equals for the sake of liberty, and human freedom thereby.

May the people who have gathered together under one hope know with assurance from above that God is a deliverer of the meek, and He alone will make a way for those who search diligently the word of God who has paved the way for life and salvation by the proclamation of the Gospel message of hope, which He has prepared for those who lean unto the law of love for their neighbour's sake, for the Lord is not a kinsman unto hatred, but unto love instead. God in Heaven has set apart the weak from the strong in order that their glory should be seen from their suffering for others, for the strength of the Spirit is not according to the flesh, but according to love. So may faith in love abound for those who search diligently the word of the Lamb for the Lord alone is their peace, and their restitution of Spirit. May God bless America as they venture into a future based on human rights and equality, that all may know that God in Heaven has set apart the United States as a symbol of hope, and of glory. Amen

A Prayer for the United Kingdom:

Blessed art Thou O' Lord our God above all creation for you have set apart in Your heart the people of the United

Kingdom whom You have loved by the giving of Your Spirit. May the people of the United Kingdom be united forever under one love, and under one rule, for the law of love has been fulfilled by the faith of our Lord and Saviour, Jesus Christ, who withstood the crowds and defeated the devil upon the Cross of Calvary by the might of His eternal Spirit, and by the power of His spoken word. May the United Kingdom be ushered into a land of milk and honey for their faith in Him who alone is worthy to receive our prayers, and who alone has taken the suffering of the world unto Himself that He may be glorified in the Kingdom to come as a child who leads the Lamb and the Lion by the way of the river in the Heavens above.

We thank You dear Heavenly Jesus this day and hour where all things shall work towards good who love You in Spirit, for the Spirit of the meek is a Spirit of grace and humility by the proclamation of the Gospel message of hope and salvation that the wicked should turn away from Thy wrath in repentance of sin, for it is by the wicked that Your Church is persecuted day and night. May those who are suffering under the yoke of persecution know with assurance from above that God is a deliverer of the people who have been set apart in His heart for the redemption of blood, and for Heaven's sake. Let all the world bear witness to the testimonies of truth, and of salvation, that derive from the Spirit of the Lamb who is with us through our trials and tribulations that each should receive their reward according to what they have done, so that the least may be called great in the Kingdom to come.

Lord, Almighty God;

We thank You Lord God in Heaven for Thy Commonwealth system of common law, which has been a grace and a service to the Kingdom of Heaven that the people should look to the United Kingdom as a source of hope and restitution of Spirit in Jesus' worthy name, for the people who are called by Thy name have received a Spirit of justice, and of mercy, that all may find in them a loving neighbour, and a hero at heart, for the people of the Commonwealth have fought a terrible enemy that sought to rule the known world by force. May the brave acts of the righteous within the United Kingdom be remembered today, and forevermore, for they gave their today that we may see tomorrow as a light that cannot fade, nor shall it pass away into the darkness of night, for they have lightened the way to victory and liberty, and human freedom thereby. May those who have established their hope in our Lord our Saviour, Jesus Christ, be revealed in the Heavens above as a rose blooms in the garden that their love for You shall never perish, nor shall it end, for the people of the United Kingdom are under Thy grace as a beacon of hope, and of glory. Amen

A Blessing to the Poor in Spirit:

Blessed is the one who does not take the Lord's name in vain, for they are like a pillar that was positioned at the entrance to the temple, and their mind is for the Lord and all that is good. God in Heaven has blessed the poor with justice from above through the provision of human rights and equality, because their poverty was not their fault, but the fault of others who do take the Lord's name in vain, and who do corrupt the ways of justice by taking advantage of the weak.

The Lord is a Good Shepherd, and He tends to His flock by day with love and mercy for they are the joy of His Spirit, and the apple of His eye, and He watches over them by night, for He is a terror unto those who prey upon the least who are called great in the kingdom to come.

Therefore, fear the least here on Earth, for God has placed honours and affections upon them that they should not fear evil, nor shun the poor, for the spirit of the meek is a spirit of grace.

Let all the world bare witness of the salvation of the Lord by His Gospel message of peace and liberty, which is without end unto those who have been persecuted day and night for defending the Lord's faith, and His name. May peace be upon you, and may restitution of spirit come to those who search diligently the word of God, which is revealed to all who love Him, for He has set apart in His flesh a day and an hour where all things shall come to an end, save those who have been found worthy before the throne of God. Amen

A Little Bird Wept:

A bird has wings, the little ones chirp, but what of the snake? Does he ever fake?

The zebra gallops, he crosses the plains, but what of the tiger? Is he in pain?

The salmon waits for the tide, but what of the bear? And his prize?

Death will lurk, death will reign, but what of love? Is it our bane?

We speak from each other, we speak for ourselves, we long to be heard like a small bird.

The zebra has stripes and so do we, a pattern of shame, we aren't to blame.

The salt of the Earth a salmon seeks, the word of God, it preserves the meek.

We must work together against the tide, a work of love, for the least we strive.

Love conquers death with a breath, so speak from love, as Jesus wept.

The Test of Faith:

Time is the essence, faith is endowed, an eternal love has
moved the crowed.
They wept for joy, they wept in pain, the love of God
removes our shame.
Tears are water, and so are the waves, they rise, they fall
but that is not all.
Emotions are deep, and so is the ocean, darkness is low, but
love helps us grow.
We rise above, we call together, a day of worship shall be
forever.
A day of rest, a day that's best, our faith, our love, for here
is the test.
We are tested in works, we are tested in love, the test of
faith belongs to His grace.
His love is pure, His love is kind, He gave His life for all
of mankind.
He opens the way, He opens the door, His path is clear
because there is no fear.
His ears are open, He reigns from above, the faith in me
is an eternal love.

The Ways of Water:

The spirit wells, the spirit speaks, a fountain of tears
removes my fears.
His love is kind, His mercies remind, I am not alone nor
left behind.
My mind is troubled, my heart is broken, but the spirit of
God, I have awoken.
He sees my sin, He dwells within, His kingdom, His
majesty reigns with Him.
Water is a stream, the river its friend, it turns it wavers at
every bend.

I sing a new song, one of hope, the love within me helps me cope.

His spirit is word, His ways are true, He created the Earth and made it blue.

The ocean's roar, the valley's sink, the Lion of Judah helps me think.

Tears are water, and so is the dew, a reflection of love, that's why the Earth is blue.

ARTICLE 7

Summary

The sole purpose of this book is to defend the Holy Bible and to warn the people of a great deception that is tied in heavily with the teaching of evolution, Secular Humanism, and occult Freemasonry. According to the Holy Bible, the end times deception will involve the mark of the beast, which is why the theory of evolution is tied in heavily with this end times deception. Evolutionary scientists are attempting to merge human DNA with animal DNA in order to try and vindicate the evolutionary theory. But the problem here with this type of practice, is that if man is to merge himself with the beasts of the field, then mankind will one day be extinct, which is self-explanatory.

So, for this reason, the evolutionary theory is the world's most dangerous theory bar none due to the science of cloning animals with humans, which must stop immediately for the safety of humanity, because all that is at stake here is our God given humanity. Our Commonwealth system of common law has been blessed with grace and humility by God in Heaven so that peace and justice should preside over the acts of terrorism in accordance with the Biblical teachings of moral law. If the theory of evolution continues to be taught from public education, then human equality will one day be lost in obscurity, because the entire purpose of the evolutionary theory is to cause the individual to deny morality as universal, as well as Biblical, by the reinterpretation of conscience.

The theory of evolution is by definition a racial theory that requires dismantle and removal in order for students to be properly educated concerning human rights and equality, so that each person is made fully aware of a lawful obligation within society, and so that no student is indoctrinated with a racial theory, and then tested based on a racial theory, which is a crime against humanity, because racism is illegal, rather than intellectual. And until the theory of evolution is removed from public education, we will continue to be faced with the horrors it produces that are relative to moral and social decay, as well as human-animal exploitation through experimentation and indoctrination, because if there's one thing that cannot be avoided when teaching the evolutionary theory to students, is the racial philosophy of survival of the fittest.

Evolution, as a theory, is also the philosophical basis for Scientific Atheism and Secular Humanism due to its materialistic and secular interpretations of life and morality, and is therefore essential to any atheistic system of belief. And this is a problem for society as a whole, because it is atheism that will be responsible for the final social cataclysm according to those who are in control of the global conspiracy to one day rule the world with Satanism, (such as Freemasonry) thereby ushering in the final days mentioned in Scripture. The sole idea behind the evolutionary theory is to espouse some form of freedom from morality by the denial of the human conscience in favour of the term, consciousness, when nothing can enslave mankind faster than the theory of evolution in practice due to the evolutionary definition of man. The evolutionary definition of man is doing more to enslave humanity by equating mankind with the animal kingdom, rather than freeing the people by the truth concerning their God given right to be defined as a created human being, which forms the basis for human rights and equality.

The evolutionary theory is the greatest threat to mankind that the world has ever faced, because the evolutionist will instinctively attempt to try and mutate everything they touch in order to achieve a desired effect, which not only includes both man and the animals, but also, law. The United States Supreme Court decision to prevent Biblical creation from being taught to every school student through the public education system in favour of the evolutionary theory, is by definition, a mutation of the said Constitution, because the United States Constitution was never to be interfered with in order to protect a pet theory by equating a human being as an animal in order to deny a person their God given humanity.

The United States Constitution was never to be interpreted using secular ideology alone, but with a correct theology due to the rights of conscience, which is protected as inalienable, while the ability to govern is by definition a privilege, rather than a birthright. Protection of person is at the cornerstone of law and order so that each individual should be convicted by their conscience to do what is right in the sight of God, which does not include granting protections to a theory in science that denies our humanity by the reinterpretation of conscience to being that of an animal instinct.

The sixth sense is a moral sense that perceives injustices, of which, the animals do not share, because human beings will actively engage a problem if the moral cause is seen as sufficient, while the animals do not. This dispute between Biblical creation and philosophical materialism is an issue that cannot go unabated from the premise of law, nor can we allow scientists to dictate the law on our own behalf, because the practice of modern science involving the empirical method has derived from the practice of law, the same as the word, science, has derived from the lawful term, conscience.

This issue has occurred as a relationship between Secular Humanism, occult Freemasonry, and the theory of evolution, because all three systems of belief are by definition, unconstitutional, whilst remaining opaque in regards to their own intentions through legal proceedings, and their theoretical system of belief that denies our humanity. If the evolutionary theory is to bring our humanity into question before the law by attempting to define man as a lower animal, then it is the evolutionary theory that must be brought into question by the law, rather than our God given humanity, which is self-explanatory.

According to the United States government, science is for the express purpose of investigating, critiquing, and analysing the theory of evolution, which is the main reason why evolution, as a theory, is the greatest theoretical set back in all of modern science, because the government will not endorse any form of critique that goes against the theory, and because every investigative effort against the theory will always be subjected to an automatic dismissal regardless of the merit of the discoveries presented. So, for this reason, the theory of evolution is by definition a philosophical dogma, because the only thing that can be analysed using the evolutionary theory, is evolution itself.

So, for this reason, it is not the creationists who are biased in favour of religion, but rather, it is the evolutionists who are bias against religion for theological reasons, because the official reason why evolution must be investigated, according to the United States Supreme Court, is because the government is secular. So, in order for science to be educational, and therefore profitable for everyone, then the ban on creation science must be lifted along with the secular standard for public education. Otherwise, the students cannot reach their full potential as creative individuals who are endowed with conscience by their Creator, because they are being taught that man is animal through the public education system with the consent of law, which is against the principles of universal law, whereby the right to be defined as a created individual is protected under international law in accordance with international agreement.

Under international law, a human being has the inalienable and universal right to be defined as a "living soul" before the law, and it is international law that is of a higher legal standard than scientific theory. While international law is subject to a higher authority in itself, such as moral law, which must derive itself from a system of morality that is by definition, universal for ethical reasons. And the one thing that atheism cannot offer, is a system of morality that is by definition, universal, due to the correct definition of atheism. The rights of conscience is a religious liberty that has been used by international law to define human rights and equality for the benefit of an individual's protection within the system. So, in order to be consistent with international human rights legislation, then a correct theology is also required, which must derive itself from Biblical creation as a legal standard for the good of the people, and for the good of the common law.

If religion is to be replaced by science, then there will be no universal basis for morality apart from what scientists think, when science is not governed by scientists, but by ethics instead. So, in order for ethics to be understood as a legal obligation, then a universal system of morality is required first, which must derive itself from the Holy Bible under the common law, otherwise, there will be no moral obligation by the individual to carry out a lawful instruction, because the evolutionary theory is being used openly to oppose the common law by the denial of conscience, and by setting a new legal precedent that is in denial of Biblical creation as a legal standard. Biblical creation, as a legal standard, is in place so that we should each have protection of person before the law in accordance with human rights and equality, and by a correct interpretation of conscience, which forms the basis for human rights and equality.

The just liberties of the people are to be protected by the rights of conscience, and with a correct theology, because the lawful term, conscience, is a theological term from the Holy Bible, rather than a secular term from philosophical materialism. National security is relative to a national trust that forbids us from abandoning the common law precedent that all men are created equal, which is a direct consequence of the evolutionary theory in practice from law and order, known formally as Social Darwinism. Thus, the United States Supreme Court decision to grant Constitutional protections to a theory in science is against the law, because no theory in both science or law can be defined as self-evident on the basis of theory.

The theory of evolution from a secular premise is assumed to be true, rather than literal, while the Biblical definition of the human conscience is protected under United States Constitutional law as not-without-standing in its legal defence, thus disqualifying the evolutionary theory through the due process of the law. The due process of law is for the purpose of equal opportunity between both parties in a dispute, whether it be a natural person, or legal fiction, the principle remains the same under the common law so that laws should protect our basic freedoms in accordance with due process. The United States Supreme Court decision to grant Constitutional protections to a theory in science raises reasonable suspicion on the grounds that a judicial verdict was reached that encroaches heavily upon the just liberties of the people to be defined as created human beings with a human ancestry.

A secular government cannot stand upon the laws they have created without first recognizing the freedom of the voting constituency, because it is the democracy that makes up the people, and the people are not secular according to their God given conscience, which forms the basis for the United States Constitution, and our Commonwealth system of voting, because you vote according to your conscience. While the United States government is secular according to its founding principle of separation of Church and State, which was enacted in order for a Christian democracy to be protected by so that each person should be convicted by their conscience in regards to a moral obligation by the law to uphold the Constitution when called upon, because it is the Constitution that protects the people's liberty on the basis of Biblical creation as a legal standard to interpret inalienable rights, and human freedom thereby.

Corporate dominance has led to the creation of Legislative Acts that attempt to cater to all from a secular premise, when a legal fiction is without a conscience before the law, and is thereby subject to the people in a civil dispute, because the rights of conscience is for the voting constituency to be protected by, rather to operate in favour of corporate dominance over the just liberties of the people. Corporate dominance is relative to social and moral decay due to false advertisement that is designed to deceive the laity into purchasing more and more expensive goods until the debt becomes unbearable, which then leads to the collapse of a nation's security when the debt cannot be repaid, just as we've seen in both Greece and Iceland when their economic system failed due to corporate dominance by banking institutions that were engaging in an unsafe financial practice based on usury loans.

Thus, national security is relative to the rights of conscience in that the people must decide through a voting system as to whether their elected government is operating fairly in accordance with the will of the people, which is not to be dictated by corporations and banking institutions whose purpose is to profiteer from the public sector. The public sector is to be well informed of the danger caused by government legislation that is in favour of corporate dominance over small businesses, which is engineered as a social experiment that is designed to fail, thus leading to a collapse of the global stock market, which then leads to the inevitable consequence of human slavery by the mark of the beast, as foretold by John the Apostle, beloved of God.

The purpose of Biblical creation, as a legal standard from law, is to liberate the individual from subjugation, whether it be a foreign rule, a domestic legal clause, or a theory in science, the principle remains the same, because it is Biblical morality that defines our human freedom by the rights of conscience. The purpose of the Gospel message of hope, as defined by the Holy Bible from the Beatitudes of Jesus Christ (Matthew 5:1-12) is to free the individual by deliverance and prayer, so that each person should be convicted by their conscience to do what is right in the sight of God, who has established His promise to all that the meek shall be called first in the kingdom to come. Evolution, on the other hand, is a theory in science that has caused a great deception upon the Earth in a time of global crisis, because nothing will enslave mankind faster, and oppress the weak, than the philosophical dogma of survival of the fittest.

In order for students to be adequately informed concerning the correct definition of what a person is, and what the endowed human conscience is for, then the secular standard for public education must be lifted, because it is the universal law of human equality that is of a higher legal standard due to international agreement. According to international law, the burden of proof is upon the individual who is challenging a lawful instruction, such as the lawful definition of person, because a human being is not to be denoted as an animal from the viewpoint of Linnaean taxonomy and the evolutionary theory before international law for reasons relating to protection of person, which is also relative to national security.

The idea that a secular society owes its allegiance to a secular government, is in fact, Communism; and as we move forward in history, it will be those who speak the truth in regards to basic moral principles that will lose their right to freedom of speech through a cancel culture, because the United States Constitution has been overruled in order to pave the way for a secular society, which is a pathway that leads to moral decay, social conflict, and global rebellion. And the world will follow suit to Americanized public education due to America's influence around the globe, and due to Communist revolution involving Scientific Atheism, which is the reason why the evolutionary theory has become dominant from public education. But the problem with the theory of evolution being taught by the State, is that the individual cannot determine the difference between a man and an animal once the theory has been accepted, which is a direct result of evolutionary terminology having been put into effect through the public education system with the consent of the law.

The only way for America to combat religious terrorism, Communism, and lawlessness, is with a correct theology, and to educate the people concerning their inalienable right to be defined as a created human being, because the day that the correct interpretation for inalienable rights fails, will be the same day that Communism succeeds; and the fastest way for inalienable rights to fail, is by a system of non-belief. So, the only way to fight the issue of Communist revolution from minority groups who question basic public morals, is to apply a correct theology in return, which was the founding fathers greatest achievement by the introduction of the rights of conscience, which cannot be overruled under the common law without detracting from the necessity of a clean testimony, because it is a clean testimony that is essential for determining the facts of a matter before the law, rather by a judicial decision alone.

Any judicial system that believes it can protect the people by protecting a pet theory, is by definition, an unjust system, and the more the system we live under continues to be based on the evolutionary theory, the more the system will fail those who deserve the truth, which does not derive from the teaching of evolution, but from a correct theology instead, because the truth of a principle will always be determined by honesty first, rather than by suppressing the truth that sets us free. And the one form of suppression that the United States Supreme Court has perfected against the good of the people, is the lie that the evolutionary theory cannot be contested for reasons relating to an educational standard that is secular, which is the very thing that prevents the people from learning about their Creator, as from a responsible source of information.

Any theory that attempts to define man as a lower animal before the law, whilst requiring the protection of the law at the same time in order to be considered as a valid theory, is to take advantage of the law for unlawful reasons, because the law is in place so that we each have protection of person, rather than to vilify a particular theory in science. If the judicial system within the United States declares protections for a theory in science that is challenging our God given humanity by defining man as a lower animal, then the people will have nothing in which to protect themselves with from the law, because it is the law that happens to be the problem now due to protections in place that disqualify any testimony that goes against the evolutionary theory in order to protect the theory, rather than the people's just liberties.

Any claim that the evolutionary theory cannot be contested or cross-examined before the law due to a Supreme Court decision, is by definition, a claim to infallibility, because any law in place that is designed to protect a given theory requires merit the same as any other law or theory. When the truth is that there is no merit, nor justification by the law to protect the evolutionary theory as incontestable by definition of the fact that a theory will always be questionable before the law. So, in order to cross-examine the evolutionary theory before the law, then there needs to be a Constitutional protection in place first, otherwise, the theory cannot be contested due to a Supreme Court decision. And it is for this reason that the Declaration of Independence acts as a Constitutional protection for the rights of conscience in that the declaration defines each person as a created human being, rather than an animal of some description that has derived from the swamps.

The evolutionary theory has caused a great deception upon the people of the Earth in a time of global crisis, because the theory of evolution attempts to define man as beast, when according to the United Nations, no human being is to be equated with the animals via their ancestry in accordance with international agreement. According to the universal law of human equality under the UDHR, all human beings have been endowed with conscience in order to be reasoned with as an individual, which is the very thing that separates mankind from the beasts of the field in accordance with international law under the agreement of 192 nations. If the evolutionary theory is to bring the universal law of human equality into question by attempting to define a person as a type of animal, then it is the evolutionary theory that must be called into question by the law, rather than the individual's God given humanity, which is self-explanatory.

The Universal Declaration of Human Rights and Equality is in accordance with peace here on Earth, while it is the work of Satan to remove peace from the Earth by the rise of war, and by failed political negotiations within the chambers of the U.N. So, in order to build a case for the purpose of defending the universal definition of man, as from a Biblical premise, then evidence is required, which is why defining yourself, or others, as an animal, constitutes as evidence that is self-incriminating, and therefore, cannot be used as a defence before the law. And the reason why it is self-incriminating to define yourself, or others, as having derived from the animals, is because the animals are legally defined as property the same as nature is defined as property. So, because of this legal status, it is unlawful to regard a human being as a type of animal so that each person may exercise their basic rights as a free individual under God.

587

Every human being here on Earth has a basic right to be informed about their Creator through the public education system on the basis of morality and conscience, with good reason, so that we are not enslaved by the laws we create, because nothing will enslave mankind faster than the adoption of rules that simply do not apply. And the one rule that simply does not apply, is the rule that the evolutionary theory cannot be contested before the law due to a secular standard for public education, which is neither right nor safe on the basis of reason and conscience. Without a system of morality that is universal in its interpretation, then there will be no legal standard in place for laws to be made universal, as well as just. God the Creator has set His moral laws upon His creation so that all shall acknowledge one another as equal in rights for the sake of human rights and equality, and equal justice thereby.

The universal law of human equality is not just a concept, but a self-evident reality instead, because all human beings have been endowed with conscience by their Creator, and it is from the conscience that our convictions derive from, which is how we make a moral decision, and our decisions are subject to the Biblical principles of universal morality, which cannot be justified by nature alone, because nature is defined as property, legally speaking. If inalienable rights derive from nature, then man is thereby the property of the State, because both nature, and the animals, are defined as property, which forms the basis for human slavery. But if inalienable rights derive from the Creator, then man is thereby independent of the State in terms of ownership, and is therefore, sovereign. And it is human sovereignty that delivers a fair outcome whereby the worker is paid in full, and the company produces a product, thereby allowing for human creativity, as well as protection of intellectual property.

A Communist industrial system has robbed the people of every nation to their intellectual property by copyrighting every idea, product, and public service, including a democracy, thereby infringing upon the just liberties of the people in order to funnel global commodities into a Communist industrial scheme that is set to fail over time, of which, we should not play a part. So, unless trade reform between the United States and China occurs, then America's manufacturing base will continue to decline, which is by definition a danger to humanity, because it is the United States that has led the world to human independence by the correct interpretation of human sovereignty under God. The right to your intellectual property is by definition an inalienable right under the universal law of creativity, which is the very thing that calls the evolutionary theory into question by definition of the word, create. If all things great and small belong to nature, then all things great and small belong to the highest bidder due to the legal definition of property. Thus, it is the legal system that is currently leading humanity into a new age system of human slavery by the reinterpretation of conscience.

If inalienable rights, such as the right to be defined as a created human being who is endowed with conscience by their Creator, and the right to a fair hearing are denied on the basis of legislative intervention, and the evolutionary theory, then it is the universal definition of man under international law that shall preside over the Legislative Act, because inalienable rights are not to be interfered with as defined by international agreement. The United States Constitution, and their Declaration of Independence is a universal statement of truth that cannot be misconstrued on the basis of the Supreme Court's authority to pretended legislations that attempt to cater to all from a secular premise, whilst at the same time, denying a person their basic right to be defined as a created human being with a human ancestry.

The United States government, and the Supreme Court, are not infallible when it comes to the interpretation of the law, because a lawful obligation must be defined by a moral obligation first, which means that morality is above the law from a Biblical premise, because it is Biblical morality that defines basic public morals under the common law, rather than secular science. Yet the United States government, and the Supreme Court, have acted as infallible the same as the Popes, past and present, because one cannot contest the Supreme Court on matters relating to religion. The United States Supreme Court has acted as a religious authority with a religious test in place that is designed to deny Biblical creation with an automatic dismissal, which is a violation of the First Amendment that prohibits the government from conducting a religious test in order to deny the Creator, and religious freedom thereby.

The United States founding fathers never created Biblical Christianity, but rather, Christianity and Biblical creation is a legal standard within the U.S before Social Darwinism became mandatory through the public education system by the teaching of evolution by the State, which has now paved the way for total enslavement by the denial of conscience, and Biblical creation. If the United States government refuses to acknowledge the Creator, and the Holy Bible by citing the limitations of Secularism as their right and justification, and continues to teach that man is animal through the public education system, whilst denying the Constitutional interpretation of man, then the rights of the people will one day be lost in obscurity due to an evolutionary definition of man that was false from its own assertions, and therefore, gave little value to the students who are entering a legal system with their own experience that holds to a Biblical definition of man due to the use of the theological term, conscience, to define a person as distinct from the animals.

If the evolutionary theory cannot be challenged before the High Court of the United States, then Communism will inevitably defeat America, and the rest of the world will follow suit thereafter due to a shift in culture if Biblical creation cannot be taught to students through the public education system, because without an acknowledgement of the Creator who has blessed America with wealth and security, then America will lose their wealth and security as we are seeing today by the rise of Scientific Atheism, and by a rise in the cost of living due to the Federal Reserve Act, which are both a core Communist tenet, rather than an American liberty. America is not a theocracy, but a democratic republic instead, and it is the democracy that makes up the republic, so that the republic is servant to the democracy, while the democracy is servant to the Creator, because it is the Creator who has endowed each person with conscience and with rights, and has thereby established His system of moral law with good will so that all should acknowledge their maker with love and humility according to the Spirit of grace.

The wicked on the other hand are not so, because it is the wicked who seek to undermine the course of justice by having their voice heard on high by force, rather than by reason or merit. And it is for this reason that New Atheism and the theory of evolution is a problem for our global society, because the one thing that cannot be reasoned with here on Earth, is a nihilist who has rejected the Creator in favour of a pseudo-definition of man. If America does not turn back to its former glory of Biblical authority then they will lose their authority within the world, because the spirit of humanity is a spirit of freedom that cannot be suppressed by a racial theory that robs the people of their God given humanity by the injustices they create.

If there is any justice to be had here on Earth, then it will have to come from faith, because it is a correct theology that defines what is just, rather than secular science. Science and law are governed by ethics, which in turn, is governed by morality, and it is the unethical conduct by evolutionary scientists in their attempts to try and merge man with the beasts of the field that constitutes as an abomination before the Lord who has set apart His image with honours and distinctions that none! should merge themselves with the beats of the field, for the image of the Lord is eternal without end. May the Lord our God who is one with the people by the breath of God be established in all righteousness through the laws we create, for He alone has established His system of moral law that all should acknowledge one another as equal in rights for the sake of human rights and equality, which is a commandment from the heights of the Heavens in accordance with the Gospel message of truth and of salvation that liberates the people from all injustices and subjugation.

May the Spirit of the Lamb, and of peace and salvation, rest upon you as you read this message from above, for the Lord is not a kinsmen unto hatred, but unto love instead by the preaching of the Gospel message of hope and liberty that all should receive a measure of truth, and of justice, each, according to what they have done. Let not your heart be troubled by the acts of terror from those who despise the Creator, and His Godly ways, for it is the will of the Father in Heaven that each person should be tested in their faith. For it is by faith alone that we are saved, and it is by God's grace alone that we are made righteous in Him by the love we have received, for God is love, and God is mercy, and He alone will avenge His people who have been established by their faith as the foundation of liberty, and justice for all.

*Citations, Online References, and External Links:

Online Historical Resources for the Genealogy:
https://en.wikipedia.org/wiki/Kenneth_Moir
https://en.wikipedia.org/wiki/Joseph_Moir
https://en.wikipedia.org/wiki/A_J_Moir_Stakes
https://en.wikipedia.org/wiki/Graham_Berry

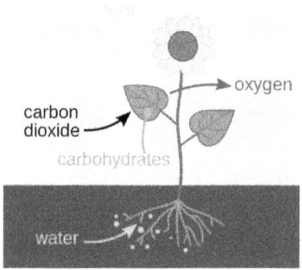

https://simple.wikipedia.org/wiki/Photosynthesis#/media/File:Photosynthesis_en.svg

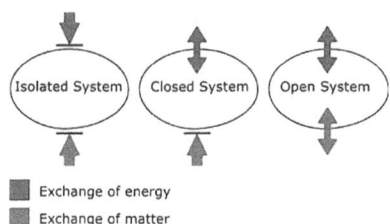

https://en.wikipedia.org/wiki/System#/media/File:Diagram_Systems.svg

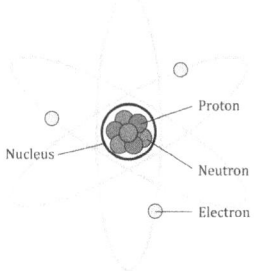

https://upload.wikimedia.org/wikipedia/commons/8/80/Atom_Diagram.svg

https://en.wikipedia.org/wiki/Experiments_in_the_Revival_of_
Organisms#/media/File:Experiment1940.jpg

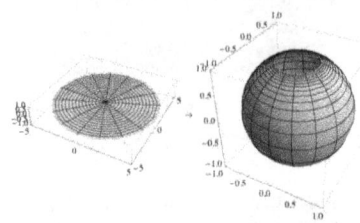

https://en.wikipedia.org/wiki/Stereographic_projection#/media/
File:PolarStereoProj.png

https://en.wikipedia.org/wiki/Magnetic_mirror#/media/File:Basic_
Magnetic_Mirror.jpg

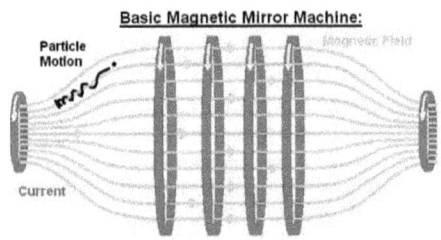

https://en.wikipedia.org/wiki/Napoleon#/media/File:JacquesLouis_David_
The_Emperor_Napoleon_in_His_Study_at_the_Tuileries_-_Google_Art_
Project.jpg
https://en.wikipedia.org/wiki/George_Washington#/media/File:George_
Washington,_1776.jpg

https://en.wikipedia.org/wiki/Karl_Marx#/media/File:Karl_Marx_001_(rotated).jpg

https://en.wikipedia.org/wiki/Hand-in-waistcoat#/media/File:George_B_McClellan_-_retouched,_cropped.jpg

https://en.wikipedia.org/wiki/List_of_knights_and_dames_commander_of_the_Royal_Victorian_Order_appointed_by_Elizabeth_II_%281978–2002%29#/media/File:GCVO_star.jpg

https://upload.wikimedia.org/wikipedia/commons/6/6d/San_Giovannino_dei_Cavalieri_stemma_Cavalieri_di_Malta.JPG

https://en.wikipedia.org/wiki/Theosophy#/media/File:Emb_logo.png

https://en.wikipedia.org/wiki/Wehrmacht#/media/File:War_Ensign_of_Germany_(1938–1945).svg

(Personal photograph taken by Adrian Moir of a Shriner's emblem purchased on Amazon.com).

https://www.amazon.com/Mason-Shriner-Masonic-Emblem

9 798765 200421